THE '80s ARE BACK!

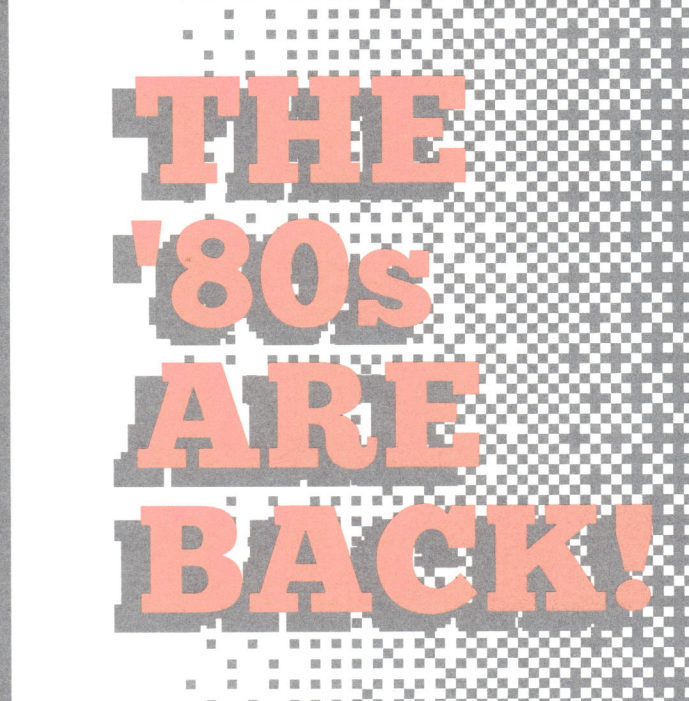

sendpoints

CONTENTS

- CITY POP
- RETRO-FUTURISM
- PIXEL ART
- DECO ART
- NEW UGLY

	CHAPTER 1	4-43
	INFLUENTIAL ART MOVEMENTS SHAPING 1980S GRAPHIC DESIGN	
7-9	1. FUTURISM: A BOLD DANCE WITH MODERNITY	
10-15	2. POP ART: A CELEBRATION OF CONSUMER CULTURE	
16-19	3. OP ART: THE NEW FRONTIER OF VISUAL PERCEPTION	
20-25	4. FROM RADICAL DESIGN TO MEMPHIS MAGIC: IMAGINATION OD AVANT-GARDE DESIGN	
26-33	5. FROM SUPERGRAPHICS TO NEW WAVE: PUSHING EXPERIMENTAL DESIGN FORWARD	
34-38	6. THE NEO-EXPRESSIONISM SURGE: EMBRACING RAW EOMTION AND URBAN VITALITY	
39-41	7. DIGITAL REVOLUTION: A FUSION OF TECHNOLOGY AND CUTTING-EDGE DESIGN	
42-43	◊ STRETCHING THE BOUNDARIES OF DESIGN–IGOR GUROVICH	

	CHAPTER 2	44-59
	ECHOES OF THE 1980S: NOSTALGIA AND THE ART OF GRAPHIC DESIGN	
47-49	1. WHY WE YEARN FOR THE 80S—NOSTALGIA	
50-59	2. A JOURNEY BACK TO THE 80S	

	CHAPTER 3	60-397
	THE EXPRESSION OF RETRO DESIGN STYLE IN CONTEMPORARY TIMES	
64-95	1. CITY POP	
96-149	2. RETRO-FUTURISM	
150-183	3. PIXEL ART	
184-245	4. DECO ART	
246-285	5. NEW UGLY	
286-343	6. SHŌWA	
344-393	7. THE DESIGNER DECADE	
394-397	◊ 1980S CHAT ROOM	

INDEX	398-399

THE DESIGNER DECADE

SHŌWA

Chapter 1
INFLUENTIAL ART MOVEMENTS SHAPING 1980S GRAPHIC DESIGN

9 PLAYING WITH VISUAL PERCEPTION

6 POPULAR CULTURE

1 A FANATICAL LOVE OF SPEED, TECHNOLOGY, AND VIOLENCE

7 VIBRANT COLORS AND GRAPHICS

2 PAINTING WITH RAW EMOTIONS

8 TEXT EXPERIMENT & DIGITAL TOOLS

4 ITALIAN ANTI-DESIGN

5 PRACTICING MORE DESIGN CONCEPTS

3 POSTMODERNISM IN ARCHITECTURE

CROSSWORD PUZZLES

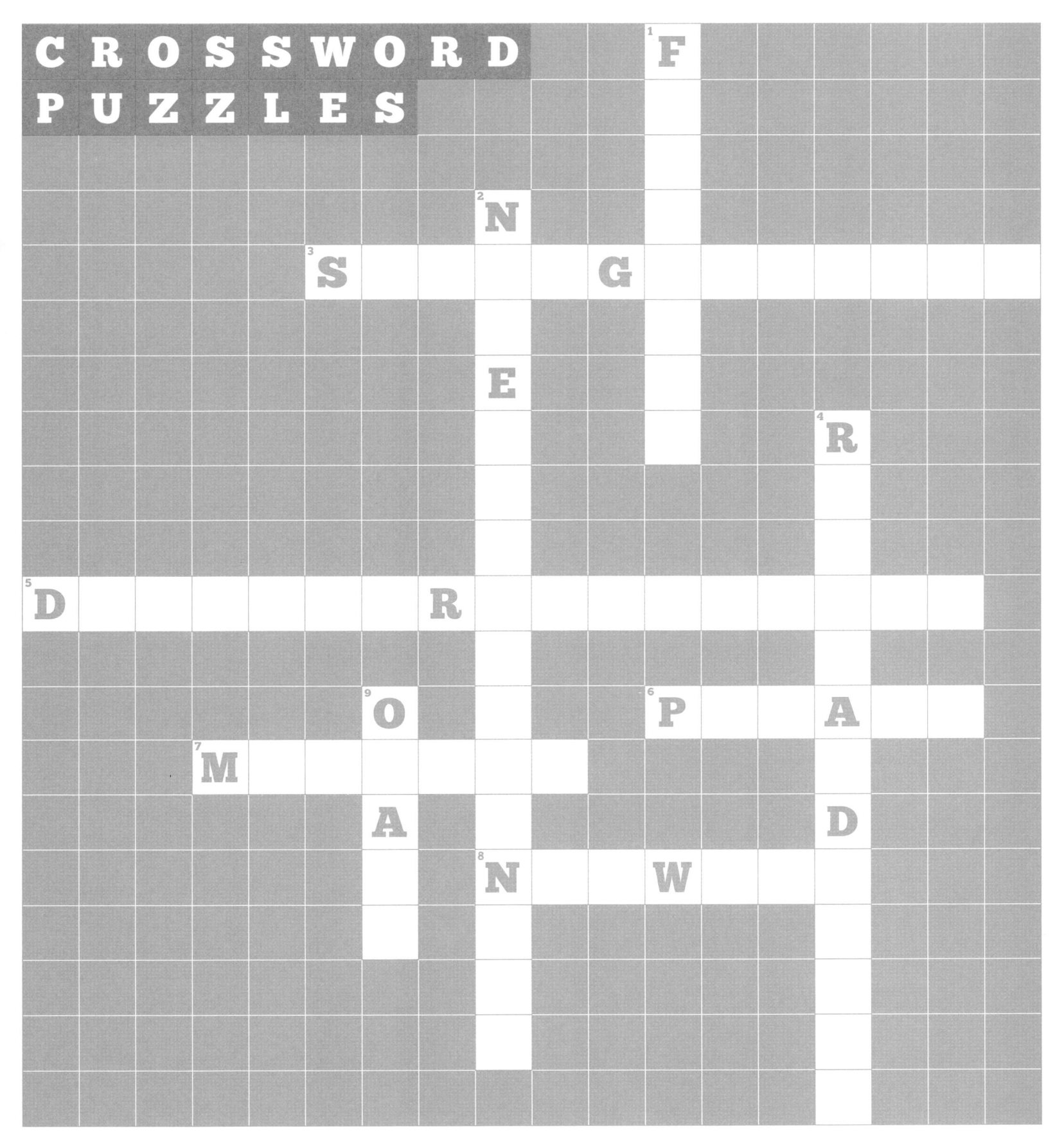

In the annals of recent history, the 1980s emerged as a resplendent epoch characterized by an explosion of vivid palettes and the birth of indelible subcultures. This luminous decade, etched into the collective memory of Generation X (born 1965–1988) and resurrected by the discerning eyes of Millennials (born 1981–1996) and Generation Z (often shortened Gen Z, born late 1990s–early 2010s), has left an indomitable imprint on our cultural tapestry. It was an era marked by audacious design experimentation, flamboyant aesthetics, and a fervent celebration of individuality, particularly within the vibrant sphere of retro graphic design. As we delve once more into the archives of the 1980s, we unearth a veritable trove of creative inspiration, a testament to the dynamic design currents that once coursed through our visual landscape.

ART MOVEMENTS CHAPTER 1

The society, culture, and technology of the 1980s were rapidly changing. With the acceleration of globalization and the swift development of information technology, people's lifestyles and aesthetic sensibilities has experienced profound changes. As a crucial medium of visual communication, graphic design was deeply influenced by these shifts naturally. Designers began to break away from traditional constraints and explore more diverse and individualized design languages.

When discussing the development of graphic design in the 1980s, it is essential to mention the movements and genres that profoundly influenced the art direction of this era. These art movements not only brought visual innovation but also advanced graphic design on cultural and aesthetic levels. This chapter will focus on Futurism's forward-looking visions, the revival of Pop Art, the visual exploration of Op Art, the transition from Italian Radical Design to the Memphis Group, the evolution from Supergraphics design to the New Wave graphic design movement, the wave of Neo-Expressionism, and ultimately, the fusion of technology and avant-garde during the Digital Revolution. Each artistic movement or style encapsulated a unique aspect of the decade's aesthetics and conceptual evolution. By examining their development, we can delve into the rich artistic influences of the time and capture the trend of design, which becomes a powerful language of culture and innovation.

Originated in Italy in the early 20th century, Futurism was an avant-garde movement that glorified modernity, speed, technology, and the dynamic energy of the future. The Futurists embraced industrialization and mechanization, seeking to break away from traditional forms and celebrate the motion of objects, the power of the machine, and the chaos of urban life. Their radical approach to art and design, with its fragmented forms, bold colors, and aggressive lines, laid the groundwork for modern graphic design. The impact of Futurism on 1980s design can be seen in the embrace of Retro-Futurism aesthetics, where technology-driven imagery and the bold, kinetic spirit of early 20th-century visions became a powerful influence on typography, architecture, and product design.

Pop Art, emerging in the mid-20th century, introduced a new visual language and a mode of expression to graphic design with its bold, vibrant colors and direct references to popular culture. By challenging traditional artistic norms and embracing diverse images from consumer society, Pop Art made designs that resonated more closely with public tastes easier to be accepted and spread. In the 1980s, Pop Art's influence began to seep into graphic design, with designers incorporating elements of popular culture to create works that were both visually impactful and widely accepted. This style not only captured the attention of a broader audience but also tightly wove graphic design with popular culture.

In the 1960s, Op Art was a visually striking movement that manipulated geometric shapes and color contrasts to create illusions of movement and depth. Op artists experimented with visual perception, using abstract patterns to evoke a sense of instability and vibration in their work. This exploration of optical effects challenged viewers to actively engage with the artwork, as static forms appeared to shift and morph in front of their eyes. In the 1980s, Op Art experienced a revival, influencing both fashion and graphic design. Its emphasis on visual trickery and disorienting effects echoed in the bold, neon-infused aesthetics of the decade, offering designers a playful, kinetic language that meshed with the era's digital and psychedelic revival.

Radical Design and the Memphis Group represent a period of self-reflection and exploration in Italian design history. By challenging functionalism and traditional design, they inspired designers to reconsider the relationship between form and function, significantly influencing 1980s graphic design. Designers broke away from the constraints of functionalist design, emphasizing freedom and personalized expression. This design philosophy sparked innovative thinking, propelling graphic design towards greater diversity and individuality. Additionally, the Memphis Group's unique use of color and composition introduced whimsical and distinctive designs to the market, bringing a new visual experience to 1980s graphic design.

Supergraphics and the New Wave graphic design movement further advanced the modernization of graphic design. By bridging postmodernism from architecture to graphic design, the artists broke away from conventional design thinking and added decorative elements to the clean, restrained International Style, leading to more intuitive and visually striking designs. Supergraphics design reinterpreted elements of the International Style, using exaggerated treatments to create highly recognizable and impactful work. Meanwhile, the New Wave graphic design movement emphasized playful and personalized styles, reworking and experimenting with different elements to make designs more experimental and innovative.

The Neo-Expressionism wave, an art movement that originated in the field of painting, emphasizes the expression of raw emotions and concepts. Under the influence of Neo-Expressionism, graphic design began to incorporate more emotional and personalized elements, making works more compelling and profound. Designers started to focus on the diversity and complexity of human nature, attempting to convey deeper emotions and meanings through their designs. This influence extended beyond the art world, resonating with broader cultural audiences across different eras.

Lastly, we cannot overlook the profound impact of the Digital Revolution on graphic design. The 1980s marked a significant turning point in the digital era, enabling designers to use advanced software and technology to realize more complex and intricate design concepts. Digital technology not only improved design efficiency and quality but also provided designers with a broader creative space, fostering a flourishing of artistic creation. With the support of digital technology, graphic design gradually moved towards greater diversity, personalization, and interactivity, bringing the potential of digital media art to the forefront.

The selected art genres and movements in this chapter have had a profound and widespread impact on 1980s graphic design. They introduced new visual languages and modes of expression, driving the evolution of design concepts and techniques. In the following sections, we will explore each of these art movements in detail, examining their characteristics and how they specifically influenced various aspects of 1980s graphic design. Through this discussion, we hope you will gain a more comprehensive and indepth understanding of the development of graphic design during this transformative decade.

FUTURISM: A BOLD DANCE WITH MODERNITY

As we look back on the 1980s, a decade renowned for its vibrant and eclectic art styles, it's impossible not to think of the futuristic aesthetics that defined much of the visual culture of the time. The rise of Cyberpunk, with its neon-lit cityscapes, digital grids, and dystopian visions, stood out as a hallmark of the '80s art, capturing a fascination with technology and the future. These psychedelic, forward-looking artistic expressions, though emblem of the 1980s, actually have their roots in an earlier modern movement: Futurism.

Futurism, which emerged in the early 20th century, was the first art movement to wholeheartedly embrace modernity and the concept of the future. It celebrated speed, technology, and the energy of the industrial age, laying the groundwork for many of the futuristic themes that would later reappear in the 1980s. The movement's emphasis on dynamic forms, movement, and the transformative power of machinery can be seen as a precursor to the neon-soaked, technology-obsessed aesthetics of Retro-Futurism and other 80s art trends. By tracing the evolution of these ideas from Futurism to the 1980s, we can better understand how the fascination with the future has continually shaped artistic expression across the decades.

1 Defining

Futurism was an experimental movement that began in Italy in the early 20th century, around 1909. It was initiated by the Italian poet Filippo Tommaso Marinetti[1], who introduced the movement through his publication *Manifesto of Futurism*. This movement celebrated modernity, technology, speed, and violence, aiming to break from the past and embrace the dynamism of contemporary life. Futurists sought to capture the energy and motion of the industrial age, often focused on themes like machines, urban environments, and the experience of speed and power.

In the visual arts, Futurists aimed to create a new artistic language that reflected the dynamism of the modern world, distancing themselves from traditional art forms. They were fascinated by the power of machines, the energy of industrial cities, and the belief that war could rejuvenate society—an idea that today appears contrary to the ideals of modernity. Futurist painters, including Umberto Boccioni, Giacomo Balla, and Gino Severini, used techniques like simultaneous contrast, divisionism, and abstraction to convey the sensation of speed and the fragmentation of objects in motion. Their work frequently depicted scenes of modern life, such as bustling cities, racing cars, and mechanical equipment, featuring dynamic compositions and fragmented forms to evoke a sense of movement and energy.

2 The Journey of Futurism

As early as 1907, *Sketch of a New Esthetic of Music* by Italian composer Ferruccio Busoni's[2], is often considered a precursor to Futurist. This marked the prototype of Futurist thinking, which soon began to flourish in Italy. Futurism was officially launched with the publication of *Manifesto of Futurism* by Filippo Tommaso Marinetti in 1909, which appeared on the front page of the French newspaper *Le Figaro*. Marinetti, a poet and theorist, argued that the development of science and technology has changed man's conception of time and space, that the old culture has lost its value, and that the concept of aesthetics has changed greatly. He called for a complete rejection of the past and an embrace of the future, war, machinery, and the fastpaced life of modern cities. He envisioned a new art that would capture the energy and dynamism of the modern world.

Marinetti subsequently traveled to England, France, Germany, and Russia to promote the ideas of Futurism, igniting its spread across Europe. The movement soon expanded to various art forms, including painting, sculpture, architecture, music, and literature. In 1910, a group of Futurist artists, including Umberto Boccioni, Giacomo Balla, and Carlo Carrà, published their manifesto, which called for a new art that would break away from traditional forms and capture the speed, motion, and energy of the modern world. In Russia, Futurism evolved well beyond its Italian origins, taking on a revolutionary social and political dimension. This development pushed Futurism in an even more fervent and extreme direction.

Some of the most fervent proponents of Futurism took its ideals to the extreme, believing that modern warfare was the ultimate expression of art due to its destructive power and capacity to reshape society. This radical view led many Futurists to become staunch supporters of Fascism, seeing in it a revolutionary force that aligned with their desire to break away from the past and create a new order. This alignment with fascist ideology and the glorification of war resulted in many Futurist artists losing their lives in the two world wars. The devastating impact of these conflicts, along with the discrediting of fascist ideals, caused the Futurist movement to fade away after World War II, leaving behind a complex legacy marked by both innovative artistic contributions and controversial political associations.

3 The Enduring Echoes

Futurism's legacy is a rich and intricate tapestry, woven from both visionary brilliance and controversial affiliations. Although the movement is indelibly marked by its association with Italian Fascism and Marinetti's later alignment with the fascist regime, its artistic and intellectual contributions extend far beyond these ties. The Futurists' early 20th-century fascination with technology, future, space, and industrialization fostered a fertile ground for imaginative exploration. Their aesthetics and conceptual innovations left an enduring mark on the art world, influencing a wide array of artistic practices throughout the 20th century, including Art Deco, Constructivism, Dadaism, and Surrealism. Furthermore, Futurism's impact extended into the 1980s, inspiring Retro-Futurism genres such as Cyberpunk and Steampunk.

KEY ARTISTS & THEIR ICONIC WORKS

Futurism rippled through various artistic movements, leaving a profound impact on the evolution of modern design. Art Deco, which emerged in the 1920s and 1930s, encapsulated the Futurist fascination with modernity and technology in its sleek, ornamental designs that celebrated progress and luxury. The dynamic forms and streamlined aesthetics of Art Deco reflected Futurist ideals, though with a more refined and commercially viable approach. Similarly, Constructivism, arising in Russia during the 1910s and 1920s, adopted Futurist themes of industrial materials and geometric abstraction to channel them into a vision of modern technology and socialist ideals. In contrast, Dadaism and Surrealism, which developed after World War I, engaged with Futurist concepts in more subversive ways. Dadaists, reacting against the mechanistic and dehumanizing aspects of modernity that Futurists had celebrated, embraced chaos and randomness, while Surrealists explored the unconsciousness and irrationality, extending the Futurist fascination with new and uncharted territories into the realm of the psychology and fantasy.

The 1980s saw a resurgence of Futurist influence through Retro-Futurism styles such as Cyberpunk and Steampunk, which echoed Futurist themes in their futuristic visions and nostalgic reinterpretations of industrial design. Both Cyberpunk's gritty, high-tech aesthetics and Steampunk's reimagined Victorian machinery reflect the enduring legacy of Futurism's celebration of technology and mechanization.

Notes:

1. Filippo Tommaso Marinetti (1876-1944), founder of the Futurist movement, outlined the core principles of Futurism in *Manifesto of Futurism* (1909). His radical advocacy for technology, violence, and speed as central themes in art influenced various avant-garde movements throughout the 20th century.

2. Ferruccio Busoni (1866-1924), an Italian composer and pianist, is best known for his work *Sketch of a New Esthetic of Music* (1907), where he advocated for innovation in musical composition, including the early concepts of electronic and atonal music. His theoretical ideas influenced later composers and movements such as Futurism and electronic music.

Umberto Boccioni
(1882-1916)

He is an influential Italian painter and sculptor who played a central role in the development of the Futurist movement. Boccioni was deeply inspired by the dynamism, energy, and technological advancements of the modern age, which he sought to capture in his work. His paintings and sculptures are characterized by a sense of movement and speed, often depicting the human figures and objects in a state of flux to convey the sensations of a rapidly changing world.

1. *Unique Forms of Continuity in Space* (1913)

Boccioni's work often explores the human figure in motion, and *Unique Forms of Continuity in Space* is one of his most famous sculptures. It depicts a striding figure that appears to be in motion, with its body fragmented and fluid, as if it is being shaped by the forces of speed and motion around it. The sculpture captures the essence of Futurist ideals, with its dynamic forms and celebration of the human figure as a machine-like entity.

Giacomo Balla
(1871-1958)

He is an Italian painter and a leading figure in the Futurist movement. Initially influenced by Pointillism and Divisionism, Balla's early works focused on capturing the effects of light and color. He became a founding member of the Futurist movement in 1910, embracing its emphasis on the dynamism and energy of modern life. Beyond painting, Balla also experimented with sculpture, design, and stage sets, consistently pushing the boundaries of visual expression to reflect the industrial and technological advances of the time.

2. *Dynamism of a Dog on a Leash* (1912)

Balla is a leading figure in Futurist painting, known for his depictions of movement and light. In this work *Dynamism of a Dog on a Leash*, he captured the rapid motion of a woman walking her dog, with the dog's legs, tail, and leash shown in multiple overlapping images to convey a sense of speed and dynamism. The painting exemplifies Balla's interest in capturing the energy and motion of the modern world.

Carlo Carrà
(1881-1966)

He is a prominent Italian painter and a key figure in the Futurist movement, as well as a later advocate of the metaphysical art movement. Initially influenced by the energy and dynamism of modern life, Carrà's works in the Futurist period celebrated movement, technology, and the industrialization of the early 20th century. His later works are known for their emphasis on the quiet, poetic aspects of reality, diverging from the aggressive dynamism of his earlier Futurist phase.

3. *The Funeral of the Anarchist Galli* (1910-1911)

Carrà is another prominent Futurist painter, known for his bold and dynamic compositions. This work depicts a chaotic street scene during the funeral of an anarchist, with the crowd shown in fragmented, angular forms that convey a sense of violence and unrest. The painting reflects the Futurist fascination with political and social upheaval, as well as their embrace of violence as a means of renewal.

Gino Severini
(1883-1966)

He is an Italian painter and a prominent member of the Futurist movement, known for his dynamic and rhythmic compositions that capture the essence of modern life. Severini's early works were influenced by Divisionism, but he turned to embrace Futurism after meeting its founder, Filippo Tommaso Marinetti, in 1910. His contributions to the movement are characterized by vivid use of color and focus on the themes of motion and speed.

4. *Armored Train in Action* (1915)

Severini enjoyed depicting the war and conflict. This work is a dynamic portrayal of a train speeding through the countryside, with soldiers firing their guns from the carriages. The fragmented forms and bold colors convey a sense of motion and energy, while also reflecting the Futurist's glorification of war as a purifying force.

Luigi Russolo
(1885-1947)

He is an Italian painter, composer, and an influential figure in the Futurist movement, best known for his pioneering work in the field of experimental sound art. Although he is often overshadowed by his contemporaries in the Futurist movement, Russolo made significant contributions to both visual and auditory art.

5. *The Revolt* (1911)

Russolo was known for his work on the Futurist concept of "noise music." In painting, *The Revolt* is one of his key works, depicting a chaotic and energetic scene of uprising. The painting's swirling forms and intense colors capture the Futurist spirit of rebellion and the breaking of traditional boundaries.

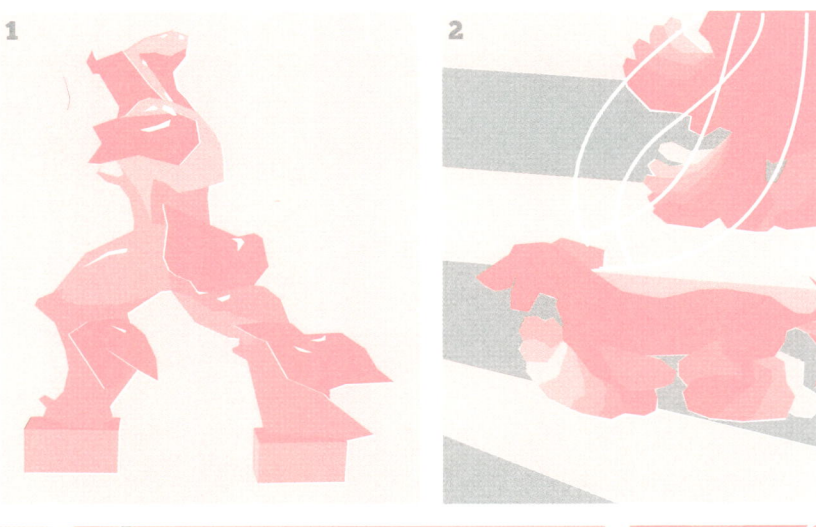

POP ART: A CELEBRATION OF CONSUMER CULTURE

After World War II, the Western world enjoyed an era of extraordinary wealth and stability, marked by the fast expansion of mass consumer culture. Economic recovery and technological breakthroughs fueled the rise of mass media. Television, radio, periodicals, and advertisements proliferated, spreading consumer culture and popular trends to households everywhere. In this atmosphere, the consumption patterns and lifestyles changed dramatically, with fashion, enjoyment, and entertainment emerging as the new social norms.

The art world was quick to capture these societal shifts. Even before World War II, mass production and consumer culture began to flourish alongside industrialization. Artists started to incorporate elements of popular culture into their work to reflect various aspects of industrial society. You have likely heard of the infamous 1917 piece **1** *Fountain,* a ceramic urinal purchased from a hardware store that influenced many later art forms. Henri-Robert-Marcel Duchamp[1] pioneered the idea of recognizing the inherent beauty in mass-produced objects, elevating them to the status of art and prompting both aesthetic contemplation and moral outrage in the visual arts. Long before Pop artists explored the world of brand logos, Edward Stuart Davis[2] was integrating images from logos, commercial signage, and modern packaging into his paintings. His 1924 works featuring **2** *Lucky Strike* cigarette boxes and **3** *Odol* mouthwash suggested a disposable culture, with advertising and brand symbols becoming sources of artistic inspiration, showcasing the close connection between art and everyday life. Furthermore, the famous Surrealist painter Salvador Dalí[3], after encountering American popular culture, praised comic strips for their profound expression of the public's psychological state and foresaw the immense potential of media in information dissemination.

However, Abstract Expressionism, the dominant form of art at the time, appeared to be at odds with the increasingly popular consumer culture. With its emphasis on individual expression and emotional catharsis, Abstract Expressionism's works were often esoteric and obscure, making them difficult for the general public to grasp and appreciate. In the context, the art world was in dire need of a new form of expression that better reflected and adapted to the environment of mass consumer culture. Naturally, Pop Art arose in the mid-20th century as a vibrant celebration of consumer culture and everyday objects. It boldly incorporated images of mass media, advertisements, and all kinds of consumer goods into its artistic creations, presenting the various phenomena of a consumer society in an accessible way. Pop Art not only pushes the boundaries of traditional fine art, but also challenges people's existing perceptions of art with its diverse forms of expression. Although this art style was controversial at the time, it marked a departure from the Abstract Expressionism that dominated the postwar art world, and could even be said to be an embrace of the new era.

In the 1980s, Pop Art enjoyed a renaissance. Pop Art in this period was not only a nostalgic tribute to the past, but also a powerful reaffirmation of the movement's enduring influence and creativity. It not only influenced traditional art fields such as painting and sculpture, but also expanded into a variety of fields such as film, music, and fashion, forming a crossover art phenomenon. With its unique charm and wide influence, Pop Art during this period has become an indispensable part of contemporary art history.

1 Defining

Pop Art, a revolutionary artistic movement, can be defined as a vibrant celebration of popular culture and the ordinary, often portrayed in a bold and colorful manner. The art movement rose to prominence in Britain in the late 1950s and early 1960s, and then flourished in the soil of the United States. It represented both a profound departure from traditional artistic conventions and an emphatic and enthusiastic celebration of pop culture and the commonplace, injecting unprecedented vigor and creativity into the art world.

One of the defining features of Pop Art is its rejection of the notion that art should be enigmatic or exclusive. Instead, it revels in the familiarity and relatability, often employing a touch of irreverence and humor. It bridges the gap between art and everyday life, making artistic expression accessible to a broader audience and enabling more viewers to connect with it. This art form challenges the elitism of high art by embracing the imagery and symbols of contemporary consumer culture. In Pop Art, everyday and mass-produced objects, such as canned goods, celebrity portraits, and comic strips, are elevated to the status of art. Artists transform these elements into bold, vibrantly colored paintings and sculptures, inviting viewers to rethink their meaning within the context of art.

Pop artists often employ reproducing and collage techniques to create works that recreate images and symbols from popular culture, reflecting their engagement with and critique of society. The monumental legacy of Pop Art continued to influence subsequent art, advertising, fashion, and society's perception of creativity and everyday objects. This movement demonstrated renewed vitality in the development of art in the 1980s, once again leaving a monumental impact.

2 Awakening Pop Art

The birth of the Pop Art movement is closely tied to cultural and social transformations, particularly the rise of mass consumer culture since the 1920s. This culture emerged early in the West, driven by the Industrial Revolution, technological advances, economic prosperity, and media proliferation, all of which contributed to its evolution. The Industrial Revolution significantly increased productivity, leading to the mass production of goods, making consumer items more plentiful and diverse. Concurrently, rising disposable incomes supported the widespread availability of consumer goods. Items ranging from TVs and cars to household appliances entered the homes of ordinary people, who began to pursue fashion, taste, and individuality. Consumer goods gradually became symbols of identity and status. Innovations in business models also spurred the development of mass consumer culture. For example, the emergence of self-service retail supermarkets, like [4]"Piggy Wiggly," revolutionized traditional shopping ways, making them more convenient and efficient. Additionally, the widespread use of credit cards provided people with more purchasing convenience, further fueling the popularity of consumer culture.

The mass media played a crucial role in the process. With the rise of television, radio, periodicals, and newspapers, information and advertising were disseminated more rapidly and widely than ever before. People were constantly exposed to various advertisements, images, and stories through the media. TV programs such as [5]*I Love Lucy* and other sitcoms attracted large audiences, showcasing the lifestyle and consumption habits of the middle class and subtly influencing viewers' consumer perceptions. In the mid-20th century, movies had become one of the important forms of entertainment, and the Hollywood film industry in the United States developed rapidly during this period, producing a large number of movies reflecting consumer culture and the American dream. The fashion, lifestyles, and consumer goods depicted in these films became objects of public imitation, serving as a form of "soft advertising" that stimulated consumers' desire. This, in turn, inadvertently promoted the rise of mass consumer culture.

[4]

The logo for Piggly Wiggly

[5]

American Television Sitcom *I Love Lucy*, 1951–1957.

As society evolves, art resonates with these changes in unique ways. In the mid-20th century, Abstract Expressionism was the dominant art movement. Most Abstract Expressionists were dedicated to creating art that delved into the subconscious, emphasizing core values such as spirituality, emotion, seriousness, intellectual sophistication, and authentic experience. Artists like Paul Jackson Pollock[4] didn't even use brushes for their paintings; instead, Pollock poured or splashed ordinary household paints onto large canvases spread out on the floor. His paintings lacked traditional composition, consisting instead of grids of color. Pollock explained his technique by saying, "The painting has a life of its own, and I try to let it come through." Their work often expressed reality metaphorically. For example, Robert Motherwell[5] created a series of more than 200 abstract oil paintings to allude to the deaths of individuals during the Spanish Civil War, using black-and-white imagery to express artistic solidarity with humanity. However, in the postwar West, as people gradually emerged from the shadow of the wars, they moved away from subjective spiritual fanaticism and began to embrace a life rich in material comforts. The lofty values of Abstract Expressionism started to clash with the growing materialism of mass consumer culture, prompting artists to seek new paths. Abstract Expressionism itself flourished with the publication of "Avant-Garde and Kitsch", and later the essay "Towards a Newer Laocoon" of Clement Greenberg[6] pushed the movement towards Minimalism. This progression led to an extreme purity of abstraction, which ultimately contributed to its decline.

Against this backdrop, Pop Art began to flourish, reflecting cultural shifts and psychological states with its unique perspective and expression. While Abstract Expressionism focused on individual emotional expression and the meaning and purpose of human existence from a personal standpoint, Pop Art diverged by emphasizing the social nature of emotion. Using techniques like repetition and collage, Pop artists highlighted the inner detachment of people within an industrial society, underscoring the inner emptiness in such a society. In this sense, Pop Art represented a higher level of pursuit—after breaking free from absolute social reality, it returned to critically engage with it. If Abstract Expressionism was the final flourish of modernist art, then Pop Art successfully achieved a postmodern transformation. Pop Art emerged both as a response to the changing landscape of postwar America and the broader Western world, and as a critical commentary on consumerism and mass media. Artists sought to capture the zeitgeist of their time by drawing on the images, symbols, and products of burgeoning consumer culture. They aimed to highlight the inner alienation of individuals within an industrial context and, in doing so, emphasized the nihilistic nature of such a society. Recognizing the power of mass media to shape public consciousness, Pop artists began incorporating media images into their works, constantly challenging the boundaries of traditional art.

3 The Birth of Pop Art

As mentioned earlier, the origins of Pop Art can be traced back to the 1950s. Influenced by the ever-changing cultural landscape of a consumer-driven society, artists sought new ways to engage with contemporary life. In the late 1940s, British artist [6]Eduardo Luigi Paolozzi[7], heavily influenced by Surrealism, began to create a set of highly inventive and tongue-in-cheek collages combining popular magazine covers, advertisements, cheesecake photographs. It is clear that his mind had absorbed the imagery of popular culture and applied it to art and design. Subsequently, in the mid-1950s, he created creative collages incorporating images of graphic machines, which again clearly pointed to these possible future changes. Subsequently, Richard Hamilton's 1956 poster design collage entitled "Just What Is It That Makes Today's Homes So Different, So Appealing?" is a key point in Pop Art that must be mentioned. The work brought together a number of images and objects that would soon be explored by others, including a large number of household objects and ancient artifacts that would later be used as source material in Pop Art. Later, in a private letter a year later, Hamilton listed the qualities needed for the new Pop Art, but it is clear that later Pop creations have evolved beyond these basic rules and regulations.

After gaining ground in Britain, Pop Art began to flourish in the United States, where mass culture was prevalent, particularly in New York City. Many artists started creating "everyday" art, drawing caricatures, street signs, light bulbs, and objects found on supermarket shelves, gradually gaining attention in the art world. It was in 1962 that American Pop artists gained significant notoriety through the interest of galleries in the United States. Galleries such as the [7]Ferus Gallery in Los Angeles and the Sidney Janis Gallery in New York showcased the works of Pop artists, solidifying the movement and introducing it to a global audience. These galleries featured artists such as Andy Warhol, Roy Lichtenstein, Claes Oldenburg[8], and Robert Indiana, among others.

Arguably the most renowned figure in Pop Art, Andy Warhol is known worldwide for immortalizing everyday consumer products and celebrities. In 1962, he made a significant mark by exhibiting his iconic *Campbell's Soup Cans* at the Ferus Gallery, marking his West Coast debut in Pop Art. The same year, he showcased his paintings at the Stable Gallery in New York, featuring Campbell's Soup Cans, Coke bottles, Marilyn Monroe, and Elvis Presley. Warhol's art was characterized by relentless reproduction, aiming to strip away meaning with the statement, "The more you look at the same exact thing, the more the meaning goes away, and the better and emptier you feel." Concurrently, he embraced new techniques like screen printing, exploring the variations that arose from different pressures, angles, and conditions of the squeegee. This method not only suited his artistic vision but also resonated with the culture of the 1960s—fast, simple, cheap, and mass-produced.

Roy Lichtenstein, another prominent figure in Pop Art, pioneered the transformation of comic book imagery into iconic art accessible to the general public. Recognizing the potency of war comics' imagery, he briefly commented on contemporary political and military developments. The 1950s and 1960s were marked by a complex political landscape in the United States, entangled in the Cold War and escalating involvements in conflicts like those in North Korea and Vietnam. Lichtenstein's paintings, such as *Balm*, exhibited at the Sidney Janis Gallery, aptly reflected these real-world concerns. In addition, Claes Oldenburg further exemplified the spirit of Pop Art by integrating pop culture references into his creations, notably through oversized sculptures of everyday objects. Together, these artists blurred the boundaries between art and everyday life, reshaping the artistic landscape. Pop Art's accessibility allowed it to swiftly establish itself as one of the fastest-spreading movements in art history, making it become a cultural phenomenon and enduring artistic movement that continues to influence art and design today.

4 Pop Art Revival

Pop Art's signature fascination with consumer culture and the omnipresence of everyday objects became a wellspring of inspiration for graphic designers. They leveraged the movement's playbook to infuse their work with a playful irony and a fascination with the mundane. In the world of advertising and branding, this translated into campaigns that transformed familiar products into icons of artistry. Richard Hamilton, a pivotal figure in the Pop Art movement, exemplified this approach through his innovative artistic collage techniques. His iconic artwork, *Just What Is It That Makes Today's Homes So Different, So Appealing?*, masterfully combined images from magazines and advertisements to comment on the allure of consumer goods in postwar Britain. Hamilton's collage not only set the stage for the Pop Art movement but also encapsulated its core characteristics: a celebration of consumerism, a critique of materialism, and a fascination with the visual language of popular culture. In many ways, Hamilton's work became a bridge between fine art and graphic design, where the blurring of these boundaries would continue to evolve and shape the visual landscape for decades to come.

Therefore, we can say that one of the most striking and enduring takeaways from the Pop Art revival of the '80s is the elevation of logos

I was a Rich Man's Plaything, Eduardo Luigi Paolozzi, 1947.

Cover of *Ferus*, Gagosian Gallery, 2002.

POP ART
From 1950s To 1960s

The '80s saw a resurgence of imagery drawn from popular culture, including references to celebrities, comic books, and consumer goods. Designers reimagined these cultural touchstones, creating a visual language that was at once familiar and subversive. Magazine covers, album art, and movie posters were adorned with vivid, larger-than-life portrayals of pop icons, exuding an air of both reverence and irreverence. Moreover, the revival of Pop Art ushered in a renewed focus on the democratization of art. It celebrated the notion that art could be accessible to all, and this ethos extended to the world of graphic design. The '80s graphic designers, inspired by Pop Art, sought to bridge the gap between high art and commercial design, redefining the boundaries of creativity.

and slogans into the realm of high art. This transformation of familiarity corporate symbols and brand logos into the central focal points of graphic compositions was nothing short of revolutionary. It celebrated the power of advertising, consumerism, and mass production, recognizing these elements not merely as commercial tools but as profound reflections on contemporary culture. This embrace of logos and slogans extended far beyond the realm of fine art. It infiltrated advertising, fashion, interior design, and even architecture. Logos became fashion statements, emblazoned on clothing and accessories, transforming brand loyalty into a form of self-expression. Interior designers integrated iconic logos into home decor, blurring the lines between consumerism and domesticity. Architectural forms took cues from the bold and graphic nature of Pop Art, infusing buildings with a sense of playful irony and contemporary relevance.

It is worth mentioning that color played a pivotal role in the Pop Art revival of the '80s. Vibrant and audacious, color palettes drew from the Pop Art tradition, showing bright primaries and bold contrasts to grab attention. This color-centric approach wasn't limited to print; it spilled over into fashion, interior design, and even architecture, transforming the visual landscape of the entire decade. The influence of Pop Art's vibrant color schemes extended far and wide, with artists like Andy Warhol, known for his vivid and repetitive use of color in works like *Campbell's Soup Cans* and *Marilyn Diptych*, serving as a beacon of inspiration for designers and artists alike. Warhol's unabashed embrace of color not only defined an era but also reinforced the enduring impact of Pop Art's chromatic exuberance on the creative world.

KEY ARTISTS & THEIR ICONIC WORKS

Andy Warhol
(1928-1987)

He is one of the most renowned figures in Pop Art, found new avenues for his artistic career as the movement emerged. He famously remarked, "The artificial fascinates me, the bright and the shiny." As Pop Art roared to life in the United States, Warhol not only participated in its explosion but swiftly rose to become its most celebrated artist. His Pop Art creations vividly portrayed his fascination with celebrity culture and consumerism, often replicated images to mirror the repetitive nature of labor, production, and marketing during that era. Meanwhile, Warhol's mastery extended to new techniques, notably screen printing. While he had previously used methods like slide projection onto canvas, screen printing offered him a quicker method to achieve similar effects in just minutes. Beyond his prominence in Pop painting, Warhol actively explored sculpture, film, and various other artistic disciplines, using each medium to express his creative vision.

1. *Campbell's Soup Cans* (1961-1962)
This series marked Andy Warhol's pioneering venture into Pop Art and remains among his most iconic contributions to the movement. Featuring 32 distinct varieties of Campbell's soup, these paintings challenged traditional notions of high art by transforming everyday objects into artistic subjects. Each canvas meticulously replicated a soup can, emphasizing the repetitive and mass-produced character of consumer goods.

2. *Marilyn Diptych* (1962)
In this iconic work, Warhol proposed a creative treatment. He reproduced a photograph of Marilyn Monroe as a star, showing perfect skin, hair, flesh, and lip gloss to make her look as much like a manmade product as possible. In contrast, the right side displays a fading grayscale image, symbolizing the ephemeral nature of fame. This juxtaposition suggests a contrast between Monroe's colorful public persona and her fading private self, hinting at deeper societal themes. Warhol, however, maintained his stance of separating art from personal meaning, refusing to attribute specific intentions to his subject choices.

3. *Brillo Boxes* (1964)
This was Andy Warhol's exploration into sculpture, a classic example of his fascination with consumer goods. Due to his preference for visible everyday items, Warhol planned to use screen printing on plywood boxes. These sculptures were nearly indistinguishable from actual Brillo boxes, blurring the boundaries between art and everyday objects. He also prompted viewers to question the value and authenticity of art.

4. *The Factory*
Warhol's studio, known as "The Factory" to emphasise the artist's assembly-line approach, is a work of art in its own right. It was a center of creativity and experimentation, bringing together artists, musicians, and celebrities. *The Factory* is as much a part of Warhol's legacy as Warhol's personal work, and embodies the collaborative spirit of the Pop Art movement.

Roy Lichtenstein
(1923-1997)

Renowned for his comic book-style paintings, Roy Lichtenstein's work is characterized by their use of Ben-Day dots, bold lines, and primary colors. Like many other artists contributed to the sensitivity of popular and mass culture art, Lichtenstein initially explored Abstract Expressionism in a mundane and dissatisfied manner. His breakthrough came in June 1961 when he painted *Look Mickey*, based on a Mickey Mouse cartoon, triggering a realization. From then on, he continuously utilized imagery from war comics to respond to and critique the complexities of politics and military affairs of the time, and aptly and humorously satirized the reality, producing a series of highly distinctive works.

5. *Drowning Girl* (1963)
In this work, Lichtenstein explored themes of love and melodrama. The central character, a distressed woman, declares, "I Don't Care! I'd Rather Sink—Than Call Brad For Help!" Lichtenstein's depiction of emotional turmoil through the lens of a comic book aesthetic is both humorous and thought-provoking.

6. *Wham!* (1963)
The work was created by Lichtenstein from an image in the 1962 DC Comics *All-American Warrior*. *Wham!* is perhaps Lichtenstein's most famous work. It depicts a fighter jet firing a missile, capturing the drama and action of comic book art. The use of bold primary colors and onomato-poeic text ("Wham!") are signature elements of Lichtenstein's style.

Richard Hamilton
(1922-2011)

He is a renowned British artist often hailed as the founding figure of Pop Art. His multifaceted career spanned painting, collage, photography, and film, making significant contributions to the evolution of Pop Art. Infused with humor and irony, Hamilton adeptly drew inspiration from everyday life, dismantling and reassembling images and symbols from popular culture to forge innovative visual narratives. Known for delving into themes of consumerism, media culture, sex, and politics, he used distinctive artistic techniques and visual effects to provoke profound reflections on contemporary society.

7. *Just What Is It That Makes Today's Homes So Different, So Appealing?* (1956)
This iconic collage was considered one of the earliest works of Pop Art and a seminal piece of Hamilton's career. The collage features a male bodybuilder holding a lollipop surrounded by images of various consumer products and pop culture. Each element is carefully cropped from magazines and adverts, highlighting the prevalence of consumerism in everyday life. The work satirises the appeal of consumer goods and the obsession with material wealth in postwar Britain.

8. *Swingeing London 67* (1968-1969)
Hamilton's fascination with celebrities and media comes to the fore in this diptych. It features two photographs of Mick Jagger, the frontman of the Rolling Stones, taken during his 1967 trial for drug possession. One image captures Jagger in the courtroom, while the other shows him seated in a police car. Hamilton's choice to incorporate these photographs from newspapers underscores the media's influence on public perception and celebrity iconography. The use of screen printing, a hallmark technique of Pop Art, enhances the visual intensity and contemporary relevance of the artwork.

Robert Indiana
(1928-2018)

He is an American artist closely associated with the Pop Art movement, celebrated for his bold and iconic use of text and symbols in his artwork. Robert Indiana's artistic journey began in 1954 upon moving to New York City, where he integrated elements from mass media, popular culture, and commercial advertising into his works, imbuing them with a poetic and narrative quality. His artworks are characterized by striking graphic compositions that often feature simple and clear motifs such as "EAT," "HUG," and "LOVE." These letters and numbers not only are easily comprehensible but also possess a profound impact within the realm of art, acquiring new meanings while simultaneously subverting their original contexts.

9. *The American Dream* (1961-1962)
This series of paintings by Indiana explores the concept of the American Dream through a combination of text and image. Each painting has a central word or phrase, such as "EAT," "DIE," or "TILT," surrounded by symbols and numbers. The works invite viewers to consider the cultural and social significance of these words and phrases in the context of the 1960s American society. Indiana's fascination with language and its impact on culture is central to this series.

10. *LOVE* (1965)
Undoubtedly, Robert Indiana's most famous and iconic work *LOVE* is a simple yet powerful work that has become a recognized symbol of love and solidarity. The word "LOVE" is represented by a bold capital letter with the "O" tilted 45 degrees to the right. The message of love is amplified by the use of bright colors, especially deep red and blue. Reproduced in various forms, including sculpture, paintings, and prints, *Love* has become an enduring symbol of the Pop Art movement. Indiana's exploration of language and its emotional impact is evident in this work.

OP ART: THE NEW FRONTIER OF VISUAL PERCEPTION

Following the explosive rise of Pop Art in the 1950s, a new artistic movement began to emerge in the Western world—one that would push the boundaries of visual perception and challenge traditional notions of art. This movement, known as Op Art, was driven by rapid advancements in science and technology that were reshaping society. Op Art focused on creating visual experiences that played with perception and engaged the viewer's sense of reality. Utilizing precise geometric shapes, vibrant colors, and optical illusions, Op Art produced striking effects that appeared to move or pulsate, transforming the passive act of viewing into an active, participatory experience. This marked a departure from traditional forms of art, inviting viewers to experience a heightened awareness of visual phenomena and reflecting the era's fascination with the possibilities of the modern age and the expanding boundaries of human perception.

Op Art's emphasis on visual phenomena also responded to the shifting cultural landscape of the 1960s. The movement paralleled the era's growing interest in perception and consciousness, mirroring contemporary explorations in psychology and the burgeoning psychedelic art[1] that questioned and expanded the limits of human experience. Op Art not only reflected these cultural shifts but also influenced them, as its immersive, almost hypnotic work resonated with the period's exploration of altered states of mind and reality.

As a result, Op Art became a significant artistic force that captivated audiences and left a lasting impact on visual culture. Its integration of science and art, focus on viewer interaction, and challenge to the conventional boundaries of painting made it a key movement of the 20th century. This section explores the origins and development of Op Art, its key figures and works, and its enduring influence on both the art world and popular culture in the 1980s.

1 Defining

Op Art, short for "Optical Art," is a style of visual art that uses optical illusions. It emerged in the 1960s as part of a broader movement that sought to explore the scientific, perceptual, and psychological aspects of visual experience, attempting to demonstrate that rigorous scientific design could also activate the optic nerve, evoking and combining visual imagery through visual action to achieve an artistic experience as moving as that of traditional painting. Artists associated with Op Art were fascinated by the potential of the visual field to create dynamic, shifting experiences for the viewer. Unlike traditional figurative art, which focuses on depicting realistic scenes or objects, Op Art is purely abstract and relies on the precise arrangement of line, form, and color to engage the viewer's eye and mind for a positive visual experience.

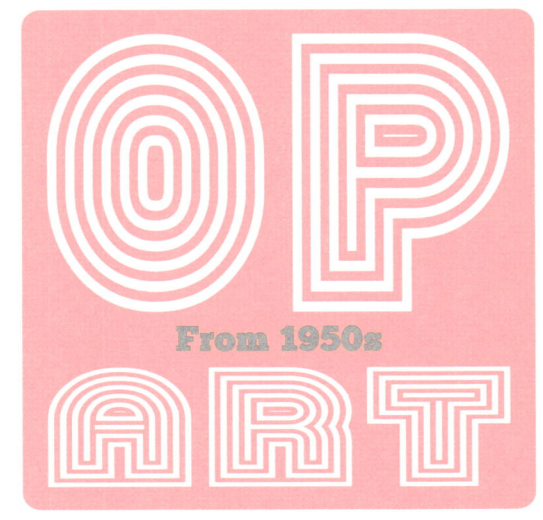

Op Art can be described as a mind game that challenges human vision, thus leading the viewer into a world of ever-changing illusions. Op artists create dynamic visual effects through the use of repetition, contrast, and precise geometric forms, often employing black and white or contrasting colors to enhance the sense of depth, motion, and dimension on a flat surface. These effects are achieved by carefully placing and arranging elements that manipulate how the eye interprets visual information to create illusions of light, shadow, and motion. Op Art compositions often feature gridlike patterns, concentric circles, and parallel lines that shift and change depending on the viewer's position and distance from the artwork.

A hallmark of Op Art is its ability to create a sense of instability and disorientation. The viewer's perception is constantly challenging as the brain tries to make sense of the conflicting visual cues. This intentional confusion invites the viewer to actively engage with the artwork, making Op Art not just a visual experience but a psychological one as well. The use of optical illusions to create dynamic visual effects aligns Op Art with the scientific exploration of visual perception, linking the movement to the fields of psychology and neurology, where the brain processes visual information are studied.

2 Exploring the Potential of Art

Op Art traces its roots in various artistic explorations of the early 20th century, particularly in Constructivism, Bauhaus, and Futurism, where artists became fascinated by the interaction between form, function, and perception. The movement truly gained momentum in the 1960s, when artists began to systematically explore the effects of color and geometric forms on the viewer's perception.

In the 1930s and 1940s, artists like Victor Vasarely began to explore the potential of geometric abstraction. Vasarely, often regarded as the father of Op Art, used simple forms and contrasting colors to create dynamic, optical effects. His early experiments with abstraction and geometry set the stage for what would later become the defining characteristics of Op Art. Other influential figures, such as Josef Albers, also played a crucial role in the movement's development by exploring the interaction of colors and the illusion of depth and movement through precise arrangements of shapes.

The 1960s marked the formal emergence of Op Art as a distinct movement. In 1965, the Museum of Modern Art in New York held an exhibition titled "The Responsive Eye," which showcased works by artists like Bridget Riley, Richard Anuszkiewicz, and Jesús Rafael Soto[2], among others. This exhibition was a pivotal moment for Op Art, as it brought widespread attention to the movement and its exploration of visual perception. The works displayed and highlighted the potential of geometric forms and optical illusions to create interactive visual experiences, captivating audiences with their dynamic effects. The public's fascination with the mind-bending illusions and the way these artworks seemed to move and vibrate cemented Op Art's place in the art world.

During its peak, Op Art became widely popular and influential, extending beyond the fine arts into fashion, graphic design, and popular culture. The movement's emphasis on optical effects and visual perception resonated with the

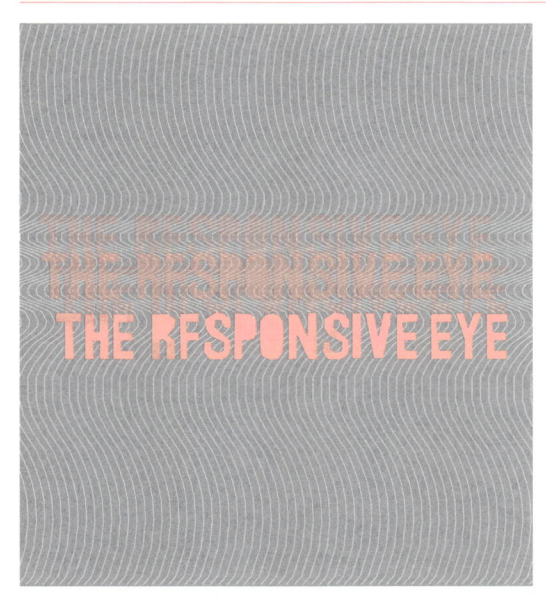

Exhibition Catalogue of *The Responsive Eye*, The Museum of Modern Art (MoMA), 1965

broader cultural context of the 1960s, a period characterized by experimentation, innovation, and a fascination with altered states of consciousness. Op Art's bold patterns and striking visual effects were adopted in various media, from clothing and textiles to album covers and advertisements, further blurring the lines between high art and commercial design. This period of Op Art's development demonstrated its versatility and its ability to engage with audiences on multiple levels, both aesthetically and intellectually.

As the movement progressed, artists continued to push the boundaries of optical illusion and visual perception. Advances in technology allowed for more complex and refined techniques, leading to a deeper exploration of how visual stimuli affect the viewer's perception. The development of computer graphics and digital media in the later decades provided new tools for Op Art practitioners, enabling them to create even more intricate patterns and optical effects. This evolution of Op Art showcases the movement's adaptability and its ongoing relevance in contemporary art, as artists continue to explore the intersection of science, technology, and visual experience.

3 Art Illusions in the 1980s

Op Art experienced a notable revival in the 1980s, largely driven by a renewed interest in visual experimentation and the expanding capabilities of digital technology. This period saw a resurgence of the optical and perceptual principles that defined the original movement, as artists and designers began to explore new ways to engage viewers through illusion and visual effects. The advent of digital tools allowed for greater precision and complexity in creating optical illusions, enabling a fresh wave of creativity that blended traditional Op Art techniques with contemporary technology. This fusion led to a dynamic reinterpretation of Op Art, where the movement's core principles were expanded to the digital realm.

One of the most significant aspects of Op Art's revival in the 1980s was its integration into various forms of visual culture, including graphic design, fashion, and music videos. The bold, eye-catching patterns and illusions of Op Art perfectly aligned with the decade's aesthetics, characterized by its vibrant colors, geometric patterns, and experimental spirit. Designers drew inspiration from Op Art's emphasis on optical effects, using its principles to create striking visual content that captured the energy and dynamism of the 1980s. This cross-disciplinary influence demonstrated the movement's adaptability and its resonance with contemporary audiences, making it a prominent feature in the visual landscape of the time.

Moreover, the 1980s also saw Op Art intersecting with the burgeoning field of computer graphics. Artists began to experiment with digital technology to create more complex and refined optical effects, pushing the boundaries of what was possible within the medium. The precision and versatility offered by digital tools allowed for a greater exploration of the movement's foundational concepts, such as repetition, contrast, and geometric abstraction. This technological advancement facilitated the creation of intricate patterns and illusions that would have been challenging, if not impossible, to achieve using traditional methods. As a result, Op Art in the 1980s took on a new life, evolving to embrace the digital age and setting the stage for further innovations in visual art.

In addition to its aesthetics and technological developments, the revival of Op Art in the 1980s was also linked to a cultural nostalgia for the 1960s, a decade known for its bold experimentation and radical approaches to art and design. The revival of psychedelic art, which shares similarities with Op Art in its use of vivid colors and swirling patterns, also contributed to this renewed interest. The combination of these elements created a unique visual style that appealed to a generation looking for a sense of continuity with the past while embracing the possibilities of the future. This blend of nostalgia and innovation not only rekindled interest in Op Art but also highlighted its enduring influence on contemporary visual culture.

Overall, the 1980s revival of Op Art marked a significant period of growth and transformation for the movement. By incorporating new technologies, expanding into various media, and resonating with cultural trends of the time, Op Art not only re-established its relevance but also laid the groundwork for future developments in visual art. This era of revival underscored the movement's ability to adapt and evolve, proving that Op Art's exploration of perception and illusion remains a powerful and compelling force in the world of art and design.

Notes:

1. Psychedelic art, emerged in the 1960s and characterized by vivid, surreal imagery, vibrant colors, and intricate patterns, often intended to evoke or replicate the mind-altering experiences induced by hallucinogenic drugs like LSD. Influenced by countercultural movements, its visual style reflects a blend of Surrealism, Abstract Expressionism, and Pop Art. Artists such as Victor Moscoso and Peter Max played pivotal roles in the development of this art form, which became closely associated with music, poster design, and underground culture. Psychedelic art's impact extends into contemporary digital art, animation, and graphic design.

2. Jesús Rafael Soto (1923–2005), a Venezuelan artist and sculptor, is renowned for his pioneering work in kinetic art and optical illusions. His exploration of movement, perception, and viewer interaction is exemplified in works such as *Penetrable* (1967), where viewers are invited to physically engage with the artwork. Soto's emphasis on the relationship between art and movement placed him at the forefront of the Op Art and kinetic art movements, making him a key figure in the evolution of modern abstract art.

KEY ARTISTS & THEIR ICONIC WORKS

Victor Vasarely
(1906-1997)

He is often regarded as the father of Op Art. His work is characterized by their geometric precision and innovative use of color to create complex optical effects. Vasarely's background in both painting and graphic design influenced his approach to visual art, leading to a career marked by a constant exploration of form and color. His creations often feel like they are in motion, reflecting his commitment to blending art with visual science.

1. *Zebra* (1938)
Vasarely created this iconic piece early in his career, using black and white stripes to produce an illusion of depth and motion akin to the stripes of a zebra. Although the first version of this artwork predates the formal conception of Op Art by 30 years, it is widely recognized as part of the movement. The final version of *Zebra* was completed in 1965. This work can be seen as a study in shape, contrast, and optical illusion. By choosing the zebra as his subject, Vasarely effectively demonstrated one of the earliest explorations of Op Art, with the zebra's curved stripes creating a dynamic illusion of motion that engages the viewer's perception.

2. *Vega-Nor* (1969)
Vasarely's subjects are often inspired by nature, which provides him with a wealth of optical illusions and emotional responses, as seen in works like *Vega*. Many of his pieces are identified by the term "Vega," but to distinguish between them, he included additional designations such as "Nor" alongside numbering. This particular work is one of his later creations and exemplifies his mastery of the Op Art style, utilizing geometric shapes and vibrant colors to create striking optical effects.

Bridget Riley
(1931-)

She is one of the most celebrated figures in the Op Art movement. Her work is renowned for their intricate patterns and optical effects that play with visual perception. Riley's early exposure to the works of modernist painters and her fascination with the interplay of light and color led her to develop a distinctive style that continues to captivate audiences. Riley's meticulous approach to creating her optical illusions reflects her deep understanding of visual perception and form. Her art invites viewers to engage actively, challenging them to experience a dynamic interaction between the artwork and their own perception.

3. *Movement in Squares* (1961)
This work features a grid of squares that progressively distort as they move from one corner to the other. The pattern creates an optical illusion of motion and depth as the squares appear to warp and bend. It demonstrates her mastery in creating visual dynamism through precise, repetitive patterns. This piece is a classic example of Riley's exploration of geometric abstraction and her interest in how shapes can manipulate perception.

4. *Blaze* (1964)
This work features a series of diagonal lines that create a pulsating effect. The pattern creates an optical illusion of motion and depth as the squares appear to warp and bend. This work exemplifies Riley's ability to evoke kinetic energy and movement through simple, yet dynamic, line patterns.

Josef Albers
(1888-1976)

He is a German-born artist and educator whose work and teachings had a profound impact on modern art and design. His *Homage to the Square* series is a cornerstone of his exploration of color theory and its effects on visual perception. Albers' work reflects his deep understanding of the interaction between colors and forms. He was not just an artist but also a passionate educator who influenced generations of artists through his teaching at the Bauhaus and later at Yale University. His rigorous approach to color and form is both analytical and deeply creative, inviting viewers to experience the subtle complexities of color interactions.

5. *Homage to the Square Series* (1950-1976)
This series consists of paintings featuring nested squares in various color combinations. The subtle variations in color and arrangement create optical effects that alter the viewer's perception of depth and color. Also, this series is fundamental in understanding color theory and its effects on visual perception. His work influenced the development of Op Art by highlighting how color interactions can create optical illusions.

Julian Stanczak
(1928-2017)

He is a leading figure in the Op Art movement. His work is known for its vibrant use of color and geometric precision, creating dynamic visual experiences that explore the boundaries of perception. Stanczak's early career as a painter was influenced by his background in design and his interest in visual phenomena. His work often feels alive, as if it is constantly shifting and evolving, engaging viewers in a visual dialogue.

6. *Accumulative* (1975)
The artwork features a series of closely packed, undulating vertical lines that seem to vibrate and shift as the viewer moves around it. Stanczak employs a technique that involves layering colors in such a way that they seem to interact and blend optically, this is a hallmark of his works. By layering squares of different sizes changing angles, the interplay creates a dynamic visual illusion, where the squares seem to move, bounce, and create a shimmering effect.

Richard Anuszkiewicz
(1930-2020)

He is a prominent American artist and one of the leading figures in the Op Art movement. He often used simple geometric shapes, such as squares, circles, and lines, to create complex visual effects. By manipulating color relationships and patterns, he created artworks that seem to vibrate, pulsate, or shift as the viewer moves around them. His paintings are often described as "color constructions," where color itself becomes the primary subject of the artwork.

7. *Magenta Square Series* (1950-1978)
This series of works is a hypnotic composition featuring the illusion of oscillating motion through contrasting color relationships. Anuszkiewicz explored the interaction between color and form through a series of concentric squares in varying shades of magenta, pink, and blue. The squares are arranged in a way that makes them appear to pulsate and shift, creating a vibrant, almost shimmering effect. The use of contrasting colors and the alignment of the radiation enhance the optical illusion of motion and depth, making the artwork seem to vibrate with energy.

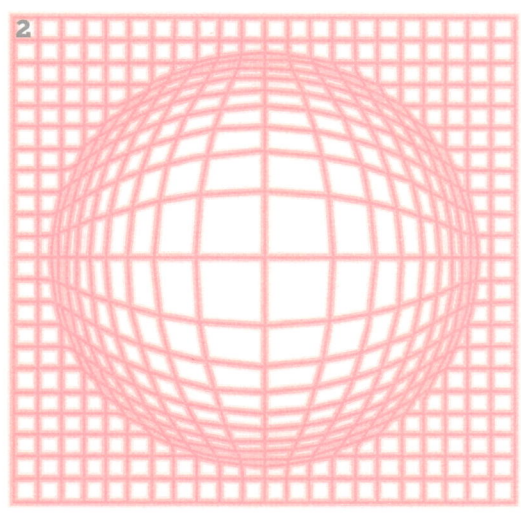

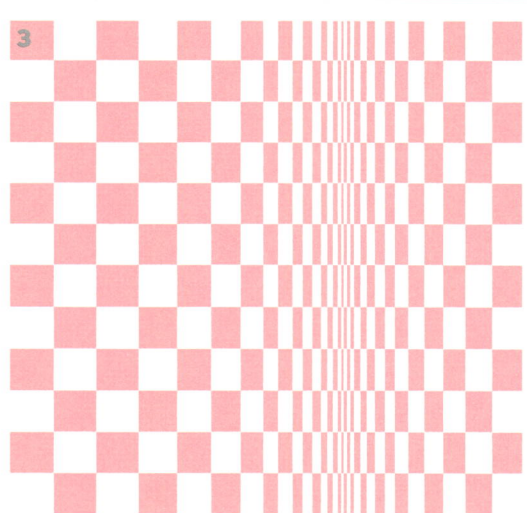

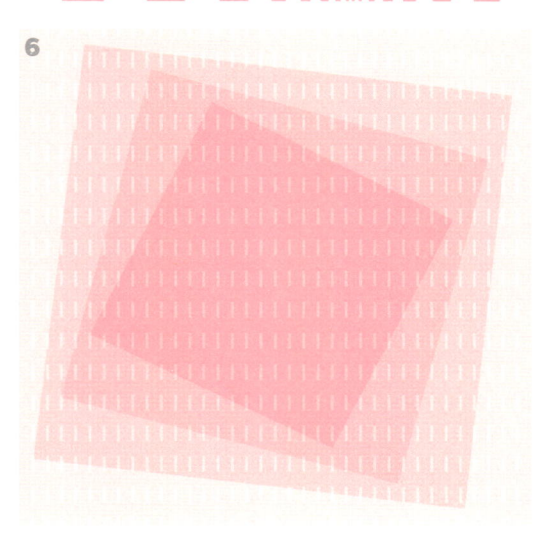

FROM RADICAL DESIGN TO MEMPHIS MAGIC: IMAGINATION OF AVANT-GARDE DESIGN

The post-World War II era was pivotal in cementing Italy's place in the global design arena. American economic aid significantly boosted Italy's recovery efforts, and the Italian government vigorously supported industrial production, expanding operations and guiding the country toward comprehensive industrialization, which reached its zenith in the late 1950s and early 1960s. During this period, architectural design made notable strides, rapidly addressing basic needs with the proliferation of public facilities and new housing. Over a decade of reconstruction led to a surge in the mass production of consumer goods, elevating living standards and making Italy one of the leading exporters of the time. As a consumer society emerged, the social structure shifted from production-driven to consumption-focused with increasingly diverse demands and consumption methods. Consequently, the design field, closely linked to consumer goods, began to spark dissatisfaction with the standardized, austere International Style[1], giving rise to a rebellious spirit in Italian design.

Designer Walter Dorwin Teague[2], in a 1950 article for the British magazine *Design*, described the postwar period as a springtime for Italy's development, with new design ideas emerging alongside the recovery and growth of the industrial economy. He highlighted a significant characteristic of postwar Italian design: its vitality and the relentless search for new paths. Concurrently, countries like the UK and the US saw a surge in Pop design trends. Influenced by Pop design, the Italian design community initiated a movement against largescale industrial production and "technical chic," known as Radical Design or Anti-Design. This movement first emerged in architectural design and then spread to other artistic fields, becoming a deeply influential trend. Consistent with the Italian style, this radical design period was primarily driven by small studios, particularly in the field of home design. Notable representatives include Alessandro Mendini, Ettore Sottsass, Superstudio[3], and Archizoom. These artists and studios aimed to challenge mainstream design by altering proportions and scales and drawing from historical styles like Art Deco and Pop Art to showcase a unique artistic character.

As the Radical Design movement progressed, Ettore Sottsass founded the Memphis Group in the early 1980s, significantly influencing the design styles of the time. The Memphis style became one of the dominant graphic design trends of the 1980s. The Memphis Group's design philosophy was heavily influenced by the Radical Design movement, incorporating new ideas and elements. They targeted the rationalization and stagnation of traditional Italian design, seeking to expand contemporary design's visual vocabulary by integrating new elements into their work. Boldly using various design elements, such as colors, shapes, and lines, they created stunning visual effects. Their work not only possessed strong artistic appeal but also demonstrated the limitless possibilities of design. The Memphis Group's design philosophy and practices profoundly impacted subsequent graphic design, becoming a milestone in design history.

From Italian Radical Design to the magic of Memphis, we witness the designers' continuous exploration and innovation amid significant social changes. Through their wisdom and talent, they presented us with design works that resonated with the times. These works enriched our visual experiences and highlighted the enduring charm and power of design.

1 Defining

Radical Design and the Memphis Group are two highly influential movements in design history, or rather, two pivotal periods in Italian design history that played crucial roles in driving design innovation and development. In the mid-20th century, as Italy experienced economic recovery and cultural prosperity, designers began to deeply reflect on traditional design concepts and actively explore new design ideas.

Radical Design emerged in the late 1960s, initially gaining traction in architectural design before influencing other fields. This rebellious and era-defining movement opposed functionalism and traditional aesthetics, instead embracing personalized and emotional expressions. The movement was primarily carried out by small Italian studios, with notable groups such as Alessandro Mendini's Alchymia Group, which pursued constant change in design through collages of various shapes and vibrant colors, liberating themselves from the constraints of mass production. Another leading figure in Radical Design was Ettore Sottsass, whose playful, anti-industrial mechanization approach propelled the movement to its peak. His establishment of the Memphis Group in the early 1980s profoundly influenced design styles of that era, nearly reshaping the entire design landscape of the 1980s. Alongside these prominent figures, numerous radical groups and individual designers emerged in Italy, such as Superstudio, [1-2]Studio 65[4], and Archizoom, reflecting on and critiquing social conditions while redefining the relationship between design, art, and society.

Building on the Radical Design movement, the Memphis Group further expanded the boundaries of design. Founded by Ettore Sottsass in Milan in 1981, the Memphis Group was an avant-garde design collective known for their whimsical and irreverent designs that broke from tradition. Their furniture and product designs not only inherited the rebellious spirit of Radical Design but also made bold breakthroughs in design concepts and practices. The group's use of color was particularly striking, boldly breaking the conventional design rule of using no more than three colors. They utilized bright and vivid hues like yellow, green, and pink, creating strong

1

Bocca sofa, Studio 65, 1970.

2

Capitello Chair, Studio 65, 1971.

visual impacts that quickly attracted market attention. The use of various geometric decorative elements was another hallmark of Memphis style. Geometric shapes such as triangles, circles, rectangles, polka dots, and wavy lines, as well as irregular shapes, made their designs lively and humorous. The bold and often clashing colors and patterns created a unique and engaging visual language. The design philosophy of the Memphis Group quickly spread and had a profound impact on graphic design styles of the time, almost reshaping the entire graphic design landscape of the 1980s.

In summary, Radical Design and the Memphis Group made a lasting impact on design history. Their rebellious spirit fueled innovation and development, highlighting the boundless possibilities of design. Even today, their philosophies and practices continue to inspire and motivate designers to explore new frontiers and push the boundaries of creativity.

2 Origins of Radical Design

After World War II, European countries faced the daunting task of rebuilding. Fortunately, with support from the Marshall Plan, Europe's economy recovered swiftly, entering a new phase of comprehensive industrialization. During this period, industrial expansion and development reached unprecedented peaks. Particularly in Italy, industrial progress was notable, with significant increases in industrial output and exports. To enhance production efficiency, Italy began adopting the "Fordism"[5] production line model from the United States. This method emphasized standardization and mass production, leading to increased product quantity and significantly reduced costs. With expanded production scales, Italy saw the rise of mass markets, making consumer goods more accessible and affordable. This laid a solid foundation for Italy's export trade, making it one of the leading export nations of the time. Alongside mass production of consumer goods, a consumer society emerged, where consumption became dominant and diversified. To meet these demands, consumer goods began to diversify in design, functionality, and materials, becoming richer and more diverse. Design played a crucial role in this development, shaping Italian products into popular examples of International Style. Characterized by simplicity, modernity, and functionality, this style maintained a consistent tone of standardization and detachment. Italian designers began to grow weary of this approach and sought revolutionary changes.

As the consumer society flourished, corresponding political shifts occurred. Despite the rapid economic growth in mid-1960s Italy, inflation became increasingly severe. While wages stagnated, prices continued to rise, intensifying pressure on ordinary citizens. Furthermore, the modernization drive left many traditional artisan workshops struggling to adapt, leading to unemployment and displacement among artisans. Against this backdrop, the New Left emerged in the 1960s. They fiercely criticized old systems, including traditional left-wing approaches, deeming them inadequate for addressing contemporary social issues. Aligned with the rebellious spirit of the postwar baby boomer generation in the West, the New Left provided a platform for young people to engage in political activism. Grown up in relatively affluent and liberal social environments, they were inclined toward personalized and liberated lifestyles, naturally resistant to traditional systems and authority. As tensions escalated, the late 1960s witnessed spontaneous large-scale worker riots and student movements in Italy, sparking a wave of rebellion. Workers demanded improved working conditions and higher wages to cope with mounting life pressures, while students protested against educational environments and quality, expressing dissatisfaction with the existing education system. This environment stimulated radical awareness among many young designers, prompting them to articulate their views on society and explore subjective emotions through design.

In response to these stimulating conditions, significant changes occurred in Italy's artistic and cultural spheres. Young designers no longer satisfied with designing solely for commercial purposes, but sought to reflect social issues, express personal viewpoints, and drive social change through design, seeking new cultural identities. Based on mass production, the Milan Triennale in 1954 affirmed the cooperation between the art world and industrial production,

announcing to the world that the development direction of Italian design was not merely practical and functional, but "artistic." Additionally, during this period, the rise of international artistic trends such as Neo-Dadaism, Surrealism, Pop Art, and the Hippie movement provided Italian artists with ample inspiration. They began employing bold design techniques, using different colors, materials, and symbolic forms to express their radical ideas to the world. Thus, the 1960s Italian Radical Design movement unfolded.

Italian furniture design has a long history, becoming a primary channel for radical designers to express their creativity. In 1969, Andrea Branzi, a key member of Archizoom Associati, designed a highly ironic chair—[3]the Mies Lounge Chair in radical design. This chair used bizarre

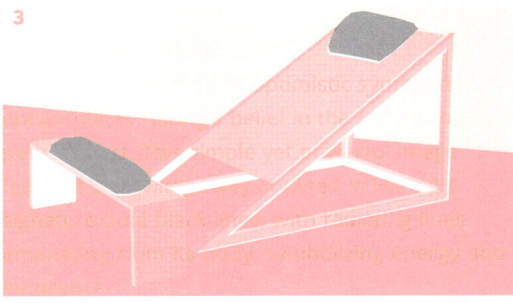

The Mies Lounge Chair, Archizoom Associati, 1969.

forms to satirize Ludwig Mies Van der Rohe's principle of "less is more," which once epitomized the core of internationalist design style. For example, the Archizoom Associati's classic *Superonda* sofa undulates like waves, combining industrial materials with nonnatural elements and challenging practical functional forms, encouraging a more flexible and avant-garde leisure approach. The renowned Studio Alchymia aimed to challenge functionality and tradition to showcase individuality in design. Its pioneering figure, Alessandro Mendini, created a chair of revolutionary significance in 1974 called the *Lassù*. Inspired by his burning cover for *Casabella* magazine, the chair's base was pyramid-shaped, a complete destruction and rebellion against functionality, yet the artist's focus was not on practical function but rather on honoring life and exploring the connection between people and objects. By destructively burning the most familiar objects, he announced the arrival of a new era in design.

In the development of Italian Radical Design, mass media also played a crucial role, with prominent Italian design magazine [4]*Domus*[6] leading the way. As Italian designers began to embrace American modernist design thinking, *Domus* emphasized the fusion of idealism with Italian traditional culture and the need for design to embody more humanistic content. Of course, this was inseparable from Italy's profound

Cover of *Domus*, Issue 373, 1960.

cultural heritage, laying the groundwork for Italy's departure from tradition and move toward postmodernism. The magazine's editor-in-chief at the time, Andrea Branzi, was also a central figure in Radical Design and the designer of the *Mies Chair* mentioned earlier. Therefore, the magazine published many Radical Design works, playing a catalytic role in promoting this design ideology, and making it a battlefield for the development of radical Italian design thinking.

3 Memphis Magic

In the 1960s, Italy initiated a comprehensive challenge to the traditional societal lifestyle and mainstream design, showcasing both cultural inheritance and integration, and highlighting Italy's unique design identity. This radical design thinking gradually evolved through collisions with mainstream design styles, and by the early 1980s, Ettore Sottsass founded the Memphis Group, which elevated Radical Design concepts to new heights, profoundly influencing the design style throughout the 1980s.

Within the wave of Radical Design in Italy, Art Deco and Pop Art provided rich inspirational soil. The Art Deco Movement, originated in the 1920s, became a dominant style in the West during the 1930s. As modernism evolved through the Dutch De Stijl and the Bauhaus, the International Style was reiterated and perfected, gradually diminishing the influence of Art Deco. With the rise of postmodernist thought in the late 1960s and the widespread application of new materials, designers began to show a renewed interest in ornamentation. This ornamentation served as a tool to counter conservative modernist design principles. Art Deco excelled in using geometric shapes and lines for decoration, employing strong colors to express exaggeration, and utilizing unconventional techniques with new materials and craftsmanship. Italian Radical Design drew extensively from Art Deco, employing distortion, exaggeration, abstraction, simplification, stacking, piecing, and integrating various decorative symbols to achieve an anti-traditional effect. Additionally, the rise of popular culture in the 1950s saw the Pop Art movement draw heavily from Art Deco ideas, influencing the development of Italian design styles. When Pop Art and design combined, they established a unique relationship, becoming tools of social resistance. They reflected the cultural and consumer concepts of the younger generation, as well as rebellious consciousness and aesthetic taste. These styles were highly sought after by radical Italian designers. For example, one of Italy's radical design groups, Archizoom Associati, located in Florence, openly claimed that their designs were directly influenced by the British Pop design group Archigram, particularly by the futuristic city forms depicted in Archigram's comic strips.

This unique blend of artistry eventually gave birth to the distinctive Memphis style in the 1980s. Founded in the early 1980s, the Memphis Group had a serendipitous start: at their first meeting, background music suddenly played Bob Dylan's song "Stuck Inside of Mobile with the Memphis Blues Again," inspiring the designers to dub themselves the "Memphis Group." The Memphis designers rejected the idea that form should strictly follow function, instead supporting the notion that design itself could be a form of artistic expression. The group's founder, Ettore Sottsass, believed that "design should be sensual and exciting." Therefore, Memphis design brimmed with vibrant hues, often arranged in unexpectedly playful combinations, challenging preconceived notions of what constitutes good design taste. This deliberate departure from pastel palettes injected vibrancy and whimsy into the design landscape. Geometric shapes and patterns were another hallmark of Memphis design. Designers embraced asymmetry and juxtaposed geometric forms in unconventional ways. This approach created a visual discordance that engaged viewers on deeper levels, while the bold use of patterns further enhanced this sense of playfulness and unpredictability.

Memphis design particularly excels in the realm of home furnishings, which challenged traditional notions of furniture and product design while breaking recognized boundaries in interior decoration. For instance, Ettore Sottsass's *Carlton Bookcase* is a quintessential example. Constructed from matte laminates and wood, its uniquely imaginative design resembles a patched mechanical figure or decorative planter. Additionally, Martine Bedin's *Super Lamp* typifies Memphis design with its unconventional and innovative approach. This lamp design exudes playfulness, resembling a portable toy full of whimsy and personal expression. Beyond its standout presence in home design, Memphis has profoundly influenced graphic design as well. In Memphis-style graphic design, designers often employ vivid colors and anti-functional elements. For example, 5 graphic designs by Christoph Radl[7]

MEMPHIS MILANO, Sottsass Associati & Christoph Radl, 1988.

lack explicit visual information, relying instead on strong color imagery that feels more like a cultural release. Meanwhile, 6 designs by William Longhauser[8] not only use vibrant colors but also incorporate grid elements commonly seen in Internationalist designs, complemented by letter forms to create a rich and colorful composition, fully embodying the postmodern graphic design style.

Exhibition poster announcing an exhibition of drawings by architect Michael Graves, William Longhauser, 1983.

The influence of Memphis design continues to resonate today, experiencing a revival in contemporary design. Designers draw inspiration from Memphis's rebellious spirit and integrate its elements into their own work. This revival is characterized by playful color applications, embracement of geometric patterns, and a commitment to challenging traditional design norms with innovative spirit. The unique style and philosophy of Memphis design will continue to inspire and influence future designers in their exploration and innovation.

Notes:

1. The International Style, a major architectural movement that emerged in the 1920s and 1930s, is characterized by its emphasis on functionalism, simplicity, and the use of modern materials such as steel and glass. Pioneered by architects like Le Corbusier, Ludwig Mies van der Rohe, and Walter Gropius, the International Style sought to create universally applicable design principles that transcended regional and historical styles. Key features include clean lines, open floor plans, and a focus on volume over mass. The movement had a profound impact on modern architecture and later extended to the field of graphic design, which also known as Swiss graphic design in 20th century.

2. Walter Dorwin Teague (1883-1960), an American industrial designer, is widely regarded as one of the pioneers of industrial design in the United States. Teague's works, including iconic designs for Kodak cameras and the Texaco service station, helped shape the aesthetics of American consumer goods in the mid-20th century. As a founder of Teague Design, one of the first industrial design firms, his contributions extended to architecture and exhibition design, including his influential work at the 1939 New York World's Fair. Teague's legacy is marked by his blend of modernist aesthetics with functional, mass-produced products.

3. Superstudio, an Italian architectural collective founded in 1966 by Adolfo Natalini and Cristiano Toraldo di Francia, was a key player in the radical architecture and design movement of the 1960s and 1970s. Known for their visionary projects and critiques of modernism and consumer society, Superstudio's works, such as *The Continuous Monument* (1969), challenged traditional notions of architecture through utopian and dystopian concepts. Their speculative designs, often presented through photomontages and films, had a profound influence on conceptual architecture, design theory, and the development of postmodernism.

4. Studio 65, founded in 1965 by Franco Audrito and a group of young Italian architects and designers, became a prominent force in the Radical Design movement. Known for its playful, avant-garde approach to furniture and interior design, Studio 65 created iconic works such as the *Bocca Sofa* (1970), inspired by Salvador Dalí's "Lips" sofa, and the *Capitello Chair* (1971), a seat in the form of a classical column capital. Their designs were characterized by bold colors, surreal forms, and critiques of traditional design conventions, contributing significantly to postmodernist aesthetics and the blending of art, architecture, and pop culture.

5. Fordism, a term coined from the practices of Henry Ford and the Ford Motor Company, refers to the system of industrial mass production and consumption that emerged in the early 20th century. Characterized by assembly line production, standardized goods, and high wages for workers, Fordism revolutionized manufacturing and contributed to the rise of consumer culture. This model, which emphasized efficiency and scale, significantly influenced modern industrial practices and economic policies.

6. *Domus* is an esteemed international design and architecture magazine, renowned for its commitment to exploring contemporary design and innovative architecture. Founded in 1928 by architect Gio Ponti and Barnabite father Giovanni Semeria, it has become a leading voice in the field, showcasing the intersection of art, design, and culture. Each issue features insightful articles, interviews, and visual essays that highlight emerging trends and celebrate the legacy of design. *Domus* continues to inspire architects, designers, and enthusiasts worldwide with its forward-thinking approach and dedication to excellence in design discourse.

7. Christoph Radl (b. 1954) is a Swiss-born designer. He grew up in Austria and moved to Milan in the seventies to work with the renowned Italian architect and designer Ettore Sottsass. Together with Sottsass Associati, he founded 1984 Italiana di Comunicazione, a creative avant-garde advertising agency. Radl's work with Memphis is characterized by its playful use of bold colors, geometric patterns, and unconventional materials, which challenged traditional design aesthetics and contributed to the development of postmodern design.

8. William Longhauser (b. 1974) is a contemporary graphic designer renowned for pushing the boundaries of graphic design and exploring new possibilities in visual expression. He holds a BFA in Graphic Design from the College of Design, Art, and Architecture at the University of Cincinnati, an MFA in Design from Indiana University, and has completed two years of postgraduate study at the School of Design in Basel, Switzerland. Longhauser's works have garnered numerous awards and featured in international publications and exhibitions.

KEY ARTISTS & THEIR ICONIC WORKS

Ettore Sottsass
(1917-2007)

He is an immensely influential Italian architect and designer, renowned as one of the leaders of Italy's Radical Design movement. His career began long before the founding of the Memphis Group, notably as a consultant for the Italian office equipment manufacturer Olivetti. In 1969, he designed the iconic Valentine typewriter, a bright red portable typewriter that showcased his ability to seamlessly integrate functionality with striking aesthetics. However, his most famous achievement came in 1981 when he established the Memphis Group, where he was regarded as the pivotal source of inspiration and cohesion. The Memphis Group was a designer collective that boldly challenged traditional design norms with its vibrant colors, geometric shapes, and playful approach to furniture and object design, starkly contrasting with the Minimalism and Functionalism trends of the time. Throughout Sottsass's career, he experimented with various materials and design methods, creating a wide range of works including furniture, ceramics, jewelry, and industrial designs. His designs often carried a sense of humor and irony, as he believed that design should evoke emotions and provoke thought, not merely serve functional purposes. Sottsass's influence in design transcended his own creations. His collaboration with the pioneering designers of the Memphis Group inspired a new generation of designers to adopt more expressive and experimental approaches, leaving a vivid and lasting impact on contemporary design.

1. *Nefertiti Desk* (1969)
This is a remarkable example of Ettore Sottsass's unconventional design. During his tenure at Olivetti in Italy, Sottsass designed the *Nefertiti Desk* as part of a broader movement to bring modernist aesthetics and functionality into the office environment. Focusing on practicality and user comfort, this desk featured built-in storage, adjustable components, and ergonomic considerations, making it highly functional. Its modular design allowed for customization to meet specific user needs. Sottsass also infused modern design principles into the desk, ensuring it both functional and visually appealing. This sleek, minimalist piece stands in stark contrast to Sottsass' later, more colorful Memphis works. Its clean lines and practical design reflect Sottsass' early interest in creating furniture that was both useful and user-friendly.

2. *Carlton Bookcase* (1981)
The most famous piece by the Memphis Group. This bold, multicolored creation defies traditional design norms with its asymmetric structure and playful use of geometric shapes. Despite its seemingly extravagant appearance, the *Carlton* incorporates stable equilateral triangles in its structure, making it practical for storing books and other items. It can be said that *Carlton* is not only a functional object but also an art piece. It emphasizes fun, spontaneity, and emotional resonance rather than mere functionality, embodying the Memphis Group's philosophy of blending form, function, and whimsy.

3. *Tahiti Lamp* (1981)
Also designed by the Memphis Group, the work is a whimsical and vibrant piece. It features a design reminiscent of a bird, with a curved long neck and a triangular base. This lamp is brightly colored and playful, exemplifying Sottsass's approach to infusing everyday objects with fun and creativity.

4. *Olivetti Valentine Typewriter* (1969)
The work is one of Ettore Sottsass's most iconic designs, also known as the *Red Valentine Typewriter*. This portable typewriter, codesigned with Perry A. King, combines functionality with visual impact. The Valentine features a stylish, portable design with rounded edges and a sleek, Minimalist aesthetics. The most striking feature is its vibrant red color, a stark departure from the typical, monochromatic office equipment of the time. The bright red plastic casing and stylish, simple form challenged the traditional notions of typewriters being purely utilitarian and monochromatic. The Valentine Typewriter quickly became a cultural icon, celebrated for its chic design and connection to the popular culture of the late 1960s and early 1970s.

Alessandro Mendini
(1931-2019)

He is an influential Italian architect and designer and a key figure in the Italian Radical Design movement of the 1960s and 1970s, which sought to challenge traditional design and architectural norms with bold and unconventional ideas. Mendini is known for his playful and eclectic design approach, often employing bright colors, bold patterns, and whimsical forms. He believed strongly in the emotional potential of design, strived to create work that evokes strong reactions and form personal connections with people. Additionally, he frequently contributed to design magazines such as *Domus* and *Casabella*, serving as editor for some time, and used these platforms to promote avant-garde design and foster dialogue within the design community. His innovative and inclusive approach to design has continually resonated within the industry, broadly influencing subsequent generations of architects and designers.

5. *Proust Armchair* (1978)
The *Proust Armchair* is one of Mendini's most iconic works. This Baroque-style chair is adorned with a pointillist pattern, blending classical and modern elements. Inspired by the Rococo style of the 18th century, Mendini combined it with vibrant modern aesthetics. The chair serves as a tribute to Marcel Proust as well as to the pointillist techniques of Paul Signac and Georges Seurat. Known for its luxurious appearance, the *Proust Armchair* merges traditional baroque shapes with playful modern colors and patterns, creating a striking visual impact with its unique juxtaposition.

6. *Lassù Chair* (1984)
The name "Lassù," meaning "up there" in Italian, suggests an ethereal or elevated experience. The *Lassù Chair* is a striking piece of furniture that exemplifies Mendini's passion for combining art and design. This chair features a lavish sculptural form and bold color combinations, merging traditional craftsmanship with modern aesthetics.

7. Groninger Museum Renovation (1994)
Mendini, along with renowned designers Philippe Starck and Michele De Lucchi, codesigned the Groninger Museum. The museum is famous for its bold, colorful exterior and unconventional forms. Mendini's contributions to the museum incorporate a blend of various artistic styles and vibrant hues, making it a landmark of contemporary architecture.

Martine Bedin
(1957-)

She is a French designer and architect known for her role in the Memphis Group, and an influential design collective established in the early 1980s. Bedin's work is characterized by its playful, colorful, and eclectic nature, often blending art, design, and architecture.

8. *Super Lamp* (1981)
The *Super Lamp* is perhaps Bedin's most iconic design. This portable table lamp resembles a toy car, with a rounded, colorful body and an exposed light bulb serving as the headlight. The lamp's playful form and bright colors embody the Memphis Group's challenge to modernist Minimalist aesthetics, emphasizing fun, creativity, and individuality.

9. *Lodge* (1982)
The work features a wooden console table wrapped in decorative laminate, showcasing an unconventional drawer system. The design integrates red and blue dots as knobs for opening and closing, adding a playful touch. This piece exemplifies the Memphis Group's blend of functionality and artistic expression.

Andrea Branzi
(1957-2023)

He is a key figure in the Radical Design movement of the 1960s and 1970s, which sought to challenge traditional design and architectural norms. As the founder of the avant-garde Italian architectural group Archizoom Associati, and a former editor of the renowned Italian design magazine *Domus*, Branzi's design approach often blends conceptual, artistic, and practical elements, pushing the boundaries of conventional design.

10. *Superonda Sofa* (1966)
Designed for Poltronova, the *Superonda Sofa* is an early example of Branzi's innovative approach to furniture design. This modular sofa can be configured in various ways, offering great flexibility. Its bold, sculptural form and vibrant colors reflect the experimental spirit of the 1960s design.

11. *Gritti Bookcase* (1984)
The *Gritti Bookcase*, part of the Memphis Group's works, showcases Branzi's eclectic and innovative approach. Designed to be both aesthetically pleasing and practical, the bookcase features clean lines and an elegant structure, often

crafted from high-quality materials like wood and metal. Its modular design allows for flexibility in arrangement, making it a perfect fit for various spaces, from home offices to living rooms. The *Gritti Bookcase* is not just a storage solution but also a statement piece, reflecting the Memphis spirit of blending art and design to create unique, expressive pieces.

12. *Domestic Animals Series* (Animali Domestici) (1985)

The *Animali Domestici* series is one of Branzi's most renowned collections, which merged furniture design with art. These pieces combine natural materials like wood and animal hides with synthetic materials, creating a striking contrast. This series challenges traditional furniture design, being both functional and highly artistic and conceptual.

FROM SUPERGRAPHICS TO NEW WAVE: PUSHING EXPERIMENTAL DESIGN FORWARD

Graphic design has continuously evolved through various transformations and innovations. From the International Style brought by the Bauhaus School to the new explorations of Swiss graphic design, and the rise of the New Wave design movement, each step in this progression reflects the spirit and aesthetic pursuits of its time. This section delves into this evolution, uncovering the logic and impact behind each design style and how they influenced and shaped the vibrant world of graphic design in the 1980s.

The Bauhaus School is undoubtedly a significant milestone in design history. It introduced modernist design concepts from Europe to the United States, leading to the birth of the International Style in architecture. Heavily influenced by Ludwig Mies van der Rohe's principle of "less is more," this movement emphasized simplicity, functionality, and rationalism, dominating architectural design of the time. As the popularity of this style grew, its influence spread to other fields of art and design, establishing a broad International Style. To align with the characteristics of International Style of cities and architecture, graphic designers began exploring design elements and techniques that complemented this aesthetics. Swiss graphic designers made notable contributions during this period. Building on the functionalist foundations of pre-WWII German modernism, Dutch De Stijl, and Russian Constructivist graphic design, they developed a new graphic design style. This style is characterized by its detached, functional, and rational approach, heavily utilizing sans-serif typefaces such as **1**Helvetica and **2**Univers, and adhering to a strict grid system to create balanced and cohesive compositions. In terms of color usage, this style is also very restrained, primarily employing primary colors, black, white, and gray, to create a clean and modern visual effect.

Since the 1960s, graphic design has increasingly integrated with architecture, often using large fonts and graphic imagery in significant architectural projects to emphasize the building's content. This trend has driven changes in graphic design. The earliest attempts were later termed "Supergraphics" style. Designers exploring postmodern architecture broke the isolation between architecture and graphic design, incorporating graphic elements into building surfaces with oversized fonts and graphic images to enhance architectural decor. This not only initiated the era of postmodernist graphic design but also expanded the applied range and potential of graphic design.

Influenced by Supergraphics, the 1970s witnessed a major transformation in graphic design—the emergence of the New Wave graphic design movement. Initiated by designers associated with Swiss International Style, the movement aimed to challenge the dominance of internationalism in graphic design. On one hand, they retained the basics of Swiss International Style, such as grid systems, but freed themselves from its constraints, focusing on innovative design for communication. Simultaneously, they re-explored typography, imagery, and layout, creating a style that was fun and highly personalized. In New Wave graphic design, fonts gained more expressiveness and decorative qualities, using fragmentation and recombination to form patterns that were both decorative and informative. Moreover, New Wave graphic design shattered the monotony and excessive rationality of previous design patterns, introducing more flexible and interesting layouts. This period saw interwoven and varied typographical elements, enriching designs with more charm and distinctive allure. Designers of this era, through innovation and experimentation, elevated graphic design to new artistic and expressive heights, laying the groundwork for subsequent design trends.

From the dominance of International Style to the rise of the New Wave movement, we have witnessed a profound transformation in the field of graphic design. These design styles have not only influenced our visual aesthetics but also reflected the evolution of societal culture and the spirit of the times. The New Wave movement, flourishing in the 1980s as part of postmodernism, continued to drive innovation and diversity in graphic design.

1 Defining

The wave of postmodernism began in the field of architecture. Under the dominance of International Style, a group of architects explored ways to incorporate graphic design elements into architecture, challenging the modernist and internationalist styles. Naturally, this challenge spread from architecture to graphic design in the 1970s, giving birth to the New Wave.

Supergraphics style, emerged in the late 1960s and 1970s, is a design approach that integrates large graphic elements with architectural spaces. These graphic styles include many of the same design elements as Internationalism, such as sans-serif fonts and geometric shapes, but the intention is to exaggerate these functional elements to achieve new decorative effects rather than abandon decoration. These graphics are characterized by their large scale, vibrant colors,

Specimen of the Typeface Neue Helvetica, GearedBull (Jim Hood), 2008.

Specimen of the Typeface Univers, Blythwood, 2015.

and seamless integration with architectural features, often wrapping around walls, floors, and ceilings. They serve not only aesthetic functions but also practical purposes such as wayfinding, branding, and storytelling, enhancing both the functionality and emotional impact of the space. Moreover, many designers pioneering this style were architects of the postmodernist movement. By employing these bold graphic images, they aimed to strongly refute the Internationalist architectural style and thereby pioneered a method and means for "postmodernism" in architecture. An important figure in this movement was Robert Venturi, and he was an early proponent of postmodernism who famously opposed the simplistic and rigid "less is more" ethos with his witty and straightforward retort: "Less is a bore." In his architectural design, he extensively used graphic design motifs and symbolic geometries to alter the stereotypical appearance of design. However, due to its ability to enhance visual appeal and strengthen brand identity, Supergraphics evolved after the 1970s into an integral part of corporate identity system design. It was predominantly applied in corporate offices, public spaces, educational institutions, and cultural venues, seemingly submerged as a design genre in history but left an indelible mark on postmodernist thought and practice.

When these postmodernist ideas ignited hope in the field of graphic design, the New Wave Typography emerged in the 1970s. It integrated the Supergraphics style that had developed in the 1960s, and incorporated various historical decorative motifs. Originated from several Swiss designers associated with the Swiss International Style movement in Basel, Switzerland, New Wave Typography was aimed to break the monopoly of Internationalism in graphic design. A key figure in the New Wave Typography movement was Swiss graphic designer Wolfgang Weingart. Initially explored graphic design at the Basel School of Design on his own, it was during his solo efforts that he met young designers upon arriving in the United States in 1972 to promote his design philosophy. These designers included Dan Friedman, 3Willi Kunz[1], and April Greiman, who formed a powerful group within the postmodernist graphic design movement and became the core force of the New Wave Typography movement. Interestingly, we find that both the Supergraphics and New Wave Typography movement were initiated by designers with backgrounds in International design. However, they each had their own views on the monotony and uniformity of Internationalism, hoping to change this situation through their design practices. It was their profound understanding and adept handling of

Columbia University, Cities on the Edge Symposium, Willi Kunz, 1991.

International Style that enabled them to find variations within the rules and bring about renewal. Weingart was strongly influenced by Constructivism, without rejecting the emphasis on visual communication functionality inherent in International Style but rather becoming tired of its singular visual effects, seeking to enliven graphic design through artistic decoration. Additionally, another characteristic of New Wave graphic artists was the use of digital technology. They employed digital tools to manipulate existing layouts and forms in various ways, maximizing the use of this new design element. Digital technology also allowed them greater freedom to explore and expand their design concepts.

2 Postmodernism from the Field of Architecture

After World War II, the International Style that had developed in Germany became the dominant style in Western countries, enjoying widespread popularity. This design approach, epitomized by Mies van der Rohe's principle of "less is more," emphasized functionality, high rationality, systematic organization, and antidecoration characteristics. By the late 1950s, it evolved into a formal Minimalism that sometimes disregarded functional requirements, in favor of complete formal simplicity. International design originally stemmed from modernist architectural principles. In 1927, American architect Philip Johnson[2] noticed the design style at the Weissenhof Housing Project exhibition near Stuttgart, Germany. He believed this style would become an internationally popular architectural style, characterized by its simplicity, rationality, detachment, and mechanical nature, which he termed the "International Style." Through efforts of architects, artists, and designers, particularly the Bauhaus movement, the International Style continued to evolve and refine. The completion of the 4Seagram Building in 1958, marked a significant milestone in the formation of Internationalist architectural style. This skyscraper, renowned for its glass curtain walls and stream-lined structure, became an iconic example of modernist architecture. Concurrently, the Perelli Building in Milan, designed by Italian architect Gio Ponti[3], also completed, contributing to the spread of International Style. These developments underscored the influence and evolution of International design from its origins in early 20th-century modernism to its prominence in postwar Western architecture and design.

As International architectural style gradually became mainstream, urban and architectural design reforms profoundly influenced graphic design. During this period, Swiss Internationalist graphic design style stood out prominently. Designers built upon the functionalist foundations of German modernism, Dutch De Stijl, and Russian Constructivist graphic design to forge a new graphic design style characterized by detachment, rationality, and strong readability. They also pioneered new typefaces like the Univers and the widely embraced Helvetica, along with innovative layout systems. These

Seagram Building, designed by Ludwig Mies van der Rohe, Philip Johnson, Ely Jacques Kahn, and Robert Allan Jacobs, completed in 1958.

designs emphasized accuracy, clarity, and depersonalization, aligning perfectly with Mies van der Rohe's "less is more" philosophy, collectively shaping the distinctive appearance of International graphic design. Joseph Müller-Brockmann[4] was one of the most influential figures in the Swiss graphic style. His work was influenced by Bauhaus and Constructivism, where typography and geometric shapes took center stage. His hallmark was a strict grid system, emphasizing rhythm and harmony within the grid, and minimizing personal emotions and feelings in favor of a universal graphical expression. One of his most defining works may be the poster he designed for the Beethoven Music Festival at the Zurich Town Hall. Viewing music as an abstract art form, Müller-Brockmann approached his poster design in an abstract manner. His composition was meticulously structured on a tight grid, where arcs were placed with their diameters doubled, and every element's position and size were deliberate. Over the years, design enthusiasts have avidly analyzed the angles and precise placements of these arcs. The use of black and white created a sense of moving circles, evoking the rhythmic nature of music. Publisher Lars Müller described Müller-Brockmann's [5]*Beethoven* poster (1955) as the ultimate example of "musicality in design."

As International Style permeated various fields of artistic design, its shortcomings gradually became amplified, unable to address diverse contexts with a uniform approach. Criticisms first arose within the architectural realm. Architects recognized that under Internationalist Style, architectural imagery was rigid, uniform, and impersonal, often lacking individuality and emotional resonance. Cities around the world started to look alike, and buildings struggled to evoke empathy or emotional connection, resulting in spaces that felt cold and sterile. In response, architects began seeking new avenues of development, turning their attention to many elements of graphic design and integrating them into architectural design. This marked a challenge to mainstream architectural design known as "Supergraphics," which can also be seen as a precursor to postmodern architecture. Elements from graphic design used in Supergraphics were typically large-scale, covering entire walls, floors, ceilings, and even building facades. These expansive images created a significant visual impact, fundamentally altering the perception of a building's environment. Furthermore, bright and bold colors were prominent features of Supergraphics, contrasting sharply with Internationalism's rejection of decoration. These colors attracted attention and served decorative purposes, also transformed architectural spaces. Additionally, Supergraphics tailored designs according to specific environments and backgrounds, reflecting cultural, historical, or functional aspects of the space to establish deeper connections with audiences. It's evident that Supergraphics borrowed many graphic elements from International Style but exaggerated and transformed them to enhance their decorative qualities. It did not reject functional emphasis but rather placed equal importance on functionality and aesthetics, infusing buildings with a unique warmth. Therefore, these design works not only achieved visual appeal but also effectively conveyed information, embodying the core principle of Supergraphics where utility and aesthetics coexist harmoniously.

Robert Venturi, a graduate of School of Architecture of Yale University, received modernist architectural education but became a pivotal figure in shaping postmodernist design. He was among the first to articulate the manifesto of postmodernism, advocated for hybrid, compromising, and distorted elements over pure, clear, and straightforward ones. Venturi famously stated, "I like elements which are hybrid rather than 'pure,' compromising rather than 'clear,' distorted rather than 'straightforward.'" Venturi's approach involved drawing inspiration from historical decorative styles and America's vibrant popular culture, challenging the rigid norms of contemporary design. This unconventional stance gained support from a group of architects and ignited the most notable architectural movement after World War II—Postmodernist Architecture movement in the 1970s. In his architectural designs, Venturi incorporated significant elements of graphic design, particularly simple geometric shapes, to achieve symbolic effects. For instance, his design for the Gordon Wu Hall at Princeton University in 1986 featured a facade adorned with numerous triangles, diamonds, arches, and circular insets, representing a quintessential application of Supergraphics style.

Another influential postmodernist architect who integrated graphic imagery into architectural design was Charles Willard Moore[5]. Moore's early experiments in the mid-1960s at Gualala in California involved collaboration with San Francisco graphic designer Barbara Stauffacher Solomon. They applied simple geometric forms and bold color schemes to the ceilings and walls of buildings, treating architectural components as elements of graphic design. This approach broke down the traditional boundaries between architecture and graphic design, marking a significant departure from conventional practices.

Supergraphics has had a lasting impact on interior design, architecture, and environmental design fields. This design style significantly alters people's perceptions of space, creating immersive and captivating environments, thereby becoming a staple tool for designers and architects alike. The rise of Postmodernist Architecture not only signaled a shift in architectural styles but also broke down barriers between architecture and graphic design, making them integrate tightly. This interdisciplinary fusion injected new vitality into graphic design, subtly influenced its development trajectory with postmodernist ideals, and fostered innovation and transformation. Under this influence, graphic design began pursuing more diverse and open forms of expression, echoing the diversity and inclusivity of postmodernist architecture, collectively shaping a more vibrant and colorful artistic world.

Beethoven Poster, Joseph Müller-Brockmann, 1955

3 The Birth of the New Wave

The development of Swiss International Style in graphic design and Postmodernist Architecture brought new opportunities to the field of graphic design, with the New Wave Typography movement being among the first to embrace this change. To fully understand the New Wave, one must delve into its historical background. The 20th century witnessed various avant-garde movements such as Surrealism, Dadaism, and Abstract Expressionism, each breaking artistic boundaries in unique ways, rejecting traditional norms and attempting to disrupt established artistic conventions. Similarly, New Wave graphic design emerged as a pioneering force in postmodernist graphic design, which can be seen as an evolution of modernism. It integrated historical and decorative elements, making them integral components of graphic design. The New Wave movement of the 1970s was not only a profound reflection on the prevailing International Style at the time but also a revolutionary innovation in the field of graphic design, and it gradually became one of the major trends in the 1980s.

Initiated in Basel, Switzerland, by designers closely associated with the International Style movement, the New Wave movement aimed to break the monotony and rigidity observed in postwar design practices. Its style was distinct and unique. Unlike the simplicity and rationality of Swiss International Style, New Wave placed greater emphasis on emotional expression and visual impact. Visually, New Wave designers boldly used various graphic elements for deconstruction, reconstruction, collage, and combination, creating vibrant and dynamic visual effects. They skillfully employed contrasts of black, white, and whitespace to enhance the depth of their designs, breaking free from traditional layout rules by manipulating fonts vertically and horizontally, and cutting and arranging them in unconventional ways. Moreover, in terms of content, the New Wave movement did not reject conveying messages but further reflected postmodernist pursuits of diversity and relativity. Designers moved beyond conveying singular messages or concepts, instead incorporating more cultural connotations and societal reflections into their works. Their designs often carried rich symbolic meanings and metaphors, guiding viewers to deeper interpretations and reflections.

Wolfgang Weingart, a pioneering figure in the early stages of the New Wave Typography movement, initially studied at the Basel School of Art in Switzerland under the tutelage of Swiss International Style master Emil Ruder. As he delved deeper into his studies, he began to feel the need to reform the rigid nature of Swiss International Style graphic design to better suit the evolving aesthetic demands of the time. Thus, in the 1960s, he embarked on explorations such as developing new typographic systems, using simple geometric shapes as the basis for font design, and employing Constructivist features in layout to achieve strong visual impacts. Beyond fonts, he creatively enhanced the interest of his designs through fragmentation, cutting, and reassembling articles and illustrations, imbuing his designs with a chaotic and lively character, and epitomizing an eclectic expression of postmodernist thought.

The New Wave Typography movement emerged on the foundation of breaking tradition, but introduced a novel element—the digital digit. Artists now had tools and technologies that transcended the physical limitations of traditional media. The digital canvas became their playground, offering limitless possibilities for creativity and innovation. Like their avant-garde predecessors, New Wave artists were not content with merely pushing boundaries; they aimed to shatter them. Weingart was particularly enthusiastic about using technology, such as phototypesetting machines. He used these tools to deform and improve already designed layouts, maximized the use of this new design element to transform the rigidity and monotony of original layouts. In doing so, he made graphic design more intriguing, lively, and occasionally infused with a touch of Surrealism.

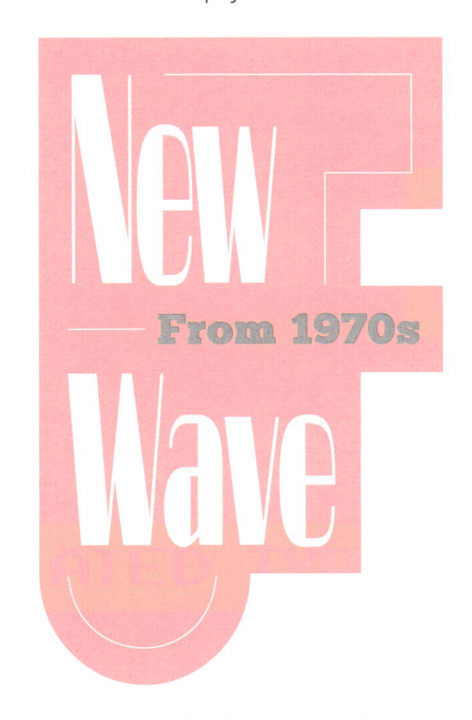

After Weingart's initial explorations in Switzerland, a trip to the United States in 1972 made him meet more like-minded designers. While postmodernist architectural trends like Supergraphics were already sweeping across America, breakthroughs in graphic design were less exciting at the time. Weingart's research undoubtedly brought fresh perspectives. These designers included Dan Friedman, April Greiman, Willi Kunz, among others, who together formed the core group of the postmodernist graphic design movement—the New Wave Typography movement. Dan Friedman used uppercase sans-serif fonts decoratively, diversified font designs, and arranged layouts in a stepped scale, transforming the overall two-dimensional image from simple and rigid to vivid and rich. He also manipulated surface textures to achieve new visual effects, integrating them into spatial layouts to create distinct personal stylistic features. April Greiman also employed similar layout techniques and effects to create a sense of three-dimensional space and motion. Additionally, Willi Kunz emphasized the conveyance of ideas and concepts through contrasting changes in layout and the symbolic significance of geometric shapes, which served as tools to aid communication. Each injected new vitality into the New Wave movement with their unique design styles and philosophies, collectively driving progress and development in the field of graphic design.

The New Wave Typography movement was a product of postmodernist thought, breaking traditional design concepts and bringing new ideas and possibilities to the field of graphic design. Its stylistic characteristics were distinct and unique, emphasizing expressive forms and design diversity. Simultaneously, the advent of digital technology completely transformed the artistic process, with computers and digital tools becoming indispensable parts of an artist's toolkit, enabling unprecedented manipulation, creation, and dissemination of art. Furthermore, the digital technology facilitated global collaboration, transcending geographical boundaries and cultural differences. This interconnectedness fostered dynamic exchanges of ideas and technologies, enriching the creative landscape. It can be said that driven by digital technology, the New Wave Typography movement profoundly influenced the field of graphic design in the 1980s, catalyzing innovation and development.

4 Feminine Power in Retro

In the 1980s, the postmodernist movement flourished, reaching new heights of popularity and influence that extended beyond galleries and museums into mainstream culture. During this period, postmodernism experienced a revival, marked by a unique turn known as "Retro Design."

Centered in New York City, Retro style actively explored and revived early 20th-century design styles. Leading figures in this movement, such as Louise Fili[6] and Paula Scher[7], distinguished female designers, based their work on historical styles, blending decorative techniques to create designs that were both elegant and rich in historical charm. [6]Louise Fili, deeply enamored by the romantic and culturally rich advertising of Italy's seaside resorts during World War II, meticulously collected and integrated elements from Italian and French graphic designs of the 1920s to 1940s into her book designs, which also preserved artisanal craftsmanship. Her books showcased how nostalgic and historical designs still possessed astonishing allure. In Retro style, illustrations, graphics, and text were not isolated but carefully arranged to form harmonious wholes, effectively conveying design themes. This layout not only held visual aesthetic value but also served as a crucial stylistic tool for thematic expression. Additionally, designers skillfully employed mixed typography, pattern combinations, and subtle color variations to create a nostalgic classical effect previously unseen in graphic design. Influenced by movements like the Vienna Secession and Art Nouveau, [7]Paula Scher utilized various typefaces and decorative patterns to transform form, color, and space, achieving a decorative nostalgic style that imbued her graphic design with distinct personalities.

This Retro Design contrasted intriguingly with the mainstream postmodernist influences of the 1980s. During the same period, postmodernist aesthetics permeated various album covers, advertisements, and posters, blurring cultural distinctions. The democratization of design allowed a broader audience to engage with these styles, challenging traditional elitist notions in art and design. For instance, designers like those from the Memphis Group, renowned for their postmodern furniture and product designs, exhibited rebellious and innovative spirits through vibrant colors, asymmetrical forms, and challenges to traditional aesthetics, further enriching postmodernist ideals.

In summary, postmodernism shattered traditional design boundaries by rejecting singular, objective truths and universal aesthetic ideals. Emerged initially in architecture, its principles and philosophies gradually matured and expanded into broader art and design domains, creating a significant cultural wave. Eclecticism, experimental approaches to layout, and an acceptance of ambiguity collectively defined this movement. Against this backdrop, Retro Design emerged as a unique branch, where its nostalgic and classical styles complemented and contrasted with mainstream postmodernist trends, collectively propelling the development and innovation in the field of design.

Best of Jazz, Paula Scher, 1979.

Cover of The *Victorian Fairy Tale Book*, designed by Louise Fili, illustrated by John Craig, 1988.

Notes:

1. Willi Kunz (b. 1943) is a Swiss graphic designer renowned for his innovative approach to typography and visual communication. His work blends Swiss design principles with a more expressive, intuitive style, challenging the rigidity of traditional grid systems. Kunz's seminal book, *Typography: Macro- and Microaesthetics* (1998), has influenced designers worldwide. His experimental use of type and structure has made him a key figure in contemporary graphic design.

2. Philip Johnson (1906–2005) is an influential American architect and also a prominent figure in the International Style. Johnson's notable works include the Glass House (1949) and the Seagram Building (1958), designed in collaboration with Ludwig Mies van der Rohe. Johnson's career was marked by his innovative use of glass and steel, and he played a crucial role in popularizing modernist principles in architecture.

3. Gio Ponti (1891–1979) is an influential Italian architect, designer, and writer. His design philosophy blended traditional craftsmanship with modern aesthetics, leading to innovative solutions in both architecture and interior design, including the iconic Pirelli Tower (1960) in Milan and the Villa Pliniana (1955) on Lake Como. Ponti's impact extended to furniture and decorative arts, and he was a key figure in promoting Italian design internationally through his role in the magazine *Domus* and his involvement in various design exhibitions.

4. Josef Müller-Brockmann (1914–1996) is a Swiss graphic designer and educator, widely regarded as a pioneer of the International Typographic Style, also known as Swiss Style. Known for his clean, grid-based designs and use of sans-serif typography, Müller-Brockmann's work set new standards in modern visual communication. His influence extended through his teaching and publications, notably was *Grid Systems in Graphic Design* (1961), which became a foundational text in graphic design education.

5. Charles Willard Moore (1925–1993) is an American architect and educator, widely recognized for his contributions to postmodern architecture. Known for his playful, eclectic style, Moore's work often incorporated historical references and vibrant colors, as seen in iconic projects like the Piazza d'Italia (1978) in New Orleans. His emphasis on human-centered, contextual architecture helped shape the postmodern movement and left a lasting impact on 20th-century architectural practice.

6. Louise Fili (b. 1951) is an American graphic designer known for her elegant and sophisticated approach to typography, branding, and package design. As a pioneer in the field of book design, Fili served as art director for Pantheon Books, where she designed over 2,000 book jackets. In 1989, she founded Louise Fili Ltd., a design studio specializing in food-related branding and packaging, with a signature style that blends European modernism with historical influences. Her work has been widely recognized for its craftsmanship and beauty, earning Fili numerous awards and a lasting legacy in the design community.

7. Paula Scher (b. 1948) is an American graphic designer and a principal at Pentagram, known for her innovative use of typography and retro-inspired design elements. Throughout her career, Scher has often drawn from historical references, integrated elements of Art Deco, Russian Constructivism, and mid-20th-century American advertising into her work. This approach is evident in her iconic branding for the Public Theater and various album covers, where she blends nostalgic aesthetics with contemporary design principles. Scher's ability to reinvent Retro Design for modern audiences has made her a pivotal figure in the graphic design world.

KEY ARTISTS & THEIR ICONIC WORKS

Robert Venturi
(1925-2018)

He is a seminal figure in architecture, renowned for his contributions to postmodernism. Trained in the modernist tradition at the Yale School of Architecture, Venturi emerged as a critical voice challenging the orthodoxies of his time. He is best known for his groundbreaking work *Complexity and Contradiction in Architecture* (1966), which argued for an architecture that embraced diversity, contradiction, and historical reference, in contrast to the purist ideals of modernism. Venturi's ideas profoundly influenced architectural discourse, advocating for architecture that communicates directly with its users and context, rather than conform to abstract ideals. His design philosophy, often summed up in the phrase "Less is a bore," celebrated complexity and visual richness over simplistic Minimalism. Venturi's architectural works include notable projects such as the Vanna Venturi House (1964) and the Sainsbury Wing of the National Gallery in London (1991), both exemplifying his playful yet deeply thoughtful approach to architecture.

1. Vanna Venturi House (1954)

Designed for his mother, this home is one of the earliest and most famous examples of postmodern architecture. The home's facade blends traditional and non-traditional elements, such as the sloping roof and oversized chimney, to create a playful and functional design. Its design challenges modernist principles by incorporating sophistication and ornamentation.

2. Guild House (1966)

This residential building for seniors exemplifies his approach of combining historical references with everyday architecture. The facade includes an oversized arch and contrasting materials such as red brick and white concrete. The use of decorative elements, such as the large antennae used as symbolic ornamentation, demonstrates Venturi's belief in the value of symbolism and humor in architecture.

3. Gordon Wu Hall at Princeton University (1986)

Completed in 1986, Gordon Wu Hall at Princeton University is one of Venturi's notable architectural projects. Designed for Butler College, it exemplifies Venturi's postmodernist style, which combines historical allusions, eclecticism, and a skillful use of graphic forms and ornamentation.

Barbara Stauffacher Solomon
(1928-2024)

She is a renowned American graphic designer and landscape architect, celebrated for her pioneering work in Supergraphics. Born in 1928, Solomon gained prominence in the 1960s for her bold, large-scale graphics that transformed architectural spaces, blending graphic design with architecture. Her distinctive style features striking, colorful geometric shapes and typographic elements, often integrated into buildings' interiors and exteriors. Solomon's work at the Sea Ranch, a planned community on the Northern California coast, remains iconic, exemplifying her innovative approach to environmental design. She studied painting in Switzerland under the famed designer Armin Hofmann, who significantly influenced her aesthetic. Solomon's contributions extend beyond graphic design to writing and teaching, making her a multifaceted figure in modern design history. Her work continues to inspire contemporary designers and architects, underscoring the lasting impact of her creative vision.

4. Sea Ranch Supergraphics (1960s)

The Northern California beachfront community of Sea Ranch Supergraphics is perhaps Barbara Solomon's most iconic work, known for its bold, large-scale graphic elements. The project consisted of remodeling the interior of the Sea Ranch condominiums with vibrant oversized geometric shapes and typography that blended seamlessly with the architectural features. This work exemplifies her innovative use of scale, color and form to create immersive environments.

5. San Francisco Ballet Building (1984)

In the 1980s, she designed Supergraphics for the San Francisco Ballet Building. Her work includes large-scale motion graphic elements that decorate interior spaces, enhancing the aesthetics and providing a unique visual experience for visitors.

Wolfgang Weingart
(1941-2021)

He is a German graphic designer and typographer, widely regarded as a pivotal figure in the development of New Wave Typography. Born in 1941, Weingart studied under Emil Ruder and Armin Hofmann at the Basel School of Design in Switzerland, where he later became a faculty member. His experimental approach to typography broke away from the rigid Swiss design conventions, embracing a more intuitive and expressive style. Weingart's work is characterized by its dynamic layouts, layered textures, and innovative use of type, which challenged traditional rules and influenced a generation of designers. His teachings and publications, particularly his influential book *My Way to Typography*, have left a lasting impact on contemporary graphic design. Weingart's contributions to the field have earned him numerous accolades, and his legacy continues to inspire designers seeking to push the boundaries of typographic expression.

6. *Typographische Monatsblätter* Covers Series (1970s)

Typographische Monatsblätter is one of the most important magazines for the successful dissemination of the phenomenon of "Swiss typography" to an international audience. In the more than 70 years since its founding, the magazine has witnessed important moments in the history of typography and graphic design. Weingart's covers for this influential Swiss typography magazine are among his most widely recognized works. These covers are characterized by bold experimental typography, layering, and geometric shapes, demonstrating his deviation from the strict grid design of the Swiss International Style and showcasing asymmetry, dynamic compositions, and interesting approaches to typography.

7. *Typographic Process NR. 1-5* (1970s)

The series posters were created in the 1970s, this series of typography transforms typography into an expressive and dynamic medium. Various elements such as graphics, numbers, and letters were processed through enlargement or reduction, changes in thickness, and exaggerated distortion to create contrasting, playful, and experimental typography that creates a sense of depth and movement.

8. The October Poster (1972)

This poster is a classic example of Weingart's ability to manipulate type and image. Utilizing photomontage techniques, he combined different fonts, proportions, and angles to create a visually stunning piece of work that broke the rules of traditional design. This poster highlights his innovative approach to typography. He also designed unique editions for each month, that is worthy of admiration.

9. Typography series (1970s)

This series of typographic experiments was conducted while he was teaching at the Basel School of Design. Weingart explored a variety of techniques, including letterpress printing, phototypesetting, and early computer graphics, to demonstrate the expressive potential of typography. These were not commercial projects, but educational works that had a profound impact on his students and the graphic design community.

Dan Friedman
(1945-1995)

He is an influential American graphic designer and artist, known for his role in advancing the New Wave Typography movement. Born in 1945, Friedman studied at the Ulm School of Design in Germany and later at the Basel School of Design under Armin Hofmann and Wolfgang Weingart. His work is characterized by its bold use of color, experimental typography, and innovative compositions that challenged conventional design norms. Friedman played a key role in bringing European design sensibilities to the United States, where he taught at institutions like Yale University and the School of Visual Arts in New York. His book, *Radical Modernism*, encapsulates his design philosophy and contributions to the postmodern design movement. Beyond graphic design, Friedman also explored furniture and sculpture, reflecting his versatile creative vision. His legacy continues to influence and inspire contemporary designers worldwide.

10. Domus Poster (1979-1989)

Friedman often designs posters for *Domus* magazine. This striking poster demonstrates his ability to combine typography and imagery in a lively and engaging way. The poster is notable for its vibrant colors and brush stroke elements, reflecting his New Wave thought.

11. Typografie (1970-1971)

Typografie is a striking example of how the boundaries of modernist design were being pushed in the 1970s. The work is notable for its dynamic and expressive use of typography. Rather than adhering to the strict rules of uniformity and clarity that were the hallmarks of the International Style, the work plays with the arrangement of letters, varying type sizes, and creating unconventional layouts that evoke a sense of energy and motion. This approach reflects the New Wave Typography's inclination towards breaking conventions and exploring new ways of visual communication.

April Greiman
(1948-)

She is a pioneering American graphic designer known for her innovative work that merges technology with visual communication. Born in 1948, Greiman studied at the Kansas City Art Institute and later at the Basel School of Design under Armin Hofmann and Wolfgang Weingart. She is a key figure in the New Wave Typography movement, recognized for her experimental use of typography, vibrant colors, and digital imagery. Greiman's embrace of digital tools in the early 1980s was revolutionary, making her one of the first designers to fully integrate computer technology into her work. Her groundbreaking projects, such as the influential "Does It Make Sense?" issue of *Design Quarterly*, challenged traditional design conventions and created new possibilities for graphic design. Greiman's contributions extend to teaching and writing, further solidifying her impact on the design world. Her work continues to inspire designers to explore the intersection of art, technology, and communication.

12. "Does It Make Sense?" Poster (1984)

Commissioned by *Design Quarterly*, this piece is one of Greiman's most iconic works. Featuring a life-size image of the artist himself, this fold-out poster was created using an early Macintosh computer. It combines bitmap graphics, layered images, and fonts to create a complex, multi-dimensional piece. This work is often cited as a seminal example of digital graphic design and an icon of the New Wave Typography movement.

13. Wet Magazine (1979-1981)

As art director of *Wet: The Magazine of Gourmet Bathing*, Greiman transformed the magazine with her experimental approach to design. Her use of unconventional layouts, bright colors, and varied typefaces embodied the magazine's avant-garde and eclectic spirit. Her work on *Wet* established her reputation as a leading figure in contemporary graphic design.

CHAPTER 1 — FROM SUPERGRAPHICS TO NEW WAVE

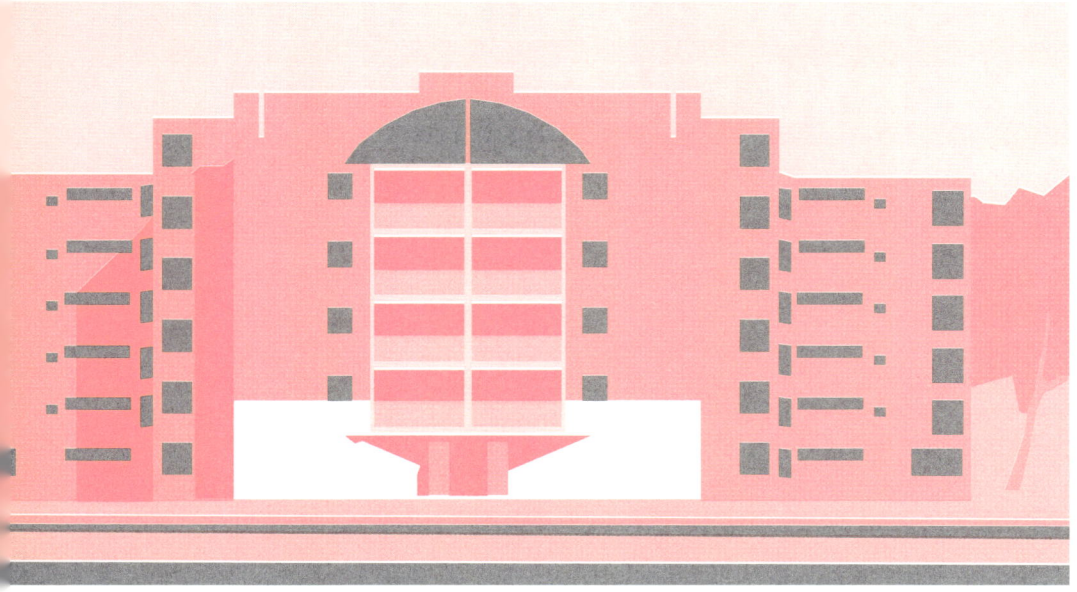

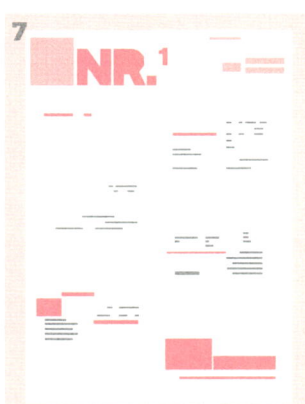

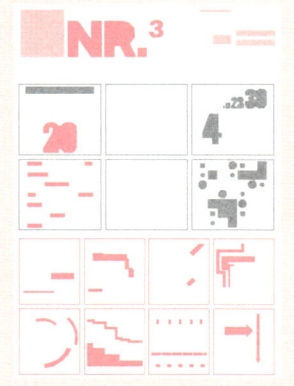

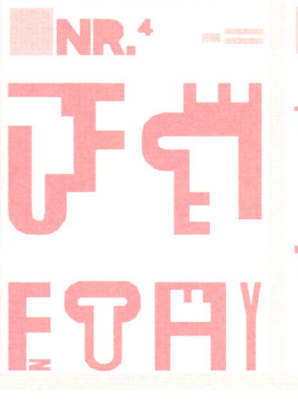

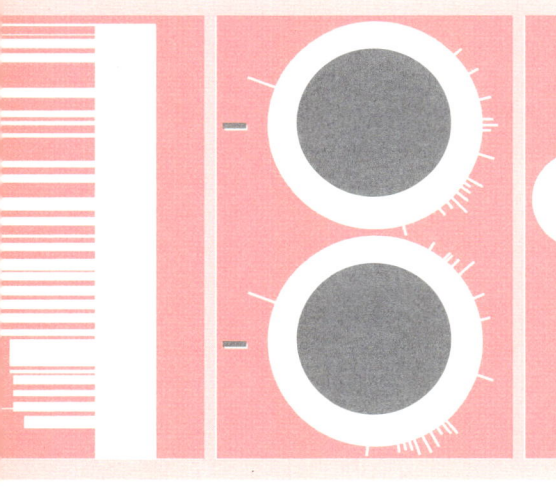

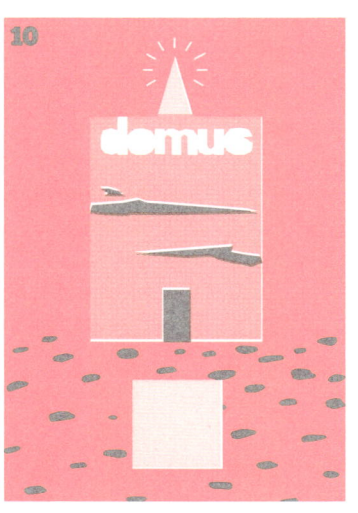

NEO-EXPRESSIONISM SURGE: EMBRACING RAW EMOTION AND URBAN VITALITY

Neo-Expressionism From 1980s

In the 1980s, the Neo-Expressionism art movement emerged as a refreshing wave, fundamentally rebelling against the preceding dominance of Minimalism[1] and Conceptualism[2]. While Minimalism and Conceptualism advocated for a cool, detached aesthetic ideology that influenced the art trends of the time, they also sparked a desire for genuine emotions and subjective expression. Neo-Expressionism was born against this backdrop, not only as an instinctive reaction to the past but also as a profound exploration within the art world. This movement is characterized by bold brushstrokes, intense emotional expression, and a deep return to the subjective realm, aiming to forefront unfiltered, raw emotions in artistic expression.

Neo-Expressionism was not just a shift in artistic style but a profound cultural movement. It fervently embraced individualism, vehemently rejected art formalism, and emphasized the inherent power of human nature. In this movement, artists' creations ceased to be cold aesthetic statements but became impassioned cries filled with warmth and emotion. Prominent artists like Jean-Michel Basquiat, Keith Haring, and Anselm Kiefer deeply influenced the core spirit of Neo-Expressionism. Their artworks often featured bold, unrestrained brushstrokes, seemingly chaotic yet powerful compositions, and a sense of urgency closely tied to the societal and political turbulence of the time. Such artworks not only touched people's souls but also, to some extent, became witnesses and records of the changes of the era.

1 Defining

Neo-Expressionism emerged as a powerful art movement in the late 1970s and early 1980s, marking a resurgence of figurative painting, vibrant colors, and themes rooted in raw emotions, aligning with broader cultural shifts of the 1980s. This movement is often seen as a deliberate reaction against the rigorous intellectualism and detachment of Minimalism and Conceptual art, forging its own distinct path. Neo-Expressionism artists often employed expressive brushstrokes and bold colors in their work, naturally evoking strong emotional responses from viewers, typically reflecting themes of anxiety, alienation, and conflict. Artists drew inspiration from personal experiences, historical events, and contemporary social issues.

Unlike previous abstract art movements, Neo-Expressionism typically focused on recognizable figures and themes, often rendered in distorted or exaggerated forms. It can be understood as a revival and evolution of the early 20th-century Expressionism movements, particularly German Expressionism. Expressionism as an artistic movement sought to convey emotions, sensations, and inner experiences through exaggerated and often distorted depictions of human forms and the world. It was a response to the turbulent socio-political conditions of the time, especially the trauma of World War II.

While acclaimed for its vitality and emotional power, Neo-Expressionism has also faced criticism for being seen as commercially driven and sensationalist, with some artworks criticized for prioritizing spectacle over substance. Nevertheless, Neo-Expressionism has had a lasting impact on contemporary art, revitalizing interest in painting and figurative art, an influence that continues to resonate with artists today.

90° village, Peter Angermann, 1984

2 The Roots of Neo-Expressionism

The roots of Neo-Expressionism can be traced back to the late 1970s, but it truly took shape in the 1980s. It was a reaction against the dominant art movements of the previous decade, particularly Minimalism and Conceptual art. These styles, with their emphasis on intellectual rigor and rejection of overt emotional expression, had once dominated the art world. However, over time, there grew a desire in both the art community and audiences for art that was more genuine, emotionally rich, and deeply connected.

To better understand the background of Neo-Expressionism, we need to look back at the social and cultural context of the 1960s. It was an era marked by various countercultural movements, including the civil rights movement, anti-war protests, and the rise of the hippie culture. These movements carried profound social radicalism, emphasizing individualism and challenging traditional social norms and authorities. This anti-establishment spirit undoubtedly found expression in later Neo-Expressionism. Against this backdrop, in the 1970s, disillusionment with art's detachment and intellectualism grew, sparking a desire for authenticity, emotional depth, and a connection to the human condition. This longing provided fertile ground for the emergence of Neo-Expressionism.

Subsequently, in the 1980s, the United States experienced significant economic growth and prosperity. This prosperity, on one hand, fostered the prevalence of consumer culture and a fascination with material wealth, while on the other hand, it exacerbated social inequalities. Especially in metropolises like New York, economic disparity and social decay coexisted with resilience, presenting a complex and diverse urban landscape. During this period, graffiti and street art stood out prominently, vividly reflected the vibrant creativity in urban life, as well as struggles and aspirations across various societal levels. At the same time, it's crucial not to overlook that the 1980s was also a time of intense international tension. The shadow of the Cold War loomed over the globe, with the arms race between the United States and the Soviet Union escalating continuously. The fear of nuclear conflict imposed heavy psychological pressure on people during this era. This international tension and inner fear to some extent influenced the direction and themes of artistic creation.

It was within such social, cultural, and political contexts that in the late 1970s to early 1980s, disillusionment grew with the detachment and intellectual styles prevalent in art. Neo-Expressionism expressed artists' emotions and ideas in a more direct, emotional, and personalized manner. It broke away from the strict frameworks of Minimalism and Conceptual art, boldly employed color, line, and shape to create visually impactful and emotive effects. The emergence of this artistic style not only satisfied people's desire for genuine emotional expression but also reflected the complex and ever-changing social realities of the time, as well as people's inner struggles and aspirations.

In conclusion, the emergence of Neo-Expressionism was not incidental; it was the result of the combined influence of various social, cultural, and political factors. From the countercultural movements of the 1960s to the economic prosperity and social inequality of the 1980s, and the tense atmosphere of the Cold War, these historical events provided crucial background and impetus for the formation of Neo-Expressionism. As a response and reflection, Neo-Expressionism became an indispensable cultural imprint of that era, characterized by its unique artistic language and profound social insights.

3 Enduring Impact

The enduring impact of Neo-Expressionism in the 1980s transcends the confines of the art world and extends into various facets of culture, leaving an indelible mark on music, fashion, and graphic design. This enduring influence reflects the movement's ability to capture and reflect the spirit of the era, resonating with audiences far beyond the gallery walls.

Music and Neo-Expressionism shared a symbiotic relationship during the 1980s, with artists and musicians collaborating to create powerful and emotionally charged works that defied conventional boundaries. Some of the most iconic album covers of the decade bore the unmistakable imprint of Neo-Expressionism, blurring the lines between music and visual art. While predating the peak of Neo-Expressionism,

David Bowie's[3] album *Heroes* is an early example of the movement's influence on music. A couple kissing near the Berlin Wall inspired Bowie to create the album that captures the raw intensity of human connection. This imagery resonates with Neo-Expressionism's focus on emotional depth and human experience. Also, U2's[4] iconic album **1** *The Joshua Tree* featured photography by Anton Corbijn, whose work was influenced by Neo-Expressionism. The cover image, featuring the band against a stark desert backdrop, evoked a sense of desolation and longing. This visual aesthetics complemented the album's themes of hope, longing, and the American landscape.

The Joshua Tree by U2, photographed by Anton Corbijn, released in 1987.

Beyond album covers, musicians like Nick Cave and the Bad Seeds[5] drew inspiration from the visceral and emotionally charged elements of Neo-Expressionism in their lyrics and performances. The movement's emphasis on authenticity and raw emotion found resonance in the music of the era, inviting listeners to engage with complex and deeply personal themes.

Moreover, the irreverent and anti-establishment ethos of Neo-Expressionism also found a natural home in the world of fashion during the 1980s. Designers drew inspiration from the movement's rejection of conformity and embraced the idea of fashion as a means of self-expression. The avant-garde fashion designer Jean-Paul Gaultier[6] was known for his punk-inspired collections that echoed the spirit of Neo-Expressionism. His designs often featured bold and unconventional silhouettes, textured fabrics, and a sense of rebellion. Gaultier's fashion shows became theatrical performances that challenged traditional notions of beauty and gender, embodying the same spirit of defiance that characterized Neo-Expressionism art. British fashion icon Vivienne Westwood[7] embraced Neo-Expressionism's punk aesthetics, incorporating elements of street culture and countercultural rebellion into her designs. Her punk-inspired collections, like the iconic collection "Pirate"(1981), celebrated individuality and nonconformity. Westwood's fashion was a visual expression of the movement's rejection of societal norms.

The influence of Neo-Expressionism in fashion extended beyond the runway, permeating street style and popularizing elements such as torn clothing, graffiti-inspired prints, and an overall sense of edginess. The movement's celebration of the raw and the authentic had a profound impact on the way people expressed themselves through clothing, challenging traditional notions of fashion and beauty.

4 Neo-Expressionism and Graphic Design

The infusion of Neo-Expressionism into graphic design during the 1980s marked a transformative moment in the field. Graphic designers, inspired by the movement's bold brushwork, fragmented text, and unapologetic emotional intensity, embraced Neo-Expressionism as a means to challenge the prevailing design conventions and to convey a sense of authenticity and urgency. This dynamic relationship between Neo-Expressionism and graphic design left a lasting impact on the visual landscape of the decade.

In the realm of graphic design, the Neo-Expressionism's influence manifested in designs that defied conventions. Layouts became more chaotic, with elements intersecting and overlapping, mirroring the fractured and fragmented nature of the era. Color palettes turned vibrant and untamed, as designers sought to convey the emotional intensity of the times.

Album cover design underwent a significant evolution during the Neo-Expressionism era. Designers sought to create visuals that not only complemented the music but also conveyed the emotional depth and rawness of the music within. Neo-Expressionism offered a natural bridge between music and visual art, allowing album covers to become powerful canvases for artistic expression. The British graphic designer Peter Saville[8], known for his groundbreaking work with Factory Records, was at the forefront of this movement. His cover design for New Order's **2** *Power, Corruption & Lies* (1983) epitomized the fusion of Neo-Expressionism with graphic design. Saville employed a color code, inspired by the works of abstract painter Giorgio de Chirico, to replace conventional typography. The result was a visually striking and enigmatic cover that challenged traditional album art norms. Saville's innovative approach blurred the lines between fine art and graphic design, setting a new standard for album cover aesthetics.

Magazines in the 1980s also embraced the Neo-Expressionism aesthetics in their layouts, departing from the clean and Minimalist designs of the previous decade. This shift reflected a desire to engage readers on a more emotional and visceral level, inviting them to connect with the content on a deeper, more authentic plane. Founded by the iconic Andy Warhol in 1969, [3]*Interview*[9] magazine was a pioneer in combining fine art with graphic design. However, it was during the 1980s that the magazine truly embraced the Neo-Expressionism spirit. *Interview* featured bold typography, vibrant color palettes, and fragmented layouts that mirrored the spontaneity and intensity of the movement. The magazine's ability to seamlessly blend art, fashion, and celebrity culture in a Neo-Expressionism context made it a cultural touchstone of the era.

Album cover of *Power, Corruption & Lies* by New Order, designed by Peter Saville, released in 1983.

Cover of *Interview*, Vol. 1, No. 1, 1969.

Neo-Expressionism's influence in magazine layouts encouraged designers to embrace imperfection and the human touch. Handwritten fonts, uneven layouts, and the use of expressive brushwork became common features in the design of editorial spreads. This departure from rigid design norms added an element of authenticity and emotional resonance to the pages of magazines. The impact of the movement also extended into art exhibitions, where posters served as promotional tools. These posters often featured works by Neo-Expressionism artists themselves, creating a symbiotic relationship between the art and its promotion. The posters, like the art they represented, aimed to provoke emotion and spark curiosity.

5 Legacy

The Neo-Expressionism movement of the 1980s was not merely an artistic trend but a cultural phenomenon that extended its reach into music, fashion, and film. Its embrace of raw emotion, individualism, and urban vitality left an indelible mark on the graphic design landscape of the decade. It challenged designers to break free from the constraints of the past and to infuse their work with a newfound sense of urgency, authenticity, and the untamed spirit of the streets.

Graphic designers of the '80s eagerly embraced the energy and rebellious spirit of Neo-Expressionism, infusing their work with a newfound sense of immediacy and authenticity. This movement breathed life into graphic design, which had, in the previous decade, become somewhat sterile and formulaic. Typography underwent a transformation, mirroring the rawness of Neo-Expressionism. Hand-painted lettering and graffiti-style typography became prominent in graphic design, injecting a sense of urban vitality and street culture into advertisements, posters, and album covers.

The '80s saw a convergence of Neo-Expressionism with the burgeoning hip-hop and street art scenes. Graffiti artists like Keith Haring and Jean-Michel Basquiat blurred the lines between street art and fine art, and their influence seeped into graphic design. Designers began to incorporate graffiti-inspired elements, bold lines, and vibrant colors into their work, capturing the zeitgeist of the inner city.

Moreover, the Neo-Expressionism surge coincided with a growing interest in outsider art and art brut (raw art)—forms of art created by individuals outside the traditional art world. This appreciation for unconventional, untrained artists further fueled the rejection of artistic formalism and the embrace of the unrefined.

Notes:

1. Minimalism is an art and design movement that emerged in the late 1950s and 1960s, characterized by its focus on simplicity, clean lines, and a reduction of form to its essential elements. It emphasizes clarity, functionality, and the removal of unnecessary features, often using monochromatic color schemes, geometric shapes, and open spaces. In design, Minimalism advocates for "less is more," aiming to create an uncluttered, serene aesthetic that allows the viewer to focus on the essential. Influential in architecture, visual arts, and industrial design, Minimalism continues to inspire contemporary design practices.

2. Conceptualism, or Conceptual Art, is an avant-garde movement that emerged in the 1960s, emphasizing the idea or concept behind a work of art over its aesthetics or material qualities. Rooted in the belief that art should prioritize intellectual engagement, Conceptualism often challenges traditional forms of artistic expression by focusing on language, documentation, and process rather than visual presentation. Artists like Sol LeWitt, Joseph Kosuth, and Yoko Ono are central to the movement, who have had exerted a profound influence on contemporary art, encouraging critical discourse and pushing the boundaries of what can be considered art.

3. David Bowie (1947–2016) was an iconic English singer, songwriter, and actor whose influence extended across music, fashion, and art. Known for his eclectic musical style and innovative approach to performance, Bowie continually reinvented himself, from the glam rock persona Ziggy Stardust to the soul-infused character of the Thin White Duke. Bowie's impact on popular culture is profound, with a career that spanned five decades, marked by his ability to blend different genres and challenge conventional norms. His legacy is characterized by his visionary artistry and enduring influence on contemporary music and design.

4. U2 is an influential Irish rock band formed in Dublin in 1976, its members include Bono (Paul Hewson), The Edge (David Howell Evans), Adam Clayton, and Larry Mullen Jr. The band's sound is characterized by Bono's distinctive voice and The Edge's innovative guitar work playing, which often incorporates effects and delay. U2 achieved global acclaim with their albums *The Joshua Tree* and *Achtung Baby*, blending rock, punk, and electronic influences with socially conscious lyrics. Their contributions to music and culture have earned them numerous awards, including multiple Grammy Awards and induction into the Rock and Roll Hall of Fame.

5. Nick Cave and the Bad Seeds is an Australian rock band formed in 1983 by frontman Nick Cave, multi-instrumentalist Mick Harvey, and guitarist Blixa Bargeld. Known for their dark, brooding sound that blends post-punk, blues, and avant-garde elements, the band has been a major force in alternative music. Albums such as *Murder Ballads*, *The Boatman's Call*, and *Ghosteen* showcase Cave's poetic lyrics, often exploring themes of love, death, religion, and existentialism.

6. Jean-Paul Gaultier (b. 1952) is a French haute couture designer with an eponymous couture label. He was the design director of Hermès, the leading French fashion and luxury brand, from 2003 to 2010.

7. Vivienne Westwood (1941–2022) is a pioneering British fashion designer and businesswoman, widely credited with bringing punk and new wave fashion into the mainstream. Her early collaborations with Malcolm McLaren, manager of the Sex Pistols, in the 1970s helped define the rebellious aesthetic of punk rock, characterized by distressed clothing, safety pins, and provocative graphics. Her collections, such as the iconic "Pirate" and "Anglomania" lines, challenged conventional fashion norms and promoted political activism. Westwood's work has had a lasting impact on

both fashion and culture, cementing her legacy as a revolutionary figure in the industry.

8. Peter Saville (b. 1955) is a renowned British graphic designer whose work, particularly during his tenure at Factory Records, shaped the visual language of post-punk and new wave music. While rooted in modernist and Minimalist principles, Saville's approach also bears connections to Neo-Expressionism in its emotive, raw, and often abstract qualities. Saville's designs for album covers—most notably for Joy Division's *Unknown Pleasures* and New Order's *Power, Corruption & Lies*—reflected an experimental, almost painterly sensibility that parallels the emotional intensity and bold visual gestures characteristic of Neo-Expressionism art. His approach blends modernist principles with a bold, experimental aesthetic, making his work instantly recognizable and highly influential in both graphic design and popular culture.

9. *Interview* is an American magazine founded in 1969 by artist Andy Warhol and British journalist John Wilcock. Known as "The Crystal Ball of Pop," *Interview* became a cultural touchstone by blending celebrity interviews, avant-garde art, and Warhol's fascination with fame. The magazine featured candid conversations with leading figures in art, music, film, and fashion, often conducted by Warhol himself or his inner circle. Its bold visual style, marked by innovative photography and design, reflected Warhol's art sensibilities and helped shape the intersection of art and celebrity culture in the 20th century.

KEY ARTISTS & THEIR ICONIC WORKS

Jean-Michel Basquiat
(1960-1988)

He is a trailblazing artist from New York City. Basquiat began as a graffiti artist before transitioning to painting. His work is characterized by a raw and frenetic energy, with chaotic compositions often featured a blend of text, symbols, and bold brushwork. Basquiat's art explores themes of identity, race, and urban life. His short but impactful career left an indelible mark on Neo-Expressionism.

1. *Boy and Dog in a Johnnypump* (1982)
This is a vibrant and dynamic painting that showcases his distinctive style and thematic concerns. The artwork features a boy and a dog depicted in Basquiat's characteristic expressive and raw manner, set against a backdrop of bold, fiery colors. The composition is chaotic yet controlled, with energetic brushstrokes and a mix of abstract and figurative elements. Central to the piece are the themes of urban life and struggle, with the "johnnypump" (a New York slang term for fire hydrant) symbolizing the artist's connection to the streets of New York City and reflecting the gritty, resilient spirit of urban life.

2. *Untitled (Skull)* (1981)
This is a quintessential Basquiat piece that exemplifies his raw, energetic style and his ability to fuse text and image. Created during a pivotal period in his career, this painting is marked by its intense color palette, chaotic composition, and the presence of Basquiat's signature motifs, including crowns, skeletal figures, and fragmented text. The work reflects his deep engagement with themes of identity, race, and social commentary, blending elements of street art, primitivism, and abstract expressionism.

Keith Haring
(1958-1990)

He is an American artist and social activist known for his graffiti-inspired work. Emerged in the New York City art scene in the late 1970s and early 1980s, Haring gained prominence with his distinct, bold lines, vibrant colors, and energetic imagery, often depicting dancing figures, radiant babies, and barking dogs. His work, which started in subway stations and public spaces, was deeply influenced by street culture and Pop Art. Haring's art carried strong social messages, addressing issues like AIDS awareness, apartheid, and LGBTQ+ rights. He ever collaborated with notable artists like Jean-Michel Basquiat and Andy Warhol.

3. *Radiant Baby* (1982)
The work is a joyful and optimistic symbol that encapsulates Haring's belief in the transformative power of art. This simple yet powerful image features a crawling baby outlined in Haring's signature bold black lines, with radiating lines emanating from its body, symbolizing energy and innocence.

4. *Crack is Wack* (1986)
The work is a mural in Harlem, New York City, that powerfully addresses the crack cocaine epidemic of the 1980s. The central image of the mural includes stylized human figures interacting with symbolic elements such as serpents and skulls, reflecting the destructive impact of drug addiction. Haring's accessible and direct visual language aims to raise awareness and provoke community action against the devastating effects of crack cocaine.

Anselm Kiefer
(1945-)

He is a renowned German painter and sculptor known for his large-scale, textured works that confront Germany's history and collective memory, particularly the legacy of the Third Reich and the Holocaust. Emerged in the late 20th century, Kiefer's art often incorporates materials like lead, straw, ash, clay, and shellac, creating a rich, tactile quality. His pieces are marked by their somber, contemplative tone and their engagement with themes of destruction, renewal, and myth. Kiefer's work frequently references literature, mythology, and history, with recurring motifs such as charred books, barren landscapes, and ruined architectures. Through his evocative and often controversial works, Kiefer challenges viewers to reflect on the complexities of memory, identity, and the passage of time.

5. *Everyone Stands under His Own Dome of Heaven* (1970)

The work reimagines the figure of the artist in a vast, snow-dusted field, isolated by a transparent hemisphere. The figure's Nazi salute is visible but shielded by the dome. Kiefer has explained that the pose acts like a "lightning rod" for our attention while the dome limits its power. In discussing this work, he stated, "Each man has his own dome, his own perceptions, his own theories. There is no one god for all. Each man has his own, and sometimes (it) overlaps with or intersects another's."

6. *Margarethe* (1981)

The work addresses themes of memory, history, and the Holocaust. Referenced Goethe's *Faust* and explored the impact of literature and myth on the human psyche, the painting is inspired by Paul Celan's poem *Death Fugue*, which juxtaposes the figures of Margarete (symbolizing German culture) and Shulamith (representing Jewish victims). He uses a palette dominated by straw and golden hues to depict the mythical German heroine, intertwining the strands of straw with the canvas to create a textured, almost sculptural surface.

Georg Baselitz
(1938–)

He is a German painter and sculptor known for his provocative and confrontational style. His work often features distorted and contorted figures, challenging conventional notions of representation. Besides, Baselitz's art also explores themes of identity and nationhood. His frequent use of inversion can destabilize familiar imagery and evoke a sense of disorientation, ultimately prompting a deeper contemplation of cultural and historical narratives.

7. *The Naked Man* (1962)

The painting features a distorted, raw depiction of a nude male figure. The figure is rendered with bold, gestural brushstrokes and a palette dominated by flesh tones, conveying a sense of vulnerability and existential angst. His unconventional approach to the human form, characterized by inversion and fragmentation, reflects his interest in exploring the psychological and emotional depths of his subjects.

8. *Eagle* (1981)

In this piece, Baselitz presents an inverted eagle, a motif often associated with power and national identity, particularly in Germany. The painting features bold, expressive brushstrokes and a vivid color palette. By turning the eagle upside down, he disrupts its traditional symbolism, challenged viewers to reconsider its meaning and connotations.

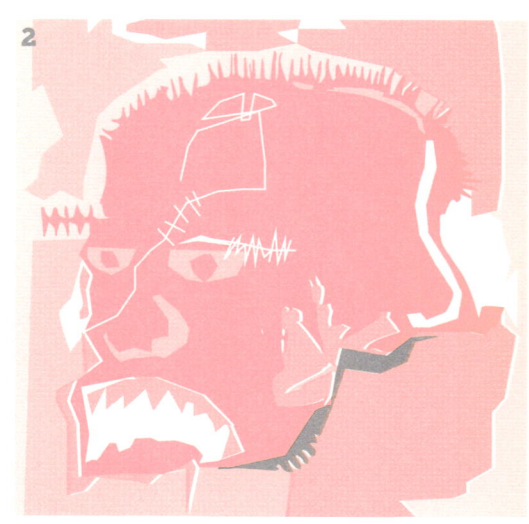

DIGITAL REVOLUTION: A FUSION OF TECHNOLOGY AND CUTTING-EDGE DESIGN

In the 1980s, the world stood at a historic turning point as the Digital Revolution quietly unfolded. This era marked the rise of information technology and the digital wave, with these emerging technologies beginning to deeply penetrate every aspect of society. In particular, the rapid development of computers and digital graphics technology not only greatly changed people's lifestyles but also had a profound impact on artistic creation.

Since the birth of computers, digital technology has rapidly transformed the global landscape at an unprecedented rate. This revolution, driven by digital advancements, has profoundly reshaped the field of graphic design. Reflecting on the origins of digital technology underscores its remarkable evolution. Decades ago, computers were colossal, expensive machines accessible primarily to research institutions and large corporations. Yet, with technological progress and cost reductions, personal computers gradually permeated households worldwide. A pivotal moment arrived with the introduction of the 1Macintosh computer. Beyond its intuitive graphical interface, the Macintosh boasted robust graphic processing capabilities, empowering non-professionals to engage effortlessly in graphic design and editing. The widespread adoption of the Macintosh significantly democratized graphic design, providing a broader platform for creative expression.

During this era, rapid advancements in computer technology provided unprecedented tools for artistic creation. The continuous evolution of digital graphics technology offered abundant creative resources and expanded possibilities for artistic expression. Previously, artists relied on labor-intensive photography and darkroom techniques for image processing, whereas designers at that time effortlessly employed these tools for intricate graphic manipulations like image compositing, color adjustments, and filter effects, leading to novel visual outcomes. The swift development of digital technology not only transformed design tools and processes but also revolutionized designers' mindsets. Pioneering designers emerged as early adopters of emerging technologies in graphic design, leveraging digital advancements to pioneer new trends. Traditional graphic design, constrained by physical media and manual techniques, often limited the realization of creative visions. However, with digital technology's support, designers' imaginations were liberated as never before. They could freely explore diverse design elements and styles, unrestricted by traditional production methods and material constraints. Their work challenged conventional design principles, daring to experiment with innovative concepts and techniques, injecting fresh vitality into graphic design in the digital age.

The impact of the Digital Revolution on graphic design was profound. It not only changed the way designers work but also expanded the boundaries and possibilities of design. Driven by digital technology, graphic design has evolved from singular visual expression to a fusion with multiple media and technologies, forming a diverse design ecosystem. This Digital Revolution has brought countless conveniences and surprises. Today, whether in print, advertising, packaging design, user interfaces, or interactive design, digital technology plays a pivotal role. It makes design more precise, efficient, and creative, while providing designers with a broad stage to showcase their talents and creativity.

The footsteps of the Digital Revolution have not ceased; the 1980s were a leap forward, and to this day, it continues to advance at astonishing speed. With the emergence of new technologies like artificial intelligence and virtual reality, the future of graphic design will present even more diverse and expansive possibilities. In the 21st century, this field still holds endless potential value and exploration space.

1 The Rapid Development of Digital Technology in the 1980s

The 1980s was a decade of revolutionary change in digital technology, marking a period of rapid development that profoundly influenced all aspects of society, particularly the field of graphic design. The emergence of personal computers, desktop publishing (DTP), digital typesetting, and advanced computer-aided design tools provided designers with new capabilities and creative possibilities. These technological advances not only transformed the way designers worked but also shaped the aesthetic perspectives of that era, giving rise to new styles and visual languages.

Among many breakthroughs of the 1980s, the advent of personal computers was undoubtedly the most striking. Personal computers introduced by companies like Apple, IBM, and Commodore empowered individuals and small businesses with powerful computing and graphic processing capabilities, making previously enterprise-only technologies accessible to all. In particular, the release of the Macintosh computer by Apple in 1984 had a profound impact on graphic design. Its user-friendly graphical interface, coupled with software like 2MacPaint and 3MacDraw, enabled designers to create and manipulate images in entirely new ways. The combination of mouse-driven interfaces and WYSIWYG (what you see is what you get) software revolutionized the design process, allowing designers to preview final print results directly on screen. This technological development not only greatly simplified the design workflow but also provided designers with ample space to explore new creative styles.

The rise of personal computers also propelled "desktop" to become a new platform for graphic designers. In the 1980s, Desktop Publishing emerged, allowing designers to directly edit and typeset in a digital environment, efficiently saving time and enhancing design accuracy. Software like 4Aldus PageMaker, released in 1985, enabled designers to lay out text and images on digital pages with unprecedented precision and flexibility. When aided by high-resolution laser printers such as the Apple LaserWriter, designers could produce professional-quality publications

Macintosh Computer, lauched in 1984

MacPrint Icon, designed by Bill Atkinson, 1983.

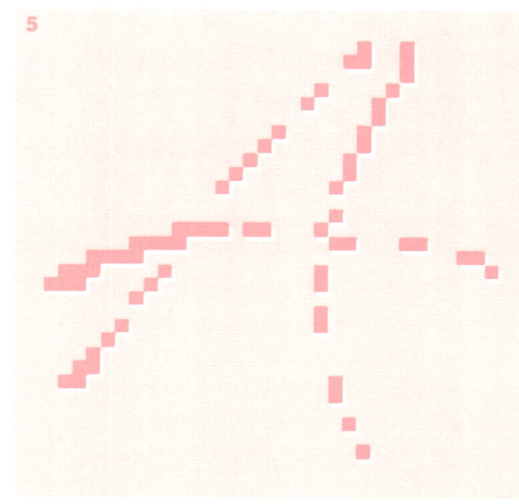

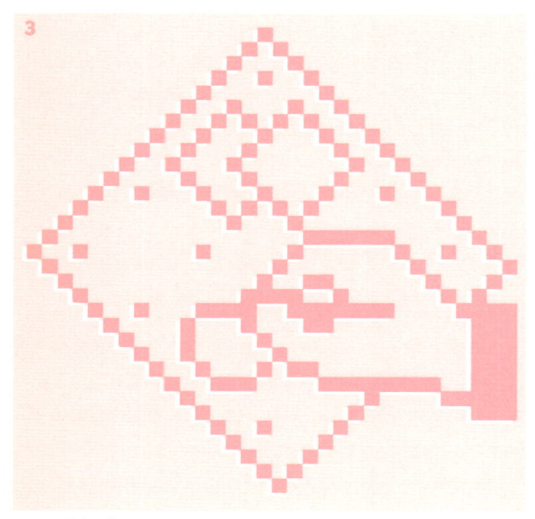

MacDraw Icon, designed by Bill Atkinson, 1983.

Aldus PageMaker Version 3.01 Image, Aldus Corporation, 1985–2001.

Adobe Illustrator Logo Version 1.0, Adobe Systems, Inc., 1987.

Adobe Photoshop Logo Version 1.0, Adobe Systems, Inc., 1991–1994.

Logo of Adobe PostScript 3, Adobe Systems, Inc., circa 1997.

Revolution spawned a wide range of digital art forms, as designers experimented with new capabilities in typography, layout, and imagery in a digital environment, each exploring the unique possibilities of digital media.

The transition from physical to digital media has catalyzed the development of digital fonts. In the past, typesetting relied heavily on physical fonts, such as metal type or woodblock printing. However, with the advent of digital technology, fonts began to be created and edited on computer screens. This transformation granted designers unprecedented control, allowing them to precisely adjust the size, spacing, and style of fonts. Adobe's introduction of 7PostScript technology in 1984 marked a significant milestone in the history of digital font design. PostScript, as a page description language, enabled fine control over the appearance of text, graphics, and images on printed pages. It quickly rose to become the industry standard for desktop publishing, facilitating the high-quality, scalable output of text and vector graphics. This technology allowed designers to create complex layouts with fine typographic details, further enhanced the quality of printed materials and the sophistication of designs.

The newfound ability to experiment with typography, layout, and imagery in a digital environment led to the emergence of new styles and visual languages. One notable example is the rise of digital typefaces and the use of bitmap fonts, which were characterized by their pixelated appearance. These fonts, such as 8Chicago and 9Geneva (used in the early Macintosh operating systems), became iconic symbols of the digital age. Designers embraced the pixelated aesthetics, incorporated it into various design projects to evoke the modernity and technological innovation of the time. Designed to match the pixel grids of early computer monitors, these fonts optimised the legibility and overall aesthetics of text in low-resolution environments. Pixel fonts played a pivotal role in early video games and computer interfaces, and have become iconic for their unique strengths.

without relying on expensive and complex traditional printing processes. This revolution not only reduced costs but also drastically shortened production times, providing more opportunities for experimentation and rapid iteration in design projects.

Simultaneously, computer-aided design tools made significant strides in the 1980s, fundamentally changing how images were created and processed. For instance, softwares like 5Adobe Illustrator, introduced in 1987, brought powerful vector graphics tools that allowed designers to create scalable, resolution-independent artworks. These tools made the precise and straightforward creation of complex illustrations, logos, and other graphic elements become possible. Additionally, raster graphics softwares like 6Adobe Photoshop (although released in 1990, its development began in the late 1980s) enabled designers to digitally edit and manipulate photographic images. These tools provided unprecedented control over image composition, color correction, and special effects, thereby fundamentally altering the landscape of photography and graphic design.

2 Digital Revolution and Graphic Design in the 1980s

The rapid growth of digital technology in the 1980s not only changed the tools and processes used by designers, but also influenced the aesthetics of graphic design. The wave of Digital

8

Chicago

Aa Ee Qq
Rr Ss Tt

Insert disk

abcdefghijklm
nopqrstuvwxyz

Specimen of the Typeface Chicago, GearedBull (Jim Hood), 2010.

9

Geneva

Aa Ee Rr
Aa Ee Rr

Electrolytes

abcdefghijklm
nopqrstuvwxyz
0123456789

Specimen of the Typeface Geneva, Brian Krent, 2015.

Besides, the emergence of large-scale font libraries also became one of the hallmarks of digital design in the 1980s. Digital type foundries such as Adobe and Bitstream began to develop and distribute digital fonts, which could be easily installed and used on personal computers. This development vastly expanded the range of fonts available to designers, fostering greater creativity and diversity in typographic design.

The use of digital tools has empowered designers to create complex and multi-layered compositions, leading to a more vivid and free-spirited visual style in the design field. Designers such as April Greiman and Neville Brody[1] have broken free from the constraints of traditional layouts and typography, boldly experimented with overlapping elements, varying font sizes, and asymmetric compositions. This approach was a key feature of the New Wave graphic design movement, and April Greiman is one of its pioneers. Greiman used a Macintosh computer to create the iconic poster *Does it Make Sense?*, published in *Design Quarterly*. This poster ingeniously combined digital imagery, pixelated graphics, and overlapping text elements, leading to a visually complex and captivating composition. Greiman's work not only demonstrated the immense potential of digital tools in creating innovative and visually striking designs but also inspired a generation of designers to explore the possibilities of digital technology more deeply.

During Japan's postwar recovery, the country rode the wave of the Digital Revolution. In this era, the works of Japanese designer Mitsuo Katsui[2] emerged as iconic symbols. Throughout his design career, Katsui tirelessly explored the fusion of computer technology and graphic design. He once remarked, "Time becomes a factor in cyberspace. Using a Macintosh, I was able to create momentary, mysterious spaces that differed from the fixed world that exists on paper." Katsui was fascinated by the interplay between new technologies and light, adeptly used the colors of light as a design language. By leveraging computer and digital technologies, he infused his designs with a strong sense of personal identity. His work not only exemplified the seamless integration of digital technology and art design, but also showcased innovative optical illusion principles in his later pieces. This inventive approach highlighted his deep understanding of digital media technology. Mitsuo Katsui continuously pushed the boundaries of graphic design form and content, providing invaluable inspiration for future designers and becoming a perpetual source of creativity in the design world.

3 Digital Art in the 21st Century

As we move further into the 21st century, the legacy of the Digital Revolution continue to shape the art world. The fusion of technology and avant-garde sensibilities has given rise to new art forms, such as virtual reality art, augmented reality installations, and algorithmic art. These forms challenge our perceptions of reality and push the boundaries of artistic expression, injecting more possibilities for artistic creation.

Looking back to the 1980s, the wave of the Digital Revolution proved that technology and art could coexist in harmony. The era not only warmly embraced the innovations of digital technology, but also challenged designers to push the boundaries of their craft. The fusion of traditional artistic influences with cutting-edge technology led to a unique visual language that was both nostalgic and futuristic. Today, digital art has found its place in mainstream culture. It is no longer confined to niche galleries but has become a recognized and celebrated form of artistic expression. Digital artists have gained prominence in the art world, and their works are increasingly being collected, exhibited, and even traded on the market alongside traditional art.

In conclusion, the Digital Revolution of the 1980s ushered in a new era of artistic innovation and creativity. The various kinds of digital art, born amidst this technological upheaval, harnessed the power of digital tools to redefine the boundaries of art. It has enabled artists to blend tradition with innovation and, transcend physical limitations and geographical boundaries. As we navigate the ever-evolving landscape of digital art in the 21st century, we continue to witness the profound impact of this fusion of technology and pioneering spirit on the world of creativity and expression.

Notes:

1. Neville Brody (b. 1957) is a distinguished British graphic designer and typographer renowned for his influential contributions to contemporary design. As the founder of Brody Associates, his innovative work has significantly shaped the visual language of modern typography and graphic design. Brody's pioneering approach to type design and his role in defining the aesthetics of the 1980s through his work with magazines like *The Face* and *Arena* are widely recognized. His impact extends through his typefaces, including the iconic FF Blur and FF Dirty, and his commitment to pushing the boundaries of design practice.

2. Mitsuo Katsui (1931–2019) was a distinguished Japanese graphic designer and a member of the Alliance Graphique Internationale (AGI). Renowned for his innovative approach, Katsui made a profound impact on graphic design during the Digital Revolution. His work uniquely blended traditional Japanese aesthetics with contemporary design techniques, leading to significant contributions to typography, branding, and visual communication. Known for his emphasis on light-centered design languages, Katsui produced numerous influential works. His career spanned the transition from analog to digital media, reflecting his ability to adapt and influence the evolving design landscape.

IGOR GUROVICH:
STRETCHING THE BOUNDARIES OF DESIGN

Igor Gurovich is a graphic designer who graduated from the Stroganov Moscow Design Academy of Design and Applied Arts in 1991 with a diploma in automotive design. However, his career trajectory shifted when he began working as a production artist in a small theater during his second phase of education.

Captivated by set and costume design, Gurovich found greater fulfillment in bringing sketches to life on the theatrical stage than in drawing cars. He discovered that while car drawings often remained on paper due to economic constraints, sketches for the theater transformed into tangible costumes and scenography pieces. Additionally, making posters for each play became his favorite aspect of the job.

At just 21 years old, Gurovich learned a crucial lesson about design: freedom of interpretation is paramount. Drawing from his theater experiences, he seamlessly transferred his skills to poster making, believing that, like a theatrical performance, a poster must tell a compelling story—a concept often overlooked in contemporary design.

Recognized for his unique approach, Gurovich's posters are likened to theatrical stages, where characters and typography take on the role of heroes. This characteristic allows him to effortlessly blend diverse styles within a single composition, from the marginal to the refined and from the beautiful to the unconventional. Inspired by the world's endless surprises and diversity, Gurovich remains committed to exploring new systems and characters for his theatrical creations.

In the dim glow of vintage arcade machines, a realm where the past and present converge, we meet Igor Gurovich, the creative mind behind the captivating posters adorning the Museum of Soviet Arcade Machines since 2008 (FIG.1). This museum, a treasure trove of retro design, showcases machines, electronics, and objects from the USSR era, spanning the early 1970s to the early 1990s. Each poster is a testament to Gurovich's profound nostalgia for the spirit of freedom and experimentation that characterized this bygone era.

Gurovich has masterfully intertwined authentic graphic components from 1970s USSR technical posters and books found within the museum's collection. These posters are not merely advertisements but portals to a time when design was an exploration, a daring journey into the unknown. He incorporates technical drawings, an often overlooked style for museum posters, skillfully blends them with other visual languages such as postcards and street typography. The result is a captivating fusion of the past and present, each piece invites viewers to embark on a nostalgic visual journey.

In his view, a poster is not merely an announcement of an event but a promise of happiness. He sees his work as creating an expectation of joy, aligning perfectly with the spirit of the museum, where in the same exhibition, one can find arcades from the 80s, old Soviet posters, Soviet furniture, and ice cream with sodas—elements that vividly remind Gurovich of his childhood. His posters, therefore, are imbued with a sense of nostalgia and emotional resonance, promising visitors an experience that transcends mere visual appeal. Through his work, Gurovich captures the essence of time when creativity flourished within the constraints of a rigid system. His designs for the Museum of Soviet Arcade Machines are a tribute to the innovative spirit of the era, reflecting a deep appreciation for the subtle nuances of Soviet aesthetics. As viewers wander through the museum, they are transported back to a world where every detail tells a story, every line and curve is a whisper of history.

Gurovich's posters serve as a bridge between the past and present, a testament to his enduring passion for the art of design. His ability to evoke nostalgia through his work is not just a nod to the past but a celebration of the timeless nature of creativity and experimentation. In his hands, the visual language of the Soviet era is reborn, offering a glimpse into a rich historical context while resonating with contemporary audiences. Through his evocative designs, Gurovich invites us to remember, to dream, and to find inspiration in the echoes of a vibrant, experimental past.

> "The most important qualities of 80s design that I consider are its freedom and experimentation."

1 THE METAPHOR

Igor Gurovich frequently draws significant inspiration from the Polish School of Posters, a movement renowned for its innovative approach to graphic design. He particularly admires the unique perspectives, methods, and practices of Henryk Tomaszewski[1], Jan Lenica[2], Milton Glaser[3], and Jan van Toorn[4]. These pioneering designers have profoundly influenced Gurovich's approach to graphic design, shaping his creative vision and techniques.

The Polish School of Posters emerged in the post-World War II era, flourished particularly from the 1950s to 1980s. This movement is celebrated for its unique blend of artistic expression, cultural commentary, and innovative design. Despite being under a tight regime, Polish poster artists enjoyed a surprising amount of creative freedom. This freedom to innovate within certain boundaries pushed artists to find clever and subtle ways to express their ideas. Polish poster designers excelled at integrating

WORKS BY IGOR GUROVICH

FIG. 10

FIG. 7 THE WHITE SQUARE

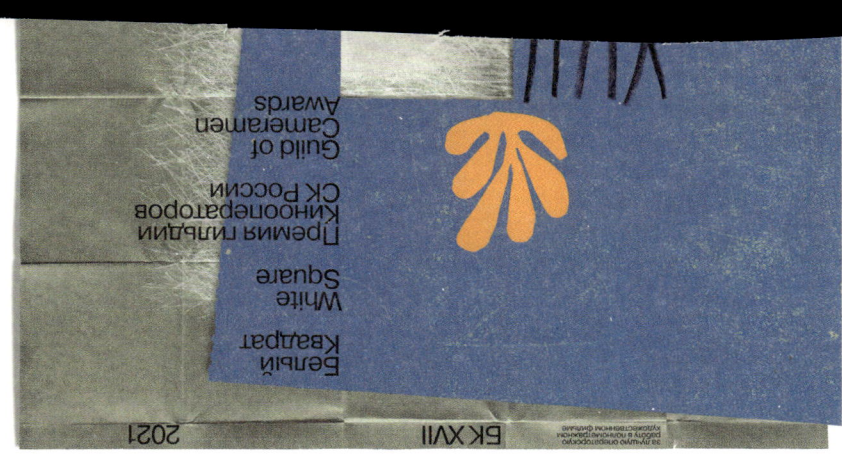

FIG. 8 CUT

FIG. 1

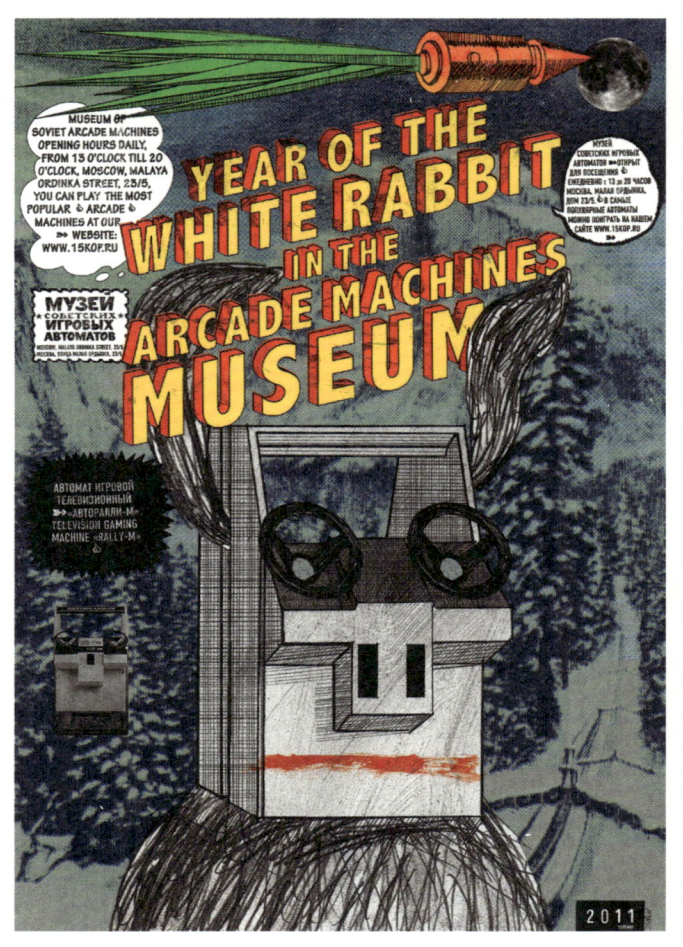

MUSEUM OF SOVIET ARCADE MACHINES

CHAMPION MUSEUM
老虎機博物館
SOVIET ARCADE MASHIN
IN 2015
АВТОРАЛЛИ·М
俄羅斯
國母
萬歲
羊的一年
ARBEITS KOLLEKTIV

museum of soviet arcade machines
2021. year of science & technology
since 2007
15 kop .ru
莫斯科博物館
★科學和技術
Газированная ВОДА

博物館
SOVIET
ARCADE
MASHIN
MUSEUM
街頭
橋梁
工匠
15KOP.RU

博物館 museum
soviet
mashines
2023

DAILY DRAWING

FIG. 9

CULTURAL CENTER DOM

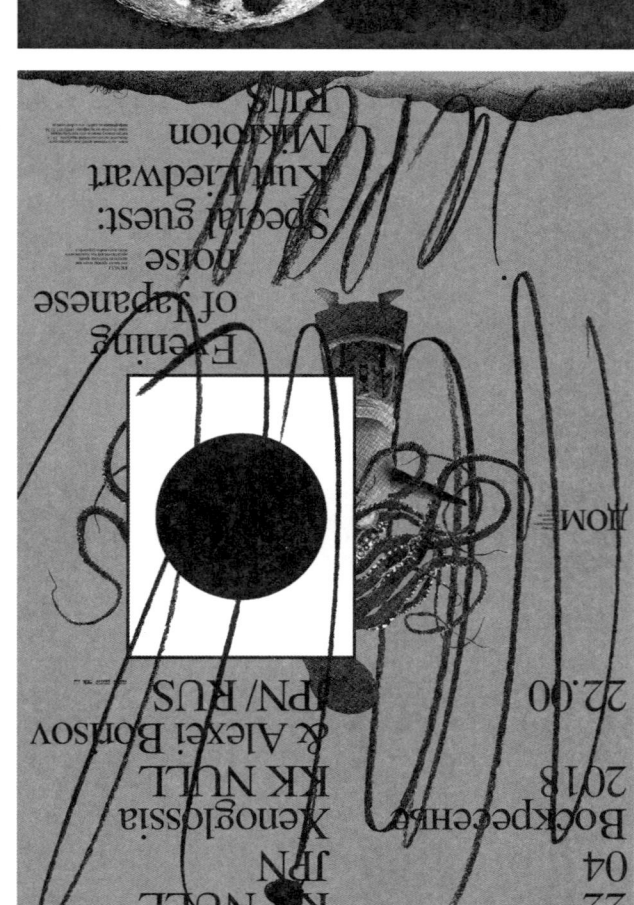

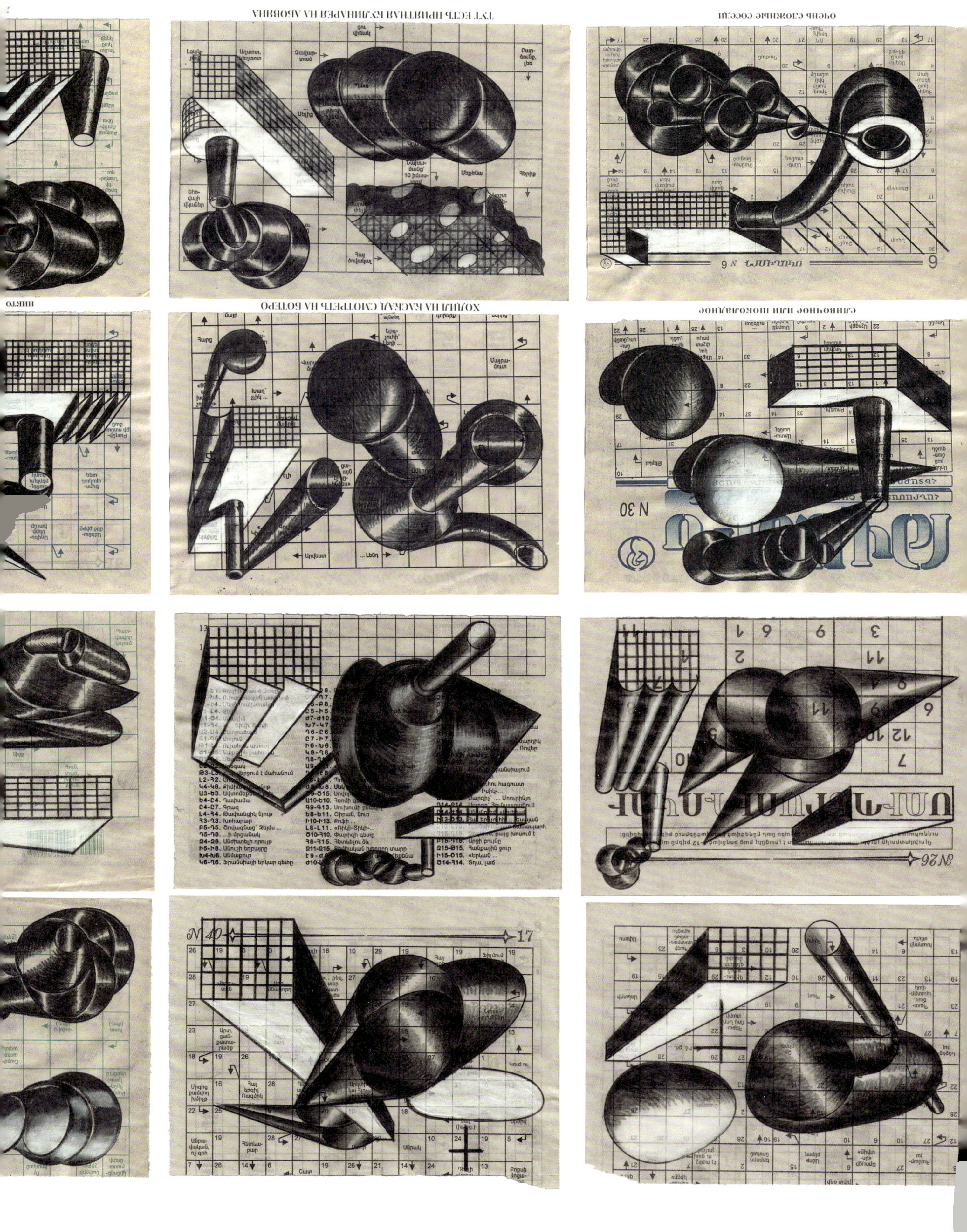
ТУТ ЕСТЬ ПРИЯТНАЯ КУЛИНАРИЯ НА АБОВЯНА
ОЧЕНЬ СЛОЖНЫЕ СОСЕДИ
НИКТО
ХОДИЛИ НА КАСКАД СМОТРЕТЬ НА БОТЕРО
СЛИВОЧНОЕ ИЛИ ШОКОЛАДНОЕ
N 30
№26
N 40

FIG. 2
BOLSHOI DRAMA THEATER NAMED AFTER G.A.TOVSTONOGOV

FIG. 3 THE INTERNATIONAL KANSK VIDEO FESTIVAL

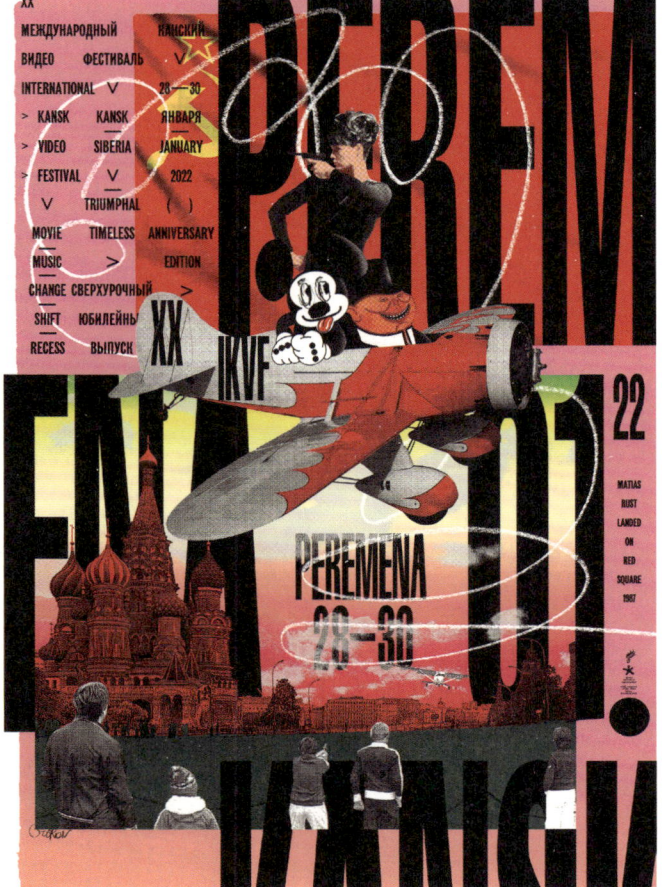

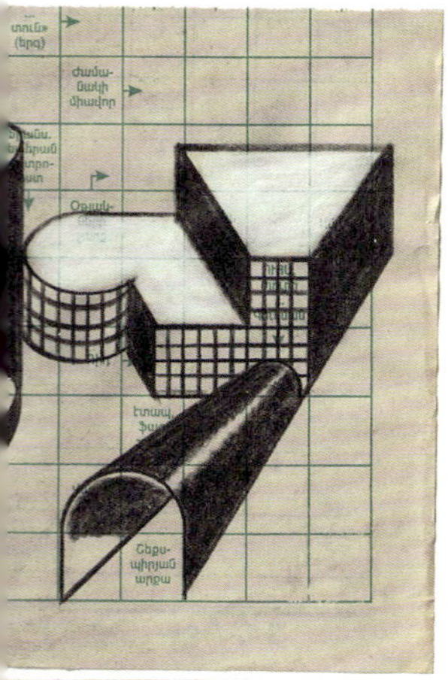

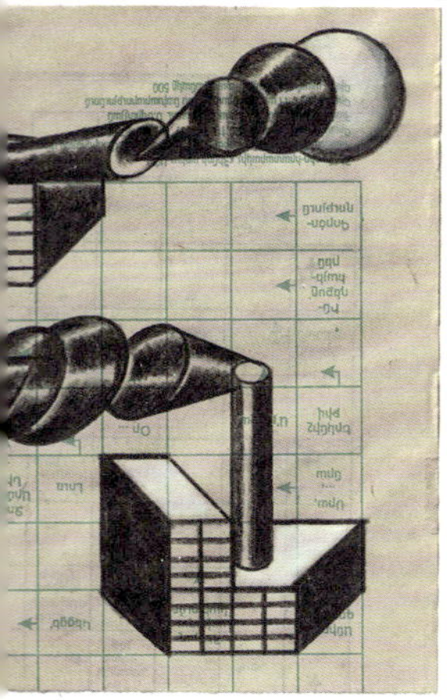

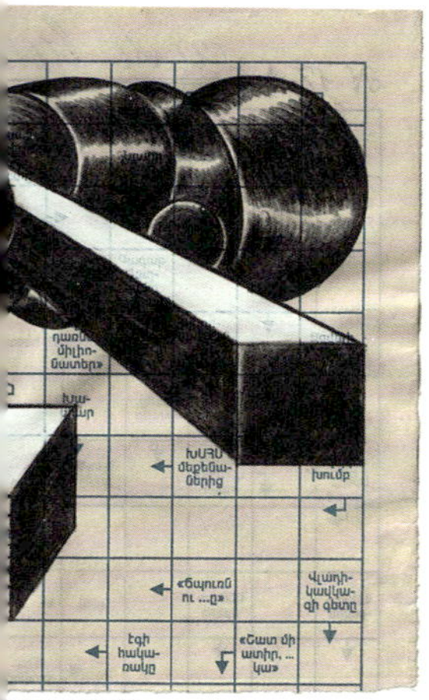

м нарвался

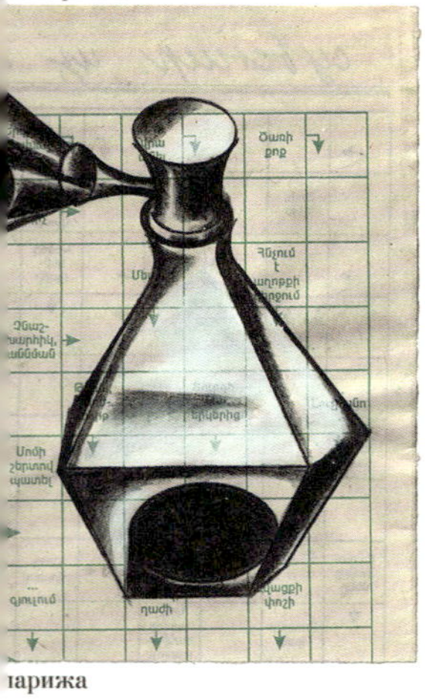

арижа

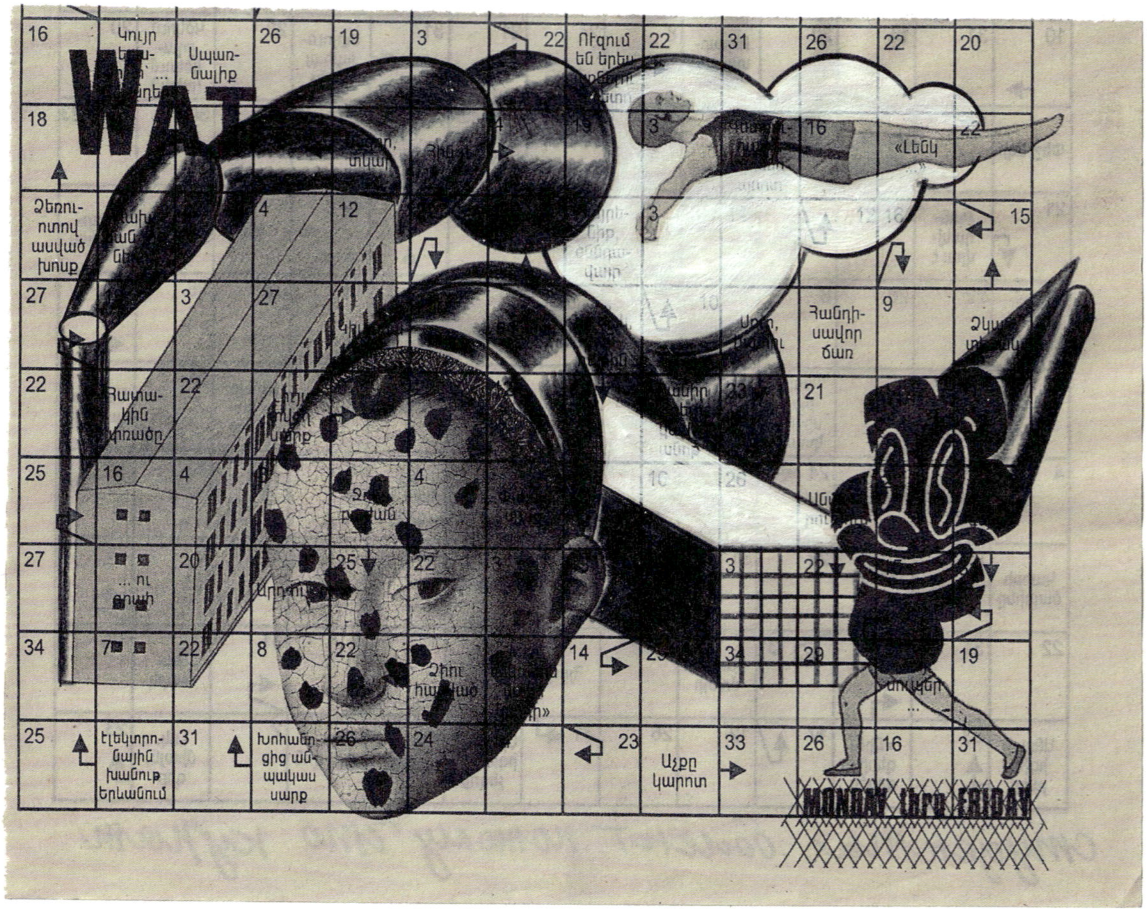

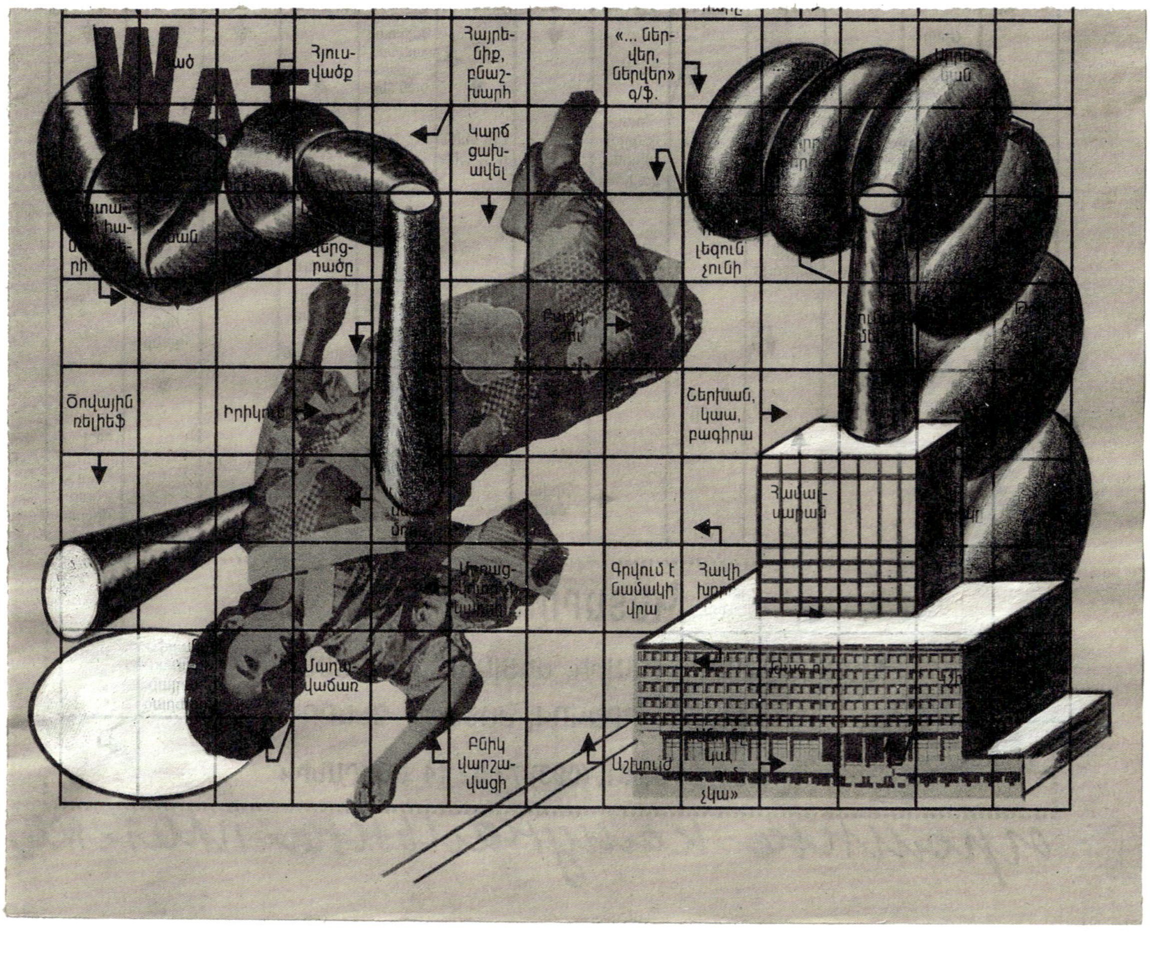

OR ELECTRO

22. 07.
22:00
2022

NEW Y
PA RTY
20 24
NOOR
ELECTRO
noor
is a
legend
bar

NOOR
ANNUAL
PARTY
BYE-
BYE
SEPT
2023
ЕЖЕ
ГОДНОЕ
ПРОЩАН
ИЕ С ХУ
ЙНЕЙ
NOOR
BAR
СЕН
ТЯБ
20
23
ANN
PARTY
男性のペニス
別れ
ファックで

noor
electro
bar & gallery
noorbar.com
2023
june

ПЯТНИЦА!10!ЛЕТ!
ИЮНЬ!TVCHANNEL
(2013 2023)NOOR!ELECTRO!
SUMMER!!FRIDAY!
FRI
DAY
POP
UP
BAR
2013
2023
TV CHANNEL FRIDAY! NOOR BAR/SUMMER/ PARTY

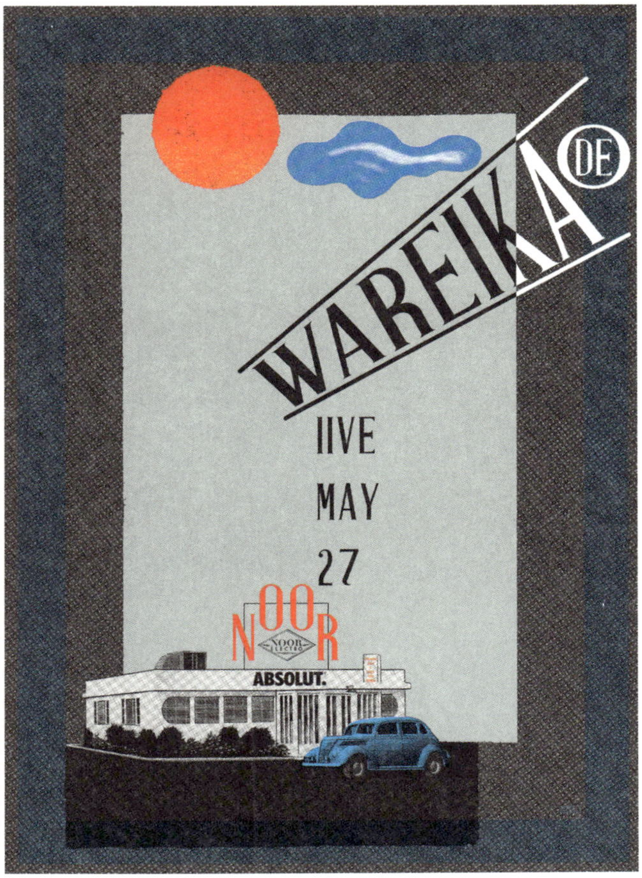
WAREIKA
DE
IIVE
MAY
27
NOOR
ABSOLUT.

FIG. 4

BIG CARTOON FESTIVAL

You can cut them out and find their place in the following text.

- NEW WAVE TYPOGRAPHY
- Metallic Shine
- VIBRANT PALETTE
- Pastel Dreams
- Graffiti and Street Art Typography
- Neon Brilliance
- PIXELATED TYPOGRAPHY
- Memphis Group Lettering
- FUTURISTIC TYPOGRAPHY.

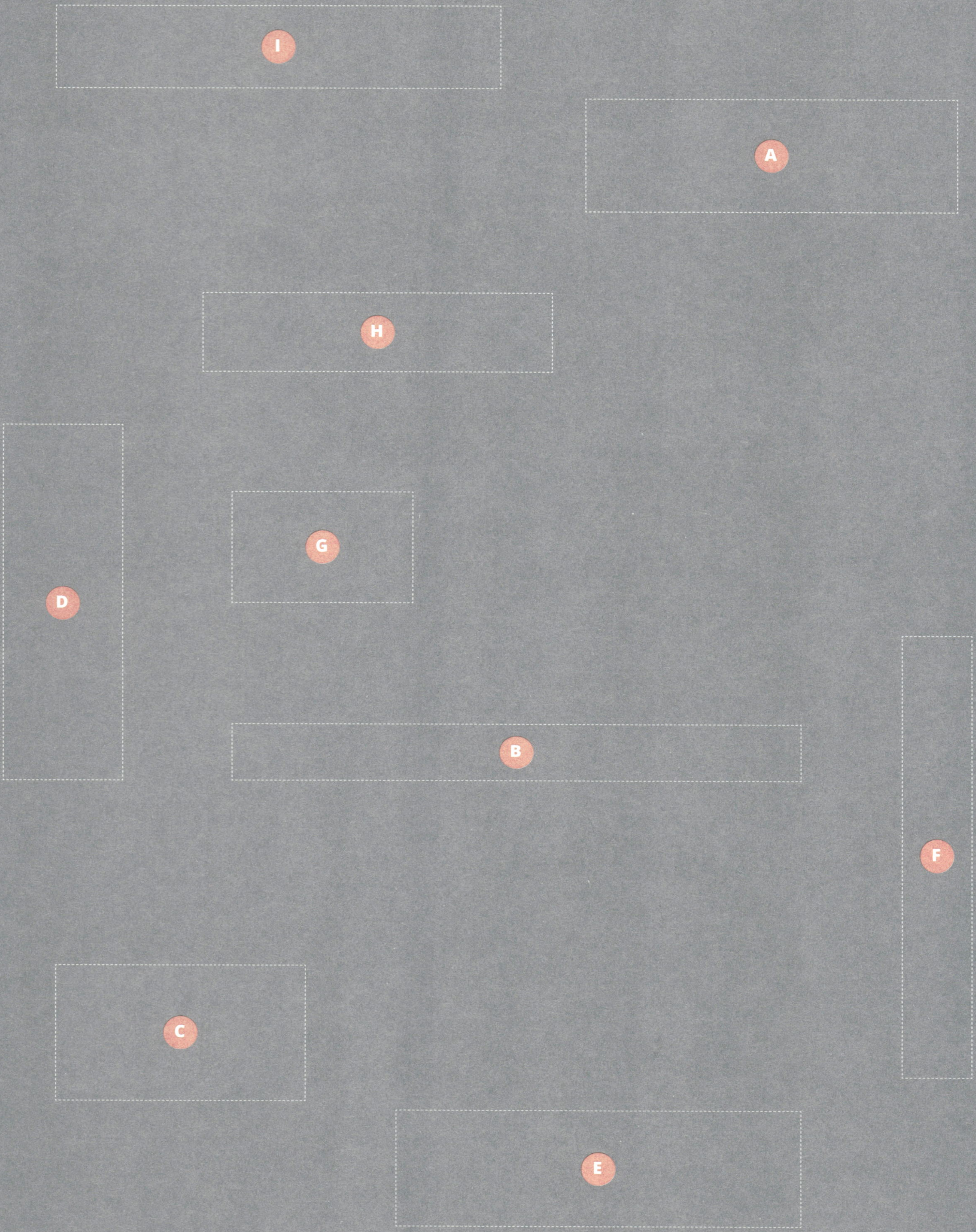
I
A
H
D
G
B
F
C
E

WHY WE YEARN FOR THE 80S— NOSTALGIA

The resurgence of 1980s nostalgia in contemporary design is far more than a superficial yearning for days gone by; it is a profound emotional connection to an era of unique cultural dynamism and technological innovation. It is a cultural phenomenon driven by a complex interplay of factors that extend beyond mere sentimentality. To understand its significance, we must first cast our gaze back to the 1980s—a decade that defied convention and embraced a spirit of audacious exploration.

From the rise of the personal computer, to the explosion of musical genres, and to groundbreaking cinema and television, the 1980s embodied a fervent spirit of experimentation and optimism for the future. Eclectic and enthusiastic, the decade left an indelible mark on the cultural consciousness. It was undeniably characterized by a sense of daring and experimentation, with artists and designers pushing the limits of their craft with unwavering courage. From the neon-lit streets of city centers to the vibrant covers of magazines and albums, design in the 80s was not a passive medium but an active force—a cultural catalyst that challenged norms and redefined aesthetics. And the embrace of technology allowed them to explore more possibilities for art. The advent of the personal computer and the rise of desktop publishing democratized graphic design, allowing the tools of creation to reach a wider audience. Designers eagerly embraced this digital frontier, experimented with digital typography, pixel and computer-generated graphics. This technological revolution changed the face of graphic design and paved the way for a new era of possibilities.

The 1980s also witnessed the emergence of subcultures that left an indelible mark on design. The punk and DIY (do-it-yourself) movements, for instance, introduced a raw and anarchic aesthetics that challenged the polish of mainstream design. This rebellion against the establishment found expression in album covers, zines, and flyers, where hand-drawn illustrations, collages, and a disregard for conventional aesthetics became the norm. It was a visual revolution that celebrated imperfection and authenticity.

A journey through time takes us to the beauty of the 80s design, which has always been associated with a vibrant spirit. Bold, saturated colors, geometric shapes, and playful patterns (often whimsical) were the hallmarks of the era. Designers were constantly experimenting with new techniques and styles, creating a visual language that was both futuristic and approachable. Influential movements such as New Wave, Memphis, Bay Area, and Retro Design continued to experiment with graphic design, challenged traditional notions of form and function to create a cohesive cultural identity. Their designs continue to show monumental appeal and vitality in the present day, and inspire contemporary design concepts.

The 1980s were characterized by major technological advances, cultural shifts, and an explosion of creativity across all fields. This decade witnessed the rise of the personal computer, the birth of iconic music genres, and breakthroughs in film and television. These innovations fostered a sense of optimism and excitement that pervaded the cultural landscape. Neon colors, Pixel Art, and digital typography came to symbolize the forward-looking spirit of the era. This aesthetics was not limited to graphic design but permeated fashion, architecture, and product design as well. Notably, the influence of New Wave music and post-punk culture brought an avant-garde sense of innovation, blending futuristic elements with retro inspirations to develop a unique Cyberpunk aesthetics.

The 1980s were a decade of bold experimentation and eclecticism, creating a vibrant and diverse aesthetic landscape. This era saw the rise of vibrant color palettes characterized by neon hues and stark contrasts, reflecting the exuberance and optimism of the time. Geometric patterns and shapes, often inspired by the Art Deco revival and the emerging digital age, flourished in everything from fashion to graphic design. The technological boom was evident in the design of sleek, high-tech consumer electronics and the growing popularity of digital art. Influential movements such as Memphis and New Wave emerged, challenging traditional design norms in playful, unconventional ways. The 80s aesthetics seamlessly blended high-tech futurism and nostalgic revival, encapsulating the spirit of an era unafraid to push boundaries and embrace new models. This overarching sense of boldness and excess defined a period that was both innovative and iconic.

However, the revival of 1980s nostalgia is more than just history repeating itself. It represents a complex exploration of the art of romanticizing the past—a nuanced journey that seeks to understand the nature of a bygone era and distill it into a contemporary design language. This chapter embarks on a vibrant journey through the graphic design of the 1980s, to explore the nostalgia evoked by the era, as well as the distinctive aesthetic traits that continue to inspire contemporary creativity.

1 Embracing the Past: The Essence of Nostalgia

The 1980s stand as a beacon of creative brilliance, a decade marked by the audacious embrace of bold colors, innovative typography, and a unique fusion of technology and artistry. This era, often romanticized in contemporary culture, evokes a profound sense of nostalgia that transcends mere reminiscence. It is a period remembered for its eclectic spirit, where boundaries were pushed and conventions shattered, giving birth to a visual language that continues to influence and inspire.

Nostalgia is a complex emotional state that arises from remembering the past, often involving a longing for what was real or imagined. Before the advent of modern psychology, nostalgia was once considered a mental illness and associated with psychological issues such as depression. However, with advances in technology and research, nostalgia is now understood as an emotion or experience, though its positive and negative components remain debated. Swiss psychiatrist Carl Jung offered a more neutral perspective, arguing that nostalgia is a way to reconnect with our past and understand our present. For Jung, nostalgia serves as a means of accessing to the "collective unconscious"—our shared human history and experience.

Nostalgia in design manifests as a yearning for the visual aesthetics, cultural references, and iconic trends of a particular era. It is a temporal reverie—a way of connecting with the past while reinterpreting it for the present. The distinctive aesthetics of 1980s design has experienced a significant revival in recent years, permeated in various media. This resurgence reflects a broader cultural nostalgia and a renewed appreciation for the bold, innovative style that defined the decade. Many television shows and movies have either recreated the look and feel of the '80s or set new content in that era. *Stranger Things* is a prime example, capturing the essence of the '80s through its sets, music, and visual style. The show's success has led to a wider embrace of the retro '80s aesthetics. Music videos and live performances often incorporate the '80s elements, from synthesizer-style soundtracks to retro visuals that pay homage to the era. Artists like The Weekend and Dua Lipa have embraced the sounds and styles of the '80s, who produced music videos that honor the decade. The Weeknd's "Blinding Lights" features a prominent synth-pop keyboard hook, a hallmark of the '80s New Wave music. Meanwhile, indie games like *Hyper Light Drifter* and *Cuphead* evoke memories of the '80s arcade games through their graphics and gameplay. These modern reinterpretations introduce the culture of the '80s to a new audience while rekindling the passion of those who lived through it.

The resurgence of 1980s design across various media demonstrates its lasting influence and broad appeal. The bold aesthetics continues to inspire and captivate, reflecting a collective sense of nostalgia and showcasing the decade's unique creativity and innovative spirit. By embracing 1980s design elements, contemporary culture creates a dynamic dialogue between the past and present, enriching our visual and cultural landscape.

Essentially, the revival of 1980s nostalgia in design is a complex and multifaceted phenomenon—a creative resurgence that invites us to reassess our relationship with the past and re-imagine its impact on the present. This journey into the heart of nostalgia brings the echoes of the 1980s into today's design, bridging different eras and reminding us of the timeless allure of creative innovation.

2 Tracing Longing: Unveiling the Roots of Nostalgia

In the book *The Future of Nostalgia*, Svetlana Boym points out that "the future of nostalgia globalization encouraged a stronger attachment to the local, a desire for some kind of community of collective memory, a yearning for continuity in a fragmented world." Pop culture seems to be a mirror of the mass psyche, resonating with the environment of the times, awakening people's common experience and sense of community, and it is an experience sometimes even created by the popularization of digital media platforms for empathy. Nostalgia for the 1980s is a powerful cultural phenomenon that has captivated generations, evoking fond memories and longing for the vibrant spirit of that era. The deep-seated reasons for this nostalgia are closely linked to the socio-economic, technological, and cultural background that characterized that era. When we delve deeper into the roots of this longing, we find that the 1980s was a time of rapid innovation, bold creativity, and major social change. From the rise of global media and iconic pop culture milestones to the emergence of unique visual and musical styles, the decade left an indelible mark on our collective consciousness. And many years later, in an era of similarly rapid development—and having survived even more epidemics of disease, antagonistic wars, increasingly closed and conservative societies and cultures, and the spreading negative influence of the Internet—we feel, to varying degrees, a certain distant similarity. By tracing the roots of the '80s nostalgia, we can discover the secrets behind its enduring appeal and understand how the period continues to influence and inspire contemporary culture.

1. Generational Memory

The cyclical nature of nostalgia is intrinsically tied to generational cycles. As Generation X, who came of age during the 1980s, and Millennials, who have a penchant for retro experiences, dominate contemporary cultural narratives, the '80s has become a potent source of inspiration. This generational overlap infuses design with an authentic connection to the era, breathing new life into the '80s aesthetics. For millennials and Generation X, who grew up in the 1980s and 1990s, the return to the '80s aesthetics represents a form of cultural self-recognition.

Nostalgia for the '80s is fueled by a desire to revisit the defining moments of youth and adolescence. It serves as a form of cultural nostalgia therapy, allowing individuals to rekindle the emotions, experiences, and memories associated with that period. The pop culture, music, fashion, and even the technology of the '80s are all evocative triggers of personal memories.

Furthermore, the '80s represented a time of rapid change and innovation, from the rise of personal computers to the advent of MTV. These technological and cultural shifts were formative for those who grew up in that era. Therefore, the resurgence of the '80s nostalgia is, in part, a generational quest to reconnect with the cultural milestones that defined their coming of age.

2. Subculture Influences

Subcultures play a pivotal role in shaping the identity and cultural landscape of the 1980s, greatly influencing nostalgia for this vibrant era. The punk, New Wave, and hip-hop movements of the '80s continue to inspire designers and artists today, providing a wellspring of creativity and countercultural authenticity that resonates with a new generation.

The punk movement, which emerged in the late 1970s and reached its zenith in the early 1980s, was characterized by its raw and rebellious spirit. Punk was more than just music; it was a subculture that embraced DIY ethos, challenging the mainstream in both music and fashion. Its distinctive visual identity, featuring torn clothing, leather jackets adorned with patches, and iconic punk band logos, remains an enduring source of inspiration for contemporary designers. The rebellious, anti-establishment ethos of punk continues to captivate those seeking a form of creative defiance.

New Wave, on the other hand, represented a departure from punk's rawness, embracing a more polished and eclectic sensibility. It was a subculture that merged music, fashion, and art into a distinct aesthetics. New Wave bands like Depeche Mode and Duran Duran embraced synthesizers and new electronic sounds, paving the way for a futuristic and visually intriguing style. The New Wave's influence is visible in today's Retro-Futurism designs, characterized by neon lights, geometric shapes, and a sense of nostalgia for the optimism of the '80s.

Hip-hop, born in the Bronx during the late 1970s, exploded into a cultural phenomenon in the 1980s. Beyond its groundbreaking music, hip-hop introduced a rich visual culture that included graffiti art, breakdancing, and distinctive fashion. The bold, graffiti-inspired lettering of early hip-hop culture has become an iconic element of the '80s retro design. Contemporary streetwear brands often draw inspiration from the baggy pants, oversized jackets, and bold logos that were emblematic of hip-hop fashion in the '80s.

From album art that blended punk's rebelliousness with the New Wave's futuristic aesthetics to streetwear that pays homage to the iconic styles of hip-hop pioneers, the subcultures of the '80s have become enduring symbols of creative defiance and authenticity. They offer a blueprint for contemporary designers and artists who seek to capture the spirit of an era marked by a relentless drive for self-expression and individuality. In today's world, where authenticity and countercultural expression are highly valued, the subcultures of the '80s not only offer a source of inspiration that transcends mere nostalgia but also give nostalgia a deeper meaning, that is, an in-depth search for identity and meaning. They constantly remind us that design is not just about aesthetics; it's a reflection of the cultural and social forces that shape our worldview and allow us to find a sense of belonging and value in niche groups. The subcultures of the '80s continue to influence and inform contemporary design, serving as a testament to the enduring power of creativity and rebellion in the world of art and culture.

3. Technological Resonance

The 1980s were a time of major technological and cultural shifts, and the digital age, with its vast archives of pop culture artifacts, has provided a platform for the resurrection of the '80s nostalgia. Social media, streaming platforms, and online communities serve as repositories of the '80s music, movies, fashion, and design, making it accessible to a global audience. This digital resonance amplifies the nostalgic revival, enabling designers to discover, reinterpret, and share the '80s aesthetics with a worldwide community.

When we dig deeper into the roots of this nostalgia, we find that it is tied to technological resonance. The 1980s marked a transformative period in the history of technology, with the widespread adoption of personal computers, the emergence of the video game industry, and the rise of digital music formats. And in the contemporary digital age, where technology is an integral part of everyday life, there is a natural fascination with modern technology. In the '80s, iconic gadgets like the Walkman and the Atari game console came out, they served as a touchstone for the digital evolution that followed. The aesthetics of early computer interfaces, Pixel Art, and neon graphics have a timeless appeal, resonating with a generation that witnessed the birth of the digital age.

The technological renaissance of the '80s is more than just nostalgia for the past; it reflects our enduring fascination with the relationship between humans and machines. This revival embodies a longing for a more intuitive, analog experiences of the past, even as we fully embrace our digital future. This fusion of past and present is what makes the digital age uniquely appealing.

4. Yearning for Authenticity

In an era marked by digital saturation and mass production, there is a palpable yearning for authenticity and a return to analog craftsmanship. The '80s, a decade where DIY culture thrived, resonates with contemporary audiences who seek to reconnect with the tangible and the handmade.

This desire for authenticity finds expression in the '80s-inspired design, where elements of imperfection and human touch are celebrated.

The '80s are perceived as a time when authenticity and self-expression were paramount. It was an era of countercultural movements, DIY ethics, and a rejection of conformity. In contrast to the curated and filtered realities of social media, the '80s represent a time when individuality and imperfection were celebrated. The music of that time was filled with a raw, natural feel, the fashion style was bold and avant-garde, and the design concepts were truly original, free from any constraints. People seek to recapture the authenticity of that era as a reaction to the polished and hypercurated images prevalent in the digital age.

The revival of the 1980s aesthetics, from music and fashion to design, allows individuals to embrace a sense of genuine self-expression. It's a rebellion against the homogenized contemporary culture, a return to an era of boundless creativity, and a celebration of imperfection and authenticity. In a world that often feels sanitized and controlled, nostalgia for the '80s opens a window to a more raw and genuine past. This was a time full of personality and creativity. By revisiting and reviving the cultural elements of the '80s, people seem to rediscover that long-lost sense of authenticity and the freedom of self-expression.

5. The Coercion of Nowadays-Crisis

The revival of the 1980s nostalgia takes on a new layer of significance in the context of contemporary events. In the age of global crises—epidemiological, war, economic, environmental—and the accompanying anxiety from unfamiliarity, we will begin share a collective yearning for the "belle époque" (beautiful age) of the '80s and early '90s. In times of uncertainty and upheaval, nostalgia serves as a comforting anchor to a seemingly simpler past. It offers a refuge from the complexities of contemporary life and serves as a reminder of the resilience of the human spirit.

Economic crises prompted a reevaluation of consumerism and excess. This introspection aligns with the counter-cultural spirit of the '80s, where subcultures questioned societal norms and consumer culture. As a response to economic uncertainty, design trends drew inspiration from the '80s, not only for their aesthetics but also for their ethos of creative resourcefulness. Global conflicts and geopolitical tensions have made the world a more complex and interconnected place. In this context, the '80s are remembered as a time when optimism and unity overcame the divisions of the Cold War. Design elements from this era evoke a sense of hope and resilience that resonates in today's uncertain geopolitical landscape. The COVID-19 pandemic, with its disruptions to daily life and isolation, has intensified the longing for a sense of community and nostalgia for simpler times. The '80s, with its vibrant subcultures and communal spirit, offer a glimpse into a world where connection and creativity flourished in the face of adversity.

In conclusion, our nostalgia for the 1980s is a multifaceted phenomenon, driven by a variety of catalysts deeply rooted in the contemporary cultural landscape. It goes beyond mere aesthetic preferences, encompassing generational shifts, technological advancements, a longing for authenticity, and the pressures of current crises. By reflecting on these reasons, we can gain a deeper understanding of why this particular decade continues to resonate so strongly in modern society and provide us with abundant inspiration and comfort amidst the complexities of contemporary life.

A JOURNEY BACK TO THE 80S

1 Radiant Hallmarks: The Essence of 1980s Graphic Design

For graphic design, the 1980s were a transformative decade during which several highly influential movements redefined the visual landscape. Among these were the New Wave Graphic Design movement, the Memphis Group, Bay Area graphic design, Retro Design in New York, and the more niche Cyberpunk style. Each contributed unique elements to the broader design trends of the era, leaving a lasting legacy and continuing to resonate in contemporary design.

The New Wave Typography Design movement began in the late 1970s and reached its peak in the 1980s. It revolutionized the clean, grid-based structure of Swiss. Led by pioneers such as Wolfgang Weingart, April Greiman, and Dan Friedman, New Wave design introduced more experimental approaches to typography and layout. Designers energetically employed asymmetry, vibrant colors, and unconventional typography, breaking away from the rigid symmetry of Swiss design and adopting more irregular layouts. This injected vitality and spontaneity into graphic design at the time. A hallmark of this movement was the diverse treatment of typefaces—stretching, slanting, layering, and more—to create captivating visual effects that captured the experimental spirit of the 1980s graphic design. This movement not only impacted graphic design but also extended its influence into fashion, music, and advertising, contributing significantly to the unique visual identity of the 1980s and reflecting a broader cultural shift.

Simultaneously, the Memphis Group, which took root in Italy, became one of the most representative and controversial design movements of the 1980s. Founded by Ettore Sottsass in Milan in 1980, it grew out of the soil of the Italian Radical Design, pushing bold, avant-garde, and uninhibited design styles to new heights. Their design was characterized by bold geometric shapes, playful colors, and eclectic material, these elements were combined in unexpected ways. The Memphis Group's use of unconventional materials like laminates, plastics, and terrazzo marked a stark departure from the Minimalist and Functionalist principles that dominated the previous decades. Instead, they embraced a more playful postmodern aesthetic, both whimsical and provocative. This design style caused quite a stir at the time, with mixed reactions from designers initially; however, its influence has grown over time, and the bold, uninhibited style became a hallmark of the 1980s design. Their impact extended across various fields, from furniture and product design to graphic and interior design, and even today, many designs still bear the influence of the Memphis Group.

Meanwhile, the ideas of postmodernist graphic design spread like dandelion seeds around the world, sparking wave after wave of graphic design movements. In San Francisco, graphic designers formed many closely-knit small design studios. When the wave of postmodernism arrived, these professional designers immediately embraced new design philosophies, forming an influential faction known as the San Francisco Graphic Design Movement, also referred to geographically as Bay Area Design. Bay Area designers broke away from the monotony and dullness of internationalism, presenting a humorous and optimistic design style. They preferred using free painting techniques to draw casual and unrestrained graphics, blending joyful and relaxed colors to create a light and free overall layout, thus forming a unique and infectious new style. For example, **1**Michael Vanderbyl's poster for California Public Radio in 1979 laid the early groundwork for Bay Area style. Abstract lines symbolized the diffusion of radio waves, and the infinitely overlapping lines seemed to create a shimmering effect. The vivid colors formed lively three-dimensional figures. At the same time, **2**Michael Cronin's poster for a Beethoven concert also typified Bay Area design style. The designer used symbolic language to express his understanding of Beethoven, with hair transformed into Beethoven's upright figure, forming organic shapes full of tension, resembling the notes of a score. The addition of contrasting warm colors expressed anger and high emotions, showcasing the personality and power of Beethoven's music.

The 1980s witnessed a revival of Art Deco. This revival was characterized by a renewed interest in bold geometric designs and luxurious details, reminiscent of the prototype Art Deco movement of the 1920s and 1930s. The revival of Art Deco in the 1980s not only paid homage to this early style but also adapted and reinterpreted it to fit contemporary cultural and design environments. The Art Deco revival of the 1980s showcased designers' renewed focus on geometric shapes and patterns, favored by movements like New Wave and Memphis. Additionally, bold and striking color contrasts were reintroduced into design. While maintaining the decorative nature of traditional Art Deco, the 1980s design incorporated a more streamlined and futuristic appearance, evident in the use of sleek lines and modern materials across various designs from architecture to fashion.

In the 1980s, there also emerged distinctive cultural and aesthetic movements that reflected the complex relationship between society and rapidly advancing technology. Cyberpunk, with its dystopian and utopian visions of the future, captured the imagination of the era and left an

Beethoven Festival poster, Michael Cornin, 1983

California Public Radio poster, Michael Vanderbyl, 1979.

indelible mark on literature, film, fashion, and art. This genre heavily drew upon the technological and social landscapes of the 1980s, such as the rise of personal computers, the advent of the Internet, and advancements in robotics and artificial intelligence, all of which became central themes in this aesthetic style. Its backdrop often featured expansive urban landscapes illuminated by neon lights, portraying grandeur tinged with loneliness. Shiny metallic elements, flickering pixel effects, and laser-focused visual aesthetics added an infinite atmosphere to this thematic style. Additionally, Cyberpunk reflected contemporary anxieties about corporate control, economic disparities, and the dehumanizing effects of technology.

The 1980s created a vibrant and diverse aesthetic landscape, particularly in the field of graphic design. During this era, graphic design saw daring avant-garde experimentation and infinite creative freedom. Movements like New Wave, Memphis, and Bay Area Design collectively challenged traditional design norms, paving the way for future innovations. The combination of embracing past art legacies with innovations in high-tech Futurism marked the 1980s as a decade of significant visual art transformation, encapsulating the spirit of an age unafraid to push boundaries and embrace new paradigms. The enduring appeal of the 1980s aesthetics and the revolutionary design principles continue to influence contemporary graphic design, demonstrating their timeless legacy. Reflecting on the history and impact of these movements provides a deeper understanding of the vitality, transformative nature, and profound influence of the 1980s graphic art on today's visual culture.

In the captivating field of graphic design in the 1980s, typography and color combinations became tools of expression characterized by bold experimentation and dynamic creativity. As we delve into this fascinating realm, we discover an era where designers fearlessly pushed the boundaries of layout and color to create unforgettable visual effects that continue to impact contemporary design. The diverse printing options and vibrant color palettes of the 1980s reveal their enduring influence on today's Retro Design landscape.

2 Typography: A Kaleidoscope of Distinctive Fonts

The 1980s, often hailed as a decade of opulence and extravagance, made an indelible mark on the world of graphic design. It was an era defined by a fearless embrace of the unconventional, a rejection of established design norms, and a celebration of individualism. Graphic designers of the time no longer adhered to convention; they sought to disrupt, innovate, and astonish. It was a period characterized by a kaleidoscope of fonts and colors, where each design choice served as a bold statement.

Typography in the 1980s was a symphony of personalities. While fonts such as Helvetica and [3]Futura had long dominated the design landscape, they faced a formidable challenge from a wave of distinctive and playful typefaces that emerged as design statements in their creators' own right. The '80s typographic palette showcased a multitude of fonts that stretched the limits of creativity and legibility. Words and letters were fragmented, deconstructed, and reassembled in unexpected and thought-provoking ways, challenging the traditional role of typography in design.

Among the most iconic typefaces of the era was the [4]Bauhaus typeface, designed by Ed Benguiat and Victor Caruso. This typeface offers a contemporary reinterpretation of the Bauhaus style, infusing it with a playful and dynamic edge. Another notable example is [5]VAG Rounded, which epitomizes the 1980s trend toward informal, rounded typefaces. These fonts were employed to inject a sense of vibrancy and movement into design work, creating a distinctive and energetic visual language that defined the decade.

Zuzana Licko's Mrs Eaves, a modern revival of the classic Baskerville typeface, introduces a whimsical and innovative twist. Its design features deliberate irregularities and eccentricities, which lend it a distinctive, experimental character. On the other hand, the Bernard MT Condensed typeface boasts bold, striking letterforms that capture the era's inclination towards attention—grabbing and impactful typography.

The typographic landscape of the '80s was a dynamic and eclectic realm, characterized by an astonishing array of fonts, each with its distinct personality and visual resonance. This era passionately celebrated the rich tapestry of typefaces, often elevated them to the status of individual artworks. In our exploration of this captivating epoch, we journey through some of the pivotal typographic choices that came to define the '80s. Remarkably, these fonts have not faded into mere nostalgia; instead, they continue to cast a significant influence on contemporary design, inspiring today's creative minds to infuse their projects with a touch of the '80s charm while maintaining a modern and relevant aesthetics.

[3]
Futura
Aa Qq Rr
Aa Qq Rr
Zuführung
abcdefghijklm
nopqrstuvwxyz
0123456789

Specimen of the Typeface Futura, Sherbyte, 2010.

[4]
Bauhaus
Aa Ee Rr
Aa Ee Rr
Tätigkeit
abcdefghijklm
nopqrstuvwxyz
0123456789

Specimen of the Typeface Bauhaus, Lebetonbrut, 2012.

[5]
VAG Rounded
Aa Ee Jj
Aa Ee Jj
Volkswagen
abcdefghijklm
nopqrstuvwxyz
0123456789

Specimen of the Typeface VAG Rounded, Connorman, 2010.

A

The New Wave Typography movement of the '80s emerged as a defiant rebellion against the rigid conventions of traditional type design. In this transformative era, the very essence of typography was redefined, transcending its utilitarian role and blossoming into an expressive art form. At its core, New Wave Typography was characterized by the deliberate distortion and deconstruction of letterforms, a fearless venture that boldly pushed the boundaries of legibility and challenged established norms.

Within this typographic revolution, visionaries like April Greiman and Wolfgang Weingart emerged as trailblazers, leading the charge into uncharted creative territories. April Greiman, renowned for her pioneering works in digital design, explored the fusion of technology and typography. Her groundbreaking *Does It Make Sense?* poster is a prime example of New Wave typography, featuring fragmented letterforms that demand active engagement from the viewer, inviting them to decipher meaning in a non-linear and unconventional way.

Similarly, Wolfgang Weingart, a Swiss typographer, embraced the principles of deconstruction, disrupted traditional grid-based layouts with an intentional visual dissonance. His experimental approach challenged the very essence of order and structure, inviting viewers to explore the interplay of fractured typography and chaotic composition.

New Wave typography's legacy persists today as contemporary designers continue to draw inspiration from its rebellious spirit, infusing their work with elements of distortion, fragmentation, and unexpected juxtapositions. It serves as a testament to the enduring power of typography and as a vehicle for creative expression, unshackled by convention and forever pushing the boundaries of visual communication.

unconventional
unshackled
distortion
chaotic
bold
CHALLENGE
deconstruction

The advent of personal computer in the 1980s brought with it a significant evolution in typography, marked by the emergence of digital and pixel fonts. These fonts were distinctively characterized by their pixelated appearance, a direct reflection of the technical constraints of early computer displays and the grid-based nature of pixel art.

One seminal moment in the development of digital fonts occurred with the introduction of the original Macintosh computer. This groundbreaking device featured bitmap fonts, such as Chicago, Geneva, Monaco, and so on. These bitmap fonts were created using a grid of pixels, with each character designed to fit within the limitations of early computer displays. The result was a set of highly legible and functional typefaces that defined the visual language of early personal computer. These fonts laid the foundation for digital typography, setting the stage for a revolution in the way we create and interact with text on screens.

The 1980s witnessed the meteoric rise of digital technology, giving birth to the captivating pixelated typography. This unique aesthetics emerged as a direct consequence of the nascent stage of computer displays, where the limitations of pixel-based rendering created a distinctively blocky and pixelated form of lettering. Despite its roots in technological constraints, pixelated typography possesses an undeniably nostalgic and retro charm that continues to captivate contemporary designers and enthusiasts alike.

During this period, digital interfaces and video games became fertile ground for the proliferation of pixelated typography. Classic video game such as *Pac-Man* and *Space Invaders* prominently featured pixelated lettering in their iconic logos and score displays, forever etching these fonts

B

into the collective memory of gamers. The low-resolution aesthetics of early computer games were emblematic of the

1980s, and pixelated typography played a pivotal role in creating the visual identity of this era's digital landscape.

Fast forward to the present, and digital fonts have evolved far beyond their humble pixelated beginnings. Yet, the nostalgia and charm of these early pixel fonts continue to resonate in contemporary design. Pixel fonts are frequently employed in the creation of retro-inspired video games, where they evoke a strong sense of nostalgia for the 8-bit and 16-bit gaming eras. Additionally, they are utilized in digital interfaces to hark back to the early days of computing, offering a playful and visually engaging element that taps into our collective memory of pixelated graphics.

Contemporary artists and designers are intentionally embracing the pixelated aesthetics to evoke a sense of nostalgia, paying homage to the pioneering days of digital design while infusing it with modern creativity. This resurgence has seen pixel fonts adorning everything from retro-style video game posters to album covers, demonstrating that even in the age of high-definition displays, the charm of pixelated typography remains as vibrant and relevant as ever.

grid
LIMITATION
digital
LEGIBLE
technical constraints
bitmap
8-bit
functional

geometric forms
BOLD COLORS
OPULENCE
glamour
avant-garde spirit

The 1980s experienced a remarkable resurgence of Art Deco-inspired fonts, a revival that transported designers and audiences alike back to the opulence and glamour of the 1920s, revealed through Memphis Group Lettering. These fonts favored by the Memphis Group were a reflection of their avant-garde spirit. These typefaces were characterized by their inherent playfulness, often featured unconventional shapes and arrangements. Geometric forms, bold colors, and an unapologetic rejection of symmetry were recurring themes in Memphis Group typography. The Memphis typeface, from which the movement took its name, encapsulated these principles with its eclectic, asymmetrical letterforms. It exuded a sense of joyful rebellion against traditional typographic norms.

One prominent example of typography from this period can be found in the opening credits of the iconic TV series *Miami Vice*. The show's title sequence prominently featured Art Deco-inspired typography that captured the essence of Miami's glamorous and vibrant culture. This choice of font was more than a design decision; it was a deliberate homage to the city's architectural and cultural history.

The Memphis Group injected its distinctive irreverence and whimsical design sensibilities into every facet of the creative landscape, including typography. At the heart of the Memphis Group's typographic approach was an unabashed celebration of playfulness and a fervent commitment to breaking free from conventional constraints. Although the group did not produce specific typefaces, their influence is evident in the design trends of the 1980s. Typography inspired by the Memphis Group's aesthetics often featured playful and unconventional shapes, bold colors, and geometric forms. These elements reflected the group's commitment to innovation and breaking free from established constraints. This approach can be seen in modern typefaces that echo the Memphis Group's irreverent spirit, incorporating vibrant patterns and varied line weights to create a dynamic and eclectic feel.

In the contemporary design landscape, Memphis Group-inspired typography continues to inspire designers to seek to inject their projects with a touch of retro eclecticism and irreverence. By embracing the playful spirit and bold aesthetics embodied by the Memphis Group, modern designers pay homage to an era of design that fearlessly broke the rules and reveled in the joy of creative exploration.

This was a transformative period where these grassroots art movements gained recognition and made an indelible mark on the visual landscape.

Prominent artists like Keith Haring and Jean-Michel Basquiat embodied the spirit of the streets, who seamlessly incorporated graffiti-inspired typography into their work. Their creations pulsated with a raw, unfiltered urban energy that spoke to the essence of the communities they emerged from. The letterforms they utilized were dynamic, often embody the urgency and vibrancy of the streets they called home.

The '80s were marked by a fervent DIY ethos that nurtured the emergence of hand-drawn and graffiti-inspired fonts. These fonts served as dynamic channels for expressing urban energy and a spirit of rebellion that resonated with the times. What set them apart was their rejection of uniformity and their embrace of irregular, often unpredictable shapes and dynamic strokes. An iconic emblem of this era's graffiti-inspired typography can be found in DIY flyers for punk bands like Ramones, Dead Kennedys, Fugazi, Minor Threat, and Bad Brains in the 1980s, exuding the raw, unfiltered energy of punk culture and reflecting the grassroots nature of the punk movement. This typography not only represented the music but also embodied the broader spirit of creative defiance that characterized the '80s.

Brush script fonts also gained prominence during this era. These fonts artfully replicated the organic fluidity and subtle imperfections of hand-painted lettering. This infusion of personality and warmth into designs set brush script fonts apart from the rigidity of conventional typography. One of the most iconic examples of the magnetic pull of brush script fonts during this era is the Coca-Cola logo. With its effortlessly flowing script, the Coca-Cola emblem encapsulated the enchanting charm of brush script fonts. It conveyed a timeless appeal, invoking nostalgia and authenticity, becoming a symbol recognized worldwide. Beyond the world of soft drinks, movie posters of the '80s often embraced brush script fonts to convey cinematic drama and emotion. For example, *American Gigolo*, *Things Change*, *Pink Floyd the Wall* and many other movie posters used brush script fonts, which add personality and charm to the posters to convey either casualness and intimacy or the raw, intense, and rebellious nature through sharp expression, causing deep emotional resonance with the audience.

The enduring legacy of hand-drawn and graffiti-inspired fonts lies in their capability to transcend time and bridge the gap between the rebellious spirit of the '80s and the contemporary urban landscape. They serve as powerful tools for conveying authenticity, energy, and a sense of cultural connection that endures in the ever-evolving world of design.

Today, the legacy of graffiti and street art typography is more potent than ever. Streetwear brands and contemporary artists continue to draw inspiration from these rebellious roots, forging a compelling bridge between street culture and the world of design. The influence of graffiti and street art typography is discernible in everything from urban fashion to album covers, underscoring the enduring appeal of the movement that originated from the streets and found its way into the very fabric of contemporary creativity.

technological advancements
innovation darkness 80
GEOMETRIC FUTURISTIC
beveled fascination

The 1980s saw a profound shift in typography, driven by a fascination with futuristic aesthetics and technological advancements. This era gave birth to two notable trends in type design: sci-fi-inspired fonts and three-dimensional (3D) and beveled fonts. These styles transformed the visual landscape, each bringing a unique sense of innovation and modernity.

Sci-Fi Fonts

The 1980s were marked by a deep interest in futuristic aesthetics, which found a significant outlet in sci-fi-inspired fonts. These fonts often featured sleek, geometric letterforms that conveyed a sense of technological advancement and otherworldly possibilities. A prime example of this can be found in the movie title fonts of the film *Blade Runner*. The film's title featured a font that seamlessly melded with the Cyberpunk genre, becoming emblematic of its visual identity. This font evoked a sense of dystopian futurism, intertwining technology and darkness and setting the stage for the film's exploration of a futuristic yet gritty world.

Today, futuristic fonts continue to play a pivotal role in science fiction branding and digital interfaces. They are invaluable tools for conveying a sense of innovation and progress. Technology companies frequently employ these fonts in their branding to emphasize their forward-thinking nature and cutting-edge products. These typefaces are also widely utilized in futuristic video games and films, instantly immersing audiences in speculative worlds where technology knows no bounds.

The enduring allure of futuristic and sci-fi fonts lies in their capability to transcend time and inspire a sense of wonder about the possibilities of tomorrow. They continue to captivate our imaginations by connecting us with the eternal human quest for progress and the exploration of the unknown.

3D and Beveled Fonts

The 1980s also marked a pivotal moment in typography with the emergence of three-dimensional and beveled fonts, ushering in a new era of depth and dimensionality in design. These fonts possessed a remarkable capability to transcend the two-dimensional plane, creating the illusion that letters were either casting shadows, leaping off the page, or even floating in space. This innovative approach breathed life into typography, giving it a tangible quality that added an extra layer of visual intrigue.

A standout example of this trend's impact can be seen in the logo for the groundbreaking film *Tron*. The film's title was rendered in a 3D font that expertly mirrored the digital realm it portrayed. This font exuded a sense of digital Futurism, perfectly encapsulating the film's narrative and visual aesthetics and becoming an iconic representation of the digital age.

In the contemporary design landscape, 3D and beveled fonts continue to be a driving force, often employed by forward-thinking designers to create visually arresting and immersive experiences in digital art, advertising, and branding. These fonts possess an innate capability to captivate and engage viewers, making them invaluable tools for conveying depth, sophistication, and modernity.

As we navigate the ever-evolving world of design, the enduring appeal of three-dimensional and beveled fonts serves as a testament to the power of innovation and the capacity of typography to shape and redefine our visual landscape. These fonts continue to be at the forefront of creative expression, adding a tangible, dynamic quality to the typography of the 21st century.

The 1980s were a transformative period for typography, with sci-fi and 3D fonts each making significant contributions to the visual arts. Futuristic fonts captured the imagination with their sleek, technological designs, while 3D and beveled fonts added a new dimension of depth and realism. Together, these styles encapsulate the spirit of innovation that defined the decade and continue to influence contemporary design.

cyberpunk

3 Color Combinations: Vibrant, Bold, and Unforgettable

The color palettes of the 1980s are a vivid testament to the era's defiance of conventional design norms, boldly embracing a chromatic landscape that has left an indelible mark on visual culture. Neon hues, with their radiant and electrifying presence, instantly command attention, and they were a hallmark of '80s aesthetics. Electric blues, often deep and saturated, evoked a sense of futuristic allure, while fiery reds imbued designs with a fiery, passionate energy.

One of the defining features of the '80s color combinations was their fearless embrace of striking contrasts. These combinations weren't just about harmony but rather about creating visual tension and excitement. Boldly clashing colors were celebrated, giving rise to designs that challenged the viewer's perception and expectations.

These iconic color schemes of the '80s continue to captivate and inspire contemporary designers. In the realm of fashion, the vibrant '80s colors find expression in bold streetwear collections. In graphic design, they infuse digital interfaces with a sense of energy and vibrancy. Brands and marketers harness the nostalgia associated with these colors to create a powerful emotional connection with consumers. As we delve deeper into the '80s color palettes, we unearth a treasure trove of visual inspiration. They serve as a reminder that design is not static but an ever-evolving dialogue with the past, where the boldness of the '80s remains a timeless source of creative vitality in the 21st century.

The '80s era was undeniably defined by the dazzling brilliance of neon colors, which took center stage in its vibrant color palettes. Electric blues, acid greens, and hot pinks, among others, lit up the visual landscape with an unparalleled sense of excitement and unbridled energy. These fluorescent hues weren't just colors; they were a visual revolution, breaking free from the subdued palettes of previous decades.

1. Neon Noir

Neon Noir design in the 1980s encapsulated a distinctive aesthetics that combined elements of film noir with the vibrant, electric hues of neon colors. This juxtaposition enhanced the brightness of the neon hues, making them appear even more vibrant and luminous against the dark background, thus creating a visually striking and atmospheric style that became synonymous with urban landscapes, nightlife, and a sense of mystery and intrigue. And the use of black as a backdrop for neon colors also lent a futuristic and edgy feel, aligning with the decade's fascination with technology and sci-fi aesthetics.

Neon Noir design drew inspiration from the classic film noir genre of the 1940s and 1950s, characterized by its dark, shadowy cinematography and gritty urban settings. Film noir often depicted crime, corruption, and moral ambiguity, setting a dramatic backdrop for its narratives. The 1980s saw advancements in neon lighting technology and the widespread adoption of fluorescent pigments, which made neon colors more accessible and vibrant than ever before. This technological backdrop enabled designers and artists to integrate neon elements into their work in innovative ways.

In graphic design, Neon Noir was characterized by its bold typography, geometric shapes, and neon color overlays. Posters, album covers, and advertisements often employed these elements to convey a sense of urban sophistication and avant-garde style. Neon Noir design found its most prominent expression in films and television shows of the 1980s. Movies like *Blade Runner* and *Taxi Driver* utilized neon lighting to create dystopian cityscapes and to emphasize the psychological states of their characters. Television series like *Miami Vice* incorporated Neon Noir elements into their visuals, using neon-lit nightclubs and urban landscapes as integral settings.

2. High Contrast Color Combinations

The 1980s saw the widespread use of high contrast color combinations, where neon colors like electric blue, hot pink, acid green, and neon yellow were paired with each other or with stark neutrals such as black and white. This approach maximized the visual impact of neon hues, creating striking, eye-catching designs that were impossible to ignore. These high contrast combinations were used extensively in fashion, where neon clothing and accessories became synonymous with youthful rebellion and energetic style, and in graphic design, where bold neon posters and advertisements captured public attention.

Album covers, exemplified by Prince's *Purple Rain*, epitomized the audacious use of contrasting colors. The bold combinations of deep purples and fiery oranges on the cover art encapsulated the very essence of the era, reflecting its unabashed flamboyance and artistic innovation. These covers were not just packaging; they were visual symphonies that set the tone for the music within.

3. Harmonious Use with Sunset Gradients

While neon colors were often used in bold, high contrast combinations, they were also employed harmoniously with gradients. These sunset-inspired gradients seamlessly transitioned from warm, fiery oranges and pinks to the cooler, more tranquil shades of purples and blues, mirroring the breathtaking hues of a picturesque sunset. This design choice was not just about color; it was a deliberate effort to capture the nostalgia and emotional resonance associated with the natural beauty of the setting sun. Album covers, in particular, embraced sunset gradients with open arms. Musicians and designers alike recognized the power of these gradients to evoke a sense of romance, emotion, and artistic depth. The sunset-inspired gradients became visual shorthand for conveying the mood and message of an album, often creating an immediate and visceral connection with the viewer.

Sunset-inspired gradients provided a natural and visually appealing backdrop for neon hues in the 1980s. This blending of the artificial brilliance of neon with the natural beauty of gradients created dynamic and visually stimulating compositions. This technique was particularly prevalent in graphic design and digital art, where neon colors and gradients were used to create immersive and engaging visuals that felt both modern and nostalgic. For example, the scene of *Miami Vice* showcased the iconic Miami skyline against a backdrop of neon-lit buildings and a gradient sunset, creating a powerful visual statement that encapsulated the era's aesthetics. Still, the influence of sunset gradients endures in contemporary digital design. Web and app interfaces frequently incorporate these gradients to create visually engaging and immersive experiences. Sunset gradients have the unique capability to convey a sense of warmth, serenity, and emotional depth, making them a popular choice in the ever-evolving landscape of digital design.

Fast forward to today, neon colors remain a powerful tool in the designer's arsenal. They are frequently used in branding, digital design, and fashion to evoke a sense of vibrancy, modernity, and, perhaps most significantly, nostalgia. Brands harness neon colors to make a bold statement, capturing the attention of consumers in a crowded marketplace. In digital design, neon hues add a dynamic and eye-catching element to interfaces, making them both engaging and memorable. In fashion, neon colors continue to cycle in and out of trends, their timeless appeal ensure them never truly fade away.

As we delve deeper into the world of neon brilliance, we uncover not only a vibrant color trend but also a cultural phenomenon that remains as relevant and captivating today as it was in the dazzling '80s. Neon colors embody a sense of unbridled enthusiasm, pushing the boundaries of visual possibility and reminding us that color, like culture, is ever-evolving and boundless in its potential.

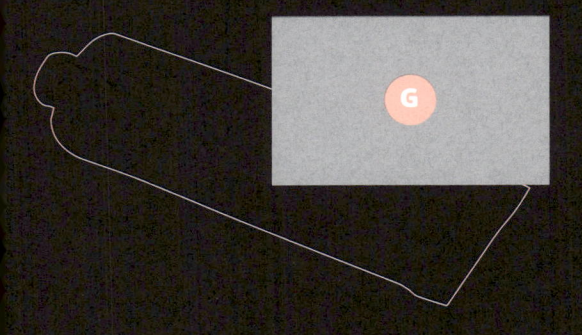

Amidst the cacophony of neon brilliance that defined the '80s, pastel colors emerged as a soothing and enchanting counterpoint. While the era reveled in the audacious vibrancy of neon, pastel pinks, blues, and mint greens offered a more delicate and understated palette that served as a visual respite from the boldness of the time. These gentle hues added an element of elegance and sophistication to the '80s color spectrum, proving that subtlety could be equally impactful.

Pastel colors found a particularly prominent place in the '80s fashion, where they adorned a wide range of attire, from pastel-colored suits that exuded a sense of casual luxury to prom dresses that encapsulated the dreamy essence of the era. These colors weren't just a fashion statement; they became emblematic of an era defined by its unique blend of extravagance and nostalgia.

Fast forward to the present, pastel color schemes have transcended their '80s origins to become enduring elements in contemporary design. They are frequently employed in branding, interior design, and digital interfaces, where they evoke a sense of nostalgia for the bygone era and inject a touch of elegance and refinement into modern aesthetics. Brands leverage pastel colors to create a sense of approachability and timelessness, while interior designers use them to craft serene and inviting spaces. In digital interfaces, pastels offer a harmonious and visually pleasing experience, making them a popular choice in the ever-evolving world of design.

As we delve deeper into the world of pastel dreams, we discover a timeless quality in these colors that transcends eras and captivates the human imagination. They are a reminder that color is a language of emotion, capable of evoking nostalgia, serenity, and a timeless sense of beauty in our ever-changing visual landscape.

pastel   delicate   understated
elegance   enchanting   soothing

A JOURNEY BACK TO THE 80S · CHAPTER 2 · 58

The '80s design ethos was an unapologetic celebration of contrast, where the art of color pairing reached exhilarating heights. Complementary colors collided with fervor, forging visuals that refused to be ignored. It was an era where boldness was the guiding principle, and this fearless approach to color yielded some of the most iconic designs in history.

The 1980s marked a departure from the Minimalist and earthy tones of the 1970s. As society moved towards a more dynamic and fast-paced lifestyle, design trends reflected this shift with brighter, more vivid and daring color combinations. This period saw a reaction against the restraint of earlier years, embracing a more exuberant and expressive approach to color. For instance, the cover design for Queen's *Hot Space* (1982) pays homage to Pop Art style by using a high-contrast color combination. The cover is divided into four quadrants, each with contrasting, vibrant background colors—orange, blue, green, and yellow. Superimposed on top are simplified, monochromatic profiles of the band members' faces, each using contrasting colors to create a striking visual effect.

In contemporary design, the legacy of the '80s bold contrast lives on. Designers across industries continue to experiment with striking color contrasts, drawing inspiration from the fearless spirit of the '80s. Whether in branding, digital interfaces, or print media, bold color combinations are harnessed to create eye-catching and memorable designs that evoke the energy and vibrancy of the '80s.

As we delve deeper into the world of bold contrast, we uncover not just a design trend but a testament to the enduring power of color in communication. It serves as a reminder that the interplay of contrasting colors is not just about aesthetics; it's about capturing attention, conveying emotions, and leaving a lasting impression on the visual landscape. In this perpetual dance of color and contrast, the '80s continues to be a wellspring of inspiration, guiding designers toward creating visuals that are both daring and unforgettable.

vibrant
unapologetic
fearless
iconic
boldness
exhilarating

The '80s was a time of unabashed opulence and an unquenchable thirst for the future, and this spirit was epitomized by the introduction of metallic colors, with silver and gold taking center stage. These metallic hues were not just colors; they were symbols of a new era, where excess and innovation converged to redefine visual aesthetics.

In the '80s fashion, the use of metallic colors was nothing short of a phenomenon. From metallic fabrics that shimmered with every movement to accessories that gleamed with an otherworldly luster, these bold and audacious choices allowed individuals to make a statement that was impossible to ignore. It was a fashion trend that transcended mere attire; it was an

4

The enduring impact of the '80s typography and color combinations on contemporary retro design is undeniable and continues to resonate deeply within the creative landscape of today. As designers delve into the visual archives of the 1980s, they draw profound inspiration from these elements to create visuals that pay heartfelt homage to the past while skillfully bridging the gap between nostalgia and modern relevance in the dynamic digital age.

The indomitable spirit of the '80s typography breathes anew in contemporary design, manifesting through the revival of distorted and experimental letterforms. It is a resurgence that celebrates the audacious nature of the '80s, where designers fearlessly pushed the boundaries of conventional type design. Today's typographic renaissance embraces the same sense of adventure, breathing life into hand-drawn lettering and custom typefaces that capture the very essence of the '80s while allowing for fresh and modern interpretations. The revival of these typographic treasures does not merely replicate the past but reimagines it, infusing it with contemporary sensibilities and relevance.

The bold and contrasting color palettes of the '80s continue to infuse contemporary design with boundless energy and vibrant personality. In the ever-evolving world of branding, digital interfaces, and marketing materials, designers often turn to the luminous neon and the soft pastel hues that characterized the '80s. These colors possess the remarkable capability to create visuals that not only catch the eye but also resonate deeply with a sense of nostalgia, transporting viewers to an era filled with unbridled enthusiasm and creative experimentation. In this way, the '80s color palettes have transcended time, weaving itself seamlessly into the fabric of contemporary aesthetics.

As we embark on an immersive journey through the intricate world of the '80s graphic design, it becomes abundantly clear that the fonts and color combinations of this era are far more than mere design elements; they are cultural artifacts, relics of a time that continue to shape our visual landscape and captivate our creative sensibilities. The '80s were a playground of artistic expression, a time when designers fearlessly ventured into uncharted territory, wielding typography and color as their primary tools to create visuals that have indelibly etched themselves into our collective memory.

Today, the influence of the '80s is not a mere revival; it's a dynamic and ongoing conversation that transcends the boundaries of time. It's a conversation that offers a rich and eclectic palette, a typographic playground, and a vivid color spectrum for the creative minds of tomorrow to explore and reinterpret. In this ever-evolving dance of design, the fonts and colors of the '80s serve as a testament to the enduring and timeless legacy of creativity, innovation, and profound impact that the aesthetics of an era can have on the art of visual storytelling. As we continue to celebrate the '80s through contemporary design, we recognize that its fonts and colors are not relics of the past but living, breathing elements that continue to shape and enrich our creative landscape, inspiring us to push the boundaries of design in our quest to tell compelling visual stories.

expression of a collective desire for extravagance and a vision of the future that was glistening with promise.

Fast forward to the present, metallic accents continue to play a pivotal role in contemporary design. They are often incorporated to infuse a touch of luxury and a sense of futuristic flair into various design elements. Whether in branding, interior design, or digital interfaces, metallic shines offer a visual richness and sophistication that resonate with audiences seeking a sense of opulence and modernity.

As we journey deeper into the world of metallic shines, we discover not just a design trend but a reflection of the human aspiration for progress and grandeur. These metallic colors are more than mere adornments; they are symbols of our enduring fascination with the interplay of innovation, opulence, and the ever-evolving narrative of design.

Chapter 3
THE EXPRESSION OF RETRO DESIGN STYLE IN CONTEMPORARY TIMES

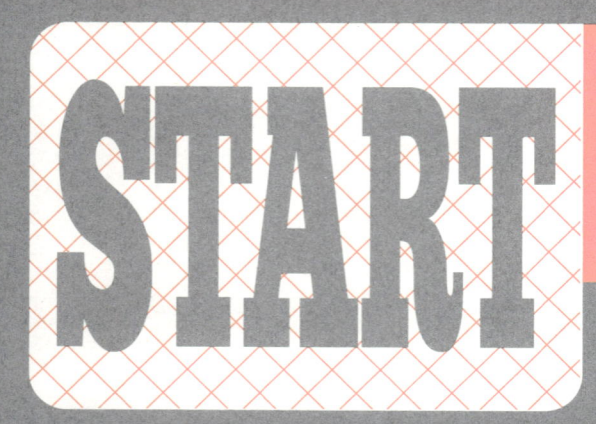

START

Unexpectedly get a large sum of money and buy a Cadillac.	**ADVANCE 2 SPACES**
Date with a Pixel girlfriend, feel very happy.	**ALL OTHER PLAYERS ROLL THE DICE AGAIN**
Trapped in a messy grid.	**SKIP YOUR TURN FOR 1 ROUND**
Wake up and feel shocked to find yourself transformed into a spiky monster.	**MOVE BACK 3 SPACES**
Pretend you're a vase and stand in the corner.	**APPOINT ANOTHER PLAYER TO ROLL THE DICE FOR YOU ONCE**
Get on the McDonald's spaceship and enjoy delicious food in the sky.	**MOVE ALONG THE PATH TO THE RIGHT SPACE**
The cells mutate and the body becomes unwell.	**MOVE BACK 3 SPACES**
Become an Internet sensation.	**STRIKE 3 DIFFERENT POSES FOR THE OTHER PLAYERS TO TAKE PHOTOS**
Obtain the Kamen Rider Belt and start transforming.	**JUMP DIRECTLY TO THE RIGHT SPACE**
Sit in a Van Thai restaurant and eat a bowl of Boat Noodles.	**ADVANCE 1 SPACE**
Spot a shooting star and make a wish.	**THE PLAYER ON YOUR LEFT GRANTS YOU ONE WISH**
Spot a clock with four limbs. Sneak up and follow it to check it out.	**ADVANCE 2 SPACES**
Live in Barbie's DreamHouse.	**ACT AS IF EATING AND DRINKING FROM THIN AIR**
Read a super favorite magazine for immersive reading.	**SKIP YOUR TURN FOR 1 ROUND**
Drink a cup of milk tea and feel energized!	**STRAIGHT TO THE FINISH POINT**
Gain the superpowers of the Maiden Warrior.	**PERFORM SAILOR MOON TRANSFORMATIONS**
Obtain a couple of exotic bouquets, but the scent is pungent.	**PINCH YOUR NOSE UNTIL FINISH**
On vacation at the beach, a coconut smacks on the head.	**MOVE BACK 2 SPACES**
Purchase a vinyl record player to enjoy music.	**PLAY THE THIRD SONG ON YOUR PLAYLIST**
Enter the graphic vortex!	**JUMP DIRECTLY TO THE UPPER SPACE**
Accidentally enter an unknown psychedelic universe.	**SKIP YOUR TURN FOR 1 ROUND**
Try new design styles, and struggle to break through.	**THE PLAYER ON YOUR RIGHT ROLLS THE DICE FOR YOU**

Top row (left to right)

- into a K-pop girl up member on the eet.
  PLAY A K-POP SONG

- Listen to a City Pop song and get inspired.
  ADVANCE 3 SPACES

- Visual fatigue: thinking black, gray, and green are gross.
  THE PLAYER WEARING THESE COLORS SKIPS THEIR TURN FOR 1 ROUND

- Accidentally eat laser food, emergency hospital.
  SKIP YOUR TURN FOR 2 ROUNDS

- See the world in pixels and need to visit an eye specialist.
  CLOSE YOUR EYES FOR THE NEXT 3 ROUNDS

- Visit an future-themed exhibition and feel amazed.
  ONCE MORE

- During the epidemic, stay home and connect with friends online.
  STEP OUTSIDE AND CALL ON ANOTHER PLAYER TO TAKE YOUR TURN

Second section

- Play with woodcut prints, and now make prints.
  LIE ON TOP OF A PLAYER UNTIL FINISH

- Play Tamagotchi, but the pet goes to heaven, feel very sad.
  SKIP YOUR TURN FOR 1 ROUND

- Post small ads on the street and is targeted by the police. Get the hell out of dodge.
  MOVE BACK 4 SPACES

- Take part in a stock car race and drive the race car home.
  ADVANCE 3 SPACES

- Eat delicious vegetables and fruits, and body becomes better.
  ALL DEBUFFS DISAPPEAR

- Invent a hyper-realistic toy and gain fame.
  THE OTHER PLAYERS APPLAUD 10 TIMES

- Jump into the pool to swim and relax while immersed in the water.
  SKIP YOUR TURN FOR 1 ROUND

- merse yourself in r work and forget ut time.
  SKIP YOUR TURN FOR 1 ROUND

- Take a Pixel ship and escape the real world.
  MOVE ONLY 1 SPACE FOR THE NEXT 2 ROUNDS

- The font design won an international award.
  STAND UP AND SPIN AROUND 3 TIMES

WIN

- Arrive at a festival and prepare to perform.
  STAND UP AND SING OR DANCE FOR 1 MINUTE

- Look at a crazy artwork that you don't understand.
  KEEP YOUR MOUTH OPEN UNTIL THE END OF THE NEXT ROUND

Bottom row

- counter an evil nster in the est.
  RUN AROUND THE OTHER PLAYERS 3 TIMES

- Transformation! Become a Lucky Cat!
  POSE AS A LUCKY CAT AND MEOW

- Transform into Mario, gain the ability to grow in size.
  ADVANCE 1 SPACE

- Consider yourself a mellow flower.
  REMAIN COMPLETELY STILL FOR 3 MINUTES

- Feel very happy with a cherry pudding.
  MAKE 3 VERY HAPPY VOICES

- Endless process pictures, very tired, and need to rest.
  LIE DOWN TO COMPLETE THE GAME (THE PIECE)

In this chapter, we will embark on an evocative journey through retro aesthetics, where the echoes of the past reverberate through contemporary art and design. This exploration unveils the dynamic interplay between nostalgia and innovation, revealing how the visual languages of bygone eras continue to inspire and transform modern creativity. Each style we delve into not only celebrates a unique historical period but also reinvents it, weaving a rich tapestry that bridges the old with the new.

The 1980s, often heralded as "The Designer Decade," were a time of vibrant aesthetics that left an indelible mark on visual culture. This era was defined by bold colors, geometric patterns, and an exuberant spirit of innovation and rebellion. The retro aesthetics not only swept through Western culture, but also had a far-reaching impact globally, expanding in a multicultural collision. Today's artists draw from these vivid elements to create works that pulsate with the energy and optimism of the 80s, using high saturation and stark contrasts to resurrect the dynamic spirit of this iconic decade in a contemporary context.

City Pop, a genre of Japanese music from the late 1970s and 1980s, transcends sound to encompass a distinctive visual style. This art form captures the urban sophistication and carefree spirit of its era, marked by bright pastels and depictions of city life and modern leisure. Contemporary artists channel these elements to evoke nostalgia, painting scenes that reflect a time when urban living was synonymous with endless possibilities and vibrant lifestyles.

Retro-Futurism art presents an intriguing fusion of past and future, imagining how previous generations envisioned the years to come. The two seemingly contradictory words, retro and futurism, create a tension in the composition. Rooted in the mid-20th-century optimism about technology and space exploration, this style features sleek, aerodynamic designs and futuristic motifs. And artists have continued to expand the boundaries of this theme, developing several sub-styles such as Cyberpunk, Vaporwave, and Acid Design, creating works that juxtapose Retro-Futurism with the advancements of the times, and providing playful yet thought-provoking commentary on humanity's ever-evolving relationship with technology.

Cyberpunk, arguably the most well-known sub-genre of Retro-Futurism, combines high-tech advancements with gritty, dystopian environments. It imagines futures where advanced technologies coexist with societal decay, creating a stark contrast between the sleek and the sordid. Cyberpunk aesthetics often features neon lights, rain-soaked cityscapes, and cybernetic enhancements, emphasizing themes of rebellion, corporate dominance, and the blurring lines between human and machine. This visual style captures a gritty yet visually striking aesthetics that has been influential in both literature and film. Vaporwave, on the other hand, is a more recent addition to the Retro-Futurism canon, which emerged from Internet culture in the early 2010s, and focuses on the nostalgia of 1980s consumerism and early digital technology. It features glitch art, pixelated graphics, and neon grids, creating a dreamlike atmosphere that critiques and celebrates the excesses of late capitalism. Vaporwave's pastel color schemes and surreal visuals evoke a sense of both irony and wistful memory.

Acid Design, influenced by the psychedelic culture of the 1960s and 1970s, infuses Retro-Futurism with vibrant, saturated colors and intricate patterns. It often uses organic and abstract forms, blending them with futuristic motifs to create a sense of otherworldly wonder. Acid Design explores themes of transcendence and altered states of consciousness, offering a dynamic and visually stimulating experience. Each sub-genre brings its own unique perspective, blending historical influence with futuristic aspirations to create an engaging and multifaceted design style. Whether through the gritty, neon-lit streets of Cyberpunk, the nostalgic irony of Vaporwave, or the psychedelic wonders of Acid Design, Retro-Futurism continues to captivate and inspire, reflecting our complex relationship with technology, progress, and the future.

Pixel Art, born from the early days of computer graphics and video games, is enjoying a renaissance in today's digital high definition, reminiscent of the glamour of 8-bit and 16-bit visuals. This style uses small, precise squares of color to create detailed, whimsical images. Contemporary artists leverage Pixel Art's squiggly limits to produce intricate and expressive pieces, celebrating the digital roots of visual culture and showcasing artistry within the pixels.

Deco Art evolved from the opulent geometries of Art Deco to the mesmerizing illusions of Op Art, a century-long quest to dazzle the eye, and is currently experiencing a vibrant resurgence in contemporary creative practices. This style of decorative art is a celebration of visual splendor and creativity, where form merges with function in a dynamic interplay of aesthetics. It encompasses a broad range of creative expressions, from intricate patterns and luxurious materials to innovative designs and striking color schemes, and even to the creation of a whole new visual experience. Contemporary works revisit and revitalize these historical styles, transforming them through a modern lens. This revitalization injects new life into classic styles, making them relevant to today's audiences while preserving their timeless elegance. Modern artists and designers are reimagining Art Deco, honoring its rich heritage while pushing the boundaries of traditional forms, blending historical influence with contemporary sensibilities to create works that are both timeless and cutting-edge.

Some unique design styles also continued to flourish and innovate in the 1980s. Shōwa art, reflecting styles from the Shōwa era (1926–1989) of Japan, blends traditional Japanese elements with Western influence. Modern artists draw from the nostalgia and cultural richness of this period, incorporating its themes and aesthetics into contemporary works that reflect a deep appreciation for Japan's artistic heritage and its evolution throughout the 20th century. In addition, the 1980s also saw the emergence of a provocative niche style that challenged conventional notions of beauty and aesthetics—New Ugly. Embracing the awkward and unconventional, this visual style pushes the boundaries of what is considered attractive or acceptable in art. It reacts against polished, homogenized visuals, offering a bold, raw alternative. Artists adopting New Ugly provoke thought and elicit strong emotional responses, encouraging viewers to reconsider their perceptions of beauty.

These styles collectively form a vibrant mosaic of retro aesthetics, illustrating the enduring appeal of past eras and their profound influence on contemporary art and design. Through this exploration, we celebrate the timeless connection between history and innovation, unveiling the boundless creative possibilities that arise when we draw inspiration from the past. This journey is not merely a look backward but a dynamic dialogue between eras, where the past continually shapes and enriches the present and future.

City Pop

DEVELOPMENT HISTORY

Early 1970s: Origins

The origins of City Pop can be traced back to the early 1970s with the release of Japanese folk-rock band Happy End's self-titled album. City Pop emerged in Japan as a response to various music genres, including funk, soul, and disco. The visual design of album covers and promotional materials began incorporating vibrant color schemes, sleek typography, and futuristic imagery.

1980s: Peak

In the 1980s, City Pop reached its peak popularity in Japan, aligning with the country's economic boom and cultural expansion. Graphic design from this era was marked by bold, vivid colors, prominently featuring neon pinks, blues, and purples. Album covers and posters often showcased stylized illustrations, geometric patterns, and a sense of urban chic. The type choices were bold and dynamic, frequently employing futuristic and angular typefaces. The design of album covers and promotional materials captured the era's sense of optimism and modernity, focusing on urban landscapes, cityscapes, and metropolitan lifestyles.

Late 1980s to the 1990s: Transition

Toward the end of the 1980s, the City Pop began to evolve and blend with other musical styles. Graphic design during this period started to incorporate more digital and technological elements while still maintaining some of the vibrant colors and geometric patterns of the genre.

21st Century to Present: Revival and Nostalgia

In the early 21st century, City Pop experienced a revival, with its music and visual aesthetics piquing the interest of a new audience. The retro graphic design style associated with City Pop garnered appreciation for its nostalgic charm, inspiring designers to revisit and reinterpret visual elements from that era. Contemporary designers draw inspiration from the original graphic design style of City Pop, incorporating it into modern designs while adding their own creative touches.

CITY POP: MODERN VISUAL STYLE GUIDE

ELEMENTS

1. Stars
2. Celebration Ribbons
3. Clouds
4. Soda Pop
5. Button Display
6. Disco Ball
7. Tropical Fruits
8. Cadillac
9. Cocktail
10. Palm Tree
11. Cellular Phone
12. Flowers
13. Vinyl Record Player

KEYWORDS

1. POP MUSIC FUSION
2. VIBRANT CITYSCAPE
3. TROPICAL & COASTAL VIBES
4. NIGHTLIFE IMAGERY
5. MANGA-INSPIRED AESTHETICS

FONTS

Airstream NF · BPscript · Morado Nib
Black Jack · New Cicle · Daisy Script · League Script
Play Ball · WC Mano Negra Bta · Dancing Script
CODE · Wolgast Script · Morado Felt · Alex Brush
Discipuli Britannica · odstemplik

COLOR

LAYOUT

ORIGINAL ILLUSTRATION BY ARDHIRAPUTRA FOR YUNG BAE THE COMPLETE BAE VINYL COLLECTION

Ardhira Putra

Ardhira Putra is an Indonesian artist renowned for his passion for blending various media dimensions and transforming nostalgic sentiments into a vibrant, contemporary universe. His illustrations and animations often feature characters, advertising labels, and popular visual elements inspired by the 1980s and 1990s. In addition to designing visuals for international musicians and music events, he collaborates independently and with global brands like Samsung on NFT projects. He is also the recipient of the Best Animated Film award at the Indonesian Film Festival.

1 City Pop Music as Inspiration

Growing up in the bustling city of Jakarta, Indonesia, in the late 1980s, Ardhira Putra was profoundly influenced by his parents, particularly in the realms of music, video games, and TV shows. The vibrant culture of his upbringing left an indelible mark on his creative outlook. During his childhood, the melodies of City Pop music became a familiar and cherished part of his life, creating one of the happiest chapters in his journey. When Ardhira immerses himself in the tunes of City Pop today, it feels like opening a nostalgic photo album, transporting him back to the carefree days of his youth and enveloping him in a wave of positive nostalgia. Crafting illustrations with a City Pop theme has become a source of immense comfort, consistently providing him with a surge of positive energy. As both a music enthusiast and player, he thoroughly enjoys exploring the design elements embedded in City Pop. Whether it's scrutinizing album artwork, magazines, or advertisements from that era, the exploration never fails to excite him. The combination of colors, graphic elements, and layout in City Pop design perpetually sparks fresh ideas in his creative pursuits.

One particular artist who has profoundly influenced Ardhira's design work is Tatsuro Yamashita. He first heard Yamashita's song "Mermaid" on a radio station in Jakarta, and the music, chords, and sounds of the instruments resonated deeply with him. This affinity may be rooted in his childhood experiences, as his parents often played Earth, Wind & Fire and Michael Jackson. Listening to Yamashita's music triggers a profound sense of nostalgia and happiness in his mind. The themes in these songs often revolve around the joys of city life, falling in love, dealing with love problems, enjoying summer vacations, and embracing beach city life, with album artwork that consistently exudes a vibrant summer beach vibe. Ardhira finds a deep connection with these themes and aspires to create artwork that resonates with others, capturing the essence of enjoying simple pleasures and being grateful for life's uncomplicated happiness. His artistic vision is always inspired by the 80s pop culture, the emergence of pop electronic music, and the captivating entertainment TV shows of that era.

2 Staying Individual in the Trend

City Pop's visual elements, including neon lights, city streets, cars, and palm trees, are iconic and instantly recognizable. However, these elements can sometimes lead to a sense of homogeneity within the genre. Ardhira Putra, a creator deeply influenced by this style, believes this uniformity is largely driven by the shared nostalgia among creators born in the 70s and 80s, who find a sense of home and happiness in the 80s aesthetics. For Ardhira, who was born in the late 1980s, these visual elements evoke a deep personal joy, making the creation of such elements highly satisfying.

According to Ardhira, the true distinction in City Pop Art lies in the soul of the work. While the fundamental elements are universally accessible, the manner in which artists deliver their creations to the audience is what truly sets them apart. Ardhira does not overly concern himself with the potential for homogeneity because trends are inherently transient. What matters most to him is that artists continuously find joy in their work. To maintain individuality and innovation, Ardhira suggests that artists immerse themselves in the creative process and experiment with different mediums. Incorporating

THE COMPLETE BAE VINYL COLLECTION

Collaborating with a musician is always a thrill, especially when that musician is one's idol. The artist first discovered Yung Bae during their university years back in 2010, at the dawn of the Future Funk and Vaporwave genres. Yung Bae was one of the pioneering artists in Future Funk, known for sampling 1980s City Pop music from Japan and America. At that time, Japanese City Pop was becoming a phenomenon.

It was truly an honor for the artist to collaborate with Yung Bae on his compilation album. The concept for the illustration was straightforward: the artist envisioned a city of music, with towering buildings adorned with signs and billboards. Each billboard and sign showcased Yung Bae's albums, from his debut to his fifth release, featuring vibrant graphics and a variety of retro advertisements.

▼ **Elements:**
The retro elements in this illustration draw inspiration from vintage images of 1980s Japan and American cities, featuring large billboards and signs scattered throughout the urban landscape.

▼ **Layout:**
The layout of this illustration is influenced by the static perspectives commonly seen in '90s anime, such as *City Hunter*, in combination with the dynamic arrangement of billboards and signs throughout the cityscape.

Client: Yung Bae

animation or motion graphics, for instance, can infuse new life into their creations. He acknowledges that every country interprets City Pop music uniquely, showcasing its expansive reach. Ardhira feels grateful for the opportunity to continually explore and find happiness in creating City Pop artworks. Gratefully, Ardhira has been given the opportunity to keep exploring the genre, and having a constant joy in creating City Pop music artwork.

Additionally, in moving away from the depiction of traditional City Pop, Ardhira has found a way to maintain individuality. His vision has shifted from conventional City Pop to a fusion with his personal visual journey. Inspirations are drawn from a wide range of interests, including graphic design, various genre books and movies, and animations such as MTV in the 80s and 90s, Beatles "Yellow Submarine," and the also psychedelic era. This eclectic mix results in a rich tapestry of influences and personal expressions within the City Pop theme. Balancing the essence of City Pop with his unique soul, Ardhira integrates personal influences from his childhood, such as video games, music videos, manga, animation, and TV shows. This fusion shapes his recent works, providing a fresh and distinctive perspective on City Pop. His primary goal is to create a personal connection rather than follow a trend. For Ardhira, the key to maintaining authenticity and distinction within the broader trend of City Pop illustrations lies in his honest engagement with familiar and cherished elements from his past.

3 Dazzle: Exploring Childhood Memories

Ardhira Putra's project, *Dazzle*, is a captivating exploration of childhood memories and a celebration of simple happiness through vintage objects. By employing vivid colors reminiscent of retro console games, Ardhira created a nostalgic yet futuristic ambiance. His approach to selecting objects for his illustrations is deeply rooted in personal emotions and a passion for retro items. He drew inspiration from his personal collection of vintage TVs, Sega Saturn and Nintendo 64 game consoles, and old magazines, while also incorporating influences from broader retro culture and vintage shops. Ardhira's imagination plays a crucial role as he crafts fictional objects and spaces, evoking a sense of nostalgia in a dreamy and surreal manner.

Initially a personal hobby, *Dazzle* has become a significant source of joy for Ardhira, illustrating his ability to balance personal happiness with broader artistic exploration. He views his artistic skills as part of a continuous learning process, with personal joy remaining a primary focus. Looking ahead, Ardhira is committed to retro artistic exploration, a path he has been dedicated to since 2017. He believes that this fusion of nostalgia and futuristic elements will continue to shape his future creative direction, maintaining a therapeutic and joyous essence in his art. Ardhira's work not only resonates with those who share his fondness for retro culture but also offers a unique and authentic expression of his creative identity.

4 Renja: A New Interpretation of Childhood Nostalgia

Ardhira Putra's artwork *Renja* uniquely merges childhood nostalgia with the complexities of adulthood, weaving together various thematic elements to create a distinctive artistic expression. Through his illustrations, Ardhira skillfully integrates psychedelic motifs inspired by personal interests alongside a deep appreciation for nature, cultivated through exploration of natural landscapes such as beaches and mountains. These elements are not mere aesthetic choices but serve as vehicles to evoke memories and emotions associated with his upbringing and cultural influences.

Titled "The East," *Renja* captures the global influence of *Tokusatsu* and the shared connection people from the 80s and 90s have with the genre, particularly in their dreams of becoming heroes. This genre, with its heroic narratives and fantastical elements, played a pivotal role in shaping Ardhira's childhood experiences. He fondly recalls how *Tokusatsu* characters seen on television and portrayed through action figures and custom masks fueled his youthful dreams and playful imagination. This personal connection imbues *Renja* with a profound sense of nostalgia, capturing the spirit of a generation that dreamed of becoming heroes.

Through his artwork, Ardhira goes beyond conventional tribute or fan art, serving as a sophisticated reinterpretation of past heroes viewed through an adult lens. *Renja* becomes a testament to Ardhira's artistic evolution, showcasing his ability to blend childhood passions with adult reflections on identity and cultural heritage. This creates a visually compelling narrative that deeply resonates, encouraging viewers to explore themes of innocence, aspiration, and the transformative power of imagination within contemporary art, celebrating both the innocence of youth and the complexity of mature artistic expression.

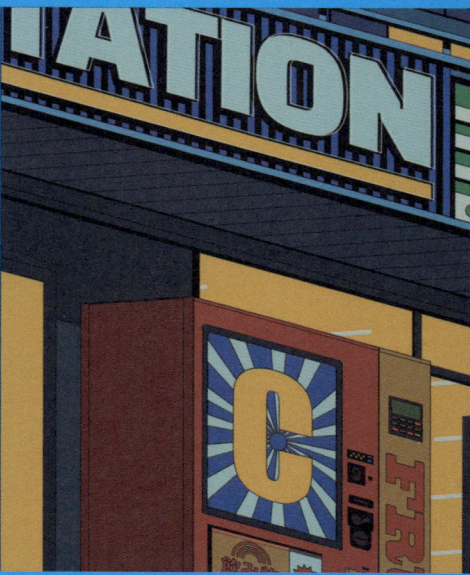

CVISION

The brief from CVISION Hong Kong was straightforward: creating a 20-second bumper that tells a simple story and ends with the CVISION logo. The directive was clear—they wanted Ardhira Putra to showcase his unique style. The artist's concept focused on capturing the fleeting, beautiful moments to breathe within the fast-paced city life. He designed a cityscape where buildings obscure the sky, but the neon lights and signs emit a joyful vibe. Given that the animation would be displayed on one of the largest high-resolution LED walls in the Asia Pacific, located in Sogo Causeway Bay's central shopping area, the artist aimed for an engaging and dynamic piece. The animation begins with a character drinking juice, symbolizing a burst of new energy or perspective. As the character moves, the surroundings become more vibrant, with lively city light banners filling the frame. The animation concludes with the character reaching the top of a building, enjoying the nighttime view as the moon morphs into the CVISION logo.

Client: CVISION — SOGO HONGKONG (China)

▼ **Elements:**

The retro elements in this project are predominantly influenced by the building shapes and window layouts of the '80s, as well as the colors palette inspired by '90s anime like *Sailor Moon* and *City Hunter*.

Most of the graphic elements in this work draw inspiration from '80s advertising city banners and LED signs.

▼ **Layout:**

The layout arrangement ideas in this work are form a more static perspective. Since the artist wanted to show the static life of people living in the city, the dynamic elements come from the color and the pattern when the animation started, so he hope it will give a unique balance in composition.

▼ Color Scheme:

| R000 G062 B137 | R000 G136 B182 | R000 G127 B065 | R199 G138 B016 | R203 G025 B043 | R100 G176 B186 |
| C100 M083 Y016 K000 | C087 M030 Y018 K000 | C091 M033 Y097 K002 | C025 M051 Y100 K000 | C018 M099 Y087 K000 | C061 M014 Y027 K000 |

Ardhira Putra · City Pop · 72

GOLDEN CIRCLE — EVENING CINEMA

The Evening Cinema approached Ardhira Putra to create the album artwork in his unique style. After listening to the album, the artist envisioned a great adventure of the band traveling abroad. Inspired by video game intros, the concept features a racing car speeding through vacation landscapes. The environment is designed to feel like home, infused with joyful energy and dreamy, surreal graphic elements. The musicians appear on TV screens as game characters, surrounded by music notes, spaceships, and fruit objects, all set in a summery atmosphere. The artist aimed to create a harmonious composition, balancing color, line, and shape to evoke a fruity, positive vibe.

Client: Evening Cinema

▼ **Elements:**

The retro elements in this project are largely inspired by his personal collection of items at home, including a vintage TV, a spaceship model, and a Casio synthesizer. Additionally, some elements are drawn from his collection of retro advertisements.

The graphic elements in this project are derived from iconic symbols found in vintage magazines. The artist reconfigured and combined these symbols to impart new meaning within the illustration.

▼ **Layout:**

The layout of this illustration predominantly features a eye-level angle, reminiscent of scenes from playing vintage video games. It reflects the perspective of a TV positioned atop a desk, surrounded by various items.

… City Pop … Ardhira Putra

MTV IDENTS

The MTV Idents project is one of Ardhira Putra's favorite projects of the year. The brief gave the creator the freedom to develop a 15-second animation that concludes with the MTV logo. Growing up, the artist enjoyed watching MTV, where he could listen to new music and view innovative music videos. The MTV idents of that era, which often featured stop motion, animation, and traditional frame-by-frame techniques, had a significant impact on the artist, inspiring his appreciation for Pop Art in animation.

For this project, the artist envisioned a narrative involving an early '90s electronic musician who created a futuristic music sound by combining sound from an old synthesizer with imagery of fruit, visual memory, and plants, using an analog computer. This retro object, associated with the birth of MTV, incorporates elements of nostalgia.

Client: MTV

▼ Elements:
The retro elements in this project were based on the 1980s, the rising era of electronic objects, including computers, synthesizers, radios, CDs, even the magazine cover style, as well as everyday items like bottles and milk cartons.

▼ Layout:
The layout of this illustration resembles a first-person perspective, as if someone is looking at their desk, aiming to create a personal and realistic vibe in the animation.

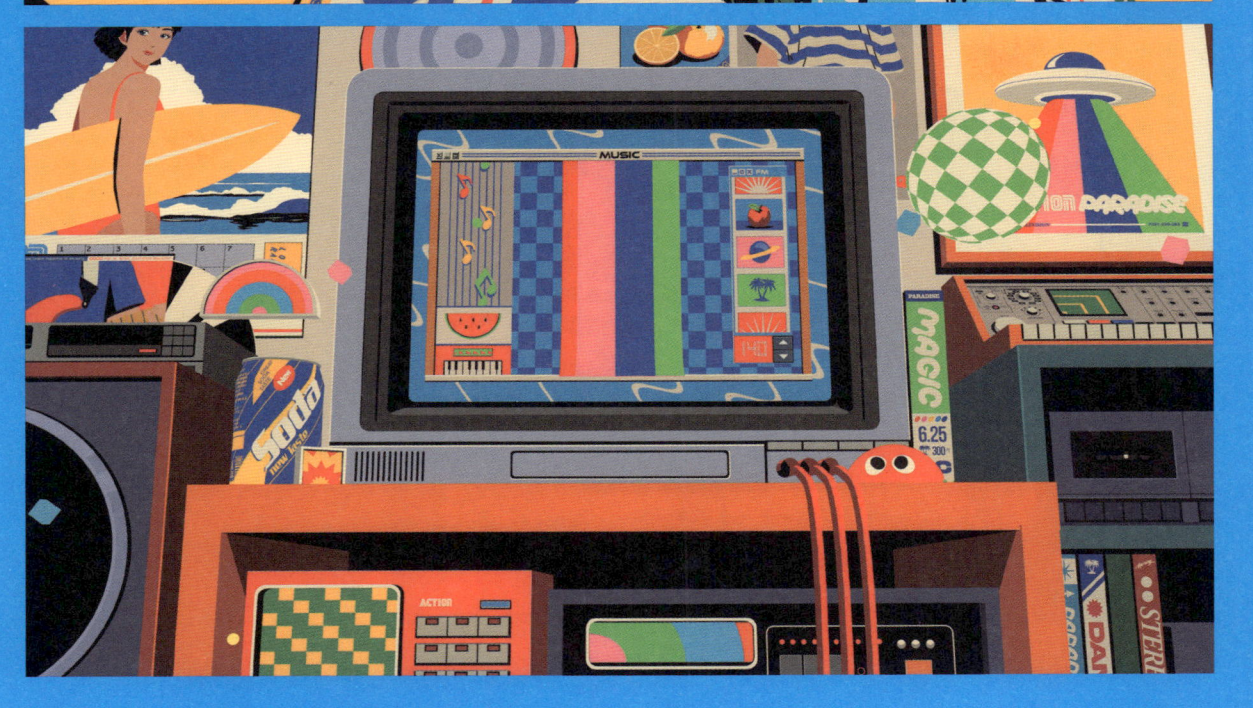

Ardhira Putra · City Pop · 74

DAZZLE

This is a personal project, reflecting Ardhira Putra's inner joy and precious childhood memories. This project serves as an exploration of retro objects such as an old TV, a VHS player, a vintage game console, and a collection of his beloved items. The inspiration is drawn primarily from the artist's memories and visits to vintage shops. This work symbolizes gratitude and simple happiness from his perspective. It resembles a still life painting with vivid colors, reminiscent of high-saturation retro console games, blending nostalgia with futuristic elements. The animation features slow movements, creating a therapeutic vibe. The artist began this project while working in an office, feeling bored with client work at the time. *Dazzle* became a personal escape, offering a sense of happiness and fulfillment.

The retro elements in this work are primarily objects from the artist's childhood, combined with items purchased from vintage and retro shops. Most of the graphic elements are inspired by the his journal entries, where he used to draw random icons, logos, and brands based on his visits to these vintage shops, as well as his daily walks to the supermarket.

▼ **Layout:** The layout arrangement in this work is primarily based on the still life painting style.

▼ **Color Scheme:**

| R237 G030 B037 | R248 G179 B000 | R115 G188 B069 | R028 G136 B059 | R000 G159 B201 |
| C000 M096 Y087 K000 | C000 M036 Y096 K000 | C058 M000 Y089 K000 | C082 M030 Y100 K000 | C083 M013 Y016 K000 |

| R024 G070 B155 | R235 G104 B141 | R246 G222 B182 | R164 G154 B138 | R000 G000 B000 |
| C093 M076 Y000 K000 | C000 M072 Y019 K000 | C004 M016 Y032 K000 | C042 M038 Y044 K000 | C000 M000 Y000 K100 |

RENJA—THE EAST

The *Renja* series is a personal illustration project in which the artist combines childhood memories with stories from adulthood. This work is not a direct imitation of past hero series; instead, the artist has created a new hero who feels more mature and richly retro. The character of *Renja* represents not just a hero but a display of the artist's fragmented memories. The illustration of *Renja* itself serves both as a statement and as a character that boldly introduces new perspectives to the environment.

The title of the illustration, "East," signifies not only the series' name but also refers to a region of the world. The world of *Tokusatsu*, originating from Japan, had a significant global impact, influencing many people born in the '80s and '90s. The artist believes that many children first experienced the feeling of being a hero while watching *Tokusatsu* TV shows. Through this work, the artist aimed to convey those emotions and connections to the audience.

▼ **Elements:**

The retro elements in the illustration are primarily influenced by vintage *Tokusatsu* posters from the 80s, combined with surreal elements reflective of the present era. And the graphic elements draw from these vintage posters, modified and interpreted through the artist's contemporary perspective on past heroes.

▼ **Layout:**

The layout in this illustration is more like a hero poster.

Ardhira Putra — City Pop — 76

COAST 2 COAST

Coast 2 Coast, the latest music album by Pearl & The Oysters, was released in early 2023. At the beginning, the band shared the album's concept with Ardhira Putra, centered around a migration journey from one island to another, symbolizing a move to a new city. They expressed their comfort with the illustration themes that the artist had previously created for their music, which prominently featured retro electronic instruments, including analog synthesizers. The artist, who had a passion for electronic music since high school, found a deep connection with the band's sound, evoking memories of relaxing summer vacations on the beach. A vintage island postcard has become one of his inspirations, which evoked a sense of nostalgia and influenced the composition of the artwork.

The illustration envisions a surreal island where electronic music instruments are scattered on the beach alongside signs of life, such as animals. In the background, another island resembling a typical city can be seen. To enhance the surreal, dreamy atmosphere, the artist added magical elements to the foreground while maintaining the layout's vintage postcard aesthetic. The color palette was carefully chosen to reflect the band's sweet, fun, and elegant tunes. Upon hearing the concept, the band responded positively and provided additional personal touches, including pictures of a green parrot from their home and their electronic instruments. These elements were incorporated into the cover to create a deeper connection to their lives and music.

Client: Stonesthrow records - Pearl & The Oysters

▼ Elements:
The instruments depicted are based on photos of the band's own equipment, and the bird in the illustration is modeled after their parrot bird. The color palette, inspired by City Pop album covers like *Pacific* (1978), incorporates dark blue hues to reflect the album's vibe. This choice aligns with the band's connection to City Pop through their use of similar musical instruments and influences. The graphic elements in the illustration draw from real life, with fictional additions like button screens and LED displays. Patterns and colors inspired by natural elements, such as mushrooms and water, are also featured, reflecting the band's use of electronic synthesizers to create nature sounds.

▼ Layout:
The artist aims to create a layout reminiscent of a vintage summer island postcard, evoking the advertisement style of inviting people to visit the island. Objects and animals in the foreground need to be noticed, as the electronic instruments in the album represent the sounds of nature, such as waves, birds, and the overall feeling of a summer vocation.

City Pop — Ardhira Putra

THE FUTURE IS FEMALE

This illustration is a personal statement on freedom of expression. In Southeast Asia, cultural norms often stereotype women as needing to become wives and mothers after high school or university, a pattern commonly seen in Indonesia and other parts of East Asia.

The illustration challenges these stereotypes, depicting a group of high school girls playing loud punk music in front of a house with explosive energy. Inspired by the Japanese film *Linda Linda Linda*, which tells the story of a girl punk band formed for a summer school festival, this work reflects a strong connection to themes of independence and self-expression.

▼ **Elements:**
The illustration is based on a Japanese movie called *Linda Linda Linda*, with a combination of surreal objects surrounding the characters. Also, many elements here reflect high school girls playing loud music, showing freedom of expression. Where there are no rules in the environment, there are a lot of surreal elements going on.

▼ **Layout:**
The layout of the illustration is like a vintage American movie, an angle from the front yard of the house to showing the activities taking place.

▼ **Color Scheme:**

■ R043 G096 B172	■ R235 G109 B165	■ R121 G189 B040	□ R255 G255 B255	■ R255 G237 B000
C084 M060 Y000 K000	C000 M070 Y000 K000	C057 M000 Y100 K000	C000 M000 Y000 K000	C000 M003 Y095 K000

ILLUSTRATIONS BY BERN FOSTER

HARLEY ON THE BEACH

Harley on the Beach:

Created for the artist's personal portfolio, this Harley-Davidson illustration is an independent project. Inspired by a vibrant vision, the artist used a Harley reference photo and applied pure imagination to the composition. The bluish hue on the metal parts reflects the sky, creating a strong contrast. The entire Harley was painted in blue to maintain a harmonious color scheme. Despite the intricacy and numerous details, completing this challenging 20x30-inch illustration took two weeks.

Windsurfers in Rio:

Inspired by Rio de Janeiro, this illustration radiates happiness with vibrant, harmonious colors, capturing a summertime vibe. The use of flat colors, akin to a vector illustration, with acrylics sets it apart.

Mels Drive in:

Featured on the cover of *Artists & Illustrators* magazine (August 2023), this illustration captures the essence of the classic American Dream and reflects the artist's values. Inspired by a desire to create a City Pop illustration with a summer feel, the Mel's Drive-in logo sparked the initial idea. Despite its simplicity, the artwork encompasses elements that have intrigued the artist since childhood: palms, the American dream, and the allure of capitalism. The color palette, dominated by pink and blues, creates a striking contrast between the darkened sky and the vibrant pink building. Painted mostly with an airbrush, the artist envisioned a location in Santa Monica while working on the piece.

Cadillac on the Beach:

Capturing west coast dreams, this illustration revolves around a Cadillac Eldorado, drawn with mechanical pencils and black paint before being painted with acrylic wash. The artist, fond of the shiny chrome parts on classic cars, used brushes for most of the painting, reserving the airbrush for the sky.

Windsurfers:

Inspired by windsurfers in Chiclana, Spain, the artist, originally from the area, aimed to capture the vibrant colors and shapes of windsurf sails. A childhood connection to the coastal city fueled this fascination with windsurfing. The illustration, completed in just two days, features windsurfers during the daytime and marks the artist's first work in 2024.

Ocean Is Calling:

This illustration began with the idea of painting a chorme Airstream, employing his typical creative process of building an illustration around a central element. Sought after for printing and licensing, the concept was inspired by an image of the

Airstream on the beach against a gradient blue sky. The sky's gradient color, achieved with an airbrush using light turquoise, cerulean blue, and purple-dark blue, stands out as the illustration's highlight. Despite its simplicity, the artwork's appeal lies in the adept use of these colors, making it one of the artist's favorites.

Planet Bass:

Crafted for Canadian funky-rock band TWRP's campaign, *Planet Bass* merges City Pop aesthetics with sci-fi elements, featuring a bass guitar, a planet, and a City Pop atmosphere. The artist reflected on the surreal concept's evolution, from a chrome sphere to a City Pop world with a hint of sci-fi. Using references, including a bass guitar photo and images of their own hands, the artist imaginatively created the unique *Planet Bass*, depicting cities, lakes, and waves within a round shape.

Bright Lights, Big City:

Inspired by Miami at night, the artist's initial motive was to paint a sunset in purple tones and experiment with different colors. The choice of Canson paper over the usual Crescent Illustration Board achieved similar results for this type of illustration.

While the reflections in the water were invented, they were painted in various tones based on building colors. The palm silhouettes were inspired by a summer photoshoot in the south of Spain. As the artist worked, two songs, "Pull the Wires" by Baltimora and "If You Were Here Tonight" by Alexander O'Neal, set the mood for the artwork, and the artist couldn't help but sing along while creating this captivating City Pop illustration.

Drink in the Beach Cottage:

Originally a personal piece, this artwork has been licensed three times. The artist invested time refining the concept, adjusting the perspective of the cottage based on a reference image. After realizing the need to add a drink in the foreground, the concept was redrawn, further altering the perspective.

The intricate creation process involved multiple elements painted with different techniques, emphasizing sharp shadow projections for a sunny atmosphere. The illustration's visual impact is striking due to vibrant colors, making it highly attractive.

Pepsi & Tropical Resort:

This illustration combines two ideas: painting a swimming pool with an exaggerated perspective to evoke a summer atmosphere and featuring a classic Pepsi soda can. The artist harbors a unique fascination with soda cans, especially the classic Pepsi design, and lamented the change in the logo. Despite the challenges of using the airbrush for large sky areas, the artist skillfully navigated the difficulties to bring both elements together in this artwork.

Illustrator: Bern Foster
Client1: *Artists & Illustrators* magazine (Mels Drive in)
Client2: TWRP band (Planet Bass)

WINDSURFERS IN RIO

▼ **Inspiration & Elements:**

Harley on the Beach: *California Dreams* TV series was in the illustrator's mind when painting this illustration. The idea of adding a cottage and the palms is to create a paradise atmosphere. He was also influenced by Japanese artist Eizin Suzuki.

Windsurfers in Rio: Japanese City Pop Artist Hiroshi Nagai has been a significant inspiration in his artistic journey. In the illustration, windsurfers are sailing in a coastal city.

Mels Drive in: The artist, driven by a fascination with late 80s and early 90s TV and magazine culture from childhood, channels these memories into their current illustrations, for example, a classic pink American restaurant named Mel's Drive-in. This artwork serves as a prime example of how the artist blends his childhood fascination seamlessly into his profession as an illustrator.

Cadillac on the Beach: The artist has been inspired by Hisao Kawada or Hiroshi Nagai. The illustration shows a Cadillac Eldorado parking in front of the beach on the West Coast.

Windsurfers: There is something magical about windsurfing; it is associated with colors and shapes, or with nostalgia. The artist was influenced by windsurfing to create this piece showing windsurfers sailing in the ocean.

Ocean Is Calling: While working on this illustration, the artist has been listening to a song titled "Carolyne" by the new age band Chi. The image and the song are connected in a way that naturally flows into the image elements: an Airstream on the beach with a palm tree.

Planet Bass: The artist was influenced by airbrush advertising illustrations from the 1980s, as shown in this illustration of a sci-fi urban pop planet playing bass.

Bright Lights, Big City: Influenced by various sunset images and artists, particularly Hiroshi Nagai, the artist drew inspiration from R&B and romantic music while creating this illustration. The perfect purple sunset over the skyline in the image shows how it feels.

MELS DRIVE IN

CADILLAC ON THE BEACH

WINDSURFERS

PLANET BASS

OCEAN IS CALLING

▼ **Inspiration & Elements:**

Drink in the Beach Cottage : The idea of making this illustration was influenced by the beach scenes of the movie *Stealing Home* (1988) with the music of David Foster. The artist constructed such a image: One drink on the handrail of a cottage with perfect views of two boats sailing in the sea.

Pepsi & Tropical Resort: The artist drew inspiration from TV and magazine adverts from the '80s and '90s. The image depicts a private resort with a swimming pool and a Pepsi on the pool coping.

City Pop — Bern Foster

BRIGHT LIGHTS, BIG CITY

DRINK IN THE BEACH COTTAGE

▼ Color Scheme:

- R216 G183 B214 / C016 M033 Y000 K000
- R149 G123 B182 / C047 M055 Y000 K000
- R000 G069 B125 / C098 M075 Y026 K010
- R014 G176 B210 / C072 M007 Y015 K000
- R158 G208 B216 / C042 M005 Y015 K000
- R070 G097 B172 / C078 M061 Y000 K000
- R155 G158 B044 / C060 M020 Y100 K005
- R000 G068 B031 / C088 M045 Y096 K053
- R012 G107 B047 / C084 M034 Y100 K026
- R000 G000 B000 / C000 M000 Y000 K100
- R235 G209 B186 / C008 M021 Y027 K000
- R193 G044 B046 / C019 M093 Y082 K007

PEPSI & TROPICAL RESORT

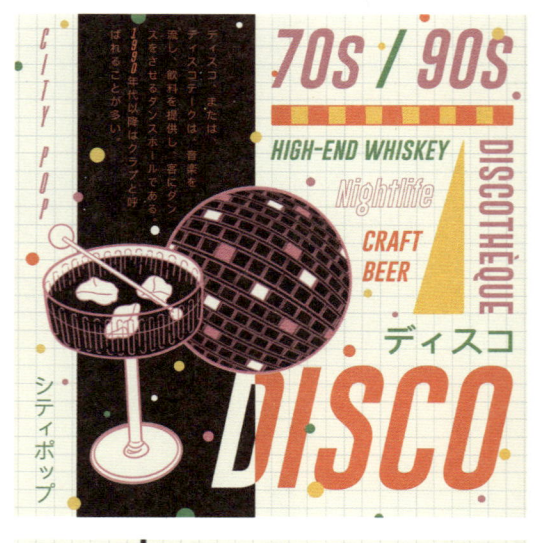

CITY POP ALBUM

The artwork aims to capture the City Pop trend of that era through postcards featuring popular items and retro colors. Designed as gifts, the postcards introduce the charm of City Pop to a wider audience. To emphasize the importance of music, CD cases are creatively used in the packaging for added meaning and fun.

Designer: LXuan

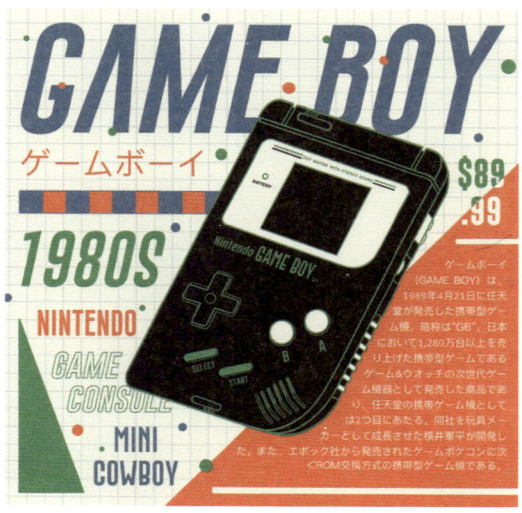

▼ **Inspiration:**

Before beginning the design process, the designer drew inspiration from anime styles, with particular reference to the iconic series *City Hunter* and *Sailor Moon*. These shows provide rich sources of illustrative techniques and character design.

▼ **Elements:**

City Pop, originating in Japan, is depicted using thick lines reminiscent of anime. There are some little graphic elements used in the illustrations, such as circles, irregular triangles, and rectangles.

▼ **Fonts:**

Gobold, Noto Sans

▼ **Layout:**

The main body of each picture is an item illustration, complemented by text and basic graphics; meanwhile, she used the vertical text typography common in that era.

▼ **Color Scheme:**

- R191 G104 B146 / C027 M069 Y018 K000
- R220 G094 B066 / C010 M076 Y072 K000
- R230 G198 B078 / C012 M022 Y076 K000
- R000 G142 B095 / C084 M024 Y076 K000
- R033 G102 B155 / C085 M057 Y020 K000
- R235 G241 B237 / C010 M004 Y008 K000
- R000 G000 B000 / C000 M000 Y000 K100

CITY POP ALBUM
シティ・ポップ　アルバム
5 FAMOUS CITY POP SONGS
WALKMAN
ウォークマン
¥33,000
WM-F77
FM-AM
AUTO REVERSE
1980S
夏
ラボ
CONVERTIBLE CAR
オープンカー
380SL
V8
LXM 59
GAME BOY
ゲームボーイ
1980S
NINTENDO
GAME CONSOLE
MINI COWBOY
$89.99
ゲームボーイ(GAME BOY)は、1989年4月21日に任天堂が発売した携帯型ゲーム機。略称は"GB"。日本において1,280万台以上を売り上げた携帯型ゲームである。ゲーム&ウォッチの次世代ゲーム機器として発売した商品であり、任天堂の携帯型ゲーム機としては2つ目にあたる。同社を玩具メーカーとして成長させた横井軍平が開発した。また、エポック社から発売されたゲームポケコンに次ぐROM交換方式の携帯型ゲーム機である。
70S / 90S
HIGH-END WHISKEY
Nightlife
CRAFT BEER
DISCOTHEQUE
DISCO
ディスコ
シティポップ
来月発売の予定
04/26
STICKER & KEYCHAIN AS GIFTS
CELLULAR PHONE
Motorola DynaTAC
80S
First Mobile Phone
$3995
限量発売
LIMITED EDITION

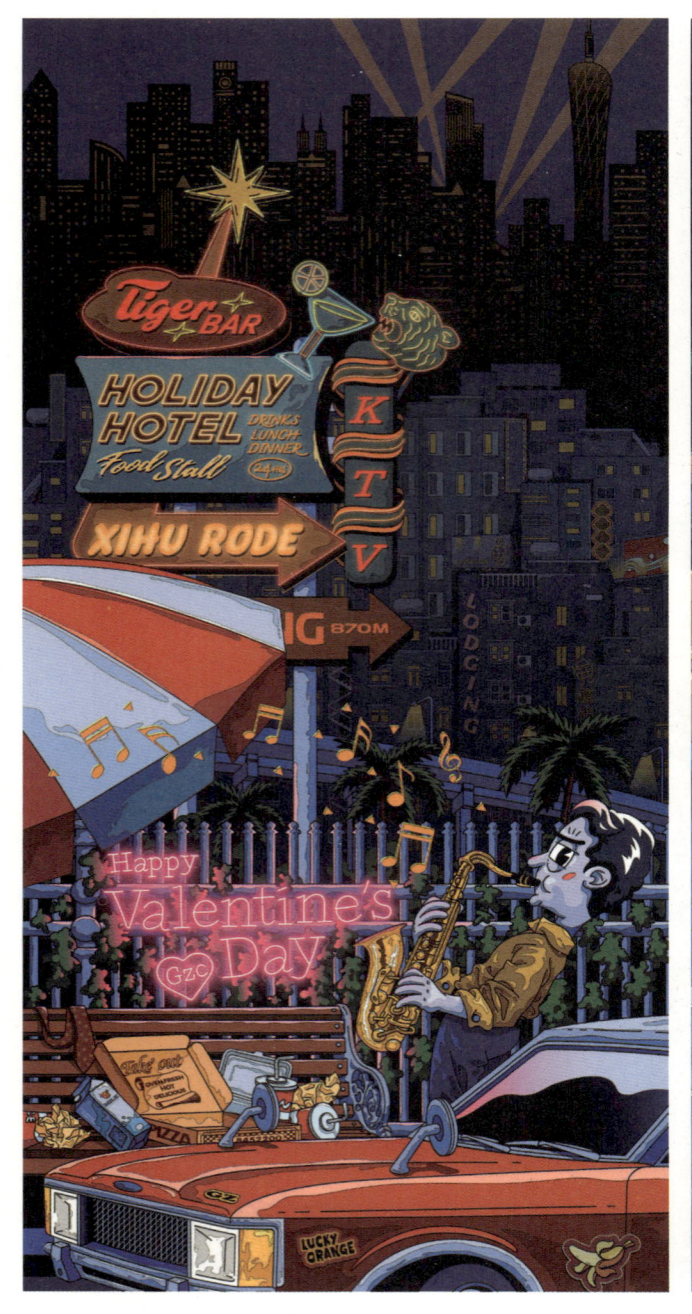

#BLACK NOSE# MR.STONE

In 2020, fresh out of the Art Academy's Printmaking Department, the artist faced rejections in the job market. Turning adversity into art, he began the "Black Nose" series, featuring Mr. Stone, inspired by a line from *Walden*: "From thence our kind hard-hearted is, enduring pain and care, Approving that our bodies of a stony nature are." This character symbolizes resilience and self-motivation.

Inspired by Japan's 1980s City Pop culture, the project captures the era's romantic and soothing essence.

Illustrator: Jun-Feng Li

▼ **Inspiration:** This project is heavily influenced by the popular City Pop style of the 1980s. In terms of music, it draws inspiration from classic works by Japanese musicians such as Tatsuro Yamashita, Eiichi Ohtaki, and Akira Terao, as well as recent Chinese emerging music groups like Sunset Rollercoaster and Metropolis. Visually, it is inspired by artists like Hiroshi Nagai, Ardhira Putra, Seizo Watase, and Eizin Suzuki. The story of this project is inspired by the 2016 film *La La Land*, starring Ryan Gosling.

▼ **Elements:** The designer objectively depicted the inherent characteristics of the objects, enhancing their connection through light, shadow, and space to create a City Pop-style atmosphere. He used the theory of light and shadow sketching, focusing on highlights, light-facing areas, inherent colors, and dark areas as the framework for depiction.

▼ **Fonts:** Source Han Sans, Source Han Serif, CJGaoDeGuo-MH, YUN FEN FEI YUN TI, HanWangKanTan, Playlist Script, Bad Script Regular, Sigmar One, Bangers Regular, Soul Handwriting, Sansita Black, Alegreya Sans, ZCOOL Addict

▼ **Layout:** The project features a protagonist from the lower social strata. To emphasize this, the designer positioned him within a small scene to evoke a sense of storytelling. Then adding mid- and long-shot background elements enhanced depth and conveyed the character's social status. Thus, the composition logic is straightforward: foreground interaction creates narrative, while mid- and long-shot background detail the character and social context.

▼ **Color Scheme:**

R203 G049 B028	R150 G060 B035	R165 G192 B228	R077 G098 B172	R027 G056 B146	R213 G190 B161
C019 M093 Y100 K000	C044 M087 Y100 K011	C039 M018 Y000 K000	C076 M061 Y000 K000	C096 M086 Y002 K000	C019 M027 Y037 K000

DAY & NIGHT

The artwork draws inspiration from the 1980s City Pop era, portraying distinct atmospheres of daytime and nighttime urban life in Japan. The scenes of a laundromat during the day and a Disco hall at night capture the unique spirit of City Pop, showcasing optimism and romance respectively.

Designer: LXuan

▼ **Inspiration:** In the booming Japanese economy of the '70s and '80s, more women entered the workforce, decreasing housewives and increasing laundromat foot traffic. The 1980s Disco craze, with its neon lights and joyful vibe, became an iconic symbol of City Pop.

▼ **Elements:** The 2D illustrations portray iconic items like radios, disco balls, and retro vending machines, with grids and polka dots for a vintage touch.

▼ **Fonts:** Gobold, Noto Sans

▼ **Layout:** Comic storyboard layouts create a unique experience.

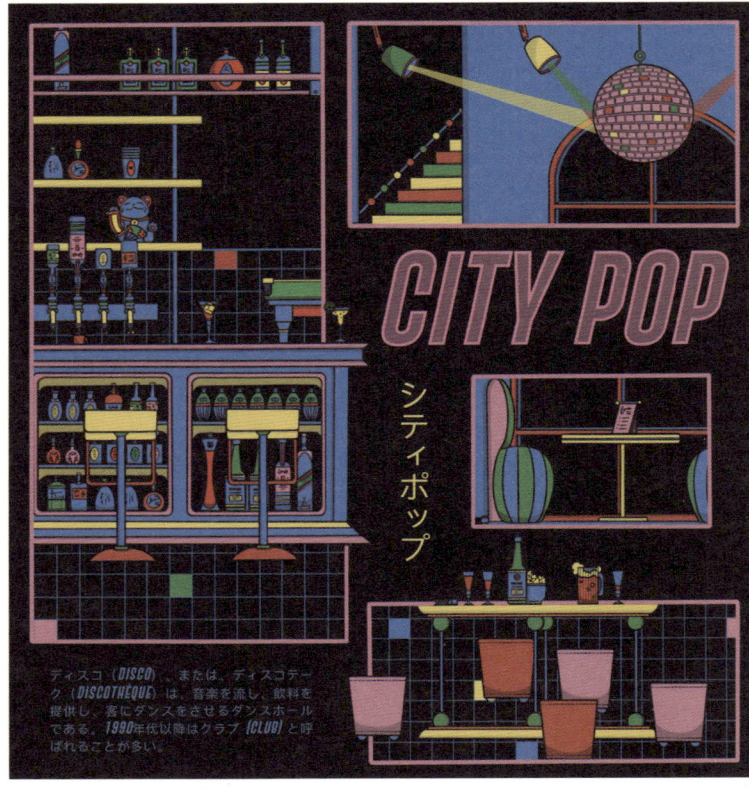

NT CITY

The artwork adopts the City Pop style to depict the room of the customer's fantasy. The items in the illustration are all Yaya's favorite things, such as Toy Story, Coca-Cola, Crayon Shin-chan, gachapon machines, rubber duckies, chocolate cookies, and more. It presents a room imagined by an adorable City Pop-loving girl.

Designer: LXuan
Client: YAYA

▼ **Inspiration:**
The work is mainly influenced by the vivid color contrasts and intricate visual style prevalent in City Pop.

▼ **Elements:**
The illustrations incorporate grid patterns, splatter textures, and snowflake screens to create a retro atmosphere.

▼ **Fonts:**
Gobold, Minecraft, Noto Sans

City Pop

TIME MISSION

In the fast-paced modern era, the design team sought to evoke nostalgia and a sense of happiness through a Mid-Autumn gift box. Mooncakes in classic tin boxes, enamel cups, and childhood puzzles are all packed in a messenger bag, with fragments of past life restored using retro illustration techniques.

To align with sustainable practices, the team chose Tyvek for the outer packaging, replacing traditional non-recyclable materials. The contents were also designed to be fully reusable, reflecting the team's commitment to environmental friendliness and circular economy.

The gift box not only served as a festive gift but also as a testament to the team's innovative and sustainable design approach.

Design Studio: CH_LAB
Designer: Meng Jiayang, Wang Zhiheng, Chen Wei, Wang Zhihong
Client: Leben, CH_LAB

▼ **Inspiration:**
The work is mainly influenced by retro objects and landscapes from the '80s and '90s, such as vintage radios, televisions, and cassette tapes, which strongly evoke a sense of "urban pop." And it is also inspired by artists such as Masuzo Watase, Hiroshi Nagai, Eito Suzuki, and Indonesian artist Ardhira Putra, and senses various visual moods in their work.

▼ **Elements:**
A significant amount of old object elements combined with urban landscapes of the 1980s and 1990s, the design aims to evoke a unique urban emotion that is exclusive to the City Pop style.

▼ **Fonts:**
Source Han Sans, Montserrat

▼ **Layout:**
The design team incorporated full-page illustrative visuals on various packaging sizes, drawing inspiration from the vibrant candy wrappers and toy packaging papers of their childhood.

BATHROOM

This series of works depicts various bathing styles in City Pop aesthetics, each characterized by unique traits and the author's conceptual interpretations. "Hot Springs" captures the experience of being in a hot spring, conveying traditional hot spring culture and relaxation through a playful narrative. While "Medicated Bath" highlights the unique elements of traditional Chinese medicine in bathing. "Turkish Bath" emphasizes the exotic atmosphere and unforgettable scrubbing experience, showcasing its indigenous nature. "Thai Massage" combines the distinctive features of Thai massage with longstanding Buddhist beliefs, expressing both the physical and spiritual aspects. Finnish "Sauna" reflects the Finnish environment and climate, merging sauna culture with Finnish characteristics and showcasing the nation's deep-rooted love for saunas. The final illustration, "Sunbathing," explores the concept of sunbathing as an attractive blend of technology and leisure.

Illustrator: Weiling Zhang

▼ **Inspiration & Elements**

Hot Springs: The artist aimed to simulate the state of the human body when taking a bath in a hot spring, extracting a lot of elements related to the Japanese hot spring culture, and comparing the bathing process to food preparation in order to achieve a certain symbolic connection. For example, a person taking a bath in a hot spring looks like Kanto being boiled in hot water.

Medicated Bath: The idea of the medicated bath is based on the concept of Chinese medicine cabinets, where the many messages of the medicated bath are transformed into visual elements and placed in the drawers of the cabinet. The animated presentation of the work uses the dynamic movement of the drawers stretching to increase the sense of dynamism and interest.

Turkish Bath: Turkey's unique way of bathing, which began with religious practices, is the source of inspiration for the design, and this illustration shows the exotic spatial characteristics of the Turkish bathing experience.

Thai Massage: In depicting a Thai massage, the artist combined the religious features of Thailand to create a Thai-inspired bathing space.

Sauna: Based on the fact that every home in Finland has a sauna, the artist incorporated the concept of a board game table, combining various forms of sauna into a large-scale game.

Sunbathing: Based on the effects of sunbathing on the human body, the artist gave the concept of a technological "sunlight laboratory" to the design, making the overall picture interesting and attractive.

▼ **Fonts:**

Gen Shin Gothic, HY Zhong Hei, Arial MT Pro Italic

City Pop — Weiling Zhang

▼ Color Scheme:

| ■ R128 G193 B195 | ■ R000 G094 B156 | ■ R164 G064 B081 | ■ R244 G171 B174 |
| C052 M007 Y025 K000 | C093 M060 Y015 K000 | C044 M087 Y062 K003 | C000 M043 Y020 K000 |

| ■ R219 G178 B081 | ■ R235 G105 B085 | ■ R247 G192 B186 | ■ R000 G070 B147 |
| C020 M034 Y074 K000 | C009 M072 Y062 K000 | C000 M033 Y020 K000 | C096 M077 Y009 K000 |

| ■ R035 G143 B201 | ■ R000 G135 B106 | ■ R221 G077 B084 | ■ R252 G239 B050 |
| C076 M030 Y005 K000 | C085 M029 Y068 K000 | C016 M083 Y059 K000 | C004 M000 Y084 K000 |

| ■ R000 G139 B184 | ■ R214 G048 B038 | ■ R013 G046 B082 | ■ R246 G169 B000 |
| C082 M030 Y017 K000 | C012 M093 Y090 K000 | C100 M091 Y051 K021 | C000 M042 Y096 K000 |

| ■ R226 G078 B132 | ■ R246 G189 B195 | ■ R006 G009 B032 | ■ R094 G131 B194 |
| C005 M082 Y018 K000 | C000 M035 Y013 K000 | C098 M097 Y069 K063 | C067 M043 Y001 K000 |

| ■ R252 G239 B050 | ■ R239 G144 B175 | ■ R233 G221 B201 | ■ R000 G161 B145 |
| C004 M000 Y084 K000 | C000 M056 Y009 K000 | C010 M014 Y022 K000 | C080 M011 Y050 K000 |

TOSHIBA TV

This project is an illustration poster for Toshiba TV on Children's Day. The visual style of the poster employs the City Pop style to capture the city's prosperity in the 1990s. The TV serves as the visual centerpiece, and the dynamic effects on the inner screen showcase the brand's classic past and refreshed present.

Designer: Bali Meng

▼ **Inspiration:**

On Children's Day, Toshiba TV, in collaboration with various brands, launched the "TOSHIBA TV FRIENDSHIP CLUB" to revisit childhood classics and relive the joy of childhood. Centered around the television, the artist explored iconic images from each brand, showcasing the nostalgic memories these brands evoke from childhood.

▼ **Elements:**

The main element is a TOSHIBA TV displaying classic images from various brands, including TOYOTA, Mizuno, RONGSHENG, CMCC, and Strong Food (Xizhilang). In the foreground, iconic products from these brands are showcased, such as Strong U.Loveit Milk Tea, a staple in the childhood memories of many Chinese people. Additionally, classic items from the era, along with fruits and plants, are thoughtfully placed as embellishments.

City Pop — Bali Meng

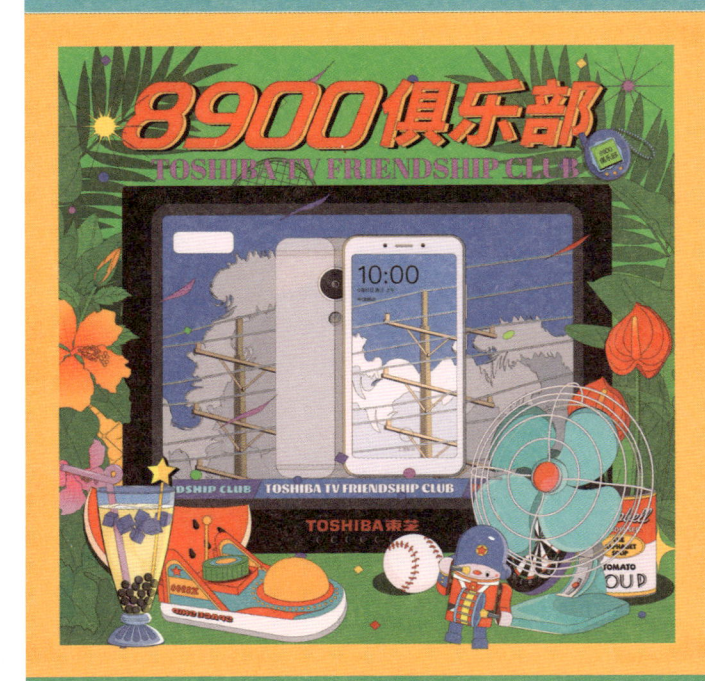

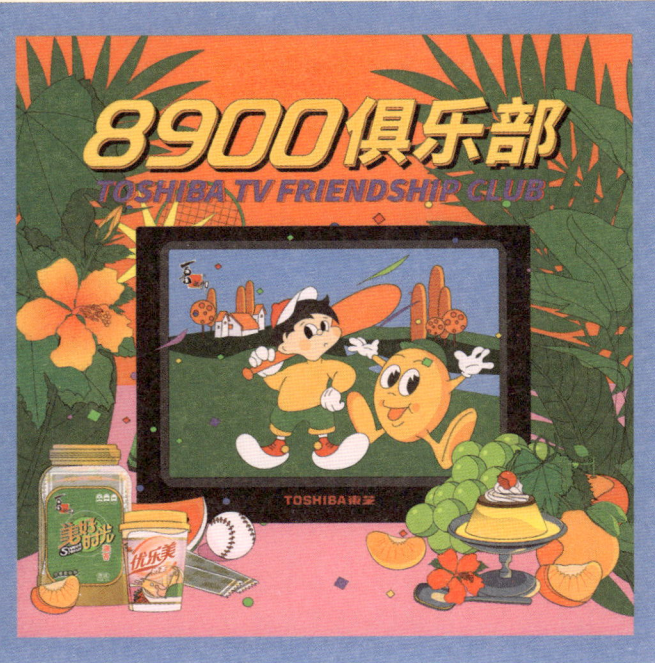

City Pop

92

ALBUM SERIES

The album series is a reinterpretation of a different music album cover, incorporating a personalized understanding of the music. "Absolute Romanticism" is the essence that the album series aims to convey.

In the summer of 2020, the artist officially began the album series inspired by the Japanese band Southern All Stars and their song "Itoshi no Ellie." The song triggered vivid summer fantasies, leading to the creation of the first artwork depicting a loving couple by the seaside at sunset. Surprisingly, the scene in the drawing resembled the music video for the song. The artwork was then transformed into what looked like an album cover, marking the inception of the album series—a manifestation of romanticism fueled by musical inspiration. While the artist didn't initially plan to continue the series, it eventually became a defining style, with each scene depicting couples as a reflection of their inner yearning for idealistic love.

Design Studio: ONO DESIGN
Illustrator: Onoitoe Yang

▼ Inspiration:

In the illustrator's artistic process, the illustrator often chooses songs with a distinct retro vibe, not limited to City Pop but including tracks from The Smiths, New Order, Yogee New Waves, and more. For example, the illustrator created "There Is A Light That Never Goes Out" by The Smiths, a widely recognized song that captures the band's signature romantic allure. The lyrics' beautiful and idealistic themes deeply resonated with the illustrator, and this sense of illumination was reflected in the artwork.

The illustrator also drew inspiration from the 1980s Japanese film and television culture, particularly for the illustration *Fly By Day*, inspired by Anri's 1982 release from the *Heaven Beach* album. Anri's sweet melodies transported the artist to the romantic ambiance of the 70s and 80s summers, which she aimed to convey through seaside scenes. Overall, these visuals represent the illustrator's intuitive responses to the emotions stirred by the music, serving as a perpetual source of inspiration.

▼ Elements:

The elements stem from creative ideas for graphic deformation.

▼ Color Scheme:

- R000 G000 B000 C000 M000 Y000 K100
- R012 G115 B179 C084 M047 Y007 K000
- R222 G161 B020 C014 M042 Y094 K000
- R209 G066 B024 C016 M087 Y100 K000
- R224 G194 B163 C014 M027 Y036 K000
- R234 G158 B174 C005 M049 Y016 K000
- R000 G125 B062 C090 M034 Y098 K002
- R017 G092 B070 C088 M053 Y080 K018

#CityPopDesignTalk

1. City Pop is a unique music genre often associated with urban life, cityscape, and the atmosphere of the 1980s. How does City Pop music inspire your creativity in your designs?

Bern Foster
It's important to highlight the origin of the term "City Pop," which emerged as the soundtrack of Japan's capitalist prosperity in the 1970s and 1980s. This unique aesthectics was shaped by Western influences, particularly from the US. My art is also influenced by the US, mirroring the connection between my art and City Pop music. I am particularly drawn to late 80s and early 90s R&B, contemporary jazz, and pop-jazz—key components of City Pop. This influence is evident in the painting process videos I shared on social media.

CH_LAB
I create while listening to music, feeling the emotions brought by the melodies.

Jun-Feng Li
City Pop music and illustrations exude a romantic urban vibe, intertwining to form our cultural image of Japan's prosperous past. When I create City Pop-style illustrations, listening to City Pop music transports me to the vibrant streets of 1980s Japan, fueling my creative passion.

LXuan
The era when City Pop emerged coincided with Japan's most prosperous economic period. Therefore, its music exudes a positive and optimistic vibe, coupled with a strong sense of romanticism. This stands in stark contrast to the recent trend of "doom and gloom" culture. I aim to infuse the vibrant and laid-back feelings of City Pop into my artwork, visually conveying these atmospheres.

Onion Design Associates
We might think the music or visual style is cool and hip today, but when I grew up in the '80s, I had never heard of a genre called "City Pop." I guess we used to call it Japanese fusion music back then. I was into hard rock, and we found City Pop boring, commercial, and associated with consumerism. However, when I listen to it today, it does bring back a lot of memories from my formative years.

Onoitoe Yang (from ONO DESIGN)
Music has always been an important medium that inspires me to create. They say it's instinctive to move to the rhythm of music, but for me, the urge to paint is just as strong when I hear a melody. Through painting, I can express what words cannot capture. In my album series, the process feels almost "unconscious"—some pieces are quick paintings I create in my downtime. The beauty of certain songs moves me beyond mere appreciation; I feel compelled to visually express my emotions. When I hear a captivating melody, my mind floods with imagery: the sea, a tent, a radio, and a red sky signaling a sunset where figures stand gazing at the world. Every moment of music translates into a vivid picture for me. Music is my catalyst for inspiration, and without it, painting becomes a challenge.

Weiling Zhang
The desire to create is very strong when listening to favorite music. In college, I liked artists like 9m88, and later on, I started listening to a lot of City Pop music, especially the song "Plastic Love" she covered. So, I dug into many Japanese singers from the 90s, like Tatsuro Yamashita.

2. Are there specific City Pop music or artists that have had a profound influence on your design work? Could you share some examples with us?

Bern Foster
Artists like Kenny G, Dave Koz, Nelson Rangell, Peabo Bryson, Johnny Gill, and Luther Vandross are often playing in the background in the studio while I am painting. This music evokes a special feeling and helps me stay connected with the illustration.

CH_LAB
There are no specific songs, but I am more influenced by City Pop musicians such as Yamashita Tatsuro, Toshiki Kadomatsu, and Happy End. As for visual artists, I am more influenced by Seizō Watase, Hiroshi Nagai, Eizin Suzuki, and Indonesian artist Ardhira Putra.

Jun-Feng Li
The work of Seizō Watase and Eizin Suzuki have deeply influenced my City Pop-style creations. Watase's unique portrayal of romantic couples adds a narrative dimension to the vibrant City Pop world, inspiring me with its relaxed yet nostalgic charm. Suzuki's vibrant scenes evoke a stunning visual impact, capturing the essence of tropical holidays with bright colors and meticulous attention to detail.

LXuan
During the preparation for my thesis, I came across the works of Ardhira Putra on Instagram, which was my first exposure to City Pop. Later, while delving into the world of City Pop, I discovered the artwork of Eizin Suzuki, particularly his album covers, which greatly inspired me. In terms of music, Miki Matsubara's "Stay with Me" and Nanidato's "Super Riser" are, in my opinion, songs that effectively represent the romantic and optimistic atmosphere of City Pop.

Onoitoe Yang (from ONO DESIGN)
Eiichi Ohtaki, Anri, Tomoko Aran, Tohyama Hitomi—the songs of these Japanese singers are a wellspring of inspiration for me. However, my favorite Japanese group, Southern All Stars, holds a special place in my heart. This pop-rock band, which gained fame in the 70s and 80s, has profoundly influenced my work. My first City Pop illustration, 「いとしのえり」, was inspired by this band. Interestingly, Southern All Stars predominantly writes and releases songs in the summer, and their music exudes a strong summer passion. As a summer lover, I continually turn to their songs for inspiration and energy.

3. City Pop's visual elements such as neon lights, city streets, cars, palm trees, and more have strong identifying features. Do you believe that this style of illustration in City Pop tends to become overly homogeneous? How do you perceive this phenomenon, and if you think the homogeneity is excessive, what strategies do you think can maintain individuality and innovation in contemporary retro design?

Bern Foster

We must remember that these elements are fundamental to the essence of capitalism and the City Pop aesthetics. In 2010, I created some 80s City Pop illustrations that gained significant traction on social media due to the scarcity of artists in this style. However, as more digital and AI artists rapidly adopted this aesthetics, it became monotonous and less impressive. Having a unique technique and aesthetics is crucial for your art, distinguishing it from the homogeneity of digital art. Eizin Suzuki, Hiroshi Nagai, Hisao Kawada, and Shohei Higushi portrayed City Pop uniquely with different techniques, contributing to its special allure. It's not about the elements used but rather the value of your style and identity.

CH_LAB

City Pop is not just a style, but more like a reinterpretation of a classic era. With diverse colors, rich elements, and various classic elements filled with "urban feel" and "emotional feel," these elements and tones constitute the unique temperament of City Pop. In the current era where design techniques are constantly evolving, designers need to use newer and more vivid design expressions to continuously develop City Pop.

Jun-Feng Li

When searching for illustrations of this style online, one is inundated with pages filled with vibrant clashes of colors and bustling urban scenes. While this homogeneity might seem concerning, it's precisely what gives City Pop its unique charm—the nostalgic reflection of a bygone golden era. To maintain individuality and innovation in contemporary retro design, designers should draw from their valuable experiences and perspectives, ensuring that their creations possess a distinct personality beyond commercial objectives.

LXuan

While these visual elements are common in City Pop works, they are essential to its culture. Altering them might dilute the essence of City Pop. However, incorporating personal flair can lead to the creation of distinctive and unique artworks within the framework of City Pop.

Onoitoe Yang (from ONO DESIGN)

It's important to understand the reason behind the homogenization of City Pop. City Pop isn't a broad design style and hasn't been popular for a very long time; it was established by only a few specific illustrators. Additionally, the urbanization of Japan and the Hawaiian immigrant boom at the time made the elements in these images universal. The key point is that without these specific elements, it becomes difficult to identify a piece as iconic "City Pop." This is where the limitations of the style come into play. However, drawing styles can be infused with personality, allowing them to be molded and evolved. As creators, we have the ability to incorporate contemporary elements and objects into our work. Otherwise, we are merely imitating an existing style without adding anything new.

Weiling Zhang

My understanding is that one needs to continuously experience life and feel a part of the changing urban culture. Afterwards, express it in one's own language and style as directly as possible. With today's social media, any work and style can become a reference. Designers need to absorb good works while cultivating their independent understanding to create a more unique and vibrant style.

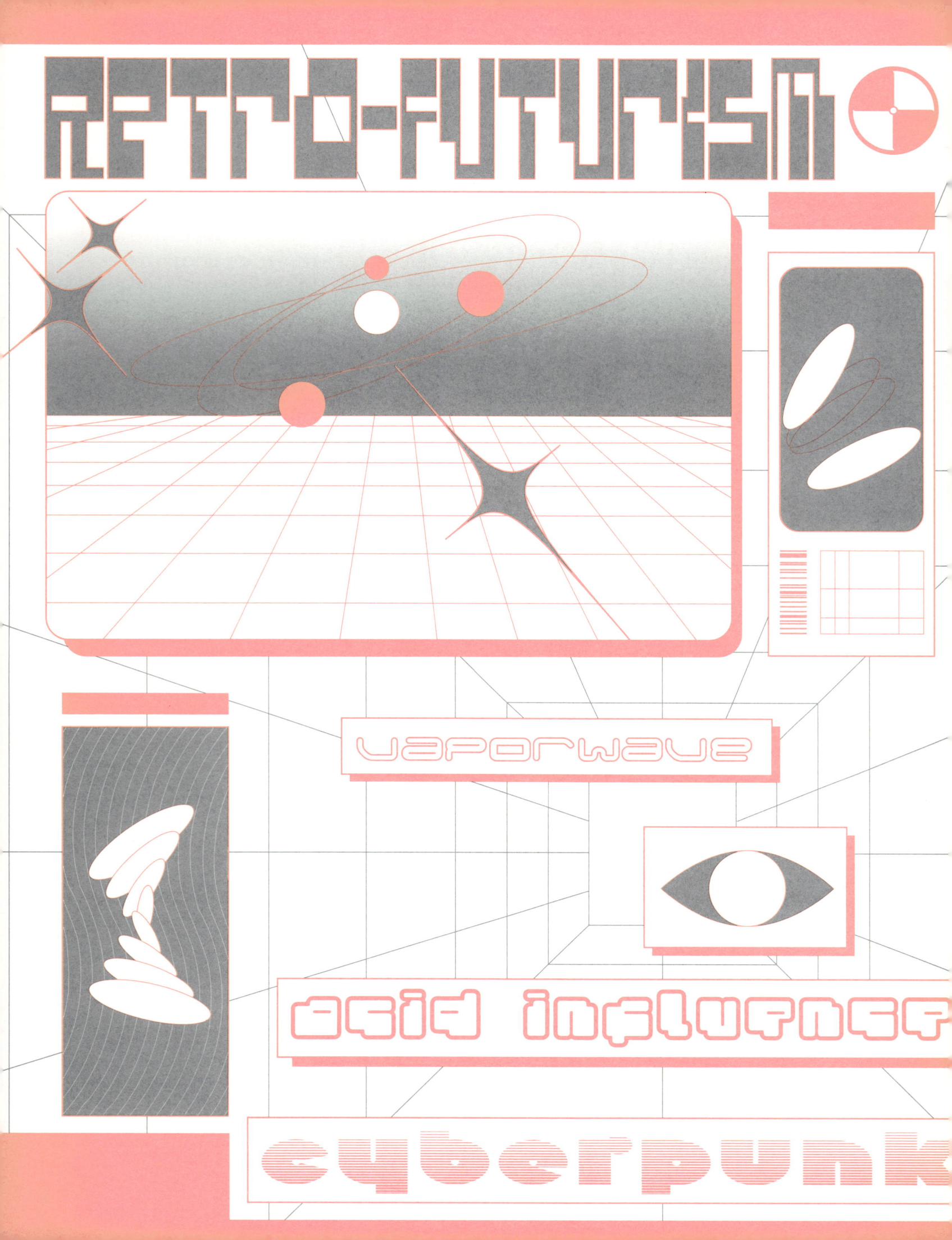

retro-futurism

vaporwave

acid influence

cyberpunk

DEVELOPMENT HISTORY

1900s-1930s: Origins in Futurism

The seeds of Retro-Futurism can be traced to the Futurist movement in the early 20th century, which embraced speed, technology, and modernity. This period also saw early science fiction, with the works of H.G. Wells and Jules Verne envisioning advanced technologies and utopian societies.

1940s-1960s: Further Imagination of the Future

The post-World War II era, especially during the 1950s and 1960s, was heavily influenced by the Atomic Age and Space Race. This period was marked by optimistic visions of the future, with flying cars, space travel, and robots prominently featured in media and advertising. Googie architecture, a futuristic style that emerged in the 1950s, is characterized by bold angles, neon lights, and space-age themes, embodying the optimistic Futurism of the time.

1980s: The Birth of Cyberpunk

The 1970s and 1980s saw a revival of earlier futuristic styles, now combined with a sense of nostalgia. Emerging in the 1980s, Cyberpunk offered a darker, dystopian view of the future, blending advanced technology with gritty urban life. This genre, characterized by its fusion of high-tech and low-life elements, featured neon-lit cityscapes, digital interfaces, and cybernetic enhancements.

1990s: The Acid Influence

The origin of this aesthetics can be traced back to Acid House flyers that were popular during the 1990s, a time when rave culture was at its peak. This style has seen a revival since the mid-2010s, introducing a psychedelic and hallucinogenic element to the Retro-Futurism design landscape. Acid Design was characterized by its vivid and distorted colors, creating a visual experience that was akin to a drug-induced trip. This style played with visual distortions, liquid textures, and a sense of unreality. When integrated into the cyber-vaporwave mix, Acid Design brought an element of chaos and unpredictability, further challenging the traditional boundaries of design.

Early 2000s: The Rise of Vaporwave

Vaporwave emerged as a distinctive style in the early 21st century from online communities, and it gained popularity through websites such as Bandcamp, Soundcloud, Tumblr, Last.fm, and YouTube. Rooted in Internet culture and a sense of nostalgia, Vaporwave reimagined the aesthetics of the 1980s and 1990s. It drew inspiration from retro computer graphics, corporate branding, and elevator music, creating a surreal and dreamy atmosphere. This style incorporated elements of consumerism and a critique of capitalism, reflecting the disillusionment with the promises of technology and the corporate world.

Mid-2010s: The Fusion

The fusion of Retro-Futurism design styles started to take shape in the mid-2010s. Designers and artists began to combine the elements of Vaporwave and Cyberpunk, creating a cyber-vaporwave subgenre. This hybrid style blended the neon-soaked, dystopian cityscapes of Cyberpunk with the dreamy, nostalgic visuals of Vaporwave. The color palettes extended to include vivid pinks, purples, and blues, while retaining the glitchy and surreal aspects of the original styles. The fusion highlighted the interplay between technology, nostalgia, and a sense of both optimism and disillusionment about the future.

Present Day: New Developments

As we move into the present day, the convergence of Vaporwave, Cyberpunk, and Acid Design styles is in full swing. Designers are pushing the boundaries of Retro-Futurism design, creating compositions that are both nostalgic and futuristic, orderly and chaotic, dystopian and utopian. The visual language includes glitch art, surreal landscapes, distorted typography, and a sense of disorientation. It's a celebration of the analog and the digital, the past and the future, the real and the surreal. This multi-faceted style reflects our complex relationship with technology, the digital age, and the ever-evolving visions of what the future may hold.

RETRO-FUTURISM: MODERN VISUAL STYLE GUIDE

ELEMENTS

KEYWORDS

1. **SURREAL FUTURISTIC MOTIFS**
2. **DIGITAL DREAMSCAPES**
3. **PSYCHEDELIC FLAIR**
4. **ACID-INSPIRED ACCENTS**
5. **MECHANICAL METALLIC SHINE**
6. **COSMIC REVERIE**

1. Planet
2. Smiley Face
3. Semi-Circular
4. Eye-Shaped
5. Human Figures
6. Rotating Light and Shadow
7. Neon Sign
8. Liquid Texture
9. Helping Hands
10. Star-Shaped
11. Checkerboard Patterns

FONTS

BB Console Astron Boy Meken Exo2 Neuropol BEBAS NEUE John Doe mega Still Time FENOTYPE foton torpedo

COLOR

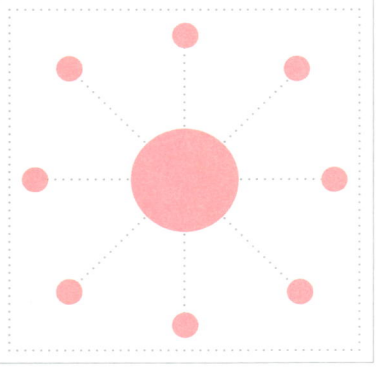

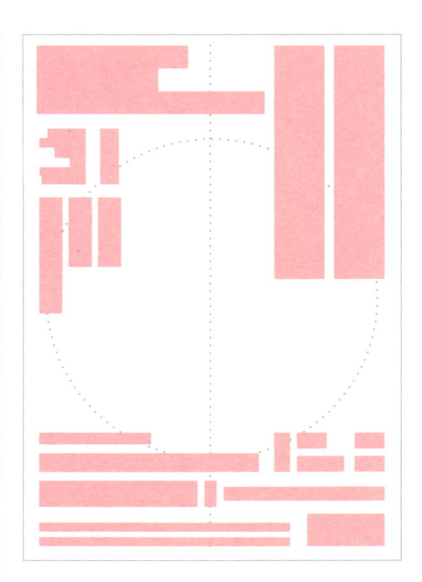

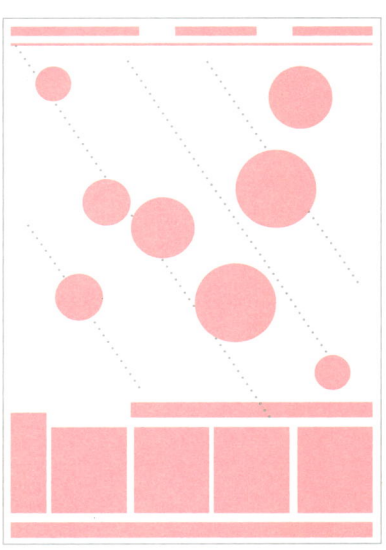

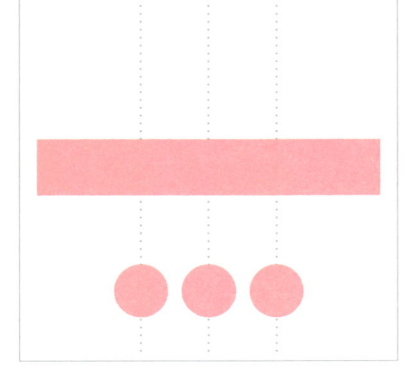

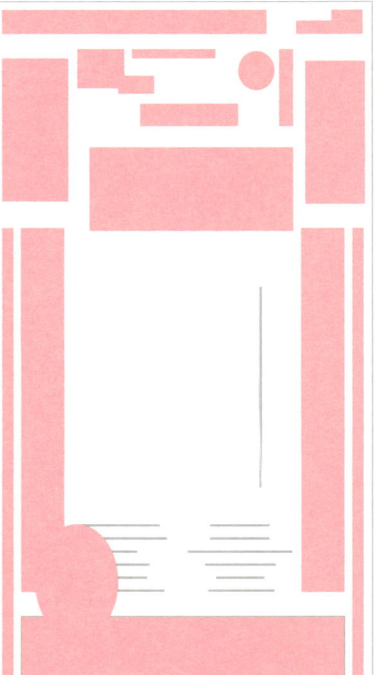

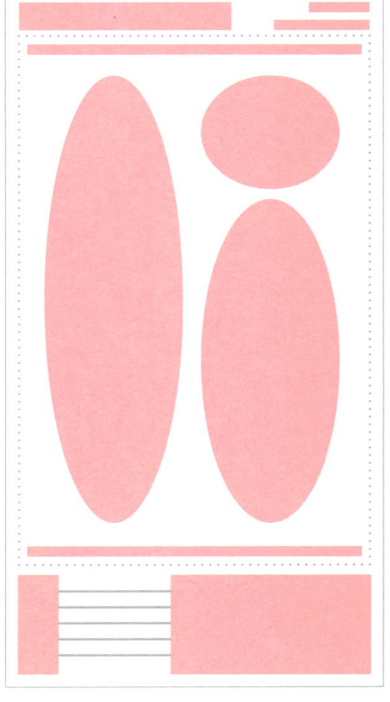

LAYOUT

Huang Heshan — Retro-Futurism

Huang Heshan

Huang Heshan graduated from the Academy of Fine Arts at Tsinghua University. With a strong academic background and deep passion, he has developed a unique aesthetic understanding of urban life design in China through research and practice. He has created a series of pragmatic masterpieces, including the *Wild Design*, which represents a down-to-earth practicality. Inspired by China's urban villages, he crafted the plastic punk world of *Too Rich City*. In 2021, during the highly anticipated Taobao Maker Festival, NFT digital artworks made their debut. Huang Heshan presented his mesmerizing NFT piece *The Unbald Garden*, which sold a total of 310 digital properties within two days, showcasing the magical realism of his work.

1 Balancing Retro and Futuristic Elements

Huang Heshan masterfully balances retro and futuristic elements in his designs, creating a compelling tension that reflects broader socio-cultural shifts. His approach is best exemplified in the *Too Rich City* series, which reinterprets artifacts from past eras within a contemporary context to construct virtual urban landscapes that bridge history and future aspirations. This series draws inspiration from the wave of postmodernist architectural trends that swept across China during the late 1980s and 1990s. During this period, numerous postmodern sculptures and buildings emerged, reflecting the socio-economic and political conditions of the time, as well as aspirations for scientific and technological advancements and visions of a better life. By integrating these elements, Huang's work encapsulates the spirit of that era while projecting it into an imagined future, creating a unique and thought-provoking dialogue between the past and the future.

2 The Timeless Spirit of Retro Elements

Huang Heshan believes that the "classic" or timeless quality of retro elements is not found in specific materials or objects, but in the "spirit" they embody. This spirit, characterized by vitality, determination, and optimism, prevailed during what is often referred to as the "golden age." It was a period when people were energetic, striving for progress, and filled with imagination and anticipation for the future. This enduring spirit, representative of the era's essence, is what truly remains timeless and continues to influence contemporary and future designs.

3 The Interplay of Retro-Futurism Design and Contemporary Socio-Culture

Retro-Futurism design is a bridge between the past and present, resonating with contemporary society and culture. Huang Heshan views this design approach as tapping into the trendy pop culture that young people find appealing, evoking a sense of nostalgia and familiarity. Retro-Futurism elements recall an era that people have lived through and hold emotional connections to, which can be leveraged to inspire innovative commercial creations. These designs often find a receptive audience on modern Internet platforms, where they evoke strong emotional responses. Some followers describe Huang's work as evoking a sense of crowdedness and oppression, blending modernity with unresolved childhood memories. This juxtaposition creates a powerful impact, reflecting both the complexity of contemporary life and the enduring allure of the past.

4 Too Rich City: Future Virtual City in China

Huang Heshan's *Too Rich City* project is a multifaceted exploration that blends cultural collisions and futuristic fantasies within China's evolving societal framework.

The artwork intricately weaves elements that reflect the daily struggles and aspirations of people living in the era, such as buildings adorned with small advertisements and washed by rain, glowing small shop signs, and exhaust fans outside working kitchen. These details evoke a sense of lived experience and cultural richness, despite the absence of human presence, thereby portraying a poignant narrative of urban existence and resilience. This futuristic cityscape, devoid of individuals yet brimming with human traces, serves as a metaphor for the interplay between past and future aspirations. This narrative of a future virtual city concept has been a long-standing theme explored by artists from developed countries through mediums like books, movies, and games, showcasing their cultural interpretations of futuristic urban landscapes. In China, however, the exploration of this concept is still in progress.

In his reinterpretation of historical products and futuristic ideals, Huang Heshan constructed *Too Rich City* as a testament to the spirit of an era marked by optimism and technological ambition. "The Top of Too Rich City" features magnificent metal sculptures, flexible mosaic tile walls, and brightly colored, uniquely styled retro buildings that embody many people's beautiful fantasies of future technology and life. By extracting and collaging these elements, Huang reconstructed a utopia where people continue to live with the spirit of that era, blending historical context with imaginative futures. This artistic endeavor bridges the gap between nostalgia and innovation, showcasing a harmonious fusion of historical resonance and futuristic vision within the urban landscape.

Huang Heshan — Retro-Futurism

TOO RICH CITY

Too Rich City is a virtual city project of magical realism that explores absurd poetry through a fictional consensus in consumer society, serving as a rebellion against the instrumental rationality of modern society.

The virtual *Too Rich City* strips away the privileges associated with objects, classes, and social status. Real fragments of China's rural-urban fringe zones are deconstructed and reconstructed into a consumer social landscape where elegance and vulgarity are fused. These landscapes will eventually transition into virtual real estate and enter the market to achieve consensus.

Too Rich City reveals the "truth" of the symbolic world through a utopian gesture. However, this truth does not arise from collage images; rather, it emerges from the consensus reached between buyers and *Too Rich City* when the trading of virtual properties. People always hold certain beliefs, whether by constructing an order of meanings through universally accepted collective imagination or by utilizing fictional concepts and symbols to create a cohesive world.

▼ **Inspiration:**
The artist drew inspirations from excellent works produced around the year 2000, resulting from the collision and integration of Chinese local culture with those of developed countries such as animated films from Shanghai Animation Film Studio, as well as films from Hong Kong and Taiwan regions of China. Additionally, Japanese animated films like *Ghost in the Shell*, *Tekkonkinkreet*, and *Red Chili Pepper* also influenced the work.

10
JP26
开业大吉
i.t
blue block
carhartt
WORK IN PROGRESS
BEAMS
KANGOL
客运旅行社

McCafé
麦劳当
McaldDon's
每周三牛肉汉堡10元3个
本店开业期间
汉堡买一送一

好望角足疗
天上人间
贵族保健
康の源足疗
大众养生大楼
保健
专业修脚
电话：18888888729
康乐保健
螺丝粉
鲜花
鲜花水果
柳州螺蛳粉
小吃
火疗养生堂
鲜花
保健
全市最低 电话：136
足浴 保健
温州休闲保健足浴
鼓浪屿
泡鸡脚
黎氏鸡脚王
好望角
良子
招待所
旅店
按摩所

秃力富 TOO RICH CITY

鸭斯克飞行器制造厂

秃力富在得了飞行幻想症后向他的好友鸭斯克先生注资成立了秃力城第一家飞行器厂

秃力富 TOO RICH

⋒ Hamburger
What an Appetite Infinity Boosting Accelerator flying at 10km high above #TooRichCity !

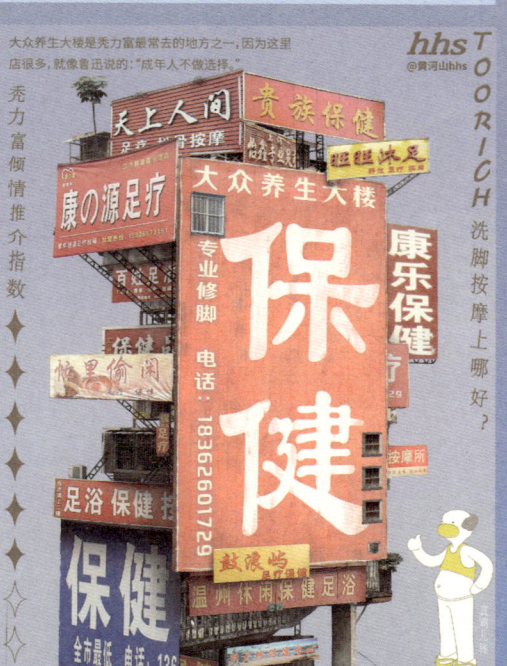

Retro-Futurism — Huang Heshan

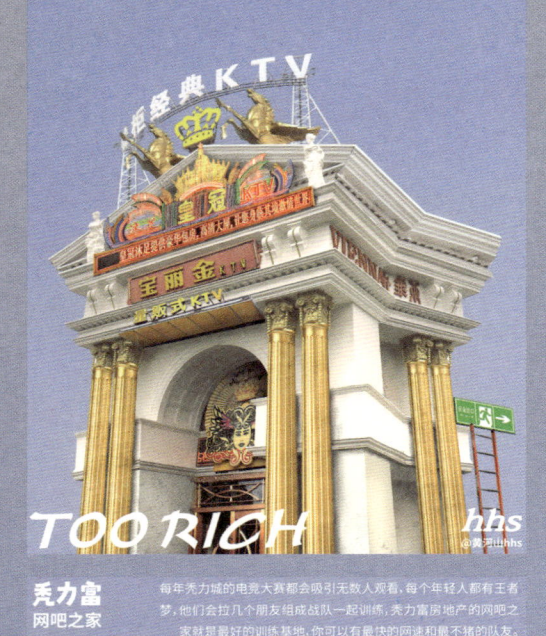

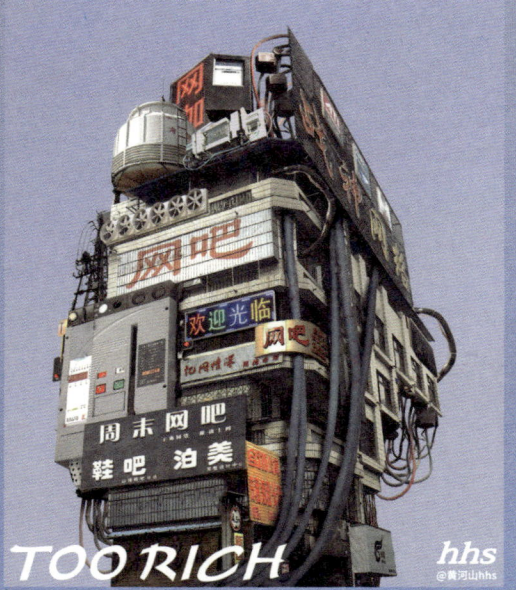

Huang Heshan — Retro-Futurism — 108

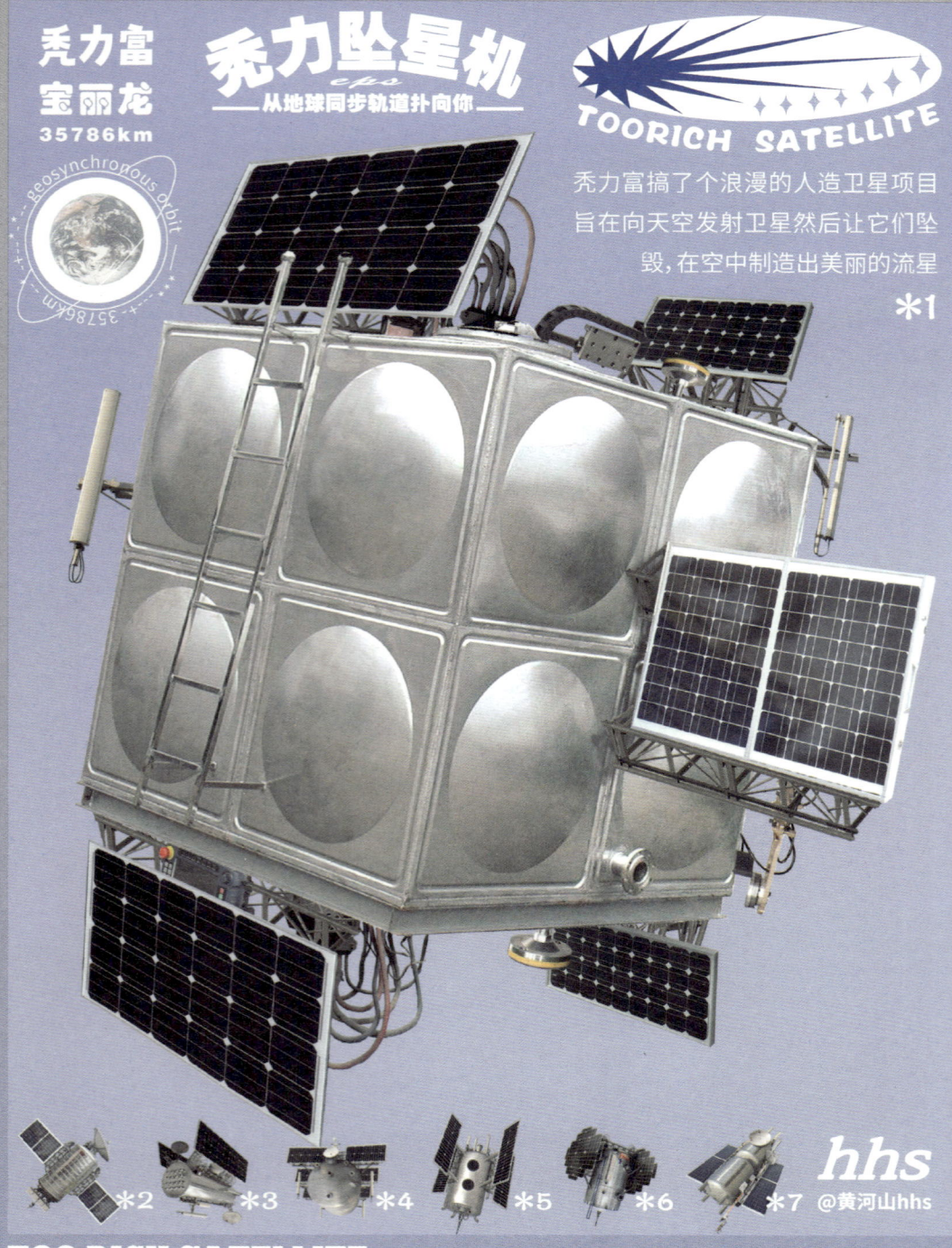

秃力坠星机

秃力富 宝丽龙 35786km — geosynchronous orbit

秃力坠星机 cps
——从地球同步轨道扑向你——

TOORICH SATELLITE

秃力富搞了个浪漫的人造卫星项目旨在向天空发射卫星然后让它们坠毁，在空中制造出美丽的流星

*1

TOO RICH @黄河山hhs hhs

做完秃力坠星机项目后，秃力富又做了个真正实用的秃力卫星，主要用来传输5G信号。

秃力富 宝丽龙 35786km — geosynchronous orbit
秃力坠星机 ——从地球同步轨道扑向你—— **TOORICH SATELLITE**

*7号机

TOO RICH TASA hhs @黄河山hhs

*2 *3 *4 *5 *6 *7

hhs @黄河山hhs

TOO RICH SATELLITE

野生设计 hhs
土味/生猛/廉价/简单/实用

WILD DESIGN

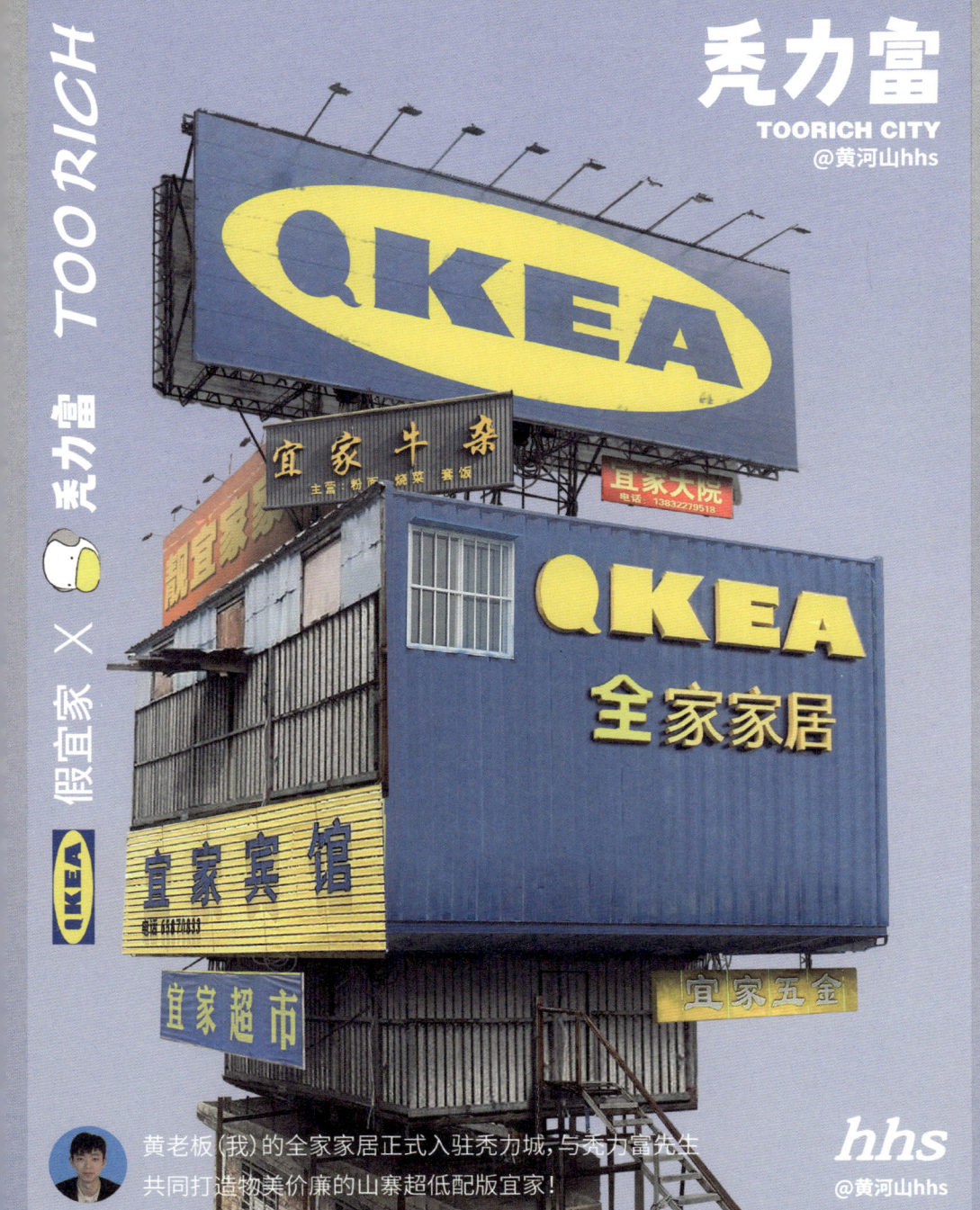

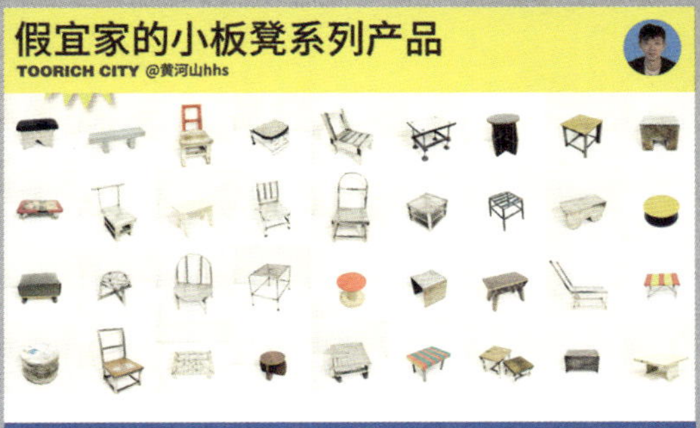

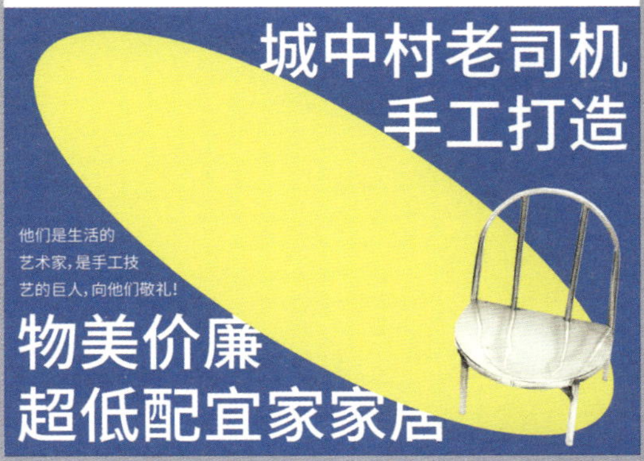

秃力富
TOORICH CITY
@黄河山hhs

假宜家 × 秃力富 TOO RICH

QKEA 全家家居

宜家牛杂
宜家大院
靓宜家
宜家宾馆
宜家超市
宜家五金

黄老板(我)的全家家居正式入驻秃力城，与秃力富先生共同打造物美价廉的山寨超低配版宜家！

TOO RICH FAKE IKEA

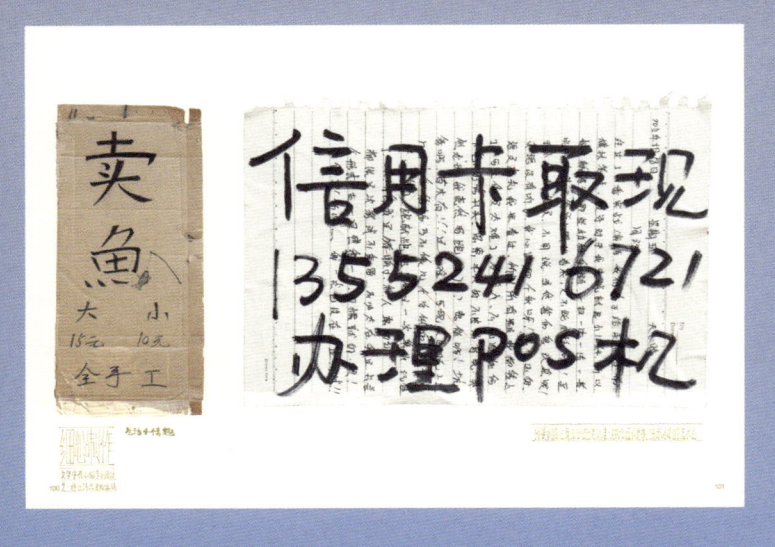

hhs @黄河山hhs

假宜家的小板凳系列产品
TOORICH CITY @黄河山hhs

城中村老司机 手工打造
他们是生活的艺术家，是手工技艺的巨人，向他们敬礼！

物美价廉 超低配宜家家居

IKEA 款式多多 每款全球限量一个！
TOORICH CITY @黄河山hhs

KOBAYASHI 小森林 ¥30.00
JACQUESHERZOG 赫尔佐格 ¥50.00
MIETVELDGO 耶特维德戈 ¥10.00
LOUISL WANG 路易斯·汪 ¥50.00
ZENGO KUMA 赠地熊 ¥50.00
JEAN NOUVELIV 让·努维尔 ¥50.00
SHANGHAI MAN 上海棒僵 ¥30.00
NIEMEYER ND 妮迈耶ND ¥10.00
NIEMEYER YE 聂迈耶YE ¥10.00

Limited Edition

卖鱼 大 小 15元 10元 全手工

信用卡取现
13552416721
办理POS机

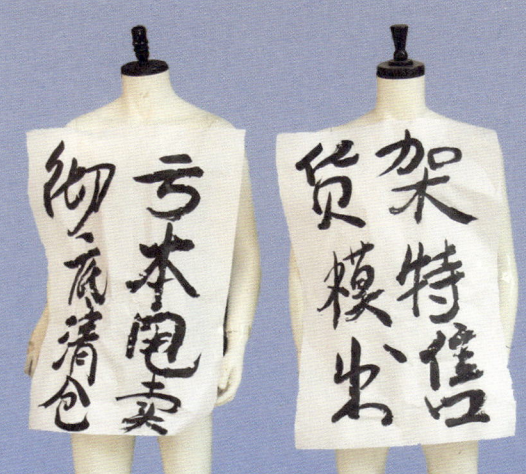

亏本甩卖 彻底清仓
货架模特僵尸出
全场99元任选

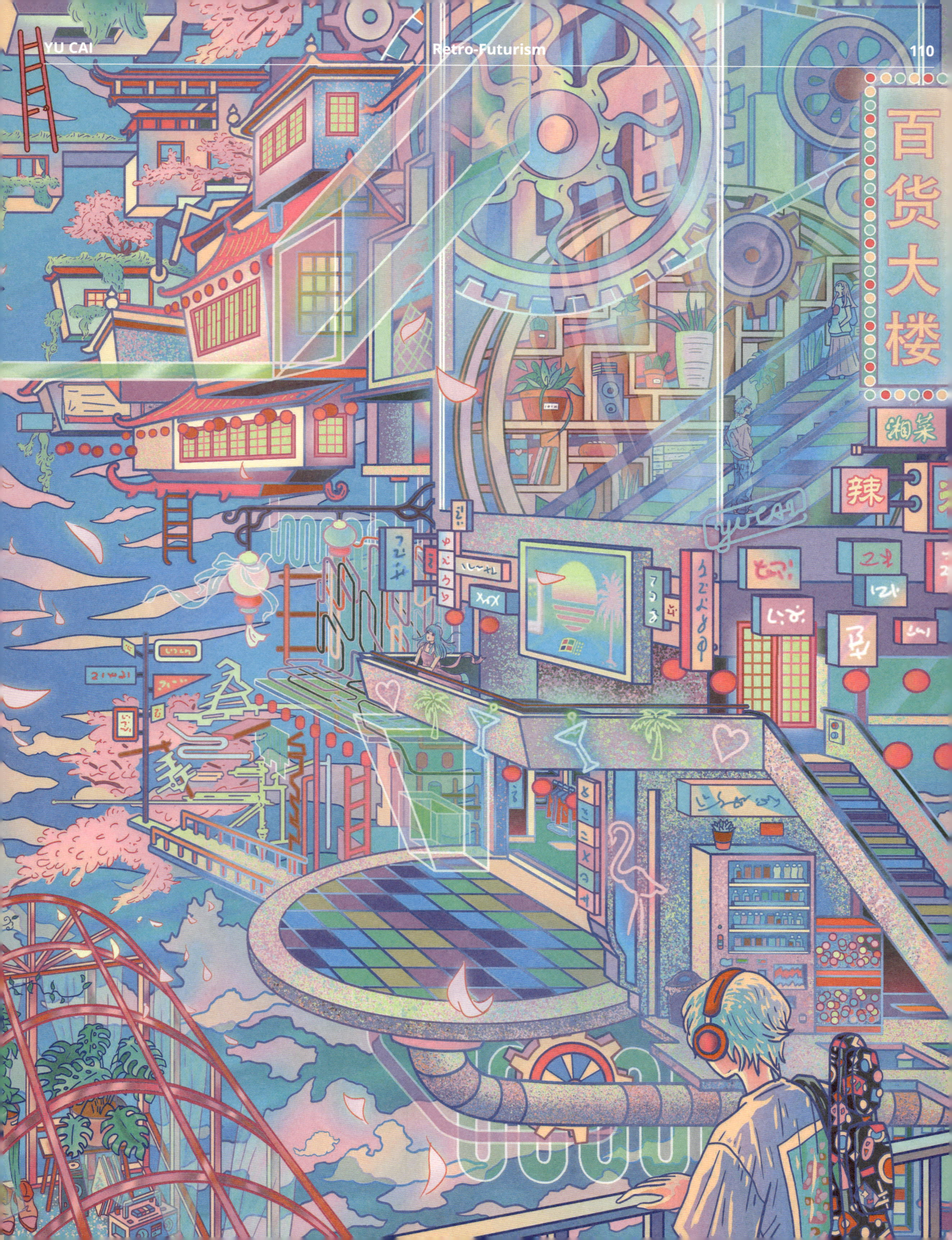
百货大楼
湘菜
辣

PSYCHEDELIC ELECTRONIC VAPORWAVE SERIES

This series is mainly influenced by Vaporwave and futuristic styles. The inspiration for the imagery comes from ordinary moments of life, quiet solitary experiences, or childhood memories from the 1990s. The lazy yet fast-paced scenes of life reveal the spiritual needs of young people in modern society. While enjoying the convenience brought by technology, people also feel languid and listless in their losses, enveloped in nostalgic emotions recalling the past. People need time and space to reconcile with themselves, the bustling city never stops for the imbalance of personal emotions. People seem to always be searching for something, yet always coming up empty-handed. Immersed in the thick smoke and neon lights of the streets, one slowly discovers a more suitable way to interact with the city.

Illustrator: YU CAI

▼ Inspiration:

The retro elements used in the design are influenced by Vaporwave, Futurism, and Steampunk. At the same time, movies have become a source of inspiration for the artist, such as *Metropolis* and *Modern Times*, Hayao Miyazaki's *Castle in the Sky*, *Spirited Away*, and *Howl's Moving Castle*.

▼ Elements:

Vaporwave: amusement arcade, Monstera deliciosa plant, sunset on screen, powder blue and pink dominate the color palette

Futurism & Steampunk: Gears, moving buildings and houses

▼ Layout:

The illustrator typically started with large square and circular frames to compose the layout, then delved into details from the basic framework. The large framework of the image is crucial; otherwise, the intricacies may become too fragmented.

▼ Color Scheme:

- R077 G186 B218 / C064 M004 Y012 K000
- R168 G206 B200 / C038 M008 Y023 K000
- R126 G150 B190 / C055 M036 Y011 K000
- R095 G091 B166 / C071 M067 Y000 K000
- R204 G167 B204 / C022 M040 Y001 K000
- R085 G187 B160 / C064 M000 Y045 K000
- R194 G227 B216 / C028 M000 Y019 K000
- R183 G178 B137 / C034 M027 Y049 K000
- R216 G231 B172 / C020 M001 Y041 K000
- R231 G172 B204 / C007 M042 Y000 K000
- R233 G087 B146 / C000 M078 Y007 K000

MACAO DESIGN WEEK 2021

Macao Design Week 2021 focuses on showcasing outstanding local and international commercial design works, guiding audiences to comprehend how the culture and narrative of a commercial brand are visually represented from various perspectives. The main visual design draws inspiration from the nocturnal ambiance of Macau. As one navigates through this city known for its tourism and lottery industries, vibrant neon lights illuminate the darkness, mirroring the rapid development of the local design scene in recent years. Through the creation of 26 individually crafted English letters, the design team employed a surreal technique to reconstruct the primary visual design, symbolizing the notion that design originates from life and becomes integrated into it. This approach aims to convey the potential and boundless creativity of Macau's design industry for the future.

Design Studio: Indego design
Designer: Lam Ieong Kun, Dan Ferreira
Client: Macau Designers Association

MACAO DESIGN WEEK 2021
MACAODA.ORG
澳門設計
MACAO DESIGN WEEK 2021
DESIGN EXHIBITION 2022.1.21-27
(M)
(MON) 3P.M.-8P.M.
DESIGN TOUR 2022.1.22
DESIGN EXHIBITION 2022. 1.21-27
DESIGN WEEK 202

WWW. MACAO DA. ORG
MACAO DESIGN WEEK 2021
澳門設計周
2022 1.21-27
MACAO DESIGN WEEK
(MON) 3P.M.-8P.M.
(TUE-SUN) 12P.M.-8P.M.
WWW. MACAO DA. ORG

MACAO DESIGN WEEK 2021
澳門設計周
MACAO DESIGN WEEK 2021
TASTING DESIGN
DESIGN TOUR
MACAODA.ORG

MACAO DESIGN WEEK 2021
WWW. MACAO DA. ORG
MACAO DESIGN WEEK 2021
澳門設計周
MACAO DESIGN WEEK 2021

▼ **Inspiration:**

The design project for Macao Design Week 2021 derives inspiration from the bustling nightlife of Macau, particularly the vivid neon lights that adorn the cityscape. While the main focus remains on contemporary commercial design, there's a subtle incorporation of retro elements within the concept. The influence of neon lights, an enduring symbol of past eras, evokes a nostalgic ambiance reminiscent of vintage signage and urban landscapes. The dynamic array of colors found in neon lights evokes a reminiscent of the neon-lit streets and vibrant cityscapes of the 1980s. Moreover, the surreal reconstruction of English letters in the design may reflect artistic movements that experimented with abstract and surreal techniques, echoing elements from the mid-20th century. Despite the primary emphasis on contemporary design, the project for Macao Design Week 2021 subtly pays homage to retro aesthetics.

▼ **Elements:**

The graphic elements are inspired by the bustling nightlife of Macau, especially its vibrant neon lights. The main visual design comprises 26 uniquely distorted English letters, mirroring the dynamic hues of neon lights. This distortion represents the lively atmosphere of the city at night and symbolizes the convergence of commerce and culture in commercial design. Moreover, the letters signify the inseparable connection between design and life, reflecting the ongoing evolution of the design industry. Additionally, the distortion metaphorically captures the rapid growth and vitality of Macau's local design scene, hinting at its boundless potential for creativity in the future.

▼ **Fonts:**

Base&Bloom

▼ **Color Scheme:**

■ R000 G139 B060 C084 M026 Y100 K000	■ R177 G209 B053 C037 M000 Y090 K000	■ R214 G140 B185 C015 M055 Y000 K000
■ R205 G079 B146 C018 M080 Y006 K000	■ R243 G164 B000 C002 M044 Y095 K000	■ R177 G209 B053 C037 M000 Y090 K000
■ R000 G124 B194 C083 M041 Y001 K000	■ R205 G079 B146 C018 M080 Y006 K000	■ R086 G064 B151 C077 M082 Y000 K000
■ R222 G025 B022 C006 M098 Y099 K000	■ R086 G064 B151 C077 M082 Y000 K000	■ R255 G255 B255 C000 M000 Y000 K000
■ R000 G124 B194 C083 M041 Y001 K000	■ R177 G209 B053 C037 M000 Y090 K000	■ R000 G139 B060 C084 M026 Y100 K000
■ R086 G064 B151 C077 M082 Y000 K000	■ R000 G139 B060 C084 M026 Y100 K000	■ R255 G255 B255 C000 M000 Y000 K000
■ R214 G140 B185 C015 M055 Y000 K000	■ R243 G164 B000 C002 M044 Y095 K000	■ R222 G025 B022 C006 M098 Y099 K000

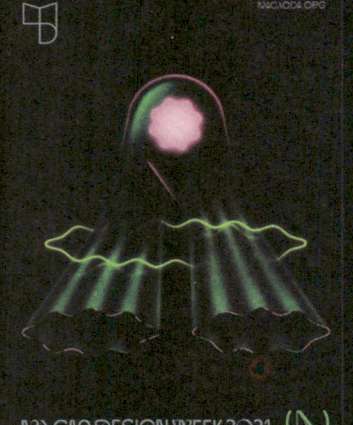

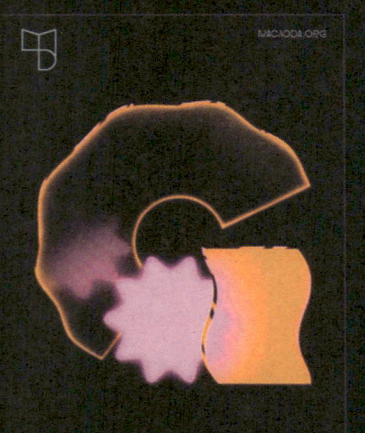

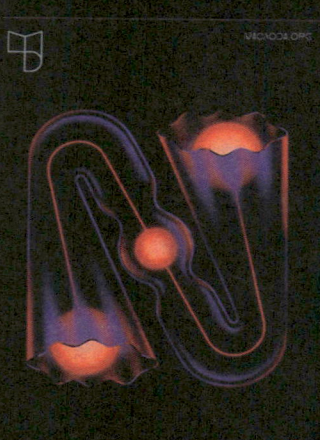

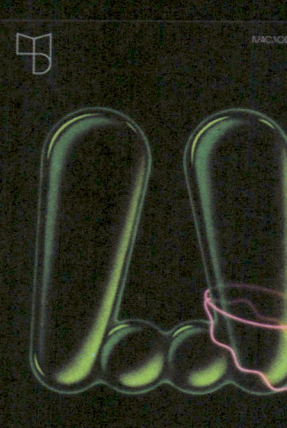

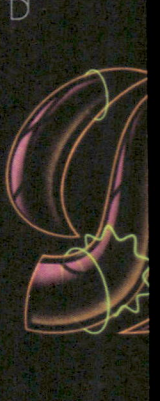

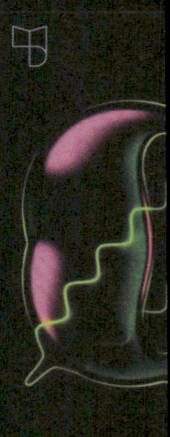

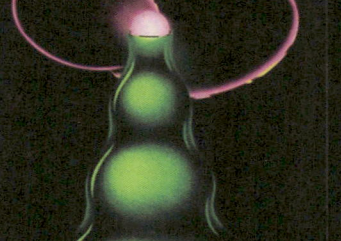

115 Retro-Futurism Indego design

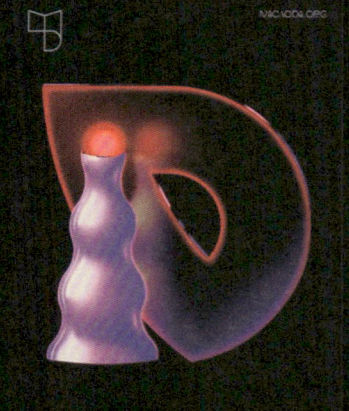

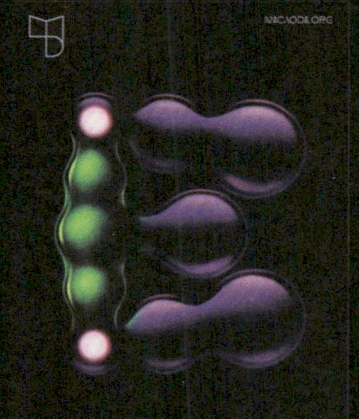

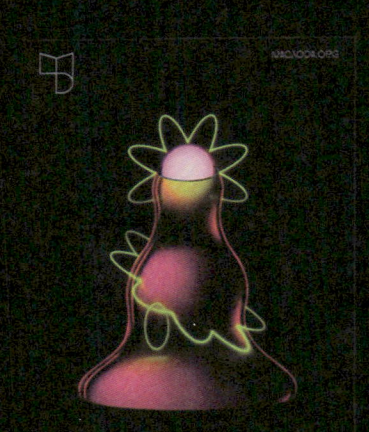

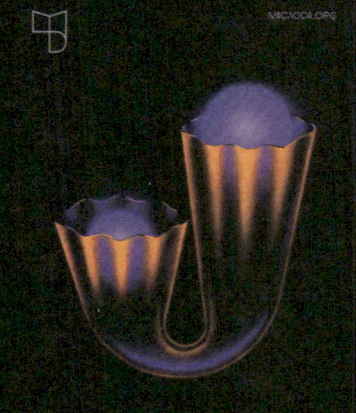

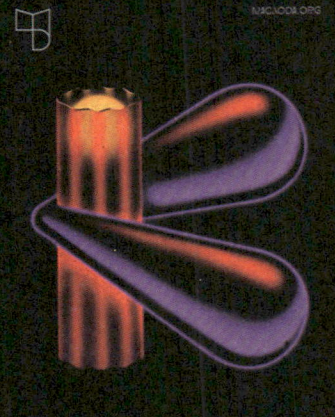

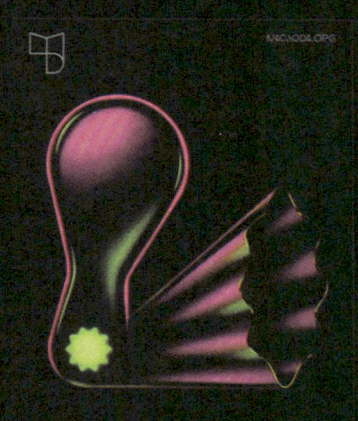

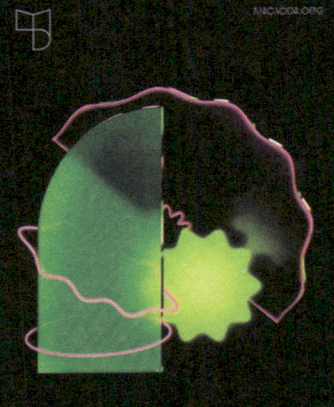

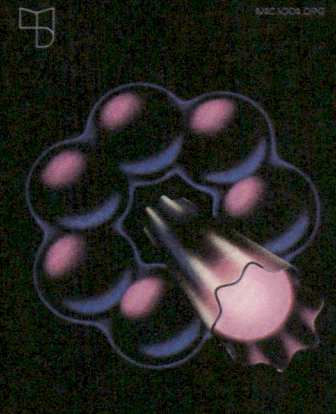

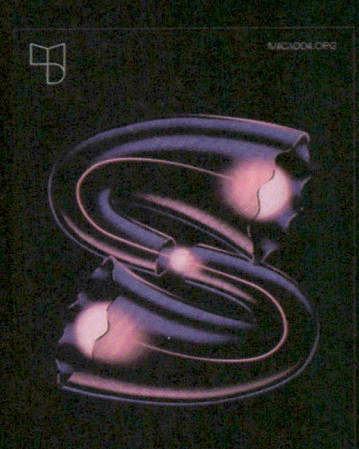

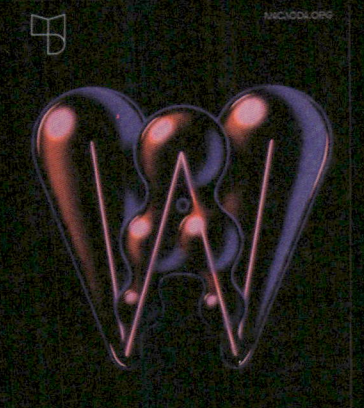

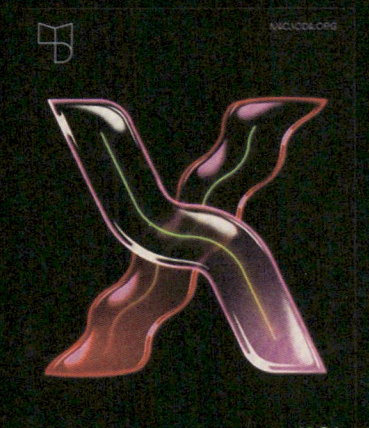

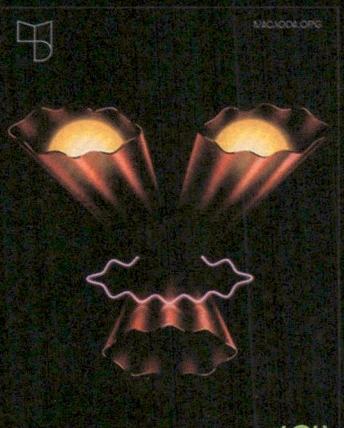

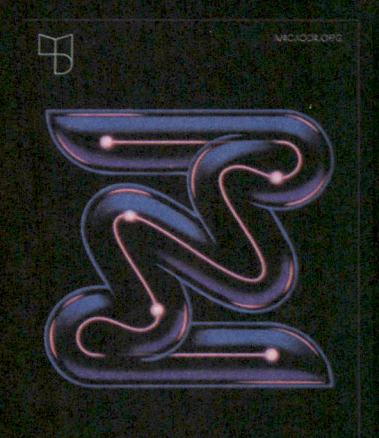

WORKS OF BRANDO CORRADINI

ACID CULTURE:

The project is an experimentation and a tribute to the Acid and rave culture of the past, present, and future, represented by the world-famous smiley face.

ZENIONE:

This is a project conceived without a specific purpose, emerging from the desire to experiment with disposable and grotesque shapes, eventually adhering them onto a blank sheet of paper.

GINOTTI TYPEFACE:

This is an experimental type that often receives criticism due to its illegibility and overall unconventional appearance. However, its uniqueness lies in its simple quirk or unusual letterforms, making it a typeface that taps into a distinctive trend.

Designer: Brando Corradini

▼ **Inspiration:**

The designer's ideal muse for creating these works is music, whether it's hip hop or house, etc. Designer expressed gratitude to Friedrich Nietzsche for the phrase "Life without music would be a mistake."

▼ **Elements:**

ACID CULTURE:

The designer used famous smiley faces stacked to spell the word "ACID."

ZENIONE:

The designer wanted to experiment with weird shapes and eventually paste them onto a piece of white paper.

GINOTTI TYPEFACE:

The designer tried to create a strange but elegant shape at the same time, commencing with the letter G, considering it the highlight of the entire project, ultimately leading to the final design of the entire typeface. At the same time, the typeface is reminiscent of the shapes used in the fashion sector, specifically for fashion brands.

GINOTTI TYPEFACE SPECIMEN

abcdefg
hijklmno
pqrs
tuvwxyz

abcdeffghi
hijklmnopqrst
stuvwxyyzz

BASELINE,
X-HEIGHT,
SIZE,
DESCENT,
ASCENT.

PANGRAM
THE QUICK
BROWN
FOX
JUMPS...

R FONT FAMILY
MBERS AND OTH
PRINTING OR FO
MOST TYPEFAC
SIZE (E.G., 24 P
BOLD), SLOPE (
ONDENSED), AN
ATIONS OF THE
FONT.

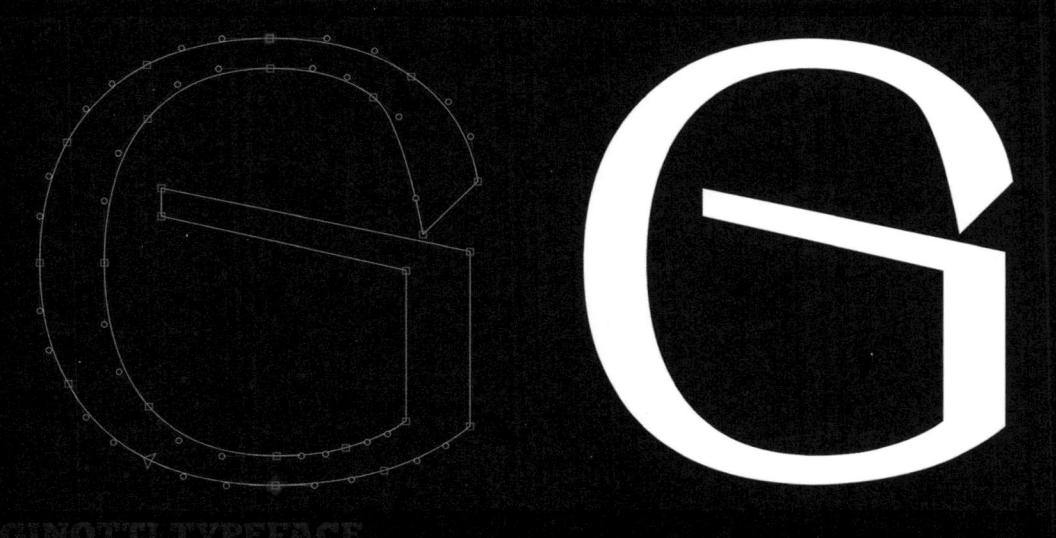

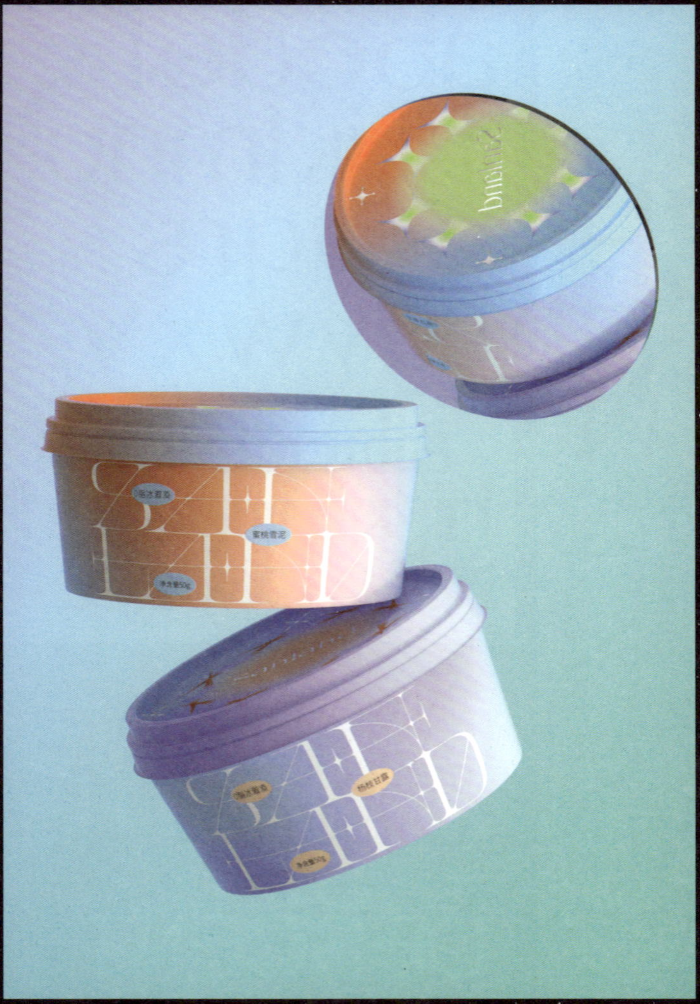

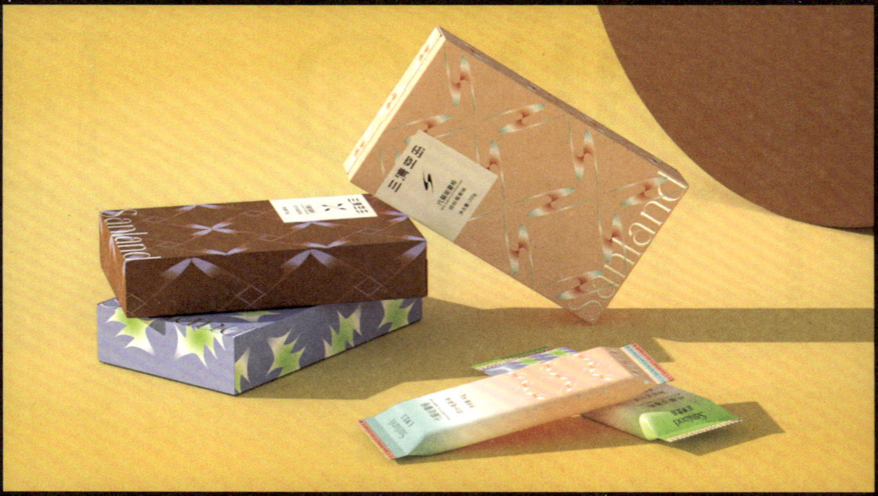

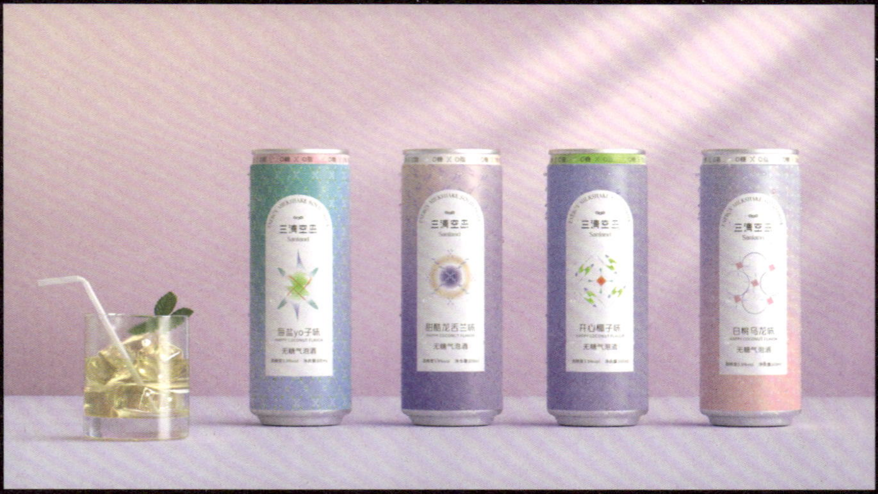

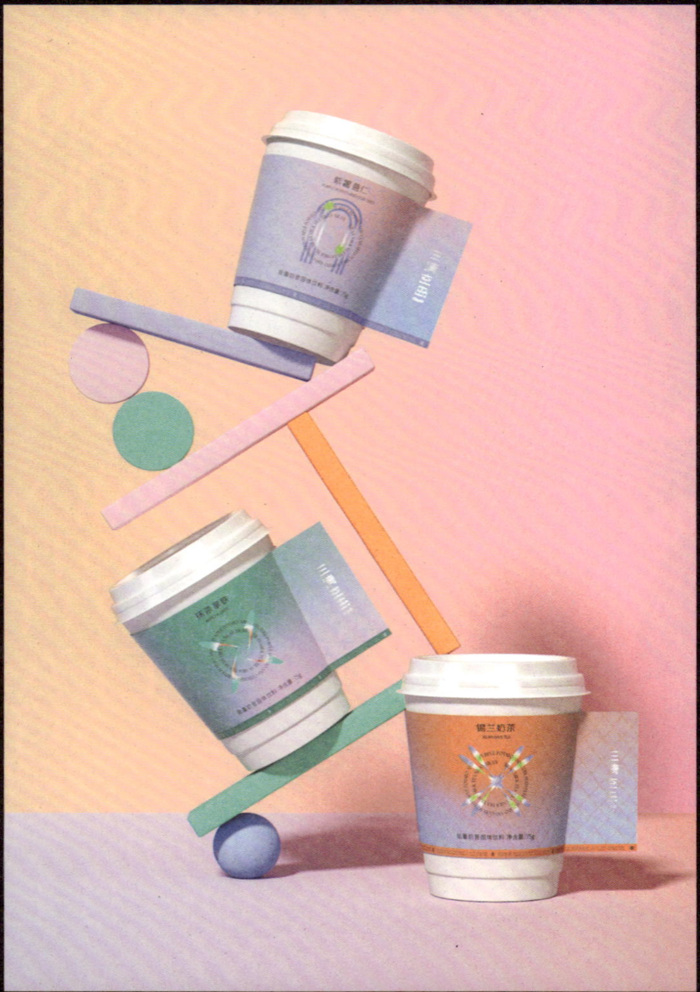

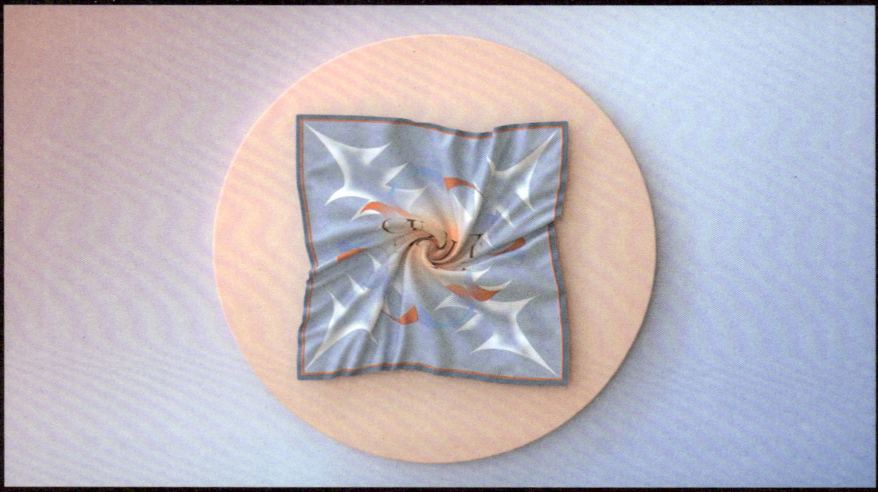

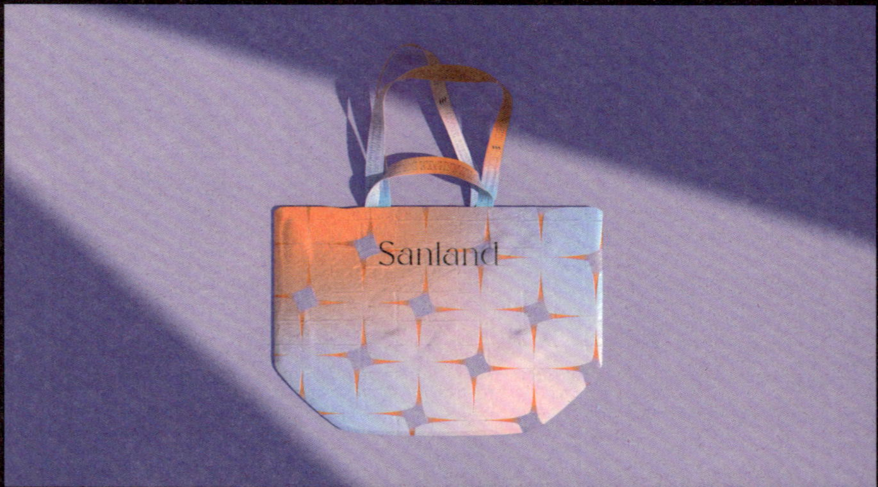
Sanland

SANLAND

The visual design of the Sanland brand aims to express the concept of natural detoxification and body control. Positioned towards young women who pursue both inner and outer beauty, the brand serves as a starting point for self-love. As a pioneer in shaping internal connections for weight loss, the brand, with a core concept of "natural detoxification and body control," provides healthy snacks for women focusing on health management and pursuing the perfect body shape. The brand aims to encourage women to regularly detoxify their lives and face life with positivity, health, and confidence. The visual design adopts a contrasting style of Chinese typography, with horizontally thin strokes to enhance recognition, overall presenting a simple and elegant atmosphere. The graphic design uses three ellipses to symbolize inclusivity and the visual sensation of zero fat.

Design Studio: Hellocean
Client: Sanland

▼ Color Scheme:

- R022 G136 B122 C081 M032 Y057 K000
- R131 G198 B194 C051 M004 Y027 K000
- R120 G137 B196 C058 M043 Y000 K000
- R083 G075 B157 C077 M075 Y000 K000
- R151 G199 B051 C047 M000 Y093 K000
- R247 G167 B175 C000 M045 Y018 K000
- R237 G118 B086 C000 M066 Y061 K000
- R169 G096 B049 C039 M071 Y090 K002

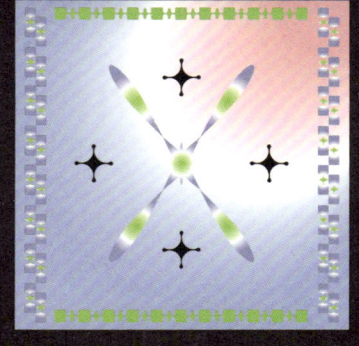

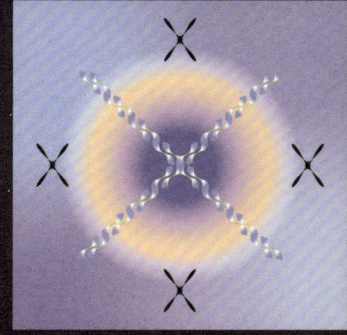

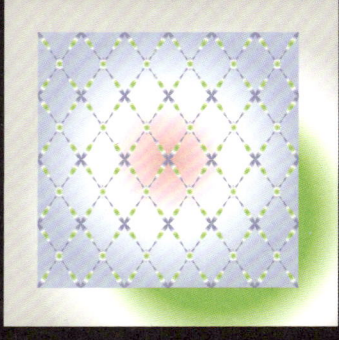

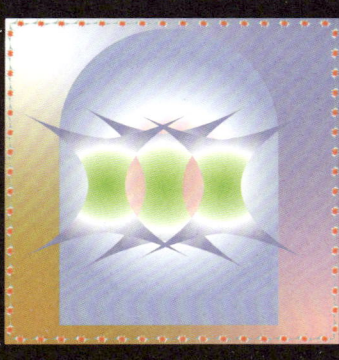

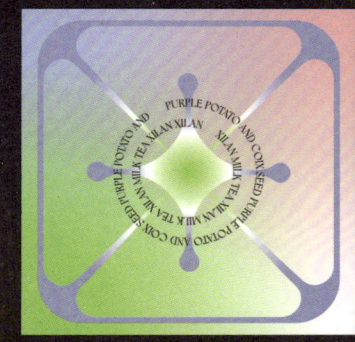

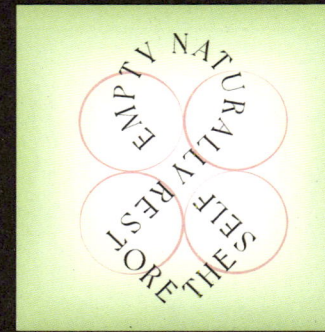

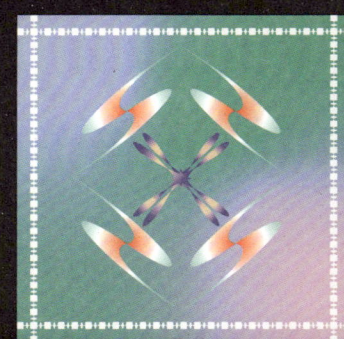

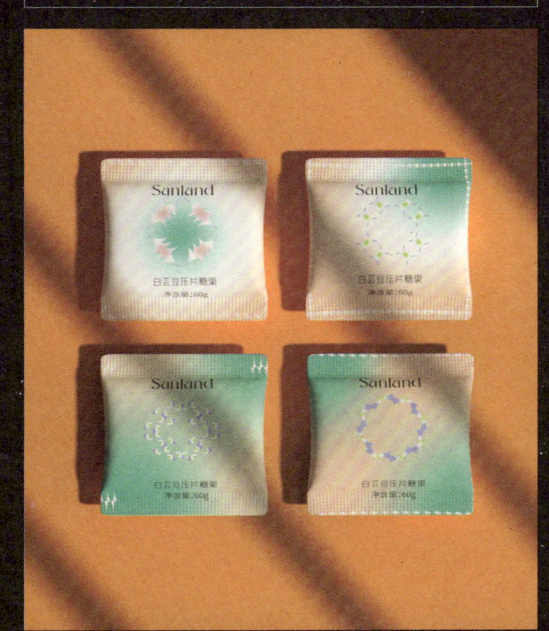

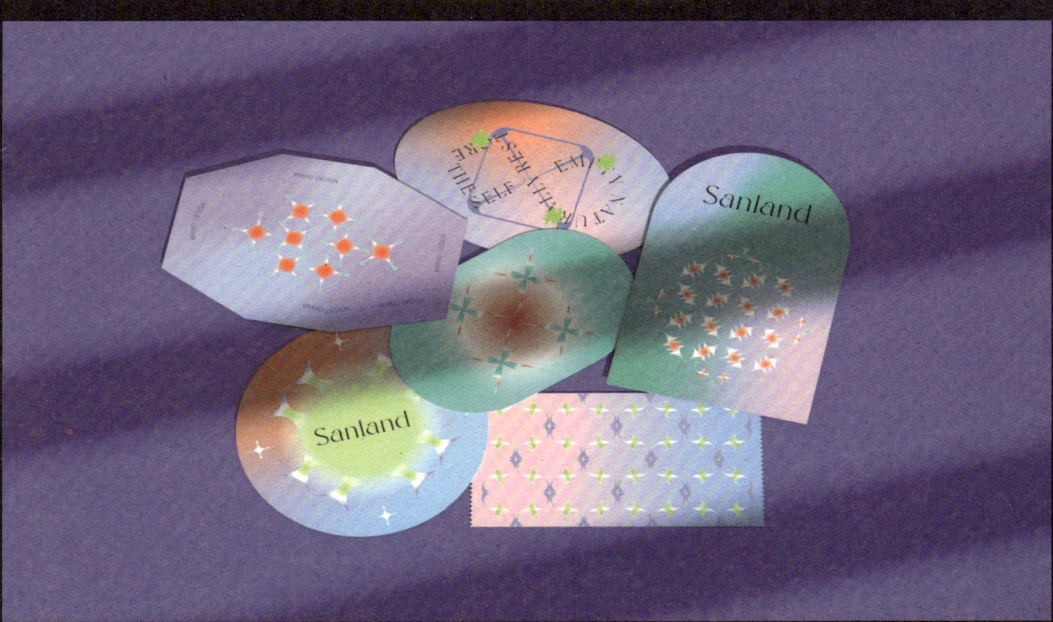

JOURNEY TO THE UNEXPLORED
IMMERSIVE DIGITAL ART EXHIBITION

Journey to the Unexplored is a digital art exhibition that brings together young artists to reimagine the fantastical realms from the East using digital media technology.

The exhibition takes the opening and closing of a traditional folding fan as its starting point, narrating the Eastern imagination of "constantly shifting between folding and unfolding, revealing a world of wonders." It extracts subtle elements or intentions from the artists' works as materials for flat creations, depicting a surreal and fantastical landscape akin to being seen through a kaleidoscope, constantly pierced, cut, and seamlessly intertwined.

Design Studio: 3% Design Studio
Designer: Deng Xiongjun, Jiang Wei, Dong Yiling, Ma Youyuan, Guo Shuwen
Client: Netease, Geeksart

▼ **Inspiration:**
In spatial decoration, mirrors are a commonly used visual element in Retro-Futurism. The sharp cutting and reconstruction of geometric shapes invisibly bring more layers of understanding and perception to a single space. Inspired by this, the design team took the "kaleidoscope" as a starting point. Through skillful slicing, it simulates the overlapping coexistence of multiple entrances to otherworldly realms, addressing the project's challenge of needing to densely present a broader and more multidimensional range of information and atmosphere within extremely limited space.

▼ **Elements:**
Interwoven throughout the design is the motif of the "kaleidoscope" within the classical Eastern context. The design team slice and rearrange the kaleidoscope to mimic the motion of rotating it, while also integrating elements from different artists' work. This approach provides a glimpse of the artists' styles without revealing too much, creating a surreal atmosphere.

▼ **Font:**
HYQihei

▼ **Layout:**
The design team applied a relatively fixed and stable layout structure to various sizes of flat materials without much variation, aiming to focus the viewer's attention on the kaleidoscopic background. This approach enhances the sense of magnificence and fantasy.

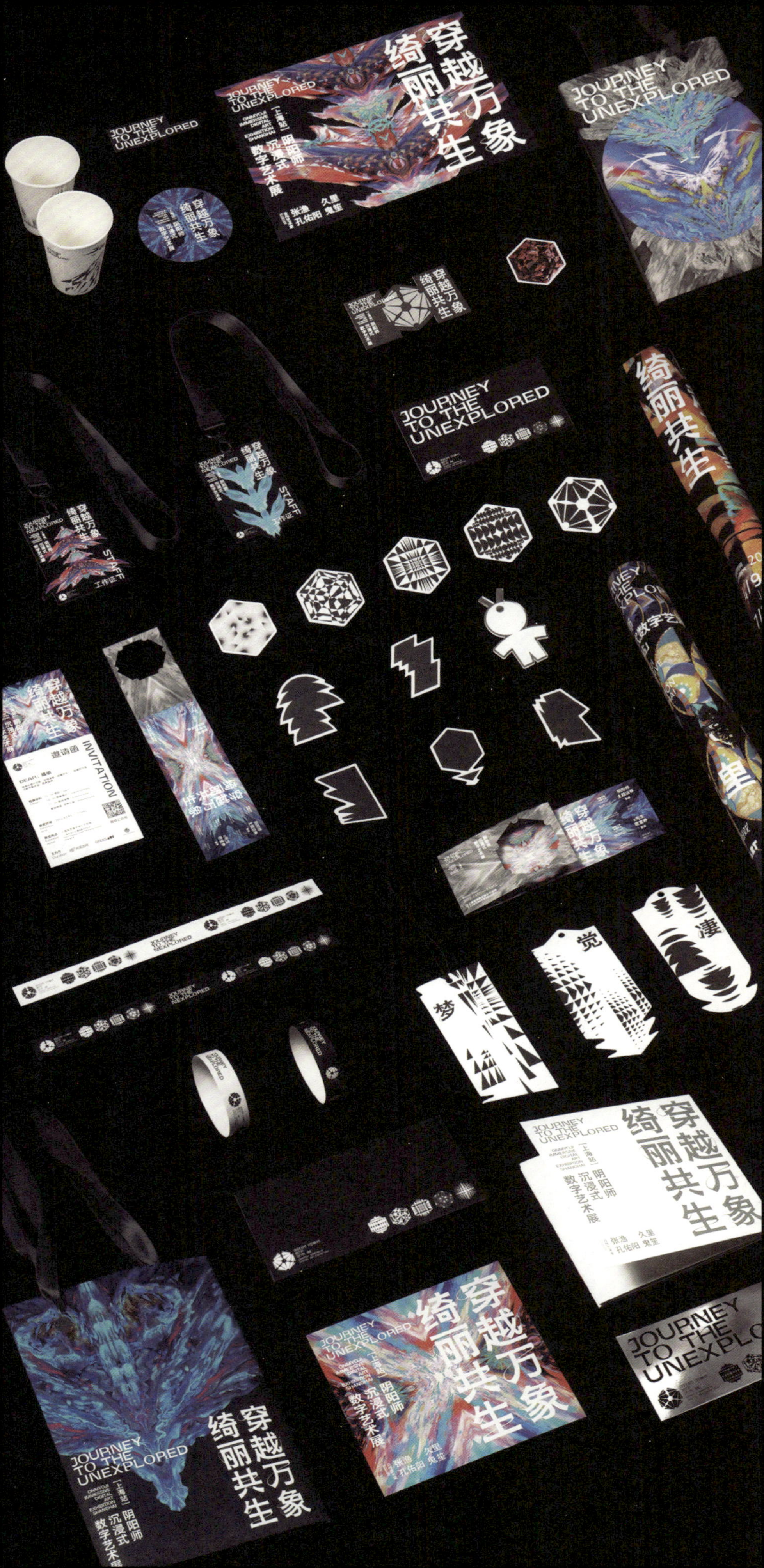
JOURNEY TO THE UNEXPLORED
穿越万象
绮丽共生
阴阳师
沉浸式数字艺术展
张渔 久童
孔佑阳 鬼笙
STAFF
工作证
INVITATION
邀请函
梦
觉
凄

JOURNEY TO THE UNEXPLORED
JOURNEY TO THE UNEXPLORED

穿越万象
绮丽共生
JOURNEY TO THE UNEXPLORED
阴阳师
沉浸式数字艺术展
「上海站」
ONMYOJI IMMERSIVE DIGITAL ART EXHIBITION SHANGHAI
2022
4/9
7/12
上海宝龙美术馆
5-6号馆
孔佑阳
网易游戏
GEEKS ART
EPSON

ORIGINAL WORKS OF GABRIEL PICARD

In the realm of digital airbrush illustration and graphic design within the music industry, the vibrant and surrealistic creations of Liorzh emerge as a captivating blend of 3D surrealism and retro geometry. The artistic vision behind these mesmerizing artworks belongs to Gabriel Picard, known by his pen name, Liorzh. Hailing from coastal northwestern France and born in 2001, Gabriel draws inspiration from the aesthetics of the 1960s to the 1980s. His expertise lies in crafting vivid landscapes infused with sci-fi elements, creating a visual experience that resonates with the nostalgic yet futuristic essence of his influences.

Designer: Liorzh (Gabriel Picard)

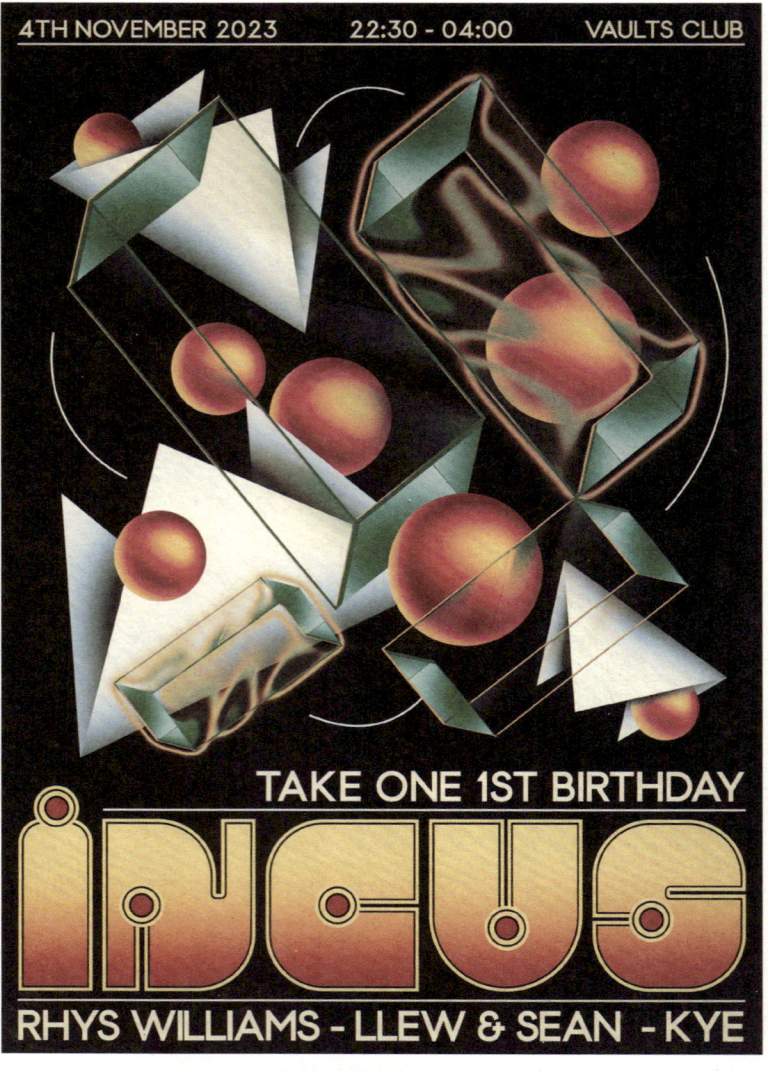

▼ Color Scheme:

- ■ R000 G000 B000
  C000 M000 Y000 K100
- □ R255 G255 B255
  C000 M000 Y000 K000
- ■ R001 G147 B085
  C081 M020 Y083 K000
- ■ R051 G069 B158
  C083 M061 Y014 K000
- ■ R228 G000 B127
  C000 M100 Y000 K000

▼ **Inspiration:**

The designer drew inspiration from Japanese designers of the 1970s and 1980s, such as Kazumasa Nagai, Koichi Sato, and Ikko Tanaka. Using magazine cutouts and stickers, they crafted collages that set the mood for the music compilation and reflected the artists involved.

The vibrant culture of the 1990s, including anime, PSX video games, hip hop, nu metal, and the electronic/trance music scene in Europe, played a significant role in shaping the project. The designer aimed to revive these influences in a fresh and contemporary form.

▼ **Elements:**

The concept aims to depict a mechanical and distorted pathway to heaven originating from a non-human or extraterrestrial entity. A detailed and intricate wireframe 3D figure descends to Earth, its complex form extending long tentacles into our atmosphere. To enhance the analog feel, various typographies and stickers inspired by VHS and DVD covers were incorporated into the design.

▼ **Fonts:**

Annonce, Glossy Display

▼ **Layout:**

The 3D mechanical wireframe object possessed inherent dynamism, making it an impressive centerpiece for the canvas. Building upon this foundation, the designer began filling gaps with typography and incorporating additional elements such as stickers and barcodes. Overlapping elements like the branches on the left top side were strategically introduced to enhance the depth of field, further enriching the overall composition.

▼ **Color Scheme:**

- R000 G000 B000
  C000 M000 Y000 K100
- R078 G095 B170
  C076 M063 Y000 K000
- R143 G124 B184
  C050 M053 Y000 K000
- R214 G069 B047
  C013 M086 Y083 K000
- R244 G205 B040
  C005 M020 Y087 K000
- R231 G195 B188
  C010 M028 Y021 K000

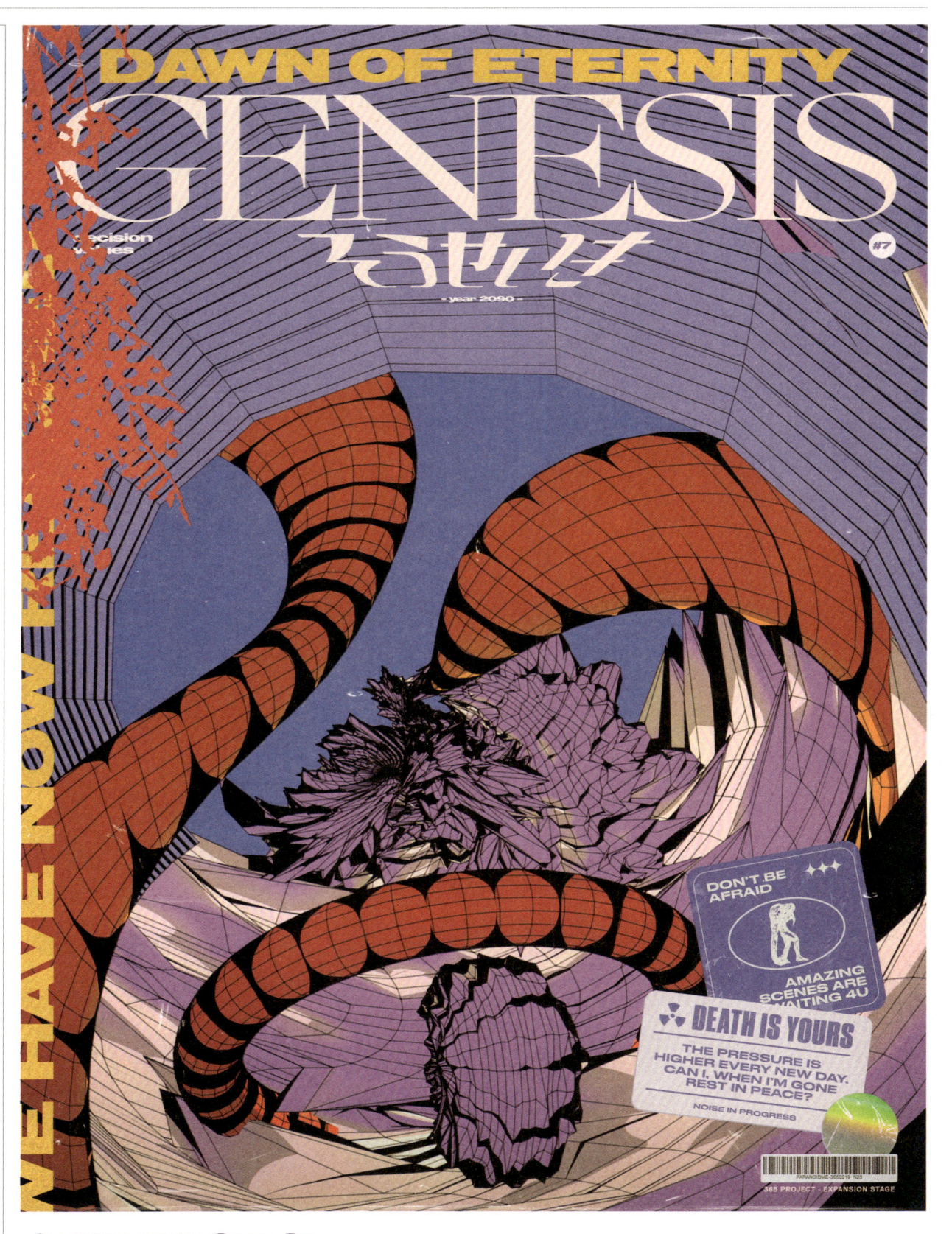

GENESIS

This poster was part of the "365 Posters" initiative undertaken in 2019, where the artist challenged himself to create something new every day. Drawing inspiration from Japanese graphics of the 1970s and 1980s, as well as retro aesthetics from the 1990s, the artist aimed to explore new creative techniques while building a collection of graphics to inspire others. To achieve an analog feel, the artist incorporated self-created assets like textures, stickers, and custom typography. The artist crafted the artworks to mimic authentic graphics found on records, films, or other products. Growing up in the 1990s, this project allowed the artist to revisit childhood memories, extracting everyday elements for creative exploration.

Designer: Diego L Rodriguez (Paranoidme)

Haruomi Hosono
MEDIUM COMPOSITIOM #2
45 r.p.m.
Angello Torres · The Whispering Sea
細野晴臣
Making of
NON
MEDIUM COMPOSITIOM; #2
MIXTURE
MEDIUM COMPOSITIOM; #2
こんどは、ふつうの愛じゃない。
Art Direction, Design
Yukimasa Okumura
Artwork
Yoshito Tada
Mastered By
Photography By
Tohru Kogure*
Producer, Mixed By, Written
Haruomi Hosono
Recorded By
Yasuhiro Terada*
細野晴臣
NON
Making Of Non-Standard Music
A Non-Standard Mixture 7:00
Making Of Monad Music
B1 Medium Composition; #1 1:10
B2 Medium Composition; #2 2:08
B3 3.6.9
STEREO 16NS-1001
DIGITAL MIX <NO-1>
STANDARD

WHISPER COLLECTION

▼ **Inspiration:**

The designer drew inspiration in collecting vinyl records of Japanese music from the '80s, particularly drawn to typographic compositions and combinations of English and Japanese words. This era's music style resonates personally with the designer. Additionally, covers, stickers, and labels serve as valuable sources of inspiration. Artists like Tatsuro Yamashita, Haruomi Hosono, and Masayoshi Takanaka, along with the band Yellow Magic Orchestra, have greatly influenced the designer's work. Furthermore, the designer is intrigued by Western music released in Japan and its interpretation in typographic compositions. Old encyclopedias featuring illustrations by Ernst Haeckel[1] or others also provide significant inspiration, offering diverse visual worlds from animal ecosystems to minerals.

▼ **Elements:**

Typography holds significant importance as a graphic element in the designer's work, envisioned as typographic landscapes that extend beyond their functional reading. Complemented by powerful imagery, the designer often delves into the surreal world, crafting unique collages depicting particular situations. These two elements serve as the foundational pillars of the designer's creations, often accompanied by diverse shapes, evocative colors, and enigmatic miscellanea to enhance their morphological appeal.

▼ **Fonts:**

Respira, Digestive, Roslindale, Sporting Grotesque, Ogg, Boogy Brut Poster, FH Giselle, Juniper, GT America, Windsor, Yu Gothic, Lÿno, Harbour, Calenda Plus, Pilowlava, Nostra

▼ **Layout:**

The typographic compositions take on an experimental and eclectic nature, prioritizing the layering of various fonts and variables. This includes combinations of Sans/Serif, Regular/Italic, Capital/Small Capitals, and even Glyphs/Jeroglyphs. Additionally, the designer mixed different languages, including English, Spanish, and Japanese, in compositions that blend Western and Eastern reading sensibilities. Playing with different reading directions, the designer created hypertextual windows that encourage free exploration and interpretation by viewers.

1. A German zoologist, naturalist, eugenicist, philosopher, physician, professor, marine biologist and artist.

The *Whisper Collection* comprises a series of personal posters crafted by the artist, drawing inspiration from a fusion of 1980s music icons and vintage botanical or animal illustrations. Rooted in a graphic style steeped in retro design, the collection pays homage to an era pivotal in shaping modern digital visualizations. During this period, known for its embrace of maximalism, the emphasis shifted towards graphic sensibility over functional communication, laying the groundwork for contemporary design aesthetics. Employing a collage-based approach in the creative process, the artist blended various visual elements such as images, typographies, compositions, and colors. The resulting pieces are akin to visual landscapes, layered with emotions and narratives reminiscent of memories.

Infused with the sensitivity of Monet and the informative richness of Hieronymus Bosch, these concepts converge in the design of posters featuring diverse subjects, ranging from musical artists to movies and animals. Each poster encapsulates a unique blend of artistic expression and thematic exploration.

Design Studio: Studio Angello Torres　　　　　**Designer: Angello Torres**

PEGGY GOU'S PLEASURE GARDENS (2019/2022/2023)

Peggy Gou's Pleasure Gardens is a stunning day festival held in Finsbury Park, curated by Peggy Gou herself. Each year, the festival embraces a unique theme, bringing fresh and exciting experiences to its attendees.

In 2019, the theme was "Utopia," featuring a tranquil and hallucinogenic color scheme with soft gradients and kaleidoscopic patterns. In 2022, the festival explored "Retro-Futurism," delving into themes of space, disco, and technology. In 2023, the theme was "The Garden of Eden," inspired by the temptation of the apple from the story of Adam and Eve.

Design Studio: Hello Rabbit Design
Designer: Helen Rabbitte
Client: Peggy Gou, Krankbrother

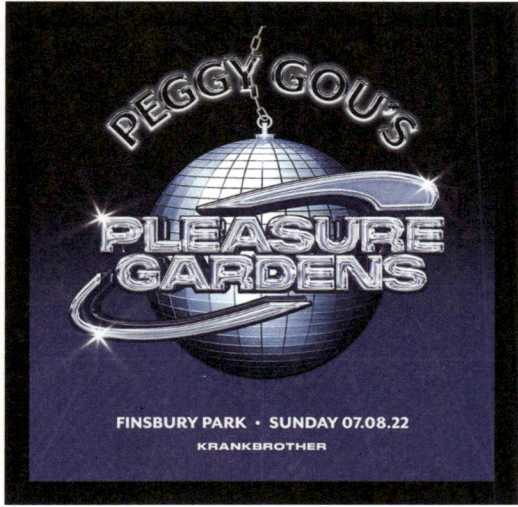

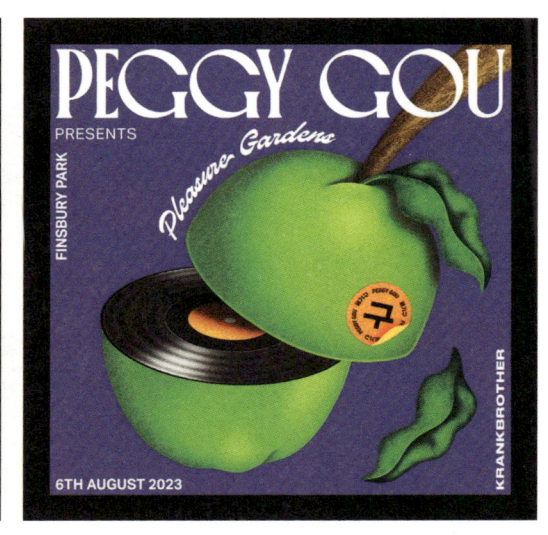

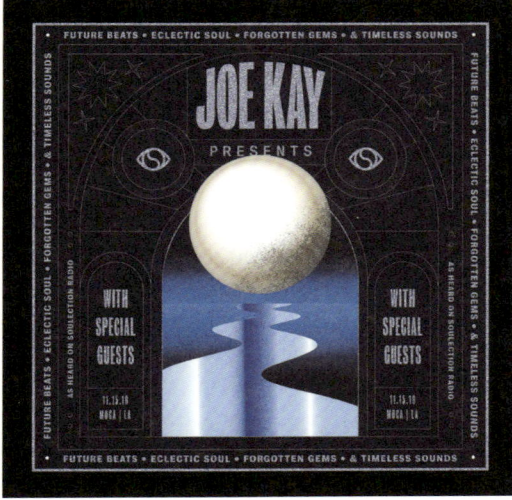

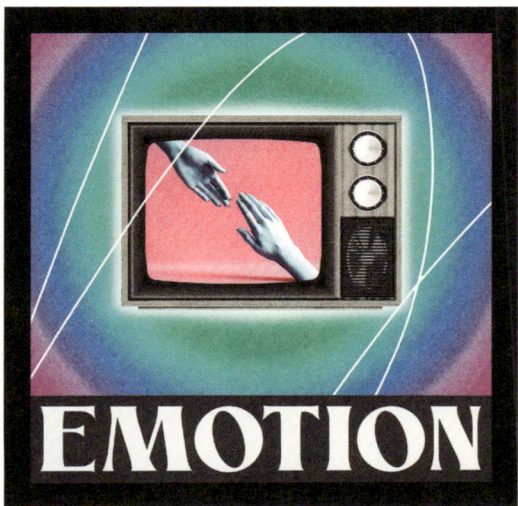

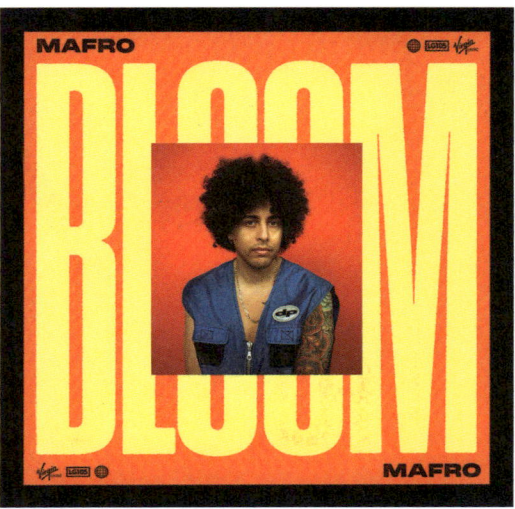

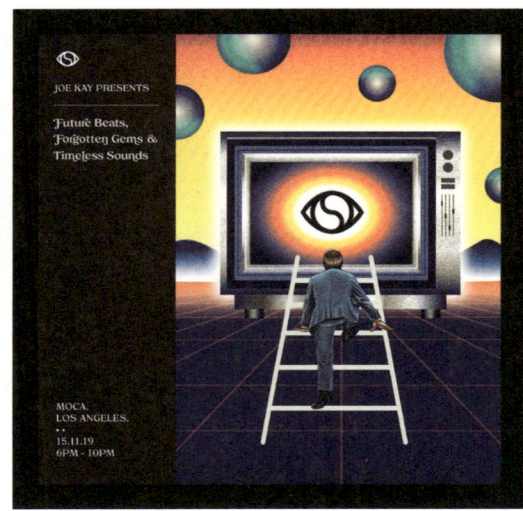

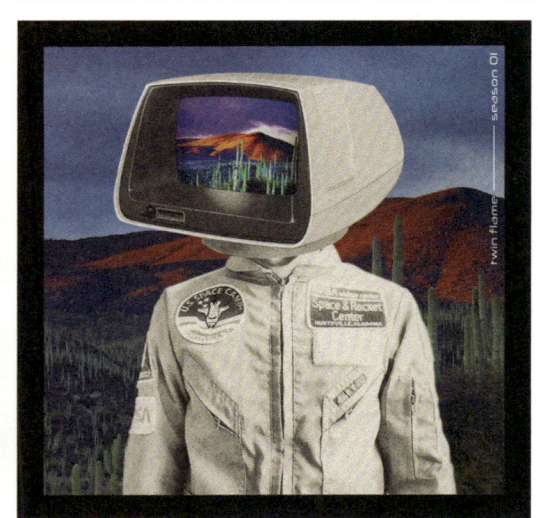

▼ **Inspiration:**

In 2019, the designer was inspired by the sci-fi graphics of the 70s, drawing inspiration from artists such as Jim Burns and Peter Haars. She also found inspiration in the vintage matchboxes of the 1920s and '30s, as she loves the cinematic romance and handcrafted elements.

In 2022, her influences included Hajime Sorayama's gynoid robots of the 1980s, as well as retro sci-fi artists such as Jim Burns and Peter Haars.

In 2023, the designer was heavily inspired by the surrealist art of Rafał Oblinski.

▼ **Elements:**

2019: An illustrated pair of hands with Peggy rising from them toward the blissful Pleasure Gardens.

2022: A chrome disco ball with a chrome typographic lock-up against a space-age dance floor.

2023: With nods to "The Garden of Eden" from the story of Adam and Eve, the work features an apple that, when cut open, reveals itself to be playing a record inside.

▼ **Font:**

Kallisto Heavy

▼ **Layout:**

2019: The layout is largely influenced by Asian street art and vintage matchbox labels.

2022: The designer aimed to make the chrome typography the main focal point, utilizing the disco ball and perspective grid to guide the viewer's eye and add tension around it.

ANTIDOTE

ANTIDOTE serves as the cover illustration for *Aranya Post*'s inaugural issue of 2022. Positioned as a remedy to the unpredictability of life, the artwork suggests the construction of a spiritual sanctuary amidst potential chaos. Whether depicting a crime scene unfolding on a breakfast table or exploring the serenity of mountain appreciation, the concept encourages reflection on the challenges endured during the pandemic while envisioning pathways to improvement. Ultimately, the artwork presents a filtered depiction of reality infused with fantasy and surrealism, thereby evoking a retro vibe.

Illustrator: Ginko
Client: *Aranya Post*

▼ **Inspiration:**
movies by Alfred Hitchcock

▼ **Color Scheme:**

- R198 G231 B249
  C025 M000 Y001 K000
- R222 G000 B122
  C005 M098 Y009 K000
- R255 G255 B255
  C000 M000 Y000 K000
- R208 G209 B206
  C022 M016 Y017 K001
- R000 G000 B000
  C000 M000 Y000 K100

SERMONS

SERMONS is a party series hosted at Heim, a dance club located in central Shanghai. Inspired by an original insight from Einstein, who wrote, "The most beautiful and profound emotion we can experience is the sensation of the mystical," SERMONS captures the irresistible feeling of submission to a higher or larger entity. Sometimes, this power is found in music, where one feels compelled to dance wholeheartedly. In these posters, the artist attempts to depict this power through four elements of life representing the mystical energy of nature, along with a butterfly signet ring symbolizing the mystical energy of culture.

Designer: Ginko
Client: Heim Club

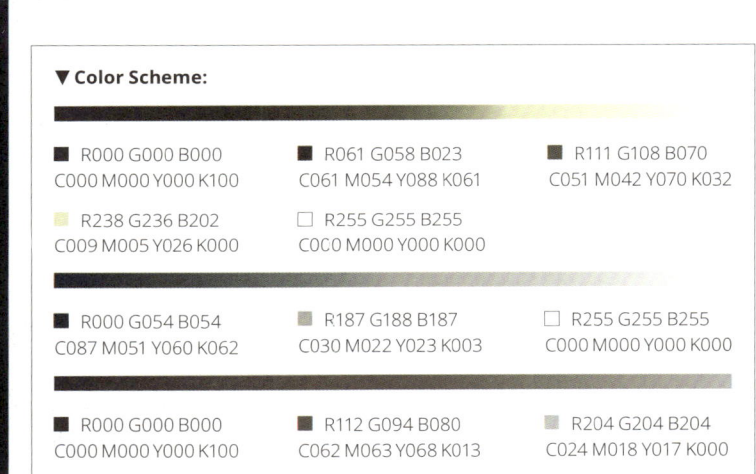

▼ Color Scheme:

■ R000 G000 B000	■ R061 G058 B023	■ R111 G108 B070
C000 M000 Y000 K100	C061 M054 Y088 K061	C051 M042 Y070 K032
■ R238 G236 B202	□ R255 G255 B255	
C009 M005 Y026 K000	C0C0 M000 Y000 K000	

| ■ R000 G054 B054 | ■ R187 G188 B187 | □ R255 G255 B255 |
| C087 M051 Y060 K062 | C030 M022 Y023 K003 | C000 M000 Y000 K000 |

| ■ R000 G000 B000 | ■ R112 G094 B080 | ■ R204 G204 B204 |
| C000 M000 Y000 K100 | C062 M063 Y068 K013 | C024 M018 Y017 K000 |

WESTERN CALLIGRAPHY ANNUAL EXHIBITION: POP & ART

In response to the exhibition theme "POP & ART," the designer team created six modern English letters specifically for the event. They invited the exhibition's artists to contribute by writing in Western calligraphy within the reserved spaces of these letters. In the accompanying video, the font evolves from a mysterious and elegant crystal texture to a metal texture, featuring strong visual contrasts and vibrant, illusory colors. This transformation showcases how traditional Western calligraphy can still exude different charms in a modern context.

The exhibition invited 17 Chinese and Western calligraphers and exhibited more than 50 Western calligraphy works created on the theme of "POP & ART." In the main part of visual font design of the exhibition, the team crafted modern style of font and reserved space boldly to invite the president of LAAOM to write in Western calligraphy, explored different presentation methods of Western calligraphy, and jointly discussed new possibilities of font design. The collision between pop and art is an interesting experiment. Classical and elegant Western calligraphy is also changing with its endless potential under the influence of pop culture.

Design Studio: Indego design
Designer: Lam Ieong Kun, Dan Ferreira
Client: LAAOM (The Lettering Artists Association of Macau)

▼ **Inspiration:**

This design project is deeply influenced by classical Western calligraphy and contemporary pop culture, presenting a fusion of styles under the theme "POP & ART" in an exhibition. Specifically designed for the exhibition, six modern English letters invited artists to write in Western calligraphy within the reserved spaces for each letter. The accompanying video presents the font's gradual transition, shifting from a refined and enigmatic crystal texture to a metallic finish, marked by striking visual contrasts and a surreal color change.

The overall design aims to explore the collision between classical and contemporary influences, drawing inspiration from the Pop Art movement of the 1960s, particularly artists like Andy Warhol. Elements of the luxurious and geometric designs from the Art Deco era are also reflected in the font's evolution. Collaboration with 17 Chinese and Western calligraphers highlights the diverse cultural impact, while the application of modern fashion trends and typography styles adds a contemporary touch.

In essence, this project serves as a creative experiment, blending classical Western calligraphy with contemporary visual art, challenging and pushing the boundaries of font design in new and innovative ways.

▼ **Elements:**

This design project incorporates dynamic graphic elements, prominently featuring six specially designed modern English letters. In a video presentation, these letters undergo a visual transformation, shifting from a "mysterious and elegant crystal texture" to a "metal texture with strong visual collision and illusory color changes." The project integrates Western calligraphy from 17 diverse artists, adding a traditional and artistic layer to the design. The deliberate deformation of the font in the video symbolizes the project's exploration of the intersection between classical and contemporary influences, pushing the boundaries of traditional design. Overall, the graphic elements aim to showcase how classical elegance can adapt and thrive within the realm of contemporary pop culture.

▼ **Fonts:**

Grand Slang, Nostra, Aeonik

▼ **Layout:**

This design project ingeniously blends classical Western calligraphy with modern visual aesthetics. The primary layout highlights six modern English letters, showcasing their transformation through a video presentation. The layout also incorporates spaces reserved for the participation of 17 Chinese and Western calligraphers, emphasizing the fusion of traditional and contemporary elements. The overall composition prioritizes visual balance and employs a video format to create a dynamic evolution effect. The design aims to challenge traditional boundaries in font design, demonstrating the adaptability and vibrancy of classical elegance within contemporary pop culture.

"BLOOMING FLOWERS & THE FULL MOON" MOONCAKES PACKAGING DESIGN

According to the designer, the feeling of "dullness" is a prevailing sentiment often associated with the Mid-Autumn Festival in recent years, there seems to be a departure from the traditional excitement and anticipation surrounding the festival. Instead, it appears that people are more inclined towards relaxation and unwinding during the brief three-day holiday period. The designer noted a shift away from traditional embellishments and excessive packaging, as well as a release from the perceived obligation to indulge in mooncakes. Consequently, the Mid-Autumn Festival has transformed into a mere illusion of "Blooming Flowers and the Full Moon." (HUA HAO YUE YUAN: A Chinese idiom for blissful harmony; the first and last characters are the Chinese words for "flower" and "circle" respectively.)

Designer: Lo.Dycha
Client: LECHATER

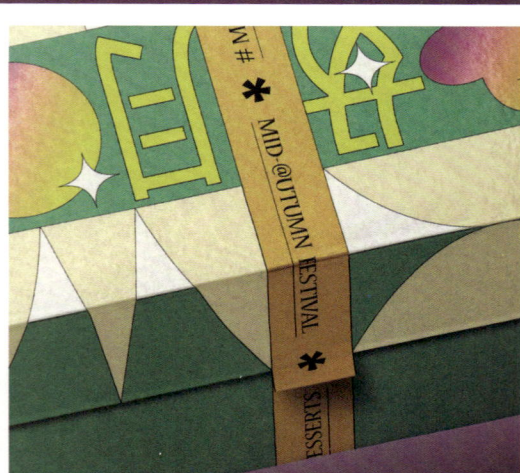

▼ **Inspiration:**
This project draws inspiration from the graphic design of the Republican era, especially concerning typography. Designers of that period often simplified characters with intricate strokes. These characters, neither traditional nor simplified, exude a unique charm that reflects the enthusiasm of creators from that era.

▼ **Elements:**
What can be conveyed graphically should not be written, which inspired the phrase "Blooming Flowers and the Full Moon" on the package.

▼ **Color Scheme:**

- R252 G240 B190 / C002 M006 Y032 K000
- R242 G172 B063 / C003 M040 Y079 K000
- R240 G234 B057 / C010 M000 Y083 K000
- R171 G084 B156 / C037 M076 Y000 K000
- R047 G172 B111 / C073 M004 Y070 K000

ALL STARS

A fun editorial design delves into the fascinating realm of stars akin to the sun. The infusion of experimental layout styles and innovative typographic placements draws inspiration from the captivating aesthetics of early 2000s science textbooks.

Designer: Osheyi.A

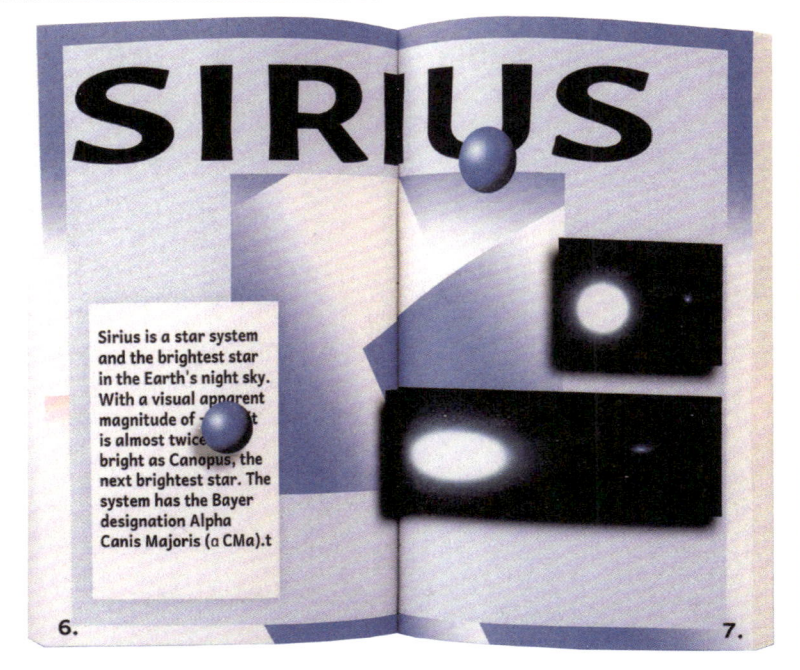

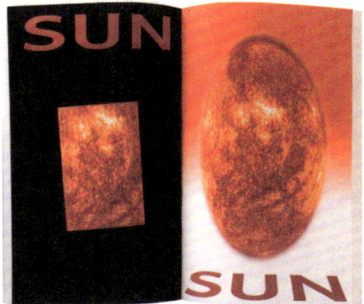

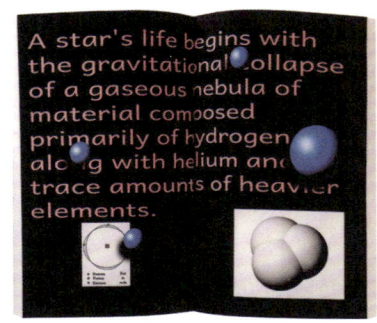

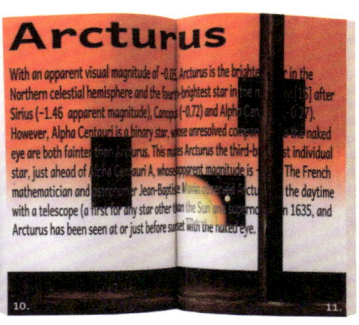

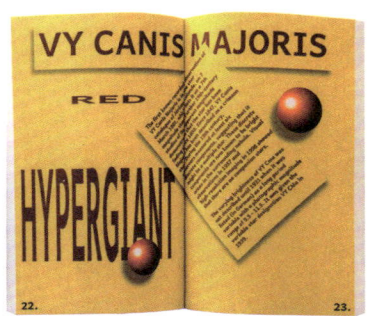

THE GROWLERS

This series of surreal retro-style illustrative posters is for The Growlers Tour in Paris in 2018. The vision for these pieces involved seamlessly blending geometric elements with a more fluid and unrestrained style of shapes, drawing inspiration from the works of surrealist artists like Salvador Dalí. The intention was to curate a visually captivating experience that paid homage to the essence of surrealism while providing a unique and compelling aesthetics for The Growlers Tour.

Designer: Osheyi.A

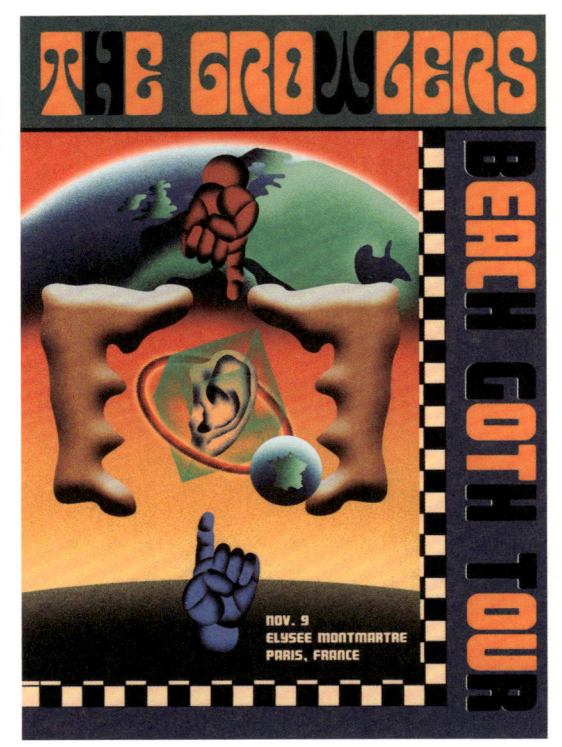

▼ Color Scheme:

■ R234 G147 B021 C006 M051 Y093 K000	■ R061 G104 B177 C079 M056 Y000 K000	■ R000 G156 B098 C083 M011 Y077 K000	■ R204 G050 B040 C018 M093 Y090 K000
■ R095 G050 B137 C075 M090 Y007 K000	■ R000 G096 B084 C093 M051 Y071 K015	■ R000 G000 B000 C000 M000 Y000 K100	

ORIGINAL WORKS BY ARRIVEDLATE

Waiting For Your Call:

The intention was to evoke a sense of nostalgia, romance, and yearning reminiscent of the 80s. It serves as a visual invitation, akin to an album cover, welcoming viewers into a world of memories.

Lovers Club:

Originally a sketch for a music client, this design wasn't selected, but the designer, captivated by its visual appeal, kept it to repurpose as a sticker.

Nostalgia Series:

This is a sticker series created to highlight forgotten yet beloved relics of the past. Once easily attainable, these items have now become coveted collectibles. The series serves as a reminder of the joy these objects once brought and how they can still evoke that same sense of nostalgia and happiness.

Illustrator: Arrivedlate

WAITING FOR YOUR CALL

LOVERS CLUB

NOSTALGIA SERIES

▼ **Elements:**

Waiting For Your Call: The designer believes that the brick telephone is an iconic technology of that era and deserves people's love and appreciation. Shell vases and whiskey glasses are decorative elements. The gridline is the primary plane, with supplementary sparkles tying it all together.

Lovers Club: The design focuses on the character, with a grid background and decorative fonts enhancing her presence without distraction.

Nostalgia Series: Each design focuses on relics with contrasting shapes, incorporating a bloom effect that enhances the overall image, creating a dreamy aesthetic.

▼ **Layout:**

Waiting For Your Call: The illustration is primarily center aligned, but to add depth, the designer split the background in two just below the center point. The grid lines all converge to the center point, tying the whole visual together.

Lovers Club: The layout is straightforward; the sticker design is centered with the text above and below wrapping around the main oval shape.

Nostalgia Series: The designer aimed to create an illusion of depth for each image by extending beyond the gridline and keeping certain parts of the design more subtle. A simple and plain background is tiled to present the collection in a cohesive manner.

ORIGINAL WORKS BY ISAIAH WORRINGTON

Isaiah Worrington, a visionary in the realm of 3D graphics, seamlessly blends spirituality, surrealism, and modernism to craft visually captivating pieces. With a keen eye for detail and a deep understanding of design principles, the graphic designer's goal is to create artworks that not only command attention but also resonate with viewers on a profound level. Each project undertaken by the designer is a unique exploration of these influences, transforming abstract concepts into tangible, captivating visuals that leave a lasting impression.

Design Studio: Cyberdreams
Designer: Isaiah Worrington

40 HAIKU POSTERS

During the height of the COVID-19 pandemic, Spain grappled with significant challenges. In response, the designer embarked on a personal challenge: creating "40 Haiku posters." This initiative aimed to transform negative thoughts into positive ones during a period of uncertainty, providing a fresh source of energy and creativity. Simultaneously, the designer sought to inspire people worldwide with the timeless beauty of haiku poetry. Originating from Japan, haiku is a form of short poetry characterized by its three-line structure and 5/7/5 syllable count. Each poem captures a fleeting moment in nature, expressing profound meaning with minimal words. Through this project, the designer endeavored to evoke contemplation and appreciation for the simplicity and depth of haiku poetry.

Designer: Diego L Rodriguez (Paranoidme)

▼ **Inspiration:**

This project draws inspiration from Japanese poster artists, anime, and comics from the 1990s-2000s. Inspired by the simplicity and depth of 1970s-1980s posters, the designer revisited childhood cartoons and comics for comfort during uncertain times. Combining this with the profound meaning of haiku poetry, the designer created *40 Haiku posters*, each blending vivid imagery with carefully chosen poems to offer moments of beauty amidst chaos.

Some posters from the 70s and 80s used very few elements to convey very complex ideas. It was important to the artists that the posters felt comfortable and fun in a time when the world was crumbling. On the other hand, the simplicity and deep meaning of haiku poetry demonstrates this aesthetic. Each poster is associated with a haiku and showcases something beautiful, using bright colors to uplift the viewer in moments of chaos.

▼ **Color Scheme:**

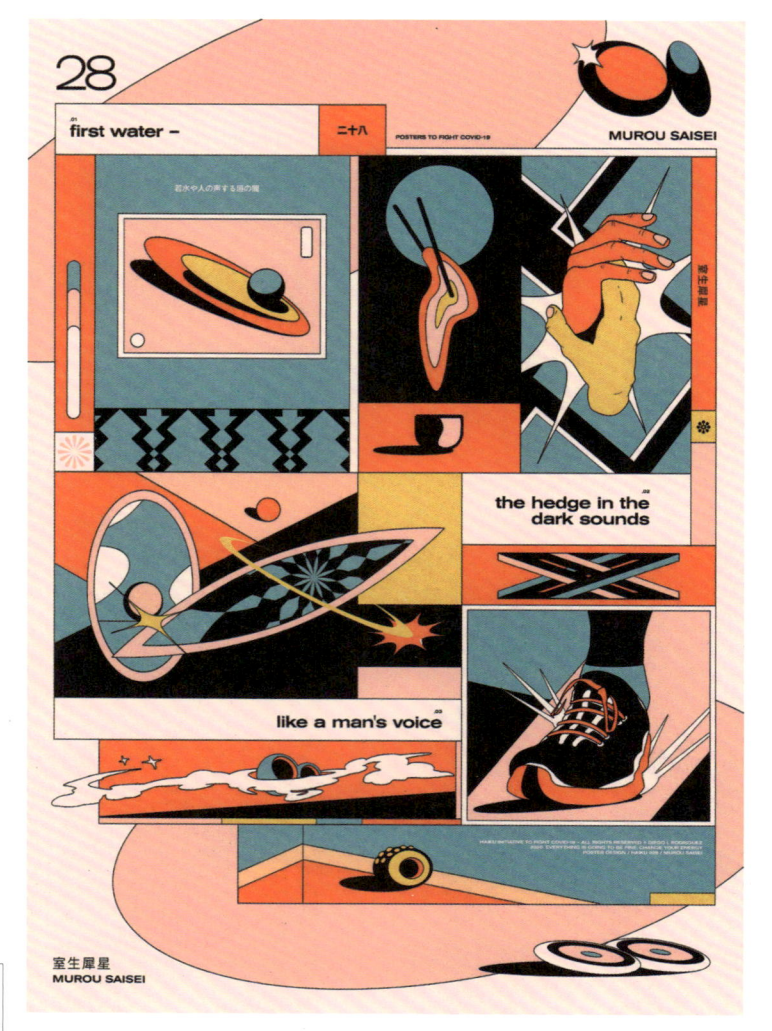

■ R063 G165 B187 C070 M016 Y024 K000	■ R235 G097 B045 C000 M075 Y083 K000	■ R245 G183 B188 C000 M038 Y016 K000
■ R232 G061 B029 C000 M089 Y092 K000	■ R099 G176 B195 C061 M014 Y021 K000	■ R233 G201 B182 C010 M022 Y029 K000
■ R071 G090 B167 C079 M065 Y000 K000	■ R237 G115 B027 C000 M067 Y091 K000	■ R212 G209 B204 C020 M016 Y018 K000
■ R141 G205 B182 C048 M000 Y035 K000	■ R232 G102 B103 C002 M073 Y047 K000	■ R246 G189 B199 C000 M035 Y011 K000
■ R237 G115 B027 C000 M067 Y091 K000	■ R048 G155 B215 C072 M023 Y001 K000	■ R221 G208 B039 C018 M013 Y089 K000
■ R093 G068 B152 C074 M080 Y000 K000	■ R134 G143 B198 C053 M041 Y001 K000	■ R237 G115 B027 C000 M067 Y091 K000

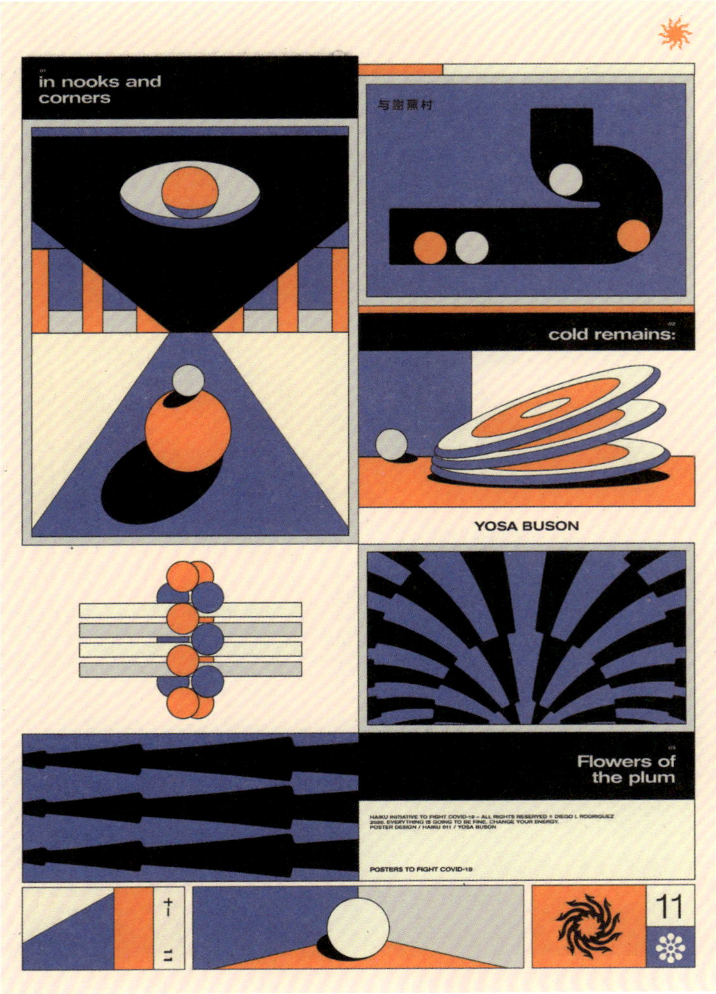
in nooks and corners
与謝蕪村
cold remains:
YOSA BUSON
Flowers of the plum
HAIKU INITIATIVE TO FIGHT COVID-19 – ALL RIGHTS RESERVED © DIEGO L RODRIGUEZ
2020. EVERYTHING IS GOING TO BE FINE. CHANGE YOUR ENERGY.
POSTER DESIGN / HAIKU 011 / YOSA BUSON
POSTERS TO FIGHT COVID-19
11

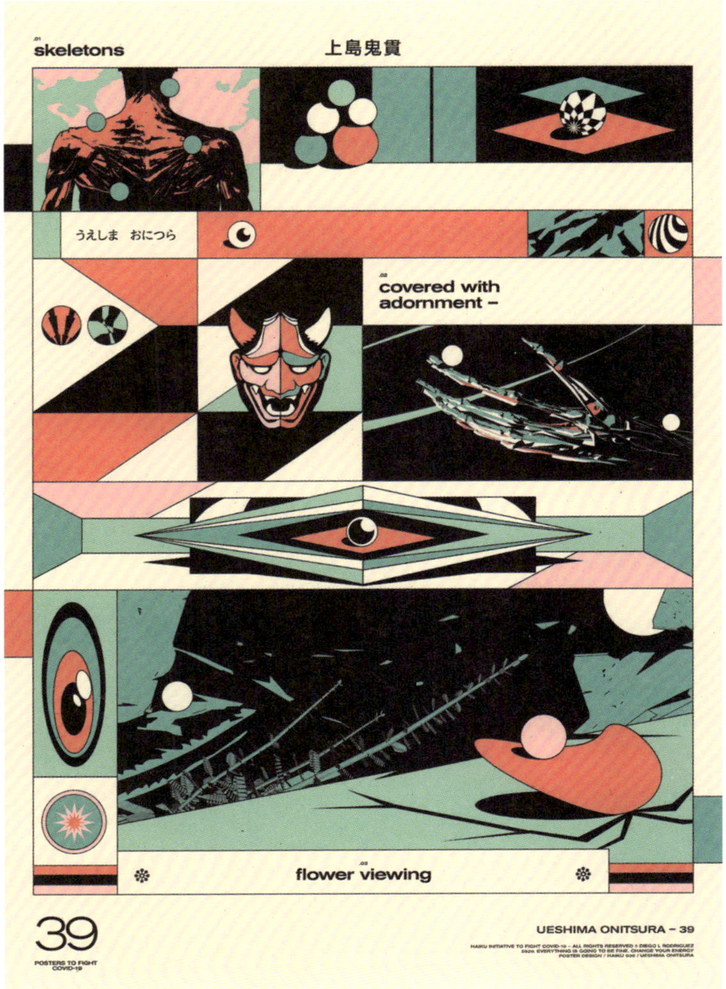
skeletons
上島鬼貫
うえしま おにつら
covered with adornment –
flower viewing
39
POSTERS TO FIGHT COVID-19
UESHIMA ONITSURA – 39

この樹登らば鬼女となるべし夕紅葉
climb up the tree
i will become a demon
三橋鷹女
MITSUHASHI TAKAJO
26
evening red leaves
POSTERS TO FIGHT COVID-19

in one rush
平押に五反田くもる時雨かな
the five ars of fields in clouds
SAKAI YAMEI 坂井野明
and then the winter drizzle
22
SAKAI YAMEI · 22

WESTERN CALLIGRAPHY ANNUAL EXHIBITION — HANDICRAFT ART IN AN ERA OF TECHNOLOGY

The exhibition invited 18 Western calligraphers from various countries and exhibited more than 60 Western calligraphic works and works of art created around the theme of "Technology in the Age of Science and Technology." In response to the theme of the exhibition, the design team boldly imagined and simulated an avant-garde "Western Calligraphy Tool Set of the Future" as part of the main vision of the exhibition, so as to echo the theme of the exhibition. In the main vision, the four future Western calligraphy tools are inextricably related to future technology and digital development, which breaks the traditional concept inherent in Western calligraphy; at the same time, the design team brought out strong visual tension in the main vision by combining Western calligraphy fonts with futuristic fonts.

Design Studio: Indego design
Designer: Kun Lam, Dan Ferreira
Client: LAAOM

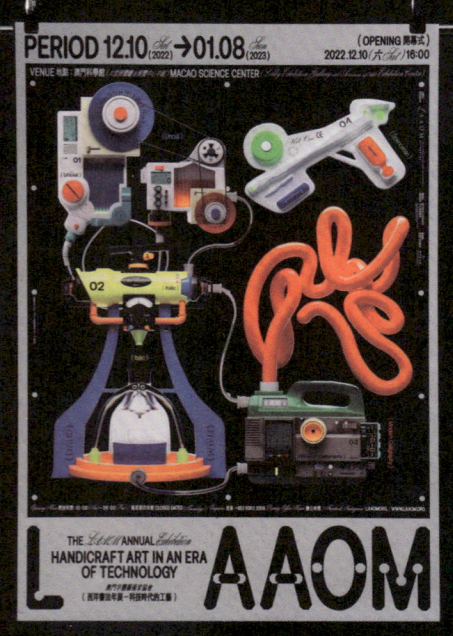

PERIOD 12.10 →01.08
VENUE 地點：澳門科學館
MACAO SCIENCE CENTER
澳門字體藝術家協會
（西洋書法年展－科技時代的工藝）
THE ANNUAL Exhibition
HANDICRAFT ART IN AN ERA
OF TECHNOLOGY
LAAOM
(01)
(Uncial)
(02)
(Italic)
(03)
(Modern Calligraphy)
(04)
(Spencerian)

SIC FILII SCITE TIBI
VI SACRA MENTU
M ERIT PRAEM
IUM SANGUINE
SANCTUM
ABSCONDITUM
PEACE
AAOM

LAAOM
HANDICRAFT ART IN AN ERA
OF TECHNOLOGY

LAAOM
Vip
Staff
Media
Artist
HANDICRAFT ART IN AN ERA
OF TECHNOLOGY

LAAOM
HANDICRAFT ART IN AN ERA
OF TECHNOLOGY

MUKANJYO

This poster was part of the "365 posters" initiative undertaken in 2019, where the artist challenged himself to create something new every day.

Designer: Diego L Rodriguez (Paranoidme)

▼ **Inspiration:** The poster was inspired by the song "Mukanjyo" by the Japanese band Survive Said The Prophet. The themes of survival, redemption, and loneliness in the song resonate with the nostalgia and past memories of the main character.

▼ **Fonts:** COM4t Drify, Verbatim

▼ **Elements & Layout:** The designer used a central image of a person in a squatting position, inverting its colors to create a more mysterious and enigmatic effect. Then he played with a ton of small typos and containers with flowers. These containers represent old photos or Polaroids, allowing the audience to walk through the character's memories.

▼ **Color Scheme:**

■ R097 G072 B154 C072 M078 Y000 K000	■ R153 G190 B057 C047 M008 Y091 K000	■ R222 G070 B014 C007 M085 Y084 K000	■ R205 G049 B120 C017 M091 Y020 K000
■ R218 G208 B207 C017 M019 Y010 K000	■ R110 G112 B136 C065 M056 Y036 K000	■ R000 G000 B000 C000 M000 Y000 K100	

LAYOUT / LOGO EXPLORATIONS & EXPERIMENTAL POSTER SERIES

The design studio KEVLAR:ESTUDIO showcases a collection of design pieces on their social media account (@kevlarestudio), offering a glimpse into their creative essence. Their inspiration spans various disciplines, rooted in themes such as nature, technology, and human experiences. By blending organic and artificial elements, they seek to evoke emotions and create visually compelling works. While their style defies easy categorization, it often leans towards a Neo-Maximalism aesthetics. Each piece carries a unique message, some aimed at fostering self-awareness, curiosity about different cultures, and challenging societal norms—both in the real and virtual realms. KEVLAR:ESTUDIO strives to depart from conventional aesthetics, providing a platform for marginalized voices and pushing beyond market-driven trends.

Design Studio: KEVLAR:ESTUDIO
Designer: Gastón (a.k.a GENDEMA) and Damián (a.k.a WIDDO)

▼ **Inspiration:**

Magazines, animated series, video games, and movies from the 2000s played a fundamental role in designers' artistic development. The music of that era, including electronic, pop, pop-punk, and nu metal genres, also left a significant impact. Notable musicians and bands such as Aphex Twin, Moby, Radiohead, Gorillaz, Bjork, and Jamiroquai have influenced them greatly. Their cultural inspirations extend beyond Argentine heritage from the province of Buenos Aires. They maintain a strong interest in diverse cultures from the Near East, Middle East, Western and Central Europe.

▼ **Elements:**

01: The concept driving this design project was to create a presentation for a self-generating operating system utilizing an extensive A.I. neural network. Key elements include icons and images, some featuring halftone or bitmap effects, along with color gradients, titles, subtitles, HUD elements, and logos.

02–04: This design project represents a broad exploration of layout concepts without adhering to a specific theme. It incorporates various elements such as icons, images (some with halftone or bitmap effects), color gradients, titles, subtitles, HUD elements, and logos.

▼ **Fonts:**

Monocode, PS-NOW-GU, Karasuma Gothic, Sitka, Saint, B612 Mono, Redaction, Geometric strokes (Illustrator), Microgramma, XEVO (modification)

▼ **Layout:**

01: For this piece, the designers departed from the rectangular format to create a more dynamic structure while maintaining a printed appearance with precise cuts and circular shapes. The main image adds an organic touch, contrasting with the technological themes elsewhere. Iconographic elements and HUD elements enhance the geometric planes, while an asymmetrical composition is balanced by varying shades of gray.

02: In this design, there is a distinct symmetry in its overall form and an internal asymmetry in its editorial and content arrangements. The structure gains organic strength from cuts made by 3D organic materials in the corners, integrated seamlessly with 2D planes through digital collage techniques. To balance the grayscale tones in the editorial design, designers compensated throughout the content. Additionally, designers enhanced the solidity of the technological and futuristic elements by employing monospaced typography.

KEVLAR:ESTUDIO — Retro-Futurism — 142

03

04

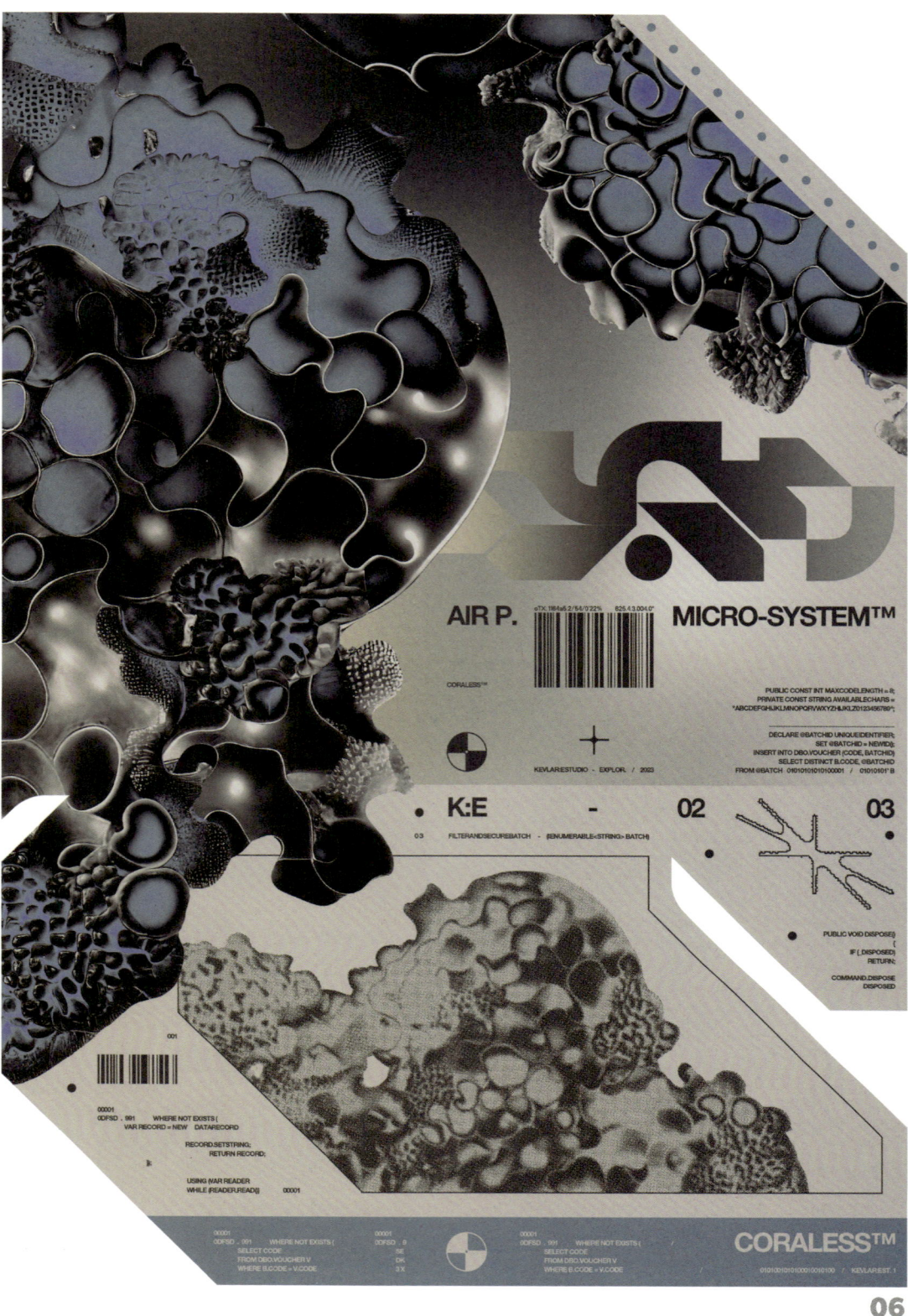

05

06

▼ Layout:

03: In this piece, there is a blend of clear symmetry in its overall form and internal asymmetry in its content structure. Organic 3D metallic materials mark the corners, framing the main planes. Grayscale balance enhances editorial coherence, while monospaced typography adds solidity to futuristic elements. Shifting the main logo off-center injects dynamism, breaking the central symmetry axis.

04–05: The designers deviated from the traditional rectangular poster morphology, opting for an asymmetrical composition that blends organic shapes with geometric planes. The layout incorporates paragraphs of monospaced typography strategically placed to fill the spaces within the geometric forms. Icons, HUD elements, titles, and subtitles guide the viewer through a visual journey, maintaining a balanced distribution of grayscale tones across the piece.

06: In this piece, the designers chose a vertical canvas with rhomboid-like cuts at 45° angles. The rigid geometric structure is softened by abstract organic forms. Short paragraphs fill the spaces within the structure, complemented by icons, HUD elements, titles, subtitles, and illustrations, ensuring a balanced grayscale distribution.

Retro-Futurism — KEVLAR:ESTUDIO

07

08

07: With a title bearing significant visual weight, the designers ensured the main image matched this prominence by adjusting its brightness. At the bottom, geometric lines were incorporated to anchor the poster while guiding the viewer's gaze back to the top. The addition of icons and small texts completed the composition within the vertical rectangle.

08: In this design, various elements were incorporated, maintaining visual balance throughout. The goal was to create a dynamic visual path without a specific reading order. To achieve this, numerous elements were used, each sharing visual weight to attract the viewer's eye to the entirety of the piece before deconstructing it. To enhance coherence, a symmetrical and centered design approach was adopted.

▼ **Color Scheme:**

■ R048 G087 B166 C085 M066 Y000 K000	■ R150 G165 B203 C046 M031 Y007 K000	■ R241 G140 B026 C000 M056 Y091 K000	■ R214 G210 B202 C019 M016 Y020 K000	■ R108 G107 B103 C065 M057 Y057 K005
■ R165 G119 B079 C042 M058 Y073 K000	■ R199 G205 B070 C028 M010 Y082 K000	■ R228 G228 B224 C013 M009 Y012 K000	■ R178 G183 B186 C035 M025 Y023 K000	■ R100 G104 B117 C069 M059 Y047 K002
■ R050 G100 B175 C082 M058 Y000 K000	■ R219 G126 B035 C013 M060 Y091 K000	■ R202 G214 B054 C027 M004 Y087 K000	■ R198 G193 B192 C026 M023 Y021 K000	■ R154 G150 B139 C046 M039 Y043 K000
■ R222 G088 B120 C008 M078 Y031 K000	■ R064 G135 B150 C075 M036 Y037 K000	■ R214 G210 B202 C019 M016 Y020 K000	■ R237 G202 B037 C009 M021 Y088 K000	■ R207 G066 B025 C017 M087 Y100 K000
■ R081 G074 B069 C071 M068 Y068 K026	■ R225 G222 B217 C014 M012 Y014 K000	■ R088 G143 B175 C068 M34 Y022 K000	■ R222 G130 B157 C010 M060 Y018 K000	■ R079 G106 B071 C074 M051 Y081 K011
■ R154 G150 B139 C046 M039 Y043 K000	■ R178 G183 B186 C035 M025 Y023 K000	■ R082 G087 B161 C076 M068 Y004 K000	■ R095 G121 B148 C069 M049 Y031 K000	■ R050 G073 B087 C085 M070 Y057 K019
■ R202 G036 B060 C019 M096 Y072 K000	■ R122 G131 B085 C060 M044 Y075 K000	■ R026 G108 B180 C084 M052 Y002 K000	■ R202 G221 B237 C024 M008 Y004 K000	■ R180 G184 B220 C033 M026 Y000 K000

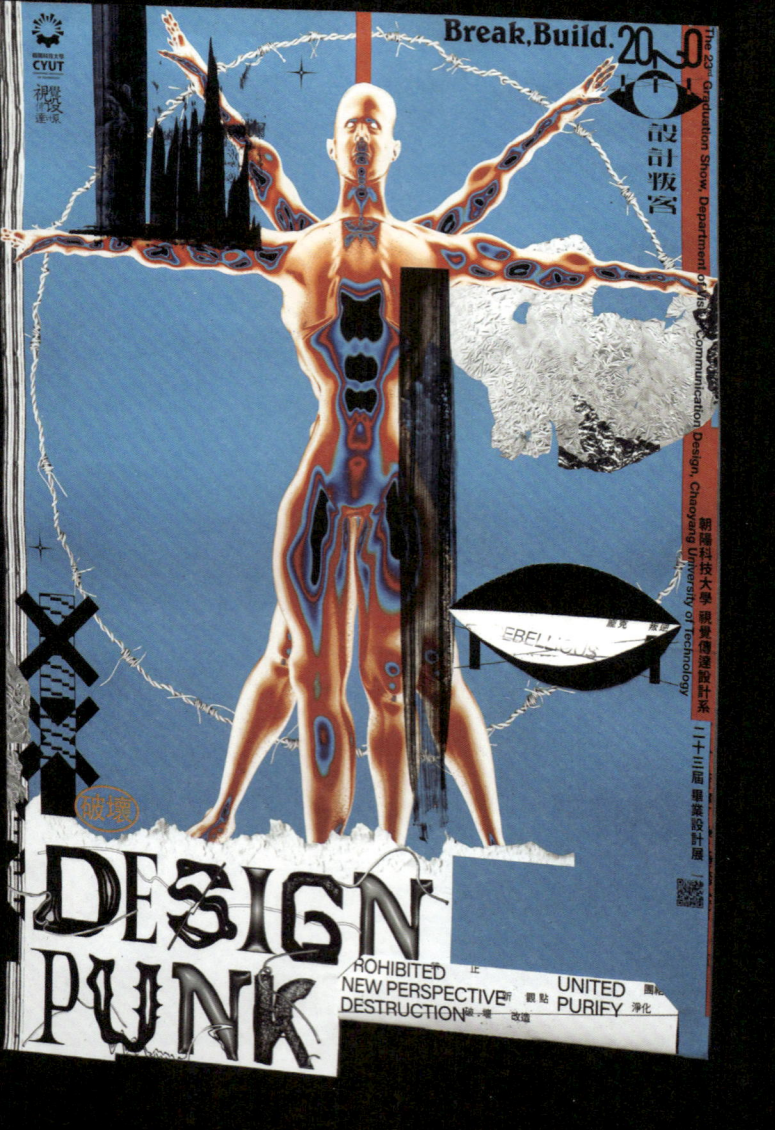

DESIGN PUNK

"Design Punk" was a mysterious emerging organization in 2020, responsible for the visual identity design of the graduation exhibition of the Department of Visual Communication Design at Chaoyang University of Technology. Their slogan, "Break, Build," embodies the concept that destruction leads to creation. The overall concept conveys that every work has its unique highlights. In this era, innovation can only be achieved by breaking away from conformity and norms and daring to think outside the box.

Designer: Yi-Ju Liao, Weiguang Wu, Ying-Syuan Lu, Hsin-Yi Shih, Chi-Chun Chiu, Tung-Nan Hu

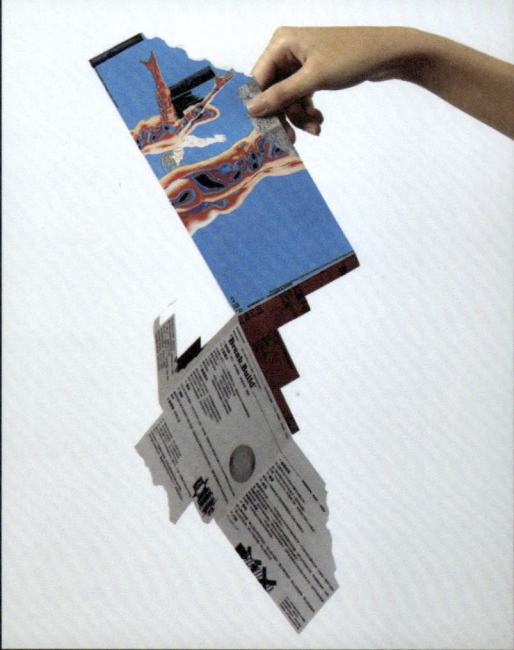

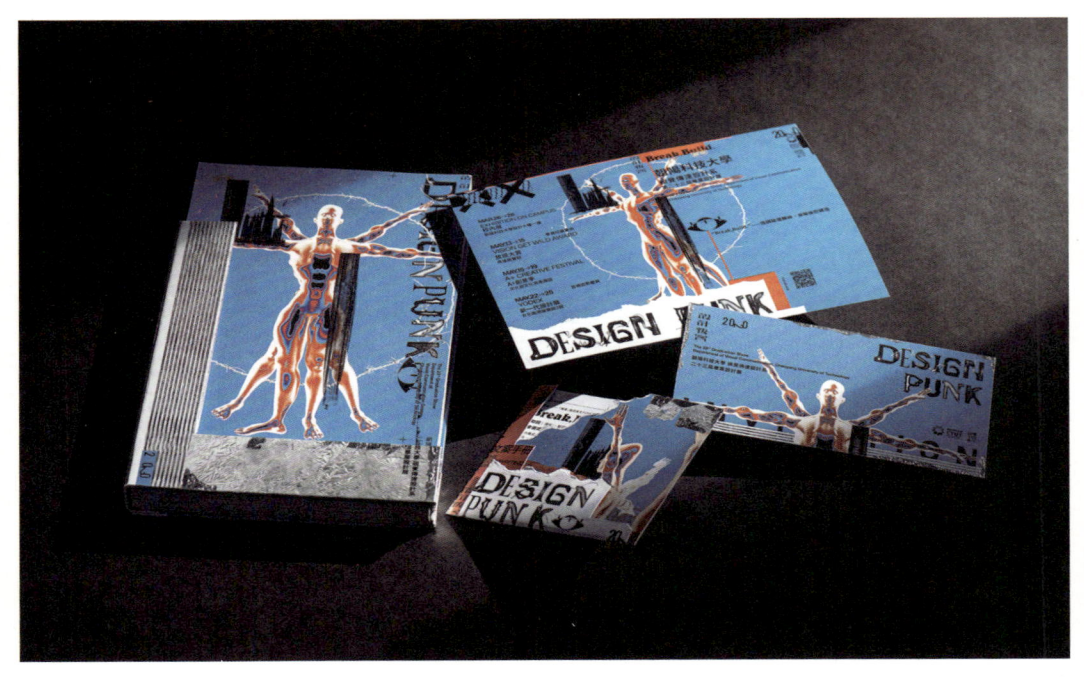

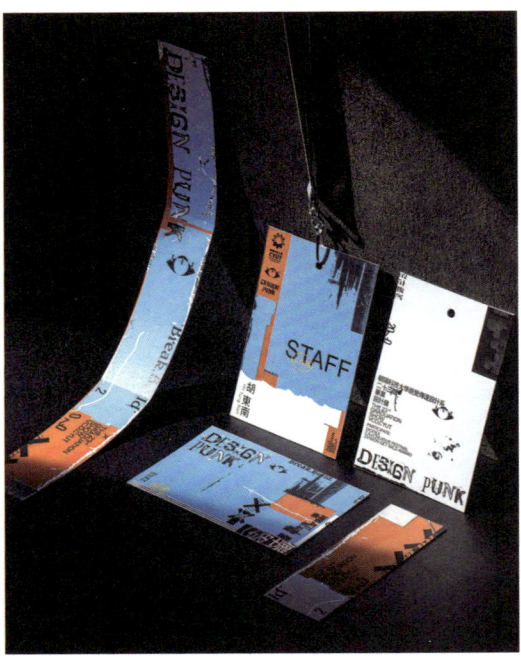

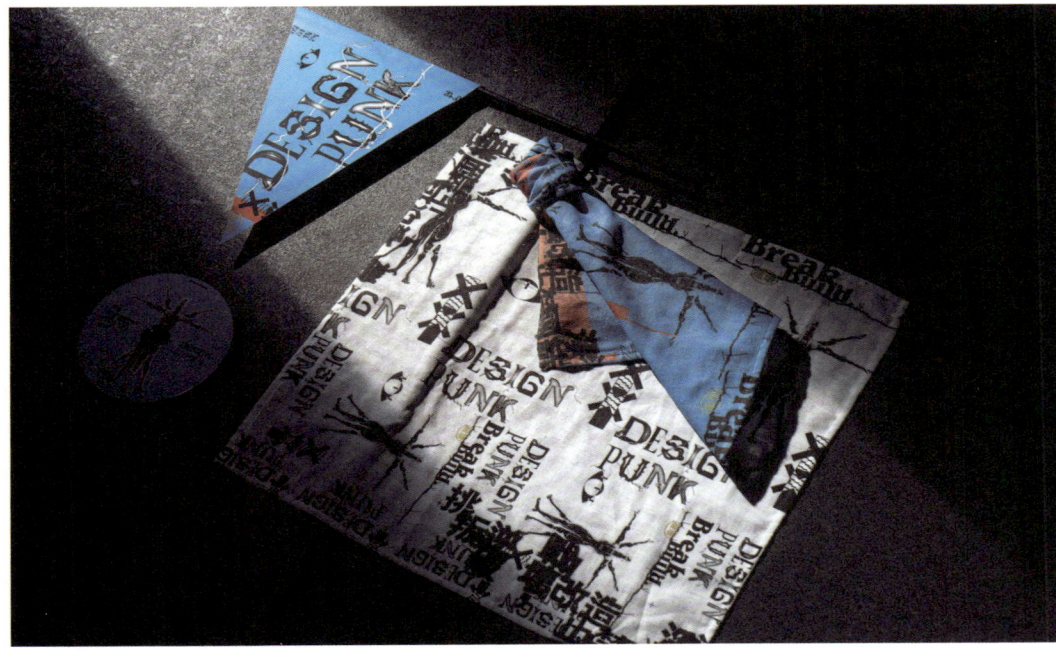

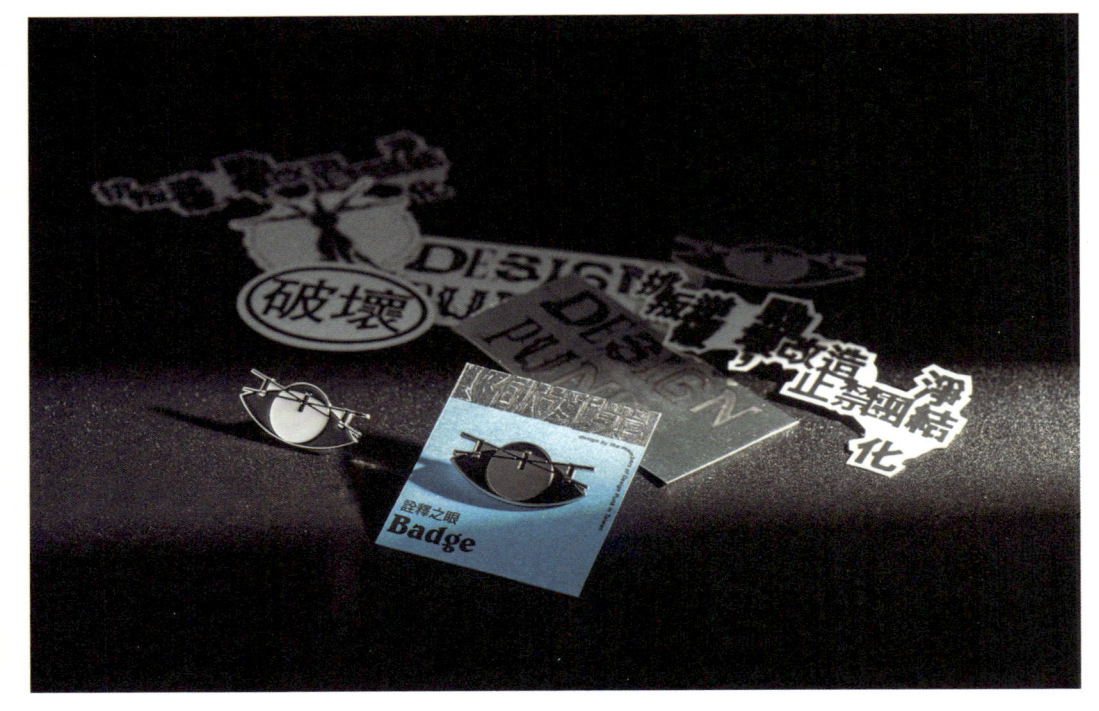

▼ **Inspiration:**
Cyberpunk, New Wave Sci-Fi from the 1960s to the 1970s

▼ **Elements:**
In production, the spirit of punk is embodied in the visual design, symbols, fonts, and layout, with a focus on breaking through conventional thinking. Materials are experimented with using computer computation, image synthesis, scratching, tearing, and other methods to create images with destructive power. Some finished pieces require viewers to tear or fold them to reveal their hidden appearance, creating different viewing experiences while breaking conventions.

▼ **Fonts:**
Source Han Sans, NOTO Sans

▼ **Layout:**
By distorting the golden ratio inherent in humanoid forms and deliberately unbalancing arrangements, the design employs principles of aesthetics while juxtaposing diverse techniques and contrasting hues. This approach seeks to achieve balance within chaos, construct new perspectives, and foster a new generation of design innovation.

#RetroFuturismDesignTalk

1. "Retro" and "futuristic" are two seemingly contradictory design elements. How do you find a balance between them in your designs? Are there specific design projects or cases that you believe best showcase the tension between retro and futuristic? Please share your insights.

Angello Torres (from Studio Angello Torres)
They are not contradictory design elements; rather, they represent different visual languages used to tell a story. I believe the literal interpretation of both concepts, "past" and "future," leads us to the misconception that they are contradictory. In design, there are numerous realms where retro and futuristic styles coexist harmoniously, such as Vaporwave, Retrowave, Steampunk, City Pop, and more.

Arrivedlate
It often depends on the client's vision, the target audience, and the overall message we aim to convey. While each one will be different and on a case-by-case basis, I find that exploring this tension in diverse projects allows for a more nuanced understanding of how these elements can complement each other. It's an ongoing exploration that evolves with the unique demands of each design endeavor.

Brando Corradini
The resurgence of retro design in new graphic trends may seem contradictory at first glance. However, it's the objects and motifs from the past that lend uniqueness and a touch of sophisticated elegance to contemporary contexts, emphasizing form over substance. Furthermore, the vintage style exudes charm and originality, offering the flexibility to mix and match graphics and motifs as desired.

Diego L Rodriguez (Paranoidme)
Since we began using the Internet as a tool to record historic events, classify and define how our world works, and connect with people from around the globe, I believe everything is blending together in a new form. "Retro" or "futuristic" are simple tags that make it easier for humans to classify something, but as a creative, I draw inspiration from everywhere. I don't mind if I fall into one classification or another, but I do believe that everything we do for the rest of this century will be defined by everything we have already done in the past. We can see this trend in fashion all the time. On the other hand, I think it's a positive sign to delve into the past and attempt to understand the messages that past generations have left for us. It's a way of recognizing creativity, innovation, and revolutionary ideas from a time when the world was not as oversaturated and people's imaginations were entirely different.

Ginko
I was portraying an imaginary scene. Mixing old and new items might be a good way to distort the sense of time and present fiction.

Helen Rabbitte (from Hello Rabbit Design)
For me, balanced Retro-Futurism design involves blending elements from the past with visions of the future. I tend to use objects, patterns, or textures from past decades but update them with contemporary typography, colors, or iconography. For example, in the *TS7-Emotion* artwork, I used a vintage television set but paired it with a vibrant gradient, scribble, and modern typeface to create tension between the past and the future. The same goes for the *Joe Kay* poster, which combines a vintage TV set with 80s-style orbs, a 70s strippling effect, and a contemporary layout and font combination. (refer to p. 127)

Indego design
Balancing retro and futuristic elements in my designs involves a strategic blend of nostalgic references with forward-thinking aesthetics. I aim to seamlessly integrate vintage and modern elements to create a harmonious fusion.

IGNORANCE1
I think that this is the challenge I face every time I want to design artwork. Sometimes I fail; sometimes I am able to put these elements together in a good way. I don't have a specific example, but trust me, some people thought that most of my artworks were real products, so I believe I've been pretty clever in finding the balance.

Isaiah Worrington (from Cyberdreams)
As a creative individual, I believe my ideas are deeply rooted in the fusion of retro and futuristic aesthetics. Drawing inspiration from various concepts of the past, I reinvent them with my unique perspective. One artist who epitomizes this delicate balance is Hajime Sorayama. His work, particularly the use of chrome material combined with robotic humanoids, embodies Retro-Futurism. In my approach to projects, I draw from this dual influence, delving into the nostalgia of retro elements while infusing a forward-thinking, futuristic twist. It's a creative journey that involves bridging the gap between the past and the future, resulting in designs that are both timeless and cutting-edge.

KEVLAR:ESTUDIO
Let's replace "retro" and "futuristic" with "organic/analog" and "artificial/computerized," concepts that better encapsulate our work. We perceive these not as opposing forces but rather as complementary elements. While embracing new technologies and information systems, we remain anchored in the material realm, emphasizing human connection and empathy. Understanding these dual realms as interconnected is essential to our approach. In essence, we hold that the future remains within our grasp. Despite concerns about the dehumanizing effects of technology, we maintain a human-centered perspective. This philosophy shapes how we integrate organic forms with geometric planes, creating compositions that harmonize both natural and digital elements.

Lo.Dycha
The theme of Retro-Futurism typically involves expressing people's fantasies about the future using styles, techniques, and mindsets from the past, such as Steampunk. However, this project is the opposite. (refer to p. 132) In the past, many designs, especially in terms of color, were limited by printing technology and could not be fully expressed. This project uses modern printing capabilities to present past graphic design aesthetics.

Onion Design Associates
While it may seem contradictory, that's what makes it interesting. In every generation, people

tend to have a romanticized vision of the future while simultaneously feeling nostalgic for the past. It's a way of escaping the present. I've also noticed that in the past, the future was always envisioned as a utopia, whereas today, people often see the future as a dystopia or a wasteland.

Yi-Ju Liao (from Design Punk)

Finding the balance between retro and futuristic elements in design is crucial for creating a unique fusion effect. This involves blending classic motifs, colors, and shapes with modern materials, techniques, and structures while retaining the core characteristics of retro design. Meanwhile, introducing contemporary nuances and carefully balancing color selection are essential. Moreover, integrating diverse cultural elements can also break traditional boundaries, resulting in designs that are both distinctive and rich in depth. By drawing inspiration from various cultures, you can create designs that are diverse and multidimensional.

YU CAI

Artworks encompass various aspects and can reflect two elements from different perspectives. The retro aspect of my work is visual and aesthetic, primarily manifested through color palettes, small elements, and details, such as the mentioned Vaporwave elements. The futuristic sense is primarily conveyed through composition, architectural structures, the direction of animation, and the scenes depicted.

3% Design Studio

The past and the future are not opposing forces, nor are they at opposite ends of time. Our contemporary perspective allows us to see both the past and future as part of our vision. They blend together, intertwining and advancing us toward higher levels. This is the essence of Retro-Futurism. Designers don't need to seek balance deliberately; our current perspective embodies that balance.

2. Are there any retro elements that you find to have particularly "classic" or timeless qualities, allowing them to persist in contemporary and future designs?

Angello Torres (from Studio Angello Torres)

The miscellanea (dots, lines, shapes, etc.) are timeless elements. While in retro styles they may be more focused on ornamentation, nowadays they are extensively utilized to create movement and depth in digital designs. Additionally, certain combinations of retro-saturated colors remain timeless. Nowadays, they are frequently employed in branding identities associated with blockchain and NFT technologies.

Arrivedlate

In my opinion, the grid is a timeless element that is typically associated with the retro aesthetics and will always help to enhance a design. Its versatility is apparent, being able to serve not only as a decorative element but also as a means to create depth in the overall design. I foresee that this retro element will withstand the test of time, transitioning into contemporary and future designs.

Brando Corradini

There is an almost limitless array of inspirations available, spanning from the 1930s to the 1980s. The choice depends on the composition you want to obtain and your tastes. However, incorporating retro aesthetics into modern contexts requires careful attention and the skill to harmonize various elements. Precisely for this reason, vintage appears to be a comfort style that allows you to face the uncertainties and evolution of the contemporary world, but it cannot be adopted in an approximate manner.

Diego L Rodriguez (Paranoidme)

I really appreciate analog noise and the textures we can observe in old books and magazines. The grainy aspect of films from the 80s and 90s is still fantastic to me as well. The depth of the colors was really rich, and I think that has been somewhat lost with so many digital advances and color grading post-production processes. We can see now how some directors—and also some music videos and commercials—embrace that approach, and I love it. I also admire how typography was treated back then. The sense of space and readability were unmatched.

Ginko

The Yin-yang symbol (Tai Chi symbol) seems to be timeless.

Helen Rabbitte (from Hello Rabbit Design)

I think classic typefaces work really well when combined with contemporary design. For example, 1920s Art Deco fonts or typefaces taken from 1950s diner signs can add a nostalgic feel, whilst classic serif fonts can add a classic, eloquent touch. Besides, retro textures that mimic old print techniques add a tactile, nostalgic quality to contemporary digital designs as well as make them feel more considered, human and hand made.

Indego design

Certain retro elements possess timeless qualities, making them enduring in contemporary and future designs. Classic typography, simple geometric patterns, and elegant serif fonts are examples of retro elements that maintain relevance and evoke a sense of nostalgia. Their timeless appeal lies in their ability to seamlessly adapt to different design contexts while consistently conveying a sense of classic sophistication.

IGNORANCE1

In my case, I believe that stamps and plastic bags are the perfect examples—and I think I was one of the first to reintroduce or invent these mockups. Most people don't use them anymore because they are no longer trendy, but I would like to stay true to my style. The fonts, when placed inaccurately and/or stretched, have a very "classic" appeal to me, with a special mention to the Chinese and Japanese characters that I love to incorporate into every artwork.

Isaiah Worrington (from Cyberdreams)

The timeless allure of chrome material is something that has endured through the ages, consistently captivating audiences. Similarly, in my own creative journey, I have a fondness for incorporating elements like skies, hearts, angel wings, swords, and more. These classic motifs, reminiscent of retro art, continue to find a place in my work, with each iteration becoming a reinvention of the familiar. The incorporation of these elements is my way of paying homage to the artistic legacy of the past while infusing contemporary energy into the mix. Skies, hearts, and angel wings evoke a sense of nostalgia, and yet, with each project, I strive to breathe new life into these timeless symbols. It's an ongoing exploration of how the familiar can be transformed and made relevant again.

KEVLAR:ESTUDIO

When encountering retro typography that adorned brands and packaging from one's childhood, a sense of safety and comfort often ensues. It harkens back to a time when options were fewer and uncertainties perhaps less prevalent. Beyond nostalgia's application as a marketing tool, it taps into a sensitive chord within individuals. By blending these nostalgic images, typographies, and color palettes with futuristic elements, an intriguing aesthetic limbo emerges. Some retro elements, in our view, stand the test of time: sans-serif Neo-grotesque typefaces, collage techniques, textured paper with its inherent imperfections, retro packaging iconography, the CMYK color system, and analog forms of photography and illustration using pigments, graphite, ink, and the like. We believe that by persisting in the use of these elements due to their nostalgic resonance, they will evolve into classics in the future we shape. However, it's crucial to recognize that new "classics" will emerge, and only those most aligned with the messages they convey will endure.

Lo.Dycha

Contemporary design heavily relies on digital products, as we are living in a digital era. If we were to define what is "classic," I would consider material things to be crucial in the creative process, whether in the present or future.

Onion Design Associates

Every design is trendy and new when it's first released. Over time, though, it becomes dated and may even seem old-fashioned. If you wait long enough, every design eventually becomes a "classic." It's a natural life cycle for designs.

Thomas Merceron

The elements that often reappear are megacities, overdeveloped vehicles, and a post-apocalyptic environment. It's overproduction at the expense of a climate that has become threatening.

Yi-Ju Liao (from Design Punk)

I believe there are no absolutes in design. Every retro element from the past has its unique significance and reasons for existence, serving as crucial starting points that influence contemporary and even future developments. Therefore, as long as one can connect their relevance with the present and future, any element can become a timeless classic.

YU CAI

I doubt the authenticity of the word "timelessness." I believe everything is subject to change, development, and flux. If there seems to be something timeless, it simply means the timeline hasn't been long enough. Frankly speaking, the style or artists I currently admire may change as my own understanding evolves.

3% Design Studio

Elements deemed classic or timeless are already solidified and static, while each of us, as tiny individuals, actually integrates into our own or our era's understanding within the retro movement. Therefore, we all contribute to the evolution of these elements. Ultimately, these changes contribute to the development of the elements themselves. Hence, they may not truly possess eternal qualities unless they have gradually been abandoned by people.

3. How do you see Retro-Futurism design interacting with contemporary society and culture? What kind of impact does it have on the audience?

Angello Torres (from Studio Angello Torres)

It is a difficult question, as in the current societal context, the general focus is on other types of interactions and concerns such as inflation or wars. However, within optimism and progress, looking at the past is always beneficial to avoid repeating the same mistakes. For designers, new AI design tools have been a great help in imagining Retro-Futurism designs directly from a screen, without the need for a large budget or extensive projects. Additionally, an aesthetics is emerging from decentralized platforms (Cryptocurrency, NFT) that utilize Retro-Futurism design to distinguish themselves from the current image of the markets.

Arrivedlate

Adapting to various facets of our culture, particularly within the multimedia realm, involves considerations of music, TV, cinema, and more. It's even starting to make its way back into consumer goods, creating an inevitable connection to design. The saying "all old things are new again" feels particularly spot-on, especially with the resurgence of "nostalgic technology" and the overall allure of familiarity. On a grander scale, I would like to see a similar impact that affects our ability to make better-informed decisions, appreciating what we already have, especially in a hyper-consumption world.

Brando Corradini

Even in the realm of graphics and design, trends can ebb and flow depending on fashion, the specific software utilized, and emerging technologies. For instance, the proliferation of video modes has facilitated the development of increasingly sophisticated animations. Among the latest graphic trends, one can observe the fusion of retro aesthetics with modern elements. Additionally, there's been an evolution of stock images towards more intricate flat design solutions capable of seamlessly integrating diverse styles, shadows, hues, and textures. Another emerging trend involves blending illustrative elements from past eras with the contemporary flat style, which are now regarded as retro details.

Diego L Rodriguez (Paranoidme)

While blending the past and the future may sound cliché, it certainly helps to communicate with millions of people, as this fusion appeals to a broader audience. What I also appreciate about it is that incorporating elements from the past may encourage a return to craftsmanship, durability, and timeless design principles—qualities that promote sustainability in today's products, which I believe is essential. By continuing to merge the past and the future, we create a bridge to educate societies and share knowledge of earlier times. Aesthetically, of course, it's very interesting, but if it also helps in learning from our mistakes, it would be a great sign to implement progress and technology to avoid certain issues. That way, I truly believe we can build a better world and a brighter future.

Ginko

The Retro-Futurism style symbolizes the desire to imagine a better future. I believe it generally conveys an optimistic spirit.

**Helen Rabbitte
(from Hello Rabbit Design)**

By blending familiar retro styles with futuristic elements, I hope to tap into a collective nostalgia, evoking memories of a "better" or more hopeful past. I think we often romanticize "the good old days," so it often gives us a sense of optimism that contrasts with current societal anxieties and offers a hopeful perspective on the future.

Indego design

Retro-Futurism design dynamically interacts with contemporary society and culture, serving as a bridge between the past and the future. It evokes nostalgia while embracing modernity, sparking both familiarity and innovation simultaneously. This duality captures the audience's attention, offering a unique visual language that reflects historical references and forward-thinking concepts. The result is a compelling blend of comfort and curiosity, engaging the audience by connecting them to the past while inspiring fascination with the possibilities of the future.

**Isaiah Worrington
(from Cyberdreams)**

I've observed a fascinating dynamic in audience reactions. On one hand, some perceive it as groundbreaking and otherworldly, akin to a journey into the unknown. On the flip side, others find it somewhat elusive, perhaps even incomprehensible. What intrigues me is that this diversity in interpretation is not a flaw but rather a feature.

KEVLAR: ESTUDIO

We believe that the impact is inherently positive in some regard, as it indicates an interest in what viewers are witnessing and prompts reflection on the hidden aspects within our pieces. In other words, it does not go unnoticed within contemporary society. Furthermore, we attribute a portion of this positive impact to the reflective nature of our work. The abstraction prevalent in our pieces creates an air of mystery, eliciting emotions and thoughts beyond the realm of familiarity for some individuals. These abstract elements possess a significant power to evoke reactions, underscoring the deliberate nature of their design.

IGNORANCE1

I think it's cool to preserve this style to let all the young designers out there know which styles have been developed in the past. The impact on society, in general, should be considered as a reminder of design roots.

Lo.Dycha

An important aspect of Retro-Futurism is "imagination," which I believe encourages people to dare to envision the future.

Onion Design Associates

People love Retro-Futurism design because it combines old memories with futuristic ideas in a cool way. It mixes the past with what people thought the future would be like, using sleek lines and bright colors. This style makes us feel nostalgic for a time when the future seemed full of exciting possibilities. Our memories of the past blend with the design's bold look, creating a comforting feeling. Retro-Futurism design takes us on a journey between the past and the future, making us rethink progress and technology. It's like a bridge that connects what was and what could be, giving us a visually interesting and sentimental experience.

Thomas Merceron

Retro-Futurism shows us what we thought we would become. It reminds us of past ideals and the anxieties that were supposed to be our reality. Retro-Futurism is an exaggerated present, serving as a point of comparison with our contemporary world. It brings nostalgia, reassurance, and imagination for the future we create.

**Yi-Ju Liao
(from Design Punk)**

Retro-Futurism combines elements from the past and the future, resonating emotionally with people by evoking nostalgia or curiosity. It blends diverse eras and cultures, breaking traditional boundaries and promoting diversity. Through reinterpreting history and imagining the future, Retro-Futurism inspires creativity and progress. This design style prompts deep reflections on the past, present, and future, offering a unique aesthetic experience and meaningful impacts on emotions and thoughts.

YU CAI

I believe this style fully reflects the current technological and humanistic environment, manifesting in various aspects of life. The rapid development of technology brings convenience to people's lives but also leads to some anxiety and discomfort. I think Retro-Futurism is a long-term artistic style because in the era of big data, technological advancements will increasingly surpass our imagination, and this aesthetics will become more relatable. However, its expression forms will continue to evolve.

3% Design Studio

I believe the sense of time is the most compelling aspect of Retro-Futurism. When designers create, they are grounded in the current perspective and the spirit of contemporary people. The designer's perspective is in the present tense. Meanwhile, the audience's attention is liberated from the present tense because of the artwork. The perspective is holographic, no longer confined to a specific narrow time range but rather sees an exit in retrospection. Time seems to form a loop, leading to endless surrealistic imaginations of the world.

Pixel Art

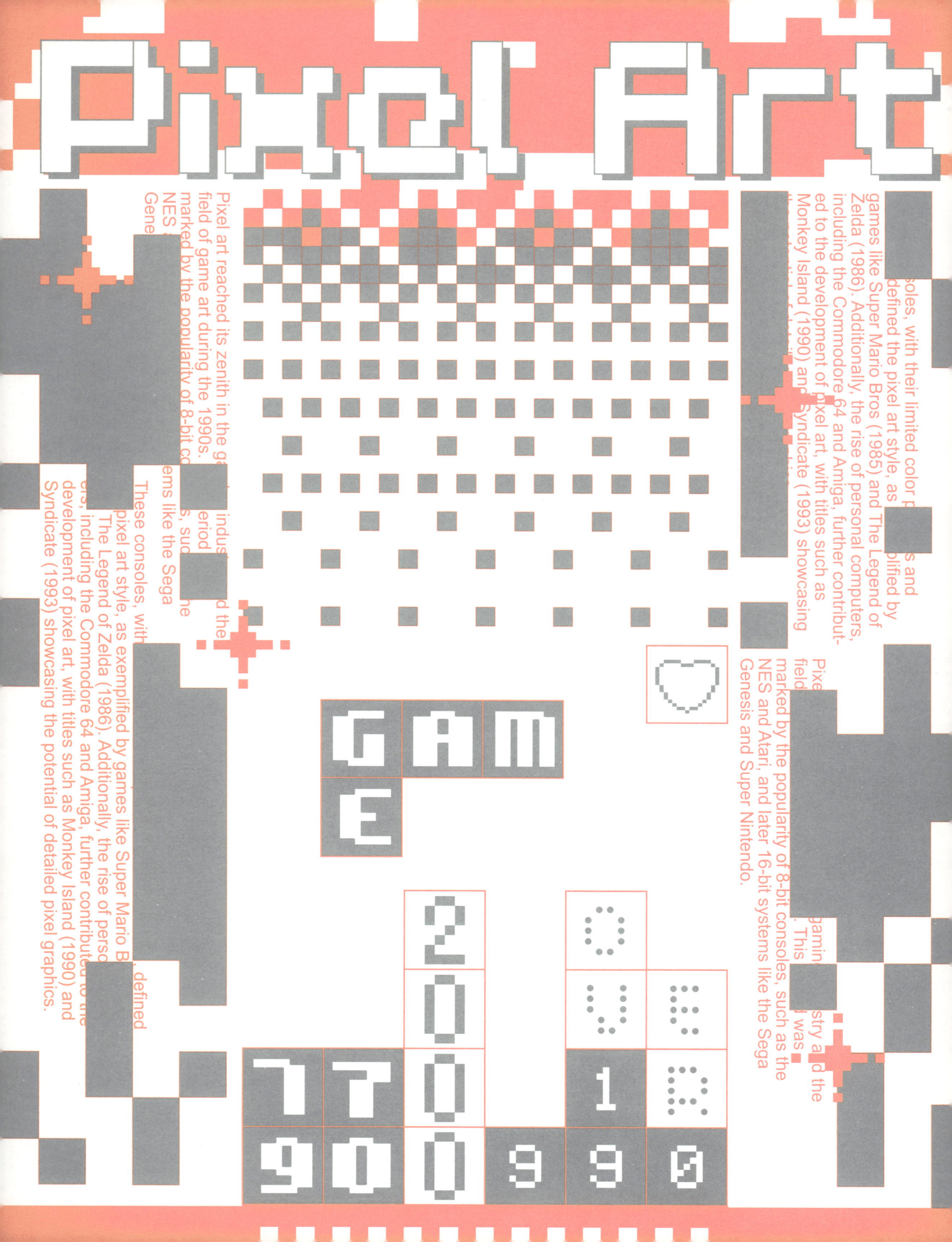

Pixel art reached its zenith in the gaming industry and the field of game art during the 1990s. This period was marked by the popularity of 8-bit consoles, such as the NES and Atari, and later 16-bit systems like the Sega Genesis and Super Nintendo.

These consoles, with their limited color palettes and pixel art style, as exemplified by games like Super Mario Bros (1985) and The Legend of Zelda (1986). Additionally, the rise of personal computers, including the Commodore 64 and Amiga, further contributed to the development of pixel art, with titles such as Monkey Island (1990) and Syndicate (1993) showcasing the potential of detailed pixel graphics.

consoles, with their limited color palettes and defined the pixel art style, as exemplified by games like Super Mario Bros (1985) and The Legend of Zelda (1986). Additionally, the rise of personal computers, including the Commodore 64 and Amiga, further contributed to the development of pixel art, with titles such as Monkey Island (1990) and Syndicate (1993) showcasing

Pixel gaming field marked by the popularity of 8-bit consoles, such as the NES and Atari, and later 16-bit systems like the Sega Genesis and Super Nintendo.

GAME

2000   1990
1990

DEVELOPMENT HISTORY

1970s: Early Beginnings

Pixel Art originated in the 8-bit and 16-bit game consoles and computers, where technical limitations necessitated the use of pixel points to represent images. Game developers and artists had to create game visuals and characters using the limited pixel resources at their disposal. Early games like *Pong* (1972) and *Space Invaders* (1978) used simple pixel graphics due to hardware limitations.

1980s-1990s: Golden Age

Pixel Art reached its zenith in the gaming industry and the field of game art during the 1990s. This period was marked by the popularity of 8-bit consoles, such as the NES and Atari, and later 16-bit systems like the Sega Genesis and Super Nintendo. These consoles, with their limited color palettes and resolution, defined the Pixel Art style, as exemplified by games like *Super Mario Bros* (1985) and *The Legend of Zelda* (1986). Additionally, the rise of personal computers, including the Commodore 64 and Amiga, further contributed to the development of Pixel Art, with titles such as *Monkey Island* (1990) and *Syndicate* (1993) showcasing the potential of detailed pixel graphics.

2000s to Present: Revival and Expansion

While Pixel Art saw a decline in popularity during the late 20th and early 21st centuries, it later experienced a revival and found new life within indie gaming and Internet culture. Artists began applying Pixel Art to various domains, including games, animation, illustration, and Internet emojis, creating unique visual experiences. For example, games like *Minecraft* (2011), *Terraria* (2011), and *Stardew Valley* (2016) embraced Pixel Art, often represent a nostalgic stylistic choice. Additionally, Pixel Art expanded to dynamic animations and 3D pixel design, further demonstrating its versatility and enduring appeal.

Contemporary Era: Diversity and Innovation

Modern Pixel Art often incorporates elements of other styles and technologies, such as higher resolutions, animations, and interactive art. As a retro and nostalgic style, Pixel Art continues to exert influence in the realms of gaming and media.

PIXEL ART: MODERN VISUAL STYLE GUIDE

ELEMENTS

KEYWORDS

1. **TECHNO RETRO STYLE**
2. **GRID-BASED LAYOUT**
3. **NINTENDO AESTHETICS**
4. **STRUCTURED PRECISION**

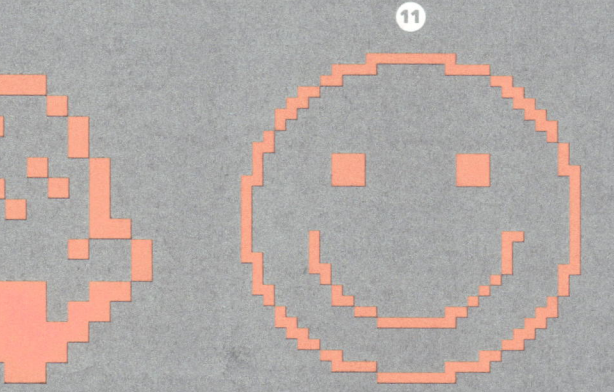

1. Heart Shape
2. Bow Tie
3. Plants
4. PC Interface
5. TV Static
6. Two-Way Arrow
7. Chat Bubble
8. Pixelated Numbers
9. Warning Sign
10. Hand-Shaped Arrow
11. Smiley Face

FONTS BPdots Grixel Kyrou WG Prophit bd TinyFont Perfect DOS VGA 437 Hannelore Karma Press Start 2P skeletor stance BPdots Condensed Square Jacquarda Bastarda 9 DIGITAL CREAM

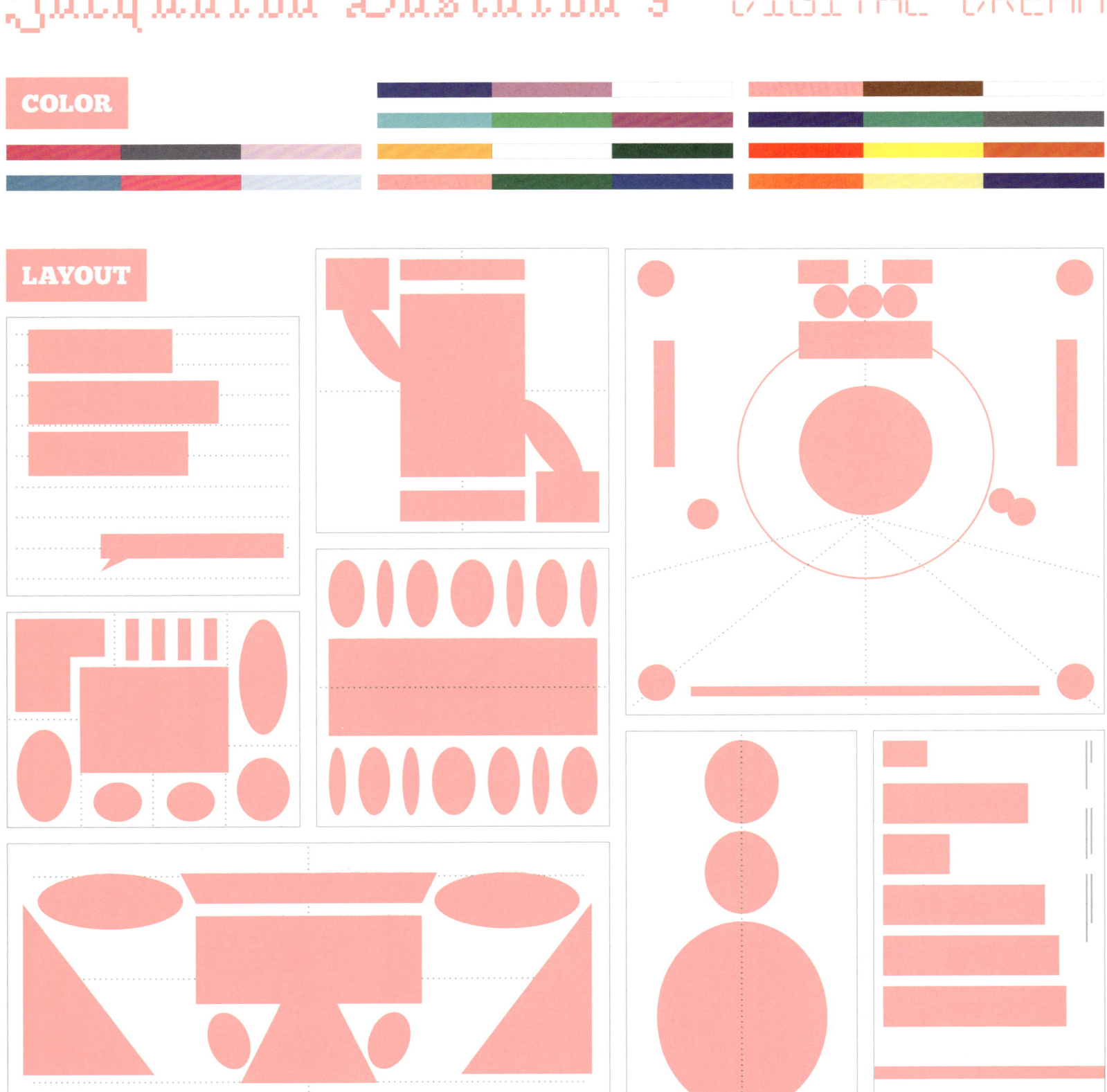

COLOR

LAYOUT

Calling

ANARRATOR

Graduated from the China Academy of Art, the artist mainly focuses on Pixel Art, encompassing digital painting and the materialization of this style. The creations predominantly feature shades of pink, incorporating diverse communication tools like beepers, cell phones, and flip phones, along with elements such as ribbons, bows, chains, and keys, symbolizing physical or spiritual connections within the artwork. The prevailing theme in the current creations is "love."

1 The Charm of Pixels

ANARRATOR, a dedicated pixel artist, initially chose pixels as the fundamental elements of her illustration work as a means to quickly capture conceptual ideas. Over time, she realized that Pixel Art offered the highest compatibility with the images she wished to present and the content she aimed to convey. Once, there was a phase where she was fascinated by creating Pixel Art renditions of Shōwa-era idol singers like Akina Nakamori and Kyoko Koizumi. Given that the Shōwa era represents retro aesthetics, using Pixel Art for these portraits felt highly appropriate. Starting from there, she began creating more works centered around the theme of "love," feeling a certain connection. This connection has inspired her to consistently engage in creating Pixel Art, treating it as an ongoing research topic.

For ANARRATOR, the unique challenge and joy of Pixel Art lie in its precision: changing the position of a single pixel can significantly alter the visual perception of the content. She often contemplates the arrangement of tens or even hundreds of pixels, a recurring source of creative dilemmas that also fuels her passion for the medium. When faced with the challenge, ANARRATO's approach is to revise repetitively until the desired perception is achieved, a method that is deliberate despite its apparent clumsiness. After completing the initial line drawing, she will create a backup, allowing her to refine other parts of the image while continually comparing and adjusting the original. For complex scenes, she will back up different sections of the line drawing to provide flexibility for modifications or rollbacks. When faced with challenging decisions, ANARRATOR will temporarily set aside the particular drawing, work on others, and return to it after some time. This methodical approach ensures that each pixel is placed with precision, ultimately contributing to the harmonious balance in her Pixel Art creations.

Besides, Pixel Art, characterized by its lack of smooth curves and the simulation of curvature through straight lines, adds a certain restraint and associative element to ANARRATOR's visuals. This technique aligns with her preference for not actively expressing enthusiasm or positive emotions in her work, resulting in creations that remain relatively calm. ANARRATOR's philosophy is to avoid burdening viewers, striving instead for a visual experience that is contemplative and serene. Through the meticulous organization of pixels, the artwork communicates a sense of calm restraint, inviting viewers to engage with her art without feeling overwhelmed.

2 The Re-Popularity of Pixel Art

Pixel Art, which originally emerged due to technological constraints, is experiencing a resurgence in the current era of high-definition visuals. ANARRATOR pointed out that the charm of Pixel Art lay in its ability to provide viewers with infinite imaginative space. The dynamic representation of pixels—where the flicker or movement of a single pixel can create different atmospheres—adds to its appeal. A few pixels, or even just one, can effectively represent a character, an object, a person, or a larger concept. The meaning conveyed by pixels depends on the creator's presentation and the viewer's interpretation, highlighting the unique and versatile nature of Pixel Art.

In role-playing games (RPG), for example, the pixelated figure on the screen, despite being less detailed than the character on the cartridge cover, becomes the player's enduring companion. This simple representation allows players to mentally associate it with the more detailed characters, enhancing their sense of immersion. According to ANARRATOR, this moderate visual association heightens the player's engagement and emotional connection. Thus, Pixel Art's re-popularity

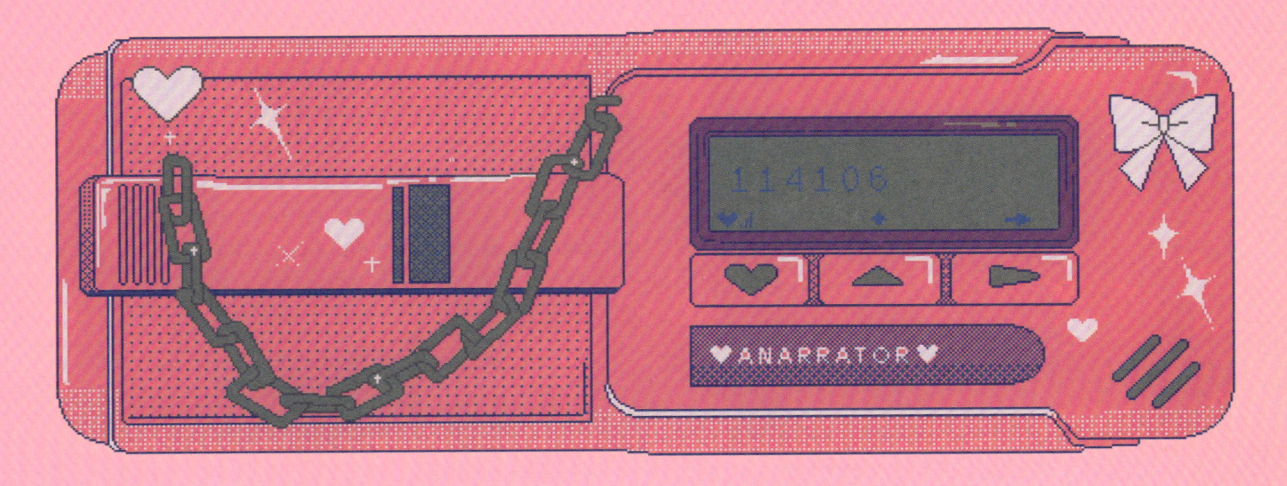

ANARRATOR Pixel Art

can be attributed to its unique ability to evoke imagination and emotional resonance through minimalist and dynamic visual expressions.

3 Loading Past Memory Card

In the design series *Save Your Love*, ANARRATOR created a nostalgic atmosphere by fictionalizing a pixel-style game and incorporating elements resembling vintage displays and floppy disks. Despite first encountering computers during the era of CDs and USB drives, ANARRATOR's childhood involved drawing on unwanted floppy disks, which felt more like playing with toys than actual use. This experience does not evoke nostalgia but instead serves as a symbol of "preservation" conceptual element for her. The limited storage space of floppy disks implies that love stored within them must be precious, encapsulating only love within that confined space. In contrast, modern phone memories, which easily reach 512GB or even 1TB, prompt ANARRATOR to question how much of that vast space is dedicated to essential content.

Meanwhile, in many of her design series, elements of past communication methods, such as flip phones and pagers, are present. She has expressed that past communication methods were more ideal, creating just the right distance between people. This nostalgic sentiment influences ANARRATOR's views on contemporary technology and social media. While modern social media allows for staying connected and communicating with more people, it also brings the drawback of information overload. ANARRATOR finds that the ease of information exchange has made not promptly checking and responding to messages a source of anxiety, making it challenging to find peaceful solitary moments. She also feels that social platforms are somewhat overused, offering excessive communication convenience, yet recognizes that this trend is unlikely to reverse. Consequently, ANARRATOR appreciates the unique restraint and romance of past communication methods, which influence her creative perspective.

This series imagines a non-existent pixel-style game called "Save Your Love," utilizing a 4:3 aspect ratio to simulate the display proportions of old monitors, serving as the foundation for the series. In the artwork, 3.5-inch floppy disks are used to symbolize the concept of "saving," with the later images expressing the theme of rescue in a simulated RPG battle style. The illustrator viewed saving and rescuing love as positive responses to the genuine and precious emotion of "love."

▼ Color Scheme:

- R231 G090 B155 / C002 M077 Y000 K000
- R085 G168 B200 / C065 M018 Y015 K000
- R194 G185 B219 / C027 M028 Y000 K000
- R248 G207 B225 / C000 M027 Y000 K000

Pixel Art — ANARRATOR

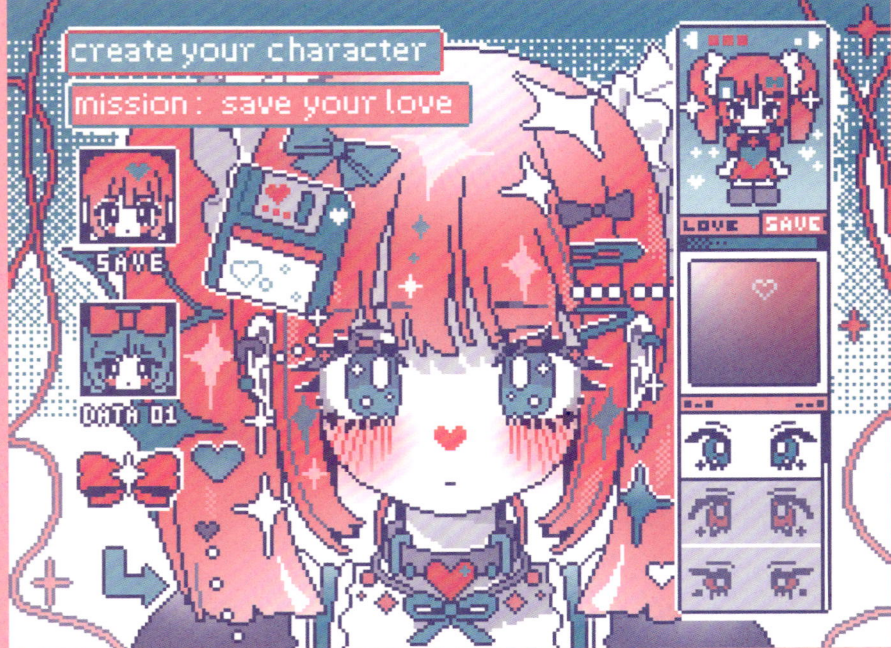

GOOD NIGHT EMAIL

PLEASE CONTACT ME

P.S. Welcome to the *family!*

They That Do

They That Do represents a cutting-edge agile studio that assembles bespoke teams from its creative community, delivering clients innovative, fresh, and exciting results. Dissatisfied with traditional studio practices and the inefficiencies stemming from multiple project managers and layers between creatives and clients, the team is dedicated to streamlined, well-researched ideas that evoke emotions. This commitment is underscored by compelling storytelling, fostering brand distinctiveness.

1 Rebranding Protein

Protein, a brand that spans multiple platforms in both the physical (studios) and digital realm (community/Discord), stands as the protagonist of this compelling rebranding project. They That Do chose pixels as the foundational elements in their design and illustration work, reflecting Protein's origins during the transformative era of Web1 in 1997. This pixelated aesthetics felt organic, especially since early client iterations were created on old devices with a naturally pixelated vibe. By revisiting the brand's roots, the team was able to craft a modern vision that remains true to its heritage.

The whole design layout departs from the constraints of early Pixel Art, embracing a more stylistic approach that intentionally overlapped certain elements, akin to the cascading and varied sizes and formats seen in modern social media emojis. This conceptual shift not only honored Protein's nostalgic 90s heritage but also positioned the brand for future growth and evolution, enhancing its visual identity to resonate with both past accomplishments and future aspirations.

Also, the pixelated aesthetics serves as an intriguing connection between the physical studio space (IRL) and the online community (URL) represented by platforms like Discord and WhatsApp. This bridging of worlds reflects Protein's desire to create a cohesive brand experience across both realms. Emotionally, the goal was to evoke joy and bring positive vibes, encapsulating all the great things that emerged from the vibrant and dynamic 90s era. The pixel style is intended to make people smile and feel a sense of nostalgia while simultaneously embracing modernity.

By adopting this pixelated art, They That Do successfully integrates the past with the present, creating a visual language that resonates with both older and newer generations. The choice to use pixels is not just about aesthetics but also about conveying a sense of continuity and evolution, celebrating the brand's journey from its inception to its current state. This approach highlights the timeless quality of Pixel Art, bridging the gap between eras and creating a cohesive brand identity that is both nostalgic and forward-looking.

2 Dynamic Visual Identity

They That Do's approach to crafting Protein's visual identity through a curated palette of assets reflects a deep understanding of bridging physical and digital spaces. The brand playbook, featuring bespoke emojis, ASCII-inspired patterns, and the thematic use of "me, you, us" to signify past, present, and future, serves as a testament to their thoughtful design process. These elements are meticulously chosen to convey the intersection of Protein Studios' physical co-working space (IRL) with its expanding online community (URL). Each component is designed not only for aesthetic appeal but also to provide a palette of elements that facilitates future growth, ensuring the brand never appears static and can be quickly grasped at a glance.

The playbook offers unparalleled flexibility and personality, akin to the customization options for phones in the 90s, where screens and downloadable assets could be personalized. In essence, the Protein playbook functions similarly—a collection of assets that possesses individual strength but, when brought together, create a sense of dynamism and movement. This mirrors the essence of Protein Studios, where diverse individuals converge to foster a vibrant community united by shared values and aspirations.

3 Timeless Appeal and Creative Flexibility

In exploring the renewed popularity of Pixel Art amidst today's high-definition visual landscape, They That Do identifies its timeless appeal and the creative freedom it affords designers. Originating as a technological limitation, Pixel Art now serves as a boundless canvas for expanding design boundaries in a structured yet flexible manner. This approach embraces "orderly disorder," allowing continual growth of the asset pack and playful experimentation with layout compositions. The pixel's inherent capability to incorporate less sharp imagery due to resolution becomes a strategic advantage, facilitating creative interpretations within the brand's design strategy.

The pixel aesthetics not only offers unique design flexibility but also evolves with the brand over time, enhancing its visual identity in dynamic ways. Beginning from a single pixel, designers can zoom in and out of layouts, refining and augmenting the pixel into a polished and progressive brand format. This approach embodies a forward-thinking philosophy, where the pixel serves as the foundational element that adapts and evolves alongside the brand's trajectory. This anti-brand sentiment encourages continual evolution rather than stagnation, enabling limitless opportunities in design while maintaining cohesion and seamlessness across brand imagery.

4 Views on Homogenization of Future Retro Design

That They Do perceives future retro design trends as a fertile ground for inspiration, provided they are approached with creativity and thoughtfulness. Retro design will pose no problem if designers learn from historical periods rather than copying them outright and presenting them as finished solutions. For That They Do, it is crucial to adapt and merge past aesthetics to carve a unique pathway and create something new. Such issue of homogenization is in fact a common problem in contemporary design, especially on certain websites where everyone seeks inspiration from the same content. This leads to a lack of diversity and originality. According to That They Do, the key to overcoming this issue lies in avoiding mere imitation and fostering creativity through a personalized design approach.

When it comes to incorporating influences from specific periods, That They Do emphasizes the importance of not merely copying past elements and assuming they'll look good. Instead, they advocate for borrowing from the past to create something relevant to the future. Their approach involves thoughtfully integrating historical elements to enhance engagement and captivate the intended audience. That They Do believes that the essence of innovation in design lies in making historical influences meaningful and resonant while ensuring the final product is fresh and contemporary. This method not only prevents the homogenization of design trends but also enriches the creative process, leading to unique and impactful outcomes.

PROTEIN STUDIOS REBRAND

Protein is an institution operating across various platforms, both physical (studios) and digital (community/Discord). The initial phase of the project involved revisiting their beginnings in '97 and envisioning their future trajectory. The outcome is a brand that seamlessly bridges the gap between the physical and digital realms, capable of evolving like a universe or ecosystem over time. Every aspect of the brand maintains a focus on the future while staying rooted in its origins. From icons for Discord to signage for their HQ, the project continues to evolve. The pixel aesthetic of the project originated from ASCII art and early computer programming research, merging with a gamification style inspired by tokens and early Atari games, encompassing both technical and playful aspects of the 80s and 90s.

Designer: Vincent Howcutt
Client: Protein Studios

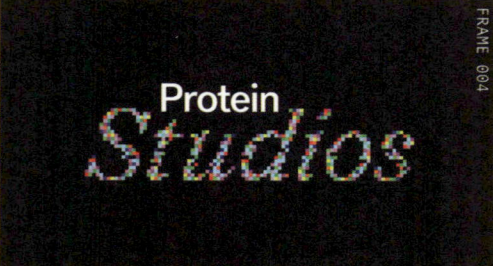

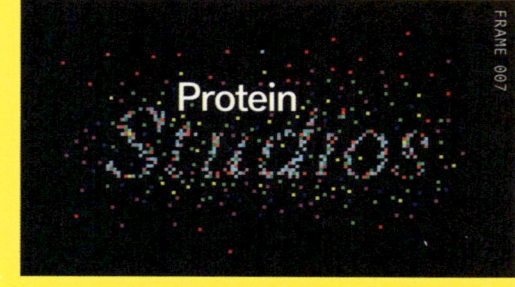

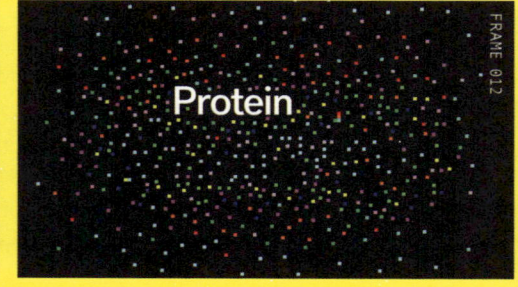

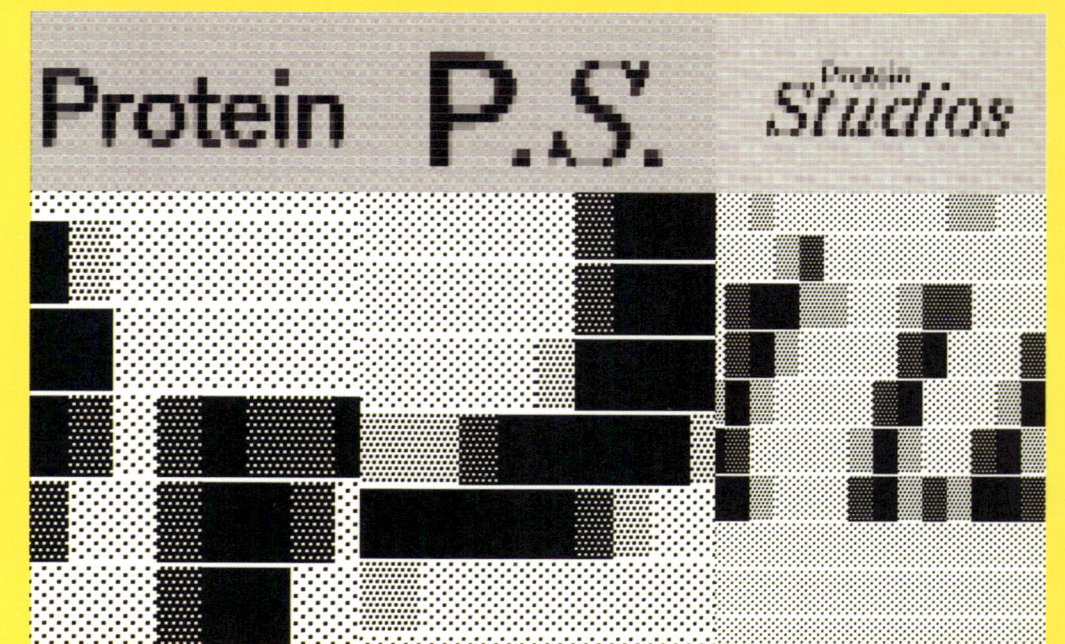

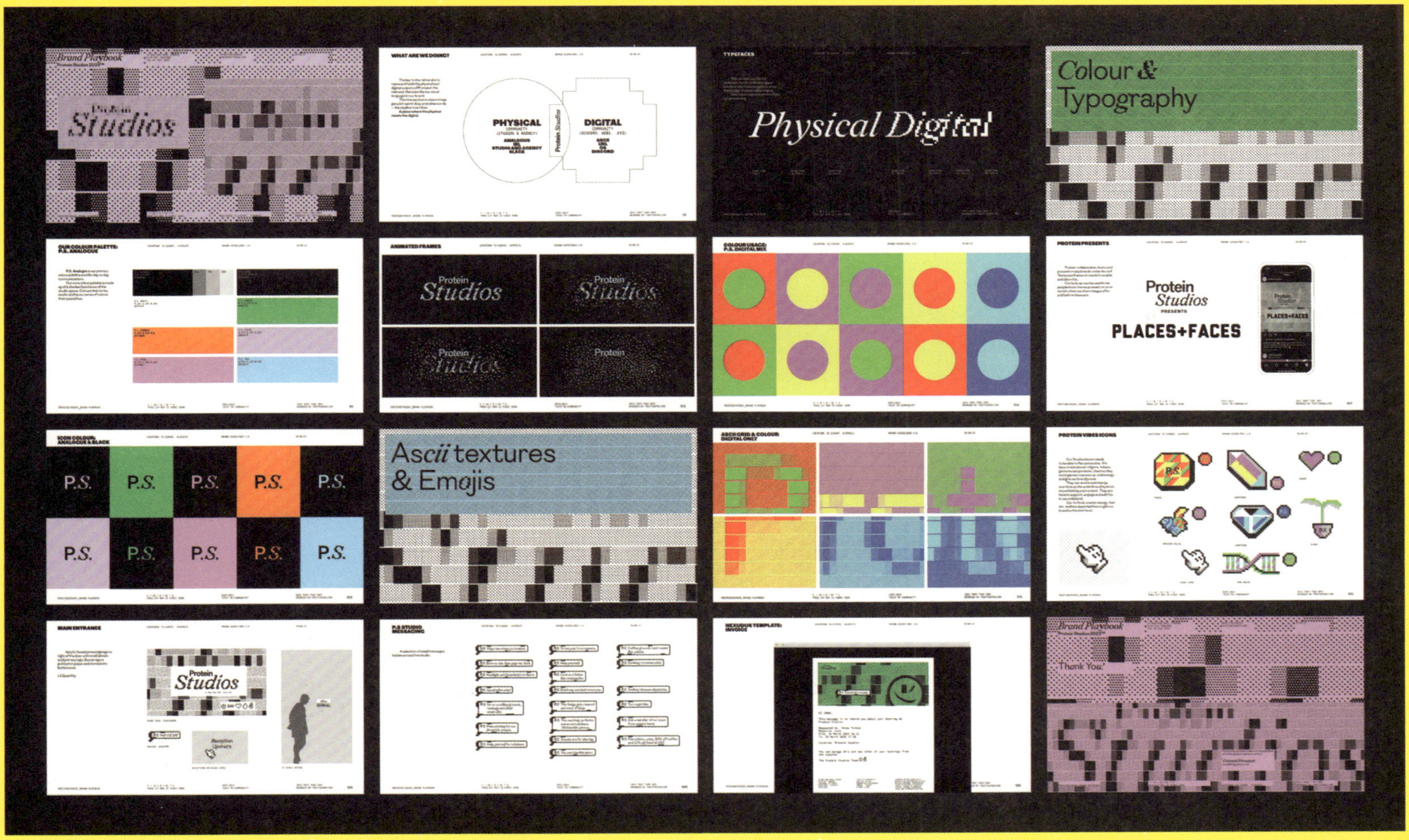
Brand Playbook
Protein Studios
PHYSICAL
DIGITAL
Physical Digital
Colour & Typography
Protein Studios
Protein Studios
PLACES+FACES
P.S.
Ascii textures & Emojis
Protein Studios
Thank You
Studios

We're HIRING!
P.S. Where people and ideas grow.
Desks available NOW!!!
P.S. Join our community.
Host your event HERE!
P.S. Good vibes only!
P.S. Event Angels.
P.S. Smiling releases dopamine.
P.S. Join our community.
100
100

Pixel Art

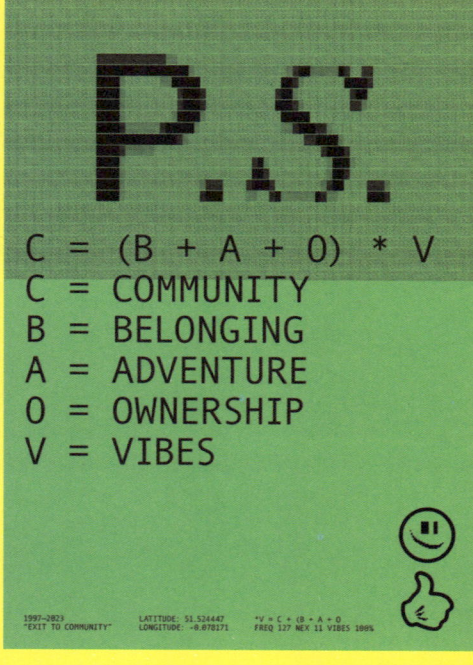

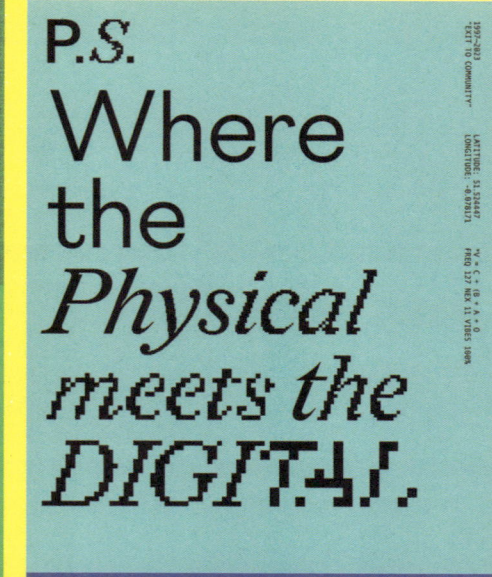

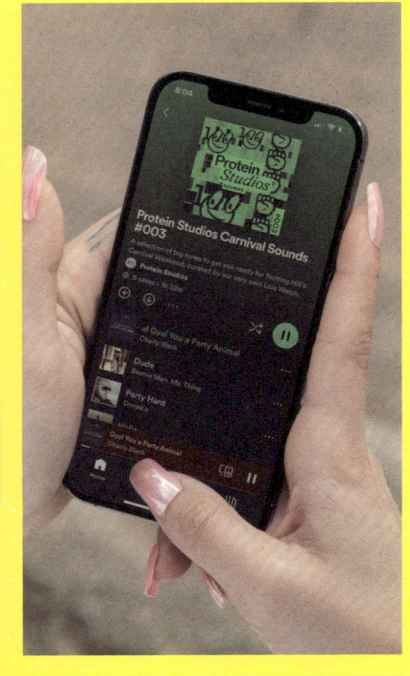

▼ **Inspiration:**

Initially, the exploration delved into the early iterations of the Protein brand, conceived in 1997 under the guidance of Protein's CEO, William Rowe. His focus revolved around color theory and early diagrammatical Web1 graphics, aiming to bring order out of disorder. Subsequently, the research journey led to an exploration of old Atari games, *Minecraft* for its tokens and iconography, and early PlayStation games like *Wipeout* for their technical details. This investigation also encompassed current-day emojis used in everyday chat. The research culminated with a study of early ASCII art from mobile devices of the time, which were downloadable for screens. These diverse learnings coalesced to form a rich tapestry of design elements for the Protein playbook—a brand characterized by ultimate fun and a good vibes attitude.

▼ **Elements:**

Design elements include emojis, chat bubbles, browser-style layouts, image frames, and ASCII pattern characters.

▼ **Fonts:**

Redaction Regular/Italic, Britain Sans Light/Regular/Black, Andale Mono Regular

▼ **Layout:**

The brand playbook enables the creation of multiple and varied layouts, akin to having numerous screens popping up in a browser or on one's screen. It thrives on overlays and visual discord, which are the elements that truly bring the brand to life.

The National
with Bartees Strange
4 October 2023
Madrid, ES
WiZink Center

Mathieu Labrecque

Montreal-based illustrator Mathieu Labrecque is acclaimed for his unique character design and exploration of evocative visual systems. His diverse portfolio includes illustrations and animations for global clients, but a recent focus on Pixel Art signifies a significant shift in his artistic journey. Formerly splitting his time between music and illustration, Mathieu decided to fully invest in illustration six years ago. He believes in dedicating 100% to one's pursuits for optimal results. His venture into Pixel Art is driven by a fascination with its "mathematical" and "puzzle"-like nature, finding joy in the grid's limitations akin to learning a new language. This digital approach injects freshness into his practice, allowing intuitive work without preliminary constraints. Drawing inspiration from music, comics, and children's literature, Mathieu sees parallels between pixel and music composition, enjoying the structured approach in both.

1. Embracing Pixel Art

Mathieu Labrecque's choice to use pixels as the foundational elements in his design and illustration work stems from his fascination with the playful experimentation of abstraction. Unlike traditional methods that can sometimes feel overwhelming and directionless, working within a grid of small, limited squares provides a structured language that one learns to navigate and manipulate. This imposed abstraction introduces a novel perspective on subjects, transforming illustrations into designs and infusing a more mathematical and puzzle-solving aspect into his creative process. Through this method, Mathieu conveys emotions that blend nostalgia with a modern design-oriented perspective, highlighting his appreciation for the unique and structured nature of Pixel Art.

2. Visualizing Technological Advancements

Pixel Art, which originated as a technological limitation, has seen a remarkable resurgence in popularity in today's era of high-definition visuals. Mathieu Labrecque attributes this revival to the pervasive digitalization and pixelation driven by various technological advancements such as bitcoins, artificial intelligence, and virtual reality. These innovations are fundamentally transforming our perceptions and interactions with the world, creating a growing demand for illustrations that reflect these shifts.

The charm of pixel graphics lies in their distinctive, abstract, and playful nature. Mathieu's approach to illustrating complex technological topics through pixel grid-based illustrations is both systematic and imaginative. The pixel grid imposes a structured approach, where the constraint of using a limited number of squares compels him to explore unconventional paths and shortcuts, transforming his work into a mathematical puzzle. This challenge aligns perfectly with the intricate systems and mechanisms associated with technological advancements, resembling a puzzle of wires and buttons. Meanwhile, Mathieu's focus on the shape of the pixel acknowledges and celebrates the forms of an increasingly pixelated world, contrasting with the smooth, high-resolution images that often seek to conceal the pixel's presence. This results in visuals that stand out, capturing the audience's attention more effectively. The abstract, impactful, and playful nature of his work resonates with the themes of technological advancement, making complex topics more accessible and engaging.

Mathieu's aesthetic preference for simple, schematic forms has always spoken to him as an engaging language. The use of pixels is an excellent example of this kind of language. For him, the "pixel grid" aesthetics

THE NATIONAL

The National commissioned the artist to design the poster for their Madrid show on October 4, 2023. Drawing from their preference for the artist's pixel designs, the subject chosen was the sunset. The challenge lay in transforming this ordinary scene into something visually captivating, prioritizing aesthetic exploration over narrative. Using rounded pixels, the artist infused the sunset with an eerie quality, reflecting The National's dual spirits.

▼ **Color Scheme:**

- R247 G200 B000
  C003 M024 Y100 K000
- R000 G124 B055
  C084 M027 Y099 K015
- R000 G000 B000
  C000 M000 Y000 K100

▼ **Inspiration:**

The portrayal of the sunset is universally acknowledged as beautiful, offering ample room for experimentation. The artist's inquiry revolved around pushing the boundaries of this form without losing its beauty or recognizability. By blending the rounded pixel treatment of the illustration with the preserved pixels for the lettering, both derived from a shared grid, the artist aimed to celebrate the pixel grid in its entirety.

▼ **Elements:**

The illustration began as a pixel grid within Illustrator. After pixelating the design, the artist rounded the corners of each shape to impart a slightly more organic appearance, making it easier on the eye.

▼ **Layout:**

In two distinct phases, the artist focused on highlighting the illustration and integrating text into the design. He enjoys the challenge of placing words within the pixel grid, achieving a sense of balance akin to winning a game when everything fits perfectly.

is not just a stylistic choice to distinguish his work from others but represents a quest for a language that conveys concepts in their simplest and clearest form. Working within a pixel-based design framework offers a molecular vision, where the artistic direction is centered around pixels striving to bring ideas to life. This method prioritizes simplicity and clarity, allowing Mathieu to convey complex concepts effectively through the unique visual language of pixels.

Through a grid of pixels, Mathieu presents the beauty of simplicity in his illustrations and celebrates the unique visual language that simplicity brings. This approach allows him to successfully capture the essence of technological developments, striking a chord with contemporary audiences. This unique approach also enhances the impact of his illustrations, skilfully blending the nostalgic appeal of retro aesthetics with the modern digital landscape.

3 Finding the Balance between Simplicity and Complexity

Mathieu's illustrations showcase a masterful blend of experimentation and conceptual clarity, deeply influenced by the modern art movement. His creative process begins with spontaneous drawing, relying on simple shapes without a predetermined plan. For instance, this approach allows him to start with a character in any position and let inspiration guide his subsequent actions, using basic geometric shapes to construct complex structures. The simplicity of this method facilitates the exploration of intricate ideas while maintaining a clear conceptual foundation.

Mathieu emphasizes the importance of responding to the drawn elements as they evolve. Overly detailed components can complicate the overall picture and hinder its development. For him, the manipulation of form and the emergence of ideas happen simultaneously, interwoven throughout the creative process. Often, his sketches serve as nearly final versions of the image, with the transition to the final illustration posing a similar challenge to starting with a written idea: the final artwork transforms into something new and distinct from the initial concept.

Textures are typically absent from his work unless they are essential to the concept, as their inclusion could disrupt the creative flow. This approach allows Mathieu to resolve both form and idea simultaneously, preserving the drawing's originality and impact. By balancing simplicity and complexity, he ensures that his illustrations clearly communicate his design ideas and explore more diverse design possibilities, thus creating a unique visual language.

4 The Timeless Quality of Art

Mathieu Labrecque believes that certain works and styles in contemporary art and design possess a timeless quality, capable of transcending eras and trends. Over the years, he has observed that clarity in conceptual and aesthetic proposals is a common characteristic among many illustrators whose work stands the test of time. These artists create images that are not only captivating but also easily understood, maintaining their appeal even when revisited after 10, 15, or 20 years.

Having delved extensively into comics, Mathieu recognizes the challenge of crafting an intelligible language that makes for a light and enjoyable reading experience. The comic book characters that resonate with him often have a simple graphic appearance, allowing for easy adaptation to various situations and emotions. This simplicity ensures that the story flows smoothly without being distracted by overdrawn or inconsistent elements. It is this fluidity and clarity that Mathieu aspires to capture in his own work, aiming to create art that remains engaging and timeless.

THE INDIGENOUS SAP OF MAPLE SYRUP (LA SÈVE AUTOCHTONE DU SIROP D'ÈRABLE)

This illustration was commissioned for a series of articles exploring indigenous heritage. The specific article delved into the legend of the discovery of maple syrup. According to folklore, maple syrup was stumbled upon by an indigenous individual who observed a dog licking a tree. Upon closer inspection, it became evident that the dog was drawn to the sweet sap oozing from the tree. Portraying indigenous people in illustrations requires a delicate approach to avoid cultural appropriation. To achieve this, the artist employed a pixel grid, allowing abstraction to maintain a respectful perspective from a distance. The initial creation involved pixelation, followed by rounding the corners of each square to impart a softer, more organic feel to the image. This technique yielded an intriguing depiction suitable for conveying the essence of a mysterious tale, capturing the theme of legend associated with the discovery of maple syrup.

Client: Le Devoir

▼ **Inspiration:**
The artist solely relied on the pixel grid to inspire more abstract images, suggesting mysterious tales.

▼ **Elements:**
The illustration began its creation process in a pixel grid within Adobe Illustrator. After pixelation, the artist proceeded to round the corners of each shape, aiming to impart a slightly more organic appearance that would be easier on the eye.

▼ **Layout:**
Each illustration in the series maintains identical square dimensions to ensure overall cohesion. The artist aimed to evoke the appearance of a family of mysterious tales through this consistent format. Additionally, the square dimensions serve as a nod to pixels, symbolizing squares within a square.

Mathieu Labrecque — Pixel Art — 170

A 163-YEAR ILLUSTRATED HISTORY OF AMERICA'S GORPCORE OBSESSION

Art Director Somnath Bhatt commissioned an illustration from the artist for an article in Bloomberg Business exploring the history of Gorpcore. The objective was to evoke a retro ambiance reminiscent of an old encyclopedia detailing the evolution of Gorpcore. Drawing inspiration from scrapbooks that blend vintage photographs with contemporary illustrations, the artist aimed to capture the essence of this aesthetics. The selected photograph, taken from the *1969 Holubar Catalog*, was chosen from a series provided by the art director.

Client: Bloomberg Businessweek

▼ **Inspiration:**
The director provided the artist with a comprehensive photo bank to reference while illustrating each phase in the evolution of Gorpcore fashion, spanning from the time of Theodore Roosevelt to the present day. The goal of the illustrations was to portray the various eras in a cohesive and whimsical style. Adopting a highly schematic approach enables the artist to emphasize specific details unique to each garment.

▼ **Elements:**
The artist initially created the illustration using a pixel grid within Adobe Illustrator. After pixelating the design, he rounded the corners of each shape to lend it a slightly more organic appearance that is easier on the eye. To enhance realism, a photograph was incorporated as a reference. The purpose of the illustrations was to evoke a retro atmosphere reminiscent of an old encyclopedia detailing the history of Gorpcore.

Photo from: *1969 Holubar Catalog*

▼ **Layout:**
The primary intention was to convey the idea of a scrapbook.

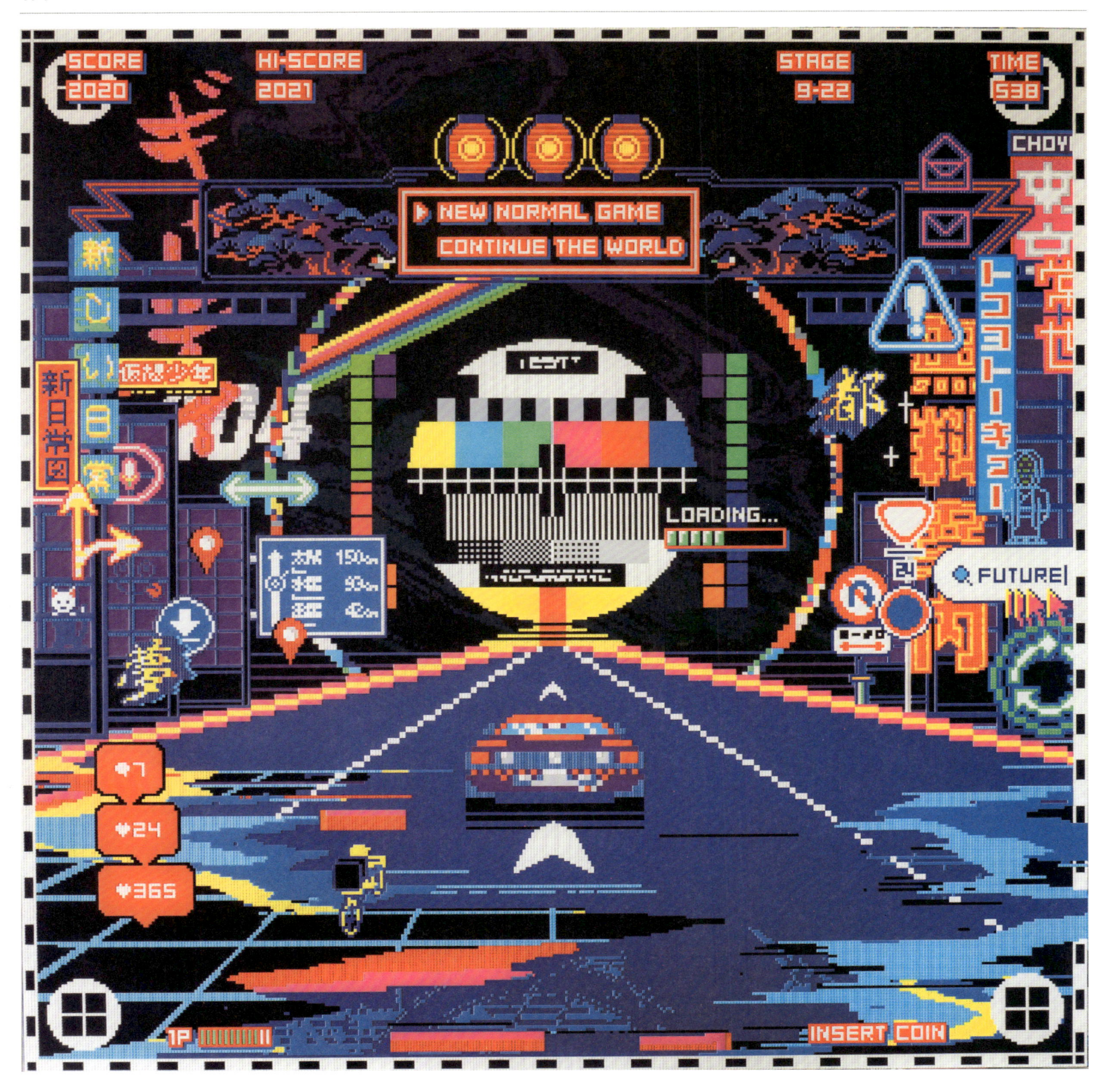

NEW GAME+

The artwork is the final piece in the *NEW GAME+* series initiated in 2020, titled "NEW normal GAME." Curiously, the *NEW GAME+* series commenced just before the outbreak of the coronavirus disease. Examining life from both micro and macro perspectives due to the existence of the COVID-19 pandemic brings a heightened awareness of what constitutes a "bug" and what is deemed "normal." In the context of the series, "NEW GAME+" implies replaying life while inheriting the status from cleared games. Reflecting on the new normal day and contemplating the future allows us, as players, to make more informed decisions in the real world.

"NEW normal GAME" delves into how we navigate this stage, centered around the theme of adapting to a new normal amid the coronavirus crisis. Despite the challenges, we must persist with our story. Initiating the "NEW (NORMAL) GAME" series is a process we can undertake multiple times, signifying our ability to embark on new beginnings in the face of change.

▼ **Inspiration:**
SEGA *Out Run* (1986) (an arcade driving video game)

▼ **Elements:**
The designers' foundational style involves a critical perspective on contemporary society. Frequently drawing inspiration from game and internet designs, words, and rules, they intricately weave Japanese and global stories and myths to articulate their ideas.

Design Studio: EXCALIBUR
Designer: Yoshinori Tanaka, Maiko Iwata

MODERN PROBLEM

The visual theme of the album draws inspiration from the musical genres of Folktronica and Retrowave, incorporating elements of electronic and acoustic folk. Given the background of the two creators in the tech industry, the music seamlessly blends cool, digital tones with warm analog vibes. The album concept explores a myriad of emotions people experience in the modern era, addressing themes such as the corporate ladder's impact on life, choices between love and career, the ambiguous feelings in modern relationships, self-reflection, the passing of things in life, intimate playlists shared between two people, the exploitation of cheap labor behind tech giants, the high cost of living in Silicon Valley, the sentiments of office workers, and contemporary behaviors like backing up romantic memories in the cloud using PDFs.

Design Studio: Onion Design Associates
Designer: Andrew Wong, Fong Ming Yang
Client: Our Shame

▼ Inspiration:

From the overall artistic perspective of the album, the visual elements incorporate Pixel Art, resonating with technology, electronics, and retro aesthetics. It pays homage to the inventions of today's tech giants, echoing the visual styles of the initial Windows 1.0 and Mac OS 1.0 operating systems. The consistent visual universe extends to adorable artwork that carries contemporary messages, resembling a collection of reissued technological artifacts.

▼ Elements:

The cover pays homage to the Sad Mac error alert icon from old-generation computer operating systems, much like the use of emojis in the communication era. The computer icon in distressed green, crying tears, interprets various anxieties, uncertainties, confusion, errors, losses, and disappearances conveyed by the 12 songs of the album's theme, "Modern Problem." The back cover echoes the front with a large computer crash screen. The outer box adopts the pure functional form of software packaging, and the printing process involves offset printing followed by screen printing to simulate the actual computer baking paint texture.

▼ Fonts:

Cubic 11, Jackey Font, Windows Command Prompt

▼ Layout:

A blue software manual filled with dense information. The cover bomb pays homage to past system errors with error warnings. The lyric design presents a breathless, overloaded operating window, resembling the overwhelming daily flood of information under the constant modern era. The extensive manual, akin to a scripture, unfolds an endless stream of message anxiety, layer upon layer, within the melancholy blue.

Pixel Art   Onion Design Associates

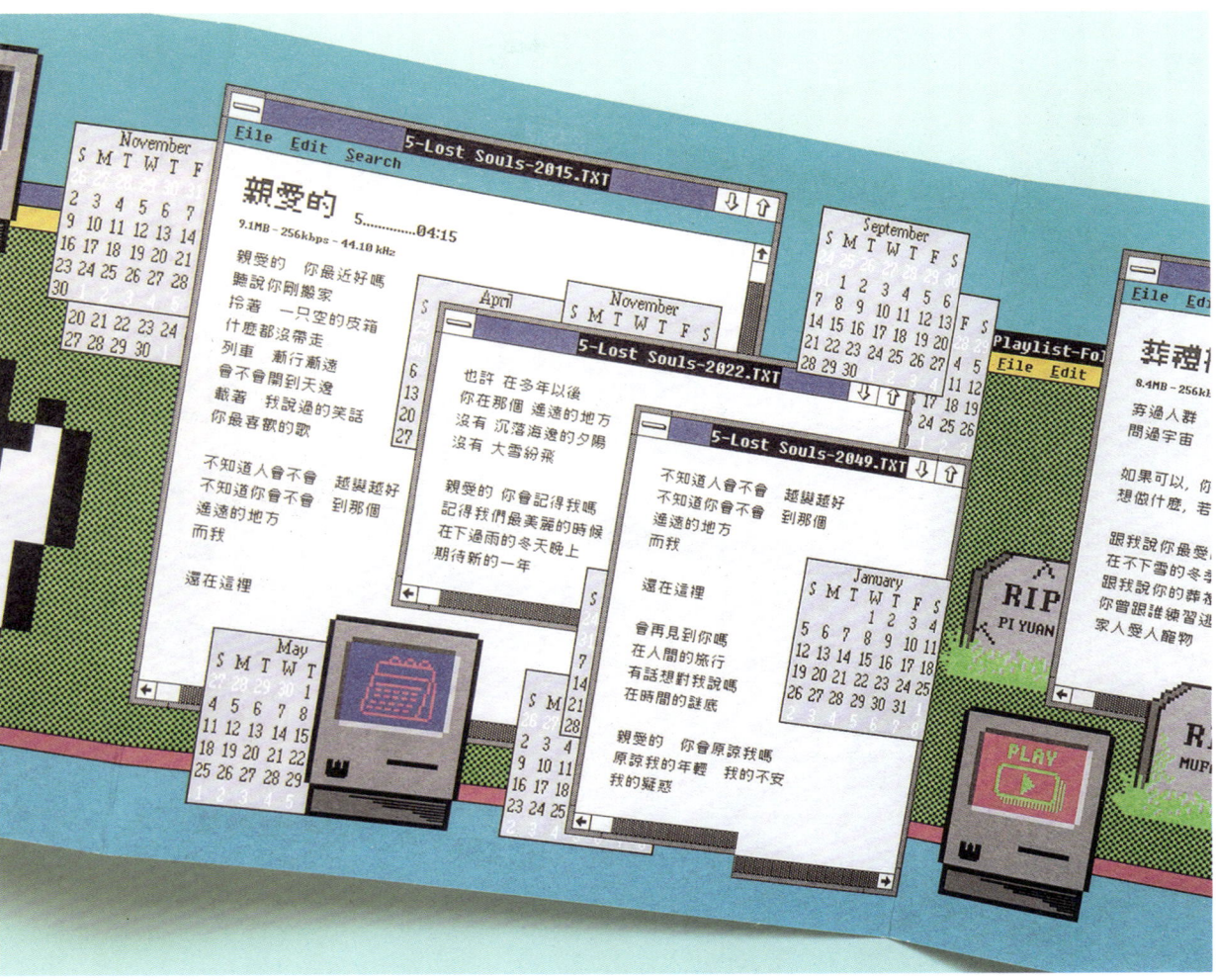

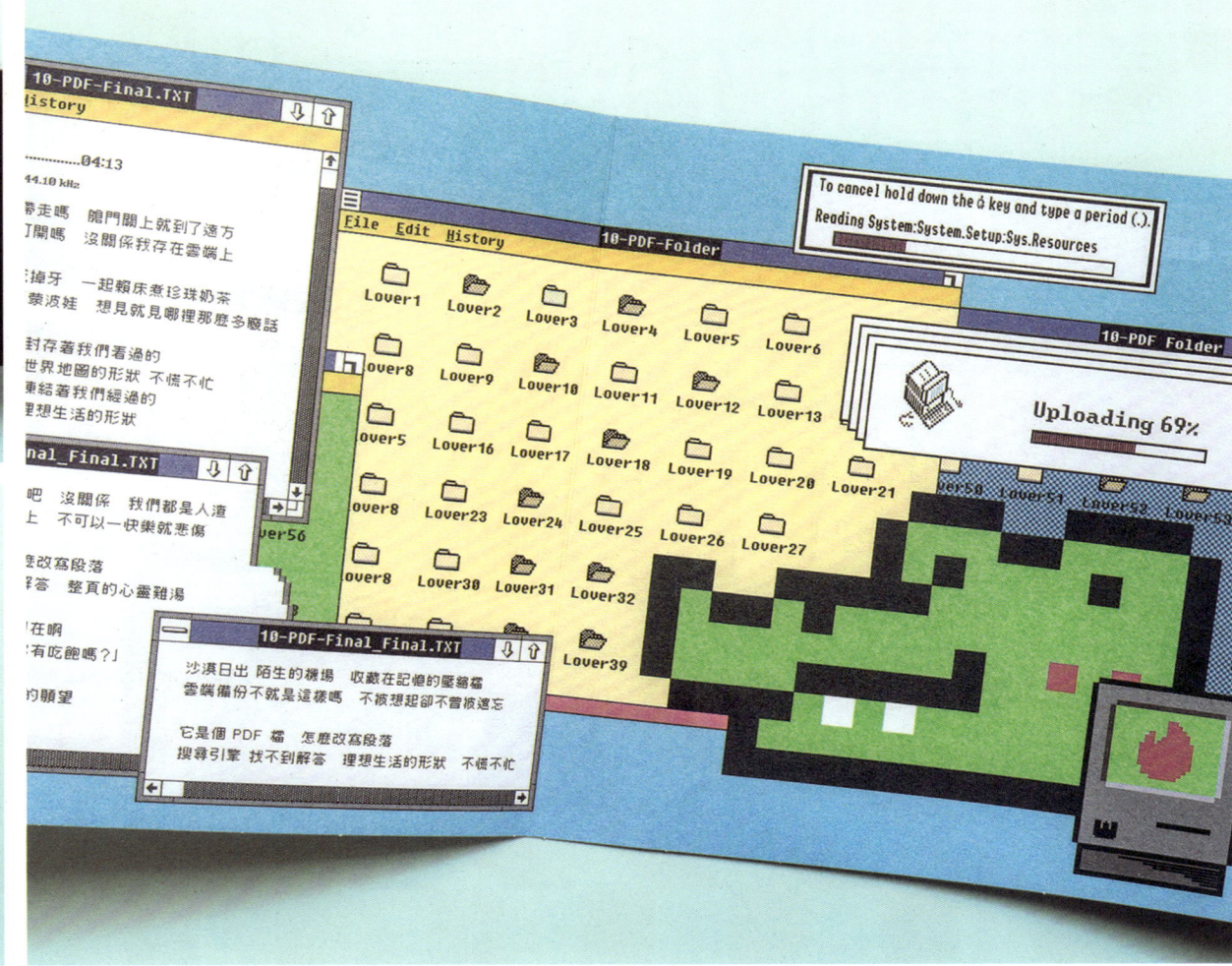

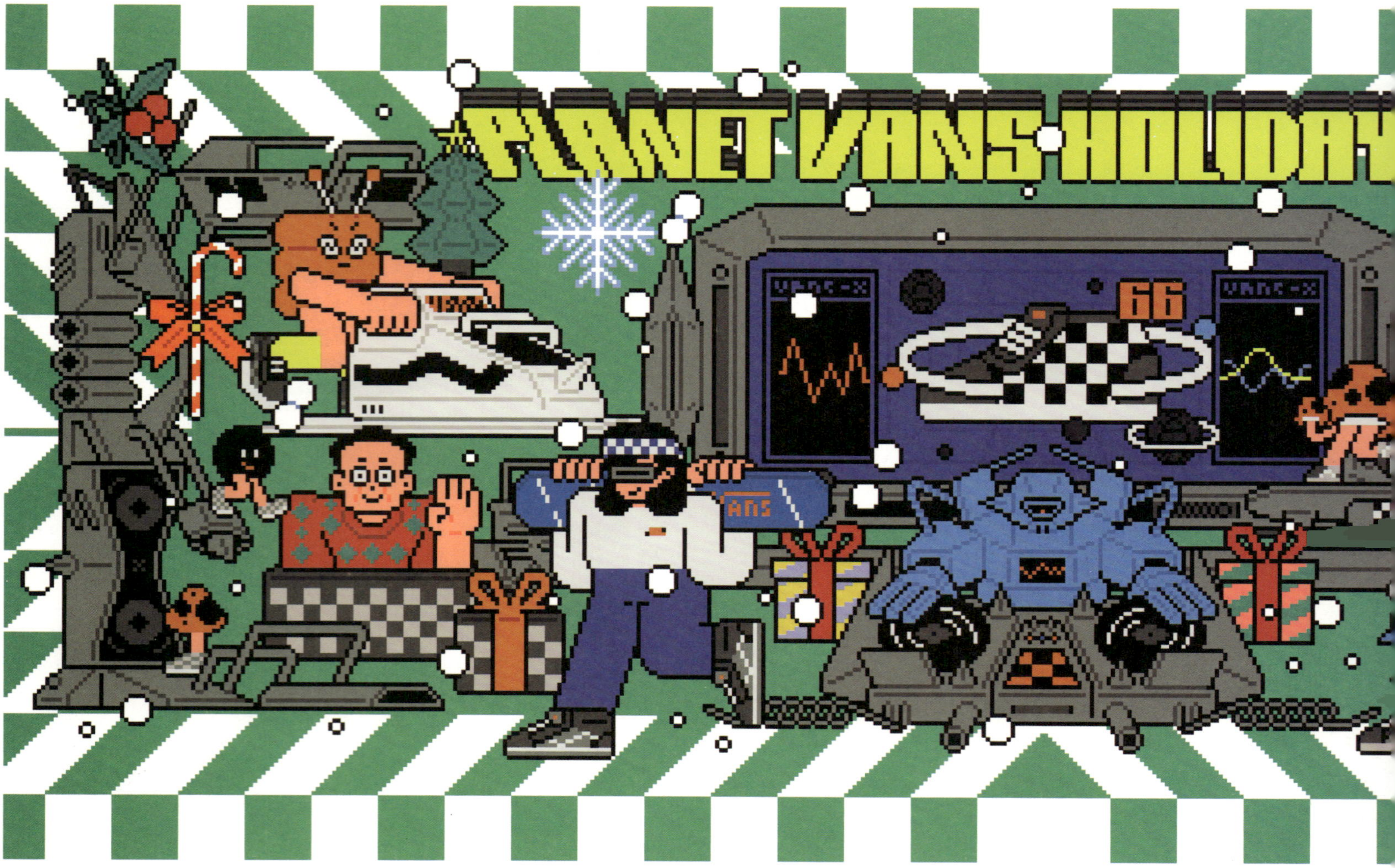
PLANET VANS HOLIDAY
66

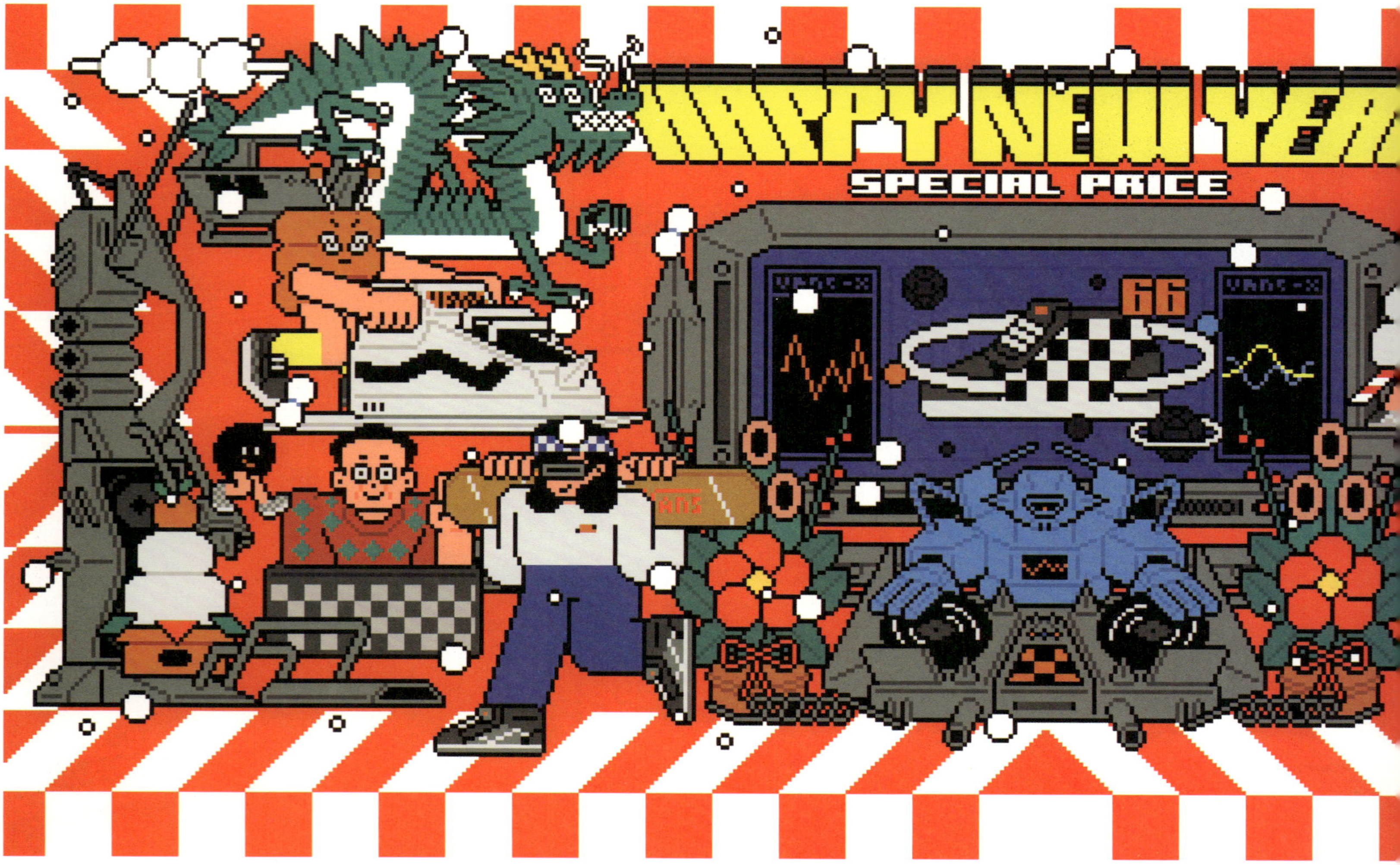
HAPPY NEW YEA
SPECIAL PRICE
66

PLANET VANS HOLIDAY JAM

Inspired by space-themed arcade games, the artwork depicts a festive gathering of astronauts inside a spaceship, immersed in the VANS planet's celebration with skateboarding, music, graffiti, and youth culture. The central symmetric composition around the monitor creates dual layers of virtual and real space. Festival-themed illustrations cater to different customs in the Asia-Pacific region.

Illustrator: Toyoya (Li Fan)

▼ **Inspiration:**

In the initial drafts, the influence of the arcade game, *The Raiden Project* (1995), is evident, emphasizing a gaming-oriented composition. The final design enhances spatial depth by combining the mechanical aspects of the spaceship to better highlight the festive atmosphere. The mushroom characters draw inspiration from the memories of the mushroom element in the game *Super Mario Bros*, and the use of floppy disk elements contributes to creating a visual scene that is both nostalgic and innovative.

PEACH BOY

This work is a 2018 manga about two scientists accidentally transformed into peach people on an evil peach planet during a space adventure. The story, told with minimal text, encourages readers to explore their own imaginative space. In 2019, the manga underwent reediting by Paradise Systems, an independent U.S. publisher. Peach Boy is now ready for a new journey in the expansive universe, accompanied by a peach companion, adding a joyful twist to the narrative.

Illustrator: Toyoya (Li Fan)

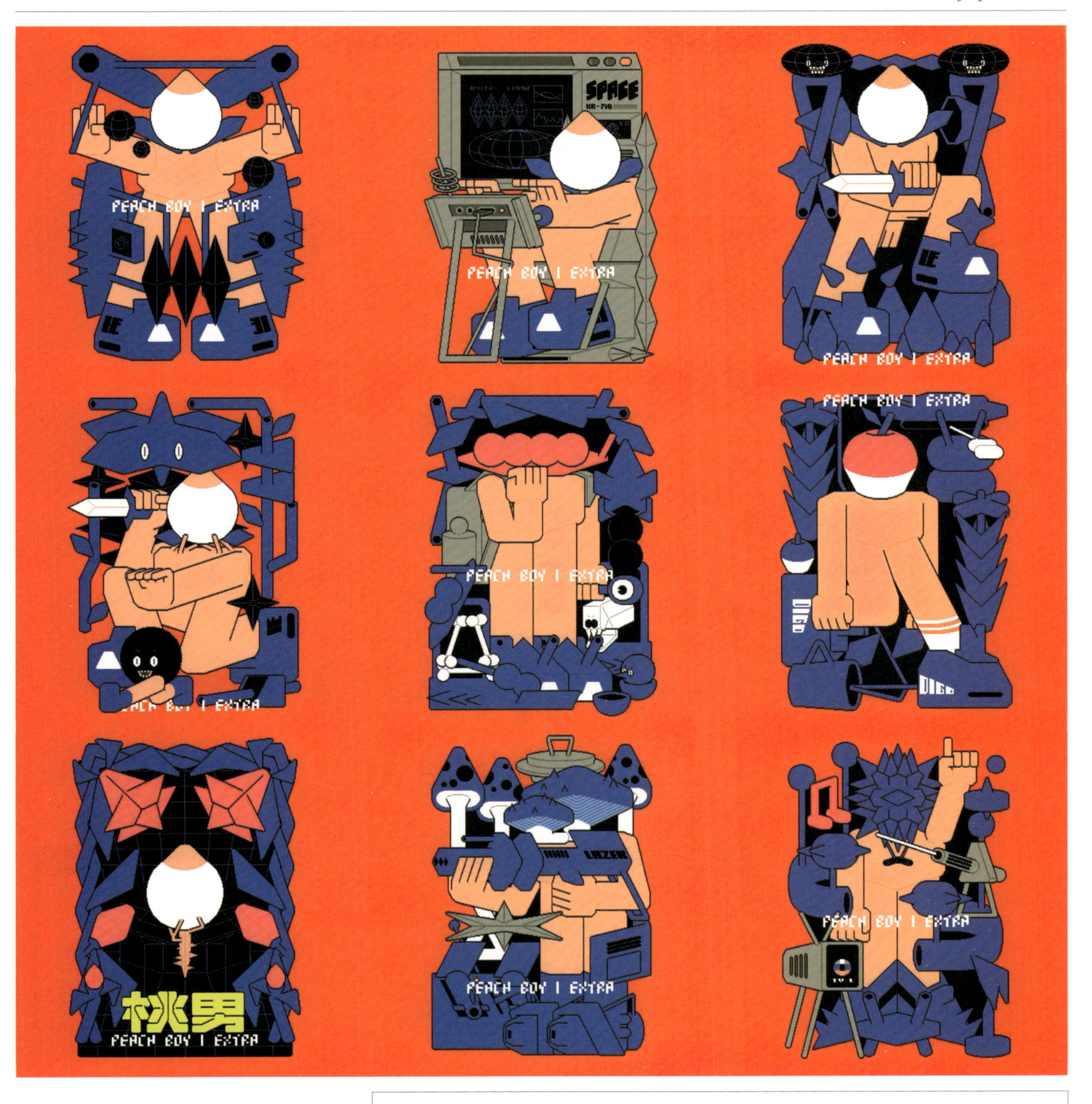

▼ **Inspiration:**

The inspiration for the work's narrative comes from the 1980s sci-fi film *Alien*. The peach elements echo the adventure tales of Momotaro, a legendary figure in Eastern folklore.

▼ **Color Scheme:**

- R241 G139 B026 / C000 M056 Y091 K000
- R076 G068 B153 / C080 M079 Y000 K000
- R230 G031 B024 / C000 M096 Y095 K000
- R000 G072 B157 / C096 M075 Y000 K000
- R248 G238 B149 / C005 M004 Y051 K000
- R159 G159 B159 / C044 M035 Y033 K000
- R243 G162 B145 / C000 M047 Y036 K000
- R156 G162 B151 / C045 M033 Y033 K000
- R244 G236 B051 / C008 M000 Y084 K000
- R231 G054 B100 / C000 M089 Y039 K000

NEURAL TRACKER

This project is a collection of works expressed through illustrations and comics, reflecting the designer's understanding of the relationship between digital mechanization and human interaction. The transformation brought about by digitization in the cognition and mode of existence of individuals symbolically reshapes the world system. The works were awarded the Excellence Award at the 2021 Shibuya Pixel Art and the Beyond Pixel Art Award.

Illustrator: Toyoya (Li Fan)

▼ **Inspiration:**

The inspiration for the artwork comes from *The Matrix* and *The Cell*, exploring the construction of virtual worlds. The visual elements draw from the flattened Windows style, while the overall composition is influenced by the style and techniques of pixel artist eboy.

▼ **Color Scheme:**

■ R230 G042 B138　　　　　　　　　　　■ R000 G146 B215
C000 M091 Y000 K000　　　　　　　　　C087 M021 Y000 K000

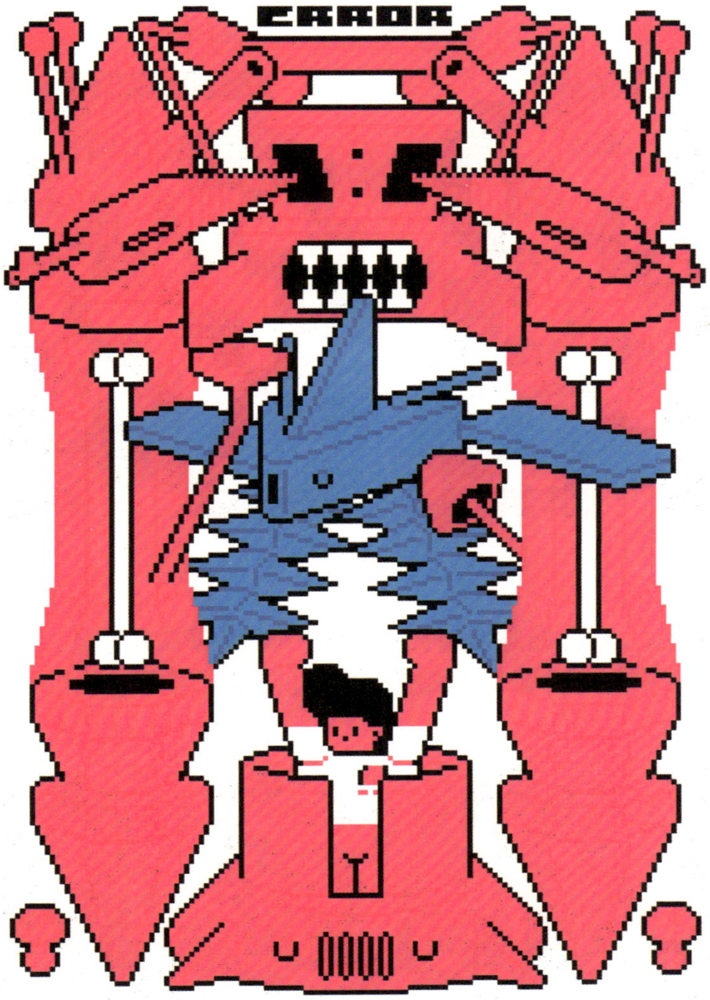
ERROR

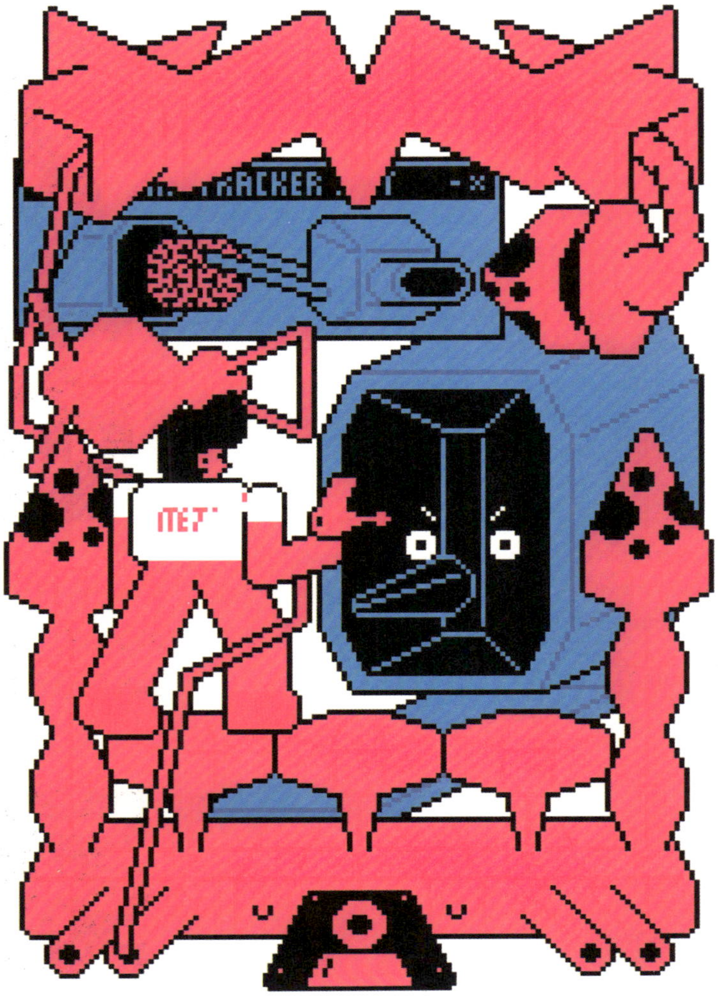

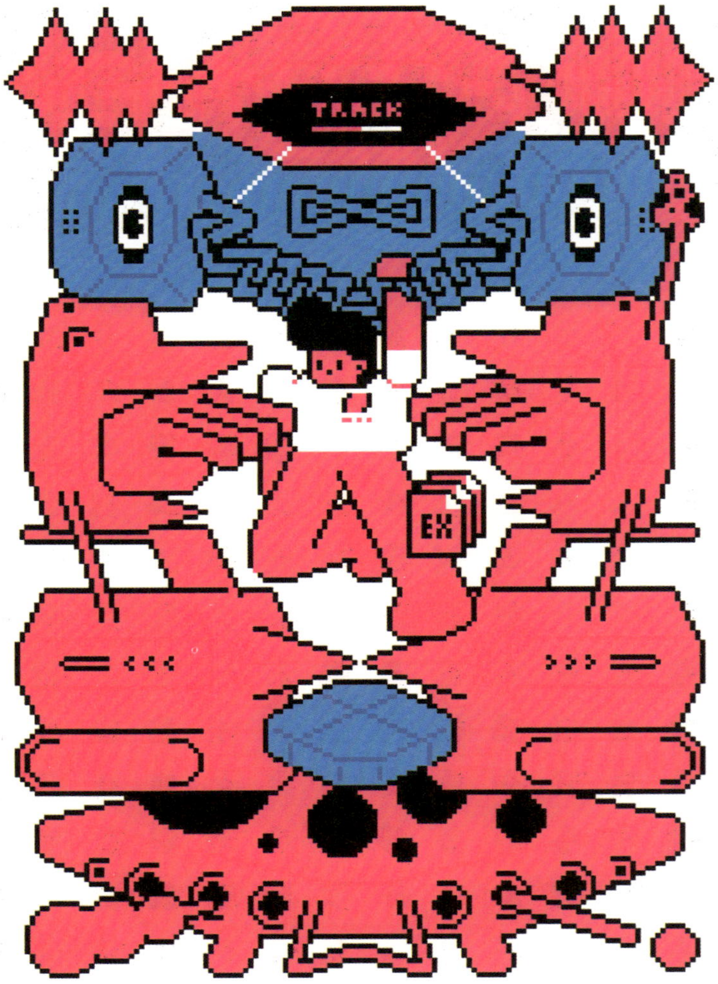
EX

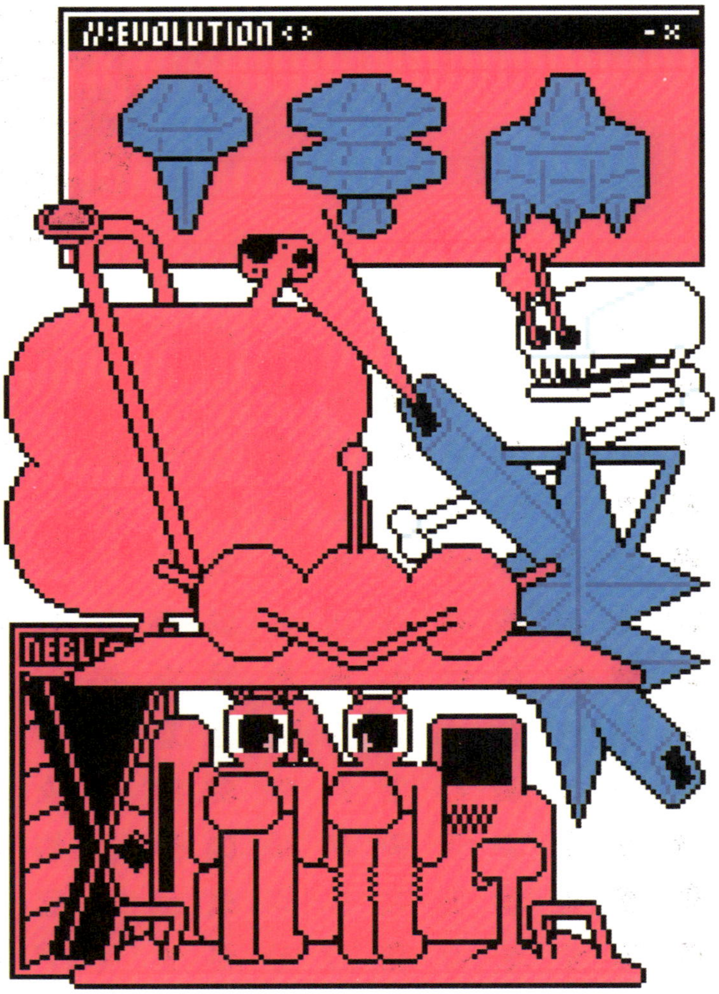
EVOLUTION

15

15 is a unique pixel character font design project inspired by the bitmap fonts of the Nintendo Era. This project creates handwritten-style Chinese characters within 15×15 dot matrix grids, aiming to weaken the haziness of bitmap fonts and strengthen the correlation and recognition between strokes. It showcases the unique beauty and diversity of Chinese characters in such a compact space. By merging the handwriting style with pixel fonts, *15* breaks traditional limitations, revealing the complex structure and beauty of Chinese characters within confined dimensions. Each character maintains its individuality in the smallest space possible, paying homage to classic bitmap fonts while infusing them with new life and expressiveness.

Designer: Junyao Chu

▼ **Inspiration:**

Taking advantage of the game typography design logic of the 1980s and early 1990s Nintendo Era (when bitmap fonts were widely used in game consoles), in which the outline of the glyphs fit snugly into the left and upper face frames, leaving a dot-matrix-width gap on the right and below for close spacing of the text, *15* was inspired by Toshi Omagari's book *Arcade Game Typography*. The book documents a wealth of design forms that emerged under numerous technological constraints, which inspired a recreation of the "strive for even the slightest" concept in the Nintendo Era, resulting in a unique style that is both nostalgic and full of the innovative spirit of modern design.

15×15 pixels

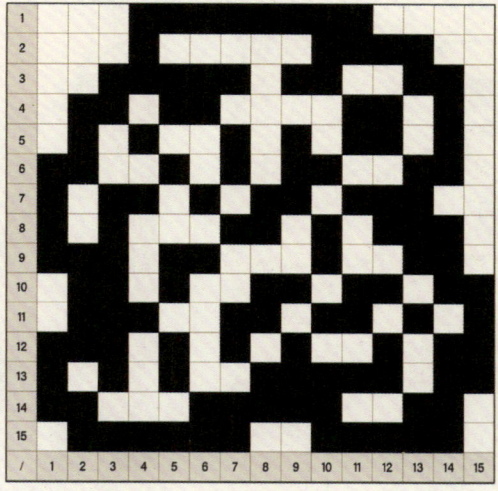

offset adjustment

Paragraph display-1

Kerning adjustment

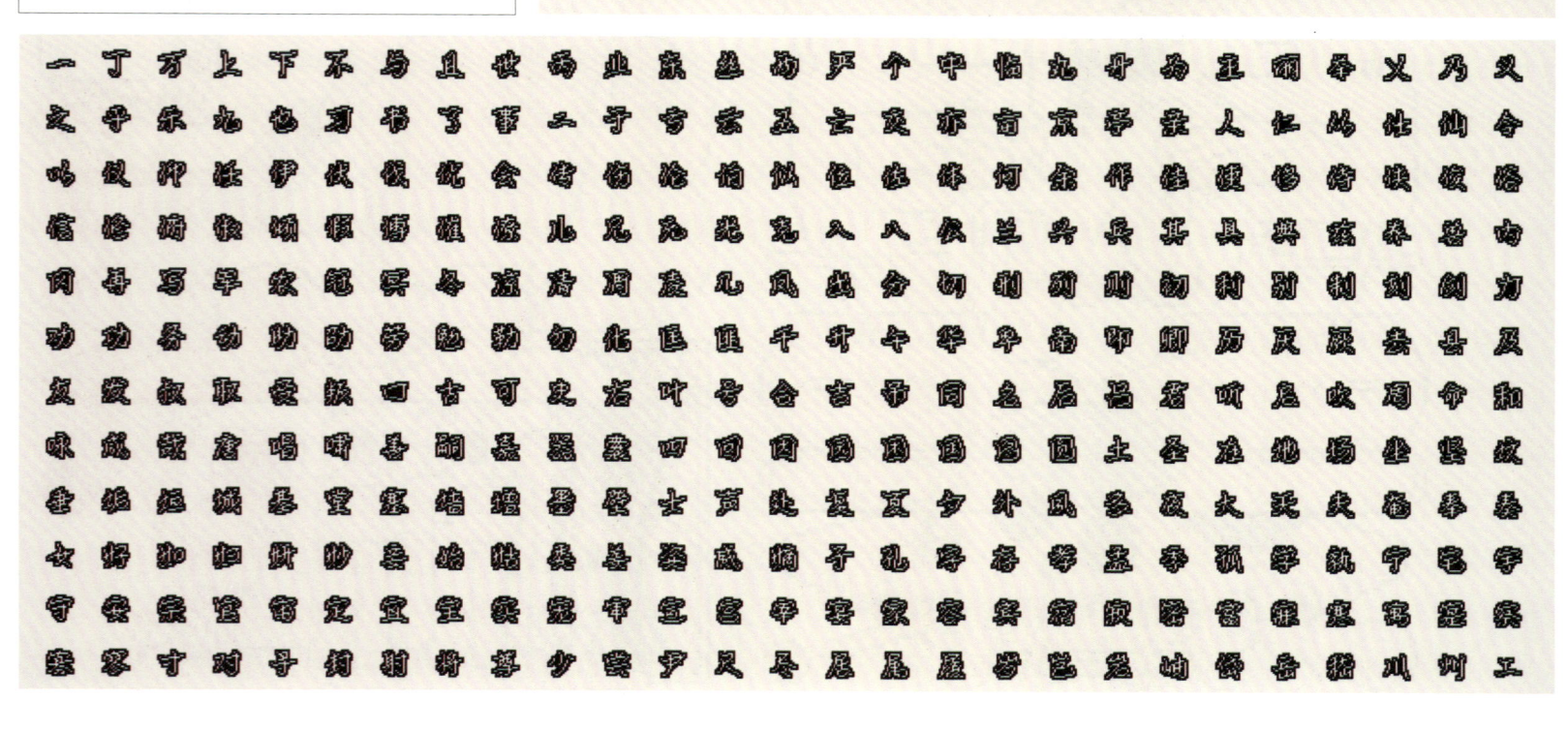

The world of fonts is more confined compared to the expansive boundaries of poster or graphic design—it often exists within the limits of a single square. However, font has its own structure, governed by numerous rules and regulations. The challenge lies in aligning these elements within a restricted space while creating thousands of unique designs.

The Story Behind

Junyao Chu had a relatively smooth process in creating his work, *15*, in general. Before embarking on the design, he began to think deeply about how to explore and convey the boundaries of typographic legibility. Based on the well-known phenomenon that Chinese characters can be recognized by their general outlines, even without looking at their specific strokes, the author focused on how to blur or omit some of the strokes in order to achieve a specific design effect. In the actual design of *15*, he endeavoured to explore the boundaries of this ambiguity, observing how different Chinese characters would take shape under this treatment. In the process of creation, he originally thought that those characters with complicated strokes would be the biggest challenge, but in fact, he found that those characters with more oblique strokes, such as the Chinese character "廉," are the most difficult ones.

As for the basis of decision-making in the creative process, Chu chose to design the text of the *Thousand Character Classic*[1], where every 16 characters are designed as a group. Since the designer tends to have preconceived notions and are already familiar with these characters, he would invite his designer and non-designer friends to view the 16 characters after they were completed. If they were able to recognize the words at first sight, the design was considered a success. On the contrary, Chu would make further changes, but he would not show the altered words to the same people again to ensure the objectivity and accuracy of the evaluation.

Legibility Boundaries for Fonts

Legibility is undeniably a critical topic in typography. When asked whether legibility is the most important aspect of typeface design, Junyao Chu suggests that it depends on the usage scenario. For example, in logo design or the main visual of a poster, a typeface can be very abstract. However, excessive abstraction across all designs may come off as arrogant, as designs need to cater to a broad audience. In contrast, for font families or designs that require to be read, legibility becomes paramount. Understanding the limits of legibility is essential for designers to create with confidence. While typography encompasses more than just legibility, it remains the foundational element that should not be compromised.

In the process of exploring legibility, he was inspired by a Chinese character typeface experiment. The experiment compared characters with the middle part dug out and those with only the middle part retained, finding that the former were more recognizable. This insight revealed that the middle part of a Chinese character is not indispensable to legibility, as in the case of handwritten characters, which are often hyphenated and omitted. Therefore, Chu believes that the core of typography is based on the ability to be recognized. His work, *15*, blends attributes of Chinese characters, handwriting, and dot matrix, with the greatest synergy being the blurring process, which has led to a number of attempts and extensions of the "legibility boundary," a concept also reflected in other works.

Exploring the legibility of a font is complex and nuanced, as each character is unique and requires careful consideration of what can be blurred and what must remain clear. Special attention is needed for similar-looking characters, such as "己," "已," and "巳," to avoid confusion. Overall, the exploration of ambiguity and legibility is a process that moves from the macro to the micro level and continues to deepen.

1. It is a Chinese poem that has been used as a primer for teaching Chinese characters to children from the sixth century BC onward.

天地玄黄　宇宙洪荒　日月盈昃　辰宿列张　寒来暑往　秋收冬藏　闰余成岁　律吕调阳　云腾致雨　露结为霜　金生丽水　玉出昆冈　剑号巨阙　珠称夜光　果珍李柰　菜重芥姜　海咸河淡　鳞潜羽翔　龙师火帝　鸟官人皇

有虞陶唐　吊民伐罪　周发殷汤　坐朝问道　垂拱平章　爱育黎首　臣伏戎羌　遐迩一体　率宾归王　鸣凤在竹　白驹食场　化被草木　赖及万方　盖此身发　四大五常　恭惟鞠养　岂敢毁伤　女慕贞洁　男效才良　知过必改

信使可覆　器欲难量　墨悲丝染　诗赞羔羊　景行维贤　克念作圣　德建名立　形端表正　空谷传声　虚堂习听　祸因恶积　福缘善庆　尺璧非宝　寸阴是竞　资父事君　曰严与敬　孝当竭力　忠则尽命　临深履薄　夙兴温凊

似兰斯馨　如松之盛　川流不息　渊澄取映　容止若思　言辞安定　笃初诚美　慎终宜令　荣业所基　籍甚无竟　学优登仕　摄职从政　存以甘棠　去而益咏　乐殊贵贱　礼别尊卑　上和下睦　夫唱妇随　外受傅训　入奉母仪　诸姑伯叔　犹子比儿　孔怀兄弟

仁慈隐恻　造次弗离　节义廉退　颠沛匪亏　性静情逸　心动神疲　守真志满　逐物意移　坚持雅操　好爵自縻　都邑华夏　东西二京　背邙面洛　浮渭据泾　宫殿盘郁　楼观飞惊　图写禽兽　画彩仙灵　丙舍傍启　甲帐对楹

#PixelArtDesignTalk

1. Why did you choose pixels as the foundational elements in your design and illustration work? Do you have a special emotional connection or story with the pixel style? What kind of emotions do you aim to convey through the arrangement of pixels?

EXCALIBUR

When we were children, the NES (Nintendo Entertainment System) was at its peak. Tanaka (one of the designers of this project) spent his elementary school breaks drawing original stages of *Super Mario Bros.* in his notebook. We witnessed the progression of those pixels, transforming into a more realistic form. Similarly, our brains appreciate the richness of the world through the electrical signals of our neurons. We believe that Pixel Art is the most fitting representation of the intersection between the real and the virtual. In the virtual realm, the accumulation of minimal data in the form of pixels excels at foreshadowing the paradox of an imperceptible, tactile reality.

Junyao Chu

One of the reasons I chose Pixel for the font design is that, while bitmap fonts have been prevalent in the design world for quite some time, there are almost no handwritten bitmap fonts, especially at such a small size. This is a gap that I aim to fill with my typeface, *15*. By designing this typeface, I hope to provide a fresh design idea for future designers. Inspired by the early days of computers and game consoles, I have combined the retro pixel style with the personalization of handwritten characters to create a typeface that allows for freedom of expression in a very small space. Through the arrangement of the pixel dots, I hope to convey the emotion of technological advancement and aesthetic heritage, while also inspiring viewers to think about and explore the possibilities of innovative design.

Onion Design Associates

Back in the early '90s, when computers were prohibitively expensive, hard disks were small, CPUs were relatively slow, and computer RAM was considered a luxury, we faced significant constraints while creating art with computers. Limited resources permeated every aspect of the process. However, these limitations gave rise to a unique aesthetics in the creation of low-tech art forms such as bit graphics, ASCII art, and text-based graphics. Early computer operating systems, including Windows systems, Mac OS, and arcade games, became popular despite their constraints. This era remains a source of nostalgia, evoking fond memories of the good old days.

Toyoya (Li Fan)

My fascination with Pixel Art stems from childhood memories of 8-bit Nintendo games and later experiences with richer graphics in arcade games. My journey into Pixel Art began in the early 2000s during my work as a designer at a web company. The limitations of Internet speed and resolution inspired my experimentation with Pixel Art and GIFs, laying the foundation for my subsequent work. I value the orderliness of Pixel Art, often incorporating symmetrical compositions. My designs emphasize electronic styles, embodying a transition from traditional to digital and virtual aesthetics. The emotional tone in my works arises from creating human diversity within the rules of programming, fostering a reciprocal influence.

2. Pixel Art originated as a technological limitation of its time. In today's era of high-definition visuals, what advantages do you believe have led to its resurgence in popularity? Is it the charm of pixel graphics, the interplay of colors, or does it convey specific emotions in artistic style expression?

EXCALIBUR

We believe that the birth of the universe and life is a superposition of nothing and being, 0 and 1. This suggests that our reality itself may be a digital world. When we digitally depict reality, we might be portraying a "retro future." The contemporary era is always the retro games of the future, and this world is continually evolving.

Junyao Chu

Today, in 2024, the world has become incredibly diverse, with various cultures co-existing and intermingling. Pixel Art, as a unique art style and design language, is no longer confined to simple technological constraints. Its retro charm and clear visual effects allow it to blend seamlessly with the multicultural background of modern design. This style not only carries a strong sense of nostalgia but also conveys diverse emotions and artistic expressions through its specific geometric and abstract features. In this multicultural context, Pixel Art showcases its unique heritage and charm, advancing alongside other design styles to enrich and innovate the language and form of contemporary design.

Toyoya (Li Fan)

Pixel Art has made a comeback in mainstream culture, and I believe it's tied to the overall trend of nostalgia and retro aesthetics. The emergence of outstanding animated games has brought pixel (broadly 8-bit) style back into the public eye. Pixel Art is characterized by its simplicity and symbolism. In an era of increasing resolutions and exquisite visuals, the raw, powerful, and primitive digital and electronic feel of pixels stands out. The charm of pixels lies in deconstructing and reshaping graphics. Whether in monochrome (1-bit) or colored Pixel Art, it requires rebuilding the visual order. Pixel graphics carry memories of electronic games and the internet, and creative work in this style is a continuation of next-generation design and visual experiences. I emphasize this expression in my work, often featuring original windows and floppy disks, as pixel style magnifies this concept.

DECO ART

Deco Art Deco Art

DEVELOPMENT HISTORY

Early 20th Century: Origin and Early Development

Art Deco emerged in the aftermath of World War I as a reaction to the ornate and intricate Art Nouveau style. Its name derives from the Exposition Internationale des Arts Décoratifs et Industriels Modernes held in Paris in 1925. Early Art Deco design embraced geometry, symmetry, and a fascination with modern materials like chrome and glass. It celebrated the machine age and the streamlined aesthetics of industry, reflecting the opulence and technological optimism of the era.

1920s-1930s: Global Spread and Diverse Influences

Art Deco quickly spread worldwide, taking on diverse influences from various cultures. In the United States, it became synonymous with the Roaring Twenties, characterized by luxury and excess. In Europe, Art Deco design was influenced by the Bauhaus movement, blending form with function. It manifested in skyscrapers, ocean liners, and the luxury of the *Great Gatsby* era.

1930s-1940s: Post-Depression and World War II

The Great Depression and the outbreak of World War II shifted priorities away from extravagance. Art Deco, however, adapted to the economic challenges, emphasizing functionality and simplicity in design. It influenced wartime poster design and rationing fashion.

1950s-1960s: Decline of Art Deco and the Rise of Op Art

As the mid-20th century ushered in new design movements like Mid-Century Modern, Art Deco's popularity waned. Many Art Deco buildings were neglected or demolished during this time. At the same time, Op Art began to gain prominence, which focused on visual effects, optical illusions, and dynamic patterns. It used precise geometric forms and contrasting colors to create a sense of motion and depth that consistently makes a visual impact on the viewer.

1980s-Present: Resurgence

The decorative elements of Art Deco saw a resurgence, influenced by the vibrant and dynamic aesthetics of Op Art. This period blends the rich, ornamental qualities of Art Deco with the optical effects and bright colors of Op Art, leading to the emergence of styles that incorporate both characteristics. Designers and enthusiasts have rekindled an appreciation for its elegance and timelessness. This resurgence has influenced contemporary design and continues to inspire architects, graphic artists, and fashion designers. The wide range of decorative art styles continues to inspire contemporary design.

DECO ART: MODERN VISUAL STYLE GUIDE

ELEMENTS

KEYWORDS

1. GEOMETRIC ELEGANCE
2. VISUAL ILLUSIONS
3. DEFORMATION & EXTENSION
4. LUXURIOUS ORNAMENTATION
5. STREAMLINED GLAMOUR
6. VIBRANT COLOR SCHEMES

1. Geometric Figures
2. Optical Illusions
3. Rotating
4. Symmetry
5. Starburst
6. Roman Column
7. Panel Patterns
8. Diamond Stripes
9. Repeated Triangles
10. Three Dimensional Panel Patterns
11. Checkered Tunnel

FONTS

Dekar **20 db** 𝕱𝖊𝖙𝖙𝖊 𝕿𝖗𝖚𝖒𝖕-𝕯𝖊𝖚𝖙𝖘𝖈𝖍

RM DECO Kingthings Sans paperclip ALGEBRA

ALT UNVEIL Metropolis

OCR A Extended bd algebra ALT AEON

ANARCH ENCYCL WeissRundgotisch

COLOR

LAYOUT

扮猪吃老虎

藏于九地之下
動于九天之上

2019 PIG
Happy Spring Festival

恭祝猪年：
可進可退 可攻可守 大智若愚

公|众|号：碧池夫人

3% Design Studio

3% Design Studio is a dynamic design agency specializing in using graphic design into brand building and management, product design, and projects within art and culture. Currently, they are delving into the intricate relationships among various graphic components such as fonts, illustrations, layouts, materials, and prints, pushing the boundaries of design potential. Their expertise extends to helping clients through the complexities of brand visual systems, intellectual property visual systems, package design, print design, merchandise design, and exhibition visual systems. At 3% Design Studio, they hold the belief that in the mode of constant making, intelligence is limited but mind exceeds.

1. 1980s Retro Aesthetics

3% Design Studio views the essence of 1980s retro aesthetics not in specific elements, but in an atmosphere brimming with excessive vigor, suggesting ambitious plans unfolding in the background. Unlike the nature-centric themes of the 1960s and 70s, the 1980s focused on human interactions and societal dynamics. Distilled elements like neon lights and Cyberpunk share a common essence—a flourishing depiction of social life and a grasp of the restless emotions behind prosperity. For contemporary design, the lesson from 80s aesthetics is to break free from digital confines, explore street landscapes, and embrace the chaotic energy of society with measured intensity, adding a touch more strength in moderation.

When working on retro-style projects, 3% Design frequently employs elements and techniques that highlight their unique creative expression. A key focus for them is the reinterpretation of "local flavor," which they see as the unadulterated essence of a particular era. They delve into small advertisements to explore the contrasts between contemporary local flavor and that of the past. Historically, advertising prioritized economic considerations, balancing cost-saving measures with the need to capture attention. However, as technology and economics have progressed, the focus has shifted toward cultural soft power. 3% Design's innovative reinterpretation of traditional retro design elements breathes new life into these motifs, offering a fresh perspective that emphasizes the evolving local flavor of our times and resonates with modern audiences.

2. Expanding the Narrative Potential of Graphics

In Art Deco style, 3% Design Studio refers to graphics as the building of a "relationship" that can be interpreted in many ways. This philosophy is deeply influenced by the free conception of space and time found in Dunhuang frescoes, which emphasizes the conveyance of ideas and intentions rather than strict narrative realism. These frescoes illustrate that if the emotional atmosphere requires it, images can be arranged freely within the composition: people can be taller than mountains, water can lack ripples, and stories can be presented without a sequential order. For instance, in Mogao Cave 257 "Deer King Jataka painting," the climax, which is also the conclusion, is placed at the center of the composition to highlight the deer's courageous speech to the king and the subsequent gaining of protection.

This insight into the capacity of images to effectively convey a message has profoundly influenced 3% Design's practice. Typically, text is relied upon to convey the majority of information, dominating the layout hierarchy, while images serve a supportive, atmospheric role. However, 3% Design has been deliberate in elevating the importance of images in messaging. For example, in their poster for Design Valley, they blurred the traditional boundaries between image and text. Here, the image assumes the primary role in conveying information, with text serving as a secondary or minimal component. This approach exemplifies their first type of "relationship building": clarifying relationships through the narrative power inherent in the image itself.

The second approach involves leveraging the inherent "disadvantage" of images compared to text—their potential for incompleteness or ambiguity. This characteristic is used to enrich the expansive realm of imagination. Dunhuang frescoes, with their unrestricted depiction of space and time, encourage viewers to actively fill in information gaps, synthesize elements, and confidently navigate the free interchange of spatial and temporal relationships within limited confines. This method continually expands the spatial and temporal dimensions within the artwork, allowing for a sense of infinite expansion in a limited space.

3. Modern Vitality of Traditional Elements

In discussing the work *Plays the Role of the Pig to Eat the Tiger*, a traditional Chinese poster for the Year of the Pig in 2019, 3% Design reviews the creative process of integrating traditional elements from Dunhuang frescoes with modern graphic composition. They extracted and vectorized elements such as the rhombus pattern, wild boar, and tiger from the frescoes. However, this approach now seems somewhat superficial, lacking deeper understanding. In their exploration of traditional expressions from the past, 3% Design Studio finds itself dynamically blending contemporary and historical perspectives. This fusion involves bringing modern insights into the past to enrich and expand traditional aesthetics and concepts, creating a realm open to new meanings. Reflecting on the poster, they recognize that their engagement with past elements feels somewhat incomplete, as they are if they are merely extracting and embracing historical elements without fully evolving them. This approach risks tethering the work to a bygone era, hindering its vitality in modern contexts.

3% Design Studio has seen a striking example of successful integration on social media—a chair inspired by Dunhuang's Flying Apsaras that fits seamlessly into contemporary spaces. Its materials and shapes reflect modern sensibilities, yet the underlying structural design and ergonomic concepts trace back to Dunhuang's origins. This juxtaposition often comes to mind when 3% Design blends traditional and modern influences in their work. This is the concept they often consider in their work—"dilution"—referring to moving beyond the concrete level of expression and artistry, focusing instead on the abstract level of chiaroscuro and developing meaning. This approach ensures that traditional elements are not merely appropriated but are thoughtfully evolved to resonate in a modern context.

4 Balancing Modern Technology with Human Touch

The Art Deco of the past focused on rich fonts, patterns, and color relationships, all filled with hustle and bustle. By contrast, the precision and detachment of modern computer work are impressive. When it comes to balancing between modern technological advances and preserving non-mechanical qualities, 3% Design Studio reflects on the inherent challenge of merging these aspects in their work. Initially, they believed that the allure of non-machine-like qualities and the hustle and bustle might stem from nostalgia or innate human tendencies. However, they soon realized that the true appeal lies not just in the immediate outcome but in the mental narrative surrounding the effort behind it. Observing a hand-drawn line involves appreciating the brushstrokes, the energy, and the vibrant individual who momentarily pauses to reflect before plunging back into thought. These intricate narratives condense into a single, refined line, capturing the grand within the minute, which forms the first source of infectious artistic appeal.

The second source of infectious artistic appeal is the dedicated investment of time. The diverse styles of the Art Deco movement were born from significant creative effort and time. Modern computer tools enable rapid completion and high efficiency due to technological advancements. However, if creators solely prioritize efficiency, they risk losing the human touch and vitality that should imbue their work.

In balancing modern technology with non-mechanical qualities, 3% Design emphasizes an inheritance of a work methodology rather than just perpetuating specific techniques. Technological advancement signifies progress in tools, but creators should prioritize the boundless creativity of the mind and the imperfect traces of handcraft. This approach fosters the creation of more nuanced and authentic works. In this context, the Japanese designer group KIGI provides an inspiring example, demonstrating how modern sensibilities can seamlessly integrate with traditional craftsmanship to produce compelling designs.

5 Embracing Freshness and Uniqueness in Trends

In navigating the cyclical nature of trends in graphic design, 3% Design Studio approaches innovation by embracing the individuality inherent in each trend cycle. While trends often suggest a convergence and universality of styles, they also risk diluting novelty and uniqueness. To counteract this, 3% Design emphasizes deep introspection and self-awareness. By continuously exploring their own strengths, talents, preferences, and biases, they uncover personalized insights that transcend the surface trends. These individual perspectives not only resonate uniquely but also contribute to the ongoing evolution of design trends. This approach ensures that their introduction of retro elements remains fresh and distinctive, anchored in a deep understanding of both personal expression and contemporary design currents.

PIGS AND TIGERS NEW YEAR POSTER

This is a poster for the traditional Chinese Year of the Pig. At that time, while perusing a catalog of Dunhuang frescoes, the design team stumbled upon geometric shapes commonly used in modern graphic design, albeit in less structured forms. This discovery prompted them to explore the integration of classical expression with modern graphic composition. They extracted decorative patterns from the Dunhuang frescoes, such as diamond patterns, and incorporated classical expression techniques, including the painting styles of pigs and tigers, along with traditional color combinations. These elements were blended with modern aesthetics and expression habits to explore a new quality of traditional expression.

Designer: Deng Xiongjun, Xiao Lv

扮猪吃老虎

恭祝猪年：
可進可退 可攻可守 大智若愚

2019 PIG Happy Spring Festival

▼ Inspiration:
The Dunhuang frescoes, dating back to the 4th century AD, captivate with their timeless beauty. In recent years, many have drawn inspiration from Dunhuang elements, though mostly at a basic level. The goal was to gradually refine and abstract these elements, blending them into personal or modern expressions.

▼ Elements:
In the less conspicuous areas of the Dunhuang frescoes, besides the classical motifs of flowers, vines, and scrolls representing landscapes, one can also observe more abstract and modern geometric patterns, such as diamond shapes. By reimagining the diamond pattern in a celestial scale and amplifying its proportion and importance in the composition, the design team aimed to find a balance between the classical and the modern. Simultaneously, they searched for hidden images of tigers and wild boars in the fresco's details, vectorizing them while maintaining the Eastern notion of pursuing resemblance rather than exact likeness.

▼ Font:
TW-MOE-Std-Kai

▼ Layout:
The design team aimed to use the layout to centralize the visual focus and concentrate their energy. They first enlarged the serrated teeth extracted from the wild boar image in the Dunhuang murals to create a central visual zone. In this central area, the wild boar and tiger, they hoped, would appear still but with a sense of movement, hence creating a dynamic contrast between the larger and smaller figures. However, they wanted both sides to be more evenly matched, so they used coloring to imbue the visually smaller tiger with a magnificent and vibrant atmosphere.

▼ Color Scheme:

■ R171 G114 B062
C031 M057 Y078 K014

■ R185 G174 B147
C032 M030 Y042 K002

■ R244 G159 B083
C000 M047 Y069 K000

■ R221 G214 B191
C016 M015 Y027 K000

■ R166 G190 B057
C040 M016 Y043 K000

■ R036 G028 B029
C069 M067 Y064 K074

YAN SPACE

Located on Shunhuang Road in Beijing, YAN Space is a multifaceted venue combining art exhibitions, themed salons, athletic competitions, co-working spaces, and coffee snacks. The logo, derived from the Chinese character "炎" (flame), creates a three-dimensional effect through the dispersion and layering of text, aiding brand recognition. Additionally, the dispersed characters symbolize rising flames, conveying YAN Space's inclusivity and endless possibilities in bringing together diverse people and activities under one roof.

Designer: Deng Xiongjun, Xiao Lv

▼ **Inspiration:**

Art Deco's lines are mechanical and geometric in form, yet they steadfastly emphasize the sensual beauty and organic nature of lines in content and spirit. The perception of both inorganic and organic sensations converges into simple linear expressions, representing a sophisticated approach. The logo also aims to accommodate these two aspects simultaneously, drawing visual parallels between the organic movement of "flames" (which, spiritually, is organic) and the inorganic

▼ **Elements:**

This graphic design doesn't adhere strictly to a systematic approach; instead, it incorporates various evolution and blends of techniques. However, regardless of these variations, there's a consistent underlying logic: to express the flickering sensation of flames through the contrast of black and white. This embodies the essence of the brand's spirit. Additionally, by utilizing black and white, the design team removed the overly turbulent and unstable sensations from the flames, creating a quieter space and enhancing

▼ **Font:**

Noto Sans Simplified Chinese

▼ **Layout:**

In the layout composition, the emphasis is placed on separating graphics and text as much as possible. This is because the project leaned towards expressing tension and dynamism through graphics, which capture most of the visual attention. Therefore, it's necessary to provide information in a less distracting environment, facilitating

MOCAI MARKET

The Mocai Market, located in Beijing, underwent a transformation within a traditional three-story red brick building. The aim was to create a unique space, catering to residents of all ages within a 5-kilometer radius year-round while attracting younger demographics. This upgrade preserved the market's grassroots charm, balancing modernization with familiarity. By incorporating elements like lines and grid patterns from traditional market baskets and posters, the design team ensured a comfortable environment for all customers. The logo, inspired by market scales and abstract dining tables, symbolizes the journey of fresh ingredients from market to table.

Designer: Deng Xiongjun, Xiao Lv, Han Yaxu

▼ Inspiration:

The most profound influence comes from the vintage posters commonly seen on the streets in the past. In the past, decorative arts, whether fonts, patterns, or color relationships, were relatively full-bodied, with a strong sense of liveliness due to the lack of deliberate pursuit of precision and symmetry. In contrast to the precision and detachment brought about by computer work today, the design team hoped to find a balance: to incorporate the modernity brought by technological advancement visually while also retaining some parts where humans are inferior to machines.

▼ Elements:

In this project, there is a high level of compatibility between graphics and text. Their lines are relatively bold and agile, with even some sharpness at the ends and turns. This contrasts with the soft lines of fresh fruits and vegetables in the market. This is partly a tribute to the retro vibe of the past but also intended to ensure a clear distinction in sensory experience between the lively branding materials and the lively natural produce, avoiding interference and allowing each to stand out independently.

▼ Fonts:

Original font, Noto sans Simplified Chinese

▼ Layout:

In this project, the design team extracted lines and grid patterns from common plastic baskets, bamboo, and woven bags found in traditional markets, experimenting with different densities and rhythms as the basis for layout design. The abstracted and simplified lines and grids create a cleaner, more comfortable visual experience, evoking a sense of cleanliness and hygiene. At the same time, the alternating red and green lines maintain a lively and prosperous visual atmosphere, infusing the market with vitality.

▼ Color Scheme:

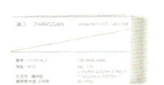

- R052 G158 B073
  C080 M015 Y100 K000
  Pantone 7739c

- R234 G147 B021
  C005 M100 Y100 K000
  Pantone 485c

- R255 G255 B255
  C000 M000 Y000 K000

YAN STORE

YAN Store is an imported affordable convenience store. The design team used a systematic arrangement of lines to form a graphic paradigm, aiming to recreate the common items found in convenience stores: buns, noodles, rice, various packaged goods, and barcodes. This approach not only addresses the diverse needs of convenience stores for individual product promotions and recommendations but also maintains simplicity and cleanliness visually.

Designer: Deng Xiongjun, Xiao Lv

▼ **Inspiration:**

The Art Deco vibe emphasizes a beauty rooted in accessibility. While it employs a plethora of straight lines, symmetry, and geometric shapes, these elements are never mechanistically applied. Instead, they are infused with a sense of sensitivity and naturalness. This approach to lines mirrors the desired aesthetic in the convenience store project. The project necessitates a systematic arrangement of lines to construct the various common items typically found in convenience stores and diverse promotional displays. Additionally, incorporating lines imbued with emotional sensitivity aims to create a welcoming and vibrant atmosphere within the space.

▼ **Elements:**

The graphic design is based on the regular deformation and displacement of lines, which form the foundation of the composition. The arrangement is diverse yet systematic. The aim was to depict the wide array of products and bustling atmosphere of the convenience store without overwhelming the visual senses, integrating the visual space to prevent it from becoming overly crowded or chaotic.

▼ **Font:**

Noto Sans Simplified Chinese

▼ **Layout:**

In the layout, color blocks are used to delineate interface sections. While conveying the vitality of the convenience store, this provides the external conditions for multi-level information transmission.

▼ **Color Scheme:**

R231 G106 B038
C004 M071 Y088 K000

R244 G205 B032
C005 M020 Y088 K000

R034 G106 B167
C084 M054 Y012 K000

YanCheng Mart
Drink Food Cigarette
Daily supplies Import *
食
Food Food
YanChengMart
炎成优品
YanChengMart
Cigarette
Import *
Chaoyang District, Beiji

炎成优品 YanChengMart
%
进口平价 *
便利店
YanChengMart.
YanCheng Mart
炎
炎成优品 YanChengMart
Drink Food
Cigarette
Daily supplies
Import *
便利店
Drink Food Cigarette
Daily supplies Import *
YanCheng Mart
饮
Drink Drink
Drink Food
Cigarette
Daily supplies
Import *
%
YanChengMart
当天制作
YanChengMart
YanChengMart 热气腾腾
食
Food Food
只卖1天
Drink Food Cigarette
Daily supplies Import *
YanChengMart

RUA DO CUNHA (17) RUA DO CUNHA (17) RUA DO CUNHA (17)

(17) RUA DO CUNHA

RUA DO CUNHA

RUA DO CUNHA (17)

CUNHRUADO

Indego design

Indego design is a renowned brand visual image design team known for its targeted and unique designs in the commercial and cultural sectors. Specializing in corporate identity, event imagery, packaging, and multimedia design, they have earned recognition both locally and internationally. Their accolades include prestigious awards such as the New York ADC Young Gun 19, New York TDC Ascenders Winner, D&AD Awards 2022 Yellow Pencil, ADC 101st Annual Awards Gold Cube, and ADC 101st Annual Awards Bronze Cube. Additionally, they have been honored with the D&AD Awards 2021 Graphite Pencil and Shortlist, ADC 100th Annual Awards Silver Cube, Bronze Cube, and Merit.

1 Innovative Power of Design

Balancing Creativity and Functionality

In the *Naughty Roll Design Show* by Indego design, the theme of imperfection is artfully embraced through a lighthearted and humorous design approach. In the project, graphics play a crucial role in conveying information and evoking emotions. Incorporating distorted and extended basic shapes adds a dynamic and playful visual appeal to these elements. Emphasizing patterns and repetition creates visual illusions that enhance the overall aesthetic quality. To effectively convey the allure of graphics, striking a balance between creativity and functionality is paramount. They must clearly communicate the intended message while aligning with the theme of embracing imperfections in a whimsical and humorous manner.

Innovation and Experimentation

In the realm of graphic design, recurring trends are common, yet experimentation and innovation are vital for pushing boundaries and fostering continual evolution. Designers can approach trends with a fresh perspective, exploring new techniques, materials, and technologies through experimentation to achieve originality. Innovation entails embracing novel ideas and melding diverse styles or cultural influences. By adapting historical influences to contemporary contexts, designers can create designs that are both nostalgic and forward-thinking. Ultimately, experimentation and innovation drive progress in graphic design, enabling designers to produce captivating and pertinent work amidst enduring trends.

2 Telling a Story through Design

In the *RE:RISO* poster project, the design team delved into Macau's past, exploring twenty streets across seven parishes of old Macau and rediscovering cherished memories. Macau, once divided into Macau City (comprising the five parishes on the Macau Peninsula) and the Island City (including the parishes of Taipa and Coloane) during the Portuguese colonial era, holds a rich and diverse history. While the current administrative divisions no longer use these city names, the parish division remains in use today. When crafting these elements to convey the charm of graphics, the team carefully considered factors such as visual impact, narrative expression, emotional resonance, attention to detail, depth, and stylistic consistency. Inspired by the city's rich history blending Eastern and Western influences, the project intricately integrates elements of colonial architecture, Art Deco motifs, and traditional Chinese aesthetics to recreate Macau's nostalgic ambiance. Through meticulous selection of shapes, colors, and lines arranged in visually compelling compositions, the design team not only captures attention but also evokes emotions and narrates a compelling story. By blending these design principles harmoniously, they aim to convey the irresistible allure of graphics within this project.

3 Commonly Used Color Schemes

In Memphis-inspired design, Indego design employs a variety of classic color combinations to evoke vibrancy and energy. These include bold pairings like bright yellow with hot pink and unconventional mixes such as turquoise with orange and purple. Pastel palettes featuring shades like pale pink and mint green, along with high-contrast neutrals such as black and white accented with primary colors, are also prominently utilized. Complementary color schemes, such as blue and orange or purple and yellow, are strategically employed to create harmonious contrasts that enhance visual impact. The emphasis is on embracing playful and unconventional color combinations to infuse designs with dynamism and aesthetic appeal.

RE: RISO

Macau, a city where East meets West, boasts a rich and diverse history. Today, Macau has evolved into a bustling global casino hub. However, in this poster project, the designers revisited the past and embark on a journey old Macau—a time marked by confusion and chaos. By skillfully combining elements from this earlier era, the designers aimed to visually recreate the perplexing streets of the city. This poster project represents the last reminiscence of old Macau, serving not only as an exploration of visuals but also as an emotional journey. It presents Macau's bewildering and chaotic scenes uniquely, evoking deep emotions and memories in its viewers. Finally, the decision to reproduce these nostalgic fragments using a Risograph printer aimed to awaken memories of the bygone golden times and revive the beautiful moments of Macau's past.

Client: Naughty Roll

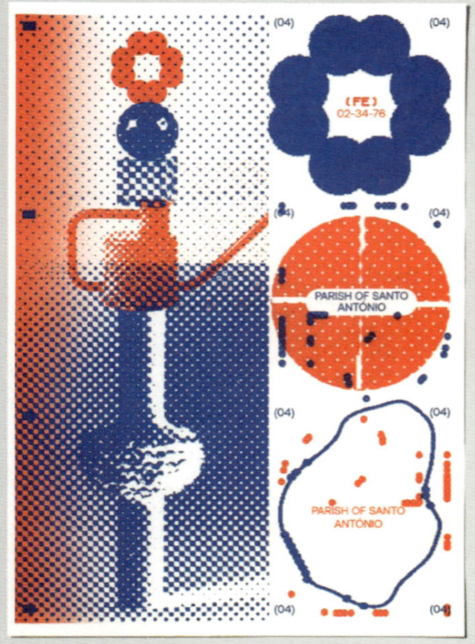
(FE)
02-34-76
PARISH OF SANTO ANTÓNIO
PARISH OF SANTO ANTÓNIO

PARISH OF SÃO FRANCISCO XAVIER
(07)

RUA DO TAP SIAC

RUA DA BARCA
RUA DA BARCA
RUA DA BARCA
(15)

RUA DA FONTE
DA INVEJA
(11)
RUA DA FONTE DA INVEJA

PARISH OF NOSSA SENHORA DE FÁTIMA
PARISH OF NOSSA
SENHORA DE FÁTIMA
(01)

(03) PARISH OF SÃO
PARISH OF SÃO
LOURENÇO
PARISH OF SÃO LOURENÇO

(06)
PARISH OF NOSSA SENHORA DO CARMO
SENHORA DO CARMO
PARISH OF NOSSA
SENHORA DO CARMO

(F&Q)
RUA DOS MERCADORES
(08)
RUA DOS MERCADORES

201   Deco Art   Indego design

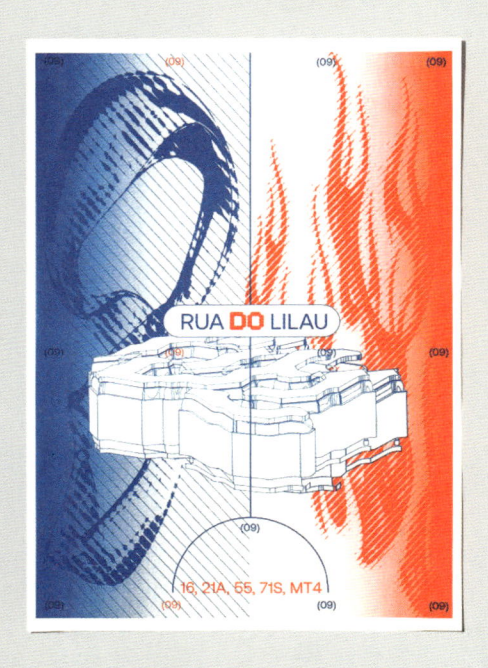

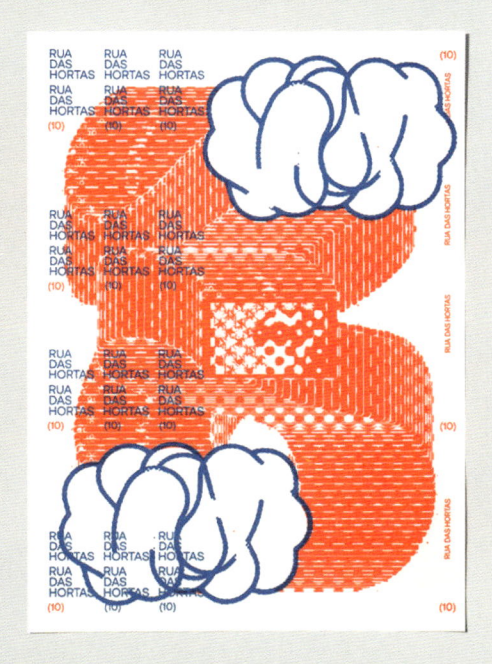

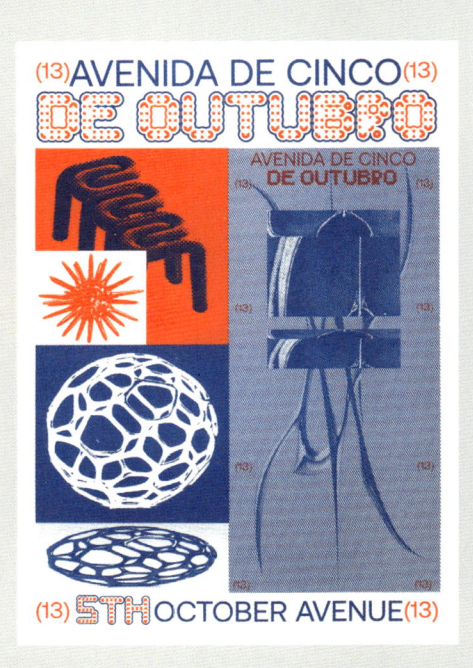

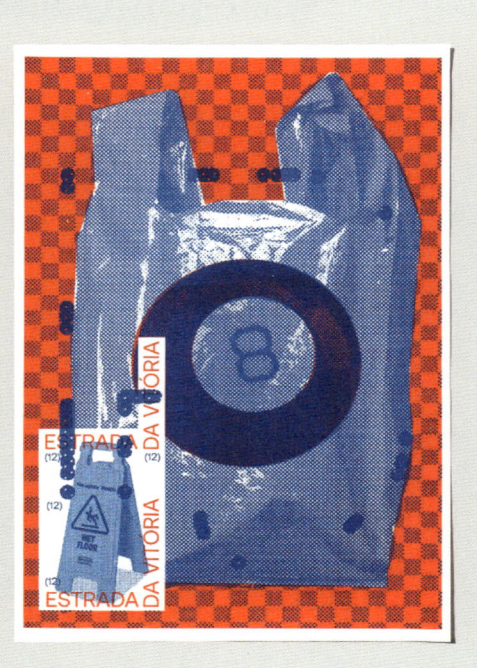

Indego design Deco Art 202

▼ Inspiration:

In this poster project, the designers drew inspiration from Macau's rich history and culture to create a nostalgic design. Influenced by the Portuguese colonial era, elements such as colonial buildings, cobblestone streets, and traditional Portuguese tiles are incorporated. The Art Deco movement of the early 20th century also plays a role, with geometric shapes, bold typography, and decorative motifs being featured. The goal was to capture the ambiance of old Macau's bustling streets, showcasing vibrant markets, colorful facades, and nostalgic signage. Vintage photographs and postcards serve as references, reflecting the street life of that era.

Retro typography, inspired by vintage signage and advertising, adds a touch of nostalgia. Elegant scripts, bold sans-serif fonts, and ornate lettering styles are used to emphasize the retro aesthetics. The design also pays tribute to Macau's unique culture by incorporating traditional Chinese architecture, iconic landmarks like the Ruins of St. Paul's, and the blending of Chinese and Portuguese traditions. These cultural references create a distinct identity for the project, connecting it to the local heritage.

Through the use of these retro elements, the design aims to transport viewers back in time, allowing them to relive the charm and memories of old Macau. It is a visual exploration that evokes deep emotions and sparks nostalgic feelings. By employing a Risograph printer, the designers sought to recreate the nostalgic fragments, reviving the golden times of Macau and bringing forth its beautiful moments once again.

▼ Elements:

The design project incorporates deformed graphic elements to create a visually captivating experience. Architectural structures, typography, and street scenes are intentionally distorted to evoke nostalgia, convey the passage of time, and create an emotional connection with viewers. The deformation adds a unique and intriguing aspect to the design, inviting viewers to interpret and engage with the visuals.

▼ Layout:

In this design project, careful layout arrangement enhances visual impact and storytelling. Key elements include balance, a grid system, layering, negative space, and flow. Strategically positioned and sized elements guide the viewer's gaze and convey themes. The grid system ensures consistency, while layering adds depth. Negative space highlights important elements, and flow brings vitality. These concepts ensure visual appeal and effective communication of the design's intent.

NAUGHTY ROLL DESIGN SHOW

Indego design — Deco Art

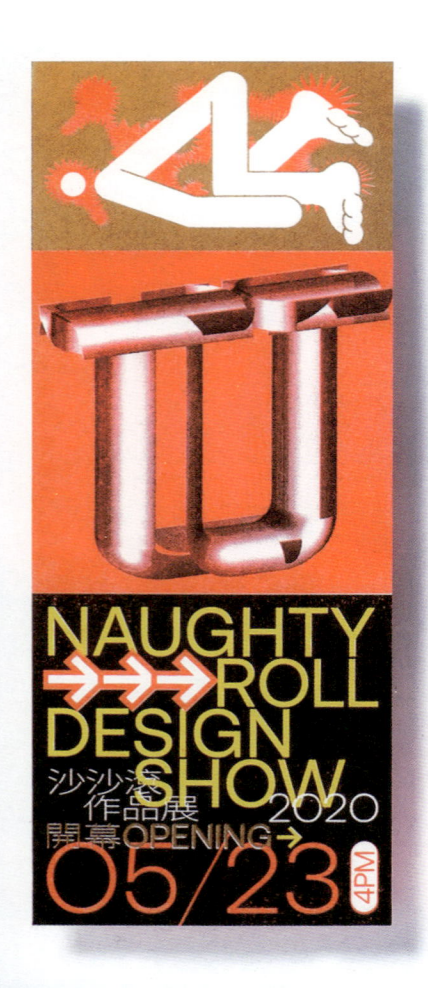

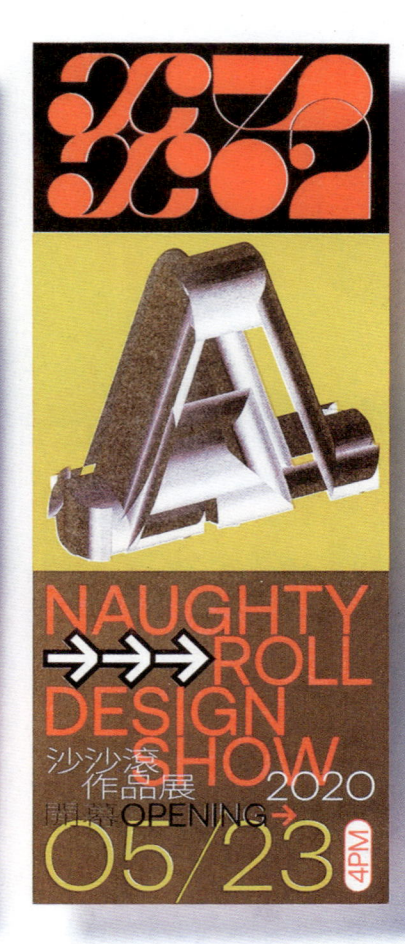

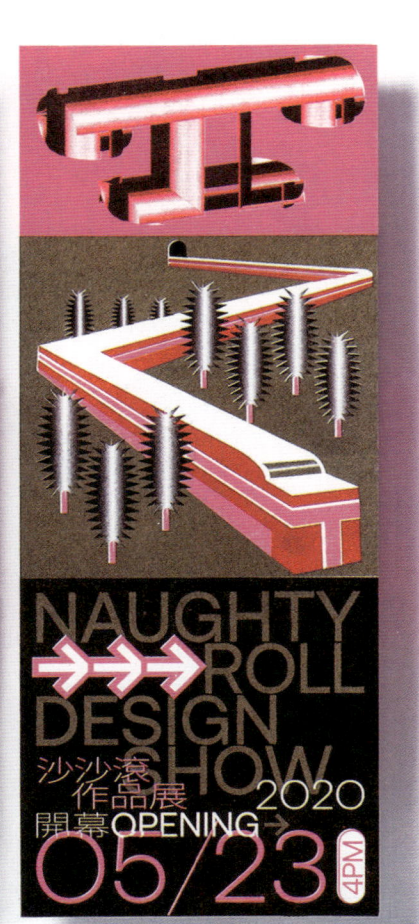

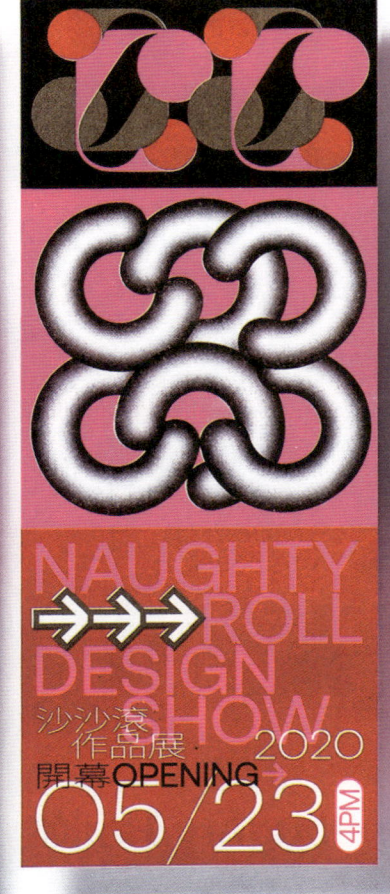

As the brand's inaugural exhibition, the *Naughty Roll Design Show* encapsulates past achievements while projecting future brand development. During the conceptualization of the show's main image, the design team recognized the imperfections inherent in progress. Both Risograph printing technology and individual lives exhibit imperfections. The theme "imperfection is part of life" was approached with light-heartedness and humor. Four letters representing "imperfection" were created in 3D modeling, accompanied by illustrated characters engaging in absurd daily actions. The combination of various techniques portrays imperfection in a humorous light, encouraging viewers to maintain a positive and humorous outlook towards life's imperfections.

Client: Naughty Roll

▼ **Inspiration:**

The *Naughty Roll Design Show*, the brand's debut exhibition, embraces an imperfection theme with a lighthearted and humorous design approach. While not explicitly stated, potential retro influences include surrealism, known for its exploration of absurd concepts, and the playful nature of Pop Art from the 1950s and 1960s. Mid-20th century retro advertising styles, featuring vibrant colors and whimsical elements, could also have played a role. Vintage typography styles like Art Deco or Mid-Century Modern may have influenced the creation of 3D-modeled letters.

▼ **Elements:**

The *Naughty Roll Design Show*'s design project explores the theme that "imperfection is part of life" in a lighthearted and humorous manner. Various graphic elements are incorporated to visually represent this concept. Four letters representing "imperfection" are created using 3D modeling and intentionally deformed to symbolize life's imperfect nature and progress. This deformation adds a playful and whimsical touch, emphasizing the exhibition's lighthearted approach.

▼ **Layout:**

The layout arrangement in the *Naughty Roll Design Show*'s design project centers on prominently displaying the four letters representing "imperfection." These letters, crafted using 3D modeling, act as a focal point, conveying the theme of embracing imperfections. Illustrated characters depicted in absurd postures while engaging in common daily actions are strategically positioned around the letters, injecting humor and dynamism into the composition. While specific layout details may vary, the overarching goal was to create a visually captivating design that embodies a lighthearted and humorous approach to confronting life's imperfections.

VAH THAI

VAH THAI Restaurant, founded in 1988, has been a staple in the lives of Macau locals for generations. Being the first restaurant in Macau to introduce classic Thai snack boat noodles, the owner crafted a unique boat noodle recipe and secret seasoning to suit the local food culture. In this design project, the focus was on highlighting the fusion of Chinese and Thai cultures and narrating the restaurant's 30-year journey, capturing the strong community bonds of Macau.

The illustrations center around the restaurant's signature boat noodles and fresh ingredients, complemented by typography that shares anecdotes from the founder's story. The brand font design blends elements from both Chinese and Thai cultures. Extensive research was conducted on fonts commonly used in Macau and Thai restaurants during the 1980s, with similar fonts being selected for the design. To showcase the history and culture of the restaurant while offering a contemporary twist, Risograph printing, popular in the 80s, was chosen for the brand posters. This choice pays homage to tradition while presenting a fresh take on the restaurant's heritage.

Designer: Lam Ieong Kun, Dan Ferreira
Client: VAH THAI

▼ Inspiration & Elements:

The design project for VAH THAI Restaurant is notably influenced by retro elements that evoke the essence of the 1980s era. The introduction of classic Thai boat noodles in 1988 serves as a foundational inspiration, aligning perfectly with the restaurant's 30-year history. The fusion of Chinese and Thai cultures further enhances the retro aesthetics, highlighting the cultural connections of Macau.

In terms of fonts, the design seamlessly integrates characteristics from both Chinese and Thai cultures, reflecting the cultural fusion prevalent in the 80s. Extensive research on fonts commonly used in Macau and Thai restaurants during that era informs the selection process, demonstrating a commitment to historical authenticity.

The choice of Risograph printing, a popular technique in the '80s, serves to amplify the retro theme. This printing method adds a nostalgic charm to the brand posters, effectively capturing the history and culture of the restaurant while contributing to the overall preservation of tradition in a contemporary context.

▼ Font:
Niveau Serif

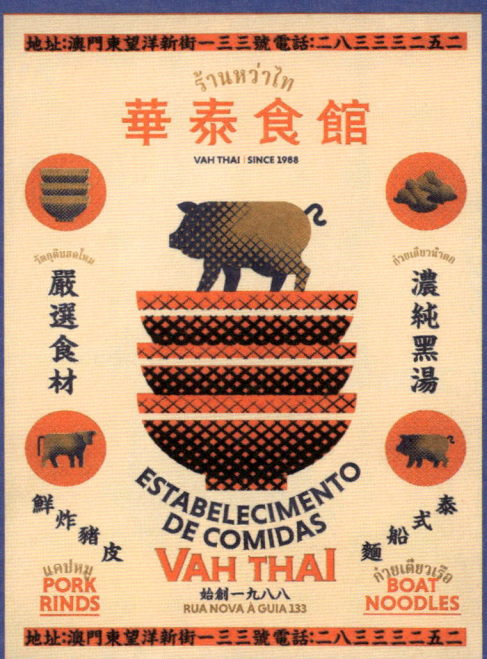

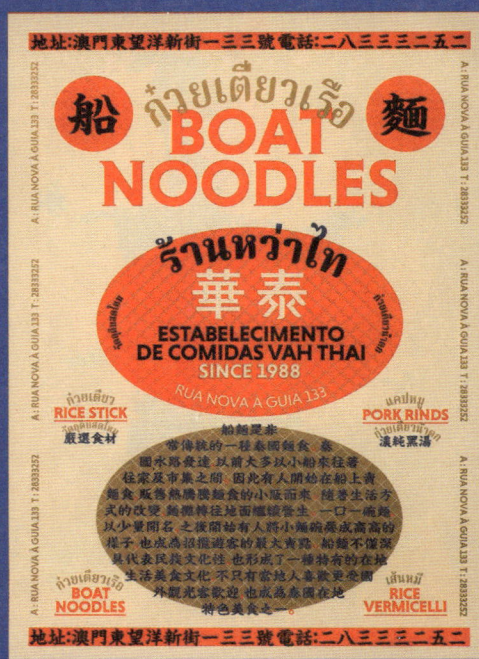

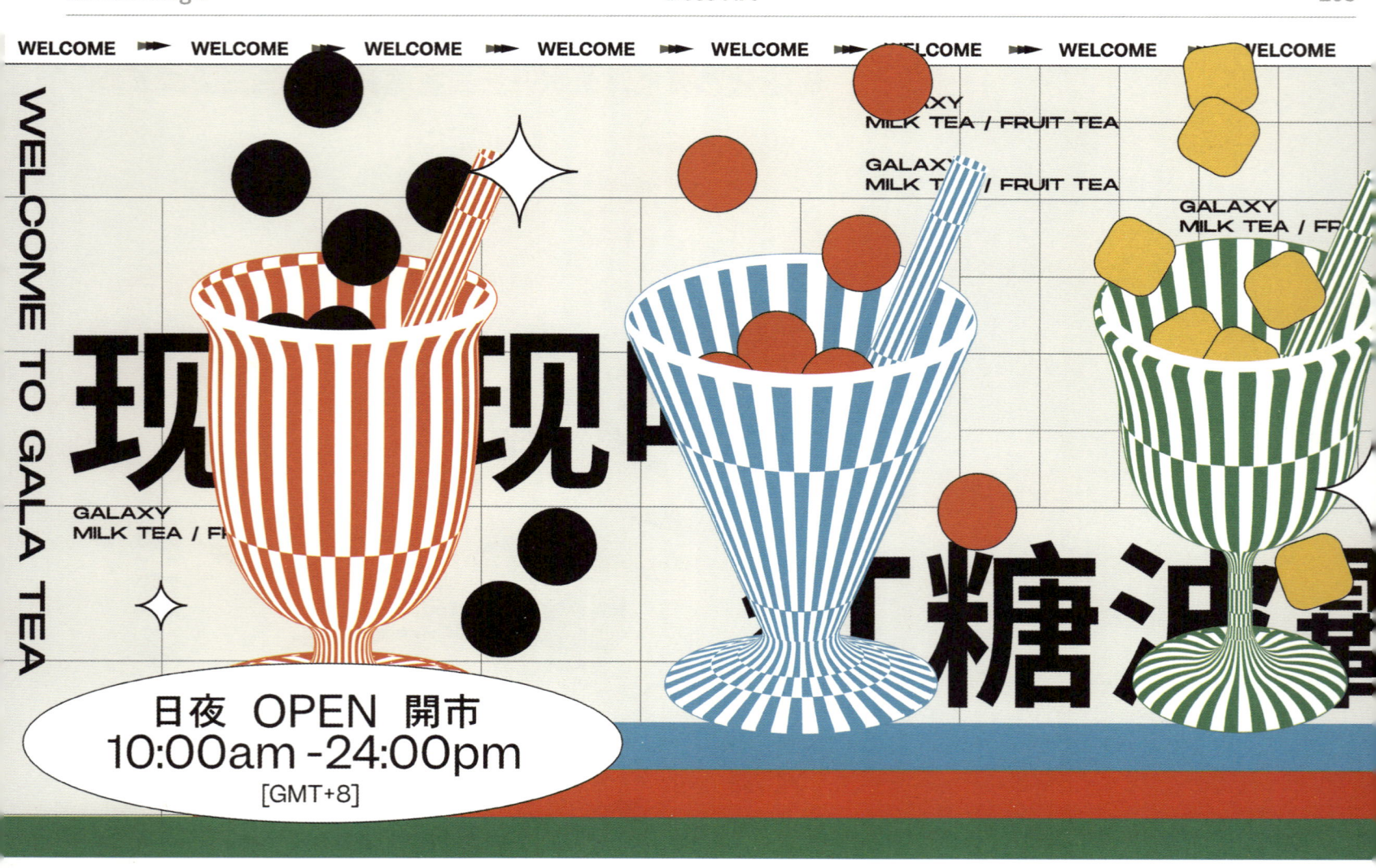

GALAXY STREET

The overall design language of Galaxy Street is built upon the concept of "Future Chinatown." The district operates under its own management organization, with a comprehensive visual system for media and public environments. Merchants within the street operate under the "G Franchising" identity. From Galaxy BBQ, Little Beer Aunt, Coffee Plantation, Jixiang Hun-tun, Gala Milk Tea, Western Street Lamb Skewers, and Urumqi Spice Company, the design team have created these independent merchants, each with rich and diverse visual designs and storytelling content, cultivating a future district filled with cultural conflicts. Considering the mixed nature of Galaxy Street's businesses, the design team aimed to create a virtual reality zone that intertwines the past and the future, blending Eastern and Western elements in a unique and engaging way, accommodating diverse businesses within the same space.

Design studio: RefleXDesign

▼ **Inspiration:**

Different parts of this project integrate elements of Cyberpunk, retro Chinatown style, Op Art, Japanese electronic gaming, as well as elements from West Asia and India.

▼ **Color Scheme:**

R221 G087 B036	R031 G158 B198
C009 M078 Y090 K000	C074 M019 Y015 K000
R018 G141 B093	R233 G232 B231
C081 M027 Y076 K000	C011 M008 Y008 K000

.COME
WELCOME TO GALA TEA

WELCOME WELCOME WELCOME WELCOME WELCOME WELCOME
Gala奶茶
歡迎
在线订座 021 64033611
日夜 OPEN 開市
10:00am -24:00pm
[GMT+8]
黑糖珍珠 專業 現煮現喝
WELCOME WELCOME WELCOME WELCOME WELCOME WELCOME

WELCOME WELCOME WELCOME WELCOME WELCOME WELCOME
New Express
Galaxy
Street 盖楽西街
歡迎光臨
WELCOME YOU
G2020
©2020 Galaxy Street All rights reserved
GO
日夜 OPEN 開市
10:00am -24:00pm
[GMT+8]
WELCOME WELCOME WELCOME WELCOME WELCOME WELCOME

WELCOME WELCOME WELCOME WELCOME WELCOME WELCOME
Galaxy
盖楽西街
LITTLE BEER AUNT
BEER
小
阿姨
G2020
Street
G2020
金光闪闪 畅饮全场
GO! GO! GO!
日夜 OPEN 開市
10:00am -24:00pm
[GMT+8]
四种生啤无限供应
生
Galaxy Street
New Express
GLXJ
GALAXY STREET

WELCOME WELCOME WELCOME WELCOME WELCOME WELCOME
Galaxy
盖楽西街
Street
G2020
金光闪闪 畅饮全场
GO! GO! GO!
日夜 OPEN 開市
10:00am -24:00pm
[GMT+8]
四种生啤无限供应
生
Galaxy Street
New Express
GLXJ
GALAXY STREET

GALAXY STREET SPICES PROVIDED
GALAXY STREET SPICES PROVIDED
Ushi Spice Company
Urumqi Spice Company Limited
乌市香料公司
EST: 2020

GALAXY STREET
SPICES
PROVIDED
Ushi Spice Company
U09
茴香
Urumqi Spice Company Limited
乌市香料公司
EST: 2020

WELCOME
NEW
盖楽西街
OPEN
ようこそ歡迎
日夜 OPEN 開市
10:00am -24:00pm
[GMT+8]
Bienvenue
Galaxy Street
©2020 Galaxy Street All rights reserved

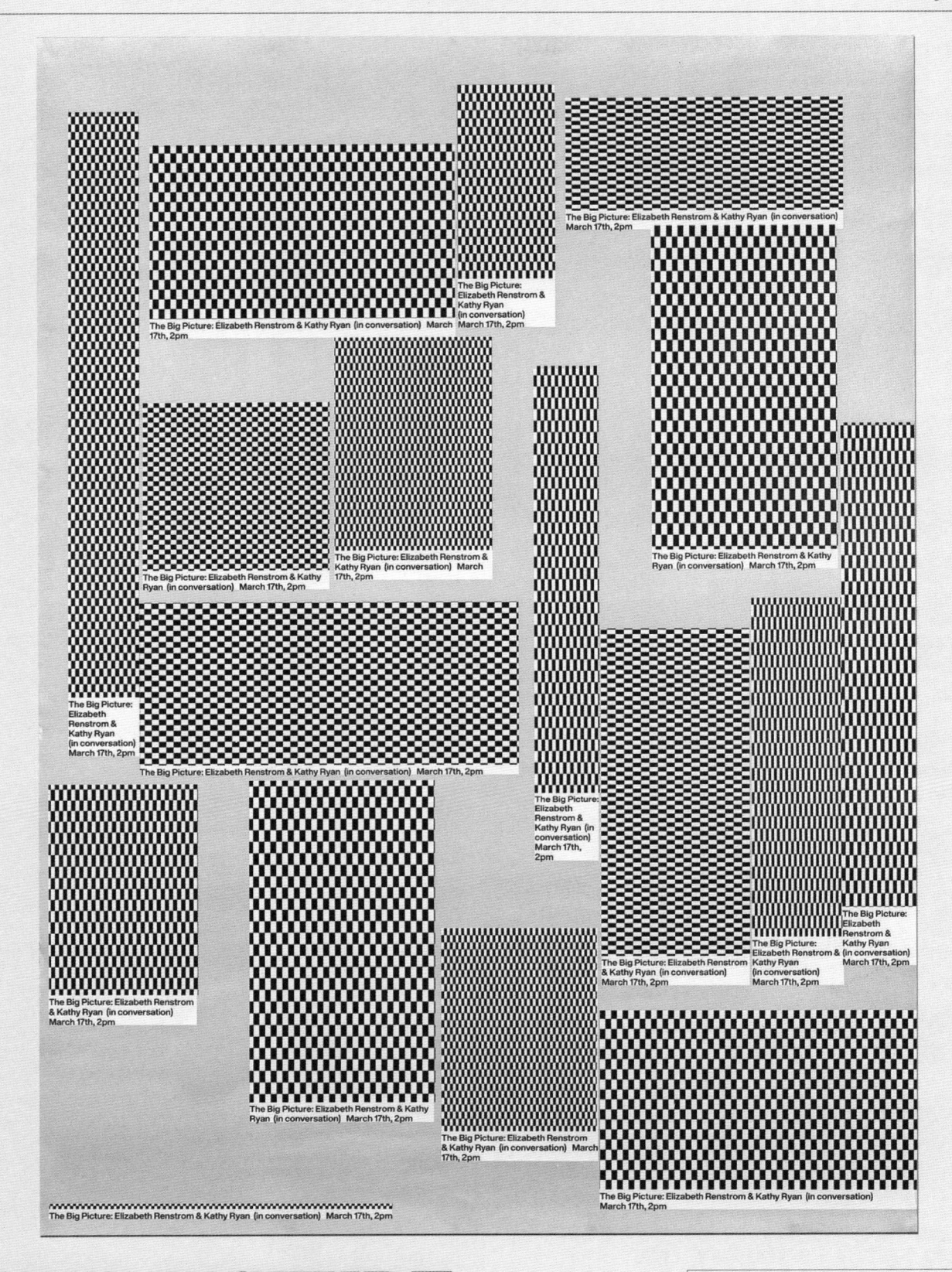

THE BIG PICTURE

Poster designed for the Yale University School of Art Photography Visiting Artist Series. The event was titled "The Big Picture: Elizabeth Renstrom & Kathy Ryan (in conversation)." The concept is to make the entire poster using repetitive elements created from the title and a pattern. Each element contains all the information that the poster should have.

Design Studio: Workbyworks Studio
Designer: Han Gao
Client: Yale University School of Art

▼ **Inspiration:**
This work is highly self-influenced, with the images forming in the creator's mind during the poster-making process. Retro references permeate the design, drawing inspiration from grids, color blocks, and vintage Olympic mark designs.

▼ **Elements:**
The graphic elements are basic checkered patterns, but by stretching the pattern, such a structure emerges.

▼ **Font:**
ABC Monument Grotesk

GLITCH CULTURE VI

The *Glitch Party VI* poster art project was a thrilling venture, focusing on Op Art and retro design to embody the dynamic spirit of Cape Town's Glitch Culture event. Inspired by Op Art from the '60s and '80s, the project aims to infuse nostalgia into a contemporary context. The core creative concept immersed viewers in Op Art's optical illusions, blending bold colors, repetitive patterns, and checkered designs. Evoking the event's moody atmosphere with underground music, black set the tone, complemented by spot colors of red and gold for a retro aesthetic. The animated poster intensified optical illusions, reflecting Glitch Culture's ever-evolving nature, adding a modern touch. The artist tiled highlighted musicians for effective event promotion. In essence, the *Glitch Party VI* poster draws from Op Art and retro design, capturing the spirit of both the '80s and contemporary Glitch Culture.

Design Studio: DTAN Studio
Designer: Julia Schimautz
Client: Glitch Culture

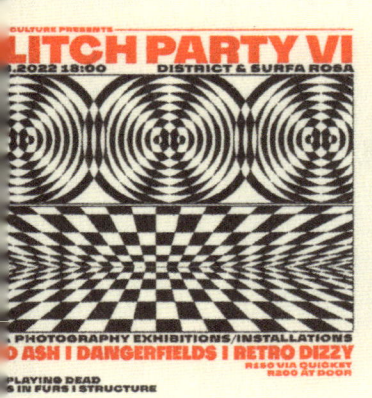

▼ **Inspiration:**

This project draws inspiration from the Op Art movement, which was prominent in the '60s but left a lasting imprint on the '80s aesthetics. Additionally, the design team incorporated elements from the moody and dark ambiance of the '80s underground music and its associated color palette. These influences, coupled with the dynamic and technological experimentation of the era, shaped the project's retro aesthetics.

▼ **Elements:**

Graphic elements like geometric shapes, repetitive patterns, and optical illusions draw inspiration from Op Art. Intentionally deformed, these elements create visual intrigue and complexity, evoking unpredictability and excitement, aligning with the Glitch Culture event's atmosphere.

▼ **Font:**

Agrandir

▼ **Layout:**

The layout features a top-oriented design with the headline at the top and detailed information at the bottom. In the middle, two containers showcase Optical Art: one with an overlaying circle and the one below with an infinity checkered pattern.

CHINESE ZODIAC

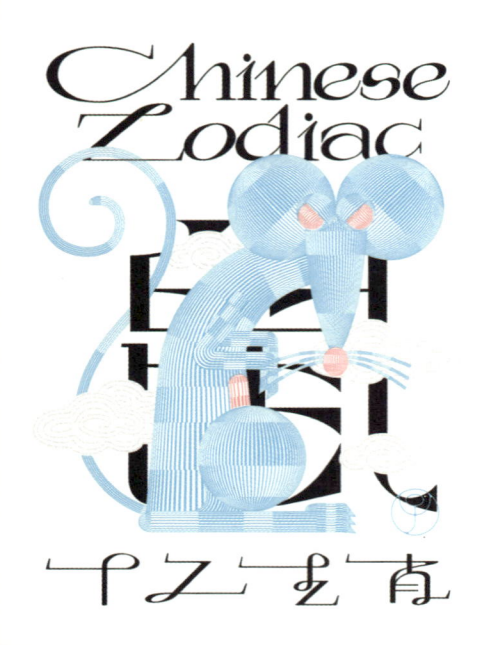

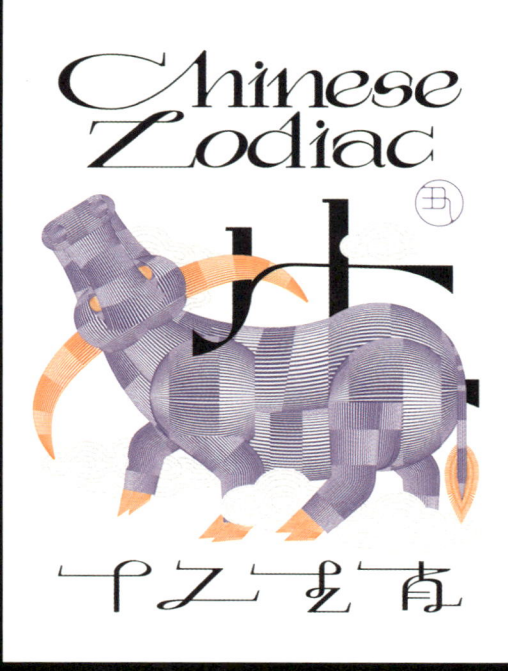

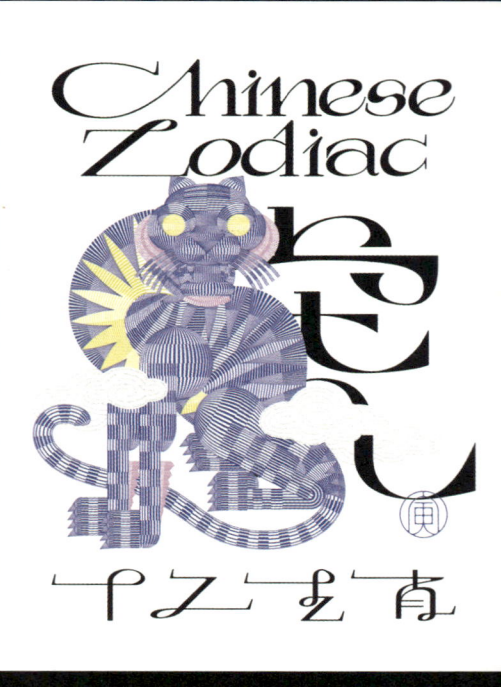

Many designs based on the Chinese zodiac signs tend to adhere to traditional forms. However, the designer aimed to explore more geometric and decorative approaches to represent traditional culture. Utilizing the repetitive, intertwining, and overlapping lines characteristic of Op Art, the goal was to make the expression of traditional culture more diverse and fashionable.

Designer: CHENBO

▼ **Inspiration:**

The work was mainly influenced by the Op Art style, which originated from an art movement in France in 1955. Victor Vasarely, known as the "Father of Op Art," was particularly inspiring to the designer. Victor's work *Zebra* had a significant impact on the designer's work.

▼ **Elements:**

Drawing inspiration from Op Art's repetitive, intersecting, and overlapping line forms, the objective was to infuse traditional representations with a more diverse and contemporary flair.

▼ **Layout:**

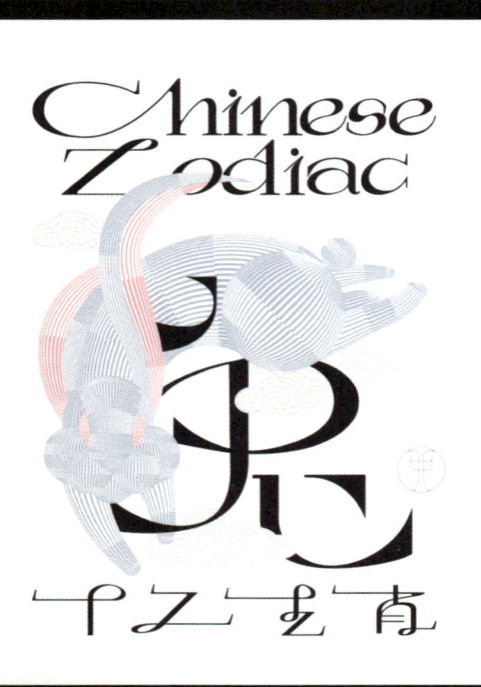

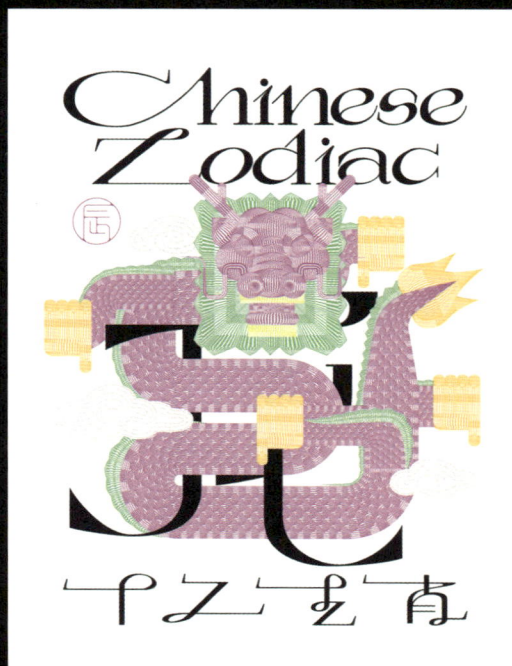

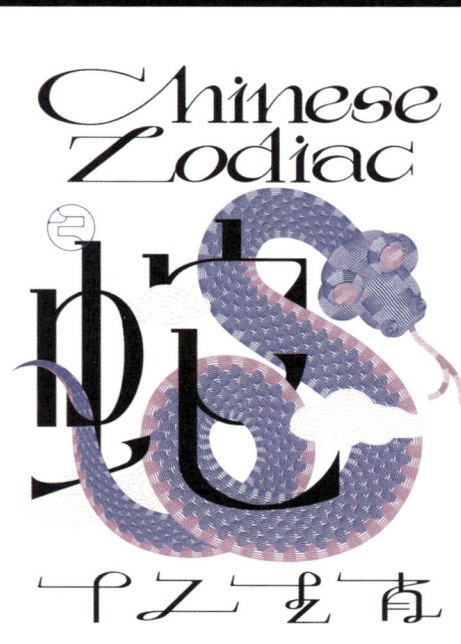

To highlight both the zodiac symbols and the text on the poster, a layout was devised that interweaves graphics and text. By employing this interplay at various levels, the relationship between the visuals and the text becomes rich and three-dimensional.

Chinese Zodiac

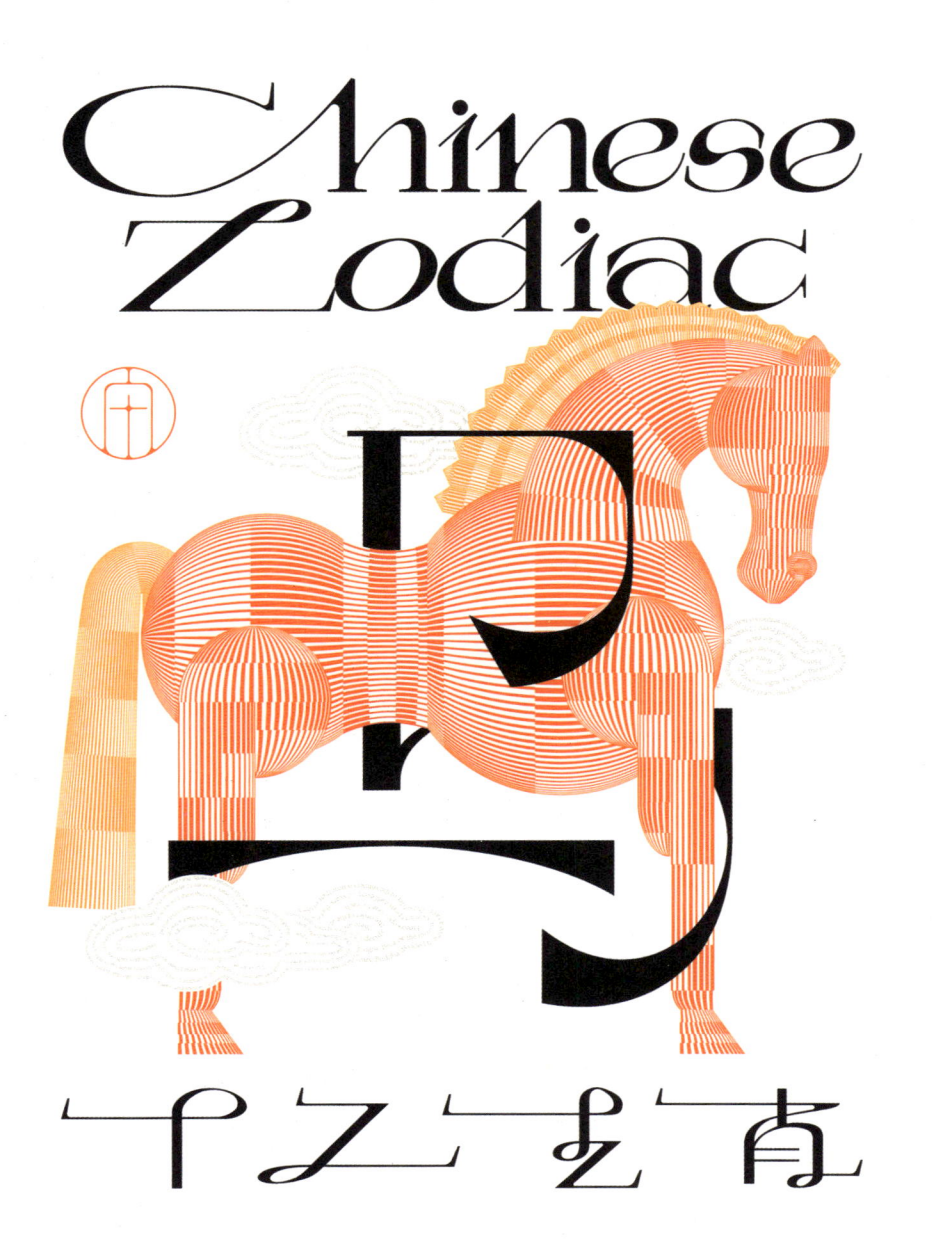

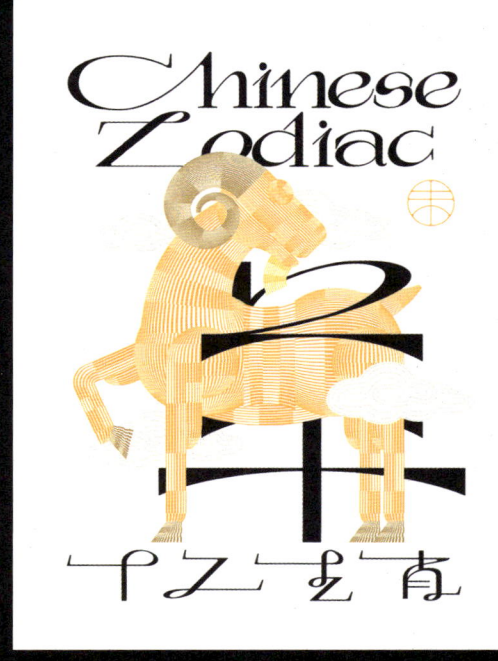

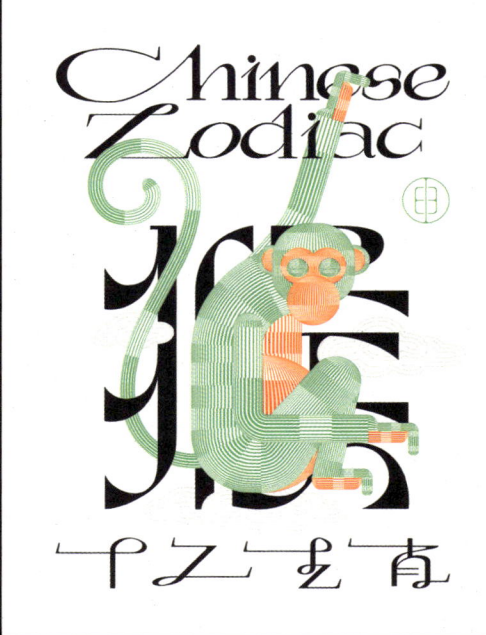

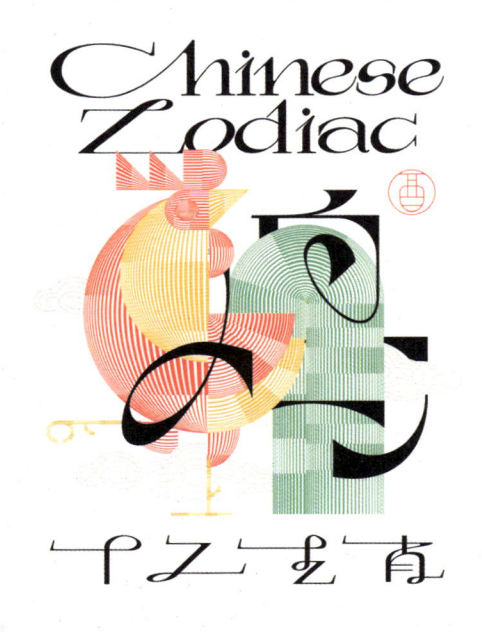

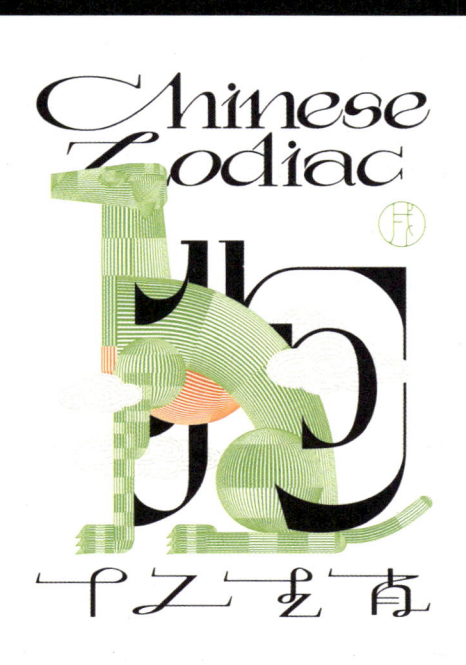

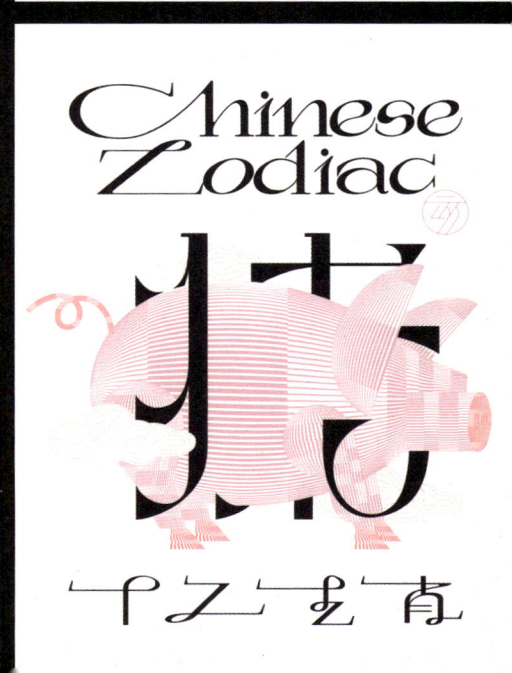

TAI SUI BACK THEN
01th OF
Yunnan Jiama
云南甲马
當年太歲

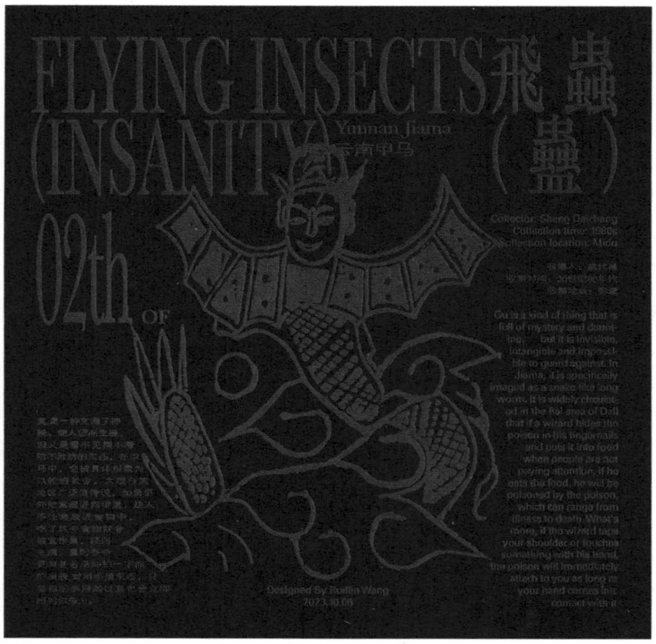
FLYING INSECTS 飛蟲
(INSANITY)
(蠱)
Yunnan Jiama
云南甲马
02th OF

03th OF

YUNNAN JIAMA

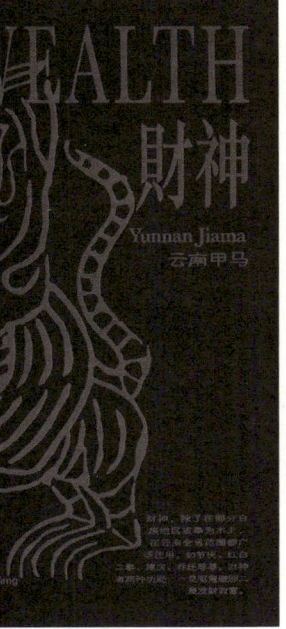

Yunnan Jiama is a woodcut print used by the Bai ethnic group for sacrificial rituals and blessings. Due to various reasons, this traditional craft is on the brink of extinction. Intrigued by the unique patterns and cultural background depicted on the prints, designers transformed these stories into posters that could be understood and shared by younger generations. Additionally, designers created a more easily carved and cost-effective rubber stamp, allowing anyone to imprint it on paper, walls, and various materials, aiming to prevent the disappearance of this cultural heritage.

Design Studio: min means
Designers: Yiyang Li, Ruilin Wang

▼ **Inspiration:**
Starting from the rustic patterns of Yunnan Jiama, the layout and communication of information are carefully considered in terms of content.

▼ **Elements:**
Extracted directly from ancient books of Yunnan Jiama, without any secondary modifications, in an attempt to preserve the original handmade, rustic, and peculiar qualities.

▼ **Fonts:**
Songti SC, Baskerville

▼ **Layout:**
The layout follows a common pattern-centric design, with the emphasis on enlarging and centering the pattern in the composition. The title interacts with the pattern through overlay or alignment, while the detailed content is arranged around the contours of the pattern.

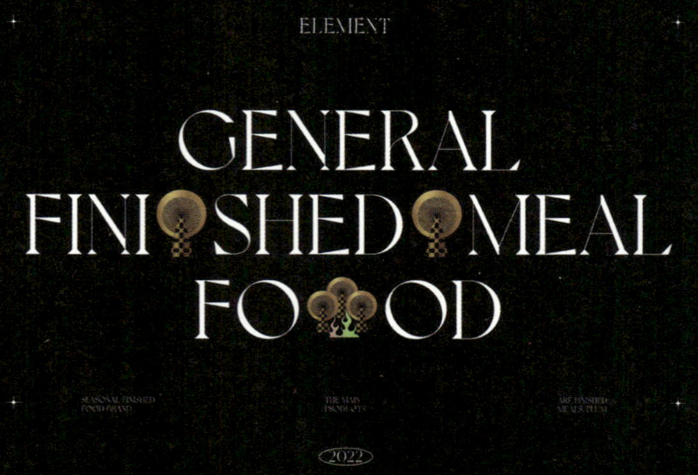

XI SHI GENERAL

Xi Shi General is a brand designed for busy yet health-conscious and quality-seeking young individuals. Embracing the concept of "Nine-to-five Simple and Luxurious Meals," the brand offers a diverse range of products, including finished meals, plum wine, Chinese cakes, and canned goods. With a focus on blending Chinese and Western culinary styles and advocating for reduced oil and salt, Xi Shi General is dedicated to innovating and developing healthy and creative food options. The brand's design features a distinctive contrast, employing bold horizontal strokes and delicate vertical lines with graphical enhancements to enhance recognition. Committed to meeting the dietary needs of the young generation in a personalized, diverse, convenient, and healthy manner, Xi Shi General aims to bring forth a taste of health and individuality through food.

Design Studio: Hellocean

XI SHI GENERAL
喜食将军
金
菇
酱
堡
喜食将军出品
SEASONAL FINISHED FOOD BRAND

XI SHI GENERAL
成品
餐食
{瑞典
肉丸}
food
{食}

XI SHI GENERAL
BROCCOLI
喜食将军
SEASONAL FINISHED FOOD BRAND

SEASONAL FINISHED FOOD BRAND
{雪山
豆腐}
喜食将军

{火山
番茄}
成品
餐食
food
{食}
THREE MEALS A DAY

XI SHI GENERAL
{三珍
瑶兔}
喜食
将军
SEASONAL FINISHED FOOD BRAND

SEASONAL FINISHED FOOD BRAND

LEMON POMELO JAR
喜食将军
柠
檬
柚
罐
POMELO JAR
和胃降逆
化痰止咳
促进消化
生津止渴
喜食将军出品

PLUM TEA
XI SHI GENERAL
SEASONAL FINISHED FOOD BRAND

Plate

清
茶
Plum tea
Tea
{茶}
喜食将军

{调味胶囊}
喜食将军
Taste
{味}

{柠檬
金菇
辣酱

YUANSHAN

远山奈何
YUAN SHAN NAI HE
远山奈何
甜柚子风味
POMELO FLAVOR

YUANSHANNAIHE
YUAN
YSNH
COCKTAIL IS A KIND OF MIXED DRINK, WHICH IS A MIXTURE COCKTAIL IS A

YUANSHANNAIHE

遠

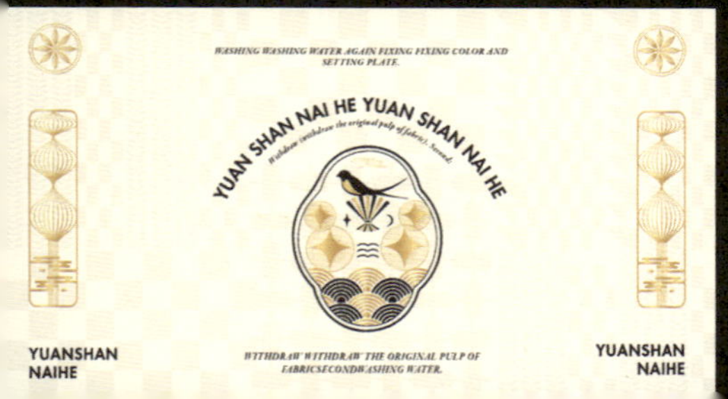
YUAN SHAN NAI HE YUAN SHAN NAI HE
YUANSHAN
NAIHE
YUANSHAN
NAIHE

YUANSHANNAIHE

YUAN SHAN NAI HE

Yuan Shan Nai He (What More Distant Mountain), an oriental-inspired contemporary liquor brand, focuses on crafting visually stunning low-alcohol cocktails, sweet wines, and sparkling wines, paired with exquisite desserts. Rooted in the ethos of "a heart longing for distance without fear," the design exudes a bold, refined, and youthful style with vivid colors, providing a striking visual impact for young consumers. The Chinese typography features bold horizontal strokes and delicate vertical lines, with an overall flattened and dignified appearance, integrating traditional and modern elements to convey the brand's unique Eastern aesthetics and lifestyle.

Design Studio: Hellocean

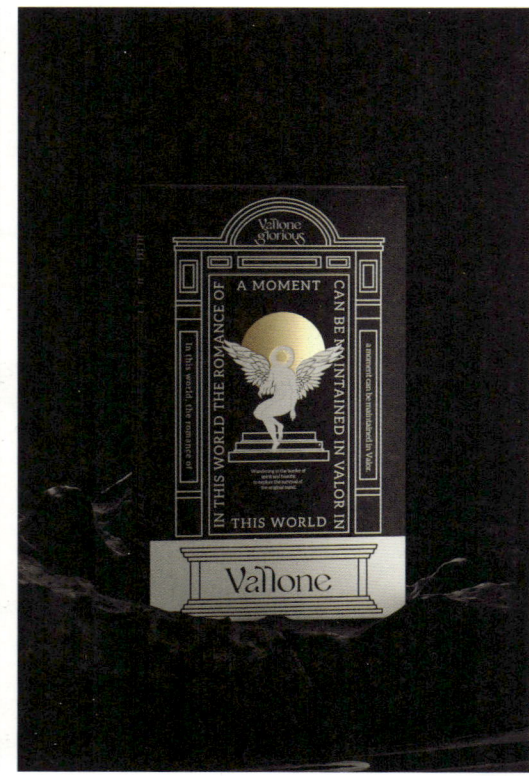

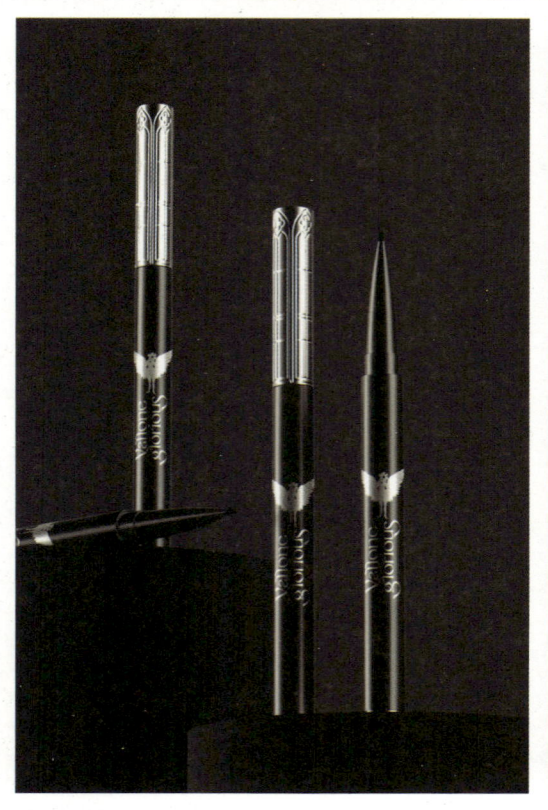

VALLONE GLORIOUS

Vallone Glorious is a unique cosmetics brand tailored for the curious and fearless young generation, blending niche, high-end, and dark-themed elements. Targeting individuals with a rebellious yet independent fashion sense, the brand transcends traditional aesthetics, creating a makeup philosophy that challenges norms and remains true to intuition. Going beyond color, Vallone Glorious emphasizes trendsetting and cultural definition. Encouraging consumers to break free from narrow aesthetic norms, the brand invites exploration of uncharted territories, moving towards the light while coexisting with it.

The design philosophy combines classical, gothic, and edgy elements with understated yet captivating colors, creating a sophisticated and mysterious beauty. Drawing inspiration from Western religions, Vallone Glorious boldly breaks traditional boundaries, showcasing unique beauty and transforming products into works of art that transcend the ordinary, reaching a realm of mysterious and unparalleled aesthetics.

Design Studio: Hellocean

HIITO QITUO

Shanghai Hiito Qituo is committed to fostering extensive global communication and showcasing opportunities between Chinese guitar makers and creators worldwide. Through annual guitar-related events, the organization offers ample opportunities for enthusiasts to engage with makers. Focused on promoting handmade guitars globally, Hiito Qituo selectively partners with internationally acclaimed guitarists who align with the brand's philosophy, providing musicians and enthusiasts with professional choices. The design emphasizes a minimalist English font with creative guitar string integration and a sleek Chinese font incorporating right angles, rounded corners, and deliberate stroke breaks, embodying a modern and professional aesthetics.

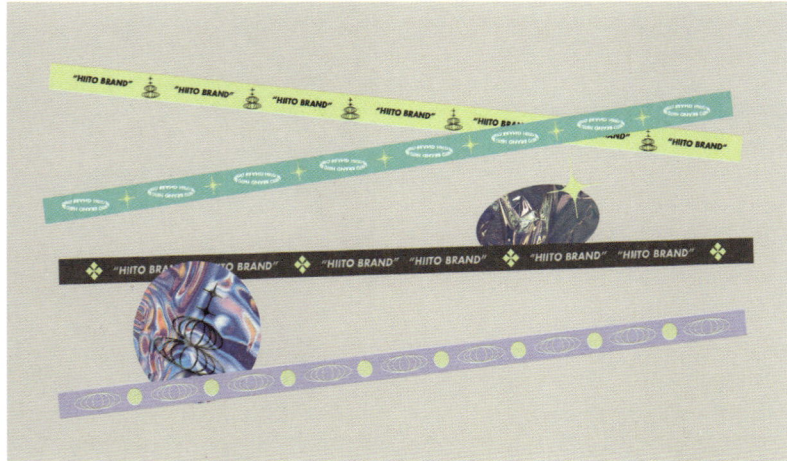

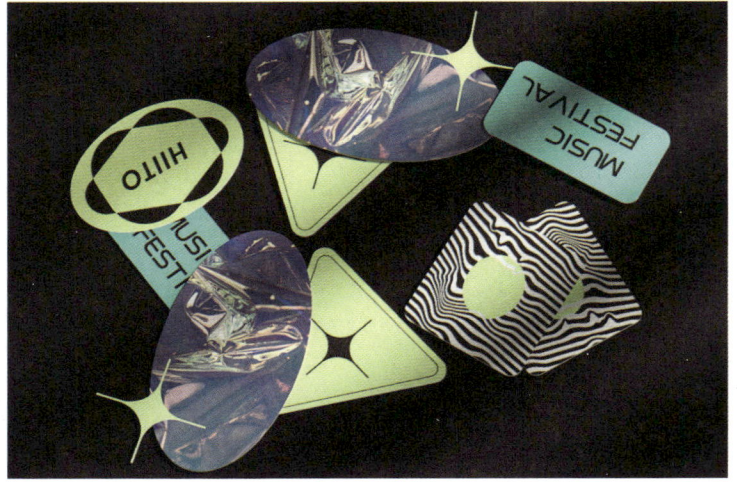

Design Studio: Hellocean

THE EVIL FOREST

The project delves into primitive biological communities, using satire to reveal the darker aspects of human civilization—greed, stupidity, arrogance, and hypocrisy. Visually, the project combines Art Deco and psychedelic poster art, employing symmetrical structures and centralized layouts with low-saturation colors for a retro printing feel.

Illustrator: Jun-Feng Li

▼ **Inspiration:**

Inspired by the influential work of musicians from the latter half of the 20th century—such as John Lennon, the Sex Pistols, Pink Floyd, and Radiohead—the artist drew upon their irony and critique to fuel his imagination and creativity. Visually, the designer drew inspiration not only from the styles of the Art Nouveau and Art Deco but also from psychedelic poster artists like Wes Wilson and Rick Griffin.

▼ **Elements:**

The graphic elements of this project need to convey strong narratives, the designer strived to depict them in a clear and straightforward manner. The designer used single lines, flat colors, and shading to represent the graphics, while adding dotted lines to enrich the details.

▼ **Fonts:**

Neo Victorian, Boecklins Universe, Sancreek, Source Han Serif, Fan Wun Ming

▼ **Layout:**

In this project, the artist introduced the concept of window frames to extend the creative process. He used the structural form of window frames as the framework for individual works, arranging the central main image, text content, and side patterns in intervals. The layout is symmetrical, imparting a sense of religious solemnity. Various font styles and effects are utilized in the text content to match different themes and atmospheres.

THE EVIL FOREST
邪恶森林

▼ Color Scheme:

- R231 G202 B199 / C010 M025 Y017 K000
- R220 G058 B077 / C008 M089 Y059 K000
- R239 G127 B066 / C000 M062 Y074 K000
- R179 G109 B041 / C035 M064 Y094 K001
- R177 G049 B085 / C034 M093 Y053 K000
- R203 G134 B168 / C021 M056 Y013 K000
- R113 G142 B149 / C062 M038 Y037 K000
- R063 G078 B150 / C083 M073 Y010 K000
- R103 G140 B092 / C066 M036 Y073 K000
- R221 G207 B202 / C015 M020 Y018 K000

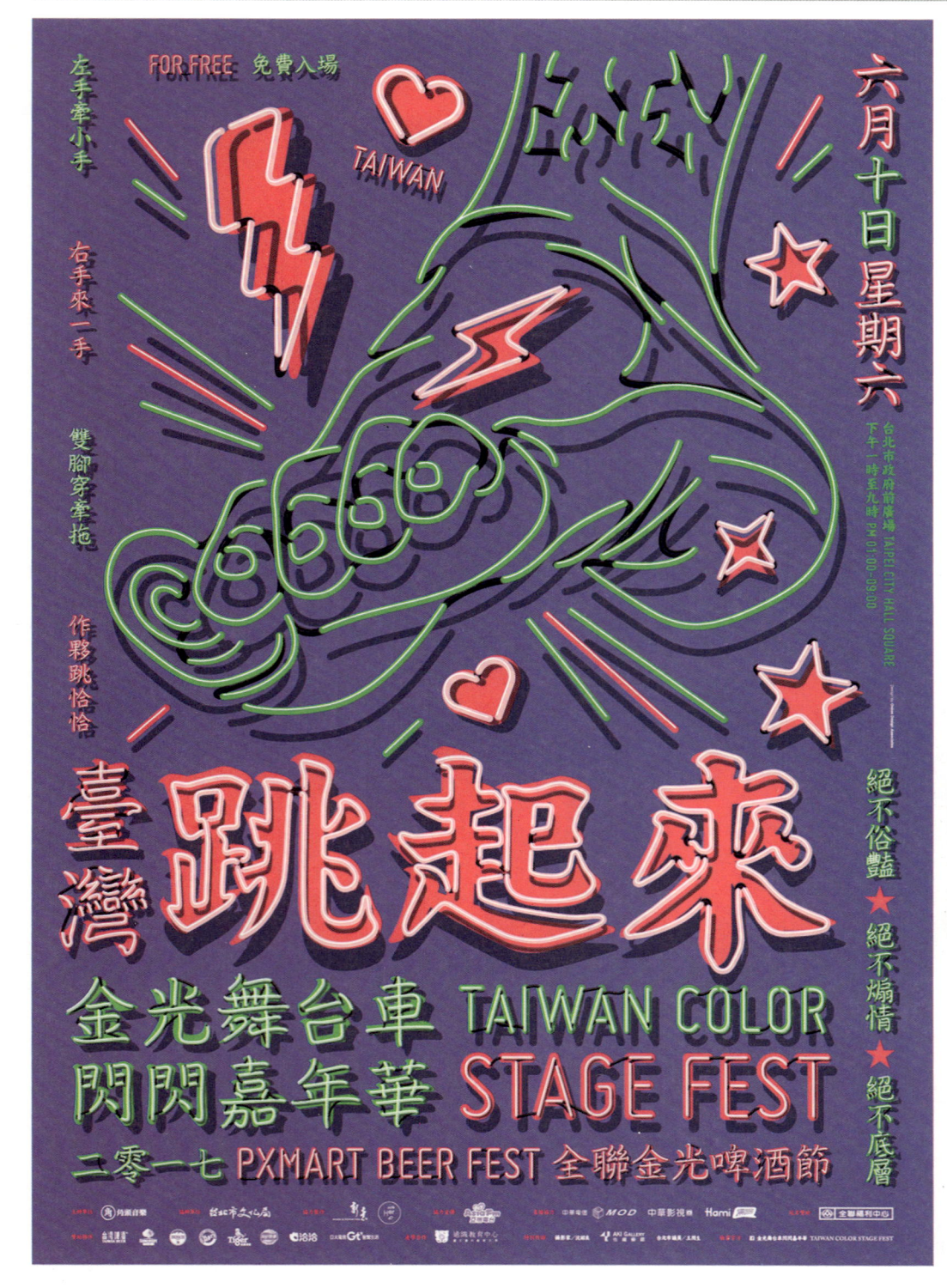

Onion Design Associates — Deco Art — 226

▼ **Inspiration:**
Electric Flower Cars are trucks that have been converted into wheeled, neon-lit platforms, typically serving as moving stages upon which strippers can perform during religious, celebratory, or funeral processions. All the typography in the poster imitates neon signs of the stage cars. The poster is also printed with four fluorescent inks to pay tribute to the colorful local subculture.

▼ **Elements:**
The project is heavily influenced by neon signs from the streets of the region and stage truck subculture.

▼ **Fonts:**
DFKaiShuStd, Miso

▼ **Layout:**
The designers embraced maximalist graphic design and try to fill up every inch of the poster, leaving no negative space, as a reference to local vernacular aesthetics.

TCM STAGE FEST

Curated by the native Music Indie Label TCM, the festival celebrates a unique local subculture of Stage Cars, also known as Electric Flower Cars. These trucks have been converted into wheeled, neon-lit platforms, typically serving as moving stages where pole dancers and singers can perform during religious, celebratory, or wedding banquets. The festival features 30 stage trucks, 30 dancing poles, stage truck singers, religious marching bands, and famous Indie bands and DJs.

Design Studio: Onion Design Associates
Designer: Andrew Wong, Fong Ming Yang
Client: TCM

KISS THE NEW YEAR CALENDAR

This project was printed with Neenah double-sided column-card stock, with the 3D glasses die-cut and folded out onto the same sheet of paper. One side is printed with metallic black ink on black, while the inside showcases two overlapping Pantone red and blue Anaglyph 3D effects.

Design Studio: Onion Design Associates
Designer: Andrew Wong, Spy Lan

▼ **Inspiration:**

The vinyl record *Shinin' On* by Grand Funk, an American rock band, came with attached 3D glasses. Given the popularity of Anaglyph 3D in the '70s, the album's image is inspired by the psychedelic era.

▼ **Fonts:**

Brothers, Latin Extra Condensed, URW, Wood Type, Buxom, Caslon 540 Std Swash Alternative Italic

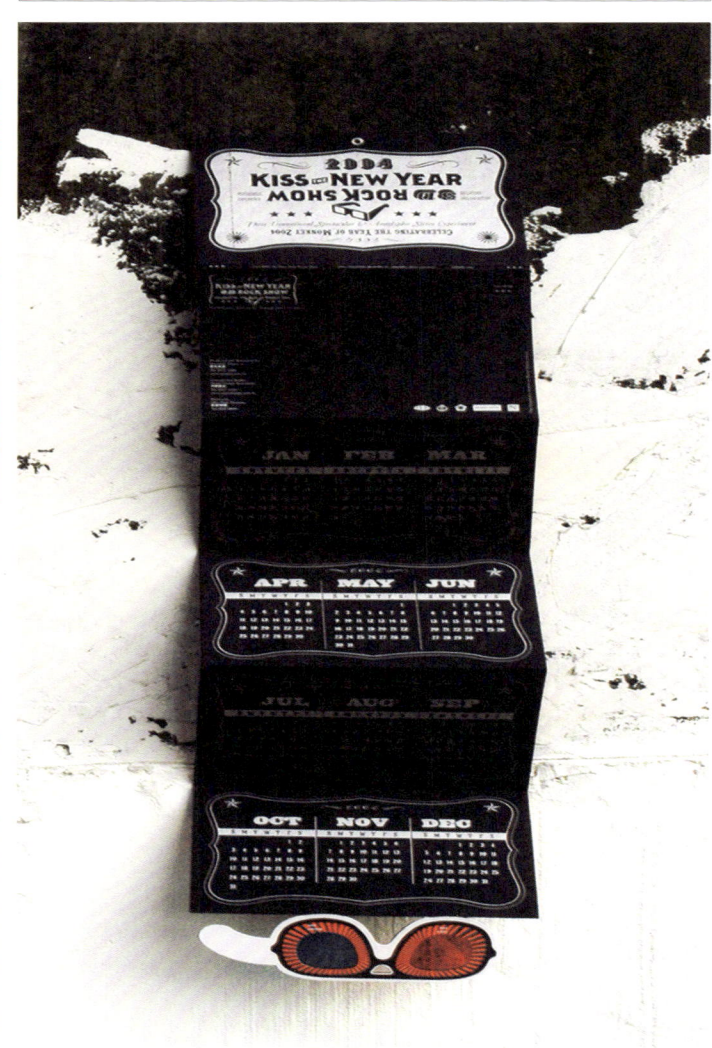

GOBLYNS CONCERT

The poster design for Goblyns encapsulates the vibrant aesthetics of the 1970s and 1980s, drawing inspiration from Op Art, psychedelic, and geometric elements. Created for a concert in Amsterdam, it adorned prominent locations throughout the city. Goblyns, an instrumental psychedelic high-energy groove rock trio, provided the musical backdrop, seamlessly blending the intensity of rock with the hypnotic ambiance of psychedelia. Influenced by Op Art and Art Deco, the retro-inspired design features a green checkered tunnel leading to a bold red heart, evoking nostalgia through a limited color palette. The chosen font reflects 70s to 80s style, contributing to the cohesive design. The poster aims to capture the feelings evoked by Goblyns' music, mirroring the immersive experience through a soft visual illusion.

Design Studio: DTAN Studio
Designer: Julia Schimautz
Client: Goblyns

▼ **Inspiration:**
Op Art is a movement from the 1960s renowned for its optical illusions and geometric patterns. It features a vibrant color palette typical of the 1970s and 1980s, particularly focusing on red and green. The typography also reflects the styles of that era.

▼ **Elements:**
The checkered tunnel serves as the main visual element, guiding the viewer's focus through its captivating design. Drawing inspiration from the Op Art movement, the tunnel's geometric patterns create a visually immersive experience, evoking the optical illusions and striking geometry that define the style.

▼ **Font:**
Geometric 231 Heavy

▼ **Layout:**
The central focus is the checkered tunnel, directing attention to the heart-shaped endpoint and emphasizing an emotional connection to the music. The symmetrical design ensures visual balance and order, while the tunnel's distortion adds a dynamic and unexpected element.

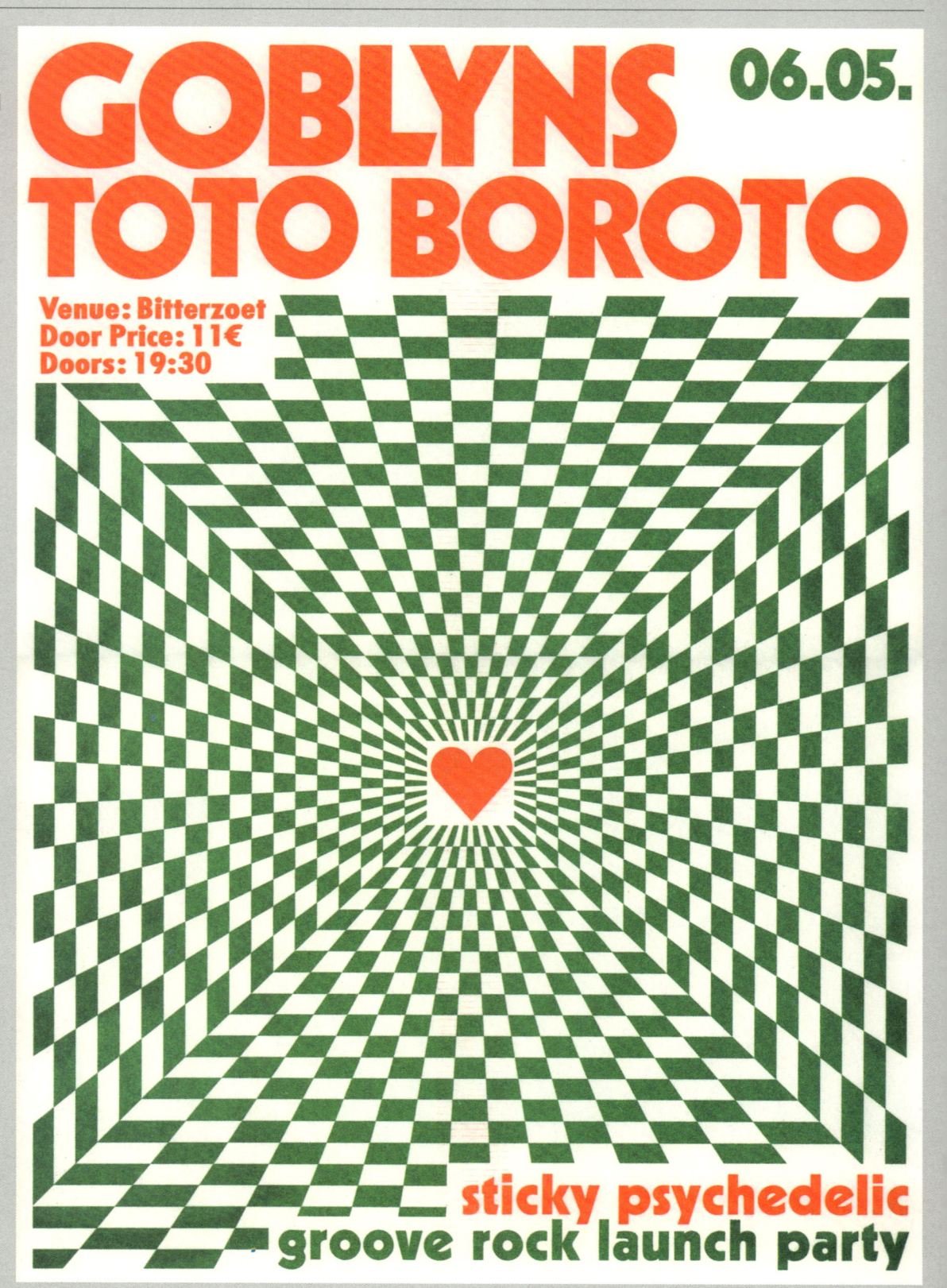

THE BACKSEAT LOVERS US TOUR

The poster designed for The Backseat Lovers US Tour project seamlessly blends retro aesthetics with an animated touch. Drawing inspiration from the Doppler effect, the design aims to evoke nostalgia with a unique twist. The Doppler effect, associated with frequency shifts in waves, inspired a series of riso animations. These animations, when played consecutively, create a visual illusion of movement. Risograph printing, chosen for its warmth and texture, enhances the retro feel and aligns with the nostalgia of past printing techniques. The color scheme, dominated by shades of pink and warmth, complements the overall vision of the project.

Design Studio: DTAN Studio
Designer: Julia Schimautz
Client: The Backseat Lovers

▼ **Inspiration:**
Influenced by a fusion of retro elements, this design project draws inspiration from the bold aesthetics of Op Art and Psychedelic Art, echoing the works of artists like Victor Vasarely and Peter Max. The free-spirited counterculture of the 1960s, characterized by events like Woodstock, infuses a sense of freedom and experimentation into the work.

▼ **Layout:**
The poster consists of a sequence of frames that, when viewed together, simulate motion. The deformation of these frames, as they transition from one to the next, creates the impression of an unfolding narrative.

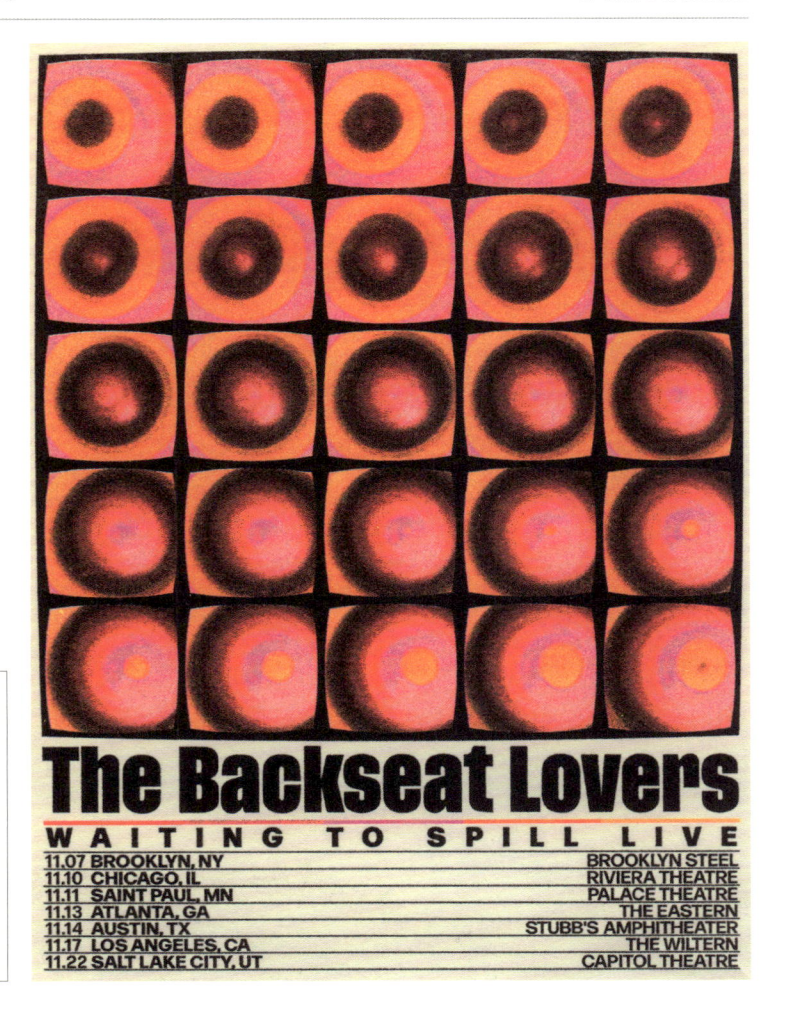

CAAMP EU/UK TOUR

This poster project explores vibrant retro aesthetics, embodying the folk rock band CAAMP's energy and live essence. Using Risograph printing for vivid colors and unique texture, the intentionally imperfect design features a central square with colorful circles and a focal black-and-white band photo. The misalignment creates playful movement, akin to Op Art's optical illusions. This fusion of retro-inspired aesthetics and contemporary risoprinting captures CAAMP's spirit and celebrates the playful imperfections of design.

Design Studio: DTAN Studio
Designer: Julia Schimautz
Client: CAAMP

▼ **Inspiration:**
The design merges the mesmerizing elements of Op Art and Psychedelic Art, utilizing optical illusions and bold colors to captivate the eye. It draws inspiration from the clean lines and geometric shapes characteristic of mid-20th century design aesthetics, blending these structured forms with a sense of whimsy. This playful approach reflects the vibrant energy found in vintage posters.

▼ **Elements:**
The design features a central square with rows of differently colored circles. Each circle is filled with a different color, and their misalignment adds an element of dynamic movement and imperfection.

▼ **Layout:**
This design project centers around the band's name at the top for clear branding. A large square below features orderly rows of circles, creating a balanced and visually engaging composition. The square serves as a focal point, contrasting with the dynamic deformation of circles, adding playfulness. Essential touring details are at the bottom, completing the comprehensive layout.

FLOWERS COMPOSITIONS

It's a series of floral visuals, existing somewhere between abstract and figurative realms. It involves working with wefts, textures, and shapes to enrich the artist's universe. It resembles a stylistic exercise, where the designer experimented with hatching, dots, and colors to discover new combinations and evolve their work.

Designer: Thomas Merceron

▼ Color Scheme:

- R176 G072 B063 / C038 M084 Y077 K002
- R049 G077 B118 / C089 M075 Y040 K003
- R043 G067 B050 / C083 M063 Y083 K039
- R111 G162 B186 / C061 M029 Y023 K000
- R101 G150 B096 / C066 M031 Y073 K000
- R171 G106 B143 / C041 M067 Y026 K000

FLEURS 2.0

Inspired by a moment on a Parisian balcony while sifting through a sketchbook, the artist conceptualized the idea swiftly, using geometrical shapes to bring the flowers to life in a digital form. The initial burst of inspiration took just half a day to translate into a visual concept. However, refining details such as colors, format, framing, and layout required several days of meticulous work. The artist adopted a process of stepping back and returning to the project to gain a better perspective, ensuring the final result meets her artistic standards.

Designer: Laura Normand

▼ **Inspiration:**

Admiring the minimalist Japanese graphic style, similar to the works of the incredible Ikko Tanaka , the designer found inspiration in drawing elements from simple and geometric shapes. Embracing this process is akin to engaging in an infinite puzzle game with numerous solutions. The artistic approach consistently yields clean, strong, and elegant designs that reflect the beauty of simplicity and geometric precision.

▼ **Elements:**

The main element is flowers, as their shapes are so fun, unique, and have infinite possibilities.

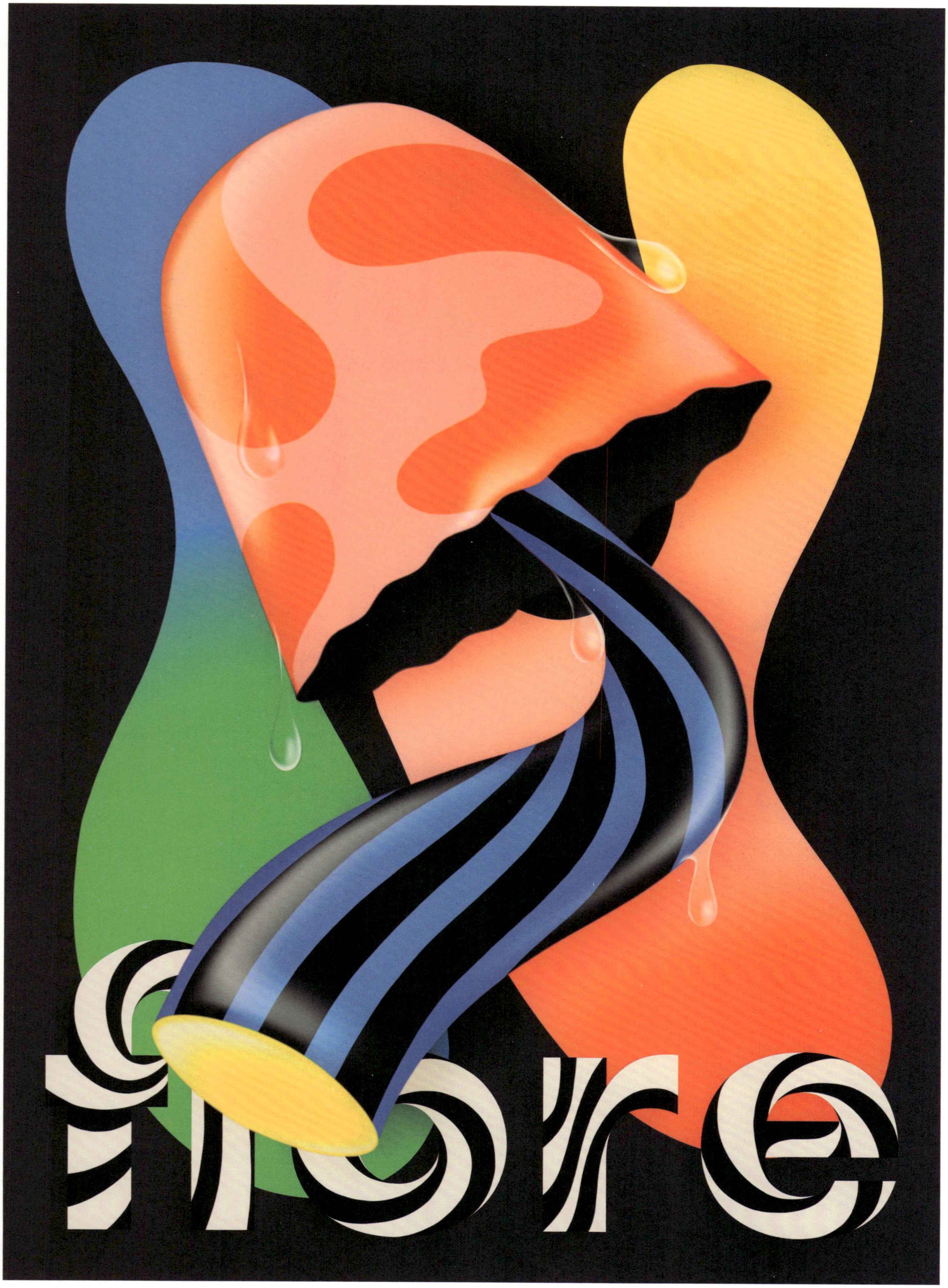

FLORE – SEXY NATURE

The process of this project involved reproducing these flowers in a more digital way, incorporating glossy textures, and infusing vibrant colors for a contemporary touch.

Designer: Laura Normand

▼ **Inspiration:**
Inspired by the Ettore Sottsass and iconic Memphis design, the designer has a deep appreciation for the movement's sexy curves, playful shapes, and positive colors. Much like Sottsass, the designer found joy in creating designs that evoke a sense of beauty, aiming for a therapeutic quality. The goal was to bring about a feeling of happiness and positive vibes when one encounters their work.

▼ **Font:**
Futura

PERFECT PRINT ITEM SYSTEM

The artist designed a visual application system for Perfect Print Studio, a Shanghai-based darkroom studio. Six different colors and graphic patterns were developed for the various services they provide. The overall aesthetic tone is inspired by traditional film-related products but created with carefully articulated contemporary design voices.

Design Studio: Workbyworks Studio
Designer: Han Gao
Client: Perfect Print

▼ **Inspiration:**

The visual elements that influence the design are akin to the film rolls from Fuji and others. There is a specific aesthetics from that era and industry, characterized by the use of color blocks and large types. These visual languages were well translated into the design of the Perfect Print visual system.

▼ **Elements:**

The graphic elements are all designed with a personal taste; many decisions are made based on personal experience and an understanding of the trend. But overall, it's using different color blocks.

▼ **Font:**

New Rail Alphabet Regular

▼ **Layout:**

The idea is simple: build up a grid system using the smallest unit of a box and align all elements to the grid.

235 · Deco Art · Workbyworks Studio

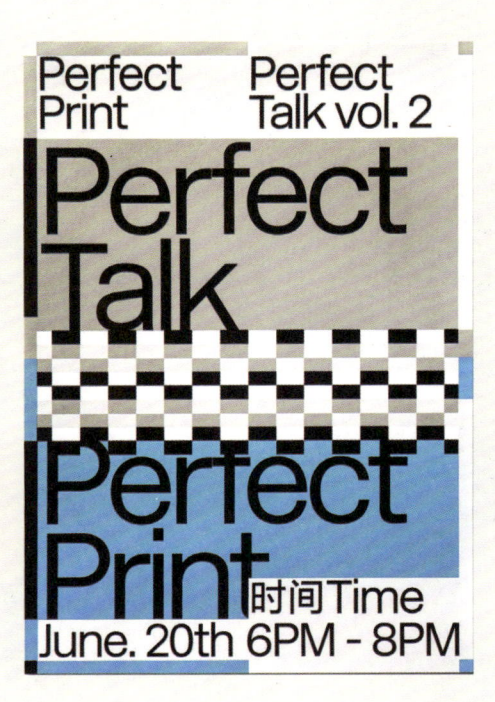

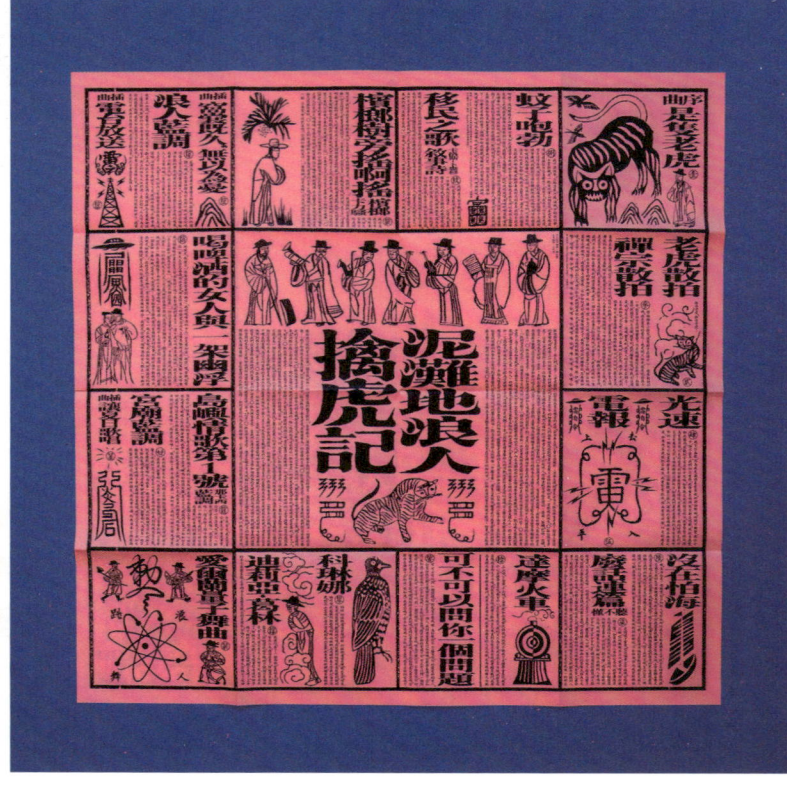

Onion Design Associates • Deco Art

HOLD THAT TIGER

Hold That Tiger is the third full-length album by the jug band the Muddy Basin Ramblers, a group of US/UK expats living in the region. To convey the complex and experimental nature of the music and its subject matter, which plays with the East/West cultural divide, the design team decided to create a visual style that combines religious folk culture and Taoist mysticism with a touch of 50s Retro-Futurism from the West.

Design Studio: Onion Design Associates
Designer: Andrew Wong, Fong Ming Yang
Client: The Muddy Basin Ramblers

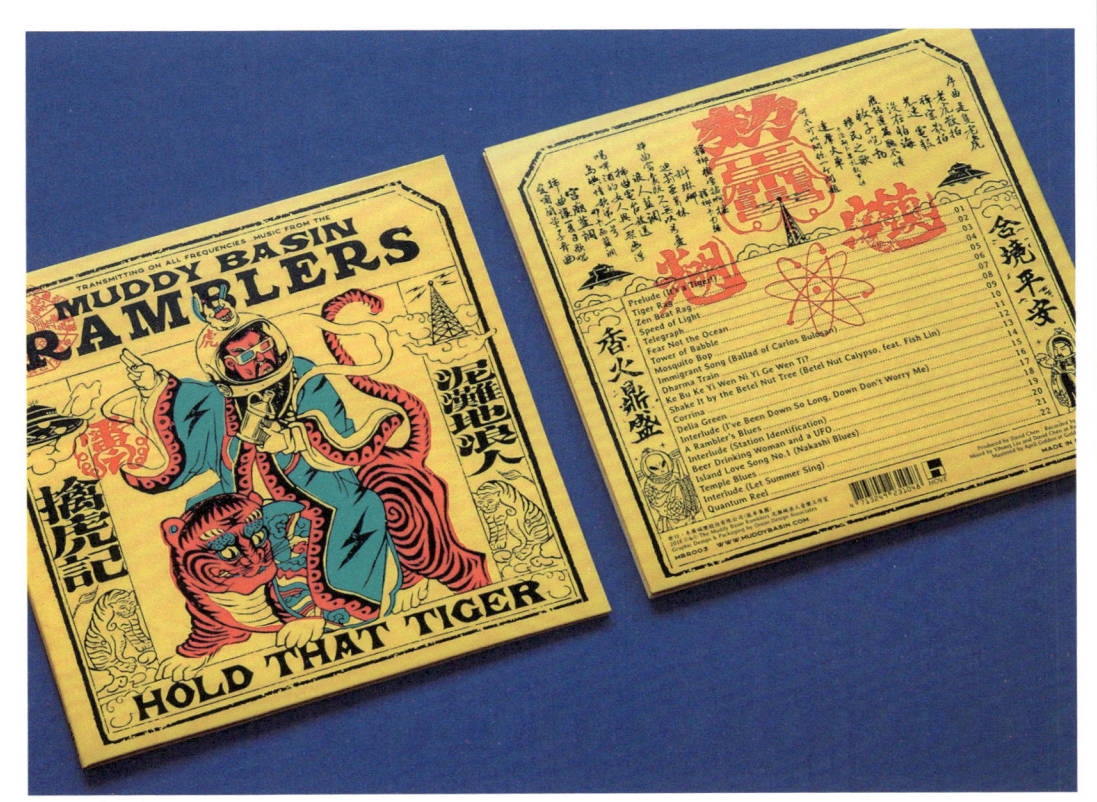

▼ **Inspiration:**

The music combines a variety of global influences, featuring mostly original tracks with styles ranging from swing jazz, blues, and ragtime to traditional temple parade music, Nakashi, Irish folk, and even local hip hop. The eclectic song lyrics cover topics like folk religion, the Asian immigrant diaspora, the Beat Generation, sci-fi/UFO kitsch from the 1950s, and jazz history. The Taoist paper talisman technique is borrowed from the artist Xu Bing's *Square Word Calligraphy*.

▼ **Elements:**

The title "Hold that Tiger" comes from a lyric in "Tiger Rag," a jazz standard dating back to 1917, which is the first song on this album. The design studio borrowed from traditional Chinese folk art, invoking an iconic image of the Taoist figure Zhang Daoling, aka "Chinese Celestial Master Zhang Tianshi," who is often portrayed with a tiger. The image is sourced from a Taoist paper talisman (符, *Fu*). The talisman is traditionally kept to ward off evil or unwanted spirits and ghosts. In keeping with one theme on the album—the mixing of traditional and modern elements—we "retro-fitted" Master Zhang with a space helmet, 3D glasses, and a jug (often used as a homemade "tuba" by jug bands).

▼ **Fonts:**

Tunesmith JNL, Primitive Tuscan JNL

▼ **Layout:**

The yellow CD cover adopts the appearance of a Taoist talisman. The printed calligraphy may seem like abstracted Chinese glyphs, but it is actually composed of Roman letters. The band's name, "The Muddy Basin Ramblers," is written on the right, and the CD title, "Hold That Tiger," on the left. This reconstruction technique is inspired by the artist Xu Bing's *Square Word Calligraphy*, where he created a system to write English resembling Chinese characters. When folded using an origami hexagon folding technique, the CD sleeve mimics the look of a traditional amulet.

GRAFIS NUSANTARA
KOLEKSI LABEL DAN STIKER
KWALITET ISTIMEWA
GRAFIS NUSANTARA
KOLEKSI LABEL & STIKER
GRAFIS NUSANTARA
2022

GRAFIS NUSANTARA
KWALITET ISTIMEWA
01
GRAFIS NUSANTARA
Vol. 01 KOLEKSI LABEL & STIKER 2022
Nusantara
LABEL
STIKER
NUSANTARA

GRAFIS NUSANTARA VOL. 1: KOLEKSI LABEL & STICKER

Grafis Nusantara Vol.1 is a book presenting a diverse collection of Indonesian product labels and stickers from the 1970s to the 1990s. Curated by Jakarta-based graphic designer Rakhmat Jaka and published by Kamengski, the book, a collaboration with Evan Wijaya, features retro vibrant colors and kitschy aesthetics. Organized into categories for easy navigation, it covers product labels from various sectors like textiles and tea, and stickers with themes ranging from erotic to religious, showcasing Indonesia's visual diversity. Additionally, the volume includes a booklet with a sticker-covered cover, five postcards, and a large tri-fold card, enhancing the reader's experience and aligning with the theme of Indonesian visual culture.

Designer: Evan Wijaya
Collection of Rakhmat Jaka

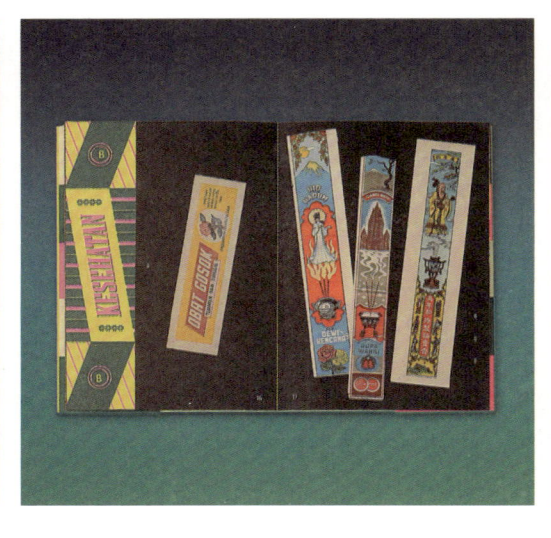

GRAFIS NUSANTARA VOL.2: LABEL KERUPUK

This project compiles kerupuk (Javanese) labels, delving into their cultural and historical significance. Featuring Atras Alwafi's collection, the book includes a bilingual interview for additional insights. With a comprehensive overview of kerupuk types, the book explores regional variations and their evolution. It also includes a sticker-covered booklet and a sample pack of kerupuk, offering a tangible connection. An essential read for food history and design enthusiasts, this project provides a thorough study of kerupuk's role in Indonesian cuisine and culture.

Design studio: Tiny Studio
Collection of Atras Alwafi

Grafis Nusantara is a collective & platform dedicated to archiving vintage Indonesian labels and stickers. The archive presents the archipelago's lavish visuals and is expected to show Indonesian vintage designs' significance as knowledge and reference materials.

ALAT KESEHARIAN
LABEL KRETEK
GRAFIS NUSANTARA
SPECIAL
ROKOK KRETEK
Pemilihan
UMUM
SLOT
KOEDOES
KONTJI
BATMAN
PEREMPUAN DAN Kretek
INDUSTRI
HOW TO ROLL YOUR OWN Cigarette
CIGARETTE Paper

Continue rolling the p
bottom edge inwards u
cylinder begins to take s
HOW TO ROLL YOUR OWN Cigarette
GRAFIS NUSANTARA

KRETEK
VOL GN 003

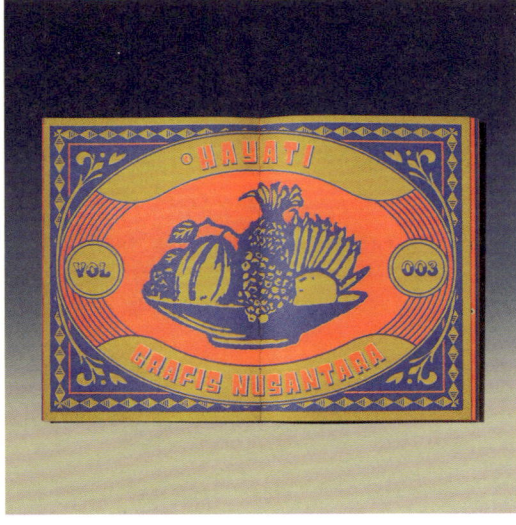

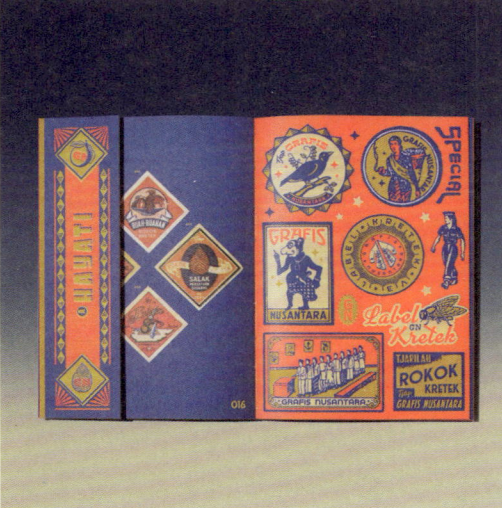

GRAFIS NUSANTARA VOL.3

This publication is an expansive collection of labels from kerupuk (Javanese), a type of Indonesian clove cigarette that is primarily produced in Java.

The labels are divided into several categories, each providing an in-depth look at the rich history and culture surrounding kretek. This book goes beyond just presenting the labels, as it also includes detailed context and explanations about each category. In addition to the book, each copy includes a booklet, lenticular graphics postcards, and kretek papers all neatly packaged in a pouch. This ensemble serves not just as an informative read, but also as a collector's item for those interested in kretek and Indonesian culture.

In this noteworthy collaboration, Grafis Nusantara collaborated with Jakarta-based design studio, Satu Collective, bringing a fresh perspective to the project without overshadowing its essence. The collaboration enhances the creative potential of *Label Kretek Vol. 3*, adding depth to the exploration of Indonesian design heritage.

Design studio: Satu Collective

#DecoArtDesignTalk

1. Decorative styles typically use various basic shapes for deformation and extension, often emphasizing patterns and repetitive elements, creating visual illusions for stimulation and freshness. So, let's have you define the next term for graphics. In your view, what is a graphic? How do you design these elements to convey the charm of graphics?

CHENBO

I believe that graphics are a language, where their shapes represent their content, and their presentation is akin to their accent. Just as we say someone's accent can influence their demeanor, I think the presentation of graphics can also affect their characters. When designing graphics, I first consider what kind of character I want them to have, what emotions they should convey, and then choose a form that matches them for the design.

Han Gao (from Workbyworks Studio)

The graphics, to me, are very fluid. They could be elements, methods, logic, or even systems. The way I see graphic design is through the lens of personal experience because different people create different work. The main job here is to understand how you can make it unique and your level of involvement in various projects. Creating those retro-vibe graphic designs, for me, is a tribute and curiosity for the graphics that no longer exist in the current period of time.

Julia Schimautz (from DTAN Studio)

In my view, a graphic is a visual creation using shapes, patterns, colors, and textures to convey a message. When designing, I prioritize visual appeal with key principles. I enjoy experimenting with shapes, patterns, and repetitive elements for unique designs. Embracing imperfections is crucial, especially with Risograph printing, which often leads to unexpected outcomes. Appreciating these imperfections adds character to the final product. Medium choice, like Risograph printing, influences my design decisions, inspiring creative solutions within constraints. My creative process lacks rigid structure, embracing serendipity and valuing mistakes for new ideas. The charm of graphics often ties to historical and cultural contexts. Retro aesthetics draw inspiration from the past, significantly influencing visual appeal.

Jun-Feng Li

If understood literally, graphics are visual elements that use a flat surface as a carrier, so I believe that all plane visual elements other than color can be called graphics. For the design of abstract graphics, I usually use points, lines, surfaces, or various inexplicable plane elements to build their aesthetically pleasing structures; for the design of figurative graphics, it is necessary to convey aesthetics from the subjective and objective narrative perspectives. I still believe that the ability to create good graphics is one of the key factors to verify whether a graphic designer's work is proactive.

Laura Normand

I like to say that I'm a freestyler because I don't like to be put in a box. I'm not only a designer, not just an illustrator, not exactly an artist—I'm just a creative person who enjoys crafting attractive visuals and beauty. This passion sometimes turns into an obsession; everything around me becomes a source of inspiration, triggering ideas. Consequently, I can rarely stop thinking about creation.

ReflexDesign

Graphics are visual representations of concrete objects or abstract concepts, often possessing a specific aesthetic form. Our approach includes extracting basic forms, boldly altering proportional relationships, incorporating graphic details, etc., fully leveraging the inherent playfulness of graphic language and the interrelationships between prototypes.

Yiyang Li (from min means)

Graphics aren't just geometric; text is also a form of graphics and can convey information more directly. When text is arranged, it forms a block of gray, which is why I now prefer using layout as my primary creative language. While I used to lean towards drawing various graphics, nowadays, I focus more on extracting and arranging visual signals.

2. Vibrant color combinations are crucial in decorative styles. Could you share some classic color combinations you use in your designs?

CHENBO

Memphis color schemes are frequently used by me, mainly employing various highly saturated colors to decorate the scene and make it lively. Another color combination I often use is the Pantone Color of the Year; because of its muted tones, it has little impact on people's emotions. It's considered to be the most comfortable color in the world. When designing scenes with a tranquil atmosphere, I would first think of this classic color scheme.

Han Gao (from Workbyworks Studio)

I love all colors; they work differently with each other. For me, I will change from time to time, but I like green, blue, gray-brown, and also dusty colors. These colors work pretty well. I appreciate it when colors understand their roles and work together as a whole.

Julia Schimautz (from DTAN Studio)

I'm particularly drawn to the vibrant color palettes popular in the 70s and 80s. Classic combinations like red and pink, or red and green, hold a special appeal for me. However, working with Risograph printing requires a thoughtful approach to color selection. I often need to get creative by mixing and overlaying colors to achieve the desired effects. Color theory plays a significant role in guiding my choices. Warm and pinkish hues prominently feature in my designs. They not only align with the retro aesthetics I adore but also infuse my work with a sense of nostalgia and visual allure.

Jun-Feng Li
I usually use low-saturation contrasting colors or complementary colors combined with aged textures to create a retro print feel. Pairing high-saturation deep blue with a warm color is also a good choice, in my opinion. Additionally, I have a fondness for the combination of yellow and black, which reminds me of the sweet and delicious taste of bananas.

Laura Normand
I can't really explain why I used this or that color. There is no hidden meaning behind the use of my colors. It's more about visual balance and contrast, creating depth, or, on the contrary, ensuring that all the elements are at the same level. In graphic design, the colors are more there to add the volume that is missing.

Onion Design Associates
Each design style throughout history has its own color palettes and combinations. By manipulating these colors, you can enhance the nostalgic feelings associated with a particular genre through the use of retro graphic elements, textures, and even subject matters.

ReflexDesign
The only rule in using colors is that there are no rules. Dare to experiment and don't be confined to specific methods.

Yiyang Li (from min means)
I don't frequently use bright colors now; the choice of colors needs to align with the brand's tone that you are serving. If I do opt for vivid colors, I lean towards using contrasting or fluorescent shades. Currently, I prefer working with the primary CMYK colors.

3. Whether it's fashion, art, or design, similar styles, colors, and shapes seem to cycle back in trend every twenty years or so. How do you believe experimentation and innovation can take place in the field of graphic design amidst these recurring trends?

CHENBO
I think although trends may come back every once in a while, each recurrence still brings some slight innovations. Every innovation in style is shadowed by other styles, so I think this trial-and-error approach is a normal "evolution" process. Even in the future, when we can use AI technology for experimentation and innovation, it will still be based on users' cognition for design.

Han Gao (from Workbyworks Studio)
I would say every recurring trend is an innovation itself because we could never recreate the same design even if we use the same color, same typefaces, and layout. Something is always missing; for instance, in fashion, there are fabrics that are similar to the old style but not the same, and then it would make everything change. So, innovation is the recurring trend; every time we do it slightly differently, it brings a new hybrid style as the current trend. That's why I am creating graphics as they are.

Julia Schimautz (from DTAN Studio)
Graphic design, like fashion and art, is intertwined with the broader cultural landscape. While styles, colors, and shapes cyclically return, I firmly believe that experimentation and innovation can thrive in this field. Drawing inspiration from both the past and our contemporary world, our designs reflect the zeitgeist. We don't merely look to history; we absorb our current surroundings, pop culture, and the evolving world, shaping our design choices. This dynamic interplay between the past and the present allows for ongoing experimentation and innovation, ensuring graphic design remains a living, evolving art form.

Laura Normand
Experimentation is very important to find your own voice and your own graphic style. Then, clients ask you to do what you love to do—what you have experimented with. These retro trends are recurring because it's sometimes hard to reinvent yourself if you're not experimenting enough on your own. So it's easier to delve into past fashions to surprise people in the present. Unfortunately, we run the risk of remaining in this infinite loop if designers fail to create new fashions.

Jun-Feng Li
Humans are creatures with nostalgic emotions, and things that were once trends have always been part of people's lives and collective consciousness. Unlike the field of fine arts, where innovation and experimentation often stand in opposition to market logic, in the realm of graphic design, designers don't necessarily need to cater to the market. The market has its own development rules. Designers can only remain faithful to design, discover their talents, and unleash their imagination. When working on design projects, besides taking appropriate steps forward, designers should also explore and consider different perspectives because there is more than one path and more than one answer.

Yiyang Li (from min means)
Not going with the flow, I absorb the logic behind classic designs and go beyond the visual aspect, persistently seeking my own unique style.

Onion Design Associates
People appreciate things that are new, fresh, and special. However, when a new style or trend becomes excessively popular, it becomes ubiquitous, losing its uniqueness. People eventually tire of it, prompting the emergence of a new style. Design, by its nature, is akin to fashion, possessing a lifespan. We are continually searching for styles that appear newer and fresher.

ReflexDesign
The development of human visual language has spanned a long time and accumulated infinite materials. We believe that different periods of content and creativity, even when combined with the same visual forms, can generate new variations. Therefore, we are constantly experimenting with combinations between the two.

NEW UGLY

CHAOS

DEVELOPMENT HISTORY

Late 19th Century: Germination

"Ugliness" began to challenge traditional aesthetic standards in the art world, as seen in movements like Symbolism and Post-Impressionism. Artists such as Vincent van Gogh and Edvard Munch rejected the pursuit of classical beauty, instead using distorted forms, bold colors, and raw emotion to explore deeper psychological and existential themes, pushing the boundaries of what was considered aesthetically acceptable.

Late 20th Century: Development Context

Visual chaos and eclecticism of the 1980s marked a pivotal era, celebrating asymmetry, clashing elements, and a disregard for conventional design norms.

2007: Emergence

Steve Slocombe's exploratory visual design for *Super Super* challenged modernist design standards and introduced the term "Ugly" to describe the departure from the norm. And then, Patrick Burgoyne, editor-in-chief of *Creative Review* magazine, published the influential article "The New Ugly."

Present Day: Continuing Development

The New Ugly design style represents an aesthetic rebellion in contemporary design, offering a fresh perspective that goes beyond surface aesthetics and celebrates the unconventional and unrefined

NEW UGLY: MODERN VISUAL STYLE GUIDE

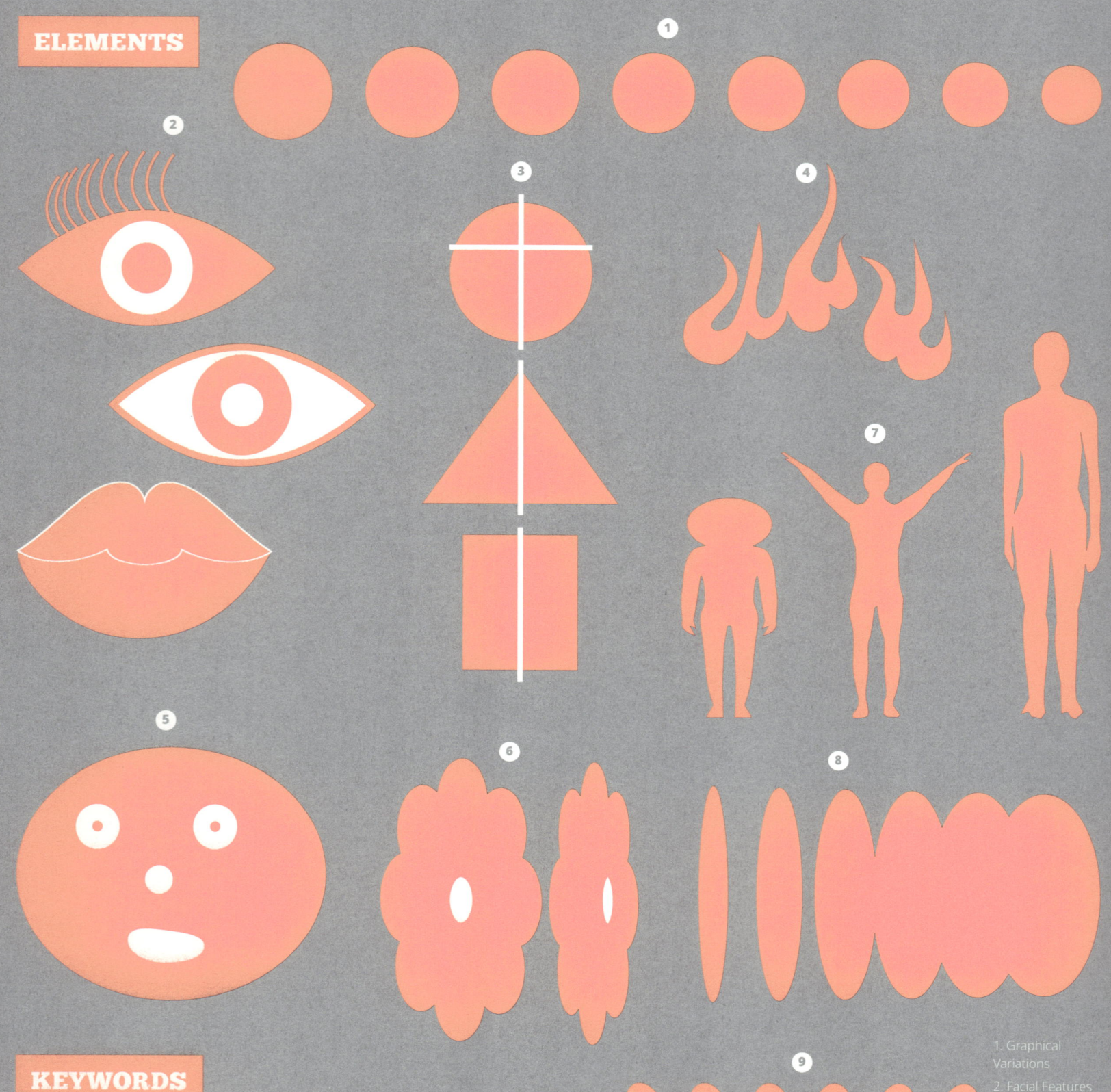

ELEMENTS

KEYWORDS

1. INTENTIONALLY DISTORTED ELEMENTS
2. JARRING COLOR COMBINATIONS
3. FRAGMENTED LAYOUTS
4. ROUGH TEXTURES
5. ANTI-DESIGN PROVOCATION

1. Graphical Variations
2. Facial Features
3. Geometric Slicing
4. Flame
5. Ugly Face
6. Morphing Flowers
7. Human Figures
8. Elliptical
9. Array of Dots

FONTS

CREEPSTER AMATIC SC LOT
Ceviche One Gandur New
BRUTALITY EXTRA BrushPen HVD ROWDY
PORTAL BLACK Antimony Blue

COLOR

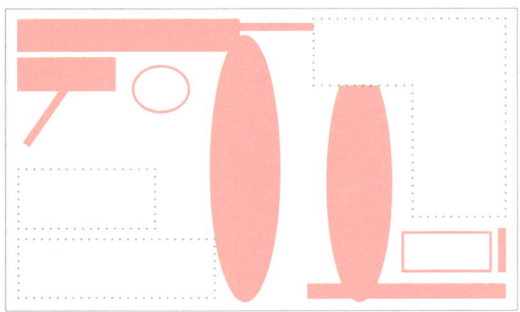

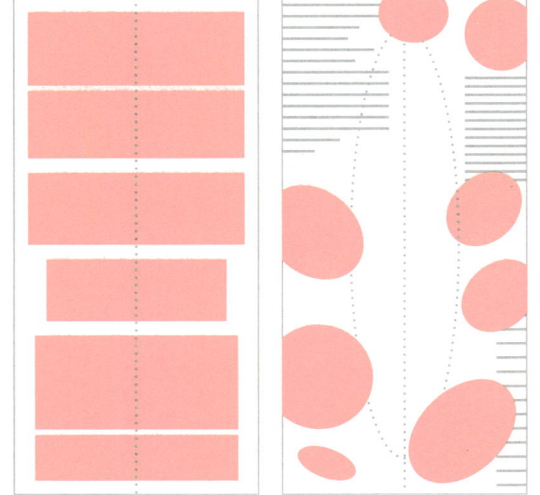

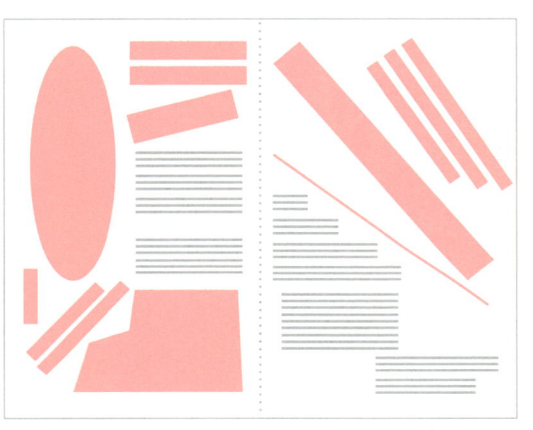

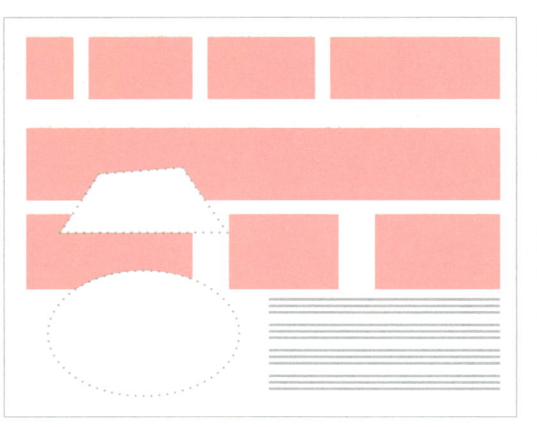

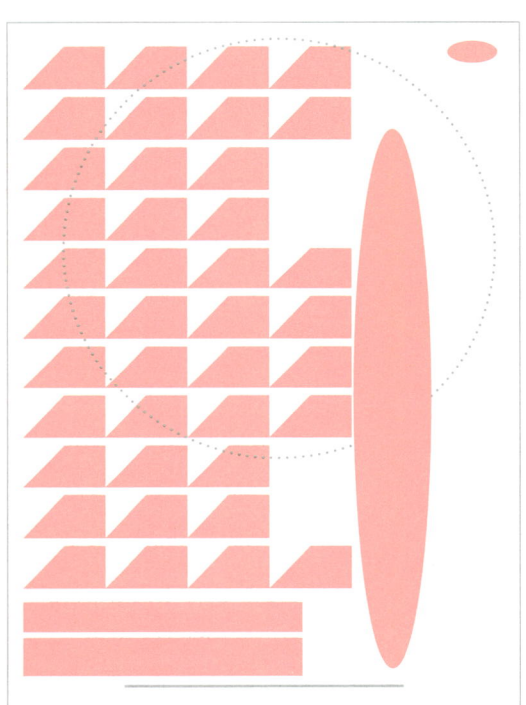

LAYOUT

Gravity
Prague #3
September 2
2023
Ankali
& Planeta Za

Clubnight
just claudia
lizwiz
Marie Pravda
Marie Montexier
NCOL

Co-funded by the
Creative Europe Programme
of the European Union

Chris Harnan

Chris Harnan lives and works in East London. He is an illustrator and artist who exhibits paintings and drawings, created both digitally and on paper using more traditional media. Chris' work attempts to simplify and reduce the world around him, often to colored dots and non-pictorial shapes. Experimenting with composition is a large part of Chris' process, and his affinity for playing with different components on a page is one of the reasons why he prefers simple geometrics and basic imagery. Through this approach, he is able to have a more direct way of communicating through color, kinetic gestures, simple symbols, characters, and words.

Past illustration clients include *Bloomberg Digital*, *Berliner Zeitung*, *The New York Times*, Nike Portland, Nike Shanghai, *Popeye* magazine, ZucZug, Lane Crawford, and the Typography Biennale in Seoul. Chris is also set to publish his second book *BIG POOL* with South London publisher Breakdown Press in 2024. In recent times, he was featured in *Lagon Revue*'s issues "Marecage" and "Plaine" with Julien Gobled. Chris graduated from the University of Brighton in 2013 and interned at HORT Berlin in 2016.

1 New Ugly Style

When observing the retro design trend of the 1980s, one notices a visual style referred to as "New Ugly," characterized by asymmetrical compositions and dissonant elements. The deliberate juxtaposition of striking colors and disorderly graphics adds an element of surprise and echoes the visually eclectic spirit of the 1980s.

Geometric Shapes and Contrasting Color Blocks

According to Chris Harnan, instead of detailed depictions, New Ugly artists prefer to use geometric shapes to distill and generalize themes, creating a repetitive and disorderly visual effect. They aim to convey information through simple semiotics and rudimentary imagery, testing the dynamic potential of a page while maintaining clarity and streamlining the design. Therefore, by focusing on basic geometry and shapes, they use color, line thickness, and position to emphasize key elements effectively.

Disorder and Repetition

Disorder and repetition serve as means of communicating emotion or mood. New Ugly artists often create a sense of speed or movement by employing multiple instances of the same image or chaotic shapes, guiding the viewer's eye and ensuring overall harmony. This approach allows them to quickly capture ideas, avoiding the loss of creative momentum as the image develops. Simple patterns or words are used to summarize thoughts, with the initial, straightforward idea often serving as the best final draft if it effectively conveys the intended message.

Emphasis on Abstraction

In their work, some New Ugly artists strongly emphasize abstraction, reducing scenes and emotions to colored dots and non-pictorial shapes. This approach stems from a desire to establish a visual language that allows viewers to interpret meaning based on the relationships between elements on the page. By making subjects less immediately recognizable, the artist creates an abstract, dreamlike, and alien tone, intriguing viewers and encouraging them to seek deeper meaning beyond a straightforward narrative. This method of abstraction serves as a powerful means of communication in both digital and traditional realms, fostering a unique connection between the artwork and its audience.

2 Exploring Personal Style

Chris Harnan's current design style developed through a combination of early experimentation and influential creators. As a young teenager, he spent evenings crafting crude music videos and cartoons. He also participated in online communities where he created some niche stuff, back when Wacom tablets and drawing pads weren't as common. This period cultivated an appreciation for low-tech aesthetics, driven by the limitations of using a mouse. Collaborating with strangers online fostered an anti-technical approach, allowing Chris Harnan to develop his style free from professional constraints and purely for the joy of creation.

While engaged in traditional paintings and still-life drawings in art class, Chris Harnan laid his true passion in creating wired symbols and simple representations for the online communities he was involved in.

Besides, Japanese comic artists and graphic designers significantly influenced Chris Harnan's approach to art, particularly in experimenting with mark-making and materiality. He draws inspiration from the artists like Heta-uma and publications such as *Garo*. Additionally, the work of King Terry (Teruhiko Yumura) and David Hockney profoundly impact his creative process, encouraging him to explore and refine his unique style.

3 Digital Tools

Chris Harnan's creative process integrates both digital tools and traditional methods, each offering distinct advantages. He primarily employs digital tools as an alternative means of mark-making and drawing. Unlike others who delve into visual effects and 3D rendering, Chris Harnan enjoys the freedom to experiment with colors and combinations quickly and neatly. While he appreciates traditional work, the often messy process can be exhausting.

Digital tools provide a more efficient way to explore ideas, enabling rapid, chaotic bursts of productivity without the hassle of physical cleanup. The convenience of being able to delete files or rename folders at the end of a session contrasts sharply with the laborious task of cleaning paint and dealing with stained clothing. This efficiency and flexibility have expanded Chris Harnan's perspective on creative expression, allowing him to experiment freely and refine his artistic vision with greater ease.

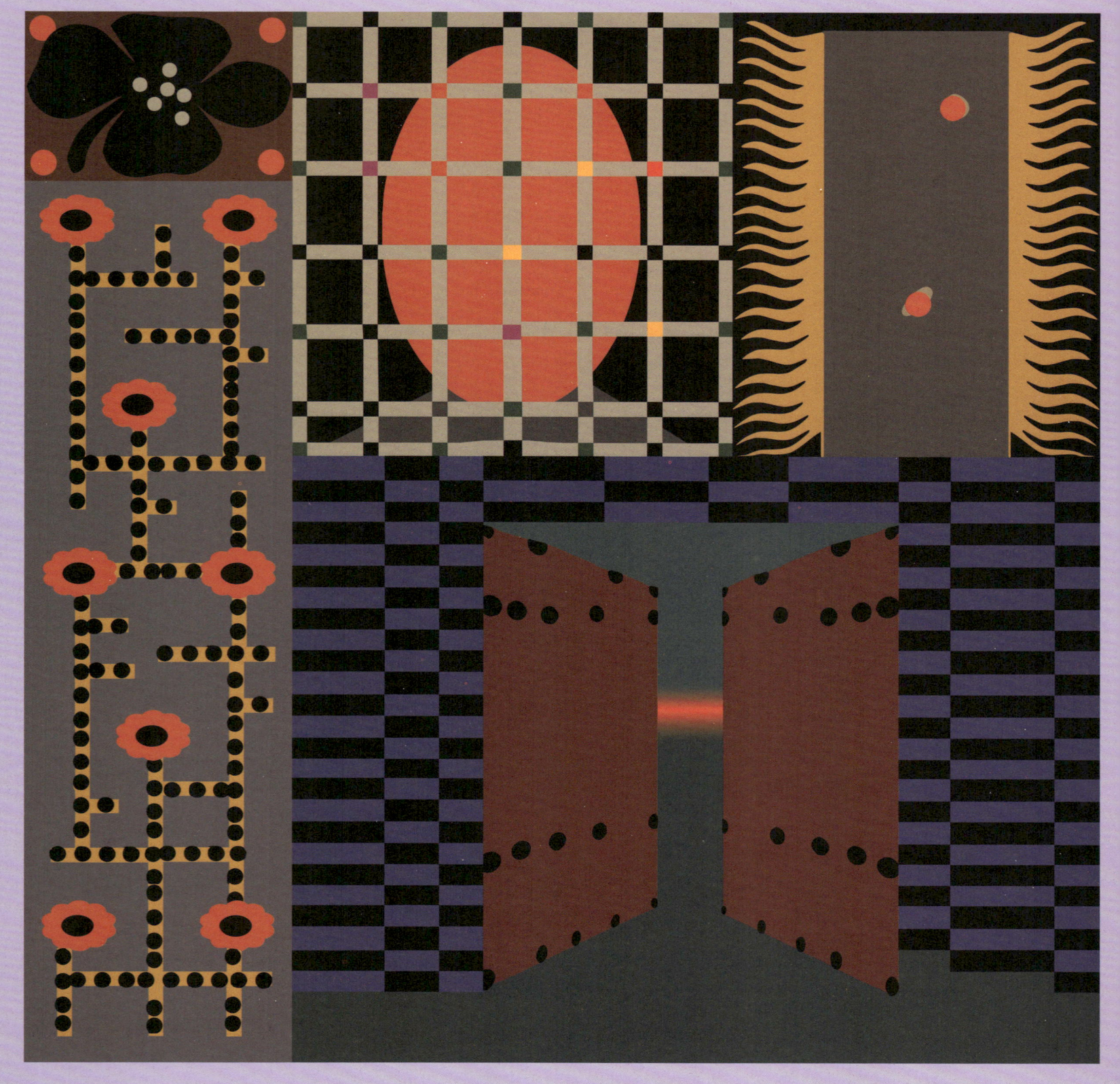

DOIS ALBUM COVER

The designer enjoys experimenting with alternative forms of communication, often using simple semiotics and rudimentary imagery to convey meaning. His aim is to explore how dynamic a page can become while remaining clear and streamlined. By stripping away non-essentials, he finds it easier to create connections between different elements on the page, especially when the imagery is straightforward. Over time, he has increasingly focused on simple geometry and shapes, using color, line thickness, and the positioning of elements to emphasize key points in a minimal yet effective way.

in March '20

ANKALI

FEEL FREE TO CLAP

HORT

HORT XMAS

Gravity
Berlin #3
September 16 2023
RSO

Clubnight
Detroit in Effect
DJ Bus Replacement Service
dzuma
Olivia

GRAVITY NETWORK

Gravity Warsaw #3
September 8 & 9
2023
Jasna 1

Clubnight
Sept 8
Galas
Glassz
Max Sinclair
Monster
Oliver Torr
Olivia

Talks
Sept 9
Dalmata Daniel
Dom Trojga
L.I.E.S. Records
Syntetyk
and more

Clubnight
Sept 9
dzuma
Elena Sizova
Facheroia
PAWEL
Ron Morelli
Taan

Co-funded by the Creative Europe Programme of the European Union

Chris Harnan   New Ugly   256

Excusez-moi, j'aimerais encaisser mes jetons s'il vous plaît

Oú est ce que j'encaisse mes jetons?

LE CASINO

▼ Color Scheme:

R143 G144 B143	R025 G086 B045	R224 G057 B021	R029 G047 B100	R000 G000 B000
C051 M041 Y040 K000	C087 M054 Y100 K025	C005 M090 Y098 K000	C100 M096 Y044 K001	C000 M000 Y000 K100
R156 G132 B047	R004 G106 B132	R065 G039 B084	R019 G134 B074	R119 G022 B027
C046 M048 Y095 K001	C088 M053 Y040 K000	C087 M100 Y053 K009	C083 M031 Y089 K000	C050 M100 Y100 K030

New Ugly — Chris Harnan

BIG POOL

Chris Harnan — New Ugly

Color Scheme:

- R000 G000 B000
  C000 M000 Y000 K100

- R018 G055 B139
  C098 M087 Y008 K000

- R248 G232 B178
  C004 M009 Y036 K000

- R193 G196 B226
  C027 M022 Y000 K000

- R255 G255 B255
  C000 M000 Y000 K000

- R055 G023 B084
  C085 M100 Y034 K031

- R000 G053 B048
  C090 M055 Y067 K060

- R023 G181 B198
  C071 M002 Y024 K000

- R025 G041 B123
  C100 M096 Y016 K004

- R140 G080 B156
  C053 M076 Y000 K000

- R166 G061 B021
  C026 M084 Y100 K021

Inflammation Vol. 1

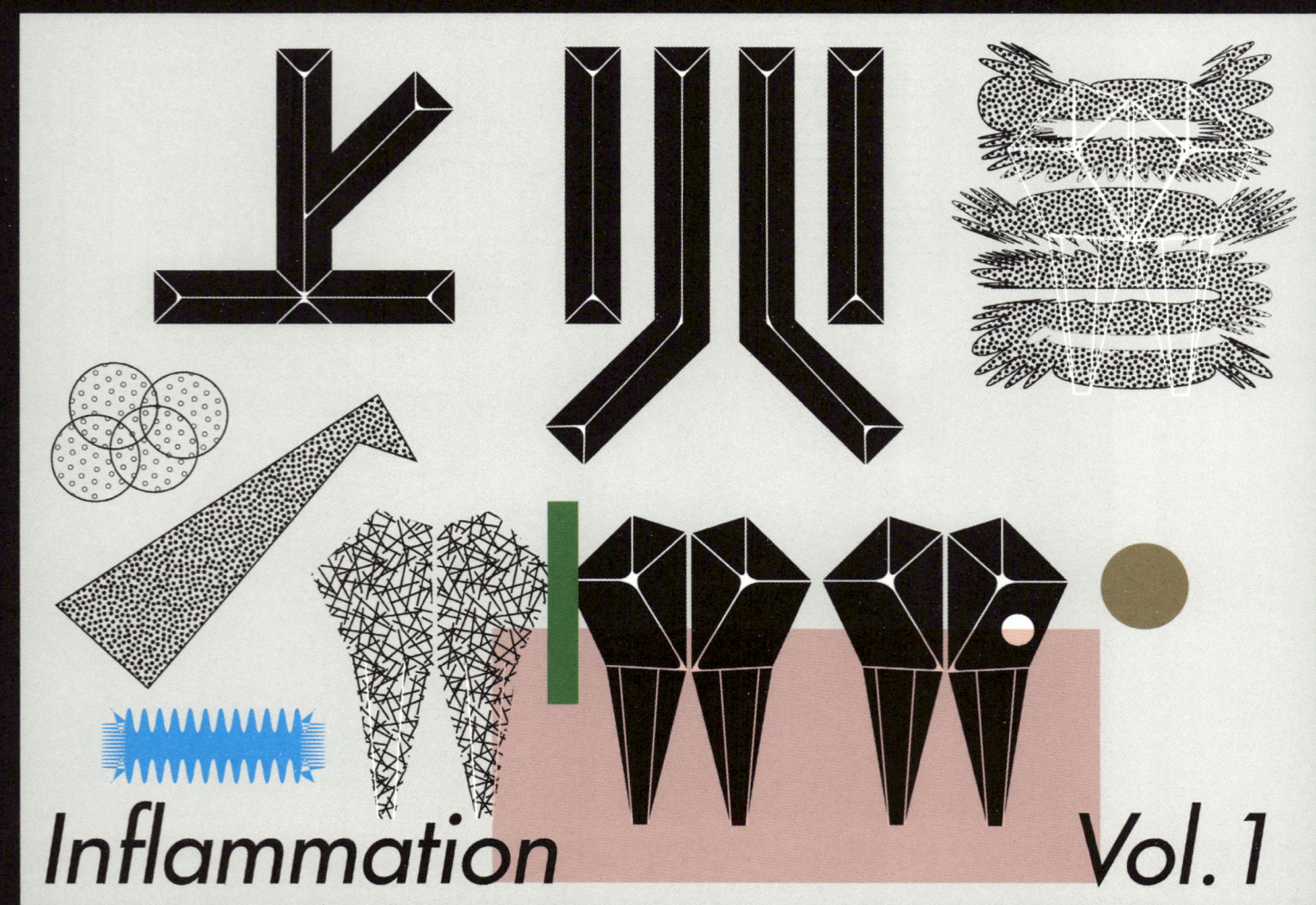

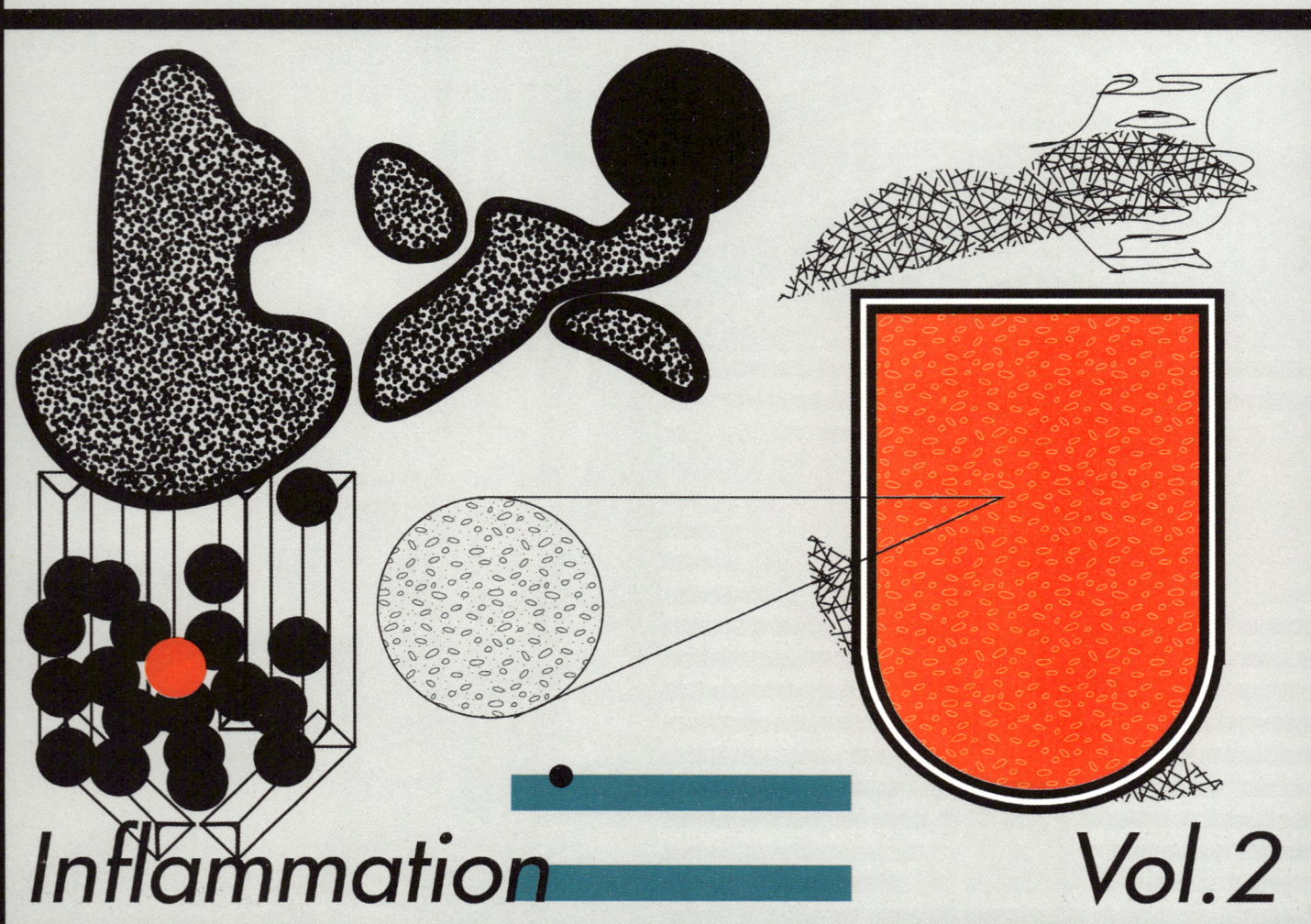

Inflammation Vol. 2

Sun Yao

A Ph.D. candidate in Design at Seoul National University with a Master's degree in Visual Design from Hongik University, he currently resides in Seoul. His work delves into the discussion of visual experiences and reading encounters in multilingual environments. He constructs diverse means of information conveyance through typography and graphic design. Additionally, he explores the balance and inclination between rationality and emotion in graphic design. His accolades include recognition from the New York TDC, Tokyo TDC, British D&AD New Blood, Moscow Golden Bee International Graphic Biennale, and the Jeonju International Film Festival's 100 Films 100 Posters.

1 Another Facet of Contemporary Aesthetics

In the realm of design, the New Ugly style boldly challenges traditional aesthetic norms through its embrace of rough print textures, unconventional color combinations, quirky layouts, and even a touch of kitsch. According to Sun Yao, New Ugly represents another facet of contemporary aesthetics where beauty and ugliness are often defined subjectively. Designers are frequently driven to break away from conventional methods, seeking to innovate at the aesthetic frontier and question established notions of beauty, much like avant-garde movements did with classical art in the past. While Sun may not exclusively identify with the New Ugly label, he acknowledges that his work often contains provocative and satirical elements that align with this style.

Regarding his approach to design, the focus is not on creating chaos but on effectively conveying content through form. For instance, in the project *Read Seoul*, which documents font application scenes in daily life, he deliberately captured the rough and irregular nature of real-world text applications. He used lines strategically throughout the book, not merely for decoration but as functional elements that delineate between main titles, text, and graphics. This systematic approach ensures that despite the appearance of visual complexity, the information remains accessible and coherent. The deliberate use of lines, varying in form and thickness, underscores his commitment to enhancing content clarity.

2 Breaking the Limits

In his design practice, Sun Yao actively challenges traditional aesthetic norms by focusing on methodologies that foster emotional resonance and the development of a distinctive visual language. In response to the increasing standardization and homogenization facilitated by Internet and computer technologies, Sun Yao seeks to carve out unique perspectives and break free from conventional design paradigms.

In the early days, Sun was a fervent advocate of grid design, and those rule-based and orderly works deeply fascinated him. However, he eventually grew dissatisfied with its limitations characterized by restraint, balance, perfection, logic, and order, and then embraced a more expressive approach. This evolution was influenced by movements like the New Wave spearheaded by Wolfgang Weingart, which critiqued stereotyped and orthodox design principles in favor of more playful and unconventional visual expressions. Embracing concepts of freedom, roughness, and controlled chaos, Sun Yao aims to establish a personal methodology that prioritizes creative exploration over adherence to established rules.

Therefore, he continues to experiment with breaking his own limits in some personal works. For instance, in the *Inflammation Guide*, he used graphic language to sensually convey the discomfort reactions generated by the organs during a week of illness. This approach reflects a deeply introspective and sensory-driven narrative style. Developing a "visual language" that belongs to oneself is a long and evolving process. He is dedicated to refining and articulating his unique creative voice with confidence and persistence.

3 Design Elements

In his design, Sun finds inspiration for elements representing New Ugly in our daily lives, such as the exaggerated stretching of Chinese characters in common advertisements. This unconventional practice, often adopted to maximize communication effectiveness despite its unrefined appearance, propels designers to reconsider typographic norms and explore alternative ways of conveying information.

Rather than adhering to predefined visual styles, Sun prioritizes unconventional thinking in his work. For instance, in the poster design for Chung-Ang University's Stage Performance major titled "生生不息 생생불식" (Life Goes On), he juxtaposed bilingual Chinese and Korean text, both characterized by square characters. Departing from the traditional square structure, Sun Yao experimented with stroke structures to find a harmonious visual language that bridges linguistic differences. The design centered around the stroke structure of the Chinese character "生," employing an artistic font style reminiscent of the 1980s. Sun embraces a preference for rough, unbalanced, and imperfect aesthetics that retain clarity and effectively convey information. Throughout his creative process, he continually seeks to integrate distinct elements and styles into compositions without compromising the primary goal of information transmission, illustrating a commitment to innovative design practices within the framework of his aesthetics.

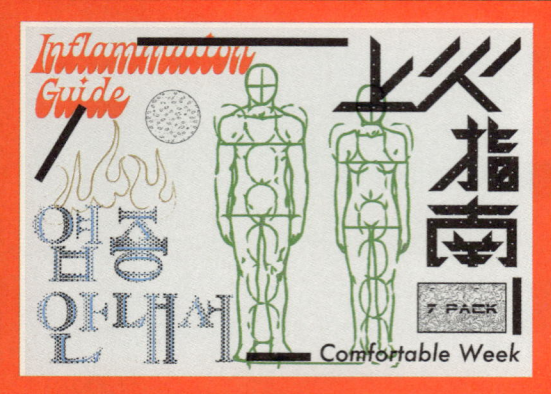

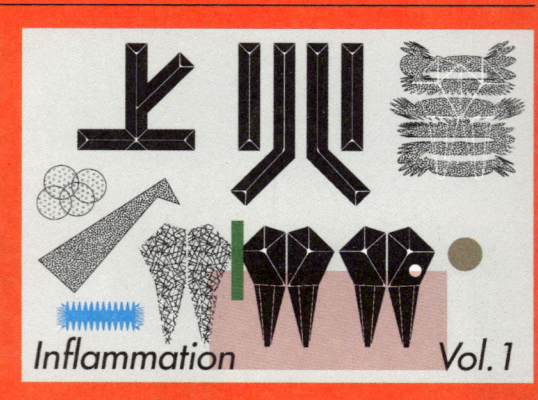

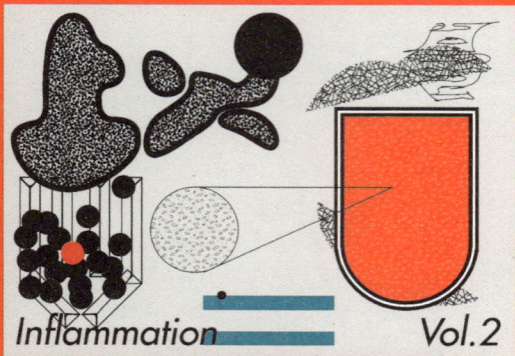

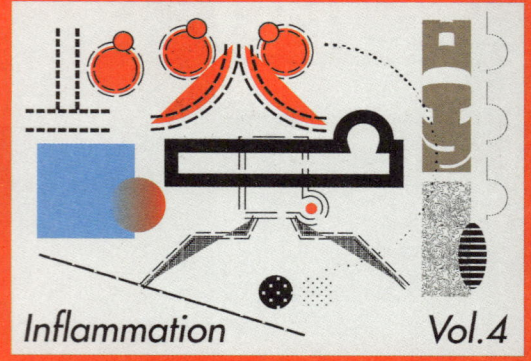

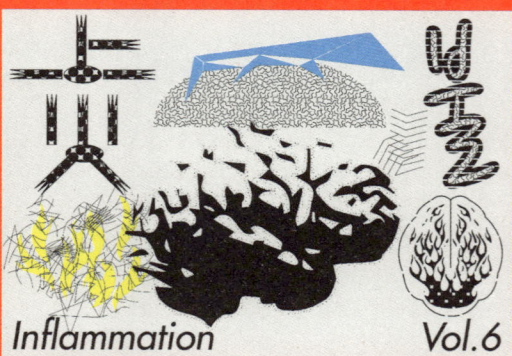

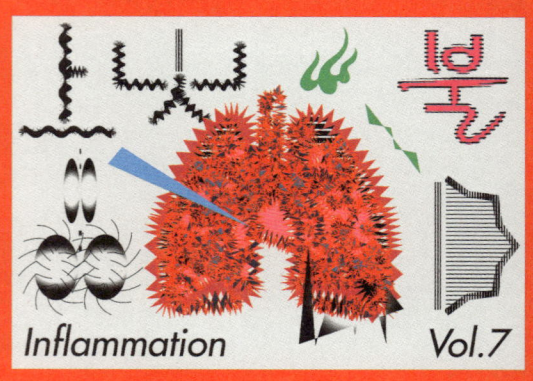

INFLAMMATION GUIDE

On Monday, the designer experienced toothache; Tuesday, he had a dry mouth; Wednesday, his eyes felt dry; Thursday, his cheeks swelled; Friday, he felt irritable; Saturday, he experienced mental fatigue; Sunday, he had pneumonia. The designer documented his weekly physical condition using expressive graphics and exaggerated retro typography, naming this series *Inflammation Guide*.

▼ **Elements:**
The designer used different shapes of graphics to express the different organ states under the condition of excessive inner heat.

▼ **Fonts:**
Chinese: FZ LanTingHei
English: Helvetica, Futura, Funkford
Korean: Noto Sans KR

▼ **Layout:** Graphics are the primary language, complemented by decorative typography.

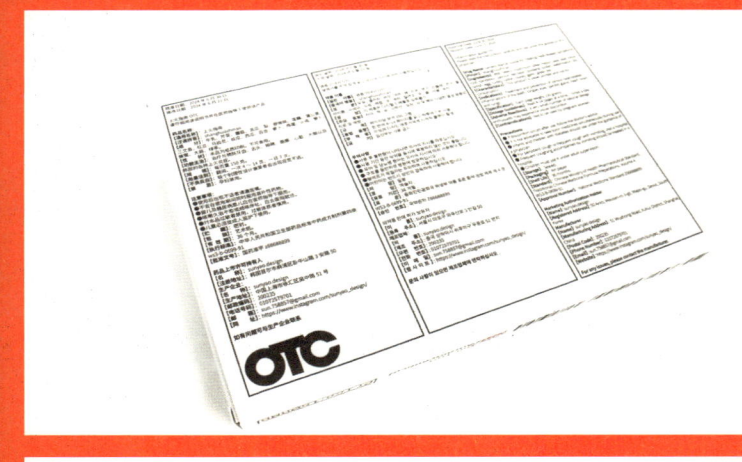

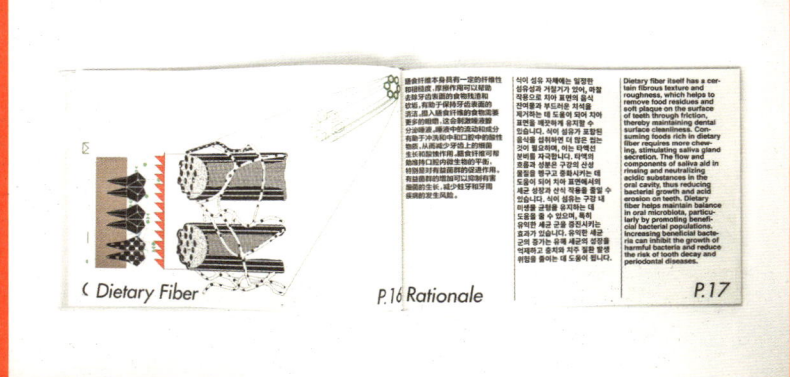

Milk P.o1	Mushroom P.o2	Celery P.o3
Bitter melon P.o7	Pears P.o9	Kiwi P.11
Salmon P.17	Radish P.18	Watermelon P.19

Dietary Fiber — P.16 Rationale — P.17

COMFORTABLE WEEK 2024
Scientific Handbook of Inflammation Self-healing and Diet

READ SEOUL

Read Seoul is an interesting discussion of textual content in different contexts. Words permeate our lives and exist in different ways. Some text applications may seem incorrect, like text stretching, while others captivate us with excellent type design, such as a store sign that piques curiosity. The book also delves into how context shapes interpretation—like how the "P" sign for no parking could be misinterpreted as prohibiting farting in Chinese culture. Living in Seoul, the designer integrates collected text from daily life and offers cross-contextual interpretations based on things, places, and events. The design concept aims to exaggerate and overemphasize, capturing the rawness of street text. To reflect the irregular use of text in daily life, fonts are stretched and distorted to varying degrees. The entire series seeks to bridge the gap between us and text in our daily lives in an engaging, unique, and mixed manner, bringing more fun and discussing the roles and different perceptions of text in our lives.

▼ **Elements:**
Irregular graphic shapes are cut through, echoing with free lines and layouts.

▼ **Fonts:**
Chinese: Source Han Sans
English: Helvetica, Futura
Korean: Noto Sans KR

▼ **Layout:**
The designer expressed the thoughts and observations of daily life through rational yet humorous writing and sensually bold layout designs.

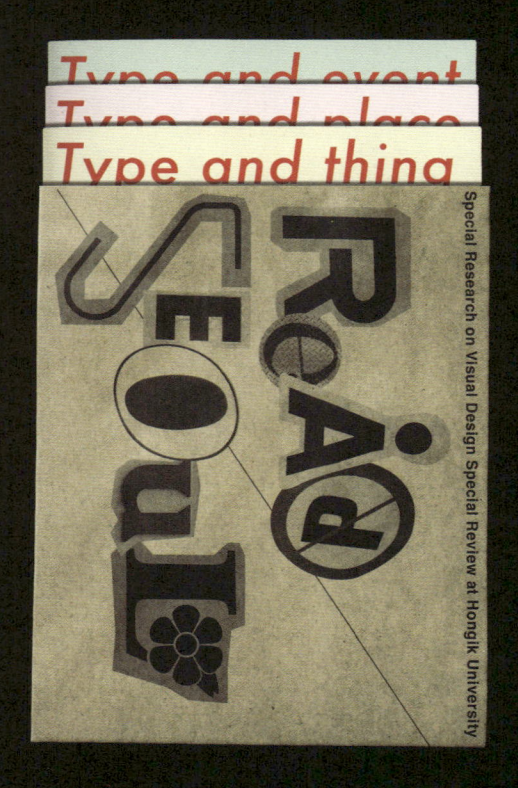

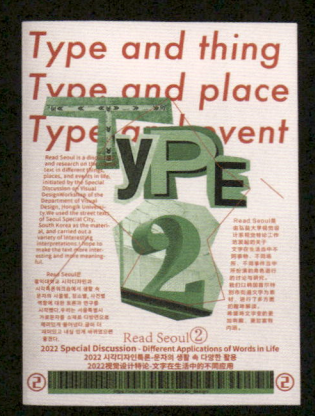

OK! Forcing the day!
Report to headquarters! Discover the Alphabet agents lurking underground.
At first I thought it was soju-flavored milk...
Helmut Schmid
헬무트 슈미트
赫尔穆特·施密德
Like a cloud, like a river, more like the old age you owe me.
It is estimated that someone
估计得有人问你这标志好注册吗。
전기·철물
好像一条看门的大黄狗。
Like a big yellow dog guarding the gate.
주차금지
ㅊa=chㅏ=茶= Tea
o(X_X)o
只有伤口
Only scratches 상처만
在韩语当中"바람"是风的意思,"피우다"是抽的意思。但是两者组合在一起的"바람 피우다"却是出轨的意思。也是,出轨的哪个不抽风?
字母散步
Alphabet Walk
走丢的部首
Lost Radical
COFFEE
No farting
禁止放P
Fart Charge
放P收费
Please fart in the area
请在区域内放P
Please fart right
Shocked me straight away!
Waited two hours
等了两个小时!
Didn't the people who gave up medicine and became literature end up being asked out of their textbooks?
Are the ads all over the world the same?
是不是全世界的小广告都一个样?
Big words! Bigger! maximum!
글자는 커야 돼! 커야 돼! 커야 돼!
字要大! 再大! 最大!
Why Hongik University so poor?
弘益大学为什么这么穷?
Awesome
대박 牛逼
Real man
真男人
No Entry
So what does this mean?
所以这是什么?
END
完
NO
谁来劝架?
지식을 버리는 하루
A day to throw away knowledge
First time seeing this.
404 Not Found
Common for a while
BEST BOOK DESIGN FROM REPUBLIC OF KOREA
한국 가장 아름다운 책
SIBF
ФАКТЫ
Tool man
I am not a virus!
病毒!
I thought it was a criminal warrant
Again please
Quite Burst
Other
기타

Sun Yao — New Ugly

LIFE GOES ON (生生不息 생생불식)

The poster was created for the doctoral graduation exhibition of the Stage Skills Department at Chung-Ang University in South Korea. In Chinese context, "生生不息" implies to grow and multiply without end. In the context of a bilingual environment, the aim was to connect Korean and Chinese in terms of font structure. The design of both Chinese and Korean characters reflects the concept of balance between yin and yang. The entire visual system of the event was constructed around the structure of the fonts, extending systematically to every aspect of the visual representation, corresponding to the concept of "the life goes on." The slanted and irregular font structures resonate with the classical essence of traditional folk dance, adding a touch of retro flavor.

Client: Chung-Ang University

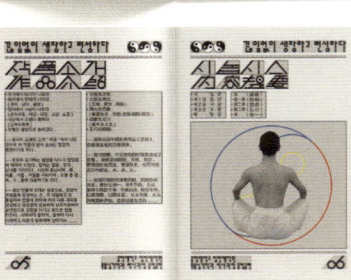

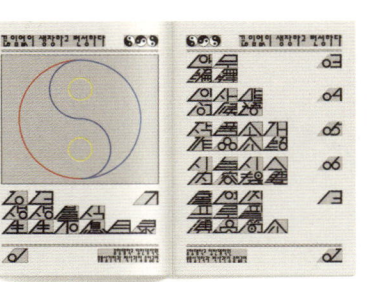

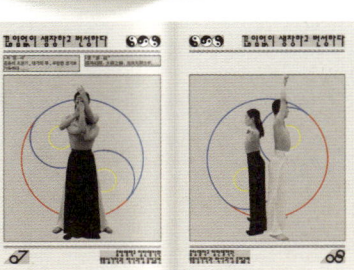

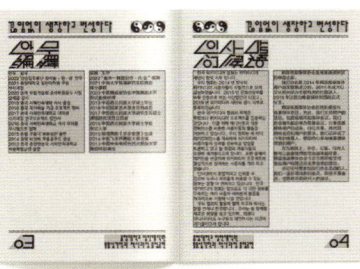

▼ **Elements:**

The inclined trapezoidal structure strives to break the traditional square form of Chinese and Korean.

▼ **Fonts:**

Korean: HY깊은샘물B, Noto Sans KR

▼ **Layout:**

The designer established the entire visual system with irregular artistic typography and extended the systematic approach to the entire visual application.

BranD
Issue 70
Simple
Clear
Memorable
BranD
Issue 70
Simple
Clear
Memorable

BRAND ISSUE 70: LOGO FACE

In recent years, as visual communication methods rapidly evolve and people's aesthetic continue to change, new design concepts emerge. Today's brand design has become more complex, prompting a deeper exploration of logo design, the first step in brand creation. In this issue of *BranD*, the editorial team delved into the theme of "Logo Face," exploring different dimensions of logo composition, studying the emotions and experiences they evoke, and analyzing the evolving and timeless design elements and laws in contemporary logo design.

Design Studio: *BranD* Magazine
Illustration and font design: Yukit Lai
Editor: Gakky Luk, Fae Kwok, Johanna Wang

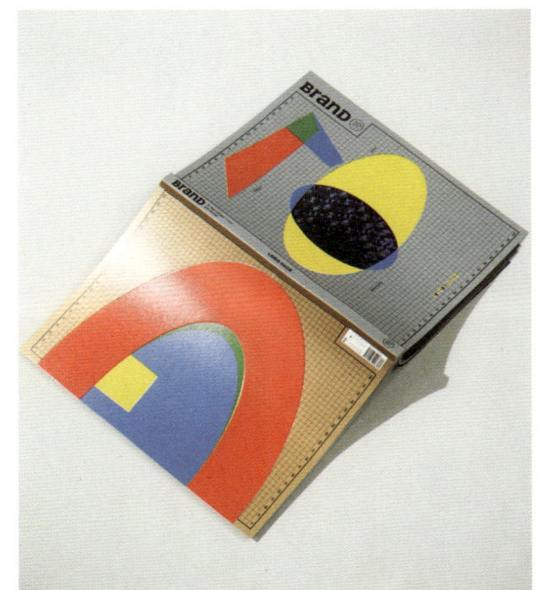

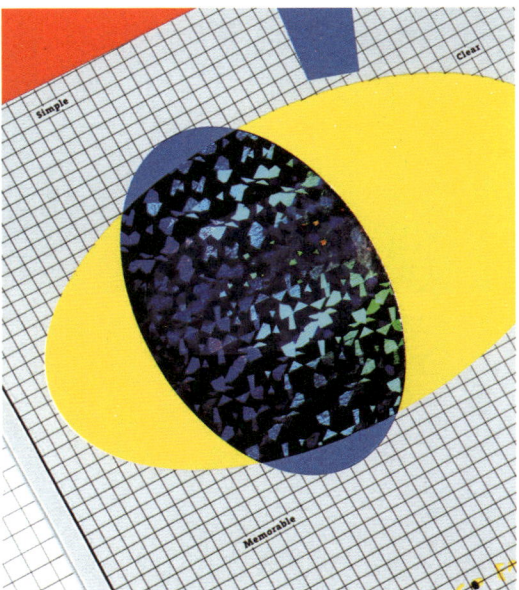

▼ **Inspiration:**

Using six-color printing, embossing, and hot stamping on the cover to create varied ink textures and gloss levels, the designer has balanced richness with restraint and added mystery with hidden blue-black fragments in laser foil. Following principles from Paul Rand to Taku Satoh, they aim for simplicity, clarity, and memorability in creating a unique logo style for the brand.

▼ **Elements:**

The designer created the "LOGO FACE" font with the most basic graphic elements, abstract eyes and a mouth are formed by changing the angle of the font. When two covers and two backs are put together, a complete face emerges.

▼ **Fonts:**

Cubic 11, Jackey Font, Windows Command-Prompt

▼ **Layout:**

Visual creativity is inspired by the design principles proposed by Sato Kashiwa, which are simplicity, clarity, and memorability. In addition to the original "Logo Face" on the cover, the designer has created 26 letters for this issue's theme and extended the elements throughout the entire magazine, thus creating a unique visual system for this issue.

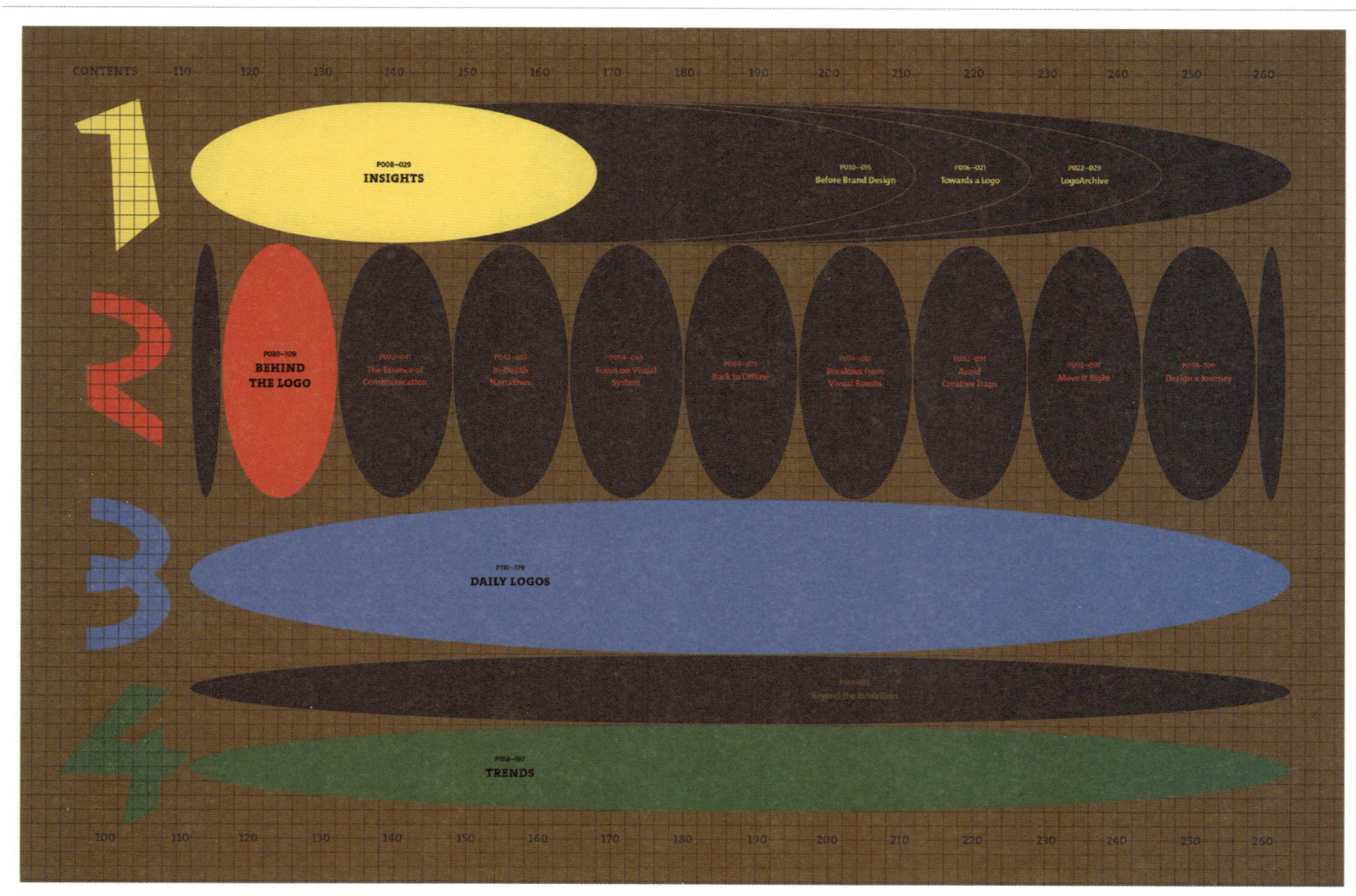

CONTENTS

1 INSIGHTS (P008–029)
- Before Brand Design (P010–015)
- Towards a Logo (P016–021)
- LogoArchive (P022–029)

2 BEHIND THE LOGO (P030–109)
- The Essence of Communication (P032–041)
- In-Depth Narratives (P042–053)
- Focus on Visual System (P054–063)
- Back to Offline (P064–073)
- Breaking from Visual Bombs (P074–081)
- Avoid Creative Traps (P082–091)
- Move It Right (P092–097)
- Design a Journey (P098–109)

3 DAILY LOGOS (P110–179)

Beyond the Exhibition

4 TRENDS (P180–187)

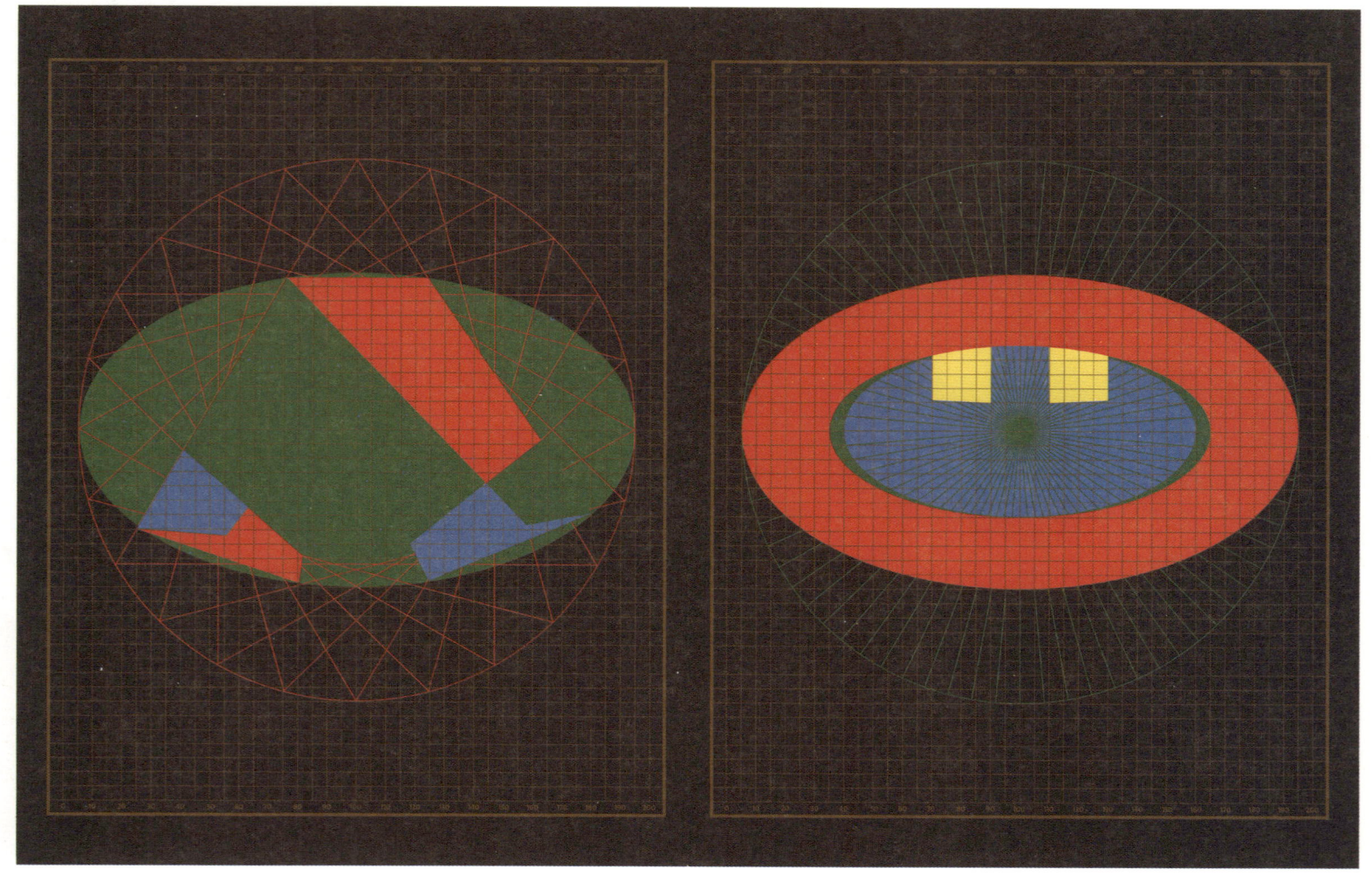

BEFORE BRAND DESIGN

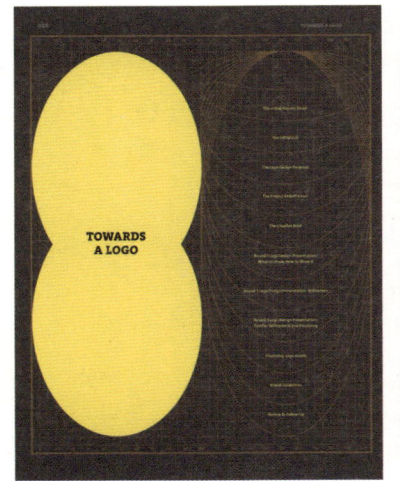

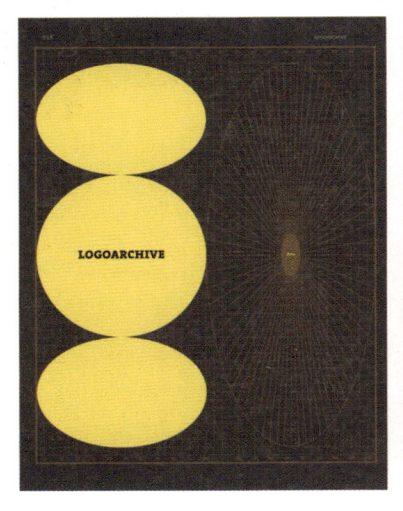

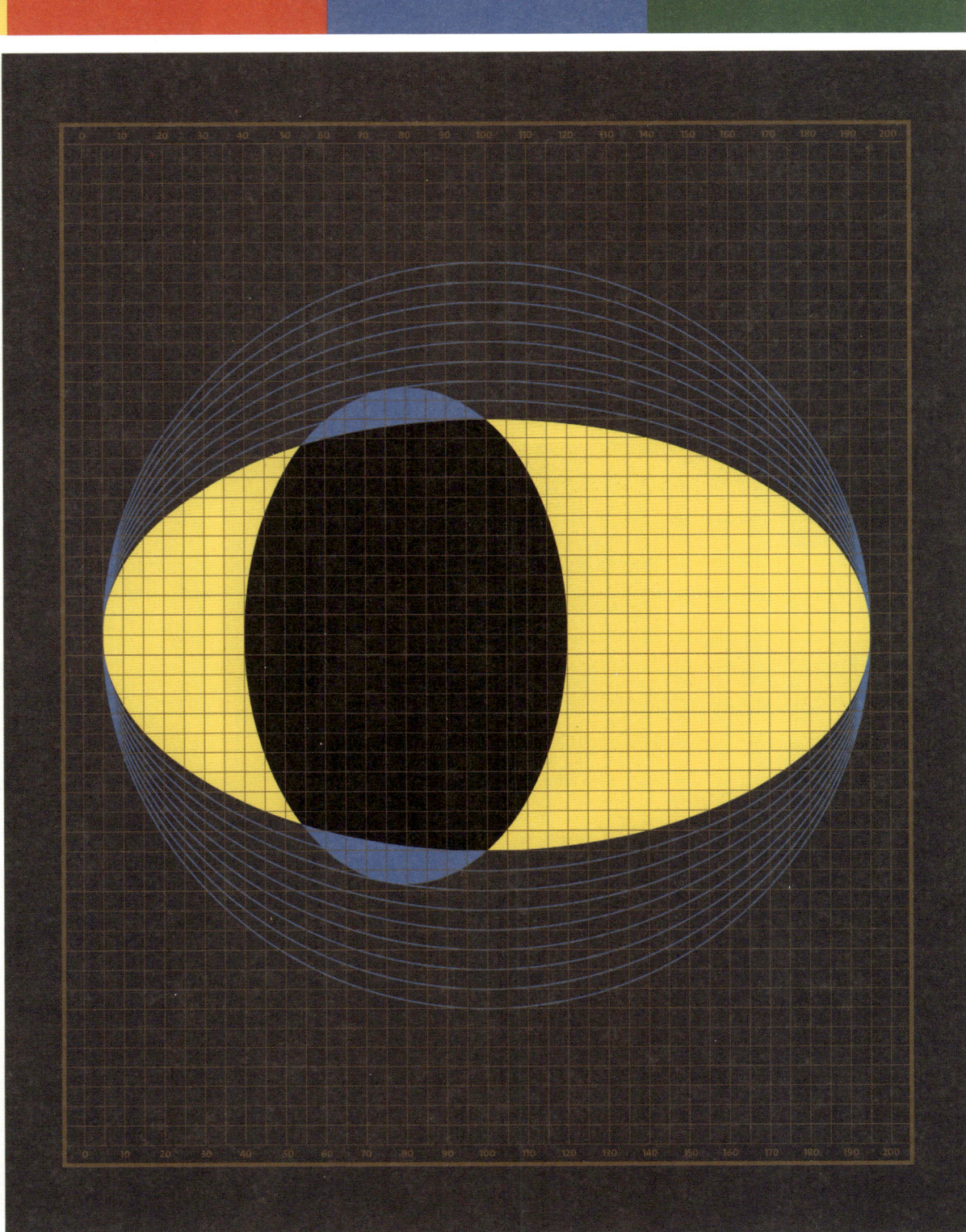

TOWARDS A LOGO

LOGOARCHIVE

Counterfeit
Tobacco

IMG_6361.HEIC
DAY 5
12345
노래방

love the cloudy weather because it might rain.

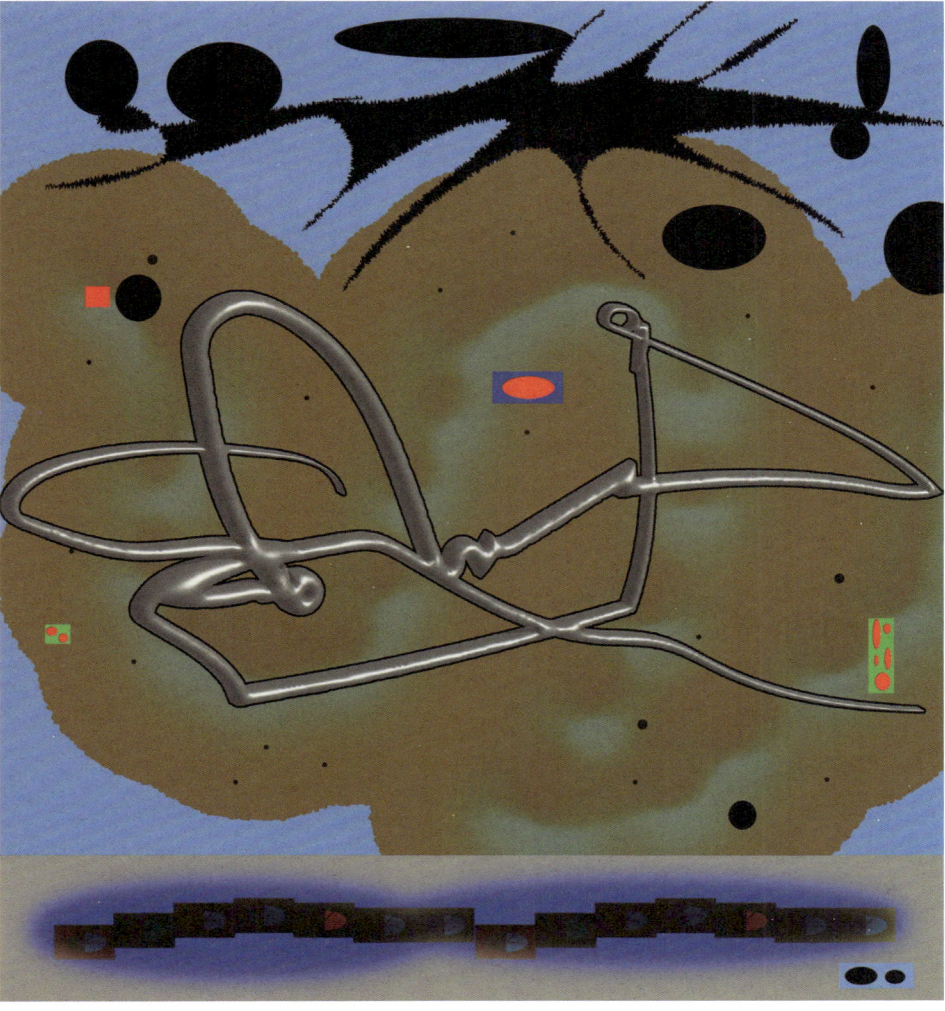

ORIGINAL WORKS BY YUNBOMU

The designer consistently uses images to represent diaries, which are inherently tied to the past. To evoke a sense of nostalgia, the designer often incorporates retro textures, such as noise and other vintage effects.

Designer: yunbomu

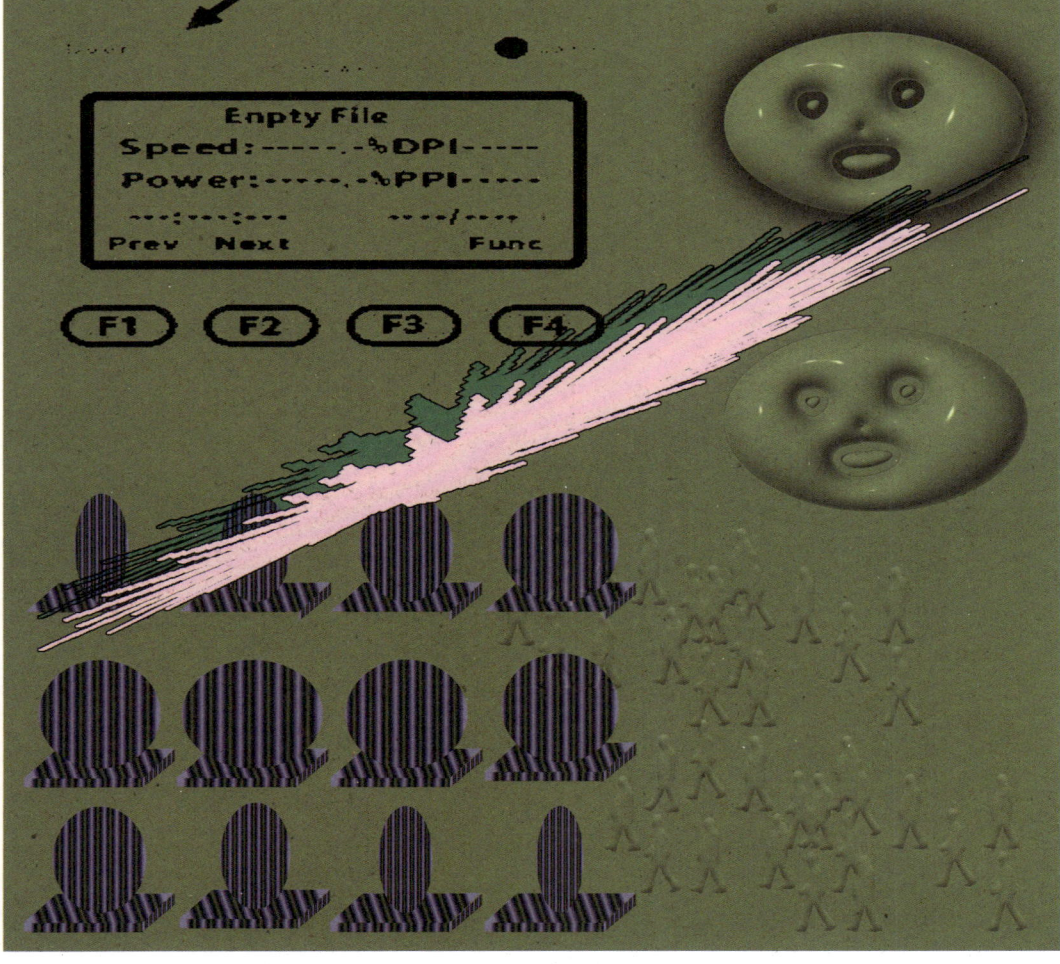

▼ **Inspiration:**
The designer really likes the old jacket design and Apple ads from the 80s and 90s, as well as the old town flyers.

▼ **Elements:**
The motif primarily reflects the designer's movements and emotions, which is why human forms and facial expressions are prominently featured. Additionally, there are many blurred shapes, representing the fluidity and constant change of these emotions.

▼ **Fonts:**
Adobe Garamond, Helvetica

XUN FENG VOL. 21:
A CENTURY OF SPLENDOR ALONG THE COASTAL RAILWAY

As a cultural and historical magazine, *Xun Feng* magazine (《薰風》) explores diverse themes like literature, history, society, and art, analyzing and presenting the texture of history in terms of time, place, people, and events. It covers specific eras, artists, cultural elements, brands, and trends. Focusing on the centenary railway culture, it depicts the coastal railway's industrial progress and modernization over the past century against the backdrop of mountainous landscapes, signifying future aspirations amid cultural and economic transformations.

Designer: Yi-Ju Liao, Chien Yi-Wen
Client: Fengyue Jinhuai Cultural Enterprise Co., Ltd.

▼ **Inspiration:**
The designers drew inspiration from the hundred-year railway culture.

▼ **Elements:**
With the railway lines spanning across the mountains as the backdrop, the scenery changes with the passage of time and space. The hundred-year-old coastal railway, winding through the mountainous terrain, has spurred industrial progress and modernization, leaving behind expectations and visions for future challenges in cultural and economic revolution.

▼ **Fonts:**
Ryumin (龍明體), Garamond

▼ **Layout:**
The magazine's design style focuses on non-representational visual elements, aiming to provide a unique visual experience. By innovatively transforming historical narratives into visual symbols, it breaks away from traditional layouts. Each cover design is inspired by historical trajectories, blending modern visual techniques with different eras to explore the interplay between history and modernity. As a cultural hub, it aims to inspire and inform readers, fostering interest in historical and social issues while encouraging contemplation of contemporary realities.

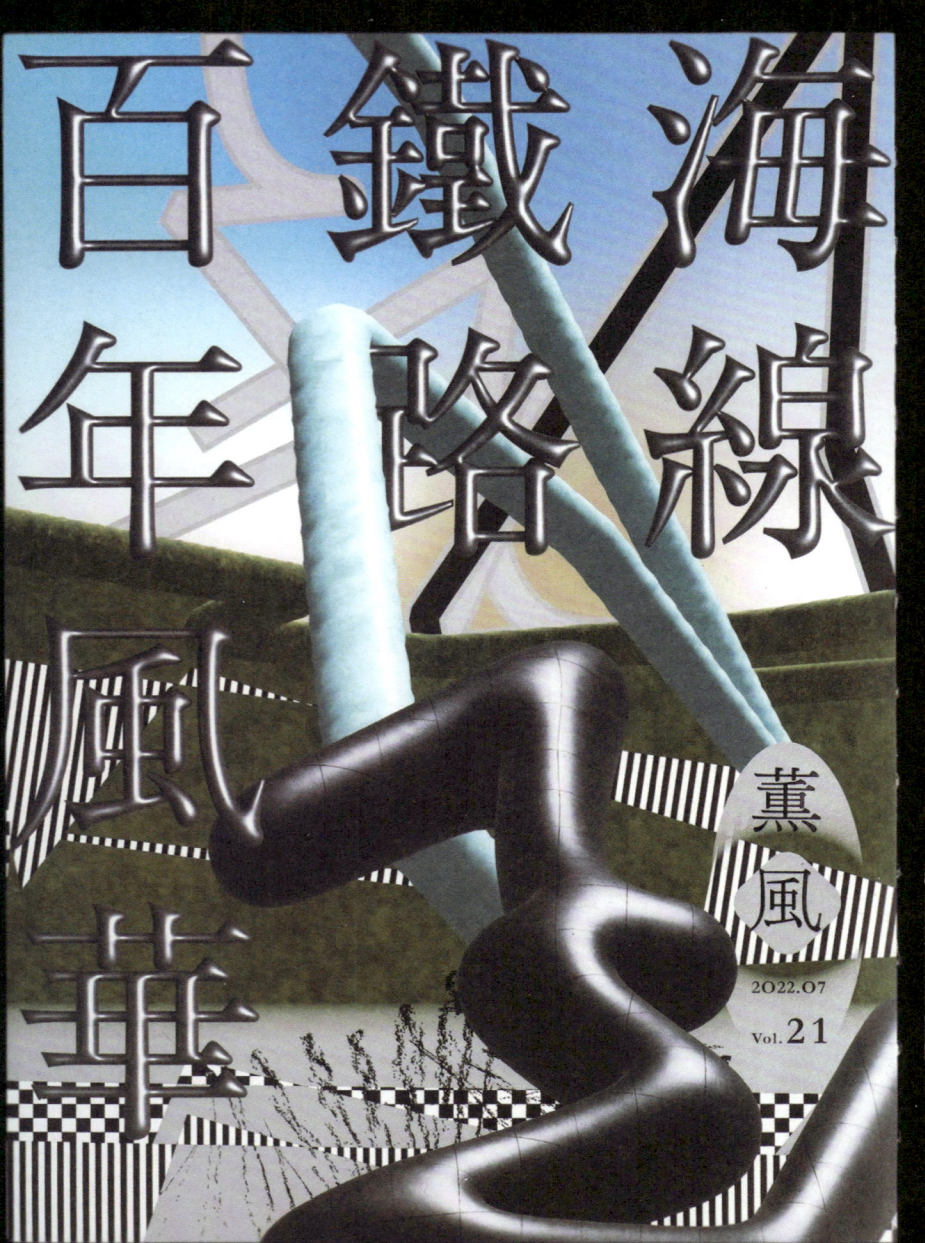

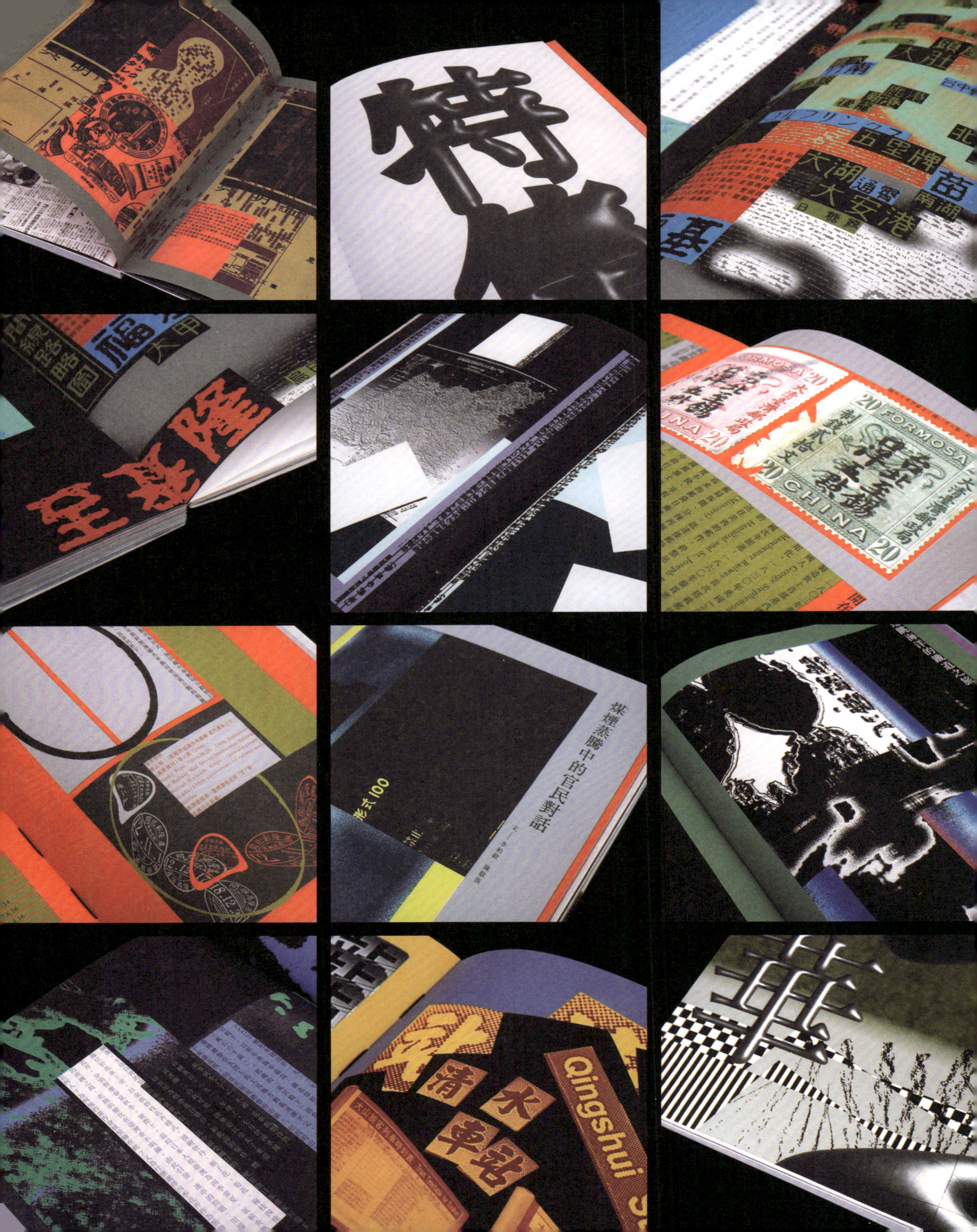
五星牌
大湖
大安港
FORMOSA
CHINA
20
媒煙蒸騰中的官民對話
形式100
清水
車站
Qingshui

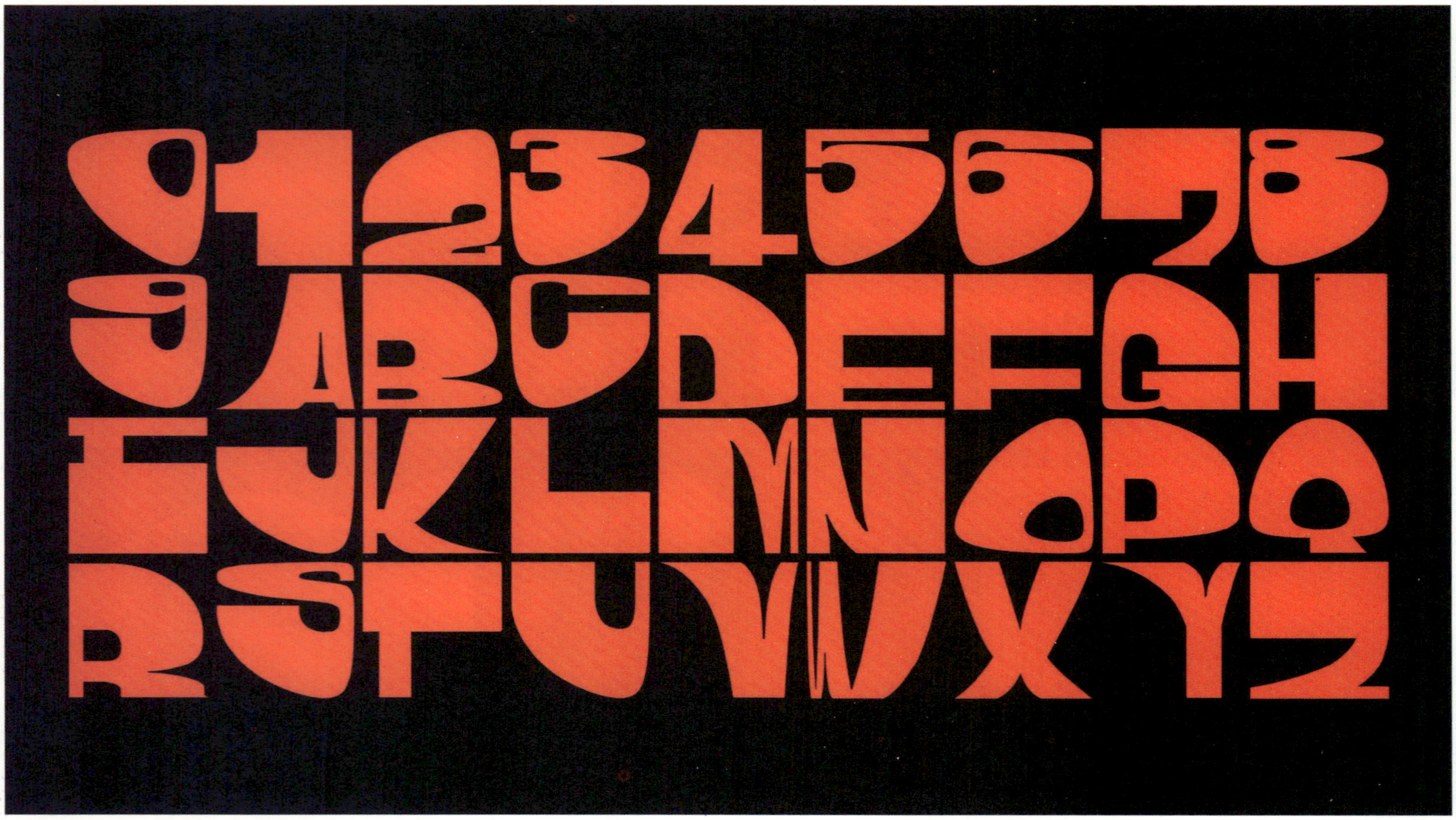
0123456789
ABCDEFGH
IJKLMNOPQ
RSTUVWXYZ

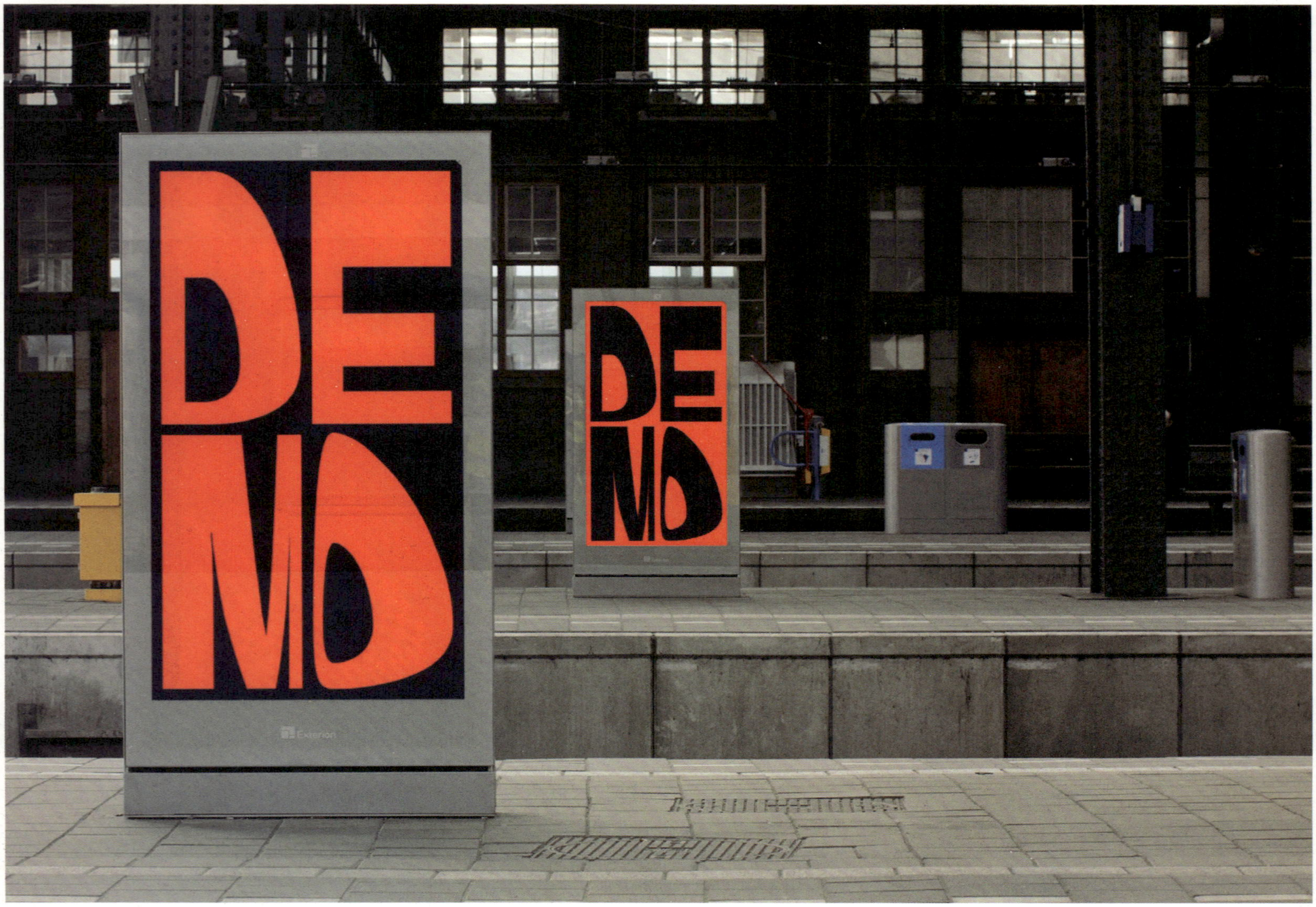
DE
MO
DE
MO

DEMO—DESIGN IN MOTION FESTIVAL

This exciting new concept, devised by Studio Dumbar in collaboration with Exterion Media Netherlands, launched with the inaugural DEMO festival on 7 November 2019 at Amsterdam Central Station. As the first event of its kind, DEMO showcased the best in motion design from studios, designers, emerging talents, and academies worldwide. For 24 hours, 80 digital screens throughout the station displayed the finest motion work, transforming the space into a dynamic, visual celebration.

Design Studio: Studio Dumbar
Client: Exterion Media Netherlands

▼ **Inspiration:**

The design concept aims to celebrate outstanding motion design in a highly visible public space. With up to 250,000 commuters passing through the station daily, Exterion Media's outdoor ad screens became the ideal canvas for this dynamic showcase. The design team sought to capture the innovative spirit and creative potential of motion design, integrating it seamlessly across all touchpoints—from the identity and website to promotional trailers and the event itself.

▼ **Elements:**

At the heart of the identity is a variable typeface, programmed with a custom script that transforms each word into its own unique animated form. The typeface remains legible while allowing the DEMO logo to be interactively distorted by website visitors: simply by moving the cursor. Paired with a striking color palette of orange and dark blue, the identity delivers bold visual impact.

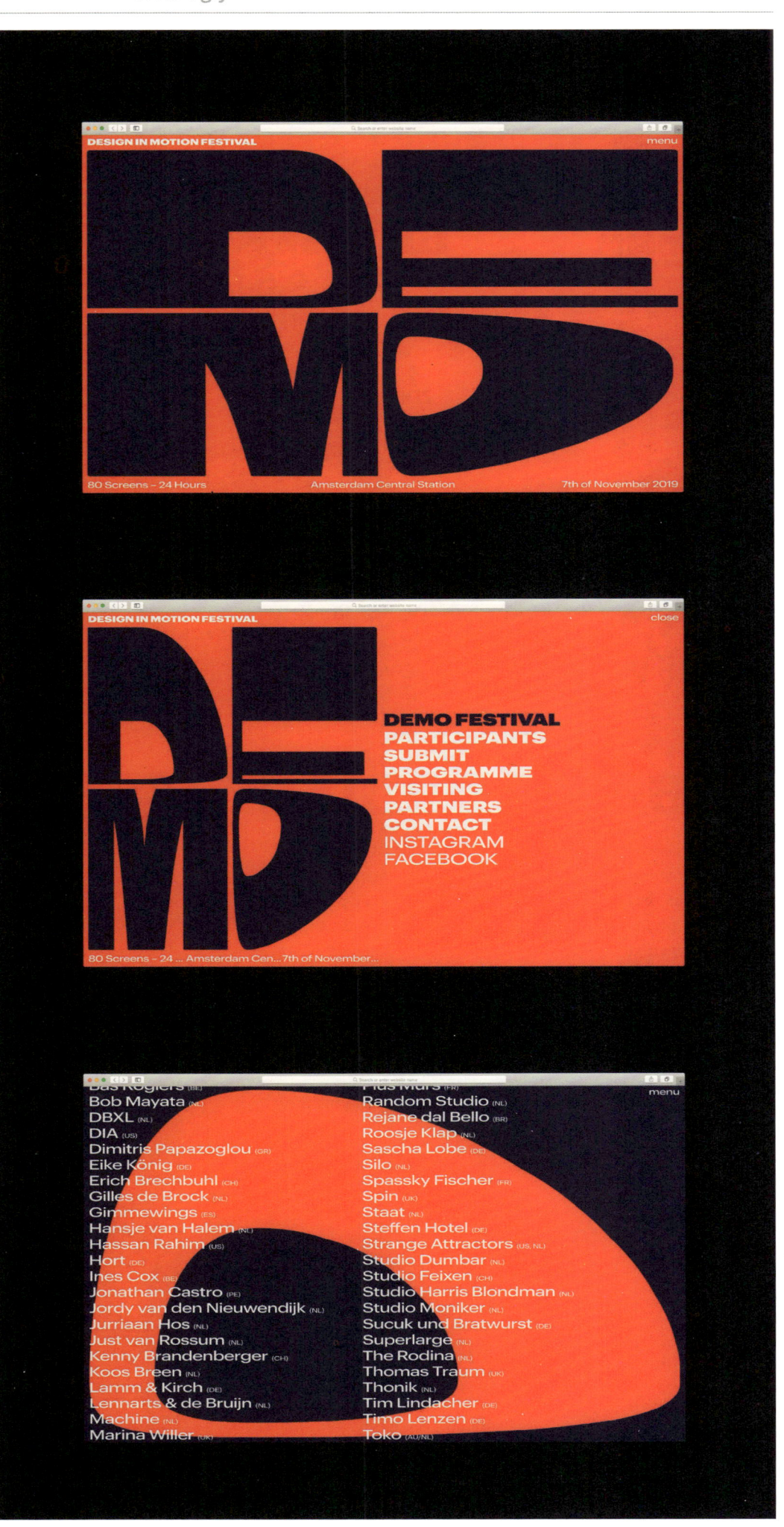

URBAN GOODIES

This project aims to improve the public perception of street vendors, transform their overall image, and encourage consumers to abandon stereotypes. By adopting a fair and friendly perspective towards this profession, it aims to instill respect and boost the confidence of street vendors. Through a series of designed visuals that resonate with consumers and creative packaging, the project enhances the value and sales of their products, providing tangible assistance to street vendors. It incorporates elements of street culture such as street signs, advertising stickers, and more. By presenting the authentic lives of street vendors from their perspective, it challenges societal stereotypes and highlights their sincerity and dedication to their livelihoods.

Designer: Yi-Ju Liao, Wei-Guang Wu, Ying-Syuan Lu, Hsin-Yi Shih

▼ **Inspiration:**
The work is influenced by street elements, such as street signs, advertising stickers, and other cultural elements found on the streets and roadsides.

▼ **Elements:**
The designer utilized street elements from the area where she lives: the inconspicuous advertisement stickers on the streets, the weathered shop signs on the left side, and even the most ordinary corners can be the trendiest and most unique hotspots.

▼ **Fonts:**
Source Han Sans, Noto Sans

▼ **Layout:**
The designers combined the unique culture of the streets and alleys by rearranging the layout of graphics and texts and expressing them through special processing methods to convey the perspective of street vendors.

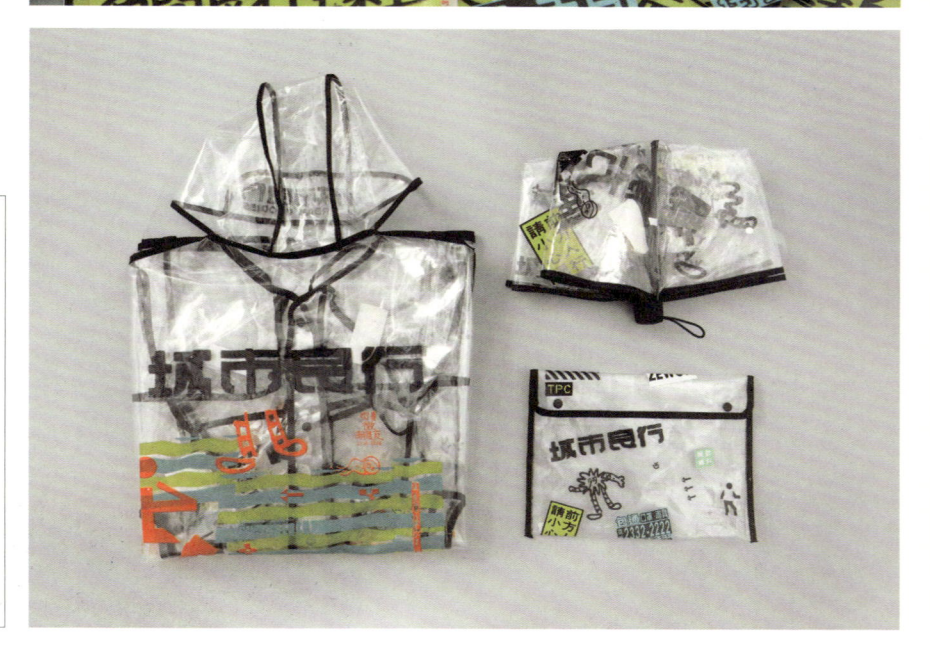

城市良行
URBAN GOODIES
TPC
ZEWOK
免用
統一發票
2 常見街賣商品

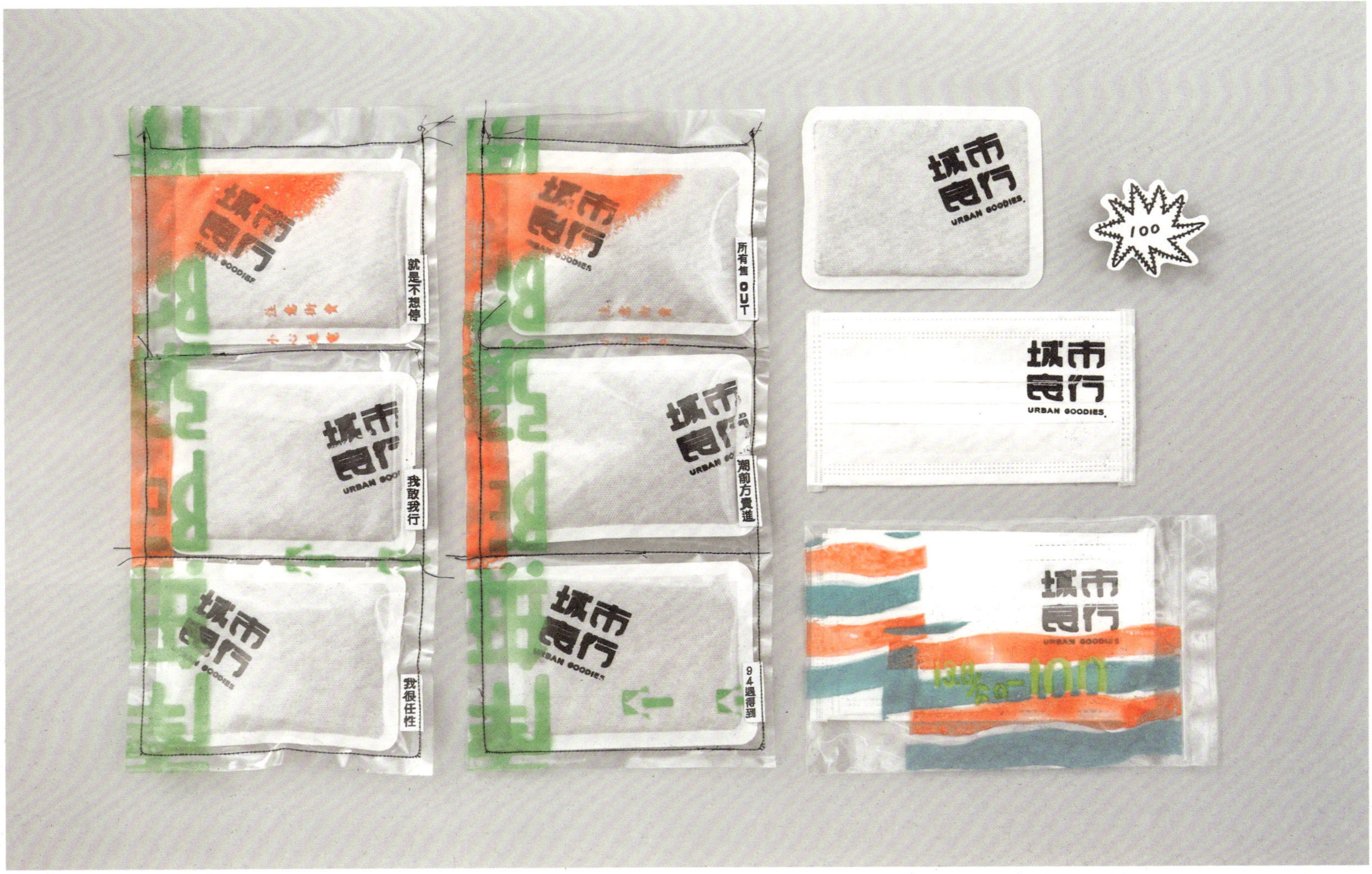
城市良行
URBAN GOODIES
就是不想停
所有攏 OUT
我敢我行
請前方實進
我很任性
94 過得到
100

SPRING SHOW 23

The poster is for the *Spring Show 23*, an exhibition scheduled for May 2023 at the Graduate School of Design, University of Seoul. It showcases the works of five designers, each pursuing their own unique approaches. The central theme of the exhibition revolves around the concept of "spring," which not only signifies the season but also symbolizes growth, renewal, and blossoming in a broader context. Various interpretations of these meanings of spring were explored in the design of the poster, aiming to encapsulate the essence of the theme.

Design Studio:
SUPERSALADSTUFF
Designer:
Haeri Chung
Graphic Assets Maker:
Haeri Chung, Sieun Kim, Misun Choi, Jiyoung Kim, Soi Hong
Client:
Graduate School of Design, University of Seoul

▼ **Inspiration:**
In fact, there was no intention to evoke a retro mood in this poster. Instead, the focus was on incorporating the latest approach and reflecting the contemporary landscape, where various styles coexist. Any perceived retro mood in the poster may arise from its complex visuals, influenced by the transition from analog to digital media and technology, as well as the blending of cultures reminiscent of the 1980s era.

▼ **Elements:**
Five designers freely explored various graphic elements under the theme "spring," experimenting with rough imagery, handmade objects, lettering, and line manipulation.

▼ **Fonts:**
Neue Haas Grotesk & heart number

▼ **Layout:**
The exhibition title sits prominently atop the poster, with diverse graphic elements below, each representing the theme of "spring" uniquely. To unify the design while celebrating diversity, a black block-like element anchors the colorful chaos below. This juxtaposition creates an intriguing yet harmonious visual.

CHINESE UGLY WORLD

In the current media environment, dominated by middle-class aesthetics, the peasant community lacks the discourse right to express their voices. The inclusiveness of emerging short video media platforms allows them to eagerly reconstruct their online identities through self-performance. This trend has given rise to a popular internet phenomenon known as "vulgar culture" or "Tuwei" (meaning "kitsch" in Chinese) culture. Both the production and consumption of Tuwei culture attract media attention, transforming it into entertaining content.

In this project, the designer created an intentionally unattractive visual world to illustrate the core aesthetic of Tuwei culture. It explores the process by which this rural online culture is increasingly becoming homogenized and formulaic. The visual representation aims to rekindle the audience's curiosity about Tuwei culture, encouraging a deeper understanding beyond the surface-level experience of vulgar symbols. Through this project, the goal is to direct the audience's attention to the underlying factors driving the emergence of Tuwei culture.

Design Studio: 2xlab design
Designer: Xinyi Liu

▼ **Inspiration:**
The designer often uses Tuwei memes in WeChat chats for humor or self-deprecation, yet is unaware of their origins. These memes were found to feature celebrities from Kuaishou, a short video community app in China, where personalities gained fame by sharing eccentric content. The designer expressed curiosity about their rise to fame. Among China's prominent short video platforms are TikTok and Kuaishou, with the latter catering primarily to users from smaller cities and rural areas. Despite Kuaishou's large user base, migrant workers remain underrepresented in mainstream media.

The designer compiled entertainment content, including widely spread memes focusing on ugliness. She drew inspiration from various sources, such as Umberto Eco's *On Ugliness* and Stephen Bayley's *Ugly: The Aesthetics of Everything*, for both design and illustrations.

▼ **Elements:**
The character graphics and typography are designed according to the text content, and the exaggerated deformations are meant to emphasize the alienated world.

▼ **Fonts:**
Most of the artwork in this project uses fonts created by the designer, except for the background blurb at the end of the book, which uses FZDeSaiHeiS.

关注
神经病
抖音记录美好生活
抖音记录美好生活
欢迎进入房间

关注
头發
HAIR

Chinese
Ugly World
喜欢主播就
我爱你!
老铁
喜欢主播就给

怪物
SOCIAL
MEDIA
经济
ECONOMY

giaogiao
deideide

SUPER
RURAL
STAR
明星

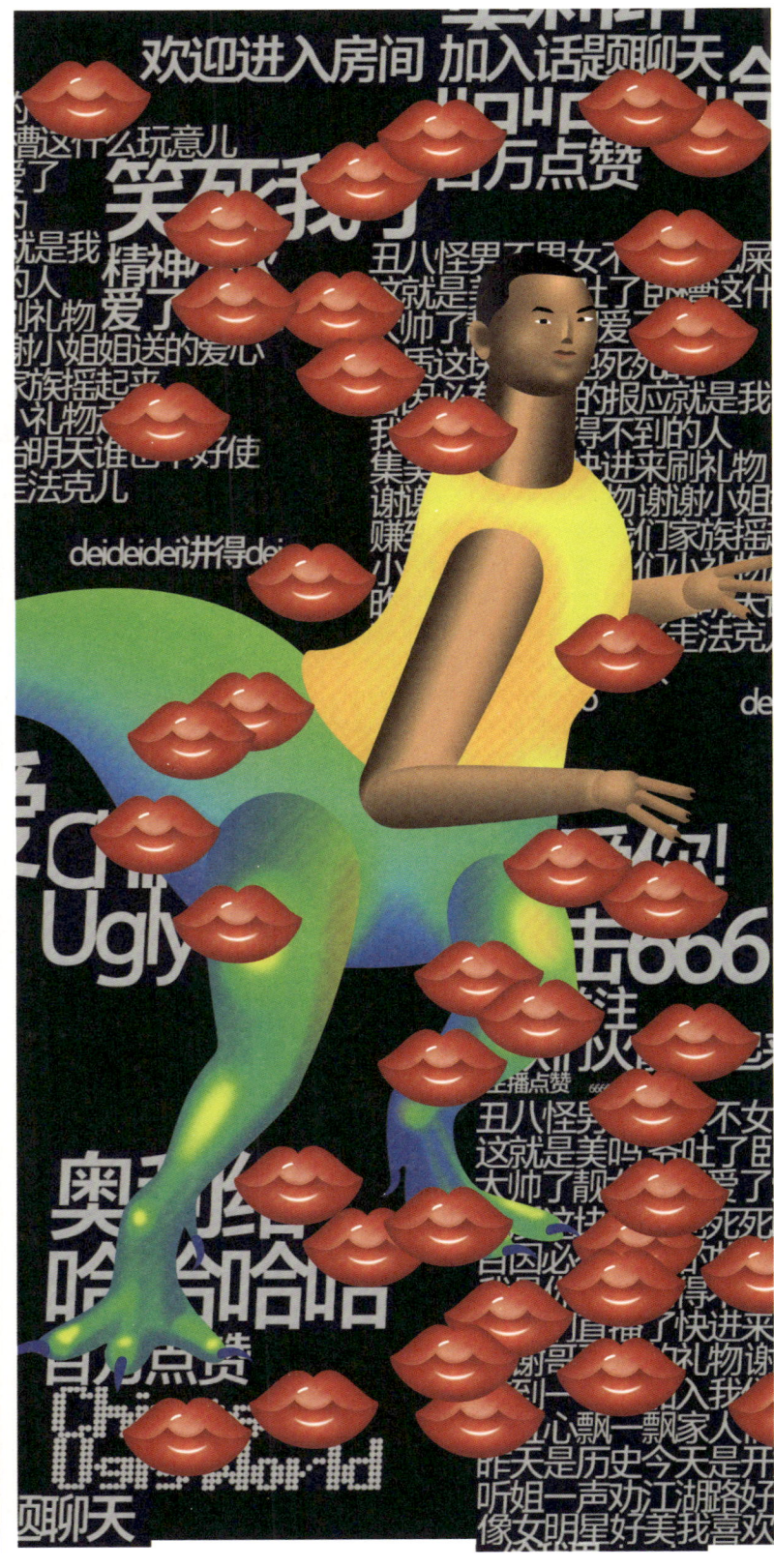

Color Scheme:

R243 G155 B076	R242 G234 B128	R214 G024 B045	R241 G140 B072	R241 G235 B056	R098 G184 B081
C000 M049 Y072 K000	C008 M004 Y059 K000	C011 M098 Y083 K000	C000 M056 Y072 K000	C009 M000 Y083 K000	C063 M000 Y085 K000
R228 G000 B127	R029 G032 B136	R000 G168 B105	R000 G144 B167	R056 G020 B052	R204 G159 B200
C000 M100 Y000 K000	C100 M100 Y000 K000	C081 M000 Y075 K000	C085 M023 Y032 K000	C080 M100 Y061 K044	C022 M044 Y000 K000

#NewUglyDesignTalk

1. The New Ugly style often challenges traditional aesthetic standards with its rough print feel, slightly conflicting colors, quirky layouts, and even a touch of "kitsch." This unconventional beauty breaks free from standard norms. How do you perceive this expressive approach, and how do you convey and structure seemingly chaotic ideas through your design work?

Haeri Chung (from SUPERSALADSTUFF)
The world we live in is not monotonous. Unexpected objects, situations, and people often intervene even in the most disciplined and organized spaces. I reflect on those experiences in my design. Nonetheless, I always try to organize things. As a result, some of the grid systems and letter positions follow traditional norms, but everything else is scattered around, or I like to set new "norms." By establishing certain constraints first and arranging everything accordingly, I can accidentally create odd visuals even if it wasn't my intention. It's a natural thing. I believe people who see the designs would feel both freedom and order simultaneously.

Onion Design Associates
The New Ugly style emerged at a time when the entire design industry was leaning towards clean and minimal modernism. With computer software facilitating the creation of clean, minimal, legible, simple, functional, and rational design layouts, akin to the Swiss typographic style, it became relatively straightforward. Subsequently, some young designers sought to rebel against this trend by experimenting with chaos, complexity, irrationality, and illegibility, embracing a messy aesthetic. This unconventional approach gained popularity and freshness. However, like any trend, it will have its moment until it becomes ubiquitous within a certain period of time, too.

Xinyi Liu (from 2xlab design)
Drawing inspiration from the imperfect yet captivating "ugly beauty," some of the content may appear slightly kitsch, but it's very lively. People always enjoy change, and new trends are always fascinating. When people become accustomed to beauty, ugliness transforms into a form of curiosity.

Yi-Ju Liao
I believe the New Ugly style is a bold and expressive design aesthetics that helps to highlight uniqueness and creativity. It challenges traditional aesthetic standards and defies audience expectations of beauty. Through rough printing effects, color clashes, and unconventional layouts, it deliberately presents a sense of chaos or unusual appearance. It conveys a certain emotion or message within the chaos and apparent disorder, creating a strong visual impact. By breaking conventional norms, it prompts viewers to contemplate and inspires different interpretations of visual expression.

Yukit Lai (from *BranD* Magazine)
This may just be a visual communication technique without going into the specific information conveyed to viewers, but it is certainly something that can initially attract people's attention. For visual communication, seizing visual attention is the foundation for successfully conveying information. In my usual design process, I first set aside the keywords from the information, organize the remaining basic information, and then integrate the focus with the overall design, blending them together.

yunbomu
I wasn't sure how much of it was design and how much was art, but I found it interesting. Breaking down boundaries intrigued me. In my case, I don't design to convey information in an easy-to-understand manner. Basically, it's a "You know it when you see it, right?" mindset. I prefer to confuse people because leaving things open-ended gives me various ideas and possibilities. I enjoy this approach.

2. Are there any traditional aesthetic concepts or habits that you deliberately attempt to subvert or reinterpret to create a unique aesthetics in your designs?

Haeri Chung (from SUPERSALADSTUFF)
I mix rules and disorder. At a glance, it might look confusing, but there's always a rule that I set in it. People tell me that my design looks free but also looks planned out, in a way that if an element is placed differently, it would be weird; therefore, everything inevitably has to be placed where it is. I think my intention is conveyed well through the rules that I set.

Xinyi Liu (from 2xlab design)
I'm not accustomed to intentionally breaking or subverting. Most of my creations are based on content production.

Yi-Ju Liao

I challenge the traditional aesthetic by incorporating innovative elements into my designs to infuse them with creativity and individuality. This includes opting for unconventional color combinations, experimenting with non-traditional materials and textures, and reinterpreting traditional cultural symbols in new contexts to create fresh cultural collisions. Through these approaches, I aim to break traditional expectations and captivate viewers with unexpected and novel design experiences.

Yukit Lai (from *BranD* Magazine)

In the current stage of design creation, I am still "standing on the shoulders of predecessors." Rather than "subverting" or "reinterpreting," I am more like climbing different trees, absorbing nutrients, and then projecting my perspective with my own experience and accumulation.

yunbomu

Maybe some cheap Asian flyer design? But that interpretation is difficult. If I recreate it myself, the fun of it will be destroyed.

3. Are there specific design elements or styles that you believe best represent New Ugly? Please share some elements you often use in your designs.

Haeri Chung (from SUPERSALADSTUFF)

I don't decide on anything before I start designing. I try to have a new approach to each and every project. It seems that a New Ugly mood might arise in the process of overlapping things with various characteristics into a layer or inserting unexpected elements.

Onion Design Associates

The New Ugly style in youth culture design emerges when one deliberately disregards conventional design and layout rules taught in design school. It involves doing the opposite—discarding concerns about legibility, grid systems, functionality, hierarchy of information, and even communication. Instead, it thrusts shock value to the forefront, challenging the audience's expectations. This style embraces strangeness, weirdness, and, most importantly, bad taste. However, it's crucial to note that New Ugly shouldn't be applied indiscriminately to every project. Its effectiveness lies in its targeted application, particularly in areas related to youth culture and pop culture markets.

Xinyi Liu (from 2xlab design)

High-contrast color schemes or high-plus-low saturation color schemes.

Yi-Ju Liao

Designs in the New Ugly style feature striking elements that break traditional aesthetic norms, creating memorable visuals. I use rough textures, bold color combinations, and unconventional layouts to grab attention and challenge viewers. Incorporating non-traditional shapes, exaggerated circles, and surreal elements adds uniqueness and sparks new interpretations of visual experiences.

Yukit Lai (from *BranD* Magazine)

I currently cannot easily give a clear definition to the New Ugly style, but personally, I quite like the classic primary colors of red, yellow, and blue, which give me a sense of purity and vividness.

yunbomu

Noise and silhouette.

Shōwa

1940

1960

1980

DEVELOPMENT HISTORY

1926-1945: Early Developmentnt

After World War I, Japan, as a victorious and economically thriving nation, entered a period of mass consumption, especially in major cities like Tokyo and Osaka. The initial phase saw a blend of traditional Japanese design elements with Western influences, particularly from the Art Nouveau and Art Deco. Graphic design during this period featured intricate illustrations and a modern sensibility.

1940s-1950s: Post-War Reconstruction

After World War II, there was a shift toward rebuilding the nation. Japanese graphic design was influenced by wartime propaganda but then embraced simplicity, functionality, and clean typography in the post-war era.

1960s-1970s: Transformation Period

The economic growth of the 1960s and 1970s marked a period of transformation in Japan. Graphic design evolved to reflect changing societal and cultural landscapes, incorporating vibrant colors, bold typography, and pop culture references.

1980s: Technological Advancements and Digital Design

The 1980s brought rapid technological advancement and the advent of digital design tools, marking a pivotal shift in the evolution of Shōwa design. This era saw a distinct fusion of traditional Japanese elements with modern, futuristic motifs, and people imagined more colorful depictions of urban life. Besides, the use of early computer software for design, along with influences from video games, anime, and electronic music, led to the creation of bold, dynamic visuals that captured the spirit of the era. Shōwa design of the 1980s reflected both the cultural optimism of Japan's bubble economy and the global fascination with technology, influencing design and culture in Japan and globally.

Present: Contemporary Nostalgia and Preservation

In recent years, there has been a resurgence of interest in Shōwa design. Designers and enthusiasts are preserving and reinterpreting Shōwa-era visuals, reflecting the enduring impact of this period on contemporary Japanese design and culture.

SHŌWA: MODERN VISUAL STYLE GUIDE

ELEMENTS

KEYWORDS

1. VIVID RETRO IMAGERY
2. WARM AND BRIGHT COLORS
3. CULTURAL SYMBOLISM
4. TRADITIONAL-MODERN FUSION
5. STYLIZED ILLUSTRATIONS

1. Vintage Television
2. Bow Tie
3. Rabbit Characters
4. Folding Fan
5. Red Fruit
6. Maneki-neko (Lucky Cat)
7. Heart Shape
8. Camellias
9. Circles and Triangles
10. Pretty Girl
11. Four-Pointed Stars
12. Cream
13. Pudding

FONTS

Sniglet Kingthings Clarity Gilroy TGL 0-17 Alt *Playball* Airstrip four vAL HVD Comic HELSINKI Signika

COLOR

LAYOUT

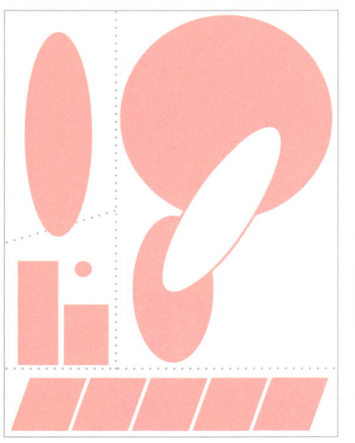

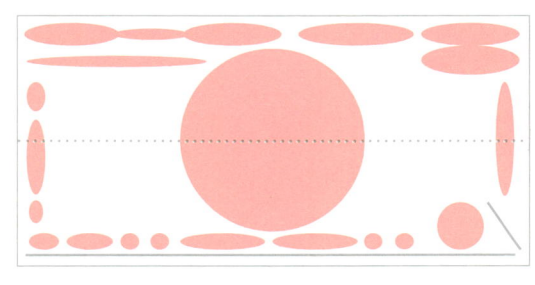

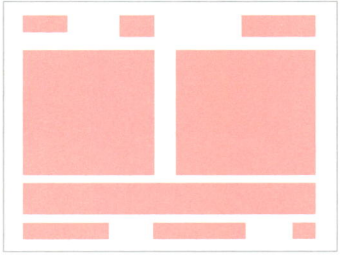

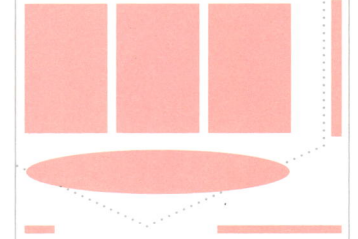

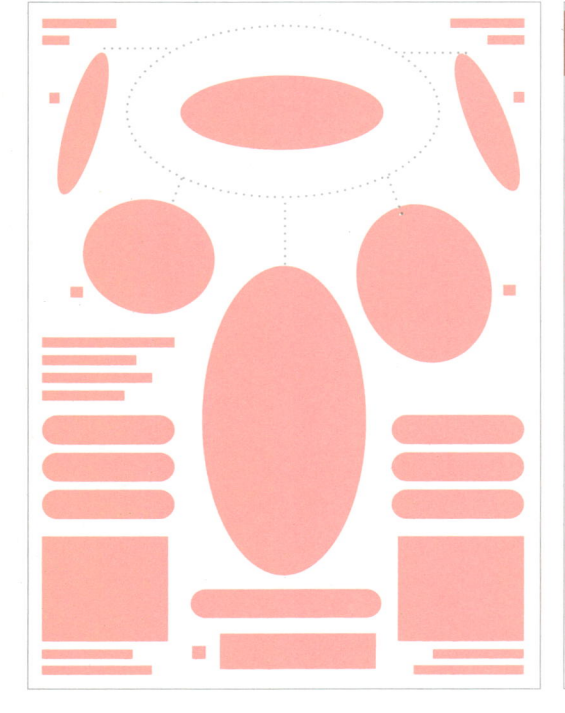

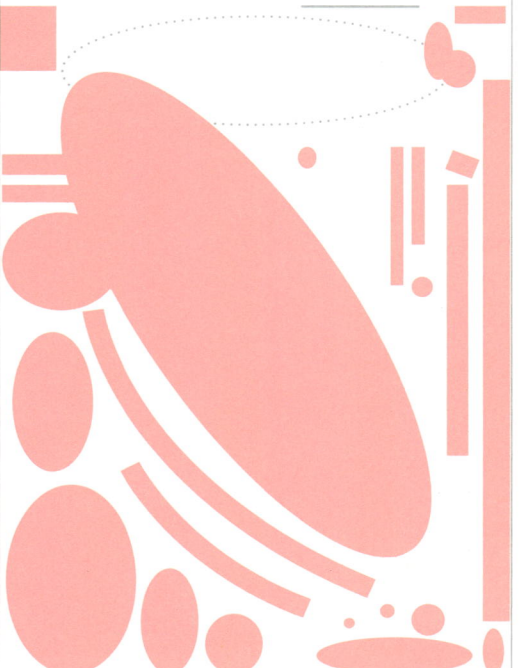

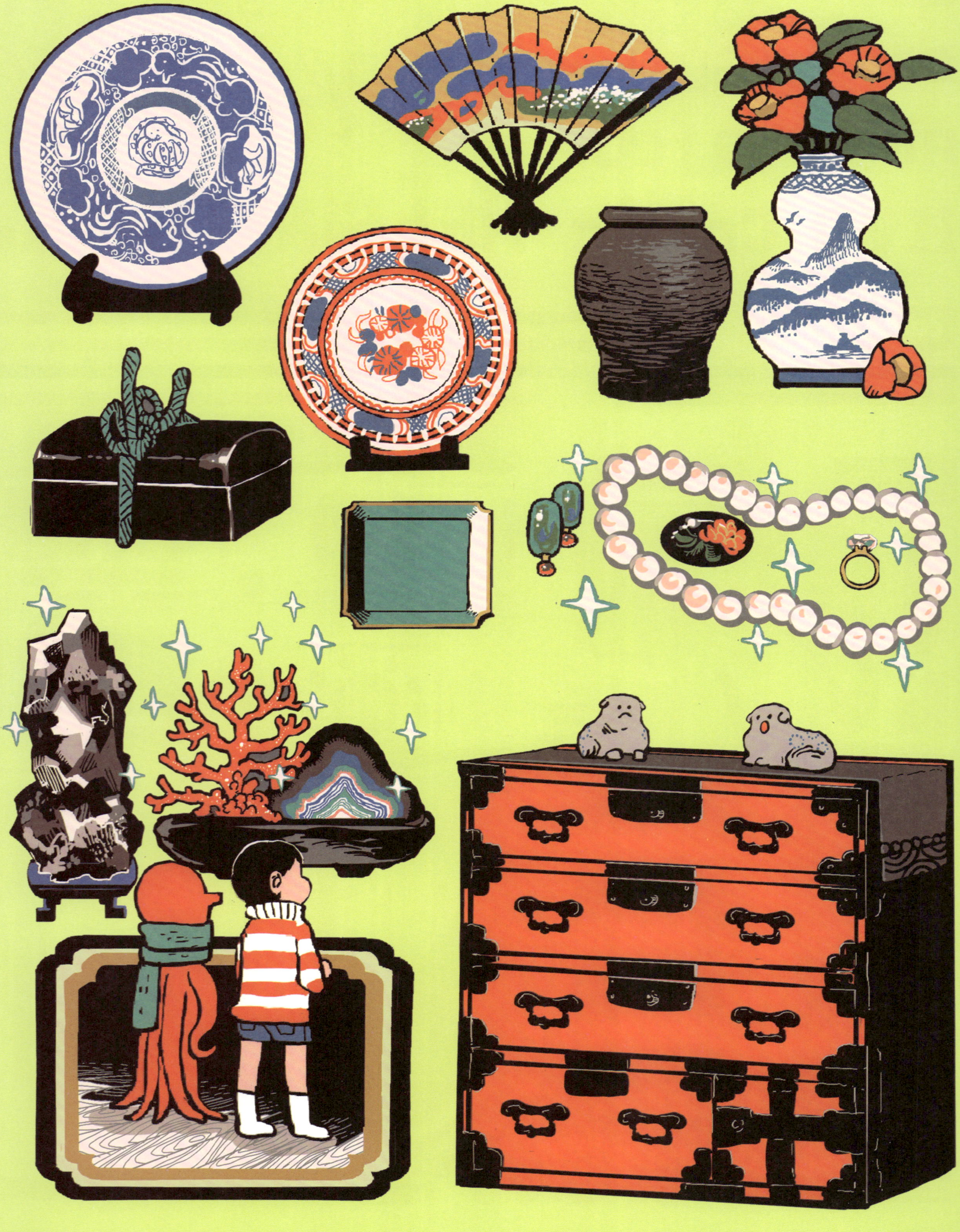

Tomii Masako

Tomii Masako, born in Saitama Prefecture and currently residing in Tokyo, Japan, is an illustrator specializing in book illustrations. In her personal artworks, she enjoys blending the essence of everyday life with a touch of fantasy.

1 Exploring Color and Style

Tomii Masako's visual expression is defined by a carefully curated palette featuring subdued colors with slightly low saturation, such as vermilion, lapis lazuli, and wild golden yellow, complemented by dark hues for enhanced visual impact. Embracing a return to her artistic roots, she now focuses on conveying images through deliberate "lines" and opts for illustrations with a reduced color scheme, facilitating efficient selection and shorter production times. Her current palette of 20 colors reflects those frequently used throughout her artistic journey.

This shift in approach has significantly streamlined Tomii's artistic process, eliminating previous challenges associated with extensive color selection and allowing her to derive greater enjoyment from her creative endeavors. Tomii draws inspiration from her experiences with the "Oekaki BBS," a simple drawing platform popular on the Japanese Internet in the 2000s. The drawing tools available on this platform were remarkably simple, primarily consisting of pens, buckets, and brushes. Some bulletin boards even lacked a color dropper function, but they provide a space for individuals to express themselves freely and have immense joy with these basic drawing tools based on the theme of the posted drawing. This influence has shaped her current style, which focuses on "lines" and emphasizes the fun and spontaneity integral to her artistic journey.

In the realm of color palettes, Tomii navigates the technical nuances of RGB and CMYK modes, consciously selecting colors that maintain integrity across different printing processes. Despite drawing illustrations in RGB mode, Tomii often encounters a sense of disappointment when converting colors to CMYK mode due to unexpected alterations. To mitigate this, Tomii consciously chooses colors from the outset that exhibit minimal changes between RGB and CMYK, taking into account the desired color tones for printed illustrations. This meticulous approach ensures that her artworks retain their intended vibrancy and visual impact, reflecting her evolving expertise and commitment to quality.

In her series *Tomidoron*, Tomii's color palette decisions are informed by collaborative input, particularly from designer Hiroko Sakai of coton design. The vibrant yellow background chosen by Sakai for the art book's binding serves as a striking departure from Tomii's usual palette, imbuing the illustrations with a newfound radiance and vivacity. Subsequently, she developed a strong affinity for this color. This saturated yellow backdrop not only transforms the atmosphere of the artwork but also establishes a visual identity closely associated with the *Tomidoron* series. Tomii's deliberate use of desaturated colors alongside this bold backdrop underscores her meticulous approach to maintaining continuity in her visual storytelling while embracing opportunities for creative evolution.

2 Shōwa-Inspired Art in a Nostalgic Reverie

In Tomii Masako's artistic endeavors, the aim is to evoke joy and fascination through the Shōwa retro style, a reflection of her enduring passion for entertaining viewers. The defining characteristics of the Shōwa era for her encompass a distinct expressiveness characterized by wooden and tatami structures, Japanese-style rooms, and vibrant tiled roofs, enriched by Western influences that imparted a unique warmth. These elements evoke nostalgic memories, contrasting with contemporary urban landscapes that she perceives as lacking vitality. Despite this contrast, Tomii acknowledges the functionality of modern life but focuses her illustrations on crafting a unique worldview that amalgamates multiple motifs, avoiding singular themes.

Central to Tomii's artistic expression is the pursuit of expressive and attractive Shōwa elements, which immerse viewers in a world where intricate details resonate emotionally. Her illustrations draw from cherished memories of childhood, including evenings filled with play, arcade streets, and late afternoons on tatami mats. These memories manifest in her art through enchanting depictions of shadows cast through shoji screens, the vibrant signage of local stores, and the nostalgic charm of wooden architecture in back alleys. Her illustrations serve as visual diaries, preserving and sharing the memories that have shaped her identity over time, inviting viewers to share in her nostalgic journey through art.

Tomii believes that works infused with Shōwa elements resonate deeply due to the era's transformative impact on Japanese society, marked by economic prosperity and a sense of optimism during the early 1980s. The pervasive influence of Shōwa-era media, including magazines and television, continues to foster a collective nostalgia, creating a lasting emotional connection for viewers drawn to the unique essence of that time. Tomii's art not only reflects this nostalgia but also captures the spirit of community and shared experiences that defined an entire generation, making her work a bridge between the past and present.

The image on the left is sourced from Tomii Masako's work, *Ancestral Collectibles*.

TOMIDORON: THE ART OF TOMII MASAKO

Client: PIE International

TOMIDORON: COVER

Shōwa — Tomii Masako

ILLUSTRATION

Tomii Masako — Shōwa — 294

PLAYFUL SERIES

CAT THAT TURNS INTO A BICYCLE

▼ **Inspiration:**
Rumiko Takahashi's manga work *Ranma ½* The characters, as well as their fashions and accessories, were cute, cool, and full of charm. The influence she got from this work was immeasurable, and the illustrator used to copy the pictures many times every day. Incidentally, her illustration expression influenced by this, which remains deep-rooted, is to add various colors to people's hair. The inhabitants of *Rumic World* by Rumiko Takahashi are colorful and cheerful to look at.

▼ **Color Scheme:**

- R049 G097 B173 / C083 M060 Y000 K000
- R224 G073 B015 / C006 M084 Y100 K000
- R197 G180 B177 / C026 M030 Y026 K000
- R000 G137 B060 / C084 M027 Y100 K000
- R036 G174 B148 / C073 M005 Y050 K000
- R245 G226 B167 / C005 M012 Y040 K000

WHERE TO FIND SNAKES

HAKUJADEN T

REST

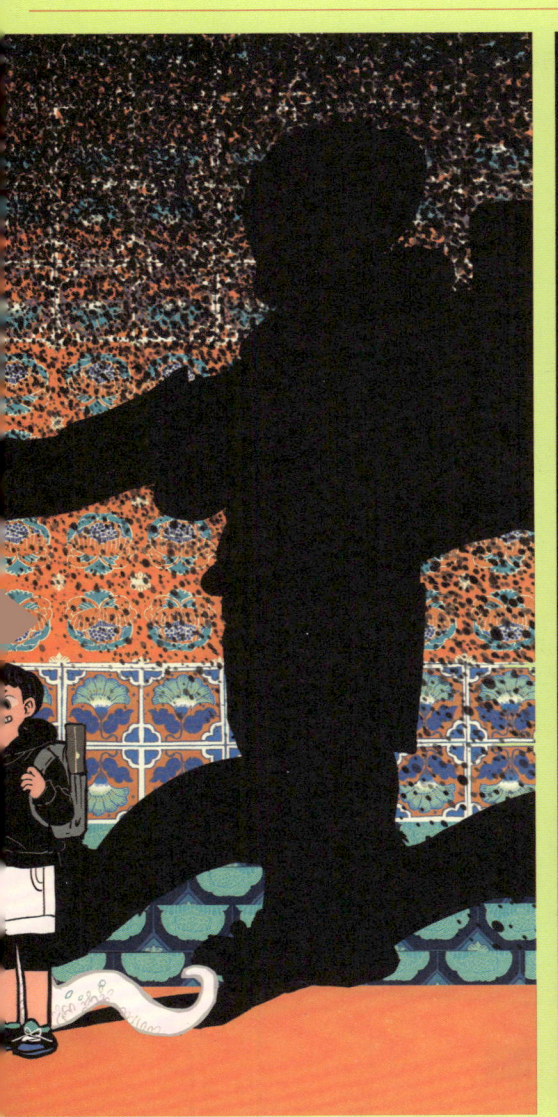

GLOWING LUMINARIES

Jentwo — Shōwa

Jentwo

Janejira Taechakampu, an illustrator based in Bangkok, operates under the pen name "Jentwo," derived from her double nickname, Jen-Jen. Following her graduation with a degree in graphic design, she ventured into the creative industry, earning acclaim, notably featured on "It's Nice That: The Next Generation 2021." Jen-Jen's distinctive artwork is characterized by dark outlines and vibrant colors, drawing inspiration from culture, travel, and retro collectibles. She boasts collaborations with renowned brands and publications such as *Today at Apple*, *The Washington Post*, and *WIRED* Japan, among others.

1 The Charm of Nostalgic Handcrafts

Jentwo's artistic style can be described as fun, bright, and maximal yet somehow minimal, infused with humor, and highly flexible. Rooted in the belief that each piece should effectively communicate its message, Jentwo is open to adapting her style to fit the work at hand. Despite potential shifts in her artistic approach, each piece retains her distinctive touch. In her personal projects, she prioritizes self-satisfaction, trusting that genuine enjoyment of her work will resonate with others rather than imposing her feelings onto viewers.

Jentwo does not rigidly adhere to a particular style but often incorporates certain elements, such as a preference for organic, textured looks achieved with rough brushes and halftone. This preference adds an analog, handcrafted feel to her digital art, blending retro aesthetics with contemporary techniques. She finds joy in the serendipity of unexpected imperfections, such as overlapping colors from Risograph printing or spontaneous grain textures, which introduce an element of unpredictability and charm, turning the digital creation into a delightful exploration with a handcrafted feel.

Her fascination with the neat, almost computer-like outcomes achieved by past artisans without digital tools fuels her passion for retro aesthetics. This passion inspires her to explore ways to make digital designs appear handmade and vice versa. Jentwo's approach is characterized by a unique blend of modern digital precision and nostalgic handcrafted imperfection, making her work distinctively engaging and visually compelling.

2 Discovering the 1980s

Jentwo's illustration *Since 1986* draws inspiration from 1980s workplace aesthetics, particularly the use of color stripes commonly seen in corporate designs of that era. Her approach involves using these stripes as pattern fills within shapes and leveraging the unique capabilities of the Risograph printing process. By adjusting opacity levels and employing a gradual color scheme when colorizing objects in sequence, she achieved a distinctive look. The Risograph, which resembles a photocopier but functions like a screen printer, produces textures such as grain and halftone, resulting in a hand-printed, tactile finish. This process, despite being digital, introduces imperfections that impart a unique quality to each piece, evoking a nostalgic feel. Besides, Jentwo finds the interiors, stationery, tools, computers, and furniture design of the 1980s workplace particularly interesting, and these elements may influence her future creations.

3 Back to The Shōwa Era

In her illustration series *Staying Home in Shōwa Era*, Jentwo explored a hypothetical Shōwa-era Covid-19 pandemic outbreak, focusing on evoking a sense of nostalgia. She incorporated modern people's nostalgic emotions by recalling missed activities from the Shōwa era, such as making calls with a telephone, playing video games, and watching television. By centering her designs around these familiar objects, she creates a bridge between the past and present. Despite today's technological advancements, Jentwo highlights that fundamental human desires and feelings remain unchanged. This enduring craving for social interaction allows elements from the Shōwa era to resonate deeply with contemporary audiences, balancing historical context with the relatable emotions experienced during quarantine.

4 Nostalgic × Futuristic Aesthetics

Jentwo's illustration style masterfully draws inspiration from the Shōwa era, City Pop, and Japanese anime, creating a nostalgic yet futuristic aesthetics. She navigates the balance between these seemingly contrasting elements by incorporating a nostalgic drawing approach characterized by the use of rough

PLAYTIME

The designer finds workplace aesthetics fascinating, particularly the concept of cubicles. While some may perceive them as stressful, she sees a certain charm in these enclosed spaces. Cubicles create personalized areas that distinguish individuals from one another. In this project, she is using the cubicle as a unit, duplicating it endlessly. Each unit is designed with unique details on stationery and office supplies, and she is also experimenting with 80s color stripes. The designer uses the term "playtime" to emphasize that work can be enjoyable. This project, for her, has been a source of creative play, involving experimentation with colors and textures and drawing inspiration from her favorite era.

▼ **Inspiration:**

Fascinated by Retro-Futurism, a movement in the creative arts showcasing the influence of depictions of the future produced in an earlier era, the designer drew inspiration for this image from the same title, *Playtime* (1967), by Jacques Tati. The film is set in a futuristic, hyperconsumerist Paris, perfectly encapsulating the essence of Retro-Futurism visions. The movie envisions modern life, coincidentally reflecting the 1980s era with its plate glass and steel structures, endless corridors, workstations, and elevators and escalators.

brushes and halftone patterns. Simultaneously, she integrates informative elements and scientific diagrams to infuse her work with a modern touch. This unique combination stems from her affection for vintage aesthetics and her enthusiasm for sci-fi movies, reflecting her appreciation for Retro-Futurism.

In her poster *56709*, influenced by Junko Ohashi's "Telephone Number" and the City Pop genre, Jentwo incorporated elements from Shōwa-era Japanese comics and the work of Eizin Suzuki. The commonality between Suzuki's art and Shōwa-era comics lies in their use of black-outline forms, screen-tones, and halftone textures. In Shōwa-era comics, background scenes often convey atmosphere, while Suzuki's images are characterized by pop-scattered geometric shapes. Jentwo's design choices in *56709* reflect these influences by incorporating black outlines and halftone textures to add depth and detail. Drawing from the comic tradition of dividing pages into grids, she uses geometric shapes and lines as leading elements to guide the viewer's gaze through the image. These design choices create a cohesive atmosphere and narrative, blending nostalgic and modern elements to produce a visually compelling piece.

5 Views on Retro Design Trends and Challenges

Our nostalgia often draws us to cherish memories of the past, especially the charm of the 80s and 90s, which holds a special place in our hearts. Recently, there's been a trend of reminiscing about the Y2K era, suggesting an enduring inclination to reflect on various periods of the past. Jentwo posits that in the future, designers may create works capturing the essence of the 2020s, invoking a sense of longing for the present moments.

Our attraction to designs from the past is rooted in their ability to stand out and embody the distinctiveness of their respective eras. However, Jentwo observes that even these vintage designs carry the imprint of earlier influences. She believes that evaluating a design transcends visual appeal; it necessitates understanding the context in which it was created. Factors such as the environment, time period, and media landscape significantly shape a designer's decisions. Consequently, if a present-day designer aims to encapsulate the past's essence in their work, the outcome will inevitably differ due to the infusion of contemporary elements, such as digital tools and the altered global landscape.

Jentwo emphasizes that inspiration in the creative process is drawn from one another, highlighting that no one truly owns an idea. It's a dynamic interplay of influences where each era contributes to the rich tapestry of design evolution. This ever-evolving process underscores the challenge of maintaining uniqueness within the retro design landscape while acknowledging the shared influences that shape our creative expressions.

SINCE 1986

This illustration was featured in Kamboja Press's Riso Club project for the Bangkok Art Book Fair CO-OP. They commissioned the designer to create an illustration incorporating Risograph-related elements like the machine, ink, or printing method itself.

Originating in Japan in 1980, the Risograph machine inspired the artist to evoke the atmospheric and introspective feeling of a working studio. Alongside essential equipment such as an office cabinet, personal computer, and stationery, the artist included the quintessential Risograph machine. Additionally, a rack in the background displays each color layer printed separately, highlighting the distinctive skill inherent to this method. The designer opted for three colors and adjusted their opacity. Renowned for its vibrant colors and unique textures, the Risograph method produced a delightfully nostalgic outcome.

▼ **Inspiration:**
This illustration is primarily inspired by 1980s workplace aesthetics. Elements such as gradual color stripes, commonly utilized in corporate identity designs during that era, have been incorporated.

56709

The designer loves listening to 1980s Japanese City Pop songs. They have a huge impact on her style, providing positive energy and creating a focused atmosphere. She created a poster dedicated to her favorite song, *56709* is inspired by Junko Ohashi's song "Telephone Number." The song has a catchy and memorable line, "Ah-ooooh! 5-6-7-0-9." The theme of this track is a woman worrying about a man she cares about.

▼ **Inspiration:**
The designer was influenced by the world of Shōwa-era Japanese comics and the legendary City Pop artist Eizin Suzuki.

STAYING HOME IN SHŌWA ERA

This project comprises a series of three posters, each envisioning life during a hypothetical Covid-19 outbreak in the Shōwa era and contemplating how people might spend their time in quarantine.

The first poster, titled "Television & Me," depicts a man in pajamas watching TV all day.

The second poster is named "I Want to Play a Game with My Friend." In the past, multiplayer games required all players to be in the same location to start the game. Consequently, during a quarantine period, a child might feel quite saddened.

The third poster in this series expresses the sentiment, "I Want to Meet You in Person." In the Shōwa era, communication was often limited to writing or calling. The accompanying image portrays a woman holding a remarkable gadget—a telephone—with a smile on her face. This symbolizes the hope that the quarantine will soon end, allowing her to reunite with her lover in person.

▼ Inspiration:
The designer was inspired by the vibrant advertising posters of 1980s Japan.

TELEVISION & ME

I WANT TO PLAY A GAME WITH MY FRIEND

I WANT TO MEET YOU IN PERSON

UNCLE BEN EP ALBUM — UNCLE'S CLOSET

This project was commissioned by Uncle Ben, a Thai indie-pop band under the supervision of the What the Duck label. The EP's music is steeped in a nostalgic concept. Despite being part of the new generation, the band enjoys embracing the charm of old, uncle-like elements. The overarching theme involves depicting the band members exploring their uncle's closet.

Client: Uncle Ben / What The Duck Co,Ltd.

▼ **Inspiration:**
They're dressed in the classic Preppy look: blazers, polos, chinos, Oxford shirts, tennis sweaters, and loafers. Preppy fashion, originating from Ivy League student style, draws inspiration from leisure pursuits like polo, sailing, rugby, and tennis. The choice of Preppy style evokes a vintage charm reminiscent of classic uncle attire yet maintains a playful essence associated with teenage fashion of that era. Floral patterns in the images reflect the band's lyrical themes and draw inspiration from William Morris designs, enhancing the retro vibes.

▼ **Color Scheme:**

R184 G111 B037	R143 G135 B048	R096 G067 B050	R185 G067 B040
C032 M064 Y096 K000	C052 M044 Y096 K000	C062 M072 Y081 K032	C031 M086 Y094 K000
R233 G179 B132	R222 G197 B093	R249 G233 B172	R069 G108 B130
C008 M036 Y059 K000	C016 M022 Y071 K000	C004 M009 Y039 K000	C078 M055 Y041 K000

YUM

Yum is a zine about the designer's favorite Thai dish—a spicy salad. Created from the designer's perspective, it's infused with humor and various elements of Thai pop culture. Printed using a 4-color Risograph by Two in Row press, it measures 12x18.7 cm with 12 pages. Inside, readers embark on a vibrant journey through Thai pop culture, from essential Yum party vocabulary to the secrets of Yum sauce ingredients. Inspired by her love for Yum and cultural exchanges with foreign friends, she shared jokes and stories. To enhance the atmosphere, she also created a poster and a motion of a baby angel pouring MSG.

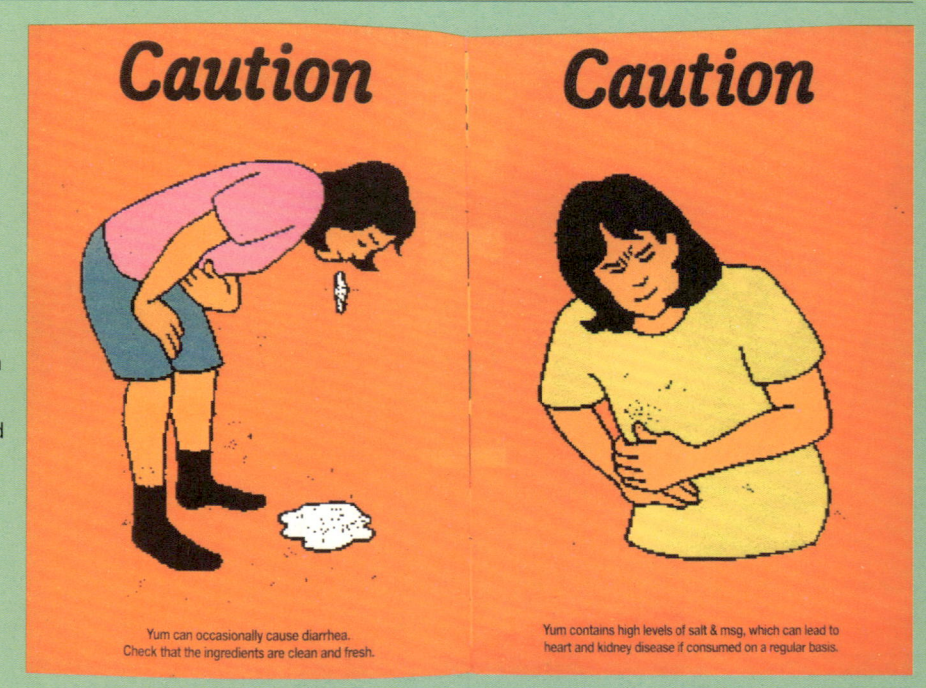

▼ **Inspiration:**
The outline of the illustrations is intentional, aiming to pixelate them because Yum shop artworks typically involve the use of broken PNG files. Additionally, she finds aesthetic appeal in Pixel Art; it evokes a feeling of nostalgia. It's kitsch and playful, perfectly mirroring the essence of Thai humor. The latest process—Risograph print—adds a vivid, grainy, and handmade quality to the zine, just as she intended. For the graphic design, she structured it like a guidebook or instruction manual, with the intention of introducing readers to the art of being a Yum beginner-eater.

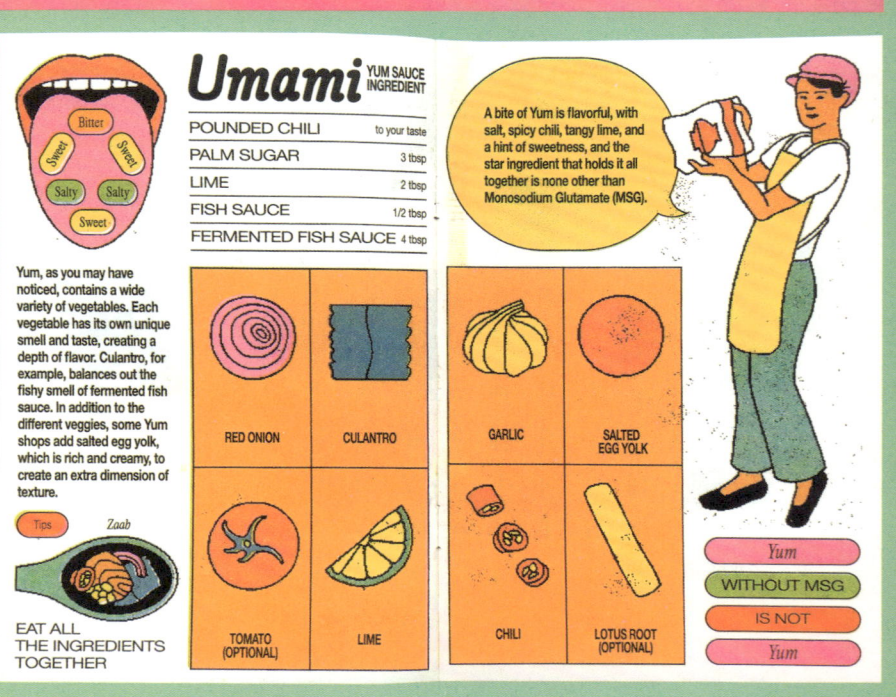

OFFICE STICKER

This set of stickers features a compilation of office-related items like telephones, coffee mugs, train tickets, radios, and more. It reflects her fascination with workplace aesthetics, taking a step back in time to a slightly older era.

> ▼ **Inspiration:**
> The sticker collection is inspired by the nostalgic charm of the 1950–1980 ephemera and stamps from Eastern Europe.

ANA TOMY

The designer collaborated with Ana Tomy, a Malaysian notebook brand, to showcase her illustrations on limited-edition notebook covers. As a museum lover, she's constantly seeking out new sources of inspiration and creativity. She drew a picture of a room filled with all sorts of different sources of energy and creativity, such as books, music, art, and more.

Client: Ana Tomy

> ▼ **Inspiration:**
> In this cover, the designer has incorporated numerous objects from the art and design world, aiming to celebrate the idea that materials for their work are found at every turn.

credit: Photo by Ana Tomy and co.

デザート会社
Totally 傘下のデザート専門店
人気アイテム
copyright (c) 2021 by Totally all rights reserved
大好きです!!!
毎日新鮮なイチゴ
純天然植物クリーム
少女の一番のお気に入り!!
最適な組み合わせ
ラテの香り

Totally
copyright (c) 2021 by Totally all rights reserved

デザート会社
Totally 傘下のデザート専門店
新発売
copyright (c) 2021 by Totally all rights reserved

甜
Totally
copyright (c) 2021 by Totally all rights reserved

デザート会社
Totally 傘下のデザート専門店
クラシック推薦
copyright (c) 2021 by Totally all rights reserved

デザート会社
Totally 傘下のデザート専門店
毎日数量限定で生産する
100個
100%新鮮な果物
季節限定発売
フルーツタルト
copyright (c) 2021 by Totally all rights reserved

Totally

A talented illustrator born in the '90s, she has a distinctive style that seamlessly blends retro and nostalgic elements with themes of teenage girls. With a penchant for creating visually striking pieces reminiscent of a sugar-coated explosion, her work strikes a balance between sweetness, a touch of darkness, and humorous satire. Each creation portrays surreal scenes detached from reality, resembling dreamlike landscapes that convey inner thoughts through the lens of dreams. Through her art, she aims to sculpt powerful and independent images of girls with distinct personalities.

1 Color and Texture in a Retro Style

Totally believes that the primary characteristics of the retro style are the high saturation of colors and the textured graininess of images. Many of her works revolve around retro themes, aiming to convey a warm sense of pleasure to the audience through a high-saturation, high-contrast color scheme combined with creative content. Even if the core of the work is dark, it can still achieve a sense of dark humor, which she finds to be a subtle way to convey the emotional content of her creations.

According to Totally, there is a relationship between visual expression and emotional conveyance, where color mainly influences emotions. Bright red, for instance, can represent heightened passion, anger, or excitement. The direction of emotions depends on the core of the artwork. When creating pieces with dark themes, she believes that creating logical contrasts is crucial. In her work *Girl and the Sea*, which features a shark trapped in a candy machine, an abandoned claw machine, and the ruins of an underwater city, the vibrant colors aim to highlight objects that shouldn't be in the ocean. The surface presents a playful combination, but the underlying message is about ocean conservation. The black humor in the retro style serves as a subtle way to express resistance, hoping to attract resonant audiences through this nuanced approach.

In her creative process, Totally often uses specific color combinations, such as deep red and pink, red and blue, pink and sky blue, and red and white. She also has a habit of adding a hazy texture to some of her works, which helps her quickly achieve a retro aesthetic. These fixed color combinations and texture treatments are crucial to her visual expression. Totally's prominent use of high-saturation color schemes and grainy textures is evident in works like *Girl and the Sea* and *Sweet Company*, creating a blurred and dreamy atmosphere for viewers. This deliberate pursuit of a retro texture did present initial challenges. Excessively vibrant colors sometimes lacked a soft texture when combined, and using grainy pixel textures risked appearing dirty if not mastered. Over time, she became adept at adjusting elements like the degree of grain and its usage, resulting in clearer and more refined compositions.

2 Nostalgia and the Future of 1980s Aesthetics

Totally's work is deeply influenced by the vibrant visual culture of the 1980s, drawing inspiration from popular shōjo manga, anime, and vintage toys of that era. Rather than specific works or characters, it is the overall visual atmosphere of the 80s that profoundly shapes her creations. She is captivated by the bright and simple colors used in toys, manga, and daily items of that time, which often avoided excessive blending. The direct expression in visuals—bold displays of personality, a carefree atmosphere, and a tangible warmth—are elements that Totally finds incredibly appealing. For instance, she admires how 80s magazines used large blocks of pure colors, placing the main subject directly in the visual center, enlarged, and full of vitality.

The piece, *Retro Girl Magazine*, is a testament to her nostalgia for the freedom and creativity of 80s culture and fashion. Inspired by vintage-themed girl fashion magazines from the 80s and 90s, this work aims to convey a sense of nostalgia for past times, invoking a resonance with childhood memories. The retro elements in her creations serve as both memories and contemporary aesthetics. She believes that each era has its own unique aesthetics, but the enduring and attractive aesthetics of the 1980s, full of vitality and allure, remain captivating even as time progresses and trends shift.

In Totally's view, the 80s visual culture offers valuable inspiration for contemporary design and art. Amidst the trend of global modernization, contemporary design often lacks the distinctiveness that characterized the 1980s. The ongoing popularity of the retro trend is attributed to its vivid individuality, which has maintained high recognition in the current era. In today's increasingly stressful social environment, the 80s color palettes visually provide audiences with a delightful sense of fun, influencing people's perception and appreciation of beauty.

THE DESSERT COMPANY SERIES

These illustrations draw inspiration from dessert shops in Japan's Shōwa era, primarily using red and white colors to accentuate the era's feel of dessert shops. The series aims to evoke sweet retro nostalgia.

Totally
Candy House
Totally Rainbow
Totally Candy House
Totally copyright (c) 2021 by Totally all rights reserved

Totally copyright (c) 2021 by Totally all rights reserved
CAUTION WET FLOOR
小心地滑

港

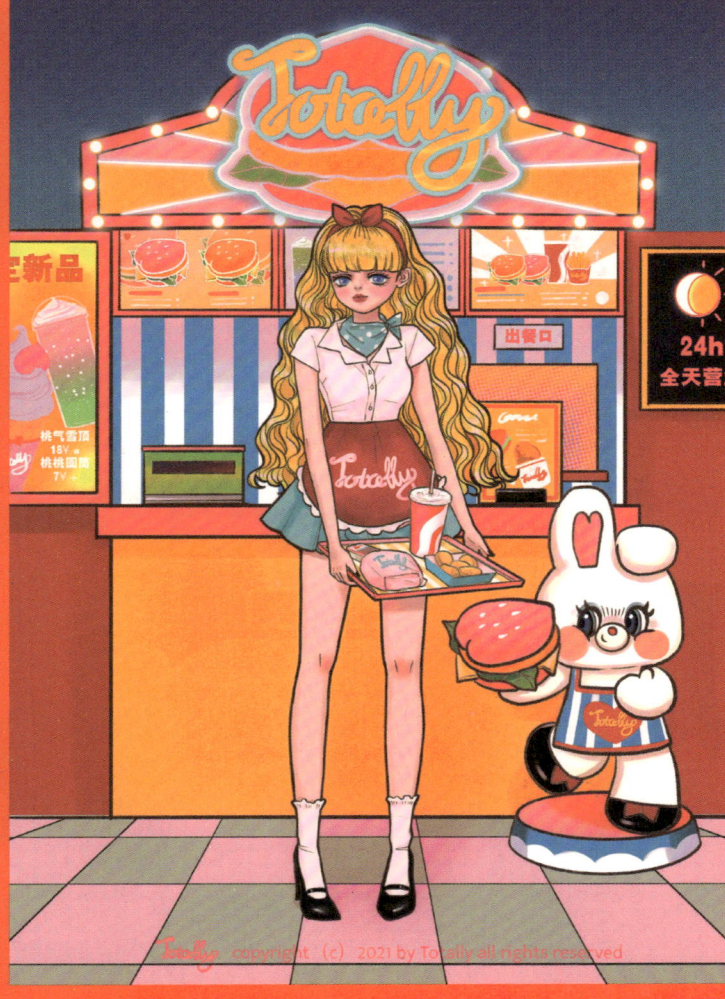

PART-TIME DIARY

Set in a retro style, the scenes depict various emotions of girls in different work environments or tasks. Mundane and tedious tasks can cause frustration, while enjoyable work brings relaxation and joy. The series uses retro aesthetics to provide a humorous escape from the exhaustion of modern life, aiming to resonate with part-time workers in a lighthearted manner.

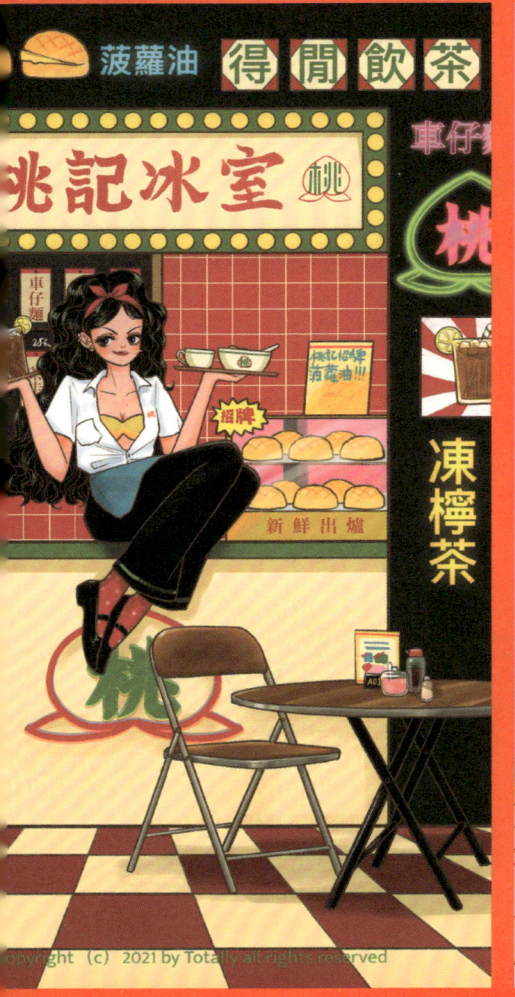

▼ **Inspiration:**
This series is inspired by the emotions the designer experienced while working.

▼ **Color Scheme:**

■ R077 G182 B113
C067 M000 Y069 K000

■ R244 G183 B210
C000 M038 Y000 K000

■ R216 G029 B056
C010 M097 Y073 K000

■ R250 G209 B080
C002 M020 Y075 K000

■ R000 G171 B213
C078 M005 Y013 K000

THE VINTAGE FANTASIES

Combining fantasy themes with a departure from reality, the series features illustrations alongside animated shorts. The animations depict music from vinyl records visualized on discs, the transformation of the ugly duckling into a ballet girl in a music box, doll snow cone machines producing doll-shaped snow cones, mischievous children turning into teddy bear toys, and innocent little girls immersed in fantasies of riding pink rabbits while on rocking horses. The aim is to create a sense of detachment from reality through vintage style, adding a touch of mystery and using whimsical methods to convey pure thoughts, hoping to encourage everyone to maintain their imagination and childish innocence.

▼ **Inspiration:**
This series draws inspiration from old-time items such as vinyl records, ballet girl music boxes, and snow cone machines.

▼ **Color Scheme:**

R163 G106 B123	R141 G192 B211	R233 G089 B122
C042 M001 Y063 K000	C048 M012 Y014 K000	C000 M078 Y029 K000
R254 G220 B109	R241 G159 B195	R230 G040 B073
C000 M016 Y064 K000	C000 M049 Y000 K000	C000 M094 Y059 K000

KEEP SWEET

The illustration series *Keep Sweet* draws inspiration from vibrant dessert candies, a central theme in the series. Utilizing a bright, highly saturated color scheme, the series features vivid color blocks to create its visuals. Transforming desserts and candies into whimsical fantasies, the illustrations reimagine cakes as soothing beds or charming stages and depict candies as whimsical characters, crafting delightful and absurd dreams. The designer aimed to invite viewers to let their imaginations roam freely through the enchanting world of this series.

▼ **Inspiration:**
The retro elements in the work are primarily inspired by popular shōjo manga (girls' comics), cartoons, and old toys from the 80s. The use of highly saturated color combinations creates a visually striking and nostalgic effect. Additionally, the grainy, hazy, and pixelated appearance, reminiscent of the limited technology of that era, plays a crucial role in achieving the retro aesthetics in the designer's creations.

▼ **Elements:**
The artwork anthropomorphizes gummy bears, jellies, and fruits to bring the desserts to life. For example, a cake box becomes a room with a strawberry girl sleeping on the buttercream, and a birthday cake celebrates her with a candle in hand. An afternoon tea jelly transforms into a noblewoman enjoying a delightful afternoon. Meanwhile, a dessert pudding evolves into a slide, with the cherries on top turning into children playing on it.

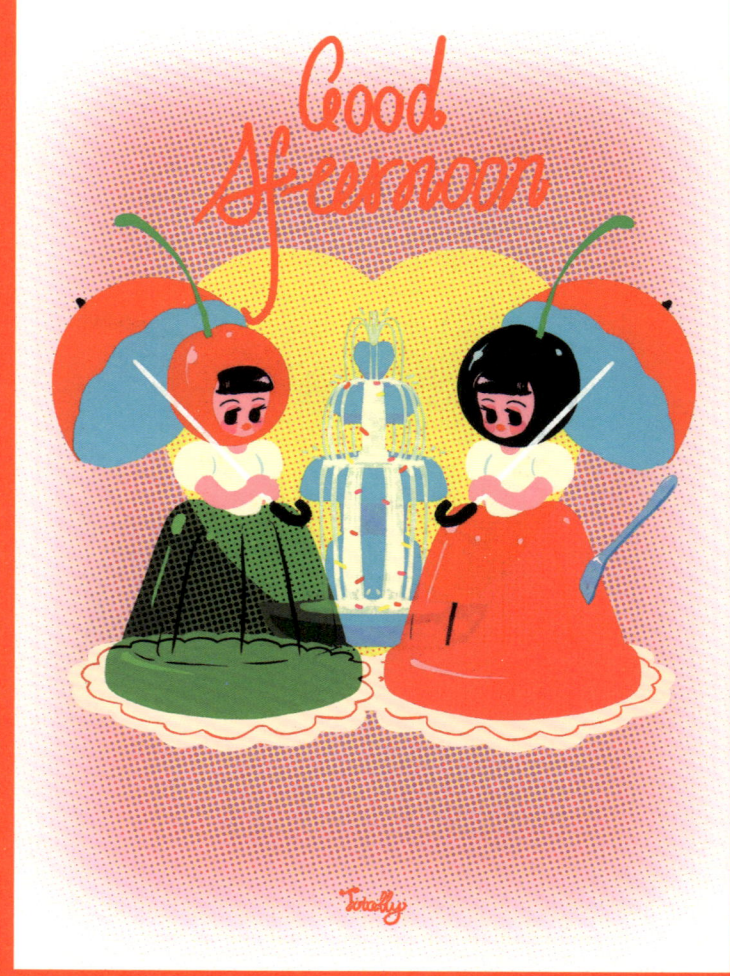

RECORD SERIES

This series is inspired by Shōwa-era City Pop music, with each artwork resembling an album cover. They convey diverse themes, mirroring the varied emotions found in music, from melancholy to light-heartedness. The illustrations are designed with grid textures, creating a swinging effect when combined with music. The packaging mimics vinyl records and CD cases, evoking a sense of nostalgia while materializing the artwork.

Totally   Shōwa   314

THE RETRO GIRL MAGAZINE

This series is inspired by vintage-themed fashion magazines for girls, blending elements from popular toys of the late 80s and early 90s (such as dress-up dolls, coloring books, and sticker photos). The goal was to evoke nostalgia for old-fashioned items through this magazine.

摩登

美容　美髮

改造前

造型推薦

劇場用の新うさぎちゃん
2021
特集
8月号
増刊
look at here!
注目
速報
紅蘿蔔的最終決定!!
正義の味方！
うさぎ美の行動
スーパーマンの誕生
原作/一億拉絲
3
Y-S
YziaSchool
東兔

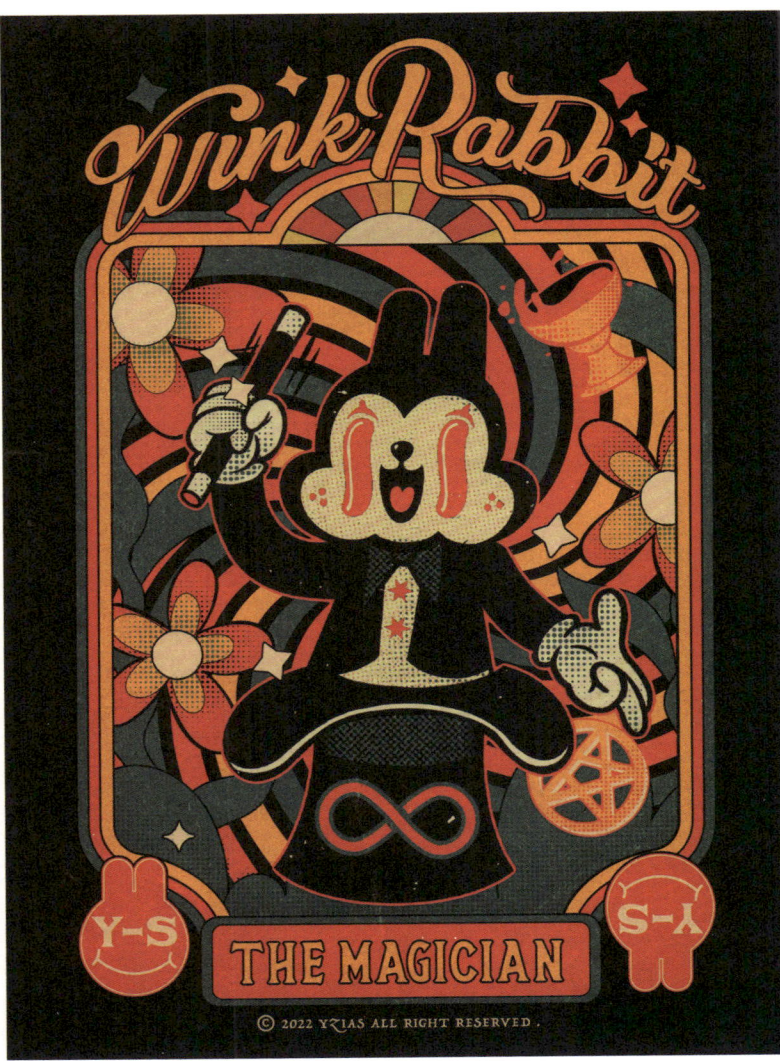

THE SERIES OF WINK RABBIT

The visual design of the illustration series *Wink Rabbit* originates from 2019, featuring an American retro style that shapes and expresses its whimsical and humorous stories and content. *Wink Rabbit* serves as a symbol of justice, embodying a young individual with courage and righteousness who is, in reality, the heir of the spirit of light, safeguarding every carrot on Earth. Whenever the skies turn gray, Wink Rabbit arrives with the gift of sunshine and joy. He is not only a talented magician but also the creator of his own magic. The style predominantly reflects a whimsical American retro vibe, often associated with an "old-school" aesthetics. While "Old School" is commonly associated with specific art forms like hip hop music and street dance, here it refers to a broader sense of tradition and vintage charm, applicable in various contexts beyond just art.

Illustrator: YZIAS

▼ **Inspiration:**

The designer was inspired by retro illustration styles from the mid-20th century to the late 20th century, particularly the 1940s, 1950s, and 1980s. The characteristics of American retro illustrations include simple yet engaging lines, giving a sense of clarity without losing complexity. Additionally, these illustrations are known for their rich and delicate colors, evoking warmth and vibrancy. Furthermore, the themes in American retro illustrations are often simple yet amusing, portraying straightforward and enjoyable subjects rather than intricate ones. This style is beloved by many for its ability to convey a rustic yet delightful feeling, offering a sense of warmth reminiscent of bygone eras.

▼ **Color Scheme:**

■ R000 G000 B000	■ R241 G214 B185	■ R231 G060 B050
C000 M000 Y000 K100	C005 M020 Y028 K000	C001 M089 Y078 K000
■ R000 G150 B182	■ R231 G091 B156	■ R055 G148 B061
C078 M024 Y022 K000	C002 M077 Y000 K000	C076 M022 Y097 K000
■ R237 G223 B075	■ R066 G058 B136	
C011 M008 Y078 K000	C085 M086 Y013 K000	

1980
XILU PARTY
2023

©CANNED
©CANNED

麻辣猪耳

DUCK'S WEB
DUCK NECK
RABBIT LEG
CHICKEN FEET

SNACKS
SNACKS
SNACKS

福兔迎春
休闲时刻，快乐食光
LEISURE TIME HAPPY FOOD
(礼盒)
2023 兔
MADE IN CHINA

XILU PARTY BRAND DESIGN

Xilu Party is a food brand specializing in marinated snacks, with its main products being marinated duck, chicken, and other ready-to-eat marinated meat products. Marinated flavors, as a traditional Chinese delicacy, boast a rich history and diverse variety, enjoying enduring popularity in the food industry. The brand's founder aims to create a delicious and enjoyable marinated snack brand, primarily targeting young consumers. Upholding a commitment to prioritizing the user experience, they strive to elevate industry standards and deliver the most delicious and entertaining marinated snacks. In terms of design, emphasis will be placed on visual appeal and brand recognition. Through unique packaging design, vibrant colors, and creative graphic elements, this brand aims to highlight its distinctive characteristics, allowing consumers to enjoy tasty snacks while experiencing the brand's fun and delight.

Design Studio: Hellocean
Client: Xilu Party

▼ Color Scheme:

■ R211 G076 B050
C015 M083 Y082 K000

■ R225 G163 B077
C012 M042 Y074 K000

■ R140 G087 B068
C052 M073 Y077 K004

■ R122 G165 B110
C058 M021 Y066 K000

■ R149 G192 B183
C046 M012 Y030 K000

■ R087 G177 B187
C064 M011 Y027 K000

IDEAFINE Shōwa

NANNIWAN APPLE PACKAGING

The spirit of Nanniwan is an important part of the Yan'an Spirit, with its core values of self-reliance and striving for self-improvement inspiring generations of Chinese people to overcome difficulties and achieve victory. The selling points of Luochuan apples, such as "sweet and delicious" and "crisp and juicy," are creatively incorporated into a vintage certificate, creating an original "New Apple Certificate."

Design Studio: IDEAFINE
Client: Nanniwan

▼ **Inspiration:**
These certificates are mainly influenced by vintage certificates from the 1930s and 1940s, reflecting the illustration and typography styles of that era.

▼ **Elements:**
The designer recreated and further developed the graphic elements from vintage certificates. The main goal was to align with the brand's characteristics and fully express its creative essence.

▼ **Layout:**
A large character "奖" (award) word is centered, while other elements and text are designed according to the layout of the certificate.

ALL WISHES WILL COME TRUE

This work was exhibited at the Anaya Poster Festival. Any wish made within 30 seconds of viewing the poster will come true.

Design Studio: 3% Design Studio
Designer: Deng Xiongjun, Xiao Lv
Client: Aranya Poster Festival

▼ **Inspiration:**

Influenced by the Maneki-neko from the Shōwa era, the design reflects the distinctive characteristics of that period's craftsmanship. Unlike modern reproductions, which often lack the handcrafted charm, these cats bear a relaxed feel with more manual involvement. The aging process has tinted them with a perpetual warmth, creating a nostalgic ambiance. Passed through various hands, they're often found among a jumble of weathered items in antique shops or markets. These Maneki-neko likely had multiple owners, their fragility tempered by careful handling over time. This human touch is subtly reflected in the font strokes and layout design, evoking a sense of cherished imperfection amidst a lively retro atmosphere.

▼ **Elements:**

There are numerous auspicious phrases in this project, such as "Good Day," "Good Luck," and "Good Health." The prefix "Good" is formed by letters arranged in a slightly arched shape, resembling the typical posture of a Maneki-neko with its raised paw. Therefore, while ensuring readability, the designers incorporated a pattern-like resemblance into the letterforms.

▼ **Font:**

Qualey Free

▼ **Layout:**

The most likely place to encounter Shōwa-era Maneki-neko is in second-hand Japanese goods stores. In the layout design, a plethora of details appears in a small, high-density format, mimicking the stacked feeling of old stores and the state of people rummaging through them.

HAPPY NEW JOBS (2023/2024)

The small cup for adding water to an ink stone, an ancient stationery tool used to adjust the intensity of ink, serves as the starting point for creating beautiful calligraphy and paintings. Since 2023, on the first working day of each year, the studio has used a "Maneki-neko" designed in the shape of this small cup as a prototype to craft a kick-off poster through various design approaches. This tradition is intended to bring good luck and a smooth creative process to the studio's endeavors for the new year.

Design Studio: 3% Design Studio
Designer: Deng Xiongjun, Xiao Lv

▼ **Inspiration:**
During the Shōwa period, poster designs often ceded grandiosity to font design, emphasizing typography. The design team also sought to explore whether achieving a synthesis was possible when typography reached the same level of complexity as imagery, combining the vitality and handcrafted involvement of the Shōwa era with the stability and vectorization of modern contexts.

▼ **Elements:**
The 2024 kick-off poster takes inspiration from the Lucky Cat font design. In Chinese, the designers relied on the outline of the "Maneki-neko" to reshape the structure of the word "开工" (kick-off), blurring the boundary between text and image. For English, they imagined a Maneki-neko that changes angles to achieve a mimetic association with the 26 letters of the English alphabet.

▼ **Fonts:**
2023: Adobe Song, MOESongUN

▼ **Layout:**
The New Year kick-off poster for 2023 focuses on incorporating a rich and varied mix of points, lines, and shapes to create a sense of spontaneity in the layout. Building upon this foundation, the rearrangement and combination of the segmented "智力开工" (ZLYX kick-off) aim to introduce more layers and randomness to the composition.

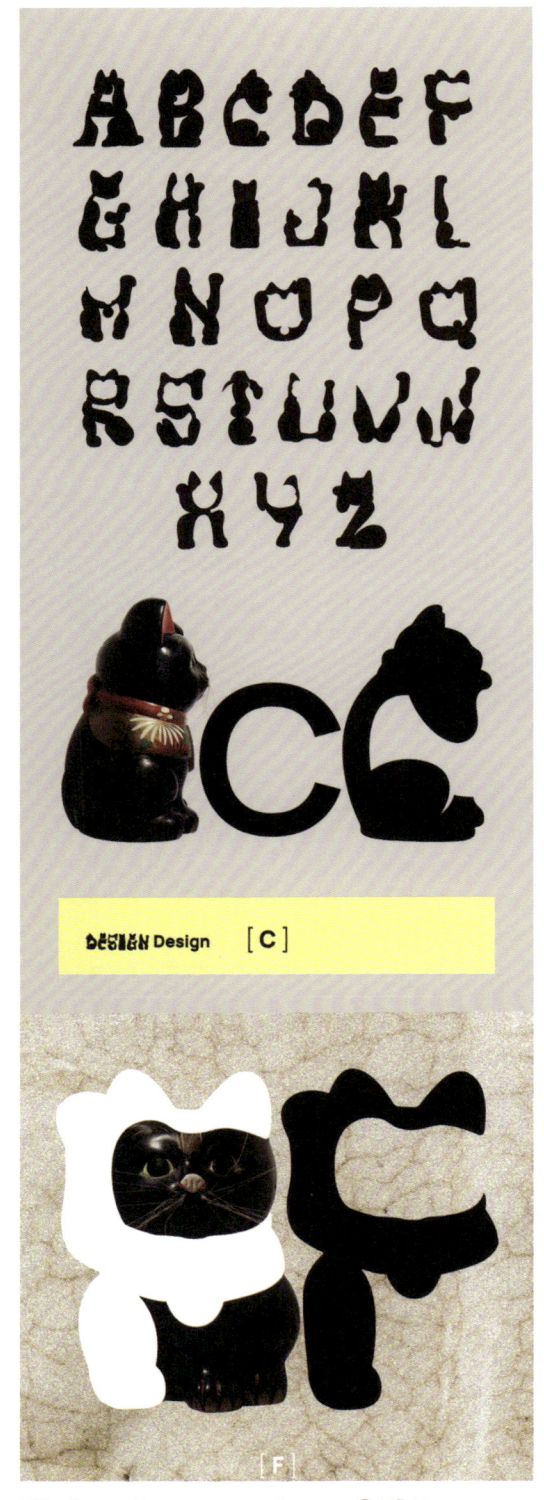

Modern Interpretations of Shōwa-era Maneki-neko

3% Design Studio often draws significant inspiration from the Shōwa-era Maneki-neko, also known as Lucky Cat, incorporating their tangible essence into their work. By collecting these items and immersing themselves in the era they represent, 3% Design Studio overlays modern visual techniques onto these traditional objects. This creates a unique collision of time periods, forming a distinct atmosphere in their designs. This approach reflects their commitment to blending elements from different cultures, enhancing their design process by integrating other cultural influences.

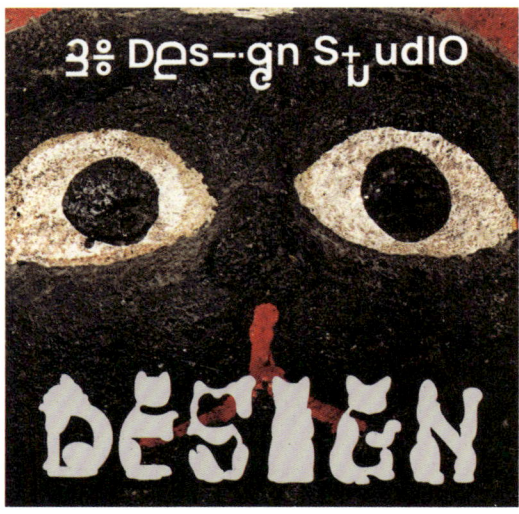

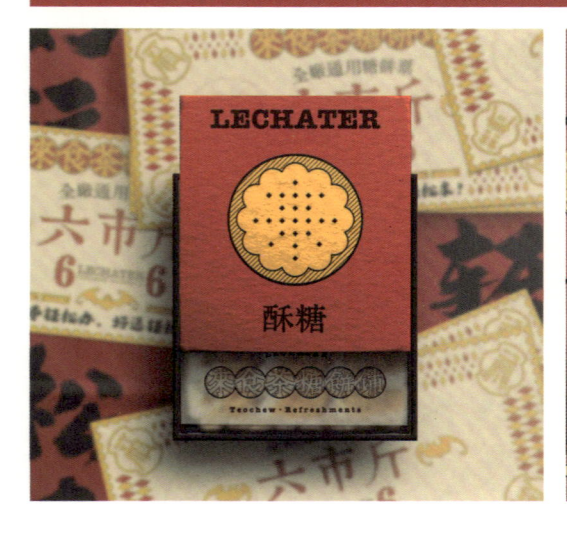

LECHATER TEA CANDY BISCUIT SHOP BRAND DESIGN

LETCHATER, meaning "Let's chatter," is derived from the Chinese Teochew[1] dialect "来食茶" (lai sik cha) which reflects the hospitality of the Teochew people. However, the complexity of Teochew customs has left more and more people feeling weary or even intimidated. "LECHATER Tea Candy Biscuit Shop" explores the branding and packaging of traditional biscuit shops, combining traditional and contemporary aesthetics to deliver "festive blessings" to consumers. It also explores the future direction of traditional biscuit shops. The brand philosophy of "good things made easy, good luck made simple" aims to allow people to enjoy the joy of good occasions more easily without the headache of complicated processes.

Designer: Lo.Dycha
Client: LECHATER

▼ **Inspiration:** The work is inspired by the local folk symbols of Teochew, as well as the signage of local stores in Japan—the packaging of KINCHO insect repellent, similar to the iconic Tiger Balm.

▼ **Elements:** Many of the graphic design prototypes in this project are derived from traditional folk customs in the Teochew region. For example, the logo of the brand is inspired by "纸节"[2] (Zhi Jie). The typography in Zhi Jie is quite unique, with only a few characters available for reference. The designer has spent a long time adjusting the strokes to the desired proportions while also ensuring readability.

▼ **Fonts:** American Typewriter Bold, American Typewriter Semibold, KingHwa OldSong (京华老宋体)

▼ **Layout:** The centered symmetrical layout chosen is a common practice in traditional packaging design, lacking complex visual focal points. Given the project's ample diversity in graphics, it was a strategic decision to adopt this conventional approach, ensuring clarity and avoiding visual clutter. Drawing inspiration from the surround layout often utilized by established brands, further solidifying the design direction.

1. Teochew: A cultural-linguistic region in the east of Guangdong, China.
2. A spirit of paper money used in Teochew.

FAKE JAPANESE VINTAGE AD CHARACTERS!

It's a series of fake vintage Japanese ad characters created just for fun. The designer was considering turning some of them into toys, and invited anyone interested to get in touch.

Illustrator: Juan Molinet

▼ **Color Scheme:**

■ R088 G014 B009 C039 M091 Y086 K062	■ R227 G036 B021 C003 M095 Y098 K000
■ R221 G089 B024 C009 M078 Y096 K001	■ R233 G180 B000 C009 M033 Y098 K000
■ R250 G241 B207 C003 M006 Y024 K000	■ R154 G201 B066 C046 M000 Y087 K000
■ R099 G159 B092 C065 M020 Y076 K003	■ R051 G159 B204 C072 M020 Y011 K000
■ R234 G156 B173 C005 M049 Y016 K000	

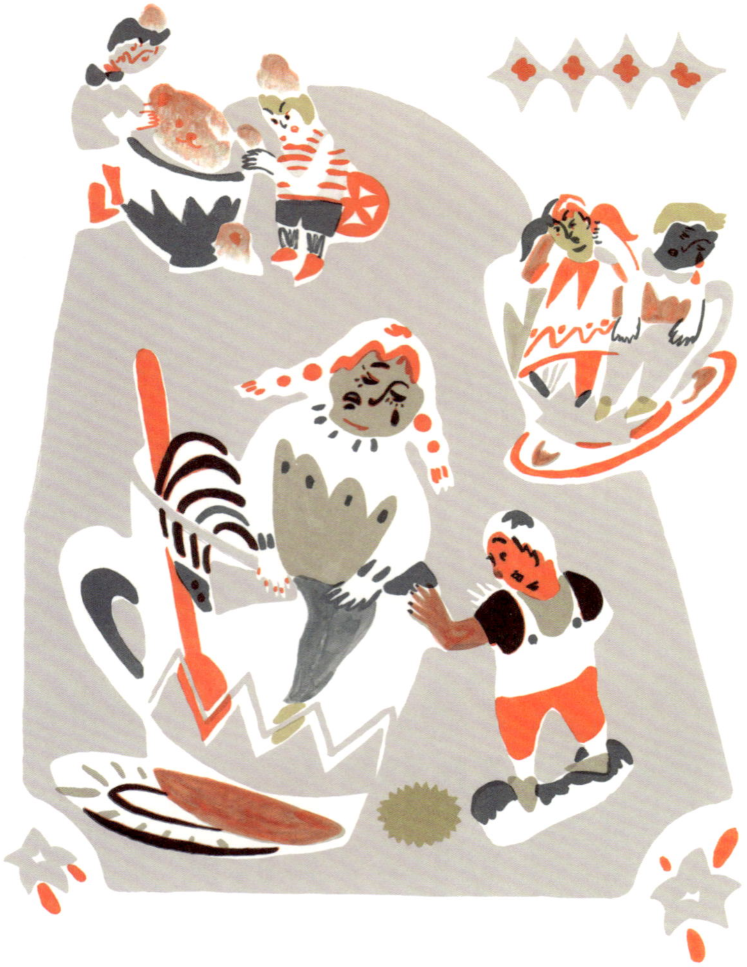

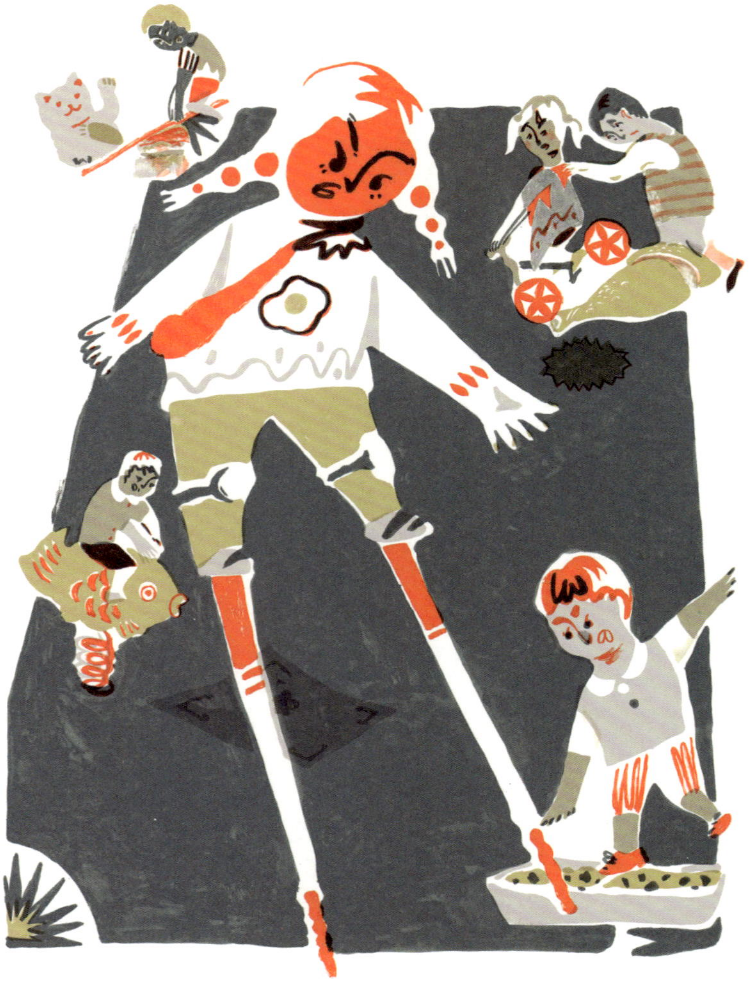

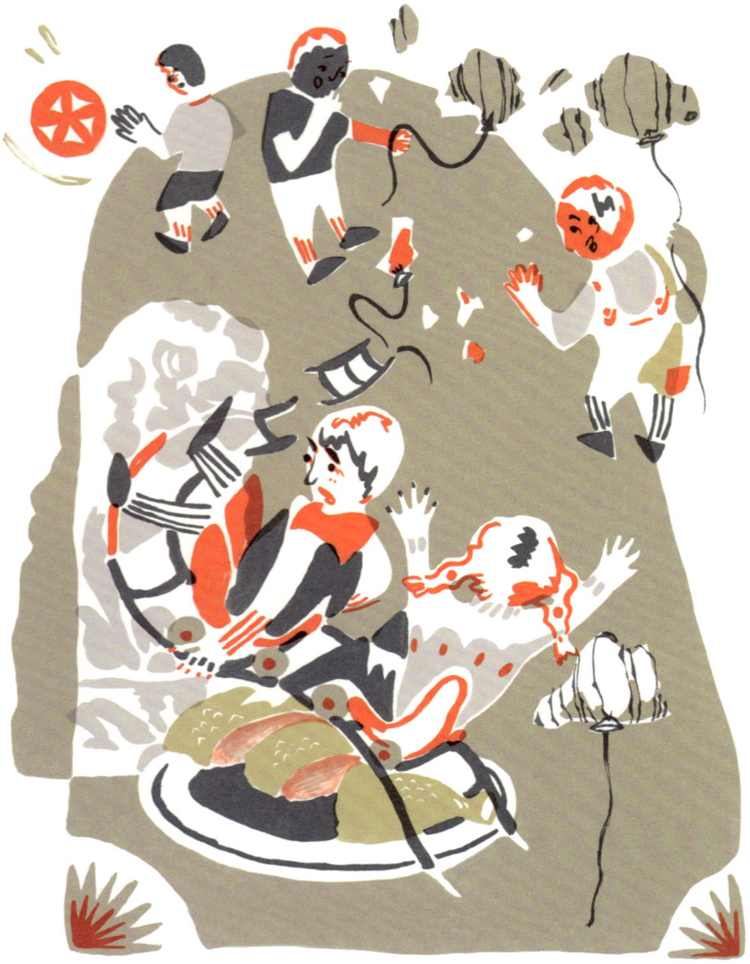

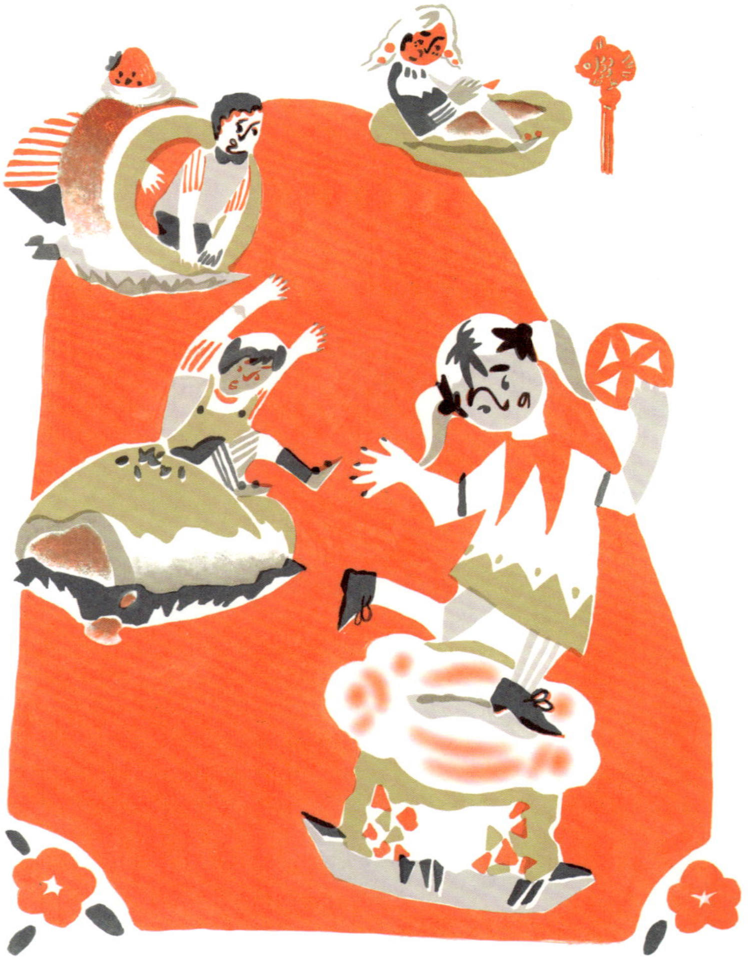

TASTE OF NOSTALGIA

This series by the designer delves into the nostalgia of the Chinese diaspora in Glasgow, UK, for food, evoking childhood memories. Through screen printing, the work aims to convey the deep connection between these memories and the flavors that are fondly remembered. The five primary colors are derived from traditional Chinese painting, linking the origins of Chinese cuisine and utensils with the current state of food among Chinese immigrants in Glasgow. These dishes, popular among the Glasgow diaspora, reveal the culinary traditions of Chinese and Southeast Asian immigrants, reminding the designer of the cherished meals of her childhood in China. The five illustrations, each using one of the five main colors, represent the flavors of salty, sweet, sour, bitter, and spicy, serving as metaphors for different memories.

Illustrator: Erin Chen

▼ Inspiration:

The design is primarily influenced by the culinary culture of overseas Chinese in the Guangdong region during the 1980s and 1990s. The diaspora from Guangdong brought their culinary traditions to the UK during that period, preserving their food culture from that era. What was once trendy cuisine has now become a nostalgic cultural phenomenon. Upon arriving in the UK, the designer encountered these 80s and 90s foods, triggering memories of their own childhood. As a result, the designer created this series to express the feeling of a dialogue across time and space.

▼ Elements:

The character designs are inspired by the characters in Chinese children's books from the 1990s, aiming to evoke nostalgic memories of childhood in China during that decade. By incorporating common Chinese culinary elements found abroad and exaggerating them, the designs serve as a means to communicate with foreign audiences.

▼ Color Scheme:

- R069 G108 B121　C078 M054 Y047 K002
- R212 G202 B142　C021 M018 Y050 K000
- R235 G090 B022　C000 M078 Y094 K000
- R218 G218 B218　C017 M013 Y013 K000
- R058 G087 B068　C080 M058 Y077 K022

RETURN TO THE WILDERNESS

The series *Return to the Wilderness* was created at the onset of the COVID-19 pandemic, aiming to explore the new relationship between urban dwellers and nature post-pandemic. Set against the backdrop of 1920, the artist presented six illustrations depicting the protagonist's journey from longing for freedom outside her confined home to various emotions and stories upon returning to the wilderness. Rather than directly depicting pandemic-related narratives, the series uses a parallel story from a different era to express certain emotions. The project's visual style combines French retro fashion with Eastern classical aesthetics.

Design Studio: Sankaramon
Illustrator: Emen Lo

▼ **Inspiration:**
As the project is set in the 1920s, extensive background research is conducted during the creative process. This includes studying clothing catalogs, fashion brands, and classic styles of the era, as well as reading literary works like *Out of Africa* and *The Three-Cornered World* that describe the cultural and natural landscapes of the 1920s.

▼ **Layout:**
Layout design often draws inspiration from ancient Chinese paintings, where blank-leaving and subtraction embody the essence of Eastern aesthetics.

▼ **Color Scheme:**

■ R014 G069 B151
C095 M077 Y005 K000

■ R172 G191 B190
C037 M018 Y024 K000

■ R233 G212 B087
C012 M015 Y073 K000

■ R221 G090 B094
C009 M077 Y052 K000

■ R217 G149 B110
C015 M049 Y055 K000

■ R089 G109 B101
C072 M053 Y060 K005

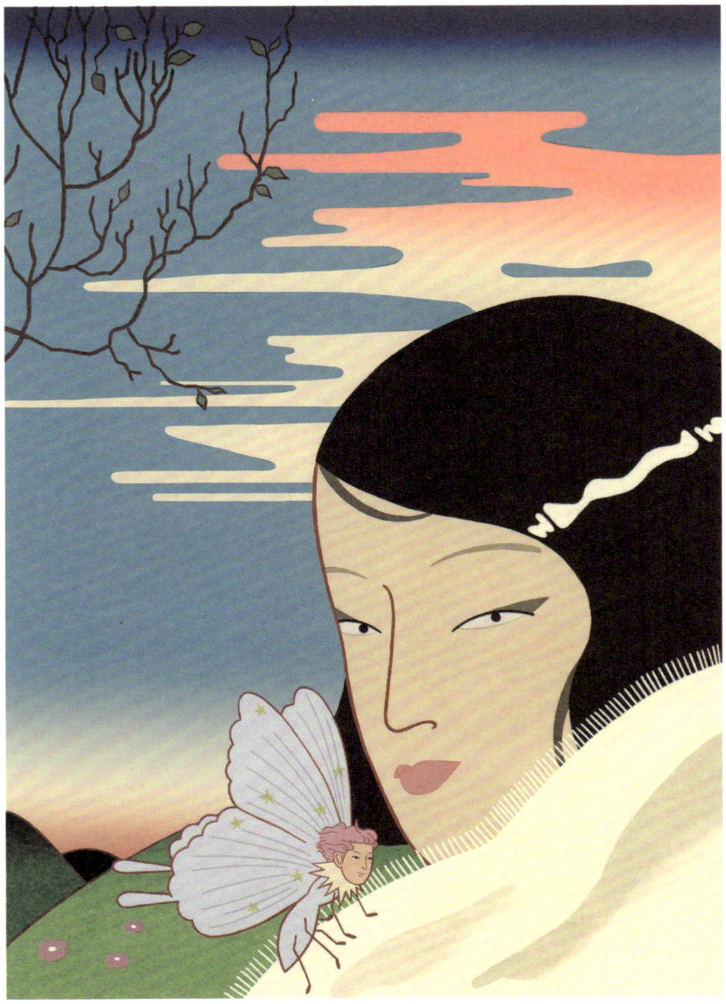

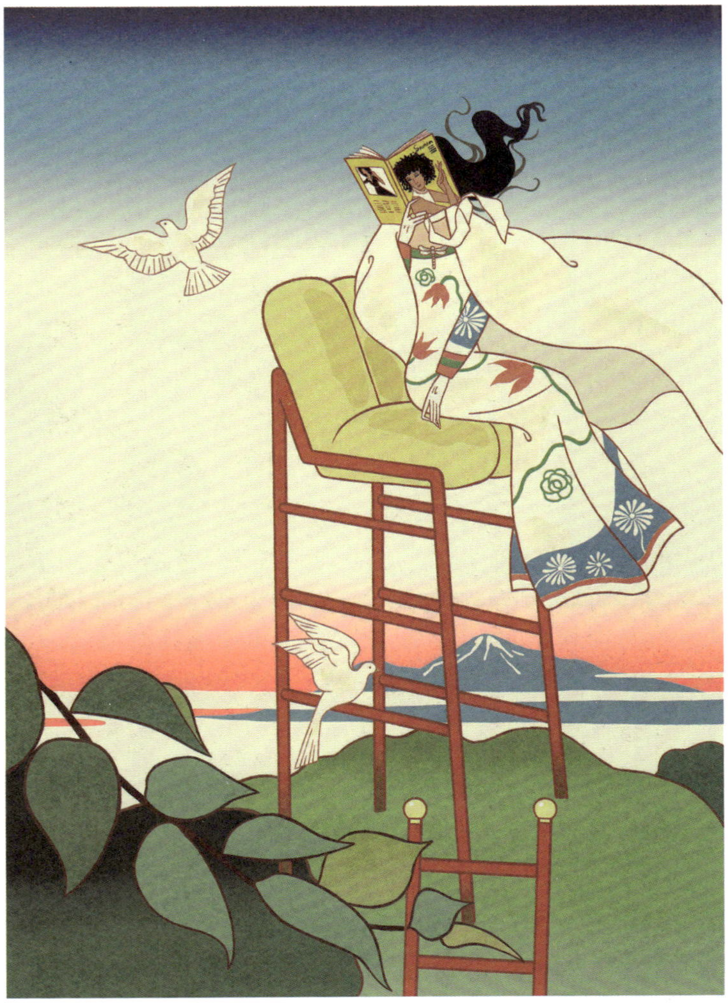

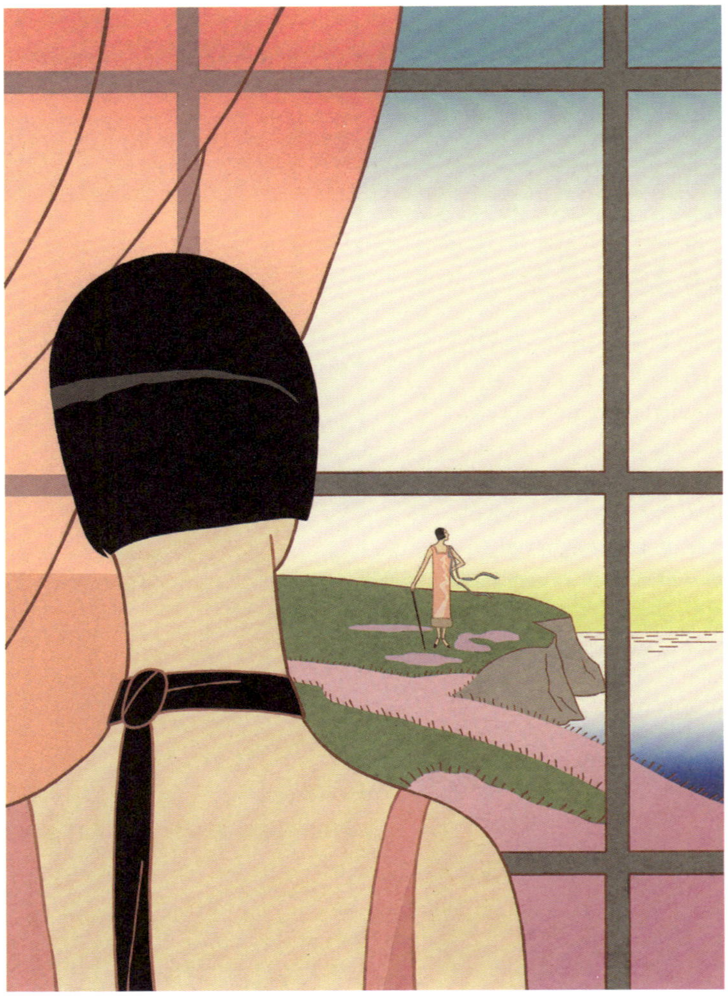

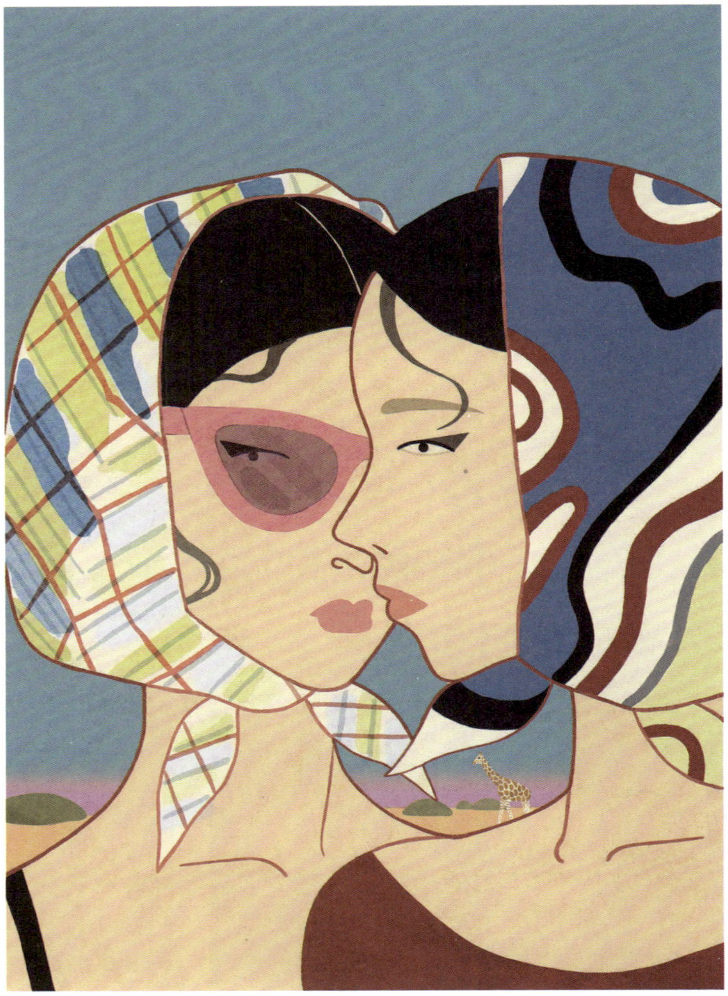

DARUMA

The *Daruma* poster draws inspiration from vintage matchbooks, placing the traditional Japanese doll in the spotlight. Created during Tatsuya Kurihara's time in Chicago, Illinois, while working at Soulsight, a brand agency, the project is designed to introduce Daruma to the people of Chicago and the agency, who might not be familiar with it. The design skillfully integrates elements from both Chicago and Japan, forging a connection between these two distinct cultures.

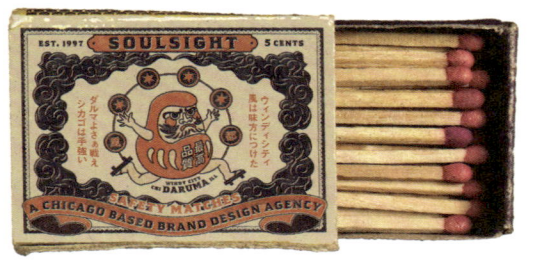

Designer: Tatsuya Kurihara

▼ **Inspiration:**

The designer's inspiration stemmed from the vintage matchbooks of yesteryear, evoking a nostalgic touch. He aimed to connect with Chicagoans by incorporating familiar visuals, like clouds and wind, emblematic of the Windy City. The inclusion of Japanese text symbolizes the merger of two cultures in one poster, reflecting Tatsuya's journey from Japan to spending nearly 8 years in Chicago. Additionally, he drew inspiration from the visual aesthetics and artistry of Fujin the Wind God and Raijin the Thunder God to infuse their essence into the Daruma character.

▼ **Font:**
Hideout Black

▼ **Color Scheme:**

R199 G081 B037
C023 M080 Y093 K000

R200 G191 B167
C026 M023 Y035 K000

R062 G070 B088
C082 M073 Y055 K017

LUCKY CAT

The roots of the Lucky Cat, or Maneki-Neko, trace back to the Gotokuji Temple in Tokyo, Japan. This poster seeks to convey the essence of this unique Japanese folk tradition to a global audience. The inspiration for the poster is drawn from vintage Japanese paper money, a nod to the belief that the Lucky Cat symbolizes prosperity and a flourishing business.

Designer: Tatsuya Kurihara

▼ Inspiration & Elements:

Every intricate graphic embellishment adorning this poster's frame draws inspiration from the architectural nuances found at Gotokuji Temple. The design pays homage to the temple's intricate details, while the messaging delves into the historical significance of both the temple and the Lucky Cat.

To captivate a wider audience and evoke interest in the Lucky Cat, the feline's visage has been artfully painted to resemble that of a kabuki actor, a nod to the traditional Japanese dramatic art form. Thoughtfully crafted messages in both English and Japanese enrich the narrative, providing a deeper understanding of the cultural and historical context surrounding the temple and its iconic Lucky Cat.

▼ Fonts:

English: Engravers MT Bold

Japanese: DNP ShueiShogoMinStd Hv

▼ Layout:

The overall layout is inspired by vintage Japanese paper money.

CHILDHOOD CONVENIENCE STORE

This is an attempt by the re-engraved series to venture into the realm of packaging. Randomly selecting products from familiar childhood favorites, and in the breakthrough spirit of the re-engraved series, the designer has invited us to embark on this new exploration.

Design Studio: pigeonstudio
Designer: GEZI

BUBBLE TAPE
Soft Bubble Gum
NEW TAB
大大卷
LONG LASTING FLAVOR
Soft Bubble Gum

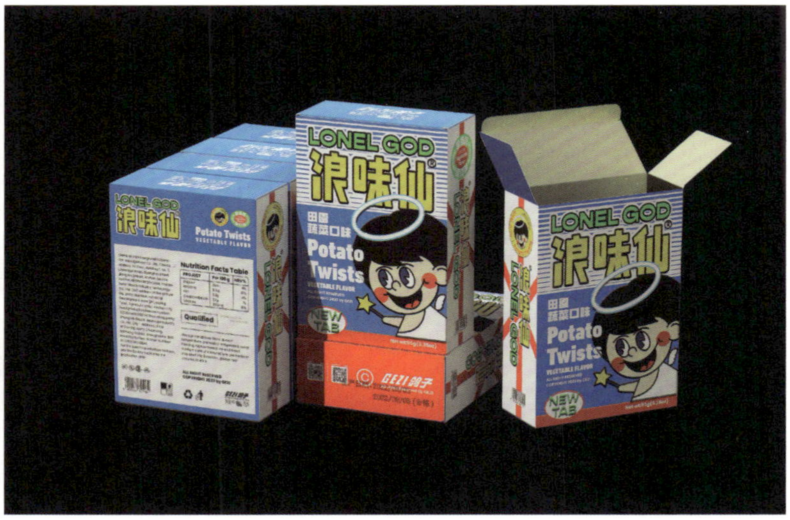
LONEL GOD
浪味仙
Potato Twists
NEW TAB

大白兔
MILK
Toffee Flavor
WHITE RABBIT
NEW TAB

儿时便利店
CHILDHOOD GROCERY STORE
欢迎光临
welcome
©2022
#
Packed—›
Coca Cola
Pepsi
White cat detergent
White Rabbit Toffee
Langweixian
big roll
202208
$2022
ALL RIGHT RESERVED
COPYRIGHT 2022 by GEZI
GEZI 鸽子

Toffee Flavor
MILK 大白兔
WHITE CAT
白猫
大白兔
MILK
WHITE RABBIT
Toffee Flavor
BUBBLE TAPE
大大卷
LONEL GOD
浪味仙
Potato Twists

BRAND REPLICA

In the brand replica in the re-engraved series, the designer selected well-known brands and redesigned them in a reproduced manner.

Design Studio: pigeonstudio
Designer: GEZI

▼ **Inspiration:**
The original intention of the re-engraved series was to explore the contrasting fun of the same brand across different eras from various perspectives, breaking some inherent frameworks and creating more unknowns and possibilities. This visual series was born out of this idea.

六神
花露水
SixGod

2022
5/18
COPYRIGHT BY GEZI © ALL RIGHTS RESERVED
徕卡
© ALL RIGHTS RESERVED
COPYRIGHT BY GEZI
LEICA
纂刻
Leica

2022/5/19
CHANEL
Copyright By GEZI All rights reserved

Copyright By GEZI © All rights reserved.
KAPPA

ChristianDior
迪奥
Copyright By GEZI
© All rights reserved
纂刻
Dior

苹果
Apple
APPLE COMPUTER, INC.
COPYRIGHT BY GEZI © ALL RIGHTS RESERVEDV

Copyright By GEZI
All rights reserved
5/16
2022

COPYRIGHT BY GEZI
© ALL RIGHTS RESERVED
mcdonald's
纂刻
麥當勞

徕卡
© ALL RIGHTS RESERVED
COPYRIGHT BY GEZI
LEICA
纂刻
LEICA

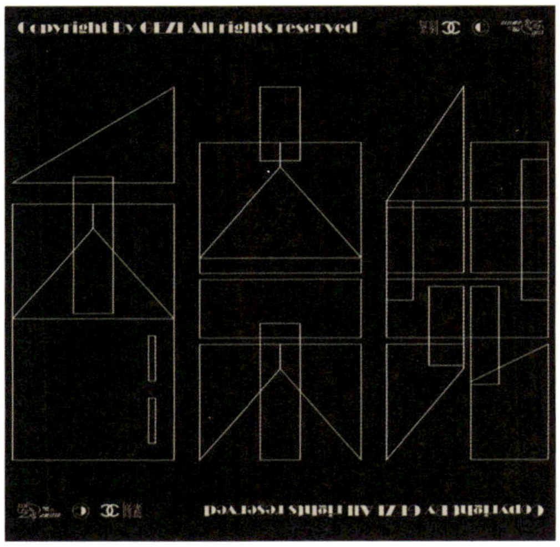
Copyright By GEZI All rights reserved

Marlboro
Classics
萬寶路
2022/5/14 © All Rights Reserved
Copyright By GEZI 纂刻 Marlboro

Copyright By GEZI
© All rights reserved
纂刻
Dior

旧物的温度
03 25 2022
zhi
纸
yuan
鸢
The Warmth of the Old
Paper Kite
重温中国旧时那些可爱的小玩意儿

旧物的温度
03 25 2022
liu
留
sheng
声
ji
机
The Warmth of the Old
Phonograph
重温中国旧时那些可爱的小玩意儿

旧物的温度
03 25 2022
bu
布
lao
老
hu
虎
The Warmth of the Old
Cloth Tiger
重温中国旧时那些可爱的小玩意儿

旧物的温度
03 25 2022
tu
兔
ye
爷
The Warmth of the Old
Lord Rabbit
重温中国旧时那些可爱的小玩意儿

旧物的温度
03 25 2022
yuan
鸳
yang
鸯
jing
镜
The Warmth of the Old
Mandarin Duck Mirror
重温中国旧时那些可爱的小玩意儿

旧物的温度
03 25 2022
zhi
纸
yuan
鸢
The Warmth of the Old
Paper Kite
重温中国旧时那些可爱的小玩意儿

The Warmth of the Old

THE WARMTH OF THE OLD

This project reflects the designer's preference for retro designs, particularly from the Republic of China era and the 1980s to 1990s. Font design, in particular, embodies the reorganization of graphics, capturing the playful essence of Chinese characters while magnifying their aesthetic appeal. Classic folk toys, such as the tangram puzzle and paper kites, blend wisdom from the past, serving as the designer's favorite "environmentally friendly and non-powered toys." Drawing inspiration from the tangram puzzle's structure, the designer geometricized and abstracted both text and graphics, using vibrant colors to recreate the beauty of retro Chinese style and evoke nostalgic memories.

Designer: PEI WEN

▼ **Inspiration:**
The work draws inspiration from the artistic calligraphy of the Republican era and the creations of Chinese cartoon master Zhang Guangyu, renowned for designing the character models in the animated film *Havoc in Heaven*. His avant-garde layout designs, illustrations, and comic style are distinctly Chinese, deeply influenced by Peking Opera. Zhang's aesthetics embodies cultural heritage, a legacy he hopes the current generation will continue to carry forward.

▼ **Elements:**
Font: Inspired by the childhood toy tangram puzzle, the theme font features shapes reminiscent of its geometric forms, such as circles and diamonds, adding playfulness with rounded corners and fluid lines.

Graphics: Retro toys and objects from the 80s, 90s, and even the Republic of China period are the basis for the graphics, simplified into a flat geometric style for a visually creative blend of retro and modern elements. And emotionally, such a design is warm, childlike, and not dull.

▼ **Fonts:**
FangZhengFangJianTi, Source Han Sans, Roboto, Adobe Song, Arial Narrow

▼ **Layout:**
The key visual layout, inspired by tangram puzzles, is arranged in a scattered yet orderly manner, integrating graphics, fonts, and vibrant color blocks effectively while retaining aesthetic appeal. Merch design elements are influenced by 1980s movie tickets and collector's cards, featuring predominantly single-color blocks with singular graphics and fonts. The poster design combines the style of old-era popular posters with a modern grid layout, blending retro and contemporary vibes.

▼ **Color Scheme:**

■ R000 G125 B079	■ R228 G115 B166	■ R053 G086 B165	■ R236 G100 B036	■ R246 G172 B001
C089 M035 Y085 K002	C005 M067 Y003 K000	C084 M067 Y000 K000	C000 M074 Y088 K000	C000 M040 Y093 K000

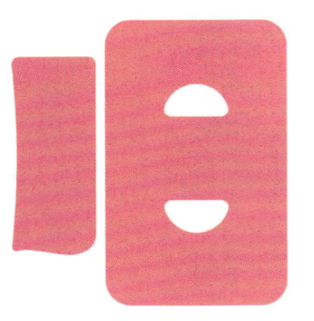

FIRECRACKERS D2020 TYPE

The "Firecrackers D2020" New Year's gift box is ready to use, with an ideal atmosphere and volume. This piece simulates the appearance and visual characteristics of real fireworks for its design, but the actual product inside is not fireworks; it's chopsticks. Due to its lifelike appearance, during the initial shipments, delivery personnel even refused to accept it, citing it as hazardous material unfit for delivery.

Design Studio: ReflexDesign
Creative Director: Cai Yi
Art Director: KaKa
Designer: Da Ming, bibi
Motion Designer: A Dai

▼ **Inspiration:**
The design language of this project mainly draws inspiration from traditional firework packaging design, as well as some retro-style cartoon comic drawing characteristics.

HOLILAND MARKET

Holiland Market is a themed bakery dessert store concept based on the flea market idea. Under the concept of a "market," different baking product lines are disguised as various second-hand shops in the flea market. Birthday cakes transform into clockwork toy forms, pastries are sold in the guise of jewelry, freshly baked bread becomes mini sofas, pre-made soft products masquerade as household robots, and so on. We have created product catalogs, market procurement guides, and a series of market-related overall visuals for these products. We even produced a promotional animation for the market, allowing customers to immerse themselves in the theme of the market.

Design Studio: ReflexDesign

▼ **Inspiration:**

This project encompasses multiple creative concepts, each adopting a different design language. A space-style English font is used in the logo design. As for the creative graphics, low-fidelity 3D models with a plastic-like feel are employed. Overall, the design team aimed to present sufficient diversity and richness to express the flea market's characteristic of offering an array of unique items.

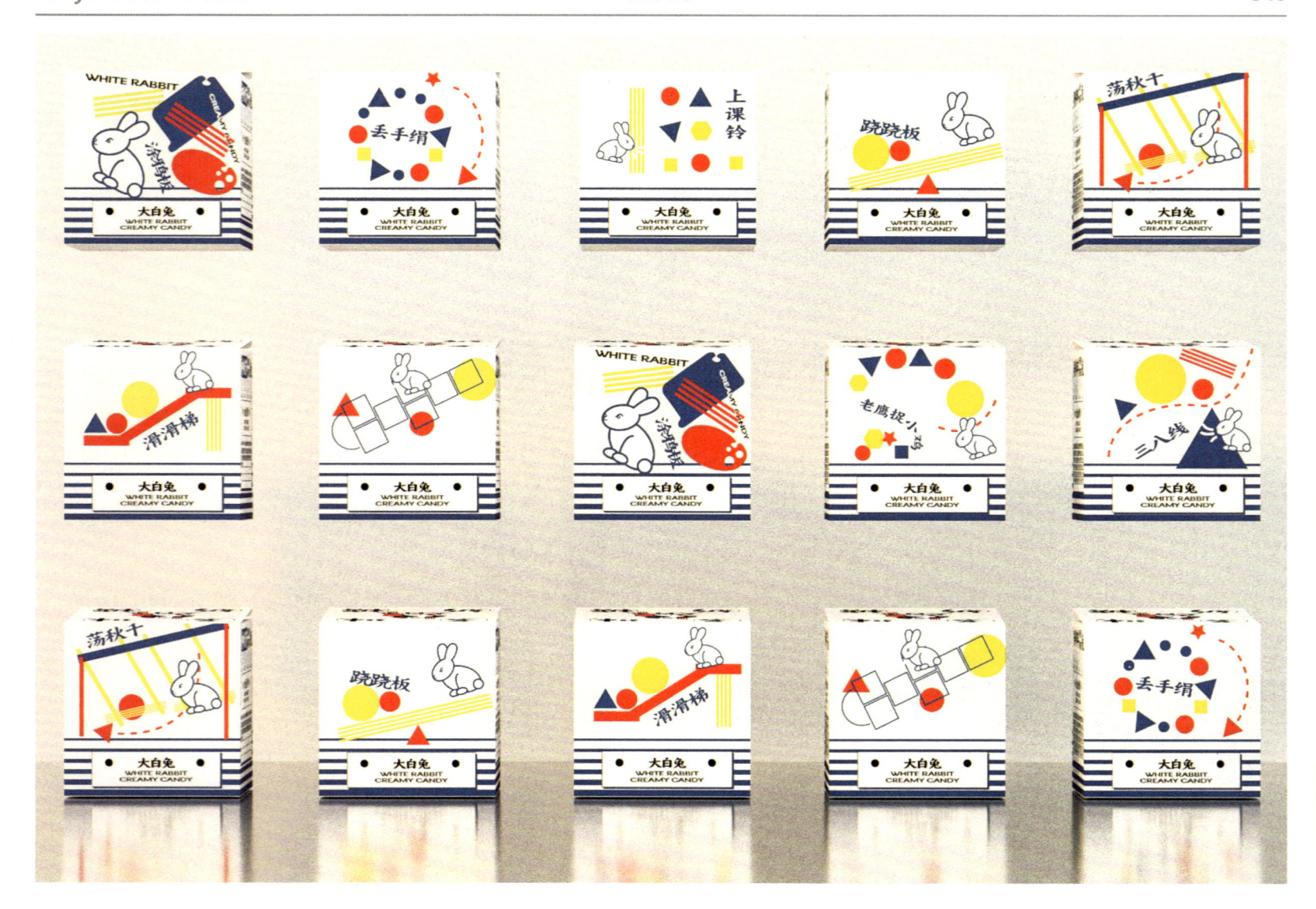

WHITE RABBIT MID-AUTUMN FESTIVAL GIFT BOX PACKAGING DESIGN

The product is the Mid-Autumn Festival gift box packaging design for the White Rabbit. White Rabbit is a classic snack product familiar to Chinese people since the 1990s, serving as the most intimate "childhood partner" for contemporary young Chinese. With the rapid development and changes in the Chinese economy, the White Rabbit still retains the "taste" of the past era in its packaging design, which may even seem outdated. As the Year of the Rabbit in 2023, it marks a milestone for the packaging upgrade of the White Rabbit. In this design, how the White Rabbit balances childhood memories and the festive atmosphere of the Mid-Autumn Festival as selling points is also a sentiment and an opportunity for designers. In terms of design expression, traditional calligraphy fonts are used for the text, and the White Rabbit graphics are simplified, expressing childhood narrative background as graphic symbols. Therefore, this project utilizes emotional and flat design to attract young people, create contemporary hot spots, and promote the brand, allowing the time-honored brand to return to the mainstream commercial market.

Design Studio: Sanyo United Studio
Designer: Liu Lei, Fu Xin

▼ **Inspiration:**
The design project primarily draws inspiration from the nostalgic experiences of childhood, where one encounters various objects that serve as unique imprints of the Chinese contemporary era's culture and characteristics. These include elements such as thatched cottages, the ringing bell signaling class time, and childhood games like hopscotch and handkerchief throwing after class. For individuals, the carefree spirit of childhood embodies the essence of "retro."

▼ **Elements:**
The packaging features a graffiti board, handkerchief throwing, class bell, seesaw, swing, slide, eagle catching chicks, desk partition, and hopscotch. These scenes are both familiar and nostalgic, evoking a sense of beauty and warmth.

▼ **Font:**
Alimama DongFangDaKai

▼ **Layout:**
The layout was arranged according to a grid system and is neat and tidy.

▼ **Color Scheme:**

R000 G101 B166
C091 M056 Y011 K000

R230 G006 B029
C000 M099 Y092 K000

R251 G238 B048
C004 M001 Y084 K000

老鹰捉小鸡

滑滑梯

荡秋千

大白兔BIG WHITE RABBIT奶糖TOFFEE 童年时光机CHILDHOOD TIME MACHINE 手册MANUAL
abcdefg
大白兔
WHITE RABBIT CREAMY CANDY
滑滑梯

大白兔BIG WHITE RABBIT 奶糖TOFFEE 中秋定制 MID-AUTUMN CUSTOM 打包袋 PACKING BAG
大白兔
WHITE RABBIT CREAMY CANDY
大白兔BIG WHITE RABBIT 奶糖TOFFEE 中秋定制 MID-AUTUMN CUSTOM 打包袋 PACKING BAG

荡秋千
WHITE RABBIT
CREAMY CANDY
老鹰捉小鸡
中秋节
辛酉月
庚寅日
八月十五
大白兔月饼
WHITE RABBIT CREAMY CANDY
大白兔
WHITE RABBIT CREAMY CANDY
中秋
WHITE RABBIT CREAMY CANDY
大白兔奶糖月饼限定
礼盒
周年限定
二零二三
节庆好礼
大白兔
GUANSHENGYUAN FOOD GENERAL FACTORY
MID-AUTUMN

#ShōwaDesignTalk

1. What do you believe are the design characteristics of Shōwa style? What emotions do you hope to convey to viewers through this style?

Emen Lo (from Sankaramon)

The characteristic of this style is to convey the personal emotions and expressions of the creator in a simple and clean manner. Since many of my creations revolve around the relationship between urban dwellers and nature, emotions like "the sea," "romance," "freedom," and "wildness" are often palpable in my work. I am not a creator who pursues "retro restoration" because it is no longer the expression of this era. Contemporary creators should pursue "retro innovation." Therefore, while conducting research on retro backgrounds for each project, more attention should be paid to expressing contemporary spirit and attitude. Constantly searching for elements in the contemporary era and attempting to collide them with retro elements to find the optimal way to present one's ideas is essential to effectively convey emotions to contemporary audiences.

IDEAFINE

How to achieve a balance between design expression and commercial viability in business projects. In the case of the Nanniwan Apples packaging (refer to p. 320), while it may seem like a mere redesign using vintage certificate elements, the true focus lies in reworking key information and highlighting selling points. We aim to make the design not only more visually engaging but also clever in its approach.

Lo.Dycha

The primary focus of my project *LECHATER* (refer to p. 324) is on promoting traditional Teochew pastries, followed by exploring how traditional culture can adapt to modern times while maintaining its essence. Unlike most traditional retro styles, which tend to be intricate and highly decorative, I opted for a more simplified approach with *LECHATER*. Combined with the slogan "good things made easy, good luck made simple," I believe that traditional culture in the modern era should embrace a more relaxed ethos rather than clinging to cultural dogma.

Sanyo United Studio

The geometric abstraction of symbolic elements allows for different interpretations of childhood scenes by each individual. Drawing upon the background of the era forms a unique language in the past tense. Additionally, during the planned economy period of the working class, products had distinct characteristics, and the clear symbolic marks made the product image vivid. The work conveys our shared growth experience. In the fast-paced economic development era, we face immense pressure. The childhood time machine allows us to understand our growth journey better, get to know ourselves, and draw wisdom and strength from it.

Tatsuya Kurihara

I perceive this style as an inspired design rooted in history, particularly evident in the frame and decorative elements. The infusion of modernity through the mascot design strikes a balance between retro and contemporary aesthetics. My intention was to convey a sense of retro-modern fusion to the audience, appealing to individuals of varying ages. Additionally, being born in Japan and raised in America, the incorporation of both languages in the art is a reflection of my identity.

3% Design Studio

The Shōwa era emerged during Japan's period of recovery and development after the war. Setting aside its methods of expression, I believe its essence, and what is most unforgettable about it lies in its warmth and enduring belief in the brilliance of life. It embodies the flip side of the war emotionally, visually striking yet devoid of outward aggression, instead inwardly stable, instilling hope and courage in life. While encountering beautiful things often leads to solitary contemplation, encountering elements of the Shōwa era makes one feel connected with the community. It confronts indifference, mechanization, and utilitarianism. The perfect balance of roughness and craftsmanship fosters a deeper appreciation for the individual's vitality.

2. Are there specific color combinations, font ideas, graphic patterns, texture treatments, or perhaps a particular designer that are crucial to your visual expression? Please share your insights.

Emen Lo (from Sankaramon)

Many people have remarked that my personal style bears shadows of early French fashion magazine illustrations, as well as some Oriental charm and elements. From the perspective of expression methods, I tend to agree with this view. I am indeed greatly influenced by fashion illustrators from the early 20th century, such as Georges Lepape and George Barbier. At the same time, I also have a fondness for Eastern art, such as Japanese ukiyo-e and paintings of China's Song Dynasty. As I matured stylistically, I absorbed these influences and integrated them into my own creation, establishing my own distinctive style. Regarding color, I believe colors should first and foremost align with the content being conveyed. Therefore, before selecting color schemes for each creation, I clarify what the project is trying to convey. While creating a visually appealing and harmonious color palette is often not difficult, finding the colors that accurately convey the emotions of the project can be challenging. This is also one of the reasons why many projects become tiresome over time. I do not limit myself to using specific colors and instead experiment with a series of attempts to find the most accurate ones.

Lo.Dycha
Shigeo Fukuda was the first graphic designer I encountered and learned from. His work is usually very straightforward, without any unnecessary graphics. I believe that every stroke in design should be emotionally expressive, rather than randomly grabbing materials or basic graphics to enrich the composition. It's definitely not about playing around or using gimmicks, which is crucial in retro-style design; otherwise, it will end up looking like just a playful gimmick.

Sanyo Design Studio
Personally, I prefer abstract graphic elements. Creative packaging design works not only focus on conveying basic messages through simple text but also emphasize cultural output behind creativity and graphics, aiming to provoke diverse interpretations among different audiences.

Tatsuya Kurihara
The design choices for both the *Daruma* poster and the *Lucky Cat* poster are deeply rooted in Japanese culture and tradition.

3% Design Studio
Our ongoing experience with the Shōwa era primarily stems from collecting Maneki-neko figurines from the mid-20th century. Out of passion, we've gathered nearly a hundred Maneki-neko figurines of different ages, materials, sizes, and styles. The closest and most impactful experience for us is being near and touching items that actually existed during that time.

On the design front, we haven't consciously attempted to mimic the Shōwa era in terms of colors, fonts, or graphics. Instead, our approach has been to use specific items from the Shōwa era as a foundation and layer our visual experiments on top of them. The visual techniques themselves are modern; we simply place them on objects that evoke a sense of the Shōwa era, hoping for a collision of these two time periods to create a new atmosphere.

THE DESIGNER DECADE

REBELLION REBELLION REBELLION REBELLION

Me

This era was defined by bold colors, geometric patterns, and an exuberant spirit of innovation and rebellion.

80

icon

YES!

energy

THE DESIGNER DECADE: MODERN VISUAL STYLE GUIDE

ELEMENTS

1. Lemon
2. Labels
3. Heart Shape
4. Sexy Character
5. Guitar
6. Orange
7. Cartoon Eyes
8. Musical Note
9. Vinyl Record
10. Irregular Starburst
11. Road Signs
12. Starburst Label
13. Doughnut
14. Cell Phone
15. Cartoon Flowers
16. Heart Wings
17. Butterfly
18. Teddy Bear
19. Cube

KEYWORDS

1. PLAYFUL TYPOGRAPHY
2. BOLD AND CONTRASTING COLORS
3. GEOMETRIC PATTERNS
4. VINTAGE POP CULTURE ITEMS
5. SENSE OF NOSTALGIA

FONTS Cabin Bevan Our Gang NF

Fjalla One Bodoni SAMARIN Cantarell

CHAPLONE Tenby Five BP Diet

Three the Hard Way advent pro Gota

ACKNOWLEDGEMENT

COLOR

LAYOUT

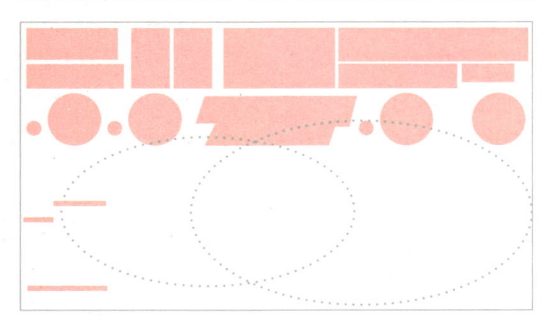

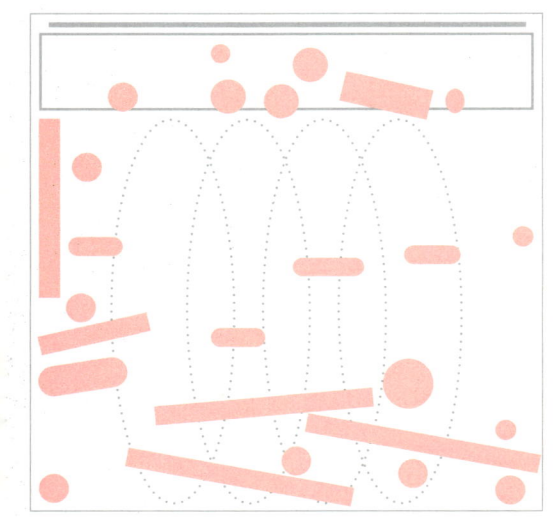

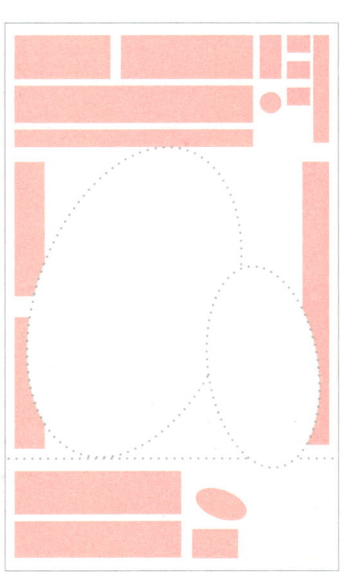

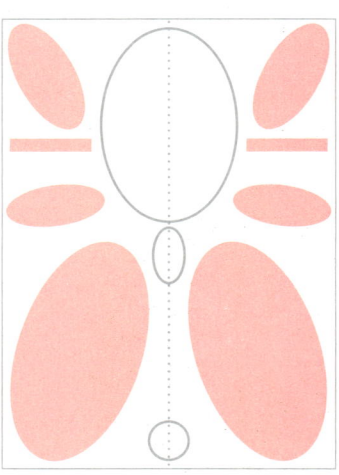

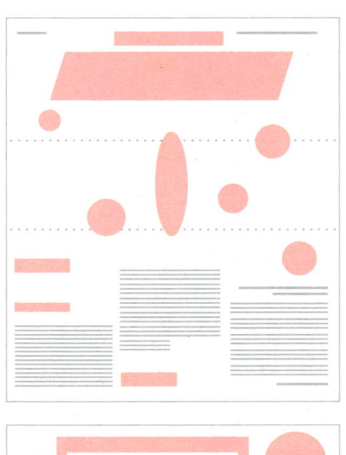

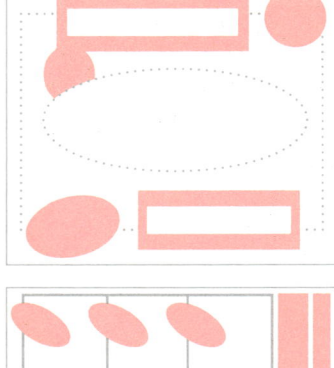

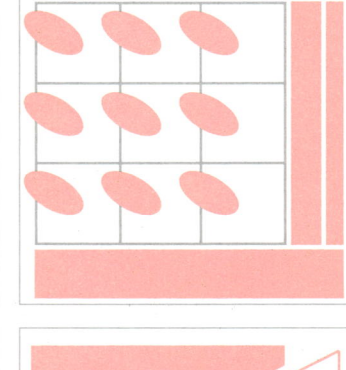

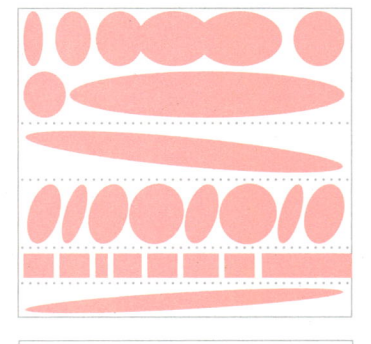

NEW JEWELRY COLLECTION

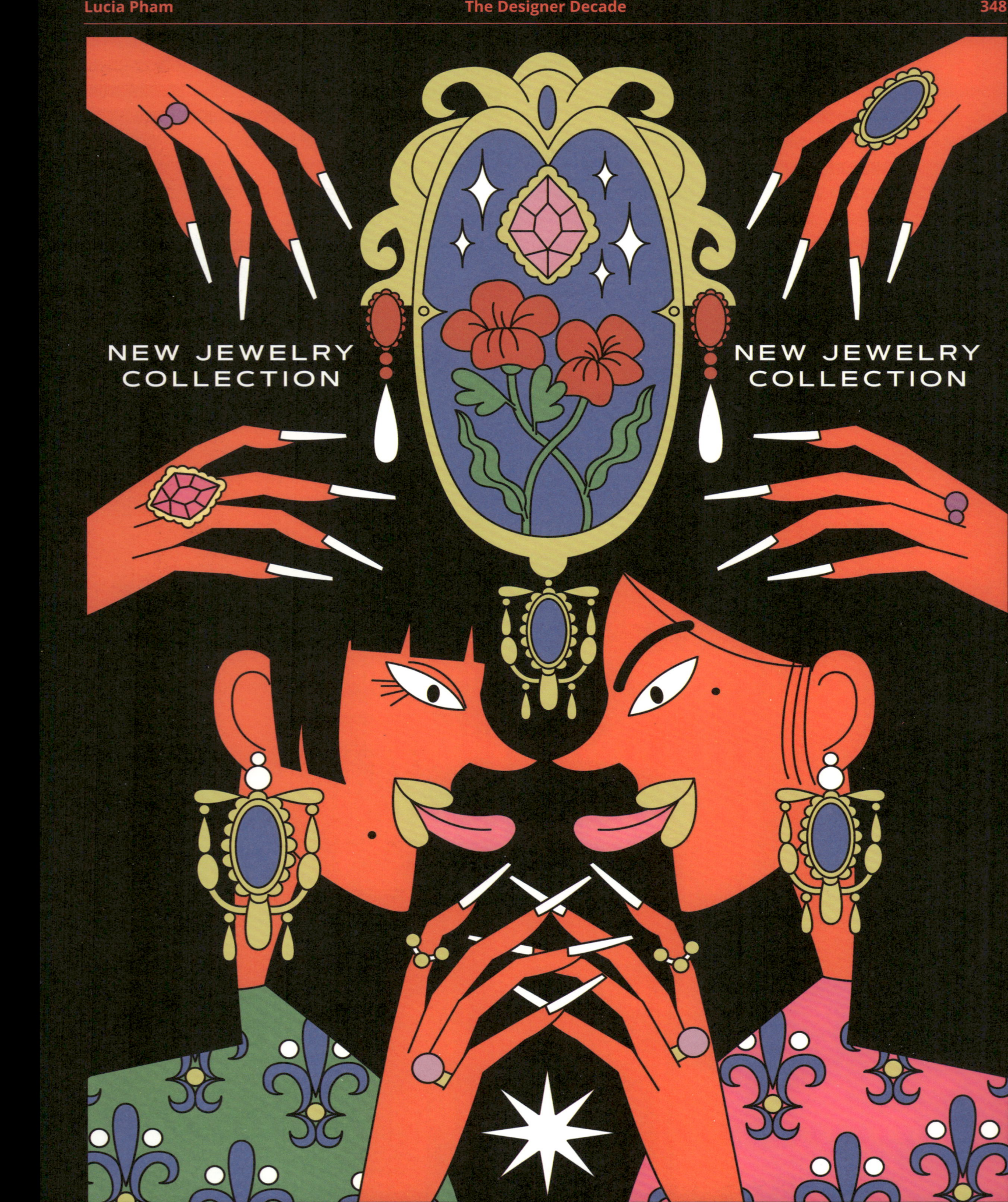

NEW JEWELRY COLLECTION

Lucia Pham

Lucia Pham, a rising independent illustrator born and raised in Hanoi, Vietnam, has garnered numerous fans worldwide with her vibrant and bold artistic style. Bright colors and clean lines characterize her work, but she also adapts her style according to the theme, resulting in pieces that can be sweet and cute or eerie and peculiar. For her, illustration is not just a tool for personal expression but also a means to connect with others because "illustration possesses the ability to transcend other forms of communication."

1 The Retro Aesthetics of the 1980s

Finding New Vitality in Retro

Lucia Pham's illustrations bear a distinct imprint of 1980s retro aesthetics, which pervade her artistic repertoire. She acknowledges that the essence of 1980s retro aesthetics lies in the bold application of typography—typically sans serif, bold, and italicized—accentuated by intricately crafted, complex yet orderly details. Color choices from that era often leaned towards low-contrast primary colors like red, yellow, green, and blue, now iconic symbols of that nostalgic period.

When working on projects with a retro style, Lucia adeptly blends diverse typefaces, integrating ideographs such as Japanese (Kanji) and Chinese alongside Latin/Roman letters. She meticulously arranges these fonts to harmonize with her illustrations, shaping unique visual narratives. To heighten visual impact, she employs higher contrasts to highlight traditional primary colors like red, yellow, and green, thereby creating a modern and compelling aesthetic that showcases her distinctive creative flair. Her design approach goes beyond the replication of retro elements; it emphasizes innovation through reinterpretation. This methodology revitalizes her work, resonating with contemporary audiences while preserving the timeless allure of the 1980s.

Global and Cultural Influences

The retro aesthetics of the 1980s not only swept through Western culture but also had a global influence. Against this backdrop, artist Lucia Pham skillfully incorporates multicultural elements into her works. As a native Vietnamese artist, Lucia has been deeply influenced by Vietnamese culture, and at the same time, her artistic perspectives have been expanded through the exchange and collision of global cultures.

During Lucia's upbringing, she was extensively exposed to and learned from cultures around the world. From an early age, she immersed herself in a variety of animated films and series—from Cartoon Network and Disney Channel to Japanese animated masterpieces such as *Doraemon*, *Sailor Moon*, and Chinese *Nezha Legend* and *Journey to the West* comics—which have greatly enriched her arsenal of artistic inspirations. Such a diverse cultural environment enabled her to effortlessly transition from the retro styles of the 1980s to the trends of the early 21st century.

Vietnamese culture is a melting pot, deeply influenced by both Asian and Western traditions. This diverse cultural background provides Lucia with a rich reservoir of aesthetic resources and visual inspiration for her storytelling. She is passionate about incorporating distinctive Vietnamese cultural symbols into her work, skillfully combining these traditional elements with modern and retro styles. This cross-cultural fusion not only adds depth and expressiveness to her creations but also fosters global understanding and appreciation of Vietnamese art. Like many young Vietnamese artists, Lucia harbors a strong desire to showcase Vietnamese culture to the world and takes pride in the progress she has made in this endeavor.

2 Transforming Interests into Art

In Lucia Pham's illustrations, we often observe a rich and diverse range of emotional expressions, spanning a broad spectrum from cheerful and bright to weird and slightly creepy. These choices of emotional direction are often influenced by the films, songs, and comics she has recently engaged with, driving her to express her inner feelings through a variety of personal projects.

She has a particular fondness for science fiction, fantasy, thrillers, and horror movies, while also enjoying light-hearted films. These diverse genres provide her with a wealth of visual material, from which she skillfully extracts unique emotional elements and seamlessly integrates them into her illustrations.

Apart from films, in her artistic process, Lucia frequently channels her emotions and thoughts into her drawings, finding a rich source of material in the music she loves. J-pop and J-rock, for example, are two styles of music that, although the Japanese language doesn't come easily to her and she sometimes struggles to fully understand the lyrics, the melodies and the musicians' approach to composing music stimulate her imagination and help her envision the unique world and story behind each song. By incorporating her personal interpretations, Lucia creates a colorful artistic experience. This approach not only allows her to be comfortable with a wide range of emotions in her art but also pushes her to explore and innovate in the creative process, ultimately creating work that touches the hearts of her audience.

Meanwhile, the highly developed K-pop industry, known for its visual sophistication, captivates her. The stunning appearance of idols on stage, in music videos, and in real life consistently provides striking visual references. As an artist who enjoys drawing female characters, Lucia finds these idols to be perfect role models and sources of inspiration for her personal projects. Their influence helps shape her distinctive style, blending musical

ABRACADABRA

Inspired by horror movies such as *The Addams Family and Charlie And The Chocolate Factory*, the designer is obsessed with the colors, styling, and the unique angles of each scene. A project was created featuring "living" frames that interact and look around. Accompanied by decorative motifs, including moons and stars, the project adopts an astrological style.

admiration with artistic expression. She noted, "Red Velvet is the girl group I admire the most." The K-pop girl group distinguishes itself through its exploration of diverse concepts, catchy music, and music videos filled with intriguing hidden stories. Each song they produce tells a unique story and evokes a range of emotions, offering Lucia a wealth of inspiration for her own creative work.

3 Unique Characters and Color Experiments

In Lucia Pham's distinctive work, we frequently encounter angular facial features, large eyes, and disordered scenes that showcase her recognizable aesthetic. These features reflect, to some extent, Asian preferences for large, almond-shaped eyes, long eyelashes, a petite nose, full lips, and thick, black hair. However, Lucia's depictions are highly personalized. Therefore, she continuously strives to refine her portrayal of diverse characters while maintaining her unique aesthetic, aiming to find the perfect balance between recognizability and innovation in her work.

In terms of color selection, Lucia has a deep affinity for all kinds of colors, particularly vibrant ones with high contrast. The color palette differs in each of her works, as she believes every piece should instantly captivate viewers and leave a lasting impact. Lucia's aesthetic journey with color has undergone a transformation. Initially drawn to softer and more refined colors, she found these did not align with her evolving aesthetic vision. Consequently, she gradually embraced more vibrant and visually impactful choices.

While subtle hues still hold significance in her compositions, they now serve as complementary accents rather than primary features, adding depth and richness to the overall piece. Lucia meticulously refines her color selections, constantly experimenting with different intensities and combinations. This approach significantly enhances the effectiveness of her illustrations, ensuring they resonate deeply with audiences. Strategically employing vibrant colors not only enhances the overall visual appeal of her work but also enriches the emotional depth of her artistic expression. This method reflects Lucia's continuous exploration and refinement of her artistic style. In her creations, color serves as a powerful tool to convey meaning and evoke sensory experiences in viewers.

▼ Color Scheme:

- R255 G001 B041 / C000 M100 Y083 K000
- R243 G173 B029 / C002 M039 Y089 K000
- R245 G208 B033 / C005 M019 Y088 K000
- R224 G202 B100 / C016 M018 Y069 K000
- R042 G151 B094 / C077 M020 Y077 K000
- R037 G078 B160 / C089 M072 Y000 K000
- R168 G126 B182 / C039 M056 Y000 K000
- R108 G068 B152 / C068 M080 Y000 K000
- R232 G077 B138 / C000 M082 Y011 K000
- R197 G061 B144 / C022 M086 Y000 K000

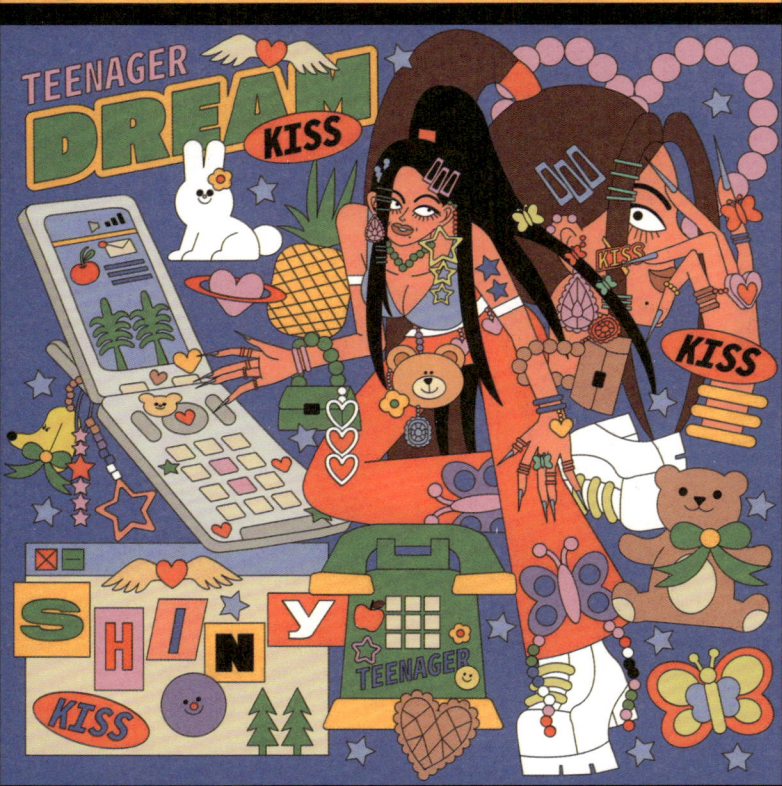

BACK TO THE 2000S

Girls are posed in a fashion magazine style reminiscent of the 1990s–2000s, with a focus on decorative accessories in clothing and makeup. Inspired by diaries, the scrapbooks are adorned with stickers. The layout is dense and chaotic, aiming to incorporate as many details as possible.

KPOP STARS

This series was created as a result of her being inspired by KPOP. As a creator who enjoys drawing female characters, she found these KPOP female icons to be the perfect source for her personal projects. At the same time, each of these Korean girl groups' songs tells a unique concept, providing her with a wealth of inspiration for the work.

▼ **Inspiration:**

The designer was inspired by the songs of different KPOP groups:

Aespa - "Black Mamba"
Aespa - "Spicy"
New Jeans - "Attention"
Red Velvet - "Queendom"

▼ **Elements:**

Elements were selected to align with various song concepts and the distinctive traits of girl groups. For example, the design for "Queendom" features a group of princesses enjoying afternoon tea, while the design for Group New Jeans includes a bunny representing the group members.

BLACKMAMBA
에스파
에스파
aespa
에스파
에스파

ATTENTION
뉴진스
NJ
NJ
NJ
NJ
NEW JEANS
NEW JEANS
HANNI
MINJI
HYEIN
DANIELLE
HYERIN

QUEENDOM
Red Velvet
레드벨벳
레드벨벳

SERIES OF POSTERS

→ 03 This small project was completed in a short amount of time. The designer allowed herself to work on this project simply, featuring fashion girls arranged in a magazine/poster layout.

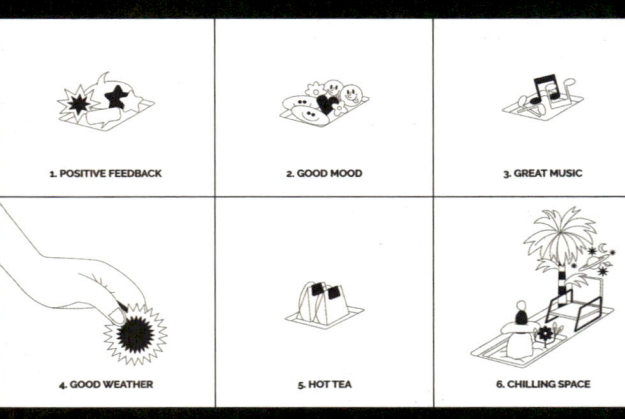

DRY & SUNNY

Taiwan Peach Tea
Oolong Black Tea
Apple Caramel Tea
Pomegranate Tea

♪ RPG SEKAI NO OWARI
▶ Baton WACCI
♪ Folktale MRS.GREEN APPLE
♪ Yesterday OFFICIAL HIGE DANDISM
♪ Amazingrace GO!GO!VANILLAS
♪ Juji No Hougaku SUMIKA

Wow! Looks great! Dope! Wonderful! Nice!

Calm, Positive, Happy, Excited

Starbuck Coffee ♥♥♥
Paris Gateaux ♥♥♥
Angel-in-us ♥♥♥
The Coffee House ♥♥♥

BEST CONDITIONAL — **FULL-TIME** — **FREELANCER**

I AM AN INDEPENDENT VISUAL ARTIST FROM VIETNAM, SPECIALIZING IN ILLUSTRATION, GRAPHIC DESIGN AND ART DIRECTION.

I LOVE TO USE BRIGHT, EYE-CATCHING COLORS AND DIFFERENT SHAPES TO ILLUSTRATE PEOPLE AND LIFE

1 → Positive Feedback
2 → Good Mood
3 → Great Music
4 → Chilling Space
5 → Hot Tea
6 → Good Weather

1. POSITIVE FEEDBACK
2. GOOD MOOD
3. GREAT MUSIC
4. GOOD WEATHER
5. HOT TEA
6. CHILLING SPACE

→ 04 Continuing to draw inspiration from posters, matchbox designs, and canned sardine packaging from the 80s and 90s, the drawings and shapes in this project maintain a retro aesthetics. However, the layout and typography adopt a more modern approach.

▼ **Font:**
Raleway

▼ **Color Scheme:**

R230 G035 B038
C000 M095 Y086 K000

R226 G225 B032
C016 M002 Y089 K000

R072 G177 B052
C069 M000 Y100 K000

R041 G082 B163
C087 M069 Y000 K000

R000 G000 B000
C000 M000 Y000 K100

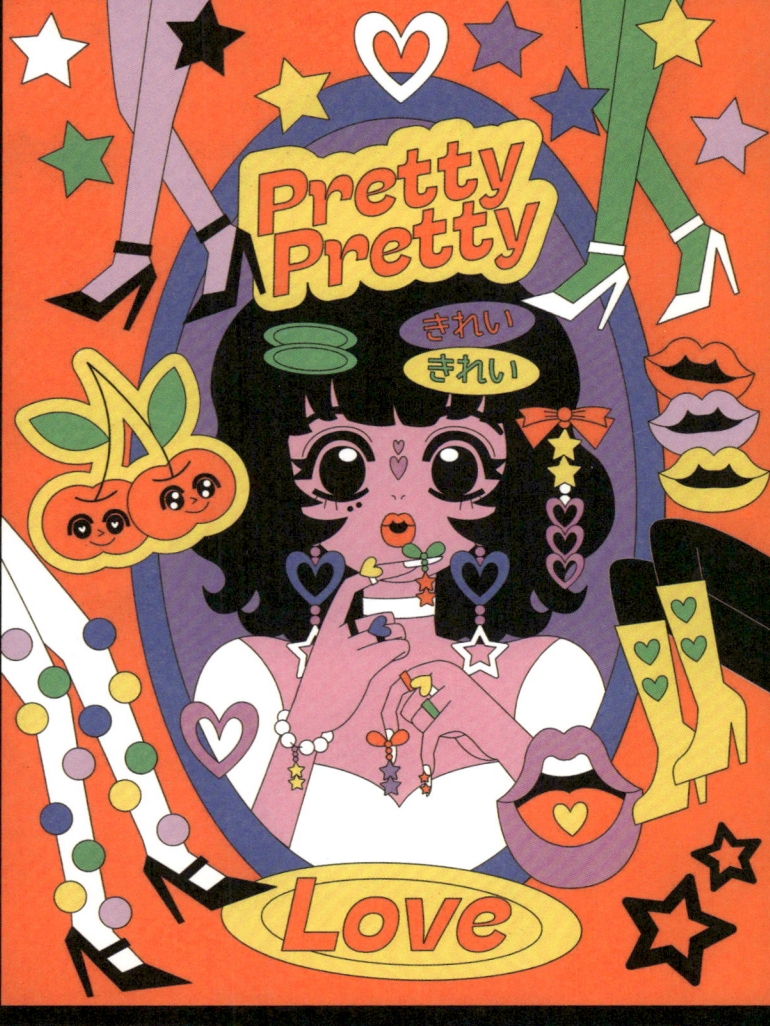

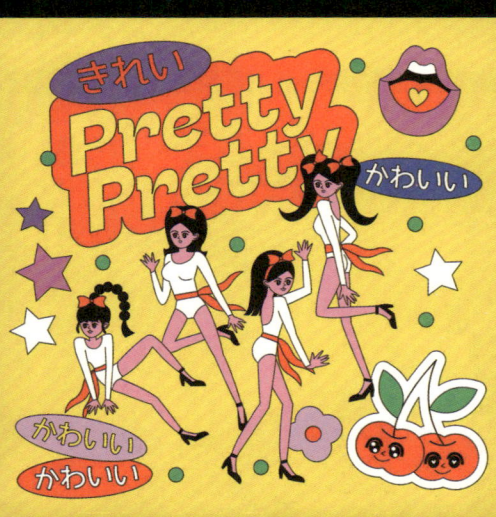

→08

Drawing inspiration from shōjo manga classics of the 80s and 90s like *Glass Mask* (ガラスの仮面), *The Rose of Versailles* (ベルサイユのばら), *Sailor Moon*, and *Full Moon Wo Sagashite* (満月をさがして), as well as Japanese teen magazines from the 2000s like *Popteen*, *ViVi*, and *Zipper*, the project features layouts teeming with text and images. The focus is on portraying cute, adorable, fashionable, and

▼ **Color Scheme:**

R053 G075 B158 C086 M074 Y000 K000	R231 G036 B045 C000 M095 Y081 K000	R248 G223 B046 C005 M011 Y085 K000	R229 G133 B179 C006 M060 Y000 K000
R231 G036 B045 C000 M095 Y081 K000	R248 G223 B046 C005 M011 Y085 K000	R130 G179 B156 C057 M076 Y000 K000	R021 G167 B103 C076 M006 Y075 K000

THE FASTEST

THE TWIN 05 悪魔 AKUMA 502-99 アクマ

FASTEST RACER

967 THE MIRROR FASTEST RACER 鏡 かがみ

KAGAMI E-25 鏡

▼ **Inspiration:**

The designer drew inspiration from different mechanical carriers, such as racing cars, large motorbikes, spaceships and flying saucers, showing endless imagination. As for the text, she drew inspiration mainly from 1980s posters, arcade games and vintage matchbox packaging style, adding suitable Japanese and English text to the illustrations.

▼ **Fonts:**

Maver, Rounded Mplus 1c, Roboto Flex

▼ **Color Scheme:**

▼ **Elements:**

In addition to the several primary carriers, the designer incorporated numerous detailed components to create a sense of ambiance and movement. Each scenario features its own distinct characteristics.

▼ **Layout:**

The horizontal composition effectively showcases the race scene and conveys a strong sense of speed. Additionally, the designer extracted elements and fonts from the main image to reconstruct a smaller picture on the right, highlighting the distinct features of the scene.

| R231 G036 B045 | R028 G249 B209 | R230 G212 B027 | R230 G212 B027 | R001 G139 B068 | R014 G018 B143 |
| C000 M095 Y081 K000 | C075 M026 Y003 K000 | C013 M013 Y090 K000 | C013 M013 Y090 K000 | C082 M026 Y094 K000 | C100 M090 Y000 K000 |

| R131 G107 B174 | R014 G018 B143 | R214 G106 B165 | R231 G036 B045 | R239 G130 B030 | R230 G212 B027 |
| C056 M061 Y000 K000 | C100 M090 Y000 K000 | C013 M069 Y000 K000 | C000 M095 Y081 K000 | C000 M060 Y090 K000 | C013 M013 Y090 K000 |

UP&DOWN
HAPPINESS
LISTEN
SUSTAIN
IMAGINATION
JUSTICE
QUEER
REPAIR
VULNERABLE
STAY HUNGRY STAY FOOLISH
KNOWLEDGE
TRAVEL
muse
X:CROSSOVER
YOUTH
GRATITUDE
EQUAITY
HTTP://WWW
ORIGIN
PLAYFULLNESS
FREEDOM

Bali Meng

Bali Meng is a freelance illustrator and designer based in Beijing. Despite a background in computer science and psychology, she has always had a passion for drawing. "Drawing" seems to open up another dimension for her, becoming a way to get along with the world and a language for self-expression. Her art, inspired by daily life, merges graphic design and illustration, employing vibrant colors to create visually striking and engaging compositions. Bali Meng's portfolio includes collaborations with clients such as Xiaomi, Toshiba TV, Wangjing Cadmium, little MO&Co, *GQ*, and *ELLE* Magazine.

1 Finding Joy in Urban Nature

Life in the city often comes with its own set of pressures and a sense of disconnection from nature. While urban living provides convenience, it also tends to make people lose sight of life's simple pleasures. Artist Bali Meng addresses this disconnection in her artwork by blending natural elements like the sun, plants, and flowers with the industrial components of rapidly developing cities. This combination allows viewers to appreciate and enjoy nature while living in the present moment, savoring the small joys often overlooked in daily life. Bali's unique approach not only highlights the beauty of everyday moments but also encourages viewers to find the joy of creation at the intersection of nature and urban life.

Bali Meng's creation is deeply influenced by the retro style of the 90s and Y2K aesthetics. In her character design, she employs classic retro elements, such as platform shoes and bell-bottoms, to evoke a sense of nostalgia. These characters are then depicted engaging in modern activities, with cartoon illustrations serving as a bridge between the audience and the artwork. Through the use of vibrant colors and playful designs, she creates a colorful world that blends the charm of the past with the vibrancy of the present. Her work stands as a testament to the enduring appeal of 90s and Y2K aesthetics, reimagined through a contemporary lens to inspire and delight audiences.

2 Modern Trends and Retro Charm

She skillfully balances elements from different eras, blending retro charm with contemporary trends. Fashion items like sneakers and computers, naturally straddle the line between retro and trendy styles. For instance, while headphones have evolved from traditional wired versions to wireless ones, there has been a noticeable resurgence of interest in classic wired headphones in recent times. And she observes that people often personalize their headphones with stickers or 3D-printed shells to enhance their fashion statement. This trend exemplifies how retro aesthetics can be reimagined to suit modern tastes. Bali observes these trends and incorporates them into her illustrations, ensuring her art remains relevant and appealing to today's audiences. Throughout her design process, Bali draws inspiration from the dynamic interplay between fashion trends and retro aesthetics. This interaction fuels her creativity, allowing her to produce unique and engaging artworks. By applying these concepts to various items of interest, Bali adds a playful and imaginative touch to her illustrations, sparking viewers' imaginations and encouraging them to envision a vibrant future. These works of art invite audiences to appreciate the beauty of different eras while also encouraging them to embrace the ever-evolving nature of style and creativity.

3 Multicultural Elements in Retro Aesthetics

Bali Meng navigates the integration of multicultural elements into retro aesthetics. She explains that her approach involves incorporating classic elements like polka dots and plaid, as well as iconic hairstyles like afros and dreadlocks from Black culture. Additionally, she also draws inspiration from Chinese elements like qipao and kung fu attire. These elements are skillfully presented with a twist, showcasing cultural nuances while influencing each other harmoniously. For instance, Bali might depict a young person with dreadlocks practicing Tai Chi, blending cultural stereotypes in a refreshing way.

Throughout her creative journey, Bali acknowledges the challenges of deeply understanding and respectfully representing diverse cultures. Particularly when incorporating religious elements, the artist needs to take great care to avoid offending religious and cultural sensibilities while effectively conveying the essence of the subject through illustration design. Despite these challenges, she finds that the fusion of multicultural elements adds vibrancy and appeal to her artwork. These creative blends not only offer a fresh perspective but also resonate deeply with audiences by conveying universal ideas and values through visual storytelling.

CHARACTERSTIC

Bali Meng   The Designer Decade   360

FRUIT BAND

This project features a fruit band performing at a music festival, drawing inspiration from hippies, rock music, and Western cowboys. Each character's actions, expressions, and attire aim to tell a story, with detailed clothing and lively appearances. Atmospheric elements enhance the mood, creating a sense of movement and evoking a unique yet harmonious feeling.

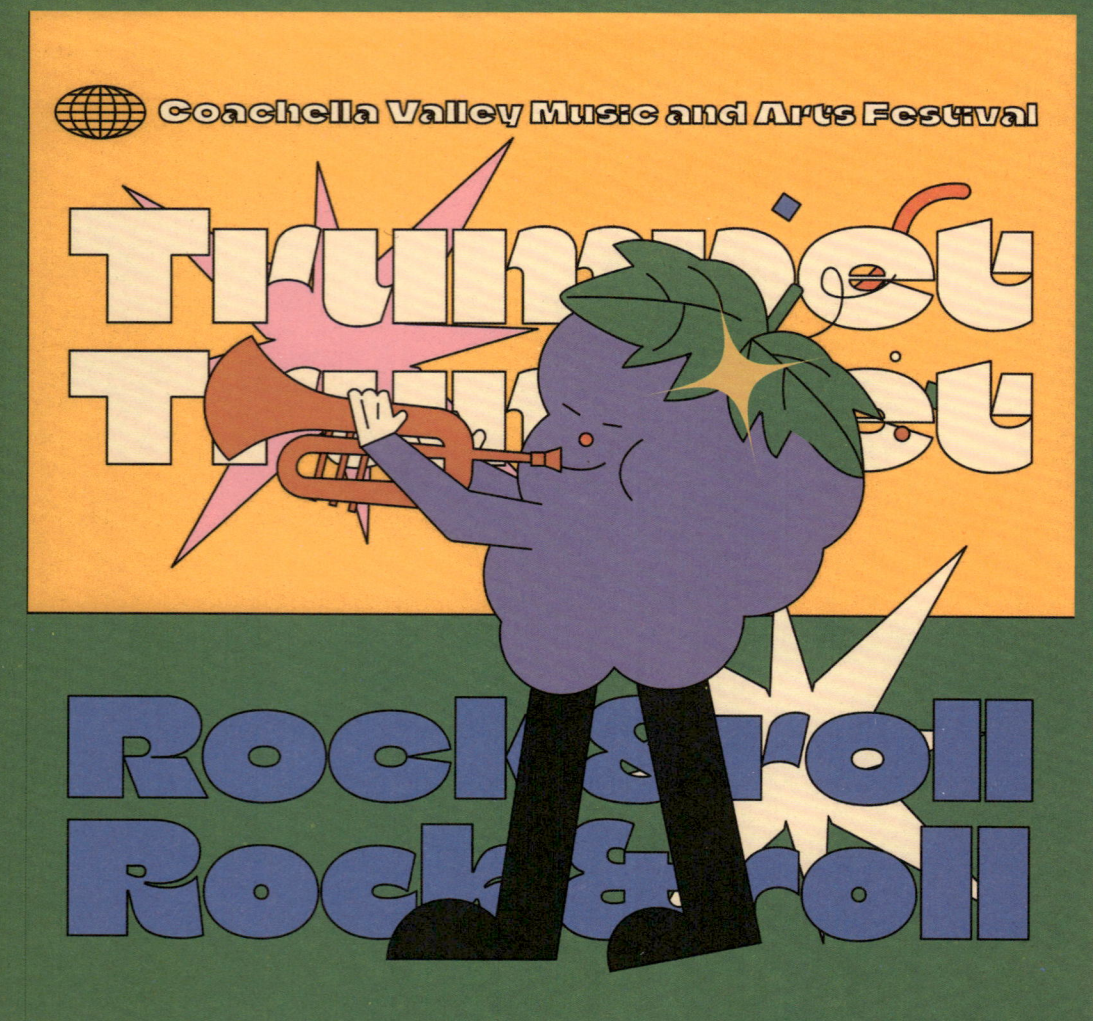

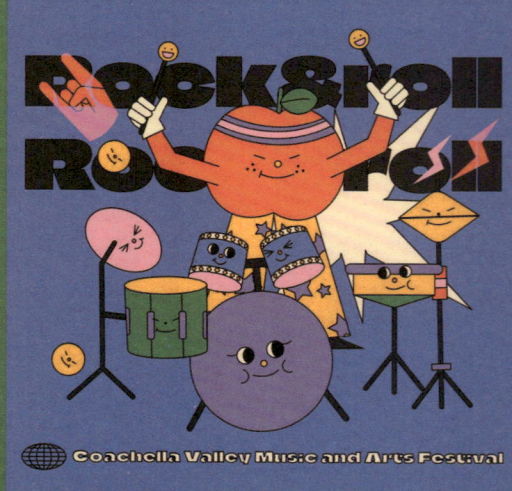

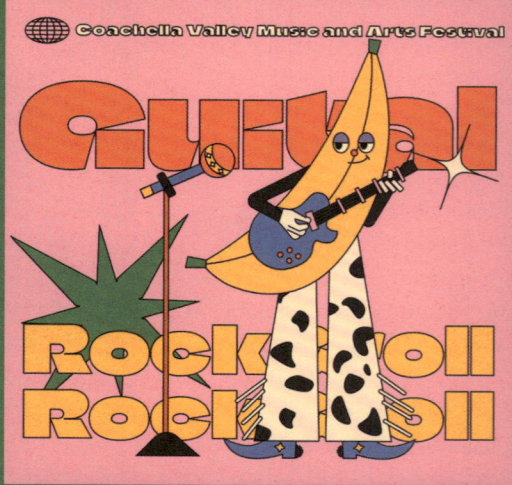

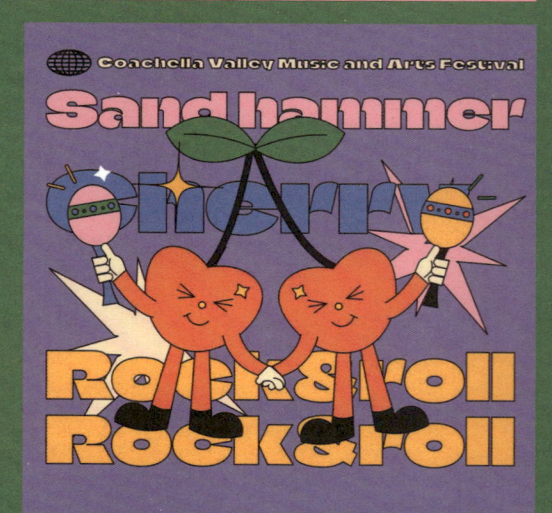

▼ **Inspiration:** Influenced by the retro style of the 90s, the illustrator enjoys watching retro films and TV shows, appreciating the era's vibrant use of color and the optimistic attitude toward the future. This unique retro aesthetic inspires her, and she also keeps an eye on current fashion trends, incorporating elements like the recent Y2K trend into her work. By infusing these elements into her art, she aims to enhance its trendiness and vibrancy, making it more lively and engaging.

▼ **Layout:** Layout design is based on a common top-to-bottom structure. It features simple, large titles and small text, with the illustrated characters in the center highlighted.

▼ **Color Scheme:**

| R229 G078 B047 | R240 G135 B022 | R020 G127 B059 | R049 G099 B168 | R119 G095 B161 | R235 G144 B178 |
| C004 M083 Y082 K000 | C000 M058 Y092 K000 | C084 M036 Y100 K002 | C083 M059 Y006 K000 | C062 M067 Y006 K000 | C003 M055 Y070 K000 |

BROOKIES COOKIES & CO

Brookies, a Brazilian brand from Porto Alegre, specializes in artisanal brownies, cookies, and coffees. With a mantra focused on bringing people happiness through their sweets, the company aimed for a new brand expression during an expansion phase. The team, guided by the vision of good and warm nostalgia appreciated by their customers, crafted an authentic, global, urban, and fun platform. Incorporating a vibrant color palette and the tagline "baking good times," they introduced a new symbol inspired by '50s cartoons, injecting a touch of acid humor with exaggerated and flashy expressions that reflect cunning and mischief.

Design Studio: Blank Design Studio
Designer: Blank Team
Client: Brookies Cookies & Co

▼ **Inspiration:**
Brookies Cookies & Co's retro-inspired VI features playful 1950s cartoons, a vintage color palette, and the tagline "baking good times." The urban and global elements contribute to a distinctive brand identity, infusing a sense of nostalgia and joy into the contemporary experience.

▼ **Elements:**
Brookies underwent a transformation, merging its heritage with modern elements: a unique handwritten font, vibrant tones inspired by ingredients, and a hint of fun. The chromatic pattern, derived from vanilla and dark chocolate, reflects the cookie-making process. The main color, vintage green, chosen through competitive analysis, exudes retro charm. The branding patterns draw from sweet stripes and urban-grunge styles.

▼ **Fonts:**
Barlow, Cooper

▼ **Color Scheme:**

R093 G189 B163
C062 M000 Y044 K000

R255 G241 B000
C001 M000 Y014 K000

R242 G186 B179
C003 M035 Y023 K000

R236 G127 B066
C002 M062 Y074 K000

NEW PLANTS COLLECTION

While visiting the Glasgow Botanic Gardens, the designer encountered a tropical plant from her homeland. Suddenly, a connection between her hometown in China and Glasgow became apparent. The realization dawned that plants, much like humans, embark on journeys and settle in new places, forming friendships and familial bonds. This narrative unfolds to illustrate how migrants adapt to life in a foreign land. For instance, anecdotes emerge about the need to be frugal in a new environment, to exercise financial prudence. In this unfamiliar setting, new aspirations emerge. Celebrations and cross-cultural relationships also find a place in the stories, mirroring the observer's own experience of celebrating with newfound friends in a new location, akin to the botanical garden's flowers enjoying a drink with her international friends.

The storytelling is further enhanced through the use of software that emulates the textured quality of Risograph printing brushes, simulating the overlapping ink textures of various colors on paper. The addition of rough paper textures, combined with gentle hues, creates a nostalgic and cozy visual atmosphere.

Illustrator: Erin Chen

▼ Inspiration:

Primarily influenced by the bold lines of American comics and the textured feel of vintage woodcut prints, the design incorporates a fusion of flat color blocks and lines to impart a personified and character-like feel to the plants. Both plants and human characters share a similar color palette, aiding readers in understanding the connection between plants and characters. The addition of woodcut-style flatness and print textures evokes a nostalgic visual experience for the audience.

▼ Color Scheme:

R179 G202 B197	R233 G233 B230	R149 G177 B175	R106 G130 B116	R122 G167 B101	R146 G177 B205	R250 G247 B192
C035 M013 Y023 K000	C011 M007 Y009 K000	C047 M022 Y030 K000	C065 M044 Y056 K000	C058 M020 Y071 K000	C047 M022 Y012 K000	C004 M000 Y033 K000

WELSBRO WATCHES

Welsbro, originally established in New York in 1926, made a meaningful return in 2021 under the guidance of Rich Reichbach and Katie Willis. The launch features four vintage watches: Lemon Lime, Orange Soda, Ketchup, and Mustard, presented in a unique "Lunch Box" packaging.

Designer: Oscar Bastidas
Client: Welsbro

▼ **Inspiration:**
Each Welsbro watch and strap draws inspiration from the food stories of Welsbro owners during their time living in New York (1980s–90s).

▼ **Elements:**
From color and illustration style to packaging, every detail in this branding project is intended to evoke the nostalgia of the 80s and 90s. The aesthetics features pop colors, bold and organic typography, and amusing characters—all presented in a lunch box reminiscent of those carried by kids to school during that era. The watch's credentials are printed on small cards, mirroring the style of baseball trading cards from the 80s and 90s.

▼ **Font:**
Hand-made fonts from Scratch

▼ **Layout:**
Handmade fonts, organic shapes, and compositions brimming with details and Easter eggs define the whimsical look and feel of this design. It aims to transport customers to a different time, where everything was simpler and infused with sweetness.

▼ **Color Scheme:**

R231 G093 B093	R255 G177 B085	R255 G231 B000	R229 G234 B111	R022 G149 B078	R093 G167 B229	R178 G124 B201	R244 G182 B216
C000 M080 Y055 K000	C000 M045 Y080 K000	C000 M005 Y100 K000	C015 M000 Y079 K000	C097 M011 Y100 K000	C059 M023 Y000 K000	C030 M060 Y000 K000	C005 M048 Y000 K000
Pantone Red 032 U	Pantone 1235 U	Pantone Yellow U	Pantone 387 U	Pantone 347 U	Pantone 292 U	Pantone 2582 U	Pantone 231 U

WELSBRO
レモンライム
LEMON LIME

WELSBRO
No.: /
LEMON LIME DIVER
MOVEMENT
VINTAGE A. SCHILD CALIBER 1913
WATER-RESISTANCE
200 METERS
LEATHER STRAP
HANDMADE IN ITALY
HAND ASSEMBLED IN JAPAN
Every Welsbro watch has a food story.
This watch is inspired by the munchies of our summers: the pool snack bar. We'd crush candy and lemon lime soda during adult swim. Then run, not walk, around the pool, high on sugar. Mmm!
DO NOT EAT THIS WATCH

ケチャップ
WELSBRO
KETCHUP

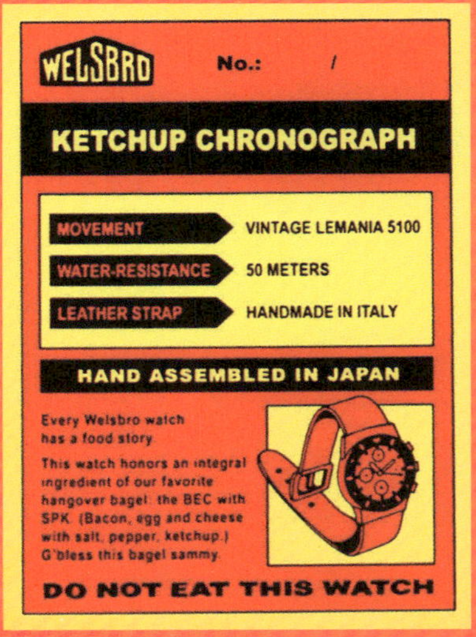
WELSBRO
No.: /
KETCHUP CHRONOGRAPH
MOVEMENT
VINTAGE LEMANIA 5100
WATER-RESISTANCE
50 METERS
LEATHER STRAP
HANDMADE IN ITALY
HAND ASSEMBLED IN JAPAN
Every Welsbro watch has a food story.
This watch honors an integral ingredient of our favorite hangover bagel: the BEC with SPK. (Bacon, egg and cheese with salt, pepper, ketchup.) G'bless this bagel sammy.
DO NOT EAT THIS WATCH

オレンジソーダ
WELSBRO
ORANGE SODA

WELSBRO
No.: /
ORANGE SODA DIVER
MOVEMENT
VINTAGE A. SCHILD CALIBER 1913
WATER-RESISTANCE
200 METERS
LEATHER STRAP
HANDMADE IN ITALY
HAND ASSEMBLED IN JAPAN
Every Welsbro watch has a food story.
This watch is inspired by the munchies of our youth: greasy pizza and orange soda from the arcade in Staten Island. Then for dessert, a trip to the comic book store. Mmm, yummy.
DO NOT EAT THIS WATCH

WELSBRO
マスタード
MUSTARD

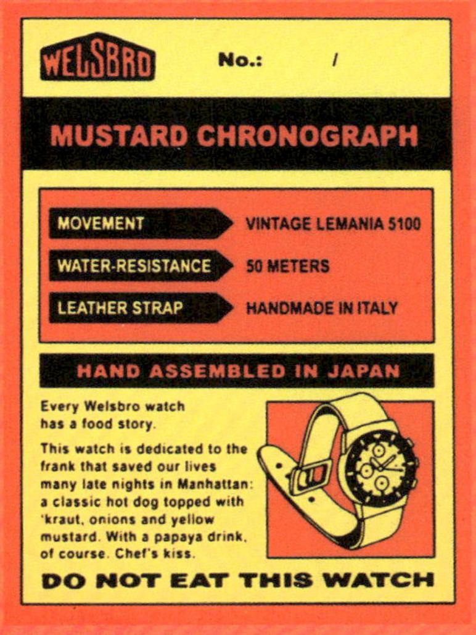
WELSBRO
No.: /
MUSTARD CHRONOGRAPH
MOVEMENT
VINTAGE LEMANIA 5100
WATER-RESISTANCE
50 METERS
LEATHER STRAP
HANDMADE IN ITALY
HAND ASSEMBLED IN JAPAN
Every Welsbro watch has a food story.
This watch is dedicated to the frank that saved our lives many late nights in Manhattan: a classic hot dog topped with 'kraut, onions and yellow mustard. With a papaya drink, of course. Chef's kiss.
DO NOT EAT THIS WATCH

モッツァレラ
MUTZ
WELSBRO
DO NOT EAT THIS WATCH
STATEN ISLAND COLLECTION

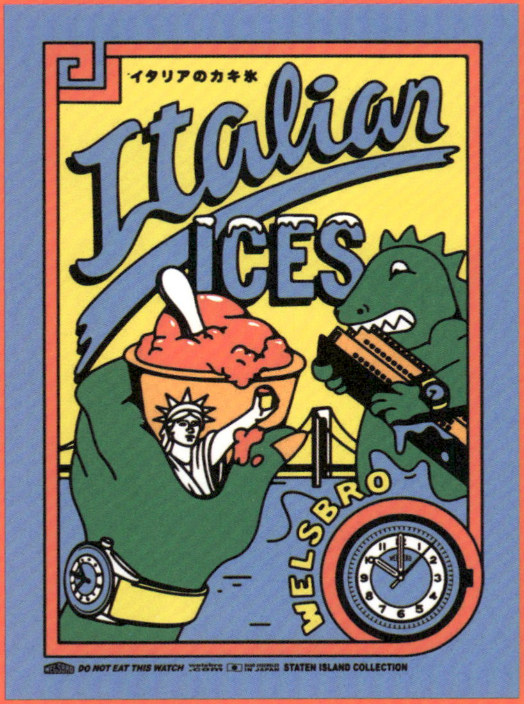
イタリアのカキ氷
Italian
ICES
WELSBRO
DO NOT EAT THIS WATCH
STATEN ISLAND COLLECTION

ガバグール
GABA
GOOL
WELSBRO
DO NOT EAT THIS WATCH
STATEN ISLAND COLLECTION

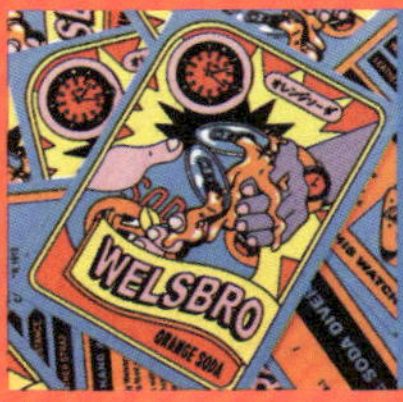

MOON COSMIC POWER

The designer, a sneaker enthusiast, blended her love for colorful, chunky footwear with childhood nostalgia for *Sailor Moon*. She aimed to recreate the magical atmosphere of the show by infusing vibrant colors, patterns, and sparkles into each sneaker design. Characteristic features of the *Sailor Moon* characters are subtly incorporated, evoking a surge of nostalgia and connection for viewers wearing these anime-inspired sneakers.

Designer: Rita

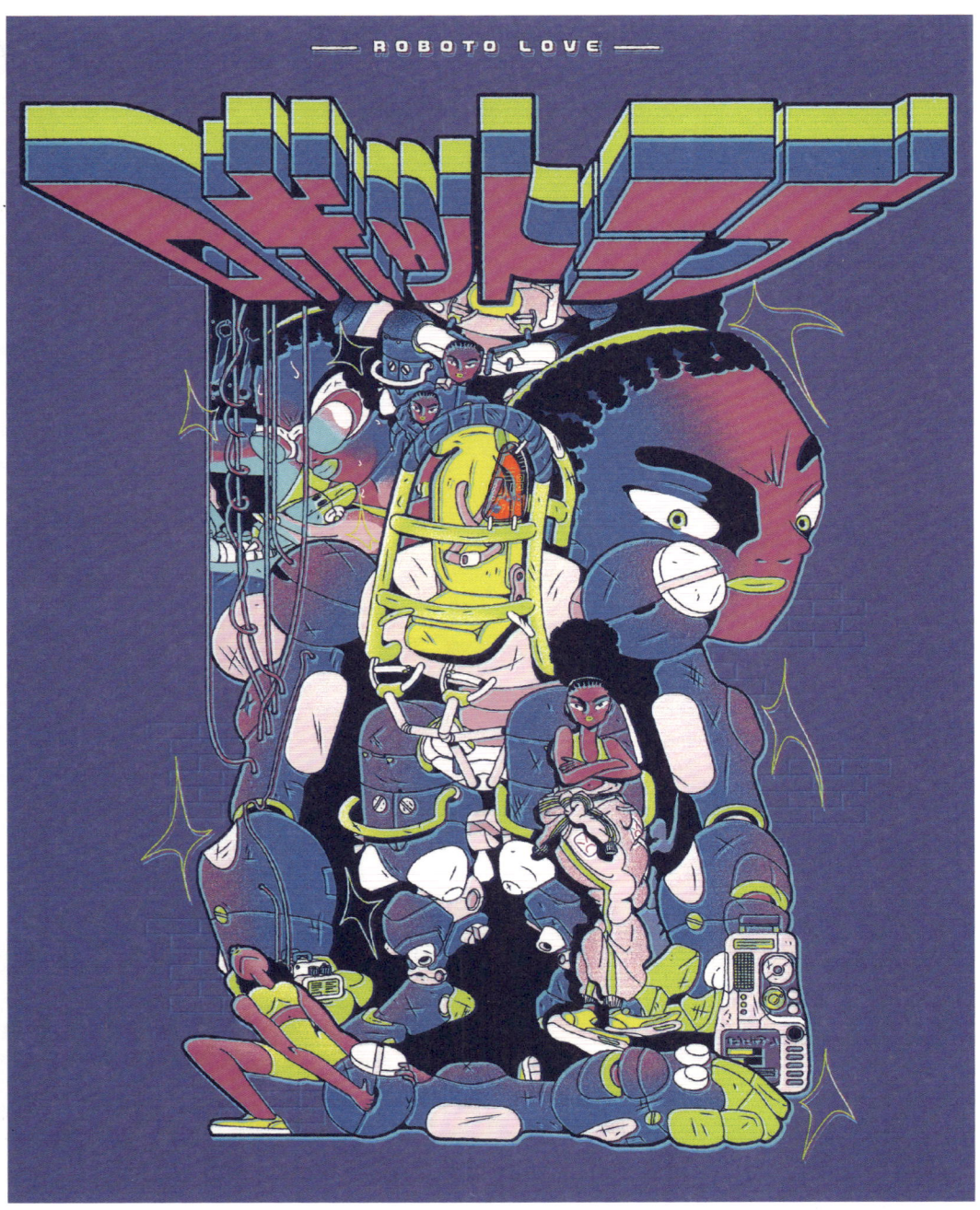

ROBOT LOVE

This project comprises a series of concept illustrations created for an animated short film. The illustrations revolve around a girl rebuilding her mom's mecha (robot). For this project, the design team developed character design, mecha design, and art direction for each scene.

Design Studio: Estudio Pum

▼ **Inspiration:**

Growing up, the love for all mecha anime illustrations inspired this project—an homage to 80s animations like *Arbegas* and *Gundam*. The neon-look color palette serves as a relatable nod to the vibrant aesthetics of that era.

▼ **Elements:**

In the process of developing characters and mechas, the design team's aim was to construct impactful scenes that vividly convey the girl's spirit as she endeavors to rebuild the mecha in her garage, all captured through compelling visual storytelling.

RELEASING FESTIVAL

The Releasing Festival project, completed in 2020, seamlessly blends '80s aesthetics with contemporary indie style, capturing the vibrant essence of a music festival. Aimed at a playful audience, the project evokes a festive, dynamic atmosphere, much like a festival featuring diverse bands. As a festival-goer and designer, he saw untapped potential in festival merchandise, creating colorful stickers, posters, tote bags, wristbands, and badges—items that people would cherish as lasting mementos of the event.

Design Studio: Helloflostudio
Designer: Florencia Leonardini

▼ Color Scheme:

- R237 G217 B032 / C011 M007 Y091 K000
- R243 G152 B000 / C000 M050 Y097 K000
- R244 G162 B176 / C000 M048 Y018 K000
- R075 G095 B239 / C081 M066 Y000 K000
- R000 G150 B064 / C084 M011 Y096 K001

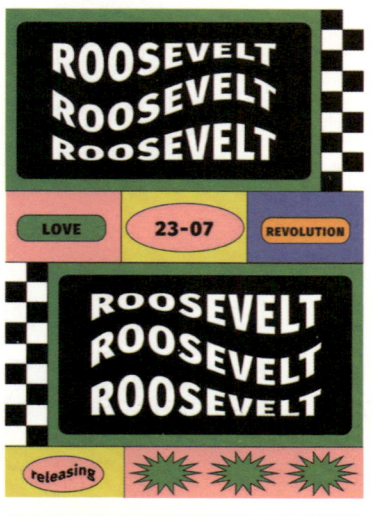

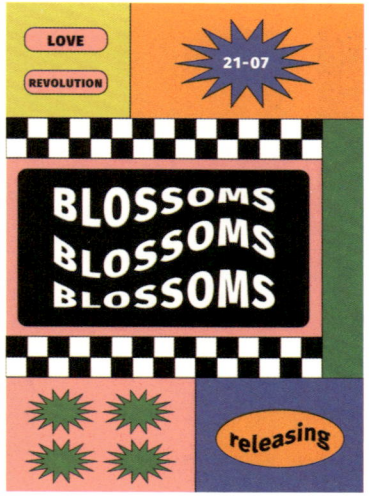

▼ Inspiration:

The aesthetics concept nods to MTV and Vans eras, inspired by retro clothing fairs and shows like *Dawson's Creek* and *Clueless*. *Derry Girls* and *Mid90s* add a modern twist.

▼ Elements:

The graphic elements in this proposal infuse a playful essence. Utilizing diverse figures, a visually dynamic system emerged, steering clear of monotony. These figures draw inspiration from the 80s/90s, transcending mere decoration to play a functional role within the created visual identity.

▼ Fonts:

Fira Sans bold, Elephant, Cooper Std black

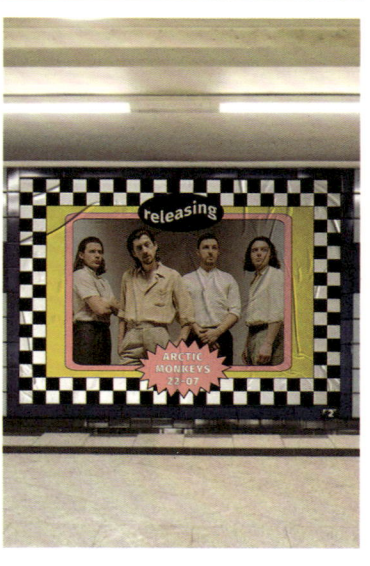

STICKERSFRUITS ANXIETY MOOD

In the vibrant world of Stickerfruits, inspiration blossoms from the overlooked beauty of branded fruit stickers. Often dismissed, these small marvels captivate with thoughtful designs. Amid the uncertainties of 2020, they became a canvas for expressing shared anxieties and offering a message of encouragement. The perspective is genuine, urging individuals to find solace in enjoyable activities and small distractions, recognizing the importance of professional help for mental health concerns. Stickerfruits embodies a creative journey intertwined with the human experience.

Design Studio: Helloflostudio
Designer: Florencia Leonardini

▼ **Inspiration & Elements**

These designs are inspired by vintage fruit labels and feature simple illustrations that evoke a retro feel through their color palette. The plants depicted were popular in the 80s and 90s and are now making a comeback. Some designs include outlined or shadowed typography, while others have line details that create an organic effect. This work blends modern elements, like bold typefaces, with a nostalgic perspective, aiming to balance past and present influences to create a unique visual style.

▼ **Fonts:**

Source Sans Pro, Poppins, Poplar Std Black, Myriad Pro, Plantin MT Bold Condensed, Oswald

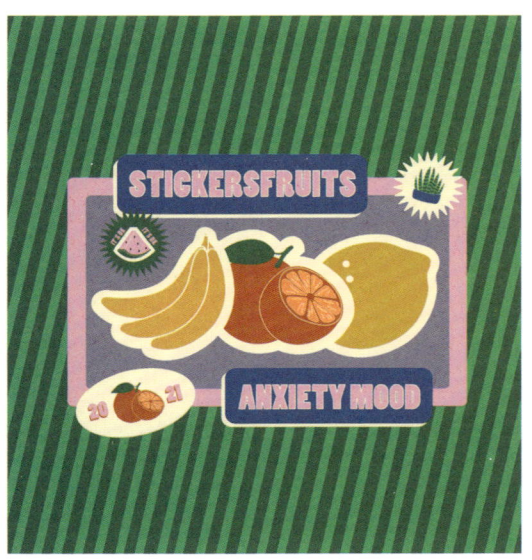

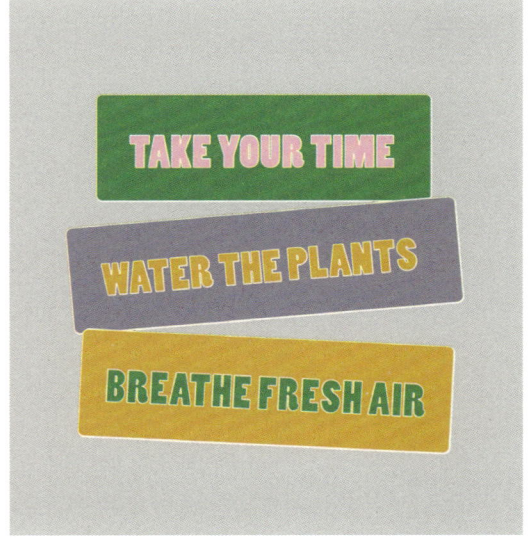

▼ **Color Scheme:**

R028 G125 B091	R050 G178 B126	R030 G193 B126	R015 G109 B073	R021 G160 B107	R003 G079 B048
C084 M027 Y072 K013	C073 M000 Y065 K000	C071 M000 Y065 K005	C087 M032 Y079 K022	C080 M008 Y072 K000	C092 M040 Y088 K044

R242 G177 B214	R211 G095 B009	R224 G185 B037	R142 G141 B178	R249 G245 B225
C035 M041 Y000 K000	C013 M071 Y100 K003	C014 M024 Y091 K002	C051 M044 Y015 K001	C004 M003 Y016 K000

RETRO AESTHETICS COLLECTION

This collection merges bold colors with nostalgic visuals, evoking the joy of childhood. Beyond retro aesthetics, it integrates functionality, tackling mental health and self-development. Focused on unique storytelling, it inspires a harmonious society. Using vivid imagery, the designs aim to positively impact viewers. The emphasis on practicality aligns with the designer's purpose, emphasizing everyone's ability to create. The collection serves as a testament to the power of unique creation without compromising functionality. It encourages individuals to contribute to building a harmonious society amidst chaos.

Designer: Michelle Chen

▼ **Inspiration:**

The designer drew inspiration from childhood animations such as *Barbie* and *The Powerpuff Girls*. Simple shapes, such as hearts, evoke a strong sense of nostalgia and are fascinating. Incorporating girly and feminine retro elements such as hearts and cakes reflects the designer's warm, sensual, playful, and soft-spoken identity. The dominant use of pink is consistent with her personality and beliefs. Although the designer is aware of retro trends, she does not completely conform; her creative direction questions and seeks ways to authentically present her designs.

▼ **Fonts:**

OffBit, Power Grotesk, Base Neue, PP Editorial Old, Bartex (often used in *Barbie*), Barbie Medium Italic (often used in *Barbie*), Acumin Variable Concept, DT Getai Grotesk Display, Cunia Bold

▼ **Layout:**

The designer maintained an organized and unique layout that is not only easy to read but also visually easy for the viewer to understand.

▼ Color Scheme:

R233 G087 B132	R248 G223 B233	R156 G241 B231	R046 G166 B217
C000 M078 Y020 K000	C002 M018 Y002 K000	C042 M000 Y009 K000	C071 M016 Y005 K000

FRUMMY

Frummy, a delightful soft caramel and chocolate product, is crafted to effortlessly melt atop one's favorite dessert. The main inspiration behind Frummy draws from mid-century advertising and retro food packaging. The creative concept is intricately woven to evoke a sense of nostalgia, transporting individuals to simpler times when sharing recipes with loved ones and spending quality time together held immense value. In reimagining these emotions, the team behind Frummy has developed a contemporary design, ensuring the project resonates with today's audience while retaining the timeless charm of the past.

Design Studio: Parametro Studio
Client: Jorge Llanderal

▼ **Inspiration:**

Inspired by various eras, a fusion of retro styles has been meticulously crafted. The main sources of inspiration include Betty Crocker and mid-century advertising. The design features groovy patterns that evoke the essence of a Pierre Cardin Collection from the 60s or the products pitched by Don Draper in *Mad Men* (a show).

▼ **Elements:**

Opting for modular pastel color blocks and a groovy shape inspired by retro patterns and melting caramel, the design team crafted a unique and eye-catching aesthetic.

▼ **Fonts:**

Customized logotype, Graphik Regular/Bold/Semi-Bold

▼ **Layout:**

The design studio created a modular layout using color blocks to segregate pertinent information without diverting attention from the design, reminiscent of a mid-century pattern. The primary graphic element is the 3D caramel effect, appearing to melt on the forefront.

▼ **Color Scheme:**

R227 G112 B072
C007 M068 Y070 K000
Pantone 1645 C

R229 G156 B155
C008 M048 Y029 K000
Pantone 5265 C

R234 G225 B208
C010 M012 Y019 K000
Pantone Pastel 9185 C

R060 G056 B091
C085 M085 Y048 K015
PANTONE Yellow U

R164 G173 B215
C040 M029 Y000 K000
Pantone 2113 C

FOUR ON THE FLOOR

NEW YORK DISCO

CHICAGO HOUSE

DETROIT TECHNO

This project explores the rich history of dance music through a series of posters, focusing on consecutive genres: disco, house, and techno. The title refers to the rhythmic pattern prevalent in much dance music, with four repetitive notes per bar creating optimal conditions for dancing. Initially inspired by early 20th-century travel posters, the project aims to examine the connection between place and music, revealing how technology, politics, and socio-economic conditions shaped these genres and their cultures.

The underlying theme reflects a profound love for dance music, which, starting underground, eventually gained mainstream recognition, occasionally reverting to its underground roots. Each genre featured pioneering sounds, unique fashion, and strong ties to social contexts challenging the status quo.

New York Disco

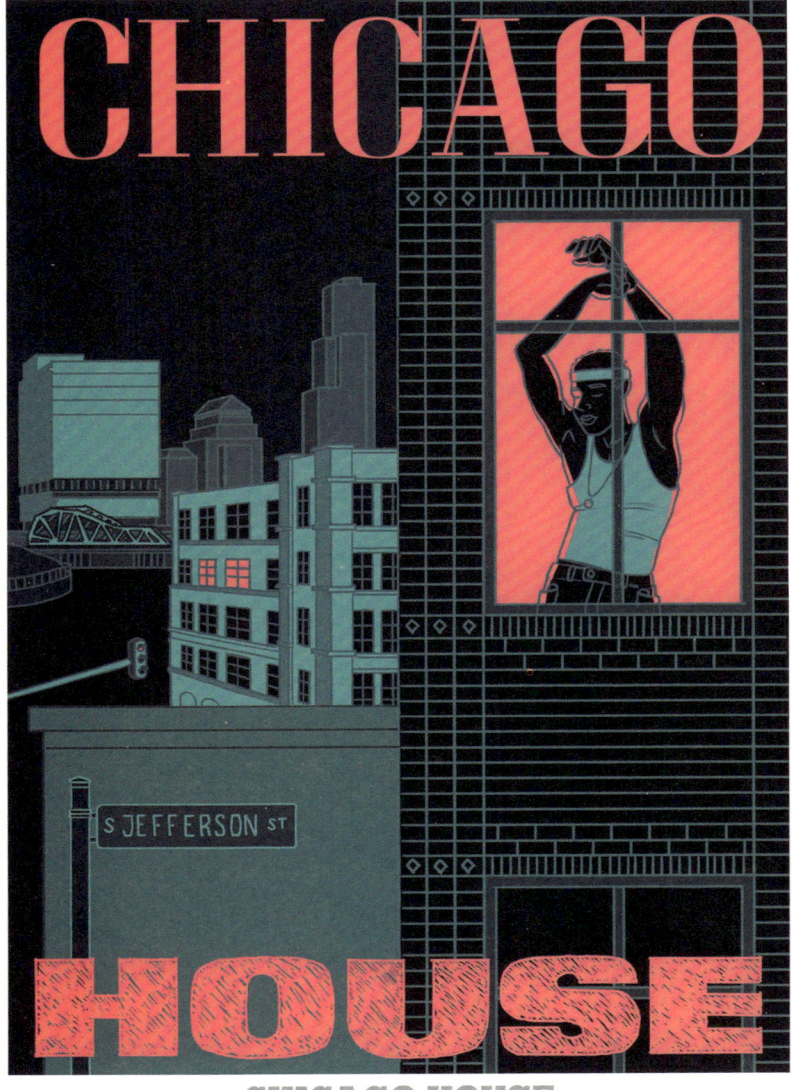

The work aims to convey the frivolity and sense of freedom fostered by LGBTQ+ nightclubs like The Loft and the Paradise Garage. It allowed marginalized communities, including Black, Latino, and Queer individuals, newfound access to exclusive nightlife.

Chicago House

The work specifically references the iconic "Warehouse" club, reflecting the latter half of the 20th century through typography, clothing, and architecture.

Detroit Techno

The work features buildings symbolizing the city's past as an industrial powerhouse, with ornate neoclassical styles recalling Detroit's economic boom as the "Motor City." However, the techno genre originated in response to Detroit's post-industrial status, using synths and drum machines to create futuristic sounds echoing the aspirations of Detroiters.

The project seeks to convey joy and expression through dance, drawing inspiration from genre-and-city-specific paraphernalia such as flyers, tickets, and posters. The *New Dance Show*, a television program established in 1988, played a major role in inspiring the use of neon, attention to fashion and hairstyles, and the overall energetic vibe of the project.

Design Studio: Megan Park Creative
Designer: Megan Park

▼ **Inspiration:**

Cultural Elements: The Second Summer of Love (a late-1980s social phenomenon in the United Kingdom which saw the rise of acid house music and unlicensed rave parties) The Paradise Garage a (New York City discotheque) Acid House (a subgenre of house music developed around the mid-1980s by DJs from Chicago)

Artists: Keith Haring, Peter Saville, David Mancuso, Frankie Knuckles, Larry Levan

Movies or TV: *Paris Is Burning, Blade Runner, The New Dance Show, The Loft*

Book: *The Hacienda*

▼ **Color Scheme:**

R085 G077 B151
C076 M075 Y007 K000

R234 G084 B032
C000 M080 Y090 K000

R000 G106 B120
C091 M051 Y049 K003

R233 G084 B123
C000 M080 Y027 K000

R233 G073 B067
C000 M084 Y067 K000

TAURUS SEASON

This project reflects a sticker sheet paying homage to the lively stickers that adorned the artist's childhood notebooks in the 1980s and 90s. Being a Taurus, the artist illustrated favorite elements like food, movies, music, nature, and a hint of 420. The collection also features beloved candies from the artist's childhood in Argentina, including Tita and Bocadito Holanda.

Designer: Marte

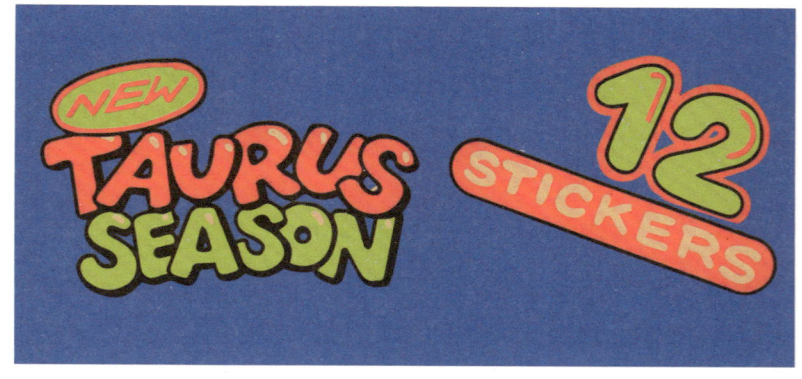

AINDA

The illustrations were crafted for two songs by the band Ainda, marking their initial exploration into a Pop sound. The artist sought to convey this transition through the selected style.

Designer: Marte

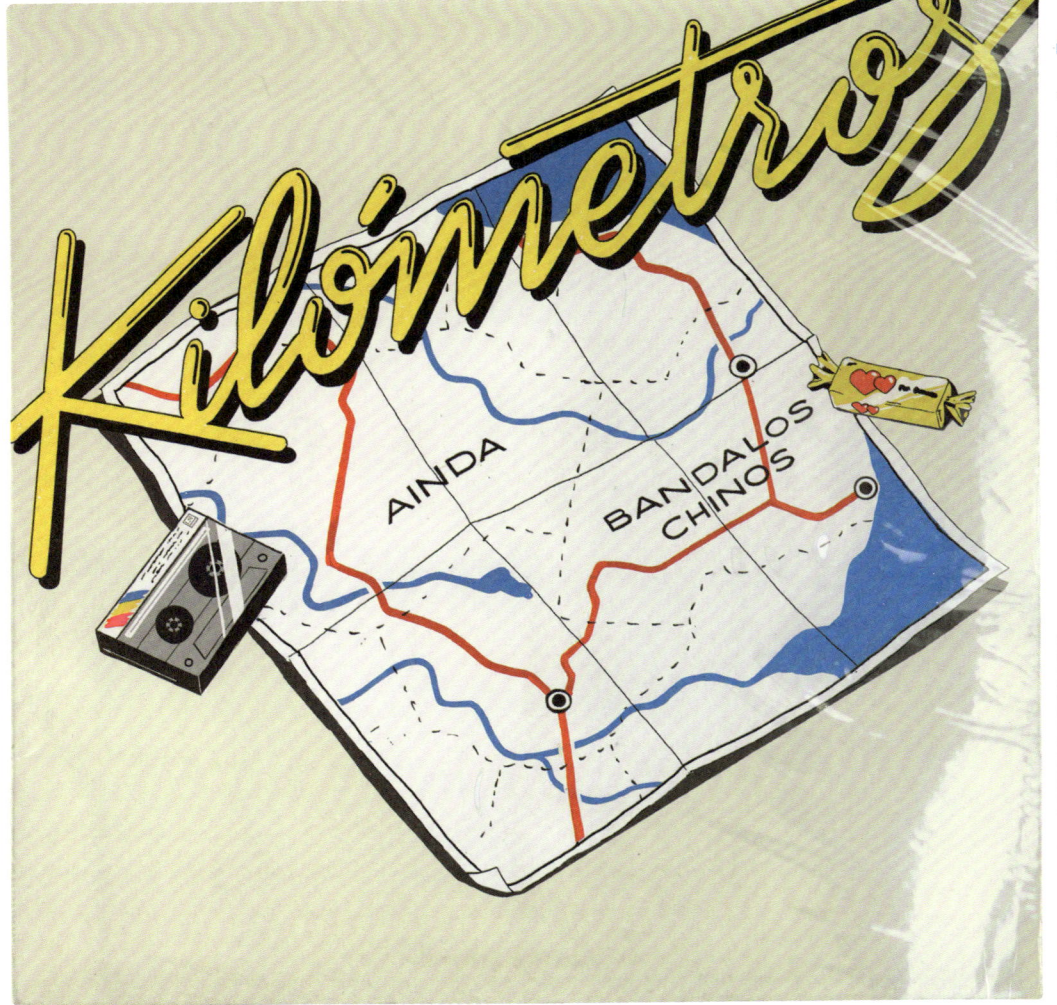

▼ **Inspiration:**
The designer was inspired by childhood things from the 1990s, such as MTV, the Nickelodeon TV channel, and candy.

▼ **Color Scheme:**

■ R047 G108 B181
C081 M053 Y000 K000

■ R041 G187 B228
C067 M000 Y007 K000

■ R244 G234 B00
C008 M000 Y097 K000

■ R232 G069 B141
C000 M084 Y006 K000

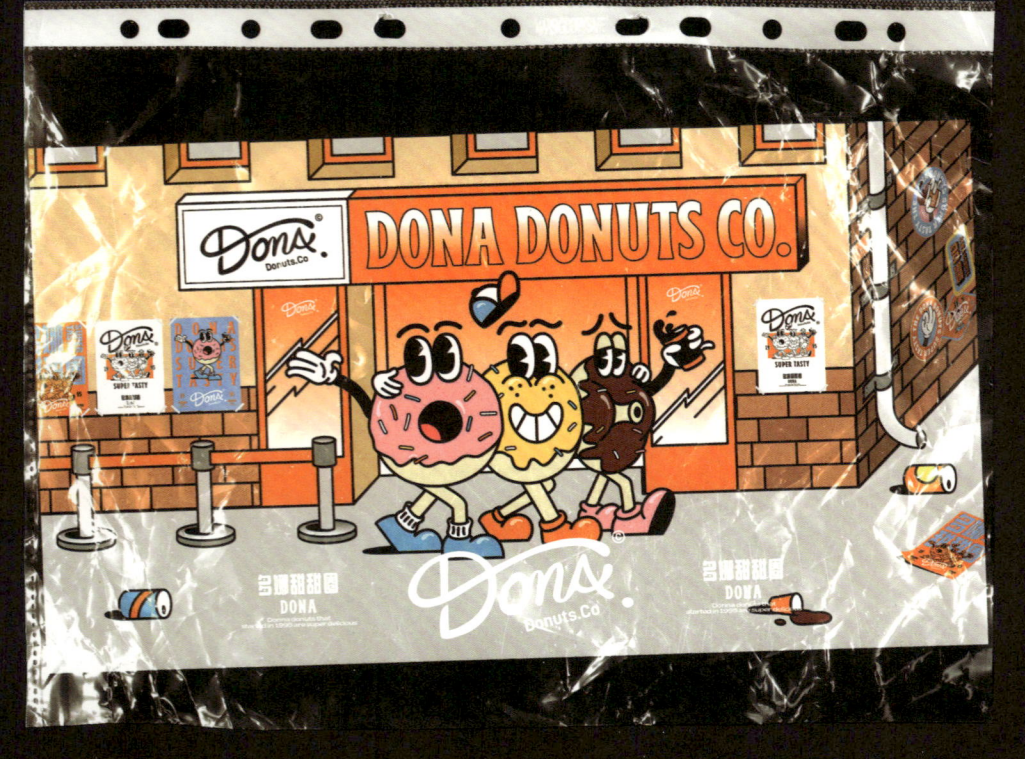

DONA DONUTS BRANDING

Dona Donuts, a sweet doughnut brand founded by a 60-year-old grandfather in the name of his daughter. He is now 75 years old. His wish is to see Dona Donuts continue in a more youthful way. The new brand manager, who took over, approached the designer with the desire to present Dona Donuts with a fresh, American retro visual. The overall brand visual centers around a doughnut as the main logo, and the packaging materials are designed in an American stickerstyle, presenting a fun, youthful, and rejuvenated American retro visual effect.

Design Studio: pigeonstudio
Designer: GEZI
Client: Dona Donuts

▼ Color Scheme:

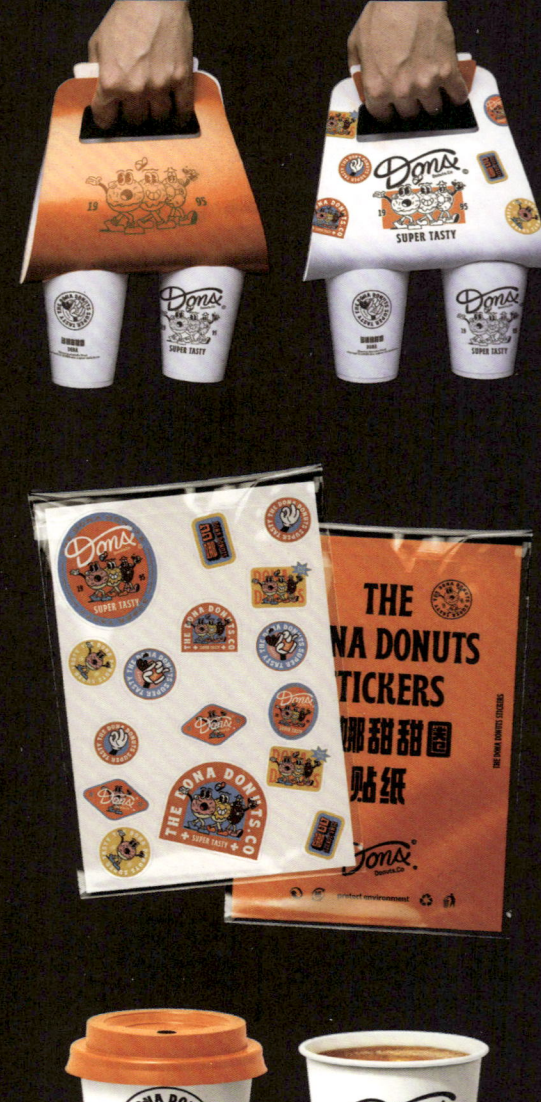

R236 G098 B023	R239 G139 B165	R253 G211 B083	R120 G023 B025
C000 M075 Y093 K000	C000 M058 Y014 K000	C000 M020 Y073 K000	C046 M098 Y098 K033

ORIGINAL WORKS BY DANIEL PELAVIN

BELT

Belt: The Belt Parkway illustration was created for *The New York Times* for a story covering a popular tourist and recreation area. The designer designed it in the style of a postcard, employing the large letter format to allow the interiors of the headline letters to showcase actual photos of the various features in the area.

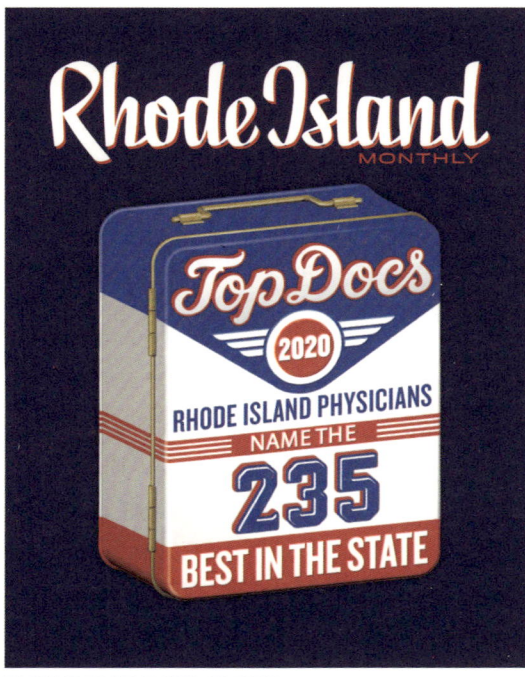

RHODE ISLAND

THE CROP CIRCLE

Rhode Island: The Top Docs cover for *Rhode Island Monthly* was designed for an article showcasing the finest doctors in Rhode Island. The designer conceptualized an image featuring a first aid kit to symbolize medicine, cleverly incorporating it to house the headline and cover lines.

The Crop Circle: The Crop Circle illustration was crafted for *Oprah Magazine* and featured in an issue addressing the prevention of waste in the farming industry. The designer designed it in the classic style of a fruit crate label, seamlessly integrating the headline and cover lines in a manner reminiscent of the text on an authentic label.

Illustrator: Daniel Pelavin

POSTERS BY FADLI RABBANI

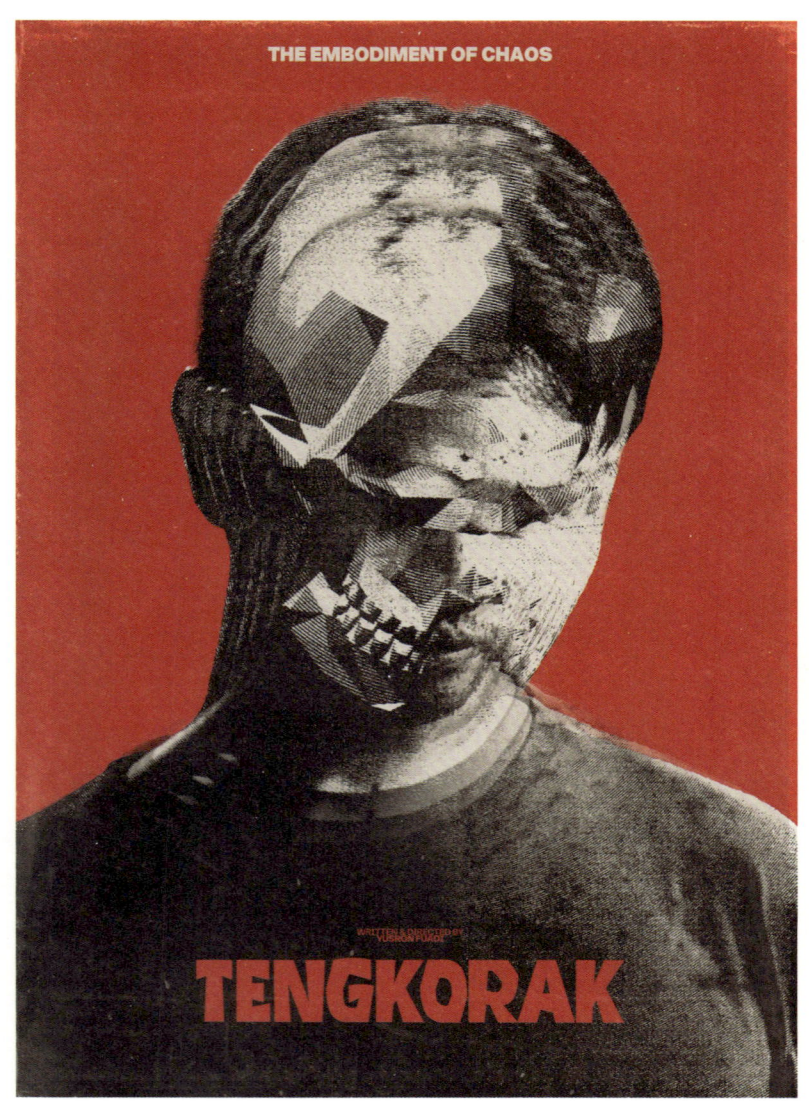

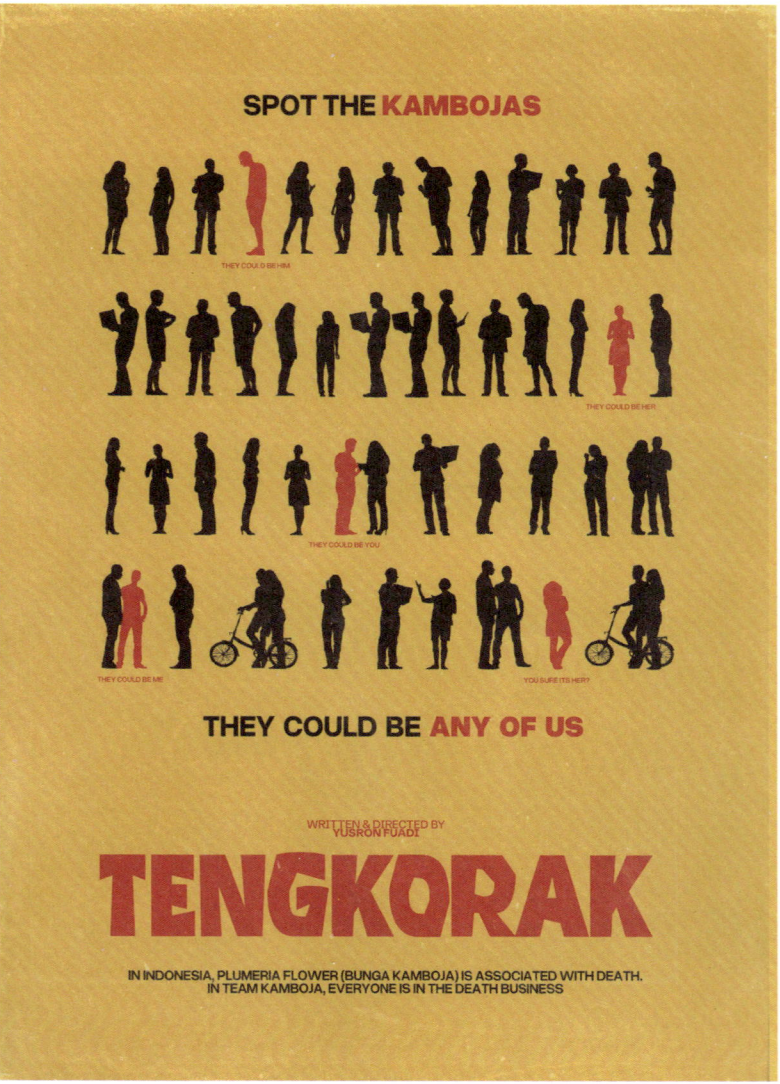

TENGKORAK

TENGKORAK

This project is a commission from Akasacara Film for their movie *Tengkorak*, released in 2018. After watching the movie for research purposes, the designer became fascinated by their filmmaking. It's raw, very "out-there," and doesn't follow traditional norms, aligning with my design philosophy.

This project is heavily influenced by Saul Bass's work and the resurgence of retro-minimalistic designs that have become a niche on social media platforms. Not to mention A24's arthouse approach, allowing their filmmakers to go wild when designing their posters and producing modern movie posters that don't play by the book.

SEE THE RED & AIR IT OUT

This project marks the first installment of his *BOLD EMOTIONS* series, where the designer will explore four emotions: anger, sadness, fear, and joy, sharing the personal experiences and how he dealt with them in daily life. In the initial piece, the designer aimed to visualize how anger affects him mentally. He depicted how he used to experience tunnel vision whenever he felt angry and now constantly question if such experiences are normal. In the second piece, the designer intended to convey how people can deal with anger by "airing it out" and emphasize that feeling anger is a normal human experience. One shouldn't suppress it, akin to how parents often advise their upset children.

The retro style of this project draws heavy inspiration from early *Thrasher* magazines and 80s editorials, explaining his preference for creating these projects in pairs. He often daydreams about seeing them showcased on magazine pages.

DEEP REST & ALONE IN A CROWD

This project is the second installment of the *BOLD EMOTIONS* series. In the first piece, the designer's aim was to show people who are currently struggling with this emotion that maybe all they need are some hugs and deep rest, and that they're not alone. In the second piece, he wanted to convey how social anxiety feels and how it can hold people's social lives back. Coming from an introvert, that's pretty ironic.

The designer took heavy inspiration from 80s magazines and how they could visualize and convey information by maximizing simple layouts.

Design Studio: Astaga Creatives
Designer: Fadli Rabbani
Client: Akasacara Film (TENGKORAK)

▼ Color Scheme:

R207 G028 B027 C016 M098 Y100 K000	R249 G195 B038 C004 M027 Y087 K000
R211 G047 B053 C014 M093 Y078 K000	R000 G000 B000 C000 M000 Y000 K100
R042 G102 B138 C085 M059 Y036 K000	R255 G255 B255 C000 M000 Y000 K000

▼ **Elements:**

TENGKORAK: The main focus of this poster is the protagonist of the movie *Tengkorak* (2018). He's an enigmatic person, and the designer tried to visualize his internal chaos by using multiple layers of his photo stacked on top of each other.

The element presented refers to a subplot of the movie that the designer found fascinating: the existence of a group of assassins who operate in the shadows and could be hiding among us.

SEE THE RED: The designer intended to visualize how he used to have tunnel vision whenever he got angry with a photo of an eye.

AIR IT OUT: The photo chosen for this design relates to the project's title. The designer wanted to convey the idea of releasing anger by airing it out.

DEEP REST: The main focus of this poster is a sketch depicting a person in distress. The designer chose a sketch instead of a normal photo to convey the raw, unfiltered emotion one might feel in such a situation.

ALONE IN A CROWD: The designer used a white block to block out everyone except the main subject (the girl), which visualizes the protagonist's social anxiety and loneliness.

▼ **Fonts:**

TENGKORAK:
Diabolik, Schibsted Grotesk

SEE THE RED & AIR IT OUT:
Libre Caslon Text, Mango Grotesque, Cygre

DEEP REST & ALONE IN A CROWD:
Schibsted Grotesk, RL Madena, Cygre

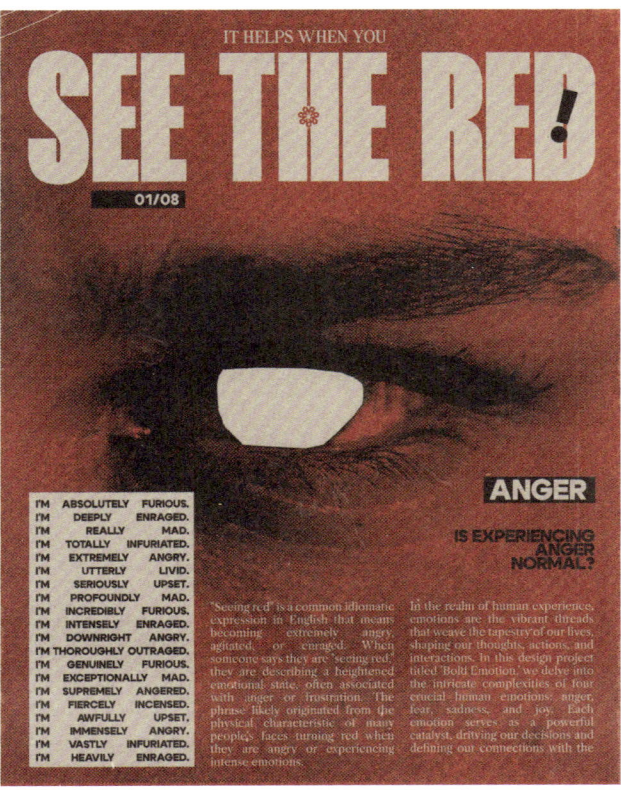

SEE THE RED

AIR IT OUT

DEEP REST

ALONE IN A CROWD

▼ **Layout:**

TENGKORAK: The layout is inspired by Saul Bass's works.

SEE THE RED: Inspired by 80s editorials, this design features bold headlines, a central subject, and smaller supporting texts, disrupted by a box with 20 sentences filled with anger.

AIR IT OUT: It is inspired by *Thrasher* magazine's use of action photographs to break boundaries and add dynamic movement to the design.

DEEP REST & ALONE IN A CROWD: The layout draws inspiration from the 80s editorial style of bold text, main subject, and smaller text, but the designer added his own twist by rearranging the smaller texts to avoid a "formulaic" look.

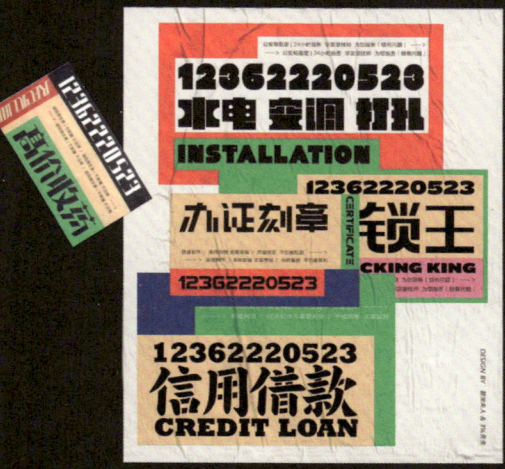

REDESIGN OF SMALL ADVERTISEMENTS

The project explores the graphic design features of urban "small advertisements" and aims to present them in a fresh way. Despite diverse owners with varying personalities and backgrounds, a universal and conventional expression is observed in the advertising forms used. The project team acknowledges that, despite being considered disruptors in an orderly environment, small ads add a vibrant, dynamic energy to the cityscape. To reflect this contradictory nature, designers experimented with unconventional design elements, such as bold color contrasts and versatile fonts. These techniques make the layout more dynamic, visually expressing the contradiction in these ads.

Design Studio: 3% Design Studio
Designer: Deng Xiongjun, Xiao Lv

▼ **Inspiration:** Advertisements, often viewed as interruptions in our living spaces, introduce a distinctive flair to everyday life. By integrating unconventional design elements such as rudimentary layouts, bold red-green color schemes, and enlarged fonts, these ads reveal a striking and simple beauty. This intriguing contrast serves as the team's primary inspiration for their exploration and creation of small ads. As the design team delved deeper into the allure of these seemingly "established crude," they were driven to discover whether the fusion of vibrant colors, innovative fonts, and unconventional layouts could create a unique aesthetic that challenges traditional design norms.

▼ **Elements:** Extracting representative actions or characteristic features from common tasks in small ads, such as unlocking, collecting medicine, drainage, hole punching, and seal engraving, serves as inspiration for font design. The intention is to incorporate visual or graphic structures into abstract fonts, allowing abstract text to convey concrete visual meanings.

▼ **Fonts:** Baltar-Regular, Five Double Zero Regular, Heron Sans SemiBold, MRockwell-ExtraBold, ROBOTECH GX, Metropolis ICG, Knockout-HTF94-UltmtSumo

▼ **Layout:** The entire layout is centered around the multi-level transmission of information. The collision of different colored blocks not only evokes a sense of retro, hustle-and-bustle atmosphere but also provides conditions for the multi-level transmission of information.

▼ **Color Scheme:**

■ R000 G188 B112	■ R243 G207 B178	■ R000 G096 B156
C081 M000 Y073 K000	C006 M025 Y035 K000	C100 M060 Y027 K000
Pantone 7480c	Pantone 475c	Pantone 3015c
■ R249 G127 B181	■ R251 G083 B115	
C002 M064 Y002 K000	C000 M080 Y037 K000	
Pantone 211c	Pantone 184c	

XIANGPIAOPIAO—BOBO MILK TEA

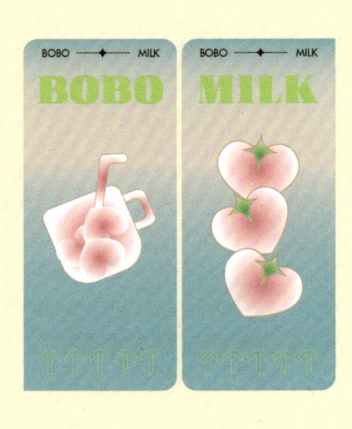

This project features captivating graphic elements and a distinct visual language. Skillfully blending lines and colors, it retains the brand's "smiling arc" signature while incorporating trendy, youthful, and innovative elements that resonate with the product's positioning as "Bobo Milk Tea." Equally impressive typeface design balances classic brand elements with subtle innovations, enhancing overall harmony. The concise yet distinctive icons effectively convey the product's core message, creating a strong visual impact. Vibrant hues in the color palette cater to young consumers' preferences, emphasizing the product's modern appeal.

Design Studio: Hellocean
Client: Xiangpiaopiao

▼ Color Scheme:

R137 G202 B167
C049 M000 Y042 K000

R244 G198 B190
C002 M030 Y020 K000

R000 G123 B089
C086 M038 Y077 K002

R252 G242 B209
C002 M005 Y022 K000

R121 G123 B185
C059 M051 Y001 K000

R090 G188 B180
C062 M002 Y035 K000

R236 G138 B111
C003 M057 Y051 K000

R185 G213 B084
C034 M000 Y078 K000

R105 G187 B200
C058 M007 Y022 K000

R123 G185 B088
C056 M005 Y080 K000

Y2K   HOLO

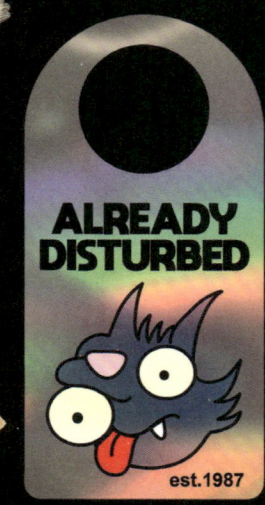

PERSONAL WORKS BY IGNORANCE1

These projects are the designer's personal works, which not only highlight his concern for current events but also infuse his emotional expression. For example, the works *XMAX* and *SUMMER* depict the emotional state of being restricted from going out during a pandemic, while *WAR* reflects his stance against any war during the Russian-Ukrainian conflict. He drew inspiration from many retro elements, such as iconic brands of the 2000s (*Y2K*) and vintage postal stamps (*STAMPS*), and reinterpreted them through a modern lens—Acid Design—breathing new life into these vintage elements. Additionally, he is actively exploring new design approaches, such as the use of holographic textures, which he extensively incorporates into his graphic experiments (*HOLO*).

Designer: IGNORANCE1

▼ **Fonts:**
Hybrid Outline, Whiskey Girls, Arial, Moon Get, Helvetica, SignPainter, DIN, AvantGarde, Heartless, Phat Freddy, PixelMix, Cooper

WAR

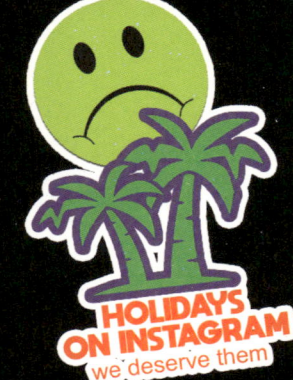

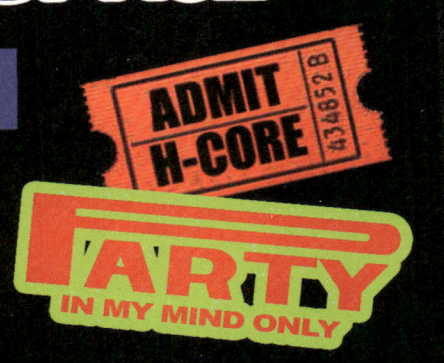

SUMMER

STAMPS

Manuel Cetina   The Designer Decade   384

90S AESTHETICS

The project is rooted in the nostalgia of elements and gadgets from the 90s, influenced by music, movies, and the vision of the near future with the arrival of 2000. The graphics are developed using the technology that accompanied individuals during the 90s and the way designers interacted with such technology.

Designer: Manuel Cetina

▼ **Inspiration:**

Futuristic movies: *12 Monkeys, Total Recall, Alien, RoboCop, The Terminator, Escape from L.A.*
Anime: *Akira, Ghost in the Shell, Neon Genesis Evangelion, Cowboy Bebop, Saint Seiya, Dragon Ball*
Culture: MTV and the Y2K tech craze

▼ **Elements:**
Vector illustration with halftone textures

▼ **Font:**
Hand-made fonts from Scratch

POSTER COLLECTIONS

A series of typographic and experimental posters, sharing the designer's daily on Instagram feed. Each piece in the collection resonates with dynamic energy, employing bold color schemes that pay homage to the vibrant and nostalgic aesthetics of 1980s–2000s cartoons, shows, and advertisements.

Designer: Osheyi.A

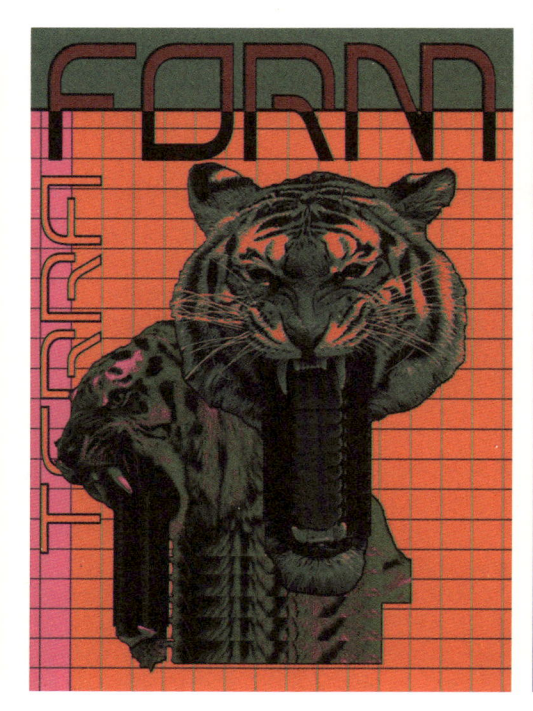

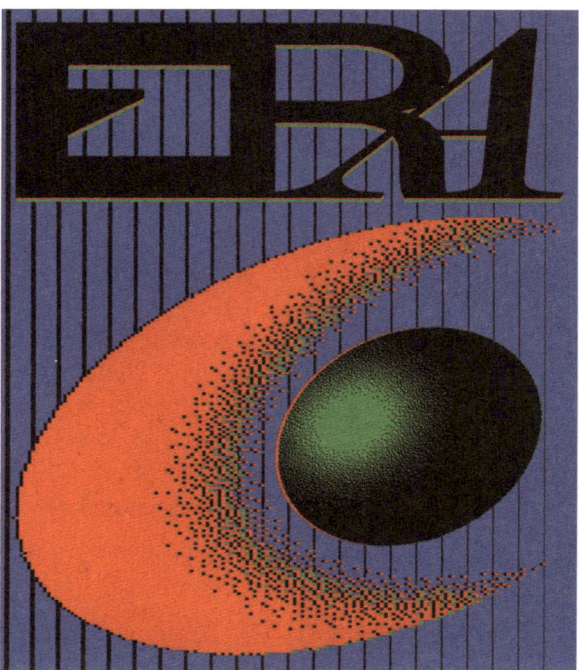

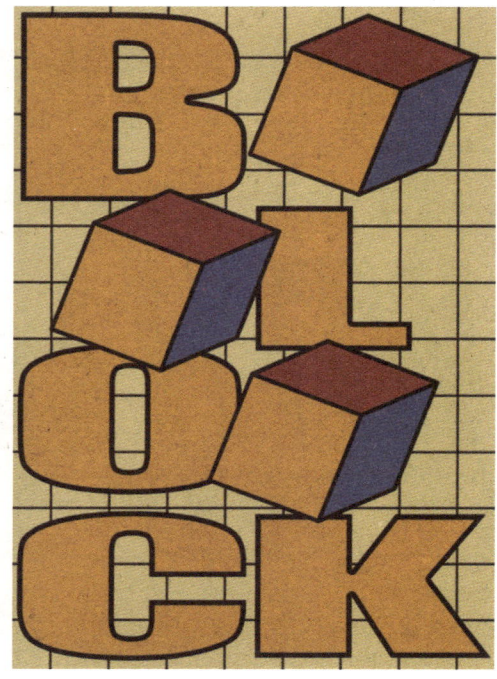

ROLLIN WITH LEON

The designer crafted experimental poster designs tailored for DJ Leon's event performances. These designs fuse a playful typographic style with a vibrant palette, creating a kaleidoscope of colors that evokes a retro ambiance. The result is a visual manifestation that authentically captures and conveys the dynamic and electric vibe of the event.

Designer: Osheyi.A

▼ Color Scheme:

R177 G031 B036 / C034 M100 Y100 K001	R248 G181 B076 / C000 M036 Y074 K000	R026 G042 B080 / C096 M091 Y049 K026
R027 G113 B160 / C084 M049 Y021 K000	R000 G084 B045 / C091 M054 Y100 K027	R216 G103 B116 / C013 M071 Y040 K000
R213 G014 B038 / C012 M100 Y089 K000	R232 G118 B065 / C004 M065 Y075 K000	R247 G206 B201 / C001 M026 Y016 K000
R038 G044 B141 / C095 M093 Y036 K000	R011 G081 B091 / C091 M063 Y057 K018	R159 G029 B062 / C042 M100 Y071 K005
R230 G109 B061 / C005 M069 Y076 K000	R058 G119 B078 / C080 M044 Y082 K003	R255 G255 B255 / C000 M000 Y000 K000
R219 G104 B163 / C010 M071 Y001 K000	R000 G145 B156 / C081 M025 Y038 K000	R000 G000 B000 / C000 M000 Y000 K100

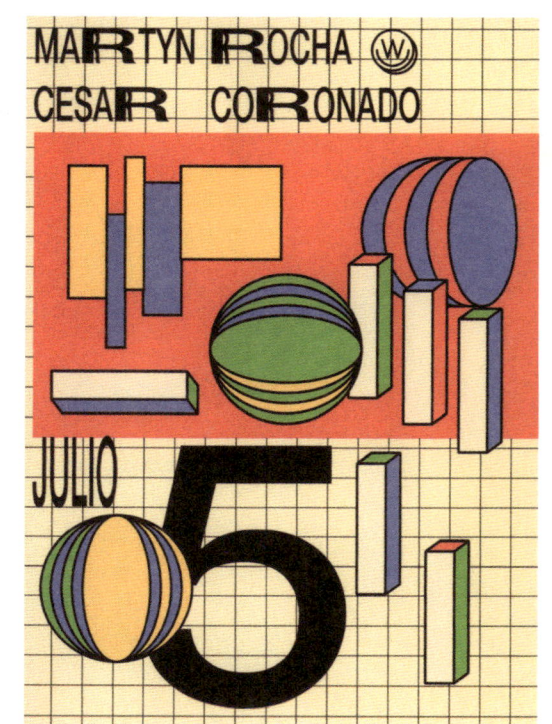

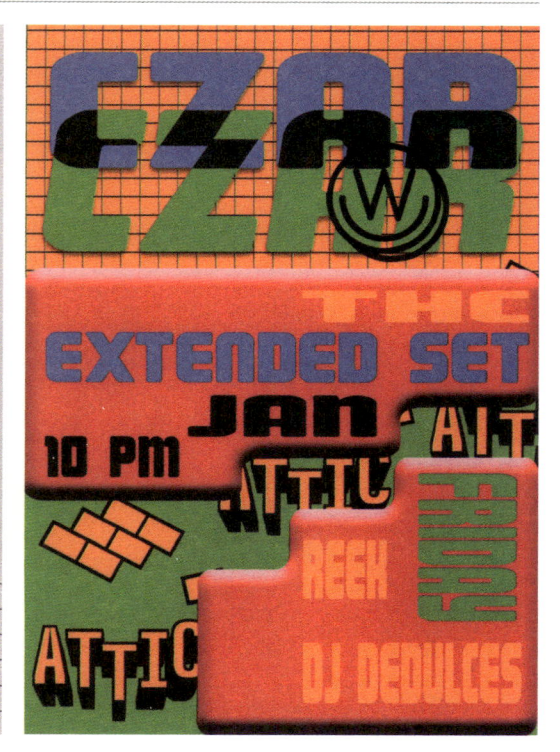

WHEREHOUSE ATTIC

These posters are for Wherehouse Attic, a music venue in Mexico. In this project, the designer delved into an experimental realm, exploring a diverse range of layout designs and illustrative elements. The resulting posters emanate a captivating retro aesthetic reminiscent of club posters from the 90s.

Designer: Osheyi.A

ORIGINAL WORKS BY JUAN MOLINET

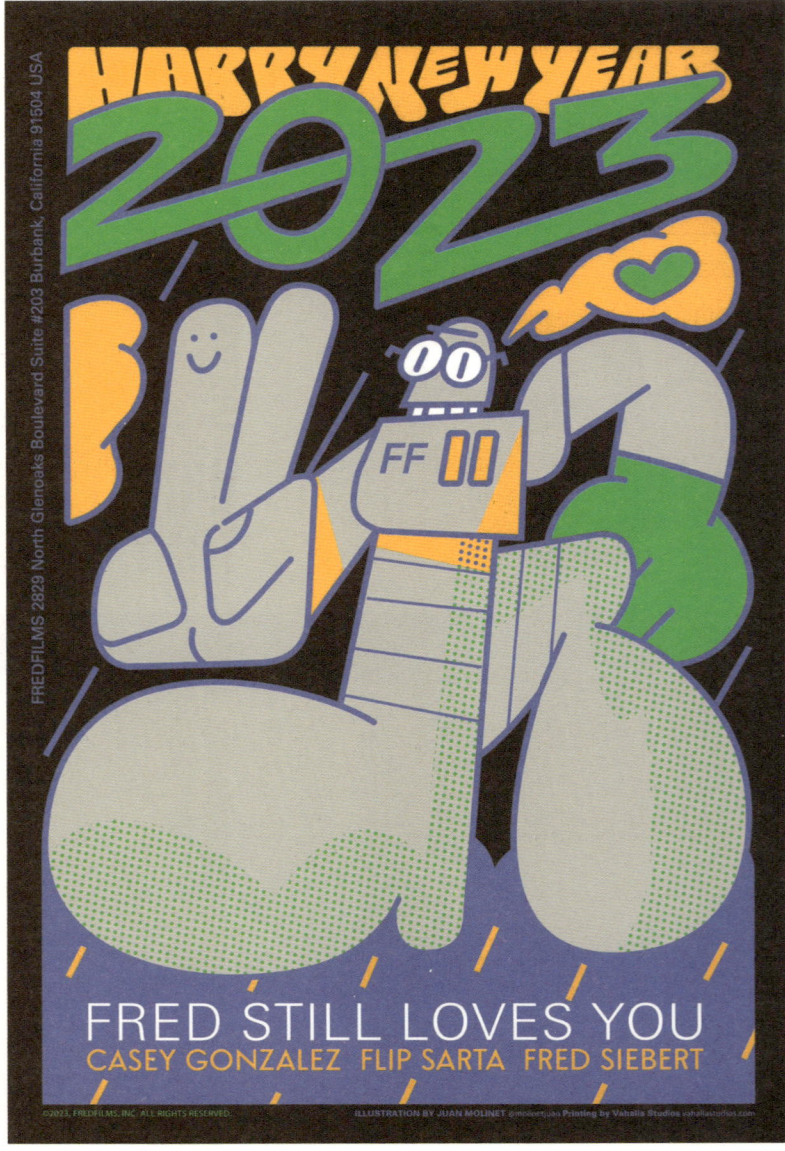

BERLIN ANIMATION FESTIVAL POSTER

FRED NEW YEAR POSTER

PING PONG MAFIA

Berlin Animation Festival Poster:

The designer was asked by Innocean Berlin Agency to produce a poster for the Berlin Animation Festival.

Fred New Year Poster:

This one is a New Year poster the designer made for Frederator Studios.

Ping Pong Mafia:

This is a spontaneous exercise project for the designer.

Designer: Juan Molinet

▼ **Elements:**

In the *Berlin Animation Festival Poster* and *Fred New Year Poster* works, the designer's distinctive and consistent style is unmistakably evident.

In *Ping Pong Mafia*, the designer introduced motion to the ping-pong ball with dynamic lines, disrupting the static nature of the image and reinforcing the "Mafia" theme.

WAUTERS

These posters are promotional flyers the designer made for various Juan Wauters Tours in various regions.

Designer: Juan Molinet

▼ **Elements:**

In addition to the unique character depictions, the artist incorporated music-related elements, like guitars and musical notes, into the poster to align with the music tours.

▼ **Color Scheme:**

- R046 G079 B022
  C072 M036 Y100 K054
- R084 G181 B087
  C066 M000 Y082 K000
- R075 G095 B170
  C077 M063 Y000 K000
- R159 G197 B233
  C041 M013 Y000 K000
- R232 G054 B015
  C000 M091 Y099 K000
- R250 G189 B000
  C000 M031 Y100 K000

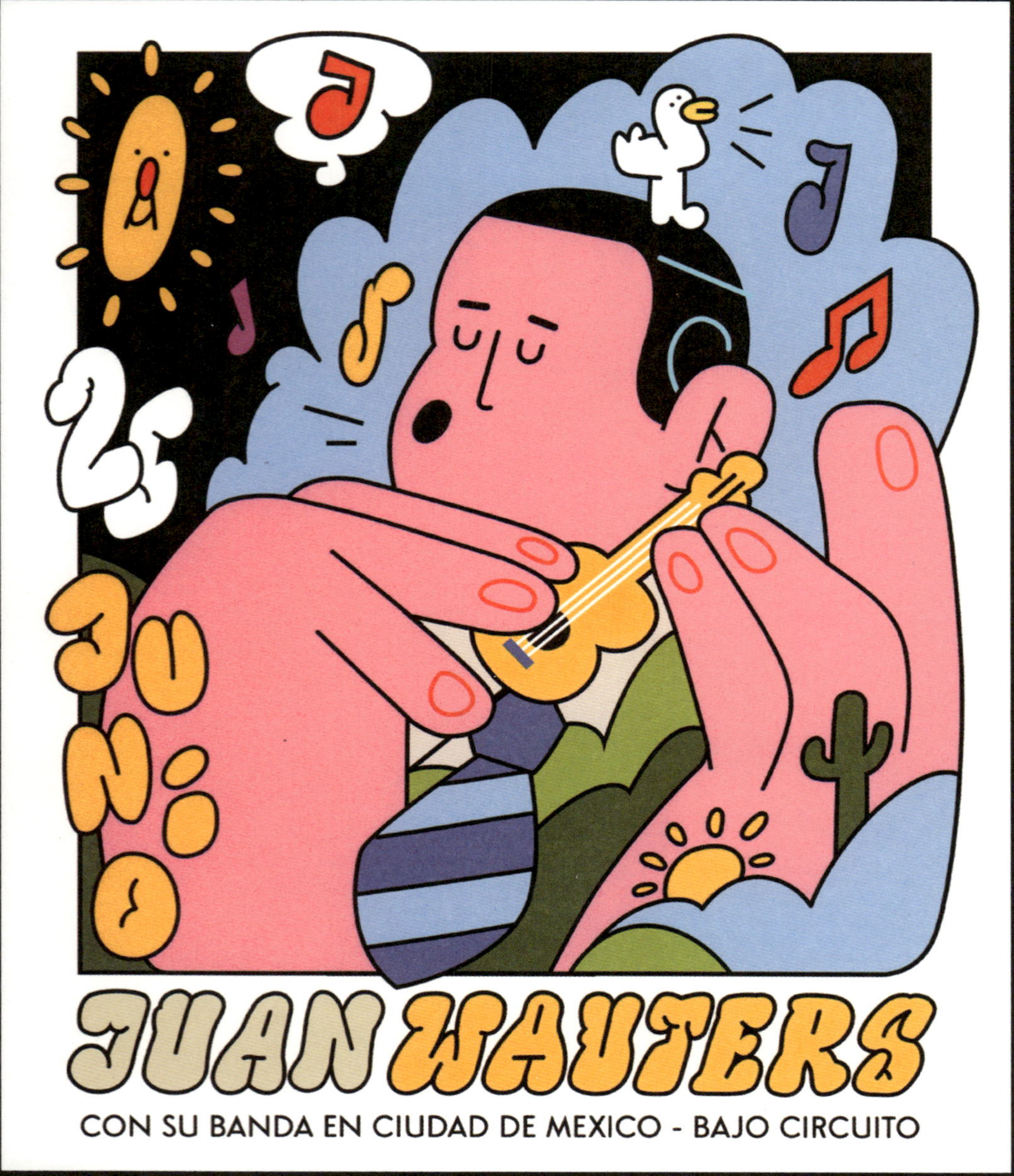

25
JUNIO
JUAN WAUTERS
CON SU BANDA EN CIUDAD DE MEXICO - BAJO CIRCUITO

CON SU BANDA
EN BOGOTÁ

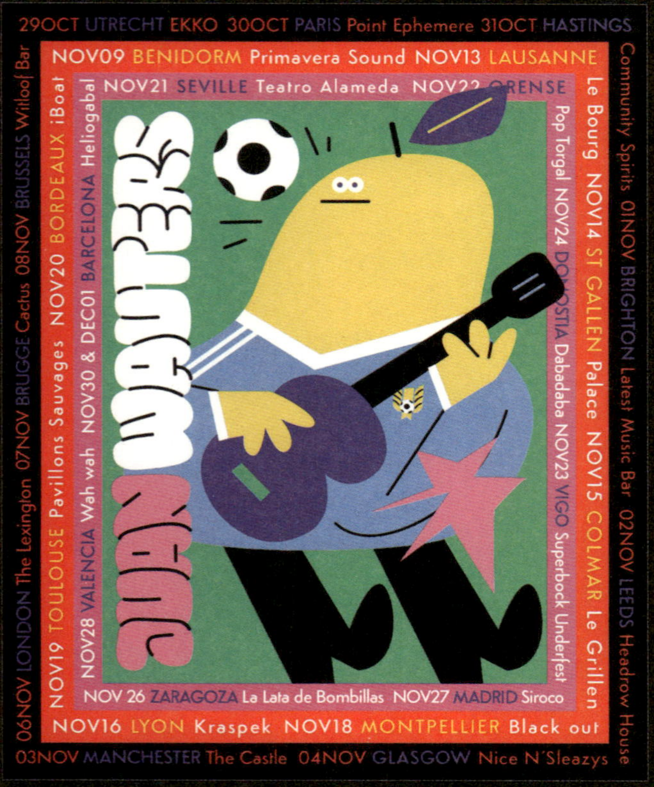

29OCT UTRECHT EKKO 30OCT PARIS Point Ephemere 31OCT HASTINGS
Community Spirits 01NOV BRIGHTON Latest Music Bar 02NOV LEEDS Headrow House
03NOV MANCHESTER The Castle 04NOV GLASGOW Nice N'Sleazys
06NOV LONDON The Lexington 07NOV BRUGGE Cactus 08NOV BRUSSELS Witloof Bar
NOV09 BENIDORM Primavera Sound NOV13 LAUSANNE
Le Bourg NOV14 ST GALLEN Palace NOV15 COLMAR Le Grillen
NOV16 LYON Kraspek NOV18 MONTPELLIER Black out
NOV19 TOULOUSE Pavillons Sauvages NOV20 BORDEAUX iBoat
NOV21 SEVILLE Teatro Alameda NOV22 ORENSE
Pop Torgal NOV24 DONOSTIA Dabadaba NOV23 VIGO Superbock Underfest
NOV 26 ZARAGOZA La Lata de Bombillas NOV27 MADRID Siroco
NOV28 VALENCIA Wah wah NOV30 & DEC01 BARCELONA Heliogabal
JUAN WAUTERS

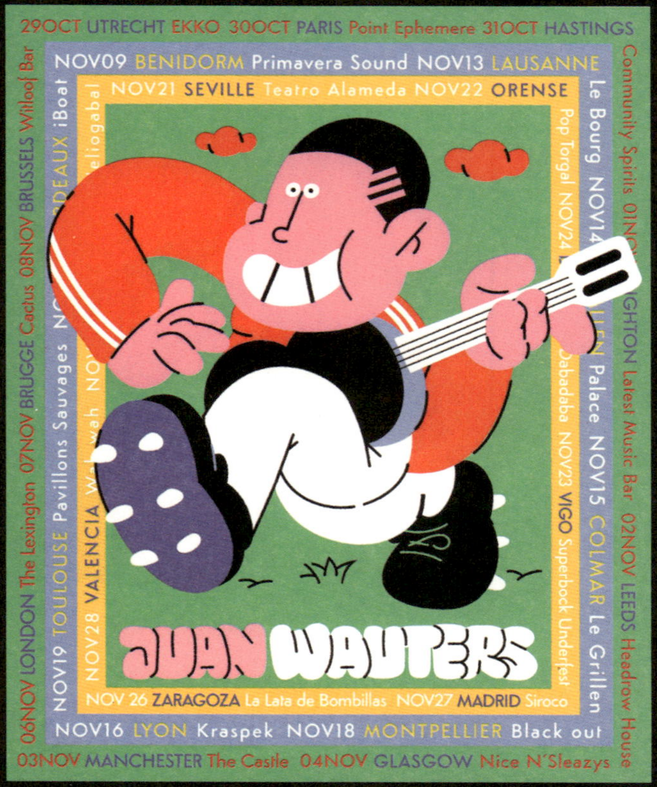

29OCT UTRECHT EKKO 30OCT PARIS Point Ephemere 31OCT HASTINGS
Community Spirits 01NOV BRIGHTON Latest Music Bar 02NOV LEEDS Headrow House
03NOV MANCHESTER The Castle 04NOV GLASGOW Nice N'Sleazys
06NOV LONDON The Lexington 07NOV BRUGGE Cactus 08NOV BRUSSELS Witloof Bar
NOV09 BENIDORM Primavera Sound NOV13 LAUSANNE
NOV16 LYON Kraspek NOV18 MONTPELLIER Black out
NOV21 SEVILLE Teatro Alameda NOV22 ORENSE
NOV 26 ZARAGOZA La Lata de Bombillas NOV27 MADRID Siroco
JUAN WAUTERS

TERS
LUB
23 DE JUNIO

Juan WAUTERS
JUNE 1st Hudson, NY The Half Moon 2 Freeport, ME Desert of Maine 3 Cambridge, MA Lilypad
4 Philly, PA Kung Fu Necktie 6 Columbus, OH Rumba Café 7 Louisville, KY Portal 8 Rock Island, IL Rozz Tox
9 Chicago, IL Avondale Music Hall 10 Detroit, MI Lager House 12 Atlanta, GA The Earl 13 Charlotte, NC Petra's
14 Washington, DC Comet Ping Pong 27 Seattle, WA Substation 28 Portland, OR Doug Fir
30 San Francisco, CA Cafe du Nord JULY 1st Modesto, CA Greens on Tenth 2 Los Angeles, CA ECHO
3 San Diego, CA Voodoo Room @House of Blues 5 Phoenix, AZ The Rebel Lounge 6 Tucson, AZ Club Congress
7 Albuquerque, NM Sister 8 Denver, CO Hi-Dive 10 Oklahoma, OK Res Head 11 Austin, TX The Ballroom
12 Houston, TX White Oak Music Hall 13 Denton, TX Rubber Gloves 14 Nashville, TN Third Man 16 Brooklyn, NY Brooklyn Made
FROM URUGUAY TO THE WORLD
TOUR
JW
JUAN WAUTERS AND HIS BAND
U.S.A
2023

J
u
a
W
a
u
t
e
r
s
JUAN WAUTERS EUROPE 2022 TOUR
MARCH 6 Dublin The Grand Social 7 Glasgow Broadcast 10 London Village Underground
12 Amsterdam Paradiso 13 Köln Acephale 15 Berlin Patchwerk 16 Copenhaguen Loppen
17 Budapest Turbina 18 Warsaw Hydrozagadka 19 St Gallen Palace St. Gallen 21 Paris Le Petit Bain
22 Antwerp Trix 23 Liege Kultur 24 Brussels Botanique 25 Bordeaux TBC 27 Madrid Sala Sol
29 Barcelona La Nau 30 San Sebastián Dabadaba APRIL 2 Valencia La Marina

Juan WAUTERS
BERLIN
LONDON
BRUSSELS
BARCELONA
PARIS
EUROPEAN TOUR
NOVEMBER SP 1 Barcelona Razz 2 2 Madrid Copernico 3 San Sebastián Dabadaba 4 Bilbao Jazzon Aretoa
5 Ourense Café Torgal FRANCE 7 Bordeaux IBOAT 8 Paris La Marbrerie UK 9 London Oslo
10 Cornwall Cornish Bank BELGIUM 12 Brussels Botanique (Witloof Bar) GERMANY 13 Berlin Franzz Club
14 Köln King Georg NETHERLANDS 16 Groningen Vera DENMARK 17 Copenhaguen Rust

#TheDesignerDecadeDesignTalk

1. What do you consider the most representative elements of 1980s retro aesthetics?

Estudio Pum
We believe that there is so much stuff that represents the 1980s, like color, pattern, type, and layout design. However, all those references are also so mixed in our pop culture today that sometimes we do not even notice them. For us, it's all about recognizing those dark references from some show, maybe some TV ads, or from some package from a toy that you instantly see and that bring you back to when you were a kid.

Fadli Rabbani (from Astaga Creatives)
I find their analog approach mesmerizing; their limitations forced them to think outside the box so they could communicate through their designs. It's pretty cool that, even with all the modern tools at their disposal, new designers are still trying to emulate that analog feel.

Florencia Leonardini (from Helloflostudio)
Among the most iconic elements of this aesthetics are easily reproducible vector shapes and vibrant colors. Contemporary design borrows from these elements, adapting them to various needs and prioritizing functionality while maintaining a lively morphology. Nowadays, these concepts influence brand identity designs, even those aiming for seriousness. The subtle nod to the '80s in these designs is commendable, illustrating the designer's ability to blend inspiration from past eras into a fresh, communicative world.

IGNORANCE1
I would say the characters, definitely. I think that when I started developing my own style, I ripped off a lot of them. Even if some of them were born long before the 1980s, they achieved success during these years. The Haribo character, Cookie Monster, Playmobil, Super Mario, Sonic, and all the others are characters from 80s video games. I think these still have a lot of influence on contemporary design, and they helped build a certain fresh style in graphic design during the last decade.

Michelle Chen
I'd say the rainbow band distortion from VHS tapes, the 8-bit designs from the Game Boy, and the UI design of the Windows 97 PC. I feel like these elements are not arbitrary but, in fact, a reminiscence of childhood and a thriving desire to bring back the "simpler times." It is one part of growing up that the majority of us share. For instance, some people might use these elements of their childhood nostalgia in their artwork to create a sense of playfulness, while others might use them to evoke a sense of nostalgia for a simpler time. This could be done by using muted colors, sepia tones, and nostalgic imagery.

Onion Design Associates
Post-modernism, New Wave, Memphis design, Wolfgang Weingart, April Greiman, QuarkXPress, grid lines, Emigre font, Mr. Keedy, skateboarding, flying geometric shapes with bright and neon colors, early 3D design, Duran Duran, Dire Straits, hair metal, cassette tapes and VHS, checkerboard patterns, airbrush, pink flamingos, *Terminator* series, *Back to the Future* series, Walkman, Game Boy, Michael Jordan, digital watches...

Oscar Bastidas
In my opinion, no specific element distinctly stands out for me from the 80s. While I could mention music and the 8-bit aesthetics, I believe that using less obvious references leads to a more successful final result. Therefore, I strive to incorporate elements of nostalgia that haven't been previously explored, aiming to differentiate the brand with a unique aesthetics.

Parametro Studio
For us, the most representative elements from the 80s include computer and video game graphics, synthesizer sounds, big hairstyles, neon colors, geometric shapes, and bold typographies. These influences have been reinterpreted in various ways, such as in music, fashion, architecture, and design, incorporating new technologies.

Rita
For me, it's all about vibrant neon colors, VHS aesthetics, bold patterns, and oversized silhouettes. Additionally, the 1980s were marked by a fascination with technology, evident in the prevalence of computer graphics, digital fonts, and pixel designs. Nowadays, these elements are experiencing a resurgence. Neon colors are making a comeback in fashion and interior design, while designers are incorporating geometric shapes, patterns, and gradients to evoke nostalgia for the 80s. Contemporary creators are blending retro aesthetics with a modern, minimalist approach, maintaining the boldness and vibrancy while refining the overall look.

2. When working on retro-style projects, are there specific elements or techniques that you frequently employ to showcase your personality and unique creative expression?

Estudio Pum
Not really. I believe it is not a specific element or technique. For us, it is about finding that reference to something that represented that "era" and stressing that thing to the limit.

Fadli Rabbani (from Astaga Creatives)
I enjoy incorporating flaws into my designs, whether it's by adding textures, halftones, or imperfections on top of the designs or incorporating flaws directly into the designs themselves. By limiting myself to what was possible in that analog-driven era, those little touches, in my opinion, really add up and elevate designs to a new level. I firmly believe that if designers start to experiment and do not restrain themselves by modern rules, they could all create interesting designs reminiscent of those from the past.

Florencia Leonardini (from Helloflostudio)
Inevitably, when selecting color palettes, I tend to gravitate towards a retro style, as it naturally aligns with my design sensibilities. While adapting to project requirements is crucial, leaving a personal mark through distinctive details or design choices is equally significant. I believe designers can consistently bring a refreshing touch to their proposals by integrating typography seamlessly with illustrations, creating a cohesive and distinctive visual narrative.

IGNORANCE1
I think that the specific elements that characterized my style the most are the artworks put inside the plastic bags and the stamps. These are elements I took from the past and reinterpreted in a modern style while preserving their vintage touch.

Michelle Chen
I occasionally pair many different typefaces in one setting as part of my go-to technique. I would normally combine serif, decorative, and script/calligraphic typefaces together to make them look unified. Apart from incorporating various typefaces, I always opt for abstract imagery visualizations using shapes and realistic objects. I feel like this gives a whole new set of perspectives to the audience and challenges them to see or think in a unique way. I believe there are some traditional retro design elements that can still be reinterpreted using different mediums (including traditional ones). Not necessarily sticking to illustrations, but it can be done using doodles, 3D, presenting them through augmented reality, or even creating multiple layers to produce a parallel effect. This way, we can bring childhood nostalgia back to life or evoke a sense of "closeness" to them.

Onion Design Associates
In fact, retro design is one of my favorite techniques. I am always interested in incorporating elements from the past throughout design history or even art history. For example, Vintorian typography, Arts and Crafts style, Vienna Secession, Art Nouveau, Art Deco, Streamline Moderne, Early Modern, Late Modern, Swiss style, Psychedelic, American Kitsch, and German Expressionism woodcut. I have been trying to pay homage to every single historical period in one project if I could.

Oscar Bastidas
I believe that the less obvious the reference used, the more successful the final result. That's why I strive to incorporate elements of nostalgia that haven't been explored before, aiming to create a unique aesthetics.

Parametro Studio
Our process focuses on conceptual exploration, adhering to the essence of what we aim to express. Understanding the social, cultural, and historical context of each design movement is crucial for its reinterpretation in the contemporary world. We firmly believe that genuine innovation arises from the interplay between the unconventional and the conventional, the raw and the refined, providing a unique perspective on current culture.

Rita
Vibrant colors and rounded shapes are signature elements of my style. I aim to create a cute and playful aesthetics, often enhancing it with glow effects and a subtle VHS aesthetics for a nostalgic feel. And traditional retro motifs like Pixel Art, cassette tapes, and video game references still hold appeal and can be creatively reinterpreted to captivate audiences with their mysterious yet beautiful designs.

3. The retro aesthetics of the 1980s were not only popular in Western culture but also had a global influence. Have you ever attempted to incorporate elements from different cultures into your designs?

Erin Chen
The 1980s were a vibrant era globally, and individuals from every country have their own memories of the '80s. Personally, I am particularly interested in and focused on incorporating retro elements from China's 1980s. While these Chinese retro elements are seldom mentioned in global popular culture, they hold significant importance for the Chinese people.

Estudio Pum
We love anime, and we are very familiar with Japanese pop culture, so we enjoy introducing logos or lettering in foreign languages in our designs and illustrations.

Fadli Rabbani (from Astaga Creatives)
As a designer who appreciates the vibrant and nostalgic vibe of 80s magazines, I find inspiration in the diverse color palettes, typography styles, and graphic patterns that were prominent in magazines from various parts of the world during that era, especially 80s skater magazines and their overall culture. Their unapologetic rawness and rebellious "not playing by the rules" attitude have genuinely sparked my recent creations and shaped my identity as a designer. Embracing these influences, I aim to infuse my work with the same energy and creativity.

Florencia Leonardini (from Helloflostudio)
In all the projects I've worked on, I've successfully adapted to the brand or project's unique world, considering they often originated from different countries with distinct visions. Designing for an audience with a different imaginative backdrop than my own is consistently challenging, yet the gratification comes when witnessing the finished result—cohesive and functional.

IGNORANCE1
Apart from the elements, I like to play a lot with the mix of different languages in my creation, such as English and Asian typography.

Michelle Chen
I've tried incorporating various elements into my designs, but I often find that they don't align with my personality or represent me authentically. When I experiment with different techniques, I feel it dilutes my problem-solving nature. I strive to keep my designs meaningful, ensuring people can take something away from them. While I'm open to experimentation, staying true to my beliefs is paramount.

Oscar Bastidas
I am from Caracas, Venezuela, a country that used to welcome people from all over the world seeking a better future. Due to this, I grew up with a multicultural heritage, and I believe that my aesthetic is shaped by the diverse influences I've accumulated over the years.

Parametro Studio
We are continually inspired by different eras, cultures, and design movements. Understanding how they perceive things keeps us inspired and open to adopting new ways of seeing and communicating.

Rita
Indeed, my art style is heavily influenced by Japanese anime and manga, which often infuse retro vibes with their own unique and captivating visuals. These cultural influences have instilled in me a love for all things cute and rounded. In essence, my design aesthetics wouldn't be complete without that characteristic chunkiness.

1980S CHAT ROOM

Please share your thoughts as a designer on the future of retro design trends and how you perceive the issue of homogenization within retro design.

Angello Torres (from Studio Angello Torres)

"Every trend eventually becomes corporate and functional for the market, and the retro style is no exception. Personally, I don't think it's healthy for design to follow the logic of visual globalization. Recently, social networks have been filled with retro designs that repeat the same colors, compositions, and effects. Luckily, there are great talents around the world who have a low profile and are managing to re-interpret from their place and culture this retro style with freshness and graphic sensitivity."

Arrivedlate

"I love the resurgence of the future retro design trend across music, photography, design, and fashion! There's a comforting joy in encountering designs and media that connect us to a familiar past, even for those who didn't live through it. The designers of that era created a timeless influence that continues to inspire today. As a society, we won't be able to escape homogenization, which is precisely why designers must persist in their craft and why publications should actively showcase and preserve these designs. Even if the trend fades from the spotlight, a fresh wave of designers and artists will emerge. It's our role to help them discover these archives so they can carry the torch forward."

Bern Foster

"I think it may turn repetitive the way new digital designers are making new retro art, as all looks are made by the same digital artist with no identity."

Brando Corradini

"Retro design has always played a significant role across past, present, and future generations. Video games keep these design trends alive and relevant, making them a visible part of our lives. With AI, the future is truly real; you can no longer distinguish fiction from reality. This is disturbing, but necessary. We hope not to return to agriculture in the future."

CHENBO

"'Future' and 'retro' are relative concepts; what we consider futuristic today may become the retro of tomorrow. The future of retro design should blend 'ancient' and 'modern' elements seamlessly. To address the issue of homogenization, the key to creating innovative designs lies in the integration of new and diverse elements."

CH_LAB

"When documenting an era or exploring a classic design style, it is inevitable that thoughts and forms will be on the same wavelength. Whether it's retro design or a new wave of creativity, the energy of a design can vary across different environments."

Diego L Rodriguez (Paranoidme)

"I believe that future trends are always hidden in the past. It's not about reviving a specific period of time; it's about how certain ideas from the past land in the future and resonate with us. The human brain and memory are powerful time machines, and we should harness this by putting our own twist on these timeless concepts."

Emen Lo (from Sankaramon)

"I believe that retro design is a tribute to the classic qualities of past eras, reflecting a deep nostalgia for their enduring artistic symbols. In our fast-paced and anxious world, the meticulously crafted products of the past are making a comeback, emerging as a new force to be reckoned with."

Erin Chen

"People are drawn to retro because it reminds them of the good old days. Contemporary visuals that reference retro reflects a tendency to look to the past for future solutions. However, many retro works simply replicate elements from the past. To stand out, retro designs should blend past elements with current trends, capturing both nostalgia and a sense of poetry."

Estudio Pum

"We're not sure if there's a homogenization in retro design. Many people are reinterpreting their 1980s pop culture references and reviving them through an idealized lens; it's a great thing to see. With so many creative reinterpretations of 80s pop culture and diverse approaches to defining design elements from that era, homogenization shouldn't be a problem."

EXCALIBUR

"It is the future to which our works will ultimately lead us. The games we played in childhood took us on a journey to different fantasies and futures, while the myths passed down to our world inspire awareness in our contemporary society. Similarly, we hope our work will empower someone to shape new realities and futures of their own. We don't see any problem with the homogenization of retro design—it is entirely superficial. Contemporary is the retro game of the future, and this world is under development."

Fadli Rabbani (from Astaga Creatives)

"People are starting to notice this design niche because modern designs often follow a predictable formula, leading to a uniform look. This trend can occur in any niche, which is why it's considered a niche in the first place. Nevertheless, there are always determined individuals who choose to break the rules and diverge from the norm. I believe these unconventional thinkers are the reason graphic design remains an intriguing form of art."

Grafis Nusantara

"We learned as an archive collective coming from a graphic design background that to keep retro designs unique, designers can use several strategies. First, they should study the history, details, and context of old styles to understand them better. Then, by bringing in ideas from different cultures, they can make their designs more interesting and varied. Using the latest technologies and materials can make old styles feel new and relevant today. Making designs that reflect individual's likes and stories is also important for creating a personal connection. Working with a mix of artists and designers can bring in new ideas, and thinking about ethics and the environment makes the designs more meaningful and responsible."

Haeri Chung (from SUPERSALADSTUFF)

"The graphic design world is highly responsive to trends, but I don't think it's a good idea to get too caught up with trends. If everyone follows trends, the whole world will create a unified style. That immediately makes the design boring and stale. Instead, I think design should always be interesting and fit the purpose."

Indego design

"As a designer, I find future retro design trends to be a captivating fusion of nostalgia and innovation. While retro design draws inspiration from the past, the challenge lies in avoiding homogenization. It's crucial to reinterpret and personalize nostalgic elements, injecting unique perspectives to prevent a generic design landscape. The key is to strike a balance between familiarity and innovation, creating timeless designs that resonate with contemporary audiences while celebrating the charm of bygone eras."

Julia Schimautz (from DTAN Studio)

"I believe future retro design should blend nostalgia with innovation. To prevent homogenization, designers must infuse fresh ideas into retro influences to keep designs diverse and creative."

Jun-Feng Li

"The homogenization of design styles is a cliché. In most cases, design work must be tested by the market and users. Creating works in styles that are well-known and accepted by the market is often an easier way to pass this test, a common practice in the design and illustration industry. I believe designers need the courage to make bold breakthroughs and innovations, along with the patience to continuously think and observe. They should strive to make each piece unique and captivating, even within constraints."

Junyao Chu

"I believe that the present era is characterized by the coexistence and collaboration of various cultures. The future trend of retro design will evolve alongside other design styles, maintaining its unique charm and lasting influence by incorporating traditional elements with modern innovations. To avoid the homogenization of retro design, designers must focus on individuality and creativity, delving deeply into cultural backgrounds and personal perspectives, thus creating works of true depth and uniqueness."

Laura Normand

"When a decade is trendy, everybody tends to do the same style. However, part of our job is to create newness. So for me, it's a bad idea to reproduce retro designs. Because you don't create for real. Instead, we should always strive for fresh thinking and new styles, drawing inspiration from design history to make it stronger, not more trendy."

Lo.Dycha

"People today are becoming increasingly sentimental, and retro design often embodies the most classic and nostalgic elements. However, 'nostalgia marketing' has faced growing criticism. It's important to consider whether there's a genuine longing for the past behind the design, as retro isn't just about 'being vintage.' Homogenization is inevitable, and like the Gold Rush, it may be interesting to look back years from now and see that aesthetics and design went through a period of retro frenzy. Personally, I believe that following design trends often overlooks the suitability of one's own attributes and style. Therefore, we should ultimately return to ourselves and reflect on 'why retro' before designing."

LXuan

"When I first started college, I had to take a basic sketching class because many of my classmates, including myself, had never touched art before. In the class, everyone drew the same object, but each drawing had a unique style and feeling. It was then that I realized the world looks different to everyone, and I didn't worry about homogenization."

Michelle Chen

"If retro designs are being used correctly in a unique way, I still think there's potential fo future retro design trends to thrive. I believe if we all just commit to trends without any clear direction, they can be diluted easily. What was once underrated can be oversaturated quickly. I believe it's important to have a purpose and 'why' certain designers commit to trends; otherwise, it can be rather meaningless."

Onoitoe Yang (from ONO DESIGN)

"Retro design is more of a niche aesthetics than a mainstream trend. It is difficult to predict its future, but I am excited about combining new trends with retro elements. The challenge with retro design is its tendency to feel repetitive, as it relies on past content. However, blending it with contemporary styles could inject new vitality."

Oscar Bastidas

"I think retro aesthetics is always going to be a trend in some way, not just in graphics but also in music and fashion. Here in NYC, teenagers are wearing Jimco pants from 1995 and listening to Nu Metal. The Cyberpunk Y2K aesthetics is super fresh right now, and it is all part of a cycle. This society's feeling is that the past is always better than the present."

Parametro Studio

"Future retro trends in design let us take advantage of the past using new technologies. It encourages us to have a balance between tradition and innovation. It is a very dynamic approach that allows for fresh interpretations reflecting technology and nostalgia."

PEI WEN

"I think our generation's cultural confidence drives us to revisit and explore designs from times we haven't experienced, which is maybe something new to us. A genuine love for retro design is essential to finding a point of exploration that aligns with your own style and develops your visual language. Homogenized retro design is merely visual self-improvement without thought. By being clear about what you want, other styles can enhance your work, making it increasingly flavorful with deeper exploration."

Sanyo Design Studio

"Art movements and genres rely on the cultural background of their times. Today, retro means repetition, and repetition means retro. To break design homogenization, we need retro combined with innovation and cultural connotation."

Tatsuya Kurihara

"It's crucial to recognize that the beautiful retro designs we admire today were themselves inspired and created within the context of their own time. Preserving the essence of retro design is significant, as it can inspire future generations of designers. But merely copying the entire retro design doesn't create something new. The key is to draw inspiration from it, blending it with modern elements that reflect the current era, thus fostering designs that are both timeless and contemporary."

Toyoya (Li Fan)

"Retro design (Pixel Art) represents the initial memories of digital virtual design, embodying both technical and artistic expression. In the future, retro design will continue to be used as a creative technique by new designers to produce fresh works. While homogenization often accompanies popularity, works with unique characteristics and styles will be more meaningful and will have an impact on the future of design."

Xinyi Liu
(from 2xlab design)

"People are often nostalgic, and trends have a way of reincarnating over time. When images are created with meaningful content and a unique perspective, rather than simply chasing form, they can avoid becoming homogenized. While it's possible to focus solely on form, pushing boundaries and establishing a distinct identity will also prevent homogenization."

Yi-Ju Liao

"As a designer, I believe retro design will persist due to nostalgia and the appeal of classic elements. However, relying too much on past styles can hinder innovation. To prevent homogenization, designers should blend retro with fresh, innovative elements, creating a style that is both nostalgic and unique."

Yiyang Li
(from min means)

"I think designers should find their own visual language rather than follow trends. Trendy visuals will inevitably become outdated, while the timeless underlying logic of classic works lies in their content and communicative power."

YU CAI

"I wouldn't worry about homogenization. 'Ancient' spans a vast range of time and space. For example, the Vaporwave aesthetics draws from the '80s and '90s in Japan and the U.S., whereas switching to the era of the Republic of China results in a very different style. Similarly, the Qing Dynasty, the Song Dynasty, and the Middle Ages each offered distinct retro styles. Furthermore, all mainstream designs today will be considered retro in the future. The discussion of homogenization exists in all periods and is not a 'problem' but a 'norm.' Many contemporaries of Beaux, like Bourguignon and Rembrandt, created similar works. Being in the present, we naturally pay attention to the work of all contemporary artists and designers. As time passes, only the best will be remembered."

Yukit Lai
(from *BranD* Magazine)

"I always believe that design is a form of service. Before addressing the issue of homogenization, if we design based on specific needs, conduct detailed analyses of particular problems, and choose appropriate design methods, we can stand out in the vast current of prevailing styles. Even in the mainstream, we can become the small fish swimming against the current."

YZIAS

"The future of retro design is expected to focus more on personalization and customization, with designers tapping into and combining elements from different eras to create unique pieces. Meanwhile, with advancements in technology, digital media, and virtual reality, future retro designs may explore new possibilities in the digital realm, blending traditional and modern technological elements. As for the issue of homogenization, designers should break the inherent patterns of traditional retro design by injecting innovation and individuality to create unique and compelling works. Additionally, relating retro design to contemporary society and culture makes it more relevant and appealing to audiences of different ages and cultural backgrounds."

3% Design Studio

"Retro design no longer settles for current popular expressions; it urgently seeks new outlets and methods by tapping into past 'zeitgeist' for content. Retro isn't an end in itself but a means to break free from present-day homogeneity. Yet, the retro movement often triggers a new wave of homogenization, which aligns with the natural rule of creative development. Initially, our minds and hands grasp basic elements like colors, fonts, and layouts, often at a superficial level of retro aesthetics borrowed from the public sphere—marking the onset of 'initial homogenization.' While many designers stop here, those who push forward go beyond mere replication. They delve deeper, distilling vintage design to its essence, stripping away overtly 'retro' elements to reconstruct new expressions rooted in personal interpretations and preferences. This journey achieves its initial goal: discovering fresh variations in contemporary design."

INDEX

A

ANARRATOR
https://www.instagram.com/anarrator/
anarrator@foxmail.com
P154–159

Ardhira Putra
https://www.instagram.com/ardhiraputra/
ardhiraputra@gmail.com
P68–77

Arrivedlate
https://www.arrivedlate.com/
helloarrivedlate@gmail.com
P134

Astaga Creatives
Fadli Rabbani
https://www.instagram.com/astagabani/
fadlirabbani27@gmail.com
P378–379

B

Bali Meng
https://www.behance.net/ziqimeng03b56d
1390246874@qq.com
P90–91
P358–360

Bern Foster
https://www.bernfoster.com/
info@bernfoster.com
P78–81

Blank Design Studio
Blank Team
https://blankdesign.studio/
hi@blankdesign.studio
P361

***BranD* Magazine**
Yukit Lai
https://www.instagram.com/brandmagazine.hk/
editorial@brandmagazine.com.hk
P268–271

Brando Corradini
https://brandocorradini.com/
brando.corradini@gmail.com
P116–117

C

CHENBO
https://www.zcool.com.cn/u/1444959
148003662@qq.com
P214–215

CH_LAB
Meng Jiayang, Wang Zhiheng, Chen Wei, Wang Zhihong
https://ch-lab.cn/
mjy@ch-lab.cn
P86–87

Chris Harnan
https://www.chrisharnan.com/
christopherharnan@gmail.com
P250–259

Cyberdreams
Isaiah Worrington
https://www.instagram.com/cyberdreamss/
hello@cyberdreams.art
P135

D

Daniel Pelavin
https://pelavin.com/
delivery@hightail.com
P377

Design Punk
Yi-Ju Liao, Weiguang Wu, Ying-Syuan Lu, Hsin-Yi Shih, Chi-Chun Chiu, Tung-Nan Hu
https://www.behance.net/q1231231346
q1231231346@gmail.com
P144–145

Diego L Rodriguez (Paranoidme)
https://paranoidme.com/
paranoidme.com@gmail.com
P123
P136–137
P140

DTAN Studio
Julia Schimautz
https://juliaschimautz.com/
julia.schimautz@gmail.com
P212–213
P228–229

E

Erin Chen
https://www.instagram.com/erinchen_illustration/
erinc2422@gmail.com
P326–327
P362–363

Estudio Pum
https://www.estudiopum.com/
hi@estudiopum.com
P367

Evan Wijaya
https://www.instagram.com/evanwijaya95/
evanwijaya95@ymail.com
P238–239

EXCALIBUR
Yoshinori Tanaka, Maiko Iwata
https://www.entaku.net/
info@entaku.net
P171

G

Ginko
https://ginkoyang.com/
info.ginkoyang@gmail.com
P128–129

Grafis Nusantara
https://grafisnusantara.com/
info@grafisnusantara.com
P238–243

H

Helloflostudio
Florencia Leonardini
https://www.behance.net/floleonardini
flodleonardini@gmail.com
P368–369

Hellocean
https://www.behance.net/Hellocean
516507153@qq.com
P118–119
P218–223
P318–319
P381

Hello Rabbit Design
Helen Rabbitte
https://www.hellorabbitdesign.com/
helen@hellorabbitdesign.com
P126–127

Huang Heshan
https://toorichcity.com/
toorich2021@163.com.com
P100–109

I

IDEAFINE
https://www.ideafine.com/
ideafine@126.com
P320

IGNORANCE1
https://www.instagram.com/ignorance1/
luis.brusciano@gmail.com
P382–383

Igor Gurovich
https://www.instagram.com/guronpics/
guron@ostengruppe.com
P42–43

Indego design
Lam Ieong Kun, Dan Ferreira, Kun Lam
https://indegodesign.com/
info@indegodesign.com
P112–115
P130–131
P138–139
P198–207

J

Jentwo
https://www.instagram.com/jen.two/?hl=en
www.Jentwo.work
jentwo.graphic@gmail.com
P298–305

Juan Molinet
https://www.instagram.com/molinetjuan/
juanmolinet@lebureau.tv
P325
P388–391

Jun-Feng Li
https://www.xiaohongshu.com/user/profile/61b5bc9d000000001000d7fd
824503480@qq.com
P84
P224–225

Junyao Chu
https://www.instagram.com/greyyy_type/
chujunyao724@qq.com
P180–182

K

KEVLAR:ESTUDIO
Gastón and Damián
https://www.instagram.com/kevlarestudio/
kevlarestudio@gmail.com
P141–143

L

Laura Normand
https://launorma.com/
laura@laura-normand.com
P231–233

Liorzh (Gabriel Picard)
https://www.instagram.com/liorzh_/
contact@liorzhdesign.com
P122

Lo.Dycha
https://www.behance.net/charleswoodlo
dycha.design@outlook.com
P132
P324

Lucia Pham
https://luciapham.com/
byluciapham@gmail.com
P348–357

Index

L

LXuan
https://www.xiaohongshu.com/user/profile/5b712fe34eacab53d5f3b092?xhsshare=CopyLink&appuid=5943ca876a6a696a0897e7a8&apptime=1725007867&share_id=4df2c79bad6946638a6beda2d3421297
kilig.lxuan@gmail.com
P82-83
P85

M

Manuel Cetina
https://www.instagram.com/el_stitch/
stitch.cetina@gmail.com
P384

Marte
https://www.martevisual.com/
hola@martevisual.com
P374-375

Mathieu Labrecque
https://mathieulabrecque.com/
monsieurmathieulabrecque@gmail.com
P166-170

Megan Park Creative
Megan Park
https://www.meganparkillustration.com/
megan@meganparkillustration.com
P372-373

Michelle Chen
https://michellecpy.com/
info.michellecpy@gmail.com
P370

min means
Yiyang Li, Ruilin Wang
https://www.instagram.com/min_means_design?igsh=MTRsNG9vcHE4Njc4MQ%3D%3D&utm_source=qr
yiyangeyoung@gmail.com
P216-217

O

Onion Design Associates
Andrew Wong, Fong Ming Yang, Spy Lan
https://oniondesign.com.tw/
hello@oniondesign.com.tw
P172-173
P226-227
P236-237

ONO DESIGN
Onoitoe Yang
https://www.behance.net/a32062717055971
onoitoe@sina.com
P92-93

Oscar Bastidas
https://www.oscarbastidas.com/
morochoscar@gmail.com
P364-365

Osheyi.A
https://osheyi.co.uk/
osheyi.as@gmail.com
P133
P385-387

P

Parametro Studio
https://parametro.studio/
press@parametrostudio.com
P371

PEI WEN
https://www.zcool.com.cn/u/15679653
961486520@qq.com
P336-337

pigeonstudio
GEZI
https://www.behance.net/pigeon_studio
pigeonstudio.info@gmail.com
P332-335
P376

R

ReflexDesign
Cai Yi, KaKa, Da Ming, bibi, A Dai
http://reflexdesign.cn/
reflexdesign@foxmail.com
P208-210
P338-339

Rita
https://www.instagram.com/moonstarlim
moonstarlimart@gmail.com
P366

S

Sankaramon
Emen Lo
https://sankaramon.cargo.site/
506779477@qq.com
P328-329

Sanyo United Studio
Liu Lei, Fu Xin
https://www.zcool.com.cn/u/23638342
15346458848@163.com
P340-341

Satu Collective
https://www.satu-collective.com/
studio@satu-collective.com
P242-243

Studio Angello Torres
Angello Torres
https://angellotorres.com/
angello.torres.dg@gmail.com
P124-125

Studio Dumbar
www.studiodumbar.com
pr@studiodumbar.com
P276-277

Sun Yao
https://www.instagram.com/sunyao_design/
sun.758857@gmail.com
P260-267

SUPERSALADSTUFF
Haeri Chung
https://supersaladstuff.com/
info@supersaladstuff.com
P280

T

Tatsuya Kurihara
https://www.instagram.com/tatsu1921/
tatsuyakurihara1@gmail.com
P330-331

They That Do
Vincent Howcutt
https://theythatdo.com/
vince@theythatdo.com
P160-165

Thomas Merceron
https://www.thomas-merceron.com/
thomas.merceron02@gmail.com
P230

Tiny Studio
https://www.t-i-n-y.com/
studio@t-i-n-y.com
P240-241

Tomii Masako
https://x.com/tomidoron
shuiro723@gmail.com
P290-297

Totally
https://www.xiaohongshu.com/user/profile/5add7bb3e8ac2b644888fb95?xhsshare=CopyLink&appuid=5add7bb3e8ac2b644888fb95&apptime=1725352018&share_id=8b9da234a559448ca9f6b3a5f8980d20
601912928@qq.com
P306-315

Toyoya (Li Fan)
https://www.instagram.com/toyoyali
toyoya8@gmail.com
P174-179

U

Urban Goodies
Yi-Ju Liao, Wei-Guang Wu, Ying-Syuan Lu, Hsin-Yi Shih
https://www.behance.net/q1231231346
q1231231346@gmail.com
P278-279

W

Weiling Zhang
https://www.behance.net/152733986266d80
15273398626@163.com
P88-89

Wind by Moon
Yi-Ju Liao, Chien Yi-Wen
https://www.behance.net/q1231231346
q1231231346@gmail.com
P274-275

Workbyworks Studio
Han Gao
https://workbyworks.studio/
info@workbyworks.studio
P211
P234-235

Y

YU CAI
https://www.instagram.com/yucai_pink
yucai.artist@gmail.com
P110-111

yunbomu
https://www.instagram.com/yunbomu/
dbsqja512@gmail.com
P272-273

YZIAS
https://www.xiaohongshu.com/user/profile/5cecac5d0000000018009fa6?xhsshare=CopyLink&appuid=5ad8bddde8ac2b39dfbb7407&apptime=1725114993&share_id=c0afd86b30f44acab6972ce121a0209a
yziasgg@gmail.com
P316-317

Z

3% Design Studio
Deng Xiongjun, Jiang Wei, Dong Yiling, Ma Youyuan, Guo Shuwen, Xiao Lv, Han Yaxu
https://zlyxdesign.com/
zlyxdesign@qq.com
P120-121
P188-197
P321-323
P380

#

2xlab design
Xinyi Liu
https://xinyiliu.works/
xinyiliu.works@gmail.com
P281-283

THE '80s ARE BACK!

English edition © 2024 SendPoints Publishing Co., Ltd.
First printing of the first edition, October 2024

sendpoints

PUBLISHED BY SendPoints Publishing Co., Ltd.

ADDRESS: Unit 23, L1/F Mirror Tower, 61 Mody Road, Tsim Sha Tsui, Kowloon, Hong Kong, China

PUBLISHER: Lin Gengli

CHIEF EDITOR: Wu Dongyan

DEVELOPMENT EDITOR: Wu Dongyan

EXECUTIVE EDITOR: Zhang Yiyu, Liang Xinyi

EXECUTIVE ART EDITOR: Zhang Zichen

ILLUSTRATOR: Zhang Zichen, Erin Chen

TRANSLATORS: Zhang Yiyu, Liang Xinyi

PROOFREADING: Zhang Yiyu, Wang Yangyu, Huang Chujun

SALES DIRECTOR: Philip Tsang

TEL: +852 6296 2246

EMAIL: sales@sppub.com

WEBSITE: www.sppub.com

ISBN 978-988-76791-6-5

All rights reserved. No part of this publication may be reproduced, stored in a retrieval system or transmitted in any form or by any means, electronic, mechanical, photocopying, recording or otherwise, without prior permission in writing from the publisher. For more information, please contact SendPoints Publishing Co., Ltd.

Printed and bound in China.

Facebook   Instagram   X

See pages 60-61 for the related content.

1
2
3
4
5
6
8
7

1 — 7: Create your pieces following the illustrated instructions.

8: Dice